I0284557

African Spirituality

Exploring Spiritual Practices from Africa, Isese, Ori, Egun, Ogun, Oshun, and Yemaya

© Copyright 2024 - All rights reserved.

The content contained within this book may not be reproduced, duplicated, or transmitted without direct written permission from the author or the publisher.

Under no circumstances will any blame or legal responsibility be held against the publisher, or author, for any damages, reparation, or monetary loss due to the information contained within this book, either directly or indirectly.

Legal Notice:

This book is copyright protected. It is only for personal use. You cannot amend, distribute, sell, use, quote, or paraphrase any part of the content within this book without the consent of the author or publisher.

Disclaimer Notice:

Please note the information contained within this document is for educational and entertainment purposes only. All effort has been executed to present accurate, up-to-date, reliable, and complete information. No warranties of any kind are declared or implied. Readers acknowledge that the author is not engaging in the rendering of legal, financial, medical, or professional advice. The content within this book has been derived from various sources. Please consult a licensed professional before attempting any techniques outlined in this book.

By reading this document, the reader agrees that under no circumstances is the author responsible for any losses, direct or indirect, that are incurred as a result of the use of the information contained within this document, including, but not limited to, errors, omissions, or inaccuracies.

Your Free Gift
(only available for a limited time)

Thanks for getting this book! If you want to learn more about various spirituality topics, then join Mari Silva's community and get a free guided meditation MP3 for awakening your third eye. This guided meditation mp3 is designed to open and strengthen ones third eye so you can experience a higher state of consciousness. Simply visit the link below the image to get started.

https://spiritualityspot.com/meditation

Or, Scan the QR code!

Table of Contents

PART 1: AFRICAN SPIRITUAL PRACTICES 1
    INTRODUCTION 2
    CHAPTER 1: GETTING TO KNOW AFRICAN SPIRITUAL PRACTICES 4
    CHAPTER 2: MAAT: BRING HARMONY AND BALANCE TO YOUR LIFE 14
    CHAPTER 3: SUPREME CREATOR GODS 24
    CHAPTER 4: THE LWA AND THE ORISHAS 33
    CHAPTER 5: SANTERIA AND THE SAINTS 42
    CHAPTER 6: HONOR THY ANCESTORS 54
    CHAPTER 7: SACRED HERBS AND PLANTS 63
    CHAPTER 8: LET'S TALK ABOUT ALTARS AND SHRINES 74
    CHAPTER 9: MOJO BAGS AND GRIS-GRIS 81
    CHAPTER 10: FESTIVALS AND CEREMONIES 88
    CONCLUSION 97
    GLOSSARY OF TERMS 99
PART 2: ISESE 104
    INTRODUCTION 105
    CHAPTER 1: WHAT IS ISESE? 107
    CHAPTER 2: OLODUMARE, THE COSMOS, AND YOU 117
    CHAPTER 3: ODU IFA, THE DIVINE SCRIPTURE 127
    CHAPTER 4: PRACTICING IFA DIVINATION 137
    CHAPTER 5: THE SEVEN GREAT ORISHAS 147

- CHAPTER 6: WALK THE PATH OF YOUR ANCESTORS 165
- CHAPTER 7: HONORING YOUR ANCESTORS 172
- CHAPTER 8: WHAT ASAFO FLAGS CAN TEACH 180
- CHAPTER 9: IWA, OR BUILDING A STRONG CHARACTER 187
- CHAPTER 10: PRACTICING ISESE EVERY DAY 194
- BONUS: AN ISESE GLOSSARY 201
- CONCLUSION 204

PART 3: ORI 206
- INTRODUCTION 207
- CHAPTER 1: BASIC SPIRITUAL CONCEPTS OF YORUBA 209
- CHAPTER 2: WHAT IS ORI? 219
- CHAPTER 3: DESTINY VS. FREE WILL IN YORUBA 228
- CHAPTER 4: OLODUMARE AND THE ORISHAS 237
- CHAPTER 5: ORI AS AN ORISHA 247
- CHAPTER 6: YOU AND YOUR ANCESTORS 256
- CHAPTER 7: LIVING WITH THE BLESSINGS OF ANCESTORS .. 265
- CHAPTER 8: EGBE, YOUR SPIRITUAL FAMILY 273
- CHAPTER 9: ODU IFA, A GUIDE TO RIGHTEOUS LIVING 280
- CHAPTER 10: ALIGNING WITH YOUR ORI 288
- BONUS: GLOSSARY OF TERMS 295
- CONCLUSION 301

PART 4: EGUN 303
- INTRODUCTION 304
- CHAPTER 1: YORUBA SPIRITUALITY BASICS 306
- CHAPTER 2: THE ORISHAS, YOUR DIVINE SPIRIT GUIDES ... 315
- CHAPTER 3: HOW TO VENERATE THE ORISHAS 326
- CHAPTER 4: EGBE, YOUR SPIRIT COMPANIONS 335
- CHAPTER 5: THE IMPORTANCE OF ANCESTORS IN YORUBA .. 343
- CHAPTER 6: THE ODUN EGUNGUN 351
- CHAPTER 7: CREATING AN EGUN ALTAR OR SHRINE 359
- CHAPTER 8: MORE WAYS TO VENERATE YOUR ANCESTORS .. 367
- CHAPTER 9: REINCARNATION IN YORUBA 376
- CHAPTER 10: ANCESTRAL CURSES AND HOW TO BREAK THEM 386
- CONCLUSION 393
- GLOSSARY OF YORUBA TERMS 395

- PART 5: OGUN 401
  - INTRODUCTION 402
  - CHAPTER 1: WHO IS OGUN? 404
  - CHAPTER 2: OGUN AS A SAINT 414
  - CHAPTER 3: ARE YOU A CHILD OF OGUN? 423
  - CHAPTER 4: OGUN IN MYTHS AND LEGENDS 432
  - CHAPTER 5: WHAT OGUN TEACHES HIS FOLLOWERS 443
  - CHAPTER 6: OGUN'S SYMBOLS AND OFFERINGS 456
  - CHAPTER 7: MAKING A SACRED ALTAR 468
  - CHAPTER 8: USEFUL RITUALS AND SPELLS 477
  - CHAPTER 9: OGUN'S FESTIVALS AND HOLY DAYS 486
  - CHAPTER 10: DAILY RITUALS TO CELEBRATE OGUN 493
  - EXTRA: GLOSSARY OF TERMS 500
  - CONCLUSION 502
  - PART 6: OSHUN 504
  - INTRODUCTION 505
  - CHAPTER 1: OSHUN - SPIRIT, SAINT, ORISHA 507
  - CHAPTER 2: ARE YOU A CHILD OF OSHUN? 518
  - CHAPTER 3: OSHUN IN MYTHS AND LEGENDS 525
  - CHAPTER 4: CONNECTING TO THE DIVINE FEMININE 534
  - CHAPTER 5: PLANTS, SYMBOLS, AND OFFERINGS 543
  - CHAPTER 6: CREATING AN ALTAR FOR THE GODDESS 554
  - CHAPTER 7: SPELLS AND RITUALS FOR LOVE AND BEAUTY 562
  - CHAPTER 8: SPELLS AND RITUALS ABUNDANCE AND PROSPERITY 573
  - CHAPTER 9: HOLY DAYS AND FESTIVALS 584
  - CHAPTER 10: DAILY RITUALS TO HONOR OSHUN 593
  - EXTRA: GLOSSARY OF TERMS 601
  - CONCLUSION 606
- PART 7: YEMAYA 608
  - INTRODUCTION 609
  - CHAPTER 1: WHO IS YEMAYA? 611
  - CHAPTER 2: THE MOTHER'S WISDOM IN MYTH AND LORE 620
  - CHAPTER 3: YEMAYA AND VIRGIN MARY 629
  - CHAPTER 4: HOW TO CONNECT TO YEMAYA 637
  - CHAPTER 5: THE GODDESS OF THE OCEAN AND THE MOON 647
  - CHAPTER 6: RITUAL TOOLS AND SYMBOLS 659

CHAPTER 7: BUILDING A HOLY SHRINE 670
CHAPTER 8: SPIRITUAL BATHS AND SPELLS 678
CHAPTER 9: SACRED DAYS AND FESTIVALS 690
CHAPTER 10: DAILY RITUALS TO HONOR YEMAYA 699
CONCLUSION 709
HERE'S ANOTHER BOOK BY MARI SILVA THAT YOU MIGHT LIKE 711
YOUR FREE GIFT (ONLY AVAILABLE FOR A LIMITED TIME) 712
REFERENCES 713

Part 1: African Spiritual Practices

The Ultimate Guide to Yoruba, Santería, Orishas, Black Spirituality, Ancestral Veneration, Maat, Haitian Voodoo, and Hoodoo

Introduction

When people think of spirituality, their minds often turn to Asian and Western practices, such as Yoga, Wicca, Paganism, and Druidism. However, there are many more spiritual practices worldwide to learn about, and the African continent is home to several vibrant and fascinating spiritual traditions.

Some of the many spiritual traditions in Africa include Kemeticism (or Egyptian neo-paganism), Isese (or the Yoruba religion), Haitian Voodoo, Hoodoo, and Santeria. Most books on spiritual traditions only focus on well-known traditions, omitting these vibrant traditions altogether. In contrast, this book highlights these spiritual traditions and explores their associated practices extensively.

This book opens with an overview of the African spiritual practices that later chapters explore in further detail. We look at how each spiritual community is structured and how rituals are conducted. We look at some of their beliefs so readers can comprehensively understand each tradition.

Next, the book explores Ma'at, Kemeticism, and Kemetic Orthodoxy and looks at ways to invite Ma'at (cosmic order) into your life. It looks at the seven principles and 42 laws of Ma'at and explains how readers can include and follow them.

After exploring Ma'at, the book delves into the traditions of supreme creator gods in African spiritual traditions and how those following these practices believe the world was created. This chapter explains how these creator gods are worshipped.

The fourth chapter explores the Lwa and the Orishas – the gods and spirits of Haitian Voodoo and Isese. It will examine the pantheons of each spiritual tradition and help readers better understand how practitioners venerated and communicated with these deities.

Next, the book looks at the mysterious spiritual tradition of Santeria and the saints that are significantly important in this tradition. It explores the links between Santeria and Catholicism, Haitian Voodoo, and Isese and helps readers to understand how to invoke each saint's powers.

The sixth chapter expands on the African continent's strong tradition of ancestral veneration. Readers will better understand why ancestors are revered and how different spiritual traditions and religions practice ancestor veneration.

After exploring ancestor veneration, the book looks at some of Africa's sacred herbs and plants and their significance in rituals and spells in African spiritual traditions like Hoodoo. We also explore the roles of altars and shrines in these traditions and help you to understand how to build your altar for personal use.

Then, we cover in detail two common talismans in mojo bags and gris-gris. It teaches you how to create and use each of these talismans, providing a source of protection and magic wherever you go.

Finally, we examine the festivals and ceremonies celebrated in these African spiritual traditions. Since African traditions remain relatively unknown, there is a limited understanding of their religious celebrations, and this chapter seeks to remedy this concern.

This book also offers a glossary of terms, making it easier to understand the spiritual practices it covers. Since these practices are often accompanied by new and unknown terms, learning about them can be challenging.

So, without further ado, let's explore the world of African spiritual practices and uncover its many secrets.

Chapter 1: Getting to Know African Spiritual Practices

Many different unique cultural and spiritual practices stem from African and African American religions. From Senegal to South Africa, these practices are often connected with spirituality, ceremonies, rituals, and other traditions varying from one area to the next. Some are still practiced today, while others have been lost to time. These practices have been passed on from generation to generation and vary from tribe to tribe. Some were practiced by all community members, while others were reserved for specific people (often those having great power or potential). This chapter examines some of the most popular African spiritual practices and their history.

African spiritual practices span all over the African continent.
https://unsplash.com/photos/Ue5kuMVmIhU

Yoruba

The Yoruba people have a rich and complex history that is still studied by modern historians. The Yoruba religion is one of the largest African diaspora groups, with members spread across the globe. From recorded documents, the Yoruba people originated in West Africa, primarily Nigeria, Benin, and Ghana, where they lived peacefully and independently for many centuries. The Yoruba faith is one of the oldest religions in the world. Over 5000 years ago, the Yoruba people came into contact with European explorers, traders, and Muslim and Christian missionaries, who influenced their practices and beliefs. Several Yoruba groups converted to Christianity during this period, while others embraced Islam. Still, many maintained the traditional practices of their ancestors, resulting in a diverse and widely practiced religion that continues as an essential part of Yoruba culture. While there has been some variation in their beliefs over the centuries, the Yoruba religion is generally defined by a polytheistic belief system (multiple deities), a focus on ancestor worship, and a central role for divination, known as Ifa. Through this divination system, followers can understand the intent of the Supreme Being Olodumare.

During the slave trade, many Africans were forced to convert to Catholicism. However, Yoruba represented their history and identity. They couldn't simply abandon their roots. They practiced their faith secretly by merging some Yoruba aspects with Catholicism, blending many of the Orishas with Catholic saints. Holding on to their faith was a form of rebellion against enslavement and the loss of their freedom.

Beliefs of the Yoruba Religion

The Yoruba people believe that their supreme deity, Olodumare, created the universe. With help from lesser spirits, Olodumare formed the Earth and everything on it, including humans. People should strive to live according to Olodumare to be blessed with good fortune. According to the Yoruba religion, Ashe represents the energy found in all natural things, including humans and deities.

The Yoruba religion primarily focuses on worshipping deities called Orishas. These deities are often associated with natural forces like animals, plants, and the environment. They are good and bad spiritual beings (egungun and ajogun). Although they are not as powerful as Olodumare, the Orisha can perform important tasks, including healing and protecting humans from evil forces. In return for gifts and offerings, the Orisha protects the people and provides them with special gifts.

Yoruba Rituals and Customs

Yoruba rituals are sacred and secular, ranging from religious ceremonies to daily life. Traditional Yoruba rituals are done for many reasons, including celebrating a person's birth, marriage, or death. They also maintain harmony and balance in the community. The most critical aspect of Yoruba rituals is respect for all people. In Yoruba culture, everyone is equal. People have different roles and responsibilities within the community, but everyone has value and worth. Rituals show respect for those who have gone before by commemorating their lives and ensuring future generations are cared for in their absence. These ceremonies have immense meaning and vary significantly across the various West African communities.

One interesting aspect of the Yoruba religion is the relationship between priests and followers. While many religions have a strict hierarchy with a few individuals (e.g., priests, ministers, etc.) at the top, Yoruba priests are typically not seen as spiritually superior to the rest of the community. Instead, priests are seen as advisors, teachers, and healers who have studied and are knowledgeable in matters of the spirit. Priests are typically chosen by their communities to lead worship and perform essential ceremonies, but they do not hold a high spiritual authority position. Moreover, there is no central organization or hierarchical leadership within the Yoruba religion. Each community is autonomous and has the freedom to practice and interpret the religion as they see fit.

While most Yoruba religion practitioners belong to one of the many distinct lineages comprising the Yoruba community, every practitioner must adhere to some basic tenets. The first tenet is that one must be initiated into the religion as a child by a community member trained to perform this task. This initiation must take place between birth and adulthood, but it is most common for initiations to occur when children are between 5 and 7 years old. After being initiated into the religion, it is vital to learn what it means to be a Yoruba person. These principles include honoring your ancestors, respecting your elders, and observing traditional laws and customs. They also include how to behave in public, such as in churches and markets, so as not to offend others or disgrace your family. However, above all else, not forgetting to live with purpose and meaning in your life is essential.

Santeria

While Yoruba is an ethnic group, Santeria is a religion developed by the Yoruba in Cuba and their descendants. Santeria is an Afro-Caribbean religion created by Atlantic slaves brought to Cuba, Puerto Rico, and other Caribbean islands between the 16th and 19th centuries. The enslaved people took many of their traditional African beliefs with them to the Caribbean, which were transformed over time into the Santeria religion. It is not just one religion but a synthesis of traditional Yoruba beliefs, Spiritualism, and Roman Catholic Christianity.

Beliefs of the Santeria Religion

There is no one set doctrine or dogma within Santeria. Instead, there are multiple sects with slightly different beliefs and practices. However, Santeria is polytheistic and revolves around the same multi-Orisha deities as the Yoruba people. It emphasizes the idea that all things have a spirit and that spirits come from the gods who created the universe. People who practice Santeria believe they can communicate with these spirits and ask them for help. The main goals of this religion are to honor and respect the spirits.

Santeria Rituals and Customs

In this religion, practitioners engage in rituals and ceremonies to connect with the spirit world. These rituals worship deities, and their ceremonies involve drumming, dancing, and chanting. They also include prayers, offerings, and fasting. These rituals are often guided by a santero (male) or santera (female). In addition to acting as a spiritual medium for its practitioners, Santeria allows followers to connect with their ancestors through rootwork and spirit possession rituals. Some practitioners believe they can communicate with their ancestors through these mediums.

The extent of participation in Santeria varies greatly. The practice of Santeria recognizes three primary deities, each with its associated ritual practices. The most important deity is the Orisha, which comes from the Yoruba people of West Africa. There are many Orisha, and some are honored in more than one form of Santeria.

The rituals of Santeria are divided into different categories reflecting the spirit being honored. Any ritual can be described as "Santeria" as long as it honors one or more deities. Each category has specific steps that must be followed to honor the particular spirit properly. For example, some ceremonies involve elaborate offerings and dances that allow participants to communicate with the honored spirit. Others focus mainly on spiritual cleansing and healing through prayer and herbs. Some ceremonies also involve animal sacrifice to appease the spirit being honored and bring protection.

Haitian Voodoo

During the Atlantic slave trade of the 16th to 19th centuries, Haitian Voodoo, also known as Vodou, developed among Afro-Haitian communities. Yoruba, Fon, and Kongo, among other enslaved West and Central Africans, came to Hispaniola with their traditional religions melded together. Over time, the religion evolved to include elements from indigenous religions and Christianity. It combines native spiritual beliefs and practices from Catholicism and is characterized by worshipping spirits and ancestors. Many people around the world currently practice voodoo. Globally, 60 million practitioners follow one of several variations of the faith. Some Haitian Voodoo practitioners trace their ancestry back to those brought to Haiti as enslaved people. Others claim direct descent from those born there or moved there after slavery was abolished. People of both backgrounds practice Voodoo, either out of belief or curiosity. The followers of Voodoo are referred to as Vodouisants.

In many ways, Haitian Vodou is similar to African religions. For example, Haitian Vodou rituals often involve foods, drinks, and herbs for healing and spiritual purposes. Like many other religions of the African diaspora, Haitian Vodou has been influenced by Christianity. Many Haitians are Christians who practice some elements of their ancestor's religion alongside their Christian beliefs.

Vodou is considered a syncretic religion because it incorporates elements from multiple sources. These sources include African religion and Christianity. One thing that sets Haitian Vodou apart from Yoruba and Santeria is their theology. In this theology, worshipping a single deity is combined with worshipping multiple deities (polytheistic).

There is a misconception that Voodoo is associated with dark magic, violence, and devil worship. However, this is an unfair representation of a peaceful religion with no relation to witchcraft. For centuries, Voodoo has suffered from many misunderstandings that led people to fear and to be curious about it. Hollywood didn't help by constantly portraying it as a method to cause people harm.

A famous incident in Haiti in 1791 could have sparked controversy and misunderstandings around Voodoo. There was a peaceful Voodoo ceremony many witnesses misinterpreted as participants making a deal with the devil. Violent slavery revolutions resulting afterward led white settlers to make these negative associations.

Voodoo dolls are also misrepresented in pop culture as tools to perform black magic and bring pain and suffering to others. Vodouisants assign specific dolls to their Lwa and use them to invoke assistance or guidance.

Beliefs of Haitian Voodoo

The religion can be challenging to define because it draws from many sources and contains many traditions. However, Voodoo is characterized by its emphasis on magic and ancestor worship. Some voodoo religions believe that spirits can possess people, animals, and objects (Loa). Others worship gods and goddesses. Also, different types of magic are part of Voodoo. Some magic rituals use animal sacrifices. Others use potions or powders believed to have special powers. Voodoo rituals often involve dancing, chanting, and drums. Offerings are sometimes made to gods and goddesses during these ceremonies.

Haitian Voodoo Rituals and Customs

Vodoun priests can be male or female. Male priests are called Oungan, while female priestesses are called Manbo. Both perform initiation rituals such as bowing, chanting, and praying in an effort to communicate with spirits or Iwa. They are responsible for administering blessings, charms, and rituals for sick people and curing illness through prayer. Besides possessing knowledge about voodoo rituals, mambos have expertise in herbal medicine, using herbs in their potions and for healing purposes.

Hoodoo

Voodoo and Hoodoo are often used interchangeably, but there is a difference.

Voodoo is a religion, while Hoodoo is not. In addition to rituals, teachers, and leaders, Voodoo has two distinct branches; New Orleans Vodou and Haitian Vodou. In contrast, Hoodoo is not a religion, has no organizational structure, and is performed by individuals claiming to possess certain magical powers, each with their distinctive style.

In Hoodoo, Christianity, Spiritualism, African religion, and Islam are combined into a syncretic spiritual system.

There are many misconceptions about Hoodoo - it is like Voodoo, or its practitioners are fortune-tellers. In reality, Hoodoo is a blend of various practices to interact with the spiritual world. It is a religion that evolved from the West African tribal religions brought to the Americas by enslaved Africans. Nowadays, it is often associated with the African-Americans culture in the South, Southwest, and Northeast United States.

Hoodoo is a southern U.S. form of magic originally brought over to the U.S. by enslaved Africans. It remained an important tradition in the southern U.S. and continues to be practiced today. The religion evolved from the West African tribal religions brought to the Americas by enslaved Africans. Although its exact roots are disputed, scholars agree that Hoodoo's development can be traced to the 19th century. Beginning in the Southern states where most Africans were kept as slaves, Hoodoo evolved from a secret (hidden from slave owners) system of spiritual practices, initially used for healing and protection, into a religion that also addressed daily life problems.

Beliefs of Hoodoo

Hoodoo is the synthesis of various African and New World folk practices and traditions. Hoodoo practitioners believe a number of mystical forces are at work in the world. These include potent entities, spirits, and supernatural forces. They also believe these forces can be harnessed and used to improve people's lives. Hoodoo practitioners use a range of techniques to connect with these forces. Some techniques include casting spells, making potions, and performing rituals. They also use charms and talismans. All these techniques aim to create a connection between the practitioner and the mystical force they are attempting to harness. Once this connection has been created, the practitioner can influence or control the supernatural force. Hoodoo practitioners believe that mystical forces can be manipulated by using certain objects. These objects include stones or bones from animals like dogs or cats because some hoodoo practitioners believe these animals have supernatural powers.

Hoodoo Rituals and Customs

Hoodoo religion is a spiritual practice focusing on using magic, witchcraft, and Botanics. There are many different hoodoo spiritualisms, but they all share common elements. These include a belief in the power of nature and an emphasis on offerings to deities and spirits. Many hoodoo religions incorporate elements from other religions, like Christianity or African tribal beliefs. No established rules or laws govern the hoodoo religion, making it difficult for outsiders to understand. However, there are some basic practices most people in the religion can agree on. For example, most practitioners agree that magic requires an element of chance and includes rituals like fortune-telling. They also agree that any worship must be accompanied by at least some form of sacrifice or offering. Some common hoodoo rituals harness spirits for various uses, use lucky charms called mojo bags or lucky pieces to bring good fortune, and perform spells to change a person's or situation's outcome, and hexes to call upon or expunge negative energy.

Hoodoo priests are known as rootworkers. Rootworkers use hoodoo practices to help people with their problems or issues in life. They are also referred to as conjure doctors or conjure masters. While these terms can be used interchangeably, rootworkers are distinct from conjure doctors, who are usually herbalists using folk remedies to heal ailments. Rootworkers focus on using folk magic and spiritual practices, like hexes or spells, to help people with their problems. The hoodoo tradition is passed down from teacher to student, and students often have to go through a rite of passage before they can begin their studies. In some cases, students might undergo an initiation or test before they can begin their studies and become fully-fledged hoodoo practitioners.

Kemetic Orthodoxy

Less of a religion and more of a theology dedicated to the exploration of truth and knowledge through worshipping deities, Kemetic Orthodoxy is a religion based on the ancient Egyptian religion and way of life. It has been adapted and changed to fit modern life and values. It is a syncretic approach combining Christianity and other world religion elements to create a new synthesis. The faith focuses on the spiritual power of ancient Kemetic elements, including Egyptian gods and goddesses, mythical beasts, plants and animals, and sacred places such as temples, cemeteries, and burial grounds. It draws on an eclectic mix of sources, including the ancient Kemetic religion, neo-paganism, animism, African traditional religions, and Western religious traditions like Christianity and Judaism. Many people practice aspects of Kemetic Orthodoxy without necessarily identifying with the entire religion. In particular, Kemetics practice ancestral spirituality alone or combined with other forms of spirituality. For example, some may practice Kemetic Orthodoxy while also practicing Wicca or neo-paganism. Others practice Kemetic Orthodoxy while also following a more traditional Christian or Jewish path.

Kemetic Orthodoxy originated in the United States and has experienced significant growth since its founding in the 1980s by Rev. Tamara L. Siuda. It is now practiced globally by individuals and groups.

Beliefs of Kemetic Orthodoxy

Practitioners, known as Shemsu, are guided through the faith by five basic tenets:

- Taking part in the community and respecting it
- The belief in Netjer (the Supreme Being)
- The veneration of Akhu (ancestors)
- Upholding the principles of ma'at (morality and ethics)
- An acknowledgment of Siuda (the founder of the faith) as the Nisut (leader)

While Kemetic Orthodoxy believes in one divine power (Netjer), it is also a polytheistic religion believing in multiple deities, similar to Yoruba and Santeria.

Kemetic Orthodoxy Rituals and Customs

The practice of the faith is divided into three categories:

- **Formal or state worship**: All members are observed by a chosen priest and perform prayers at sunrise to a chosen deity
- **Personal piety**: All members, priests, and higher clergy give praise and worship the deities in an established Senut (shrine)
- **Ancestral devotion** through offerings and prayer

These are five of the many different African religions and spiritual practices that have existed for centuries. The practices vary significantly from one region to another. Each is based on various deities and different rituals and practices for worship. They are all unique, and their histories and traditions are fascinating. They provide a fascinating look into the history of these African regions and the people who lived there for centuries.

These religions are more than traditional practices but represent the African identity and roots. Even though the Abrahamic religions found their way to Africa, many people still hold onto their ancestors' traditions.

Chapter 2: Maat: Bring Harmony and Balance to Your Life

Maat, an ancient Egyptian goddess or a concept? Maat was a goddess but represented something more. She symbolizes order and harmony. Every king's duty was to ensure that Maat or order was established to replace disorder (Isfet) and chaos. Maat represented various significant notions in ancient Egyptian cultures, like truth and justice. Yet, Maat was also a powerful and influential goddess, the daughter of the creator god and the god of the sun, Ra. When Ra was creating the universe, Maat was created out of him, meaning Maat has existed since the beginning of time and brought balance and harmony to a chaotic universe. For this reason, many treated Maat as a concept to live by rather than a deity.

Maat represented order and harmony.
TYalaA, CC BY-SA 4.0 <https://creativecommons.org/licenses/by-sa/4.0>, via Wikimedia Commons
https://commons.wikimedia.org/wiki/File:Goddess_Ma%27at_or_Maat_of_Ancient_Egypt_-_reconstructed.png

    She didn't have a story like the other goddess or a personality. She merely represented a few crucial ideas. If you become one with Maat and her principles, you'll lead a balanced life and be guaranteed a peaceful eternity in the afterlife. However, if you reject her laws and principles, you'll suffer severe consequences in the afterlife. In other words, Maat represented the ideal behavior and characteristics to abide by and on which all other deities agreed. Maat was the foundation on which Ra built his creation and represented the rules the ancient Egyptians were instructed to follow.

    Maat means *"that which is true and straight,"* which signifies everything she represented. She is depicted as a woman with wings carrying the key of life (the ankh). Maat was cherished among ancient Egyptian kings and people, and her followers called themselves "Beloved of Maat." In some legends, she was married to her brother Thoth, the God of wisdom.

Each person had the choice to lead an honorable and honest life and abide by Maat's principles, or they could ignore them and live by their own rules. In other words, everyone was responsible for their actions without any gods' interference. The gods were fair. They left each person to their own, but they should also be prepared to face the consequences in the afterlife and pay for their mistakes. However, the gods still hoped that people would care about one another as they cared for them and lived in harmony. Living in harmony with the gods meant abiding by Maat's principles.

The ancient Egyptians, similar to many other cultures at the time, believed in the afterlife. How they would spend their afterlife depended on the life they chose to lead. Every person underwent a trial and judgment, referred to as "The Weighing of the Hearts."

The Weighing of the Hearts

After death, the soul of the dead arrives at a place in the afterlife called "The Hall of Truth." Whether he was a king or a peasant, everyone had to be tried and face the gods' judgment. The gods who judged the souls were referred to as the council of Maat. During each trial, the soul of the dead stood in front of the judges while the human body remained in its grave. However, only the aspects of the human soul would make it to the Hall of Truth for the trial.

The ancient Egyptians believed nine parts made up each person's soul.

1. The Khat (the physical body).
2. The Ren (a person's secret name).
3. The Ka (a person's double form).
4. The Ab (the heart which drives the person to be good or bad).
5. The Ba (a part of the soul that took the shape of a bird with a human head and could travel between the heavens and earth).
6. The Akh (the immortal self).
7. The Sahu (an aspect of the Akh).
8. The Sechem (another aspect of the Akh).
9. The Shuyet (the shadow self).

These nine parts represented the human soul's aspects that existed on Earth. After death, the Akh and its two aspects, Shuyet and Sechem, would travel to the underworld and stand before the god of the underworld, Osiris, to await their judgment in front of forty-two judges. Some of the most insignificant gods and goddesses in Ancient Egypt were among these judges, like the Creator Ra, Horus the god of the sun, Nut the goddess of the sky, Geb the god of the earth, Hathor the goddess of love, Shu the goddess of peace, Nephthys the goddess of the dead, and her sister Isis, the goddess of life. The fourth aspect of the soul, the Ab (heart), was placed on a golden scale and weighed against a white feather. However, this was no ordinary white feather; it belonged to Maat and was referred to as the feather of truth.

Before the heart was placed on the scale, the immortal self (the Akh) had to first recite the "Negative Confession" or "The Declaration of Innocence," which was a list of forty-two sinful actions to confess they never did. The confessions were made to each of the judges. Negative confessions differed from one person to another. They were tailored for each person because people are different, and the temptations they faced and the sins they committed aren't the same. For instance, a sin like "I never ordered a kill" was appropriate for a blacksmith who would normally never be involved in ending someone's life. However, kings, soldiers, and judges had probably been in a situation where they had ordered someone's death. Therefore, this sin wouldn't be included in their confessions since, in this case, it was their job, not a sin. Also, committing all the sins presented to them had to be denied. If a warrior denied killing someone, they would be lying. Therefore, there wasn't a standard list for each person, but there were some common sins that no person should ever commit, like stealing or cursing the gods. Intentions were significant in these confessions. For instance, the confession, "I never made someone cry." No one would attest if this were true because it could never be known if their actions or words had brought someone to tears. Their confession here was based on their intention, meaning they never intended to make someone cry.

The sins represented everything that went against Maat's principles. The ones who lived by her rules were virtuous, and even the sins they committed didn't have ill intentions. The purpose of these confessions was to show that each person understood life should only be lived according to the gods' teachings, not the person's whims.

After a person listed their confessions, their heart was placed on the scale. Even if they lied during confessions, their hearts would never lie. If they pretended to be virtuous, the scale would expose them. The heart of a good person would be lighter than the feather of truth. In this case, Osiris would consult with Thoth and the forty-two judges to determine if the person was truly worthy and should be rewarded. The gods would evaluate how many sins a person had committed and decide if they were on the virtuous or sinner side. However, if the heart was heavier than Maat's feather, they would be denied an afterlife. Unlike other religions, the ancient Egyptians didn't have a concept of hell. The goddess Ammut would devour the heavy hearts, and the person would no longer exist. Maat was depicted on top of the golden scale during the trial. However, other drawings showed her by Osiris's side.

After judgment was passed, the light hearts were allowed passage to The Field of Reeds, the ancient Egyptians' equivalent to heaven. However, the journey wasn't easy. Evil forces like demons created chaos and traps to prevent the soul from reaching its final destination. Those who managed to arrive safely would be reunited with their departed loved ones and spend eternity in the enchanted realm of the Field of Reeds. Other myths don't include the demonic traps - the souls lead an easy journey through Lily Lake, where they face one last test before they reach the Field of Reeds.

Maat protected this realm and all its residences. If a person was lucky enough and had a pure heart, they would get the chance to see Maat. Her role wasn't only to weigh hearts, but she also supported the souls of the people in the Field of Reeds who abided by her rules.

Maat's Role in Kemeticism

In the myth of creation in Kemetism, before there was mankind or creation, chaos was the only thing existing. Ra emerged from the chaos to create the universe. She was created as a power against chaos. Maat's role in Kemetism was similar to her role in ancient Egyptian religion. She was the keeper of order, harmony, and truth and prevented chaos. She represented justice and truth. Hence, her feather determined the worthiness of a person's heart. The concept of Maat and everything she represented was hugely significant in Kemeticism. The worshipers performed specific rituals and prayers to honor the laws of Maat and help spread them among others.

When the upper and lower of ancient Egypt were united, the Kemetism followers became aware of the forty-two rules of Maat, which they applied in their daily lives and used in their negative confessions.

The weighting of hearts also took place in their belief in the underworld or duat against Maat's feather of truth. If Maat found that the person had abided by her laws, they were granted eternity in the Field of Reeds, where they would meet Osiris, who guarded its gates.

A Light Heart in the Spiritual Journey

A light heart will grant you eternity in paradise or the Field of Reeds. It signifies that a person has led an honest life and is in harmony with the gods. A light heart is a pure and virtuous heart. A person must guarantee their heart is light before embarking on a spiritual journey. A spiritual journey involves self-discovery, asking questions, finding answers, finding your place in the universe, awakening your spirit, and experiencing a rebirth. During this journey, you become aware of who you are and whom you are supposed to be.

A light heart is necessary on this journey. Another version of yourself inside of you'll be awakened during your spiritual journey - one who is more positive, confident, and powerful. Becoming the best version of yourself requires a pure heart that can let go of anger, greed, lying, and other vices and embraces positivity and light. Whether you take a spiritual journey to discover yourself, find your place in the universe, grow, connect with a deity, or move on from an unfortunate past, your heart has to be free of everything that ever held you back. Most people are led by their hearts, and an impure heart will prevent you from achieving your journey's purpose.

You can have a pure heart by following Maats' laws. Although these rules are ancient, they are still relatable and can still be applied. Many things have changed through the centuries, except what defines a good person. These timeless laws and principles will help you walk a straight path. They purify your heart of hate, anger, greed, envy, and everything that can taint it. You have the power to lead an honest life, even if it seems hard at times.

In Kemetic belief, applying Maat's principles is necessary to live a balanced life and have a light and pure heart.

The Seven Principles and Forty-Two Laws of Maat

This chapter has mentioned the principles and laws of Maat a few times. Here, you'll discover these principles and the laws which can be applied in modern times.

1. Order

Maat is the opposite of chaos, so it makes sense for its first principle to be "order." The universe wasn't created randomly. There is a pattern behind everything in creation. Everything is in order - the night follows the day, the planets revolve around the sun, and the moon goes through different cycles. Even in the world of the deities, there is a hierarchy, and every god and goddess knows their place. The god of the underworld won't leave his position to rule the skies or vice versa. Maat was created to bring order to a once chaotic universe and maintain its balance. Order is life, so it's the main focus of Kemeticism. Without order, the universe would succumb to chaos and perish.

You can apply the concept of order in life by keeping your environment organized, clean, and clutter-free.

2. Balance

Finding the balance between opposites in life is necessary. You shouldn't indulge in or lead a life of excess. For instance, a life with all play and no work is a waste of time, and a life with all work and no play can be hard and boring. Find balance in everything in life so you can live in harmony. In other words, coexist with nature. Don't empty its resources and only take what you need. You don't want to deprive future generations of Mother Nature's resources.

3. Justice

Justice is the foundation of life and one of the most significant of Maat's principles. Like the gods don't differentiate between kings and peasants, people should also treat everyone equally. Applying justice is living by an ethical code where you put what is right above everything else. It represents equality where no one goes hungry, and every person is allowed their basic needs - food, water, medical care, and a home. Everyone should be treated with respect regardless of their social status. If justice is applied, there will be less killing, stealing, and cheating.

4. Truth

Truth is honesty, whether you are honest with yourself about who you truly are and what you need or honest with others by sticking to the truth and avoiding lies. Living your truth requires you to see yourself for who you truly are and be your most true and authentic self without lying or faking. Everything you think, say, or do should be truthful. It is a sign of respect when you honor yourself and others with the truth.

5. Reciprocity

Reciprocity resembles the concept of karma or what goes around comes around. This concept is in many religions, like Christianity and Buddhism. If you do good deeds and treat everyone with kindness and respect, others will treat you in the same way, and good things will happen to you. However, bad deeds and disrespect will only bring negativity into your life.

6. Harmony

Harmony is achieved when people, plants, and animals live authentically and move together in alignment.

7. Propriety

Propriety is the understanding that all living creatures have the right to exist. All creatures, like animals, should also be left to live in peace without feeling threatened or harmed. It is similar to the ethical code behind vegetarianism and veganism. Propriety also implies that you shouldn't harm yourself or others with words or actions.

The Forty-Two Laws of Maat

The forty-two laws of Maat were derived from her seven principles.

1. I have never cursed.
2. I have never sinned.
3. I have never eaten more than I should.
4. I have never stolen.
5. I have never lied.
6. I have never killed.
7. I have never stolen from a deity.
8. I have never deceived the gods and goddesses with offerings.
9. I have never used violence to commit robbery.

10. I have never stolen food.
11. I have never been angry for no reason.
12. I have never ignored the truth.
13. I have never accused an innocent person.
14. I have never been unfaithful.
15. I have never eavesdropped.
16. I have never made someone cry.
17. I have never deceived anyone.
18. I have never felt sad for no reason.
19. I have never stolen someone's land.
20. I have never attacked anyone.
21. I have never violated my boundaries.
22. I have never seduced another man's wife.
23. I have never been reckless or acted without thinking.
24. I have never polluted myself.
25. I have never disrupted someone's peace.
26. I have never frightened anyone.
27. I have never been violent.
28. I have never broken the law.
29. I have never cursed a deity.
30. I have never been extremely angry.
31. I have never destroyed a temple.
32. I have never exaggerated the truth.
33. I have never been arrogant.
34. I have never committed evil.
35. I have never stolen food from a child.
36. I have never polluted water.
37. I have never disrespected the dead or stolen from them.
38. I have never spoken with arrogance or anger.
39. I have never stolen anything that belonged to a deity.
40. I have never cursed in deeds, words, or thoughts.
41. I have never put myself on a pedestal.

42. I have never used evil deeds, words, or thoughts.

You may feel guilty or discouraged that you have only just learned about these laws. However, it is never too late to start working on yourself. It doesn't matter what you did yesterday or who you were before. Now that you have learned about Maat's laws, you can start a new chapter in your life by following her rules. The rest of your life can start today.

Maat's laws will push you to be a better person, make you feel good about yourself and your life, and strengthen your relationship with others. If you aren't sure whether you need these rules or not, ask yourself:

- Am I happy with my life right now?
- Am I the best version of myself?
- Am I leading a life I should be proud of?
- Am I living an honest and authentic life?
- If I died today, would my heart be light or heavy?
- What can I do to be better and do better?

It will take time to memorize these laws to include them in your life. Help yourself by writing them in a note on your phone and reading them every day before you go to bed, and when you wake up, so they are always on your mind. You can write them as questions in your diary, like, have I lied today? Have I made someone cry? Was I arrogant? Was I angry for no reason? Or you could write each law on a small piece of paper, fold them, and put them in a bowl. Every morning randomly pick a piece of paper and do two or three things to apply the law.

Maat, as a concept or goddess, is a fascinating part of ancient Egyptian history. Everything she represented and her laws and principles can still be applied in the modern age. It will take time and effort to get accustomed to her teachings, but with persistence, you could have a light heart. Remember, having a light heart doesn't mean being perfect or committing no sins. It's about letting the good in you outweigh the bad.

Chapter 3: Supreme Creator Gods

In the belief systems of African cultures, supreme creator gods were responsible for creating people and the world. These are the most important and highest gods in the pantheon and have many commonalities. These gods have so much in common because they are likely derived from the same source. The similarities are further proof that an earlier pan-African religion fragmented over time and place as people settled, farmed, and adopted new practices. In addition to being creators, these supreme creator gods also are notably important in these cultures. For example, some are known as intermediaries between humans and other divine beings. Other supreme creator gods are less important but still have specific characteristics that make them stand out from the rest. This chapter explores the supreme creator gods in African-derived religions. For example, Yoruba religions worship Olodumare as their supreme being. Olodumare created and ruled all things. He determined the fate of humans and their characters. Bondye, another supreme being, is worshipped as the world's creator and sustainer of balance in Vodun.

The supreme creator gods are the highest order of deities.
Image_of_an_African_Songye_Power_Figure_in_the_collection_of_the_Indianapolis_Museum_of_Art_(2005.21).jpg: RichardMcCoyderivative work: IdLoveOne, CC BY-SA 3.0 <https://creativecommons.org/licenses/by-sa/3.0>, via Wikimedia Commons https://commons.wikimedia.org/wiki/File:Image_of_an_African_Songye_Power_Figure_in_the_collection_of_the_Indianapolis_Museum_of_Art_(2005.21)-EDIT.jpg

Olodumare

Olodumare, also called Olorun or Olafin-Orunis, is the supreme deity venerated in the Yoruba religion, Santeria, Umbanda, Folk Catholicism, and Candomble. The word "olodumare" is a combination of two words: "olofin" and "odumare," meaning "noble spirit" and "lord." He is the god of creation and the master of all things. In short, he's the one who made everything possible. Olodumare is neither male nor female and is often called "they." Few people know about Olodumare. But for those who do, there may be more questions than answers. Who is this god, exactly? Why should we worship him? Why would anyone want to follow him?

Who is Olodumare?

Olodumare is the supreme deity in Yoruba religious traditions. As the creator and ruler of the universe, he is the ultimate source of all power. Olodumare is usually considered a monotheistic deity. His name means *"the owner of the house," "the owner of the market,"* or *"the king of the market."* In this case, the market is the world, and he is the owner. As the supreme deity and creator of all things in the Yoruba pantheon of gods and goddesses, he lives in the sky, where gods live. All creatures and spirits of the land, air, and sea are subject to him, but he is not omnipresent and does not walk on Earth, although he does remain active and responds to prayer.

Since the Yoruba religion is passed down orally, various versions of the same myths and legends exist. Some stories describe Olodumare as an absent deity who isn't involved in the lives of mankind. They live in Heaven, far away from the people and their affairs, and cannot even hear their prayers. Therefore, they created the Orishas as intermediaries between Olodumare and mankind. However, other legends tell a different story of an attentive deity who knows the affairs of man and the Orishas.

The Symbolic Meaning of Olodumare

The Yoruba people understand the god of the sky and the heavens, Olodumare, in many ways. He created the universe and all things in it and is the ultimate source of authority, law, and order. Therefore, he is considered the Supreme Being, who cannot be disobeyed. He is the fountain of wisdom, knowledge, and understanding. Through Olodumare, we learn and grow. He is the judge of all people, and he decides their fate after death. He is the one who gives out rewards and punishments and decides whether a person should be sent to heaven or hell after death.

How Did Olodumare Create the World?

African religions believe that creation occurred on different planets in various systems throughout the universe at different times. Several versions of this creation story depend on where a person lives. One of the most well-known is the spider and the palm tree story. In this story, Olodumare first created a spider. He told the spider to spin a web strong enough to hold up the world. The spider tried for a long time but could not do it. So, Olodumare killed him and used his remains to create a palm tree. Then, he told the palm tree to bend over and form the floor of the world. The tree bent down so far that it formed a bowl-like structure on the Earth's surface. Olodumare used water from the ocean to fill the bowl, forming the oceans and seas. He used a bit of soil to create dry land, which formed the continents. He used the palm tree's trunk to create the mountains and the tree's leaves to make the forests. Finally, he bent the tree's branches down to form the sky.

Another version of the creation story involves Obatala, the sky father. After the creation of the universe, there was only sky and water. Obatala wasn't satisfied with the creation of the universe and felt it was lacking. He went to Olodumare to ask permission to create dry land, and they obliged. With the help of other Orishas, Obatala obtained the necessary tools and descended to Earth to build hills, valleys, and mountains. He spent some time enjoying his new creation, but he became lonely and bored. He asked Olodumare's permission again to create mankind, and the deity agreed. After Obatala built humans, Olodunmare breathed life into them. Therefore, every living being possesses a part of the divine inside them.

Olodumare wasn't happy with the state of the world. He felt that something was missing. The world needed a positive force to bring joy and happiness, so he created Oshun, the Orisha of love.

The Orisa

The Yoruba believe Olodumare created spirits responsible for various aspects of life and the natural world. These spirits were called Orishas. These Orishas, like Oshu, Orunmila, and other gods, are intermediaries between mankind and Olodumare. They are responsible for maintaining harmony and order in the universe. The Orishas are also responsible for the well-being of the people of Earth and act as guardians, providing advice, healing, and other help to humans. What makes the Orishas particularly special is they were believed to have been human once. This is why they can understand human conditions and help humans when they are in need. Olodumare shares a special bond with the Orishas as he trusts them with the world's affairs. However, this trust was, at times, misplaced. The Orishas have plotted on more than one occasion to kill Olodumare.

What Religions Worship Olodumare

Many religions worship Olodumare. Some include the Yoruba religion, the Ifa religion, the Obeah religion, the African traditional religions, and the Caribbean religions. Also, many New Age religions worship Olodumare. For the Yoruba, Olodumare is the supreme deity. They believe he created the world and everything in it. He speaks to his followers through his priests and priestesses, known as Babalawos. They are trained in a divination system known as Ifa. The Ifa religion is a traditional religion that has been practiced in West Africa since ancient times. It is now primarily practiced in Nigeria, Ghana, Togo, and Benin. Ifa emphasizes the importance of nature and the environment and teaches that humans can live in harmony with the world by practicing a respectful way of life. The Obeah religion is an African traditional religion primarily practiced in Jamaica and other Caribbean islands. It combines the Yoruba religion and West African religious elements with Christianity and other influences. One of its central deities is Olodumare. The African traditional religions are related religions practiced in many African countries. Most worship Olodumare, but some also worship Orungan and Obatala.

How Do Followers Worship Olodumare?

Followers of Olodumare pray to him for guidance and to help them to live harmonious and compassionate lives. They often pray for healing and guidance in health-related issues. Although no specific shrines are dedicated to him (because he didn't come to earth, we don't know what he looks like), followers of Olodumare often create shrines dedicated to him and other Orishas. These shrines are usually found in people's houses who practice the Orisha religion. They will light candles, pour out libations, and pray to the Orishas. Often, they leave gifts, like sweets or flowers, as an offering to the Orishas. Some also offer animal sacrifices to their Orishas, but this is not a general practice.

How Do Followers Connect to Olodumare?

There are many ways to connect to Olodumare. One is to follow any of the religions that worship him. Another is to meditate on his name and ask to be guided by him. Other ways are praying to him or reading about his creation and deeds. You may feel disconnected from the divine if you feel something missing in your life, like not being fulfilled or happy. You don't have to go through life feeling like a part of you is missing. You can connect with the divine in many ways, but you should do whatever method works.

Bondye

In the beginning, there was darkness, chaos, and noise. We may not know how or when the world was created, but we do know that the Haitians had a lot to say about it. Since the Haitian religion is derived from a different culture and region, their supreme god's origin story differs from Olodumare. Bondye, also known as Gran Mèt or Grand Maître, is the supreme creator of all things. Our understanding of this Vodou deity is limited as most resources only give a general overview of his role in the Vodou ritual. However, with further research, you can understand why this complex belief system provides such rich symbolism for the followers.

Who Is Bondye?

The majority of Haitians practice Voodoo, a West African-based religion that combines elements of African spirituality and Catholicism. One of the most important figures in the Vodou pantheon is Bondye, a creator god who is often equated with God in Christianity or other religions. However, there is no devil equivalent. It is often depicted as an old man with a long beard and hair that extends to the ground. He is the source of all things and the benefactor of all humanity.

The Symbolic Meaning of Bondye

Bondye is often depicted with a conch shell symbolizing his voice, which he used to create the world. He has two other symbols; a jar of fire and a blue cross. Bondye's symbols represent his power to create life and light. His colors are black and white because darkness and light have opposite qualities representing the duality of all things.

Bondye's role is to create everything that exists in the world, including people, animals, and material things like plants and minerals. From his throne at the center of the world, he oversees all that happens on Earth, giving it shape and form by making it rain and giving life by giving the sunlight to shine upon it. When someone prays to him, they invoke his power so their wishes can come true.

Bondye is also considered a protector against evil forces like voodoo curses and an oracle who helps people communicate with spirits from beyond this world. In addition, he is a judge who decides who lives and dies on Earth for good or bad deeds done in life.

The name Bondye comes from the French words *bon* and *dye*, meaning "good god." Similar to Olodumare, Bondye isn't involved in the affairs of mankind, so he created the Lwas to assist and be an intermediary between him and humans. It could be that Bondye's lack of involvement is due to his disinterest. However, Bondye, like Olodumare, represents many complexities often associated with supreme deities. He is far too complicated for the human mind to interact with or grasp. He is beyond our understanding. So, he created the Lwas, who are simple yet divine entities. Lwas are imperfect beings with many flaws, just like humans. This begs the question, did Olodumare and Bondye create the Orishas and Lwas to be imperfect on purpose? The gods probably intended for the entities people interact with daily to be relatable.

How Did Bondye Create the World?

The first things Bondye created were spirits (Lwas). These were created to help guide people get through difficult times in life.

After creating spirits, Bondye created humans. When people were born, they came out from Bondye himself. People may have had different skin colors or facial features depending on which part of Bondye they came from.

Next, Bondye made Earth. He made plants grow from seeds and placed animals on the Earth. Then he created islands and mountains to protect his creations from demons and evil spirits. Finally, he turned himself into the night and spread darkness over everything to keep evil away.

When people worship Bondye, they believe they are taking part in a cosmic dance of creation. They are creating their own world with Bondye's help. Along with Bondye, the people who worship him are also participating in their world's creation. You are making your place to live where you can feel comfortable and safe.

Lwa

The spirits belonging to Bondye are different from the Orisha of Olodumare. For example, the Lwa are ancestors who were once human. The Orishas were gods and goddesses and separate beings from their followers.

This difference also includes creating Lwa or Loa, who embody Haitian values to share their wisdom with others. The Lwa are powerful healers and protectors. They help keep people safe and guide them on their path in life. For example, if someone is having a hard time at work or school, a spirit might come along with advice about how to deal with it or protect themselves from further harm. In addition, when someone is in danger, the spirit can help them find a way out of the situation or contact emergency services to help them escape as quickly as possible. Bondye spirits can also have different personalities. Some spirits have more power than others, but it all depends on your connection to that spirit and your willingness to work with and command it.

How Do Followers Worship Bondye?

Vodou ranges from simple activities like the performance of spirit possession to more complex rituals like the consecration of an altar or an offering for a specific Lwa (spirit). Followers worship Bondye through a series of rituals, often involving drumming, dancing, singing, and a trance-like state. During this ritual, followers can communicate with their ancestors' spirits and Bondye.

How Do Followers Connect to Bondye?

Haitian Vodou followers connect to their gods or ultimate power through various methods. In some cases, these methods reflect the religious beliefs of the follower, while in others, they may be more personal or idiosyncratic. Common methods include prayer and ritualized dancing, such as the sabbat. In addition, many Haitian Vodou practitioners use herbs and herbal remedies to connect with their gods. Depending on individual followers' needs, these methods can be used alone or combined with another. While no single method is inherently superior to another, each has advantages and disadvantages. Some are more effective for people at certain times, while others could have a more lasting impact on overall spiritual well-being.

Why Is Bondye Important?

The story behind Haitian Vodou's supreme creator, Bondye, is intriguing, complex, and of great importance to those following this religion. The creation story of Bondye and his two helpers is a beautiful example of how diverse cultures can blend together and produce something unique. Bondye is the supreme creator of all things, good and evil, to the Haitian Vodou followers. The story of his creation takes us back to a time when chaos reigned. It is a story of light emerging from darkness and order emerging from chaos.

Why Do These Religions Need a Supreme Creator?

African religions follow a supreme creator for several reasons, including that these religions were likely born out of a period of social disruption. In other words, they were created to preserve cultural identity. As people were moving around and changing their lifestyles, they had to devise new ways to explain who they were and where they came from. It's also possible that Africans were naturally more inclined to believe in a supreme Creator than their non-African counterparts. Even if this isn't true, it doesn't mean that belief in a supreme Creator doesn't make sense. African cultures have always been known for their strong spiritual beliefs and connection to the land. So, it makes sense for them to believe in something like a supreme Creator.

African religions follow a supreme god for several reasons:

- These religions emerged on the continent, and African people have an affinity for their ancestral gods
- Many African gods share similarities with other world religions, making them familiar and approachable
- These religions often have a large following across the continent, providing an anchor point for people to gather and organize

These are a few of the reasons African religions follow a supreme god. Others include space limitations, lack of familiarity with other deities, and cultural influences. All these factors significantly impacted African religious development.

The supreme creator god concept comes from African religions. Their beliefs center on a single god who created all things or a group of gods who are the highest and most powerful of their kind.

These supreme creator gods are much greater than humans and often have different names in different cultures. They're almost always separate from nature. They can continue to reside outside the natural world or simply be apart from it until they reclaim it again or send their followers back to it in the future.

Mankind owes everything to the supreme deities. They created the universe and breathed life into all living creatures. Although they exist far from the people, we can never accuse them of abandoning their creation. They left the world in the care of the Orishas and Lwas, who have never ceased to provide support and guidance. Whether the gods are involved or not, they exist in all their creations.

Chapter 4: The Lwa and the Orishas

As you learn more about African spiritual practices, the terms Lwa and Orishas will come up quite often. It's easy to confuse them since they share many similarities. However, there is one key difference separating the two. The Lwa are spirits in Voodoo and Haitian religions, while the Orishas are gods in the Yoruba religion. This chapter provides detailed information about the Lwa and the Orishas and their similarities and differences.

The Orishas are gods in the Yoruba religion.
Omoeko Media, CC BY-SA 4.0 <https://creativecommons.org/licenses/by-sa/4.0>, via Wikimedia Commons
https://commons.wikimedia.org/wiki/File:Orishas_in_Oba%27s_palace,_Abeokuta.jpg

The Lwa

The word "Lwa" means spirits, but these entities are no ordinary spirits. They are divine beings who are significant in Voodoo and Haitian practices. However, unlike the Orishas, they aren't gods. The Lwas or Loas are intermediary spirits who travel between heaven and earth to deliver mankind's messages to Bondye, the creator god in Haitian and Voodoo religions. No one knows how many Loas exist. They could be infinite since there are ones we aren't aware of, but there are about a thousand Loas in Voodoo. They are divided into families, like the Guede, Petwo Lwa, and Rada Lwa. Each family differs in its music, rituals, offerings, and dances.

According to Haitian Voodoo beliefs, Loas are everywhere around us in the natural world. They exist in plants, mountains, rivers, trees, etc. Loas are helpful spirits associated with various aspects of nature, like wind and rain, and assist mankind in many daily activities like farming, fighting, and healing for the sick. However, they are more than just helpful spirits. They are powerful enough to change someone's destiny. They don't have a specific form since they are spirits. They usually appear to people by possessing a willing person during a ritual to interact with the attendees.

Some Loas were originally spirits of the dead, but many come from African gods and goddesses. They reside with the spirits of the dead in a place called the Vilokan. Legba, a prominent male Lwa, stands guard at the gates of the Vilokan. No one is allowed to communicate with a Lwa or any spirits in Vilokan without his permission. In Voodoo practices, practitioners call upon their Lwas to ask for help. They appease them by making various offerings like drinks or food.

During slavery and after the arrival of Christianity, enslaved people living in places like Louisiana and Haiti didn't abandon their pagan beliefs. They combined Lwas with some of the Catholic saints. Refusing to give up their religion was a form of rebellion against the oppression they faced. Holding on to their beliefs and history was their way of maintaining their identity.

Venerating Loas

Unlike Bondye, the Loas were more involved in people's daily lives. Although from the outside, the relationship between mankind and the Lwa seems demanding since humans serve them, it is still a very satisfying relationship. Loas significantly impact Voodoo practices, and serving them is one of the religion's main activities. Although the Loas are helpful and giving, they also have a dark side that can easily be avoided. Honoring the Loas and presenting them with offerings can protect you from their wrath and punishment. The relationship between Loas and humans is mutually beneficial. Humans present them with offerings and devotions, and the Loas provide humans with protection, favors, blessings, and healing.

Voodoo practitioners highly revere the Loas, which is clear from how they *call on them*. They give them the same respect given an elderly person by calling them "Manman," meaning mother, "Papa," meaning father, and "Metrès," meaning mistress. Practitioners hold specific ceremonies for Loas. These ceremonies have a religious nature and usually occur in a Voodoo temple led by a priest or a priestess.

The Loas ritual ceremonies usually involve drumming, dancing, songs, praying, and tracing the Veve. The Veves are specific rituals where the participants draw symbols called "Veve." There are as many Veves as there are Loas since each Loa has one symbol or more associated with it. The purpose of these ceremonies is to invite them to accept the offerings. When the Lwa arrives at the ceremony, it possesses the priest or the priestess leading the ritual. In some rare cases, it possesses one of the attendees. Possession allows the Loa to communicate with the worshipers. It is the perfect opportunity for them to ask their Loa questions or favors.

Possession isn't a negative experience or a forceful one like in the movies. The Loa don't mean any harm; it answers the people's calls and prayers and possesses a willing host. It provides guidance and healing. Since the word possession has a negative connotation, many people use the term "mount" instead.

The Pantheon of the Lwa

Loas are categorized into families with their characteristics and responsibilities. This part of the chapter focuses on the three most significant Loas families: Rada Lwa, Ghede Lwa, and Petro Lwa.

The Rada Lwa

The Rada Lwa originated in West Africa. It is a family of spirits or deities known for their creativity and calm and kind nature. Although the Rada Loas have a cool temper, some have similar aspects to the aggressive characteristics of the Petro Lwa. These Loas were highly revered among the enslaved people brought to America. Many Rada Loas were integrated into Christianity and associated with various saints.

One of the most significant figures in the Rada Lwa pantheon is Papa Legba. Although he is a very powerful spirit, he is known to be mischievous and a trickster that can even trick fate. People struggling with a difficult decision or requiring a change in their lives call upon Legba for guidance. All rituals should begin with invoking Legba since he is the gatekeeper of the supernatural world and the intermediary between mankind and the Loas. In some places in Africa, Legba is considered a fertility god. In others, he is the guardian of children. He is often associated with Saint Peter, the gatekeeper of Christianity's heaven.

Dambala is another prominent figure, and he is Legba's rival. According to African myth, Dambala was the first Lwa Bondye created, and he assisted Bondye with creating the universe. Hence, he is considered a father figure for mankind. His image is of a white serpent. Legends state that he shed his skin to create valleys and mountains. Dambala represents wisdom, healing magic, and knowledge. He lives between the sea and the earth and is also associated with Saint Patrick.

Erzulie is a female Lwa associated with the colors pink and blue. She is the goddess of love and beauty and symbolizes sensuality and femininity. She is invoked by women struggling with issues related to feminine sexuality or motherhood. Erzulie is associated with the Christianity theme Lady of Sorrows because she is constantly grieving for what she can't have and often weeps at the end of rituals.

Loco, the patron of healers, and his wife Ayizan, the ruler of commerce, are considered prominent Loas in the Rada Loa pantheon. They are the parents of the spiritual priesthood since they were the first priest and priestesses.

Ghede Lwa

The Ghede Lwa pantheon is associated with sexual desire and death. They are responsible for delivering the spirits of the dead to the underworld. These Loas are known for their obscene behavior, like making inappropriate jokes or provocative dance moves. Although they are associated with death, they are known for enjoying and celebrating life.

Baron Samedi is the superior Lwa of the Ghede Lwa pantheon. He is the Lwa of death and is extremely powerful. He greets the spirits of the dead and guides them on their journey to the other world. Baron Samedi is depicted as a corpse covered in black cloth, which is the traditional Haitian burial custom. He is the protector of cemeteries and is highly revered yet feared among Voodoo followers. Similar to his family, Baron Samedi enjoys swearing, making crude jokes, drinking, and smoking. He is known for his multiple affairs with mortal women, even though he is married to the female Lwa Manman Brigitte. He doesn't only help the dead but the living, too. He can lift curses, heal the sick, and resurrect the dead. People invoke him to help the sick and dying.

Petro Lwa

Petro or Petwo Lwa isn't as old as the other families since they originated from Haiti. They are the hot-tempered and aggressive Loas, unlike the Rada and Gehde. For this reason, they can be invoked for dark practices and magic. Categorizing Petro Lwa as evil may be naive since many of its Loas are invoked in rituals to provide assistance rather than harm.

The Orishas

The Orishas or Orisas are minor deities or spirits from the Yoruba religion. Similar to the Loas, they act as mediators between the Yoruba supreme god Olodumare and mankind. Like in Voodoo, the supreme deity isn't directly involved with people and their affairs. It is the Orishas who assist them in their daily activities. The simple human mind will never comprehend the complexity of Olodumare, so he created the Orishas as different aspects of himself. There aren't as many Orishas as there are Loas since there are only 401 Orishas. When enslaved people of Yoruba reached America and were introduced to Christianity, they combined the Orishas with Catholic Christian saints, like the Loas.

For this reason, countries like Brazil and Cuba refer to Orishas as Saints or Santos. Another similarity with the Loas is that many Orishas were once the spirits of the dead. However, these were the spirits of wise and intellectual individuals.

Practitioners invoke the Orishas to seek guidance, assistance, and enlightenment. Many people worldwide, like Wiccans, Neo-Pagans, and Santeria followers, worship the Orishas and incorporate them into their rituals. Orishas are depicted in human forms and can appear to people through possessions like the Loas.

The main purpose of Orishas is to assist mankind without selfish gain. However, Orishas have a personality and characteristics with strengths and weaknesses, which make them closer to humans than gods. As a result, they defy their purpose, and instead of assisting, they focus on their own personal gains. Neither mankind nor the Orishas are perfect, and they can succumb to their dark side and become arrogant, envious, or proud. In one legend, the Orishas rebelled against Olodumare by refusing to follow his orders because they believed they should rule the universe since they were more involved in mankind's affairs. When Olodumare found out, he stopped the rain, causing drought and death to the lands and crops. This was a tough lesson for the Orishas, who repented and begged Olodumare for forgiveness. Although their human-like qualities got them into trouble with Olodumare, these qualities made them relatable among practitioners. They aren't perfect beings detached from humanity. They are flawed, making it easy for people to identify and sympathize with them.

Similar to Loas, the Orishas exist in nature and accept offerings of food and drinks. Each Orisha is associated with a color and number and has favorite offerings. By understanding the Orishas and their personalities, you can tailor the right offering to each so they can recognize it. Orishas rule over nature, and you can learn about their personalities and temperament by watching the force of nature they represent.

Venerating the Orishas

Rituals that involve dancing and drumming help practitioners communicate with Orishas. Similar to Lwa, an Orisha will mount the priest leading the ritual, referred to as trance possession. Trance possession is largely significant in venerating the Orishas in the Santeria religion. A ceremony is held for the Orishas, called a bembé (drumming party). The purpose of these ceremonies is the same as the Loas' - to invite an Orisha to mount any attending priests.

Specific songs and dances are performed during these ceremonies to entice the Orisha to join. Whoever the Orisha chooses to mount is considered a great honor and a blessing for this person. Like Loas, Orishas only mount priests or priestesses. However, if they mount (possess) one of the attendees, it strongly signifies that this person should become a priest or priestess. During trance possession, attendees can communicate with the Orisha. Mounting is a joyful experience that leaves the person wiser and in awe of being the host to such a powerful being.

You can revere Orishas and Loas together or only the Orishas since they can replace the Loas in many rituals.

The Pantheon of the Orishas

Unlike the Loas, the pantheon of the Orishas looks different since they aren't categorized into families. This part of the chapter focuses on the most significant Orishas in Yoruba and Sanitaria.

Eshu

Eshu or Elegba, similar to Papa Legba, is the god of trickery and mischief. He has the same powers as the Norse god Loki, but Eshu isn't as evil as his counterpart and doesn't harm mankind or other gods. He acts as a messenger between mankind and the spirit world. Eshu is favored by Olodumare since he helped him during the Orisha rebellion. Eshu was the one who told Olodumare the Orishas weren't following his orders. In another story, Olodumare is terrified of mice, so the Orishas decide to take advantage of this weakness and scare him to death so they could rule in his place. Their plan almost worked, but Eshu interfered and rescued Olodumare, who punished the Orishas involved and rewarded Eshu. Eshu's reward was to do whatever he wanted with no consequences to his actions, allowing him the freedom to perform many tricks and pranks.

Shango

Like the Norse god Thor, Shango or Chango in Santeria is the god of Thunder. He controls lightning and thunder and is associated with magic, masculinity, and sexuality. He is married to three Orishas; Oba, Oya, and Oshun. Practitioners call upon him to lift hexes and curses. He is associated with Saint Barbra in Christianity.

Oya

Oya is the protector of the dead and is associated with cemeteries, ancestors, and the weather. She rules over all the dead, including animals and plants. Oya is the goddess of change and, like the weather, is constantly changing and never remains in the same state for long. Oya is also a fierce warrior, often fighting by her husband's side in battle. She is tied with Saint Teresa in Christianity.

Oshun

Oshun is the Orisha of the rivers, fertility, love, and marriage. She governs all relationships and is associated with genitals and feminine beauty. Oshun's role was crucial in the legend when Olodumare caused drought in response to the Orishas' rebellion. The Orishas repented for their actions and wept to beg Olodumare to bring back the rain. However, their voices never reached him. Oshun decided to deliver the Orishas' repentance message to Olodumare and beg him to forgive them. She transformed into a peacock and took a long journey to Olodumare. However, she flew too close to the sun and burned her wings. She succeeded in delivering the message even though she lost her wings and fell sick. Olodumare was impressed by her courage and persistence, healed her, and replaced her burned peacock wings with the wings of a vulture. He bestowed an honor upon her by making her the only Orisha to deliver him messages. Oshun corresponds with Our Lady of Charity, an aspect of the Virgin Mary.

Orunmila

Ornumilla or Ornula is the Orisha of wisdom, knowledge, and divination. He is the only Orisha who doesn't interact with mankind through Terrance's possession or mounting. Practitioners communicate with him through divination. Ornumilla is one of the oldest Orishas and has been around since the beginning of time and witnessed the creation of mankind. Therefore, he knows the fate of mankind and each soul's past, present, and future. Practitioners invoke Ornumilla to gain insight into what the future holds and to learn if their actions will help them to achieve their destiny. He is associated with St. Joseph, St. Philip, and St. Francis of Assisi in Christianity.

Yemaya

Yemaya is the protector of women and the Orisha of seas, mystery, and lakes. She is regarded as a mother figure since she is associated with motherhood. She is the mother of the Orishas, so she is one of the most revered Orishas in the pantheon. She resembles Our Lady of Regala from Catholic Christianity.

Osain

Osain is the god of nature. He governs the forests and has powers over herbs giving him the power to heal. He is the protector of homes and is associated with hunting. Osain used to look like a regular man, but after he lost an eye, ear, leg, and arm, he looked like a cyclops with his other eye in the center of his forehead. He also uses a tree branch to help him walk. He is associated with several Christian saints like St. Joseph, St. John, St. Benito, and St. Ambrose.

Obaluaye

Obaluaye is the god of miracles and healing. Although he is a healer, Obaluaye also has the power to curse people. Hence, people are terrified and respect him. Practitioners invoke him to heal the sick, especially those gravely ill.

Oba

Oba is the Orisha of rivers, and she symbolizes water. She represents energy, flexibility, manifestation, restoration, movement, and protection. She is Yemaya's daughter and one of Shango's three wives. Oba is responsible for the flow of time, which is why people turn to her when they feel stagnant and unable to achieve their goals. Oba and her sisters Oya and Oshun provide safe waters to the people they need to survive. In some places in Africa, she is the protector of prostitutes, and in Brazil, she is the Orisha of love.

The Loas and Orishas are more alike than they are different. They have human qualities and aren't regarded as perfect beings who can do no wrong. Both entities are relatable because they are guided by their emotions and have weaknesses that can get them into trouble. People feel close to them because, like us, they also suffer, struggle, fall, and get up again.

Both entities were created to help and serve humans, so they deserve to be highly revered. They must always be acknowledged for their existence and show gratitude to ensure their blessings' continuation. The Orishas and Loas need humans just as humans need them. People need assistance from the Lwa and Orishas daily; these entities depend on human acknowledgment and offerings to survive.

Chapter 5: Santeria and the Saints

Due to the similarities between the Orisha's worship and the representation of its saints, Santeria is often compared to its parent religion, Yoruba. However, unlike the Yoruba traditions regarding deities, Santeria's religious syncretism means that spirits are represented by Catholic saints. After colonization, enslaved people brought to the New World were forced to convert to Christianity. However, because there were many similarities between the deities of African religions and Christian saints, the enslaved people could maintain their beliefs by merely renaming their gods. They could continue worshiping them and also created another religion called Santeria. This chapter is dedicated to Santeria, its saints, and how they are celebrated through their different correspondences.

Santeria worship can be done through an altar or symbolization with a statue or doll. Ji-Elle, CC BY-SA 4.0 <https://creativecommons.org/licenses/by-sa/4.0>, via Wikimedia Commons https://commons.wikimedia.org/wiki/File:Trinidad-Santer%C3%ADa_(1).jpg

What Is Santeria?

Santeria is a religion born out of a combination of an African religion called "Regla Ocha de Los Yorubas" and Catholicism. Due to this, it accepts and mixes rigorous Christian traditions and free-flowing pagan Yoruba practices. Santeria means "The way of the saints" or the "the way of worshiping the saints." The saints in question are also identified as Orishas or Lwas in different African religions. However, the Orishas and the spirits (Lwas and the Santeria saints) are viewed differently, which is notable in how they are worshiped. Where Orishas are depicted as deities who only answer to the Supreme Being, the spirits have no divine qualities.

Santeria encompasses two main concepts, Ache (the divine power) and ebbo (sacrifice). By connecting with Ache, practitioners can achieve any spiritual goals. Most Santeria rituals help obtain Ache, which, in turn, helps find answers to questions, guidance, or whatever you need. On the other hand, ebbo is a sacrifice made to the Orishas (saints) when asking them for a specific favor. These favors are usually related to witchcraft and ailments. The offerings include flowers, candles, fruit, and other food and drink.

Santeria is a unique system, as it represents a decentralized religion, meaning practitioners have no specific places for worship. There are no predetermined ways to honor the deities, doctrines to follow, or rules to conduct rituals. When a practitioner has a need, they call on a saint (Orisha) and ask for guidance, assistance, or whatever they require. They also offer gratitude or make sacrifices and offerings before and after receiving the blessings. How this is done can differ from one practitioner to another, indicating that it's a highly intuitive practice.

Apart from worshiping the saints, followers of Santeria also practice ancestral veneration and believe there is a possibility to communicate with ancestral spirits and the different forces of nature. Whether you want to evoke a saint, ancestral, or other spirits, the best way is through an altar dressed for the occasion. A symbol of the saint is needed when calling on them. It can be a picture or a statute. The altar is covered with a cloth in the color associated with the saint. The other elements (candles, elements of nature, offerings symbols) are linked to the Orisha. If you're addressing another spirit, like the ancestors, the altar is dressed in their favorite colors, offerings, and symbols.

The Saints of Santeria

While the number of saints (deities) you can work with in Santeria practices is vast, a few can be particularly helpful for beginners. Below, you'll find a few you can connect with. You must approach them respectfully and follow through by thanking them when receiving their help. If you aren't sure which saint you should contact, meditate with their symbols to see which resonates with you. Reading about their powers can help determine who can assist you with your needs or requests. Once you've found the entity whose power you need to connect with, prepare to approach them. Working with Santeria saints requires practice. You need to get close to them to understand them.

Understanding them will help you prepare adequate offerings, please them, and harness their power to uncover higher wisdom.

Mary - Yemaya

Known as Yemalla and the Star of the Sea, Yemaya represents the Santerian aspect of the divine trinity. She is the goddess of salty waters, where life comes from, so she is considered the mother of the world. Yemaya also rules over the moon and guides the sailors and fishermen traveling through the seas and oceans. The goddess is associated with witchcraft, fertility, children, and women. She represents the Virgin Mary and is often called Our Lady of Rule in prayers.

Besides prayers, Mary can be invoked through meditation, visualization, and several other techniques when you need help with fertility issues, pregnancy, and children's illnesses. She can accompany you on a journey across the sea or ocean and grant you safe travel. Invoke Yemaya on the Saturday before your trip to ensure the best results. Her colors are white and blue, so use these to decorate your altar and wear them on your travels. Using white and blue crystal beads, you can make a charm that harnesses Yemaya's protective powers.

You can perform several rituals to call on Yemaya - use them for meditation, affirmation, or when asking for help, guidance, or healing. Here is a simple one:

- Make an offering of fruit - bananas, pineapples, and other tropical fruit work best, but you can also use whatever is in season
- Place the offering in a bowl (or large seashell if you can find one) on your altar
- Put a bowl of salty water next to the offering
- Place seven coins around the bowls in a circle. These represent how many days are between the moon's two phases
- Look at the water, and say the following:

   "Mary, you are grace,

   You're enlightenment,

   You are blessed among women,

   And so is the fruit of your womb.

   Bless me, mother of all

   Help me now throughout this journey."

- Practitioners often combine a similar version of the prayer to Mary (Hail Mary) with a rosary. If you feel comfortable, you can repeat this prayer several times using rosary beads.
- When you have finished with this prayer, in your words, tell the goddess what help you need
- End with an expression of gratitude for granting her power

Las Mercedes - Obatala

As the second aspect of the divine trinity, Obatala represents the male counterpart of Mary. Known as Our Lady of Mercy, Obatala was the one who brought life to earth. He was the first saint (deity) ever created by Olodumare, implying that he is the wisest of all. He can chase away negative energies and protect the fathers, just as Yemaya protects mothers and their children.

Obatala's color is white, meaning any offerings and representations would be presented in this color. Traditional offerings to this deity include rice, milk, coconut, yams, cascarilla, white hens and doves, and cotton. Offerings made and prayers requesting assistance should be recited on Sunday.

Calling on Obatala is helpful when you need to communicate your negative feelings toward others or eliminate negativity from your life. Using a white, seven-day candle will ensure you acquire purity in mind and body and obtain your goals.

You need the following:
- Yams
- Rice
- Milk
- Coconut shavings
- Cascarilla - fresh or dry
- A piece of white cotton yarn
- A white, seven-day candle
- A representation of the saint

Instructions:
1. Organize your altar or sacred space by clearing away anything not required for this ritual.

2. Place the white candle and a symbol representing Obatala onto your altar.
3. Prepare the rice, milk, coconut, and yams in separate bowls and place them on the altar.
4. If using fresh or whole dried cascarilla, tie the plant into a bunch with white cotton yarn.
5. If using chopped dry leaves, spread them around the candle and tie the yarn around the bottom of the candle.
6. When ready, light the candle, close your eyes, and prepare to call on Our Lady of Mercy.

    Then, recite the following spell:

    "Oh great Lady of Mercy, please lend me your power,

    Send me patience and knowledge.

    May I be strong and wise,

    So I can pursue my passions.

    Help me stay fair and caring,

    To treat others with great integrity."
7. The candle should burn for seven days. The best practice is to leave it burning only during the time you can supervise it and focus on gathering the saint's energy.
8. Snuff the candle out when you have finished your prayer and go about your day. Relight it when you can supervise it until it burns out.

Saint Barbara - Chango

Representing the third aspect of the divine trinity is Chango, the patron of transformation, fire, and merriment. He rules over thunder and lighting, through which he provides immense power. Saint Barbara was an innocent young woman who became the protector of souls who suffered wrongful deaths after being killed by her father when she converted to Christianity. Chango is a spirit who empowers people seeking revenge or wanting to take back something stolen from them. According to the lore, her father was struck by lightning when Saint Barbara died. Hence the connection between this seemingly unlikely pairing.

Chango's colors are white and red. Friday is the best day to pray to her or ask for her assistance. On this day, you can reclaim your power using Chango's power. Here is a practice to help you with this endeavor.

You'll need the following:
- Red and white prayer beads (98 in total)
- Paper and pen
- Red candle

Instructions:
1. Make a ring of the beads, starting with a white stone. Then add six red ones, followed by six white ones, and finish the sequence with a red one.
2. Repeat the pattern six times.
3. Write affirmations for each bead on the ring. Ensure they are positive statements and write them in the present tense as if you already had whatever you wished for.
4. Adorn your altar using white and red decorations, Saint Barbara symbols, swords, lightning bolts, a cup, and a red candle.
5. On a Friday night, light the candle and say as many affirmations as you can while remaining focused and counting down the beads.
6. Repeat the steps for 24 consecutive Fridays leaving offerings of apples, bananas, anise, red okra, and red wine to Chango.

Saint Anthony - Eleggua

Whereas Eleggua is the messenger of the deities in the Yoruba pantheon, Saint Anthony reconciles people who have lost touch or had a disagreement with each other. Eleggua can open the door to divine wisdom and make people hear what they would otherwise miss. Before invoking another saint, you must first call on Saint Anthony (Eleggua) to ensure your message will be sent. For example, you can say:

"Eleggua, I ask you to open the doors for me,

To remove the barrier between this world and the spiritual realm

So I can pass my message through."

Since Eleggua is also linked to protection, you can harness his power to ward off negative energies. His colors are red and black, so use beads, flowers, or decorations in this color to make a charm or talisman. Place this on your front door to protect your home, or take it with you to safeguard your person.

You can also offer rum, cigars, coconut, smoked fish, other red and white food and drink, candy, and toys on Mondays to evoke Eleggua. It will come in handy if you need a specific favor.

You need the following:
- A brown candle
- A representation of the saint or deity
- An assortment of canned food

Instructions:
1. Start by lighting the candle and saying the following:

   "Saint Anthony, you who are always ready to help those in trouble,

   I ask you to empower me with what I need to do.

   My request may be grand, but I have faith in you.

   Please grant me this favor, and I will be eternally grateful."
2. Visualize your message being carried upward through the candle smoke and traveling toward the spiritual realm.
3. Let the candle burn out, take the canned food and offer it to someone in need, whether a food bank or a specific person.

Saint Joseph - Osain

The husband of Mary, Saint Joseph, has a clear connection to Osain, the nature god of the Yoruba. Despite often depicted as a frail person relying on a crutch, Saint Joseph can be a powerful ally. He answers all the prayers dedicated to him, especially if coming from the heart. He is the patron of homes, carpenters, other hand laborers, fathers, those who die happy, and parents who take in children needing a loving home.

Osain is associated with nature and the forest and empowers healing herbs. According to Santeria, if you pray to him while foraging, he will help you find the plants to ward off evil spirits and their effects. However, Saint Joseph oversees everything vulnerable, so you must ask his permission before removing any plant or herb from its natural habitat.

A ritual performed in the name of Saint Joseph can help grant his ashe to assist you in protection or healing. He favors the color yellow, and offering food and other items in this color on a Thursday makes the ritual even more powerful.

For this ritual, you need the following:
- A yellow candle
- Pine incense (to represent nature)
- A symbol (picture or statute) of Saint Joseph
- Plant parts you find in a forest, like pine cones, cedar needles, blackberry thorns, etc.
- A small bag

Instructions:
1. Place the candle and the incense on your altar in front of the symbol and light them.
2. Take the symbol into your hands, and move it over the incense smoke while saying:

   "By the power of this candle's fire and the smoke of pine

   May my home be protected from evil spirits.

   Saint Joseph, please heed my prayer.

   As all green things grow

   And heal with your help,

   May I be guarded by your ashe

   Please protect my home and those who are inside."
3. Place the plant parts into the bag, and finish the ritual with this prayer:

   "Our protector, Saint Joseph,

   Grant me relief from spiritual harm

   I implore you to protect this home from evil."
4. Place the bag with the plant parts in front of your home by hanging it up or burning it partially in the ground to secure it in place.

Our Lady of Charity - Oshun

Also known as the Our Lady of Caridad del Cobre, Oshun is one of the most influential saints and deities. She is the goddess of love, fertility, rebirth, renewal, pleasure, marriage, sexuality, art, and finances. Oshun can grant you fertility in all areas of life and is known to be very charitable, which explains why she is linked to Our Lady of Charity.

Oshun is often evoked on Fridays. However, she is the most powerful on September 8 and celebrated with an enormous feast on this day. Despite being compassionate, she can be easily angered. To avoid making her lose her temper, she must be appeased regularly. She loves gold and lavish decorations, so if you want to address her, this is how you should adorn your altar. Gold-colored jewelry, gold, yellow or white candles, honey, white wine, rum cakes, pumpkins, and other yellow and white fruit and vegetables are her favorites.

Perform this ritual for Our Lady of Charity to attract love and prosperity.

You need the following:
- A piece of jewelry
- A nice metal dish
- A yellow or gold candle
- Honey
- A representation of the saint
- A piece of yellow cloth
- Paper and pen

Instructions:
1. Arrange the jewelry in the dish on your altar in front of the saint's representation.
2. Pour the honey over the jewelry and light the candle.
3. Focus on your intention and meditate on it. Think about why you want to attract that specific thing.
4. Extinguish the candle and go to sleep.
5. When you wake up the following morning, wrap the jewelry in a yellow cloth and pray to Oshun.
6. Next, write five lines reaffirming your intention (the reasons you decided on the previous night).
7. Fold the paper five times and place it beneath the candle used the previous night.
8. Light the candle again and offer another prayer to Oshun.
9. When you've finished, extinguish the candle.
10. Repeat the last step for five days, burn the paper, and bury its ashes in your garden or in a pot.

11. Be sure to thank the saint when your wishes have been granted.

Saint Peter - Oggun

Like Saint Peter is asked for help when a person needs work or wants to be successful in their workplace, Oggun provides the ashe for hard-working people. If you're willing to put in the effort, he will help you reach your professional goals. He is associated with the colors green and black. If you want to realize a new business venture or manifest a better job, adorn your altar with these colors. The best day to pray to Saint Peter is Tuesday. The best offerings for him are green food, rum, cigars, green leaves, and "hard-working" animals like a rooster that gets up early in the morning. Oggun is connected to the earth element, so you can use soil in your rituals.

For a simple ritual invoking Saint Peter, you need the following:
- A symbol of Saint Peter
- An iron cauldron or bowl
- Two keys (symbolizes the saint and the deity)
- Seven other pieces of iron (nails, small tools, etc.)
- Black and green cloth for the altar
- Black and green beads
- String
- Offerings of your choice
- Paper and pen

Instructions:
1. Make a circlet of the string and beads, starting with a black stone. Follow up with seven green beads, add seven black ones, and finish the sequence with a green one.
2. Repeat six times to have 112 beads on the circlet.
3. Write your intention on the paper, and tuck the paper under the green candle you placed on your altar.
4. Light the candle, and pray to Saint Joseph while visualizing your goal and going through the beads.
5. When you've finished, snuff out the candle and bury the paper in the soil.

The Santeria religion includes many saints represented by Catholic saints. These saints are of the highest order and demand due respect.

So, whenever you invoke them for favors or questions, you must do so with the utmost respect and gratitude.

Chapter 6: Honor Thy Ancestors

Ancestral veneration is a practice shared by various cultures. People who honor their ancestors through spiritual practices believe their loved ones exist in another realm. Most humans are only capable of seeing what is in the physical realm, and not everyone can witness spirits who have crossed the physical realm.

Honoring the ancestors is an integral part of African spirituality.
https://unsplash.com/photos/n_GkKJCGgBI

Therefore, people communicate with their ancestors through spiritual means. Of course, there are other reasons why honoring ancestors is a vital practice. This chapter thoroughly explains the nature of ancestral worship, how different spiritual practices view the ancestors, and how and why they honor them.

Ancestors: Who Are They? Why Should We Honor Them?

Defining the word "ancestors" may seem a bit absurd, but it is crucial to understand ancestral veneration truly.

When the word "ancestors" is mentioned, most people think of the family members who came before them; grandparents, great-grandparents, etc. In a strictly biological sense, to an extent, this is true. Your ancestors are the people who came before you and with whom you share a connection by blood.

However, the definition of ancestors becomes less about blood and more about connection with spiritual practices. It includes all connections made throughout a person's life, spiritual connections, connections made with guides or mentors, connections with loved ones, friends, and blood relatives.

Of course, some practitioners firmly believe that only blood relatives count as ancestors. There are no rigid rules in spirituality. Ultimately, it's about what aligns best with the practitioner.

According to African Theology, man is not just flesh. Humans have three layers, Ma, Ka, and Ba. Ma is the body, Ka is the energy force that moves the body, and Ba is the soul. However, when the body completes its earthly cycle, the soul is separated from it and returns to its divine realm. The soul of the physically dead person is still around, and you can communicate with it.

Honoring the dead is part of African culture. It is deeply ingrained. It is reflected in their spiritual practices regardless of how they vary. Dedicating specific days or hours to the ancestors is a celebration of their lives. It is how we pay respect to and honor them.

Ancestors are seen as protectors and wisdom givers. Many believe ancestors can help from the beyond. Their help can be whatever you need it to be. Are you looking to answer questions you do not have answers for? Ask your ancestors. Do you need guidance with a certain situation? Pray for your ancestors to guide you. Are you having trouble with your life lately? Ask your ancestors to help you through this difficult time.

The ancestors are perceived as divine and loving figures. They love you, and they watch over you from another realm. Trust that they have your best interest at heart. They will offer you wisdom and guidance whenever you need it.

So, it is important to keep up communication with your ancestors. Celebrating them on certain days shows you honor and respect them. It shows you appreciate what they do for you and that you are grateful. Honoring the ancestors on specific days or frequently communicating with them builds a strong relationship with them. The more you communicate or pray to your ancestors, the stronger you feel them around you. You'll feel their presence around you and feel their protection and warm embrace around you.

It is important to clarify that every African culture has its own way of honoring spirits from beyond. African spirituality is mostly viewed as a closed practice, meaning only people with African roots can engage in these practices. This also applies to practices within the culture. If you practice Haitian Voodoo, it may be best to honor your ancestors according to your beliefs.

However, some practices like Hoodoo and Haitian Voodoo allow outsiders to practice their beliefs and rituals. This only happens through a process of initiation conducted by certain priests. If you are not a member of either practice but feel connected to their teachings and rituals, it is best to research and consult the priests before joining. It is also vital to remain polite and respectful when addressing the priests. After all, these faiths are highly regarded and valued, so always be respectful.

Yoruba

Individuals who live according to the Yoruba religion, called Isese, have shrines for their ancestors. The ancestors can be related to you through blood, land, or history. Building a shrine or an altar is essential to connect with your ancestors. You'll go to the shrine whenever you need to pray for advice or guidance, as this is the designated meeting place you built for your spirit guides.

To build a shrine, you must first choose a surface. You can use a clean table or anything that can be used as a table top. It is preferable to place this table somewhere private in your apartment or home. You do not want interruptions when you are engaging with the energies.

You can place anything on it which is related to your ancestors when they were alive. It could be a piece of clothing, their favorite flower, leaves, pictures, etc. Place a clay plate or a seashell containing leaves or herbs.

Cleansing the altar physically and spiritually is vital. The place must be free of dust or clutter. It is considered disrespectful when the altar is placed in a dirty area. Spiritually cleansing the altar requires sage smoke or rosemary smoke. Set your heart and intentions in the right place as you energetically cleanse the altar. You must believe the smoke is getting rid of any wanted energies and is welcoming the spirits into a purified space. The spiritual cleansing must occur before and after your prayers.

It is also vital that you give offerings to the ancestors. The offerings could be as simple as a bowl of fruits, a white, lit candle, a cup of water, oils, etc. When you make offerings, you show appreciation and gratitude to the spirits. The offerings must proceed with a prayer. The prayer invites the spirits and lets them know these offerings are for them.

> "*E nle oo rami o. I am greeting you, my friends.*
>
> *Be ekolo ba juba ile a lanu. If the earthworm pays homage to the earth, the earth always gives it access.*
>
> *Omode ki ijuba ki iba pa a. A child who pays homage never suffers the consequences.*
>
> *Egun mo ki e o. Ancestors, I greet you.*
>
> *Egun mo ki e o ike eye. Ancestors, I greet you with respect.*
>
> *Ohun ti wu ba njhe lajule Orun. Whatever good things are being eaten in the realm of the ancestors.*
>
> *No mo ba won je. Eat my offering with them.*
>
> *J'epo a t'ayie sola n'igbale. Eat richly from the earth.*
>
> *Omo a t'ayie sola n-igbale. The children of the earth are grateful for your blessing.*
>
> *Ori Egun, mo dupe. I thank the wisdom of the ancestors.*
>
> *Ase. May it be so.*"

When you need guidance from the spirits, you must pray to them first. The prayer is done over the shrine and is part of the cleansing ritual. The prayer is said over the leaves to bless them.

> "*Iba se Egun. I pay homage to the Spirit of the Ancestors*
>
> *Emi (your name) Omo (list your lineage starting with your parents and working backward). I am (your name), child of (lineage)*

Iba se Ori Ewe. I pay homage to the Spirit of the Leaves
Ko si 'ku. Send away the Spirit of Death
Ko si arun. Send away illness
Ko si wahala. Send away all gossip
Ase. May it be so."

Burn the leaves over the shrine. The smoke can also be used to cleanse yourself. Guide the smoke to move from your feet to your head. When you feel the smoke has cleansed the shrine, say, "toe," which means enough.

Yoruba priests advise the people only to invite specific spirits to the shrine. They typically avoid inviting ancestors who struggled with or exhibited addictive behavior. The same goes for ancestors who engaged in any form of abuse. Yoruba priests say their energies could cause unwanted problems for the person who prays to them.

Finally, you must seal the shrine with a fragrance you often wear mixed with your saliva or bodily fluid belonging to you. This lets the spirits know you are at the shrine they are being invited to. When done, ask the spirits for guidance or do readings to receive answers from them.

Santeria

Santeria is similar to the Yoruba religion. People who practice Santeria also build a shrine to their ancestors. The components may be different, but the rituals are similar. Like Isese, Santeria originated in Nigeria, but it is practiced more in Cuba and the United States.

The word 'Santeria' is translated as *"the way of the saints."* The saints refer to the Orishas, known as African spirits or deities. Santeria revolves around praying to the saints and constantly honoring them. So, building a shrine to honor them is a vital step.

In Santeria, ancestors are referred to as Egun. An Egun can be related to people by blood or religion, meaning you do not have to limit your prayers to your family ancestors. You can pray to any ancestor who practiced Santeria. The shrine should include two main ingredients, sticks and offerings.

The sticks you place on your shrine come from a specific tree the priests have blessed. Ask your priest and receive nine sticks from them. Tie the nine sticks with a red cloth and place them on the altar.

Next, place the offering. The offering can be an animal sacrifice, food, or drink. All offerings must be placed around the sticks. If you are invoking a spirit, you must use an Opa egun - a straight, tall stick taken from a tree. If you are to summon a spirit, you must be male and slowly tap the floor with the stick to catch the ancestor's attention, and they can hear your prayers.

Eating after you have made your offerings is important when offering food and drink to the spirit. Otherwise, it is considered disrespectful. The offerings should always contain food and drink. The drink could be water or any alcohol or liquor. It is also tradition to sprinkle water or liquor on the shrine through the lips or fingertips.

Certain ceremonies must be conducted to honor the ancestors in Santeria. The ceremony takes a few days to complete. On the first day, people offer large quantities of cooked meals, animal offerings, and drinks. People also sing and dance to their ancestors. People sing, dance, and play drums on the second day to honor the spirits. Food is also served on that day.

During the ceremonies, the following prayer is said if a member wants to connect to their ancestor. The spirit of the ancestors mounts (or possesses) the mediums gently while a vulture flies over the ceremony like a snake. The ancestors possess power beyond the realms of death. We must sweep and clean the ground before greeting our ancestors upon their arrival.

> *"The spirit of death directs our Ori toward the ancestors who have obtained the secret of life beyond death. Today, I show the marks of my body as a hymn to the sacred oath. I offer my devotion to the ancestors through the oath. And I am blessed by your energy and your wisdom. Ashe."*

Fét Gede in Haitian Voodoo

Fét Gede, or Festival day of the dead, is an important celebration dedicated to honoring the ancestors. Haitian Voodoo believes the spirits are not seen on any other day and only appear during their ceremony.

The Gede or ancestor can be a close friend or a family member. During a ceremony, the Voodooist or Voodoo practitioner invokes their spirit and turns them into a Gede.

This festival happens every November first and second. It is usually conducted in the cemetery, and, like Santeria, it involves a lot of singing and dancing. The Gede may possess individuals during the festival.

If an individual is possessed, they will immediately be recognized because of their physical appearance. They usually dress their faces with white powder and may wear black sunglasses, and have a walking staff. They also wear purple, black, and white clothing. They drink alcoholic beverages infused with hot peppers since the Gede love spicy peppers. Many will eat or apply hot peppers to their skin during the festival.

The possessions are another way to honor the dead. It is one way, Voodooists show the spirits they are welcomed into their world, space, and bodies. Ideally, Gedes do not have bad intentions toward their person, so usually, no harm is done during the possession.

The possession also shows the strong bond between the person and Gede. Of course, not everyone is comfortable with possessions, but they are practiced, nonetheless. If you are interested in having this bond with your Gede, ask your priest to learn more.

Like Santeria and Isese, Haitian Voodooists offer food and drinks to their ancestors. The offerings must be placed on a table in the cemetery to honor and respect those who have passed to the spiritual realm.

The Haitian Voodoo celebration of the dead is similar to Santeria since they dance, sing, and drum to the dead. The priests also pay respects and eat the food offered to the dead. Unlike Santeria and Isese, possessions occur on the day of the festival.

The ceremony cannot be conducted unless permission is granted from Papa Gede, the first man ever to die. Once priests have permission to conduct the ceremony, the celebrations begin.

Hoodoo

Hoodoo is similar to Isese and honors the ancestors. A clean shrine must be established in a neat environment. It must be cleansed with salt water or sage smoke. The altar must have pictures of the ancestors or any item connected to them. Hoodoos communicate with their ancestors frequently.

Their communications can be through prayers or normal conversations. Of course, offerings must be made, and this is something Isese, Santeria, Haitian Voodoo, and Hoodoo have in common.

The offering can be a lit candle, food, drink, or a special item. The honoring ceremony might not be as loud as Santeria or Haitian Voodoo, but it is rich with deep feelings and emotions. Usually, Hoodooists ask the ancestors to take away illnesses or challenges that have been affecting their lives.

Hoodoos deeply connect with their ancestors because of their high communication level. Practitioners practice spiritual readings with their ancestors. They may get a yes, no, or maybe through a spiritual medium. Practitioners use corn shells, tarot cards, and other tools to understand what the spirits say.

They leave an animal sacrifice or a fruit basket next to a tree in the name of their ancestors. The tree should be close to the person's house and is yet another way of respecting and showing appreciation to the spirits.

Like Santeria, some practitioners sing to their ancestors. However, the songs are sung by one individual, usually during their private time with their ancestors. Practitioners light candles for the spirits and must energetically cleanse the space before and after a prayer, or a ceremony is conducted.

Honoring the ancestors is a sacred activity shared by many African Spiritual beliefs. No matter how different they are from one another, remembering the spirits is a divine practice conducted yearly or daily.

African spirituality revolves around the connection between the individual, nature, and spirits. This connection must be kept even when the living takes a different form. Therefore, it is essential that practitioners continue honoring the dead, so their connection remains strong and alive. The spirits are seen as deities who have wisdom and power. They are believed to influence your life for the better, so practitioners ask for their guidance and help.

African spiritual practices like Santeria and Isese do not see ancestors as only relatives. The ancestors can be anyone linked to the religion or the practitioner's history. On the other hand, Haitian Voodoo sees the ancestors as relatives or close friends. Isese is similar to Haitian Voodoo since it also defines ancestors by bloodline or their relationship to the practitioner.

Offerings are a common element between these beliefs. When people honor their spirits through offerings, it is seen as a way to welcome their ancestors, honor them, and show them respect. The tools used during the ceremony differ from one belief to the other. However, it does not matter what tools you use so long as your heart is in the right place when honoring your loved ones.

Whether you were born into African spiritual traditions through ancestral roots or an outsider with a deep sense of belonging, you must respect the faith's beliefs and adhere to its rules. The consequences of disrespect and arrogance will significantly impact your life negatively. These traditions have survived for centuries due to the followers' devout faith.

Chapter 7: Sacred Herbs and Plants

Herbalism is sacred knowledge, and African spiritualists are no strangers to it. Whether the root, stem, petals, or leaves, nearly every part of the plant is used in all spellwork. This chapter explains the different herbs heavily used by African practitioners. If you have been trying to find herbs for love or protection spells, you'll find them in this chapter. Other herbs are also explained to help with power, prosperity, purification, spirits, and lust.

Certain herbs and plants are considered to be sacred.
https://unsplash.com/photos/7LsyosoO0GQ

It is common to ingest certain herbs during ceremonies and spellwork. However, you must be careful what you are ingesting. For starters, it is probably best to avoid ingesting any herb or plant if you are a beginner spellcaster. If you do not know whether you are allergic to certain herbs or plants, you should avoid swallowing anything. You can always burn the herb instead of consuming it and see its power manifest.

Adam and Eve Root

The Adam and Eve root is mainly used for love spells. Its spiritual properties are associated with matters of love, connection, and lust. Practitioners anoint the root with attraction essential oils, like clary sage, lavender, jasmine, or rose.

This root is used on same-sex couples and opposite-sex couples. The Adam and Eve root can be worn as an amulet carried by the couple or anointed daily to strengthen the love and spice up the relationship.

Agrimony

Agrimony is a versatile herb. It is mainly used for protection purposes but also to remove energy blockages. This herb is typically used in protection spells and is the main ingredient practitioners use to break jinxes.

People practicing Hoodoo magic use agrimony to clear energetic blockages. They also use it to cleanse their tools before working on their spells. Burning agrimony is common for protecting themselves against the evil eye. Often, spiritualists use this herb as candle dressing when working on a spell that breaks gossip or stops people from badmouthing them. It is common for people to burn agrimony to strengthen their energetic field.

Basil

Basil is commonly used in all African witchcraft. It is associated with prosperity, luck, and happiness. Practitioners use it to invite prosperity into their lives and bring in more money. They anoint a green candle with dried basil leaves and cast a spell allowing money to flow smoothly toward them. Some people carry basil with them when gambling because it is seen as a lucky charm.

Other practitioners use basil as a healing herb. Besides curing and warding off illnesses, it also energizes the spellcaster since it helps with fatigue and brain fog. Female practitioners dress a red candle with basil oil to relieve painful menstruation.

Bay Leaves

Spiritualists from different backgrounds use this herb because of its high versatility. Some use it to draw in money, and others to cast against evil eyes, banish harmful spells, and release themselves from work and family problems. The outcome of this herb depends on the spell and how you use it.

It is common in African spirituality to wash with bay leaf water. It is believed that washing hands and feet with this water increases the chances of receiving money. Other practitioners save bay leaf water to cleanse their doors and mirrors. Why? Because it brings positive energy and gets rid of negativity entering the house.

Belladonna

Belladonna is an herb that must be used with caution. **It should not be ingested or inhaled in any way.** This herb is associated with hallucination, seduction, and magic. It is usually used in love spells and on voodoo dolls.

Beginner practitioners are advised against using it because of its power, and it is tricky to work with when you do not have enough experience with witchcraft.

Some voodooists stuff belladonna into voodoo dolls when working on a love spell. Usually, this spell involves increasing a person's allure to seduce them. Others merely carve the individual's name onto a red candle and anoint it with belladonna to attract them toward themselves.

Cedar

Cedar smoke is famous for sharpening psychic abilities and hearing from spirits. It is also known for its rejuvenation capabilities. Spiritualists use cedar to feel energized and heal from aching or tired bodies. Cedar is used for warding off illnesses, so it is common to be around cedar smoke when a spiritualist feels they are about to get sick.

Voodooists use cedar smoke to sanctify their voodoo dolls. This sanctification ritual is the last part of a voodoo doll creation. The cedar blesses the doll and protects it from any unwanted energies.

Cedar smoke is used to sharpen psychic abilities and ward off illness.
https://unsplash.com/photos/zI84PsYBODg

Chamomile

Chamomile is another highly versatile herb. Some practitioners use it to ensure their manifestations come true, while others use it to have better dreams.

African practitioners put chamomile in their Mojo bags to increase their winning chances in gambling. Others fill their sachets with chamomile and put them under their pillows to have better dreams and decrease their chances of experiencing nightmares and sleep paralysis.

Some spiritualists bathe with chamomile water to increase allure and self-love. Others sprinkle dried chamomile petals around the house to ward off negative energies and entities from their space.

Cinnamon

Cinnamon is a powerful plant associated with financial prosperity and protection. If you want to invite money into your life, follow this spell.

On the first of every month, put some cinnamon powder in your hands and blow it onto your front door. You can do the same with your shop, company, etc. When you are blowing the cinnamon powder, visualize yourself receiving money and feel the emotions you would experience with prosperity. After you blow the powder, rub it into your hands. Washing it away may lessen the intensity of the spell.

When working on a protection spell, anoint a piece of paper with your name on it with cinnamon, or dress a white candle in cinnamon and picture yourself being shielded from negativity and people who wish you harm.

John the Conqueror Root

This root is highly valuable among Hoodoos. According to folklore, John the conqueror fell in love with Lilith, the devil's daughter. The devil challenged John and promised him Lilith's hand should he successfully complete the challenges. John bravely took on the challenges, but he knew the devil would kill him. Knowing this, John and Lilith stole the devil's horse and escaped to Africa. They agreed never to use their powers again so they could not be found and murdered by Lilith's father. John put his powers into the root in the United States and escaped with Lilith.

Today, Hoodoos use this root to be blessed by John's power. Practitioners dress white candles with this root seeking protection and peace. Others anoint red and pink candles with this root to attract love. People use this root with green candles to receive money and increase their luck.

Hyssop

Hyssop is a popular herb in African witchcraft. It is mainly used in purification and cleansing rituals. It is common for practitioners to bathe in its water before and after working on a powerful spell.

Haitian Voodooists sprinkle its water on their altars, while the Hoodoos clean their mojo bags and gris-gris with the herb's smoke. Others like to clean their witchcraft tools with hyssop water or smoke before spellcasting. The tools must be purified from previous spells. Otherwise, the consequences could be dire. Spiritualists also put Hyssop's purple flowers and leaves in their mojo bags to protect themselves from evil deities and entities.

Jimson Weed

The Jimson weed was used among Voodooists during slavery. They believed this herb eased the possession process. During the ceremonies, the individual consumed this herb and would be possessed by a spirit or an ancestor.

To this day, this herb should not be consumed without supervision. Multiple witnesses have claimed the herb causes people to have a complete lack of self-awareness. Researchers, Busia and Heckles, noted that the herb causes a "bodily frenzy" during possession ceremonies.

Voodooists use this herb to reach refined consciousness levels. Not everyone feels safe taking this root, so it is best not to consume it if you are not experienced with it or are not surrounded by professionals who can ensure your safety.

Lavender

This flower has various spiritual properties, like attracting love, and beauty, increasing money, and enhancing intuition. The flower's purple hues are associated with intuition and psychic abilities. Mixing lavender with rose petals is known to draw love into a person's life and enhance their physical allure. Carrying lavender around makes the person financially richer.

If you want to partake in any of these spells, pay close attention to these instructions:

- To increase your allure and find love, draw a bath, sprinkle it with lavender and rose petals, and soak your body in the water. If you do not have a bathtub, put lavender and rose petals in a sachet and hang the sachet over the shower head. Let the water run through and shower with its water.
- If you want more money, put lavender in a green sachet with a few coins. Carry this sachet on you, especially if you are on your way to work or to gamble.
- To strengthen your intuition, burn some lavender and surround yourself with its smoke. Exercise your intuition by praying to the ancestors or practicing your psychic abilities during this time. The lavender will sharpen your intuition to achieve better results.

Lucky Hand Root

From the name, you can gather that this root's spiritual properties are related to luck. The lucky hand root is an excellent herb to have on you when competing, gambling, or taking part in the lottery.

You can wear this herb, keeping it close to your chest, or put it in your mojo bag. Many Hoodoos replace their mojo bag with a lucky hand root because it is that powerful. People who carry this root, instead of a mojo bag, usually anoint the lucky hand with essentials, like cinnamon and sandalwood, to enhance their luck and ensure their winnings.

Mandrake Root

The mandrake root is close to the Voodoo dolls' function. In other words, it can heal or harm someone. For instance, let's say you created a Voodoo doll to heal a client. Instead of creating a Voodoo doll from scratch, you can carve the client's name into the root and proceed with your healing ceremony.

This root is incredibly powerful, especially if you manifest something in your life. For example, carve your name into the root and apply herbs and oils associated with success and prosperity if you want to manifest success and wealth.

If you use this root, you must be careful with its location and ingesting it. This root can heavily influence someone's life, so you must ensure you are the only person with access to it. Also, avoid ingesting the root since it is not meant for human consumption.

Maguey Root

Santeros, Santeria priests, believe the maguey root has incredible healing powers. It is highly common to drink maguey root tea if you practice Santeria since they believe it heals illnesses and wards off negativity. Hoodoos use this root as a charm that boosts the mojo bag's power. This root is used with red candles to increase lust in a relationship or make someone fall in love with you. Maguey root is used to spiritually cleanse the self from negative spirits and energies.

Rattlesnake Root

Burning rattlesnake root with the intention of attracting love brings the right people into your life and protects you from individuals not meant for you.

Spiritualists say that this root may make people leave your life, but, in reality, the root shields you from people who are not right for you. If you have a love interest and want to know whether they are a good fit, then you use this root. However, if you do not want to experience the harsh reality the root might expose you to, then maybe this is not the time to use it.

Rue

If you think someone has cast a spell on you or has hexed you, you might need to bathe with rue water. Practitioners sprinkle rue in their bathtubs to break hexes and jinxes.

Other practitioners prefer to drink rue tea instead of bathing in it, but again, it is better not to drink any herb if you do not know what effect it will have on your body.

Spiritualists believe sprinkling rue leaves outside their houses can bring them prosperity and luck. If you want more wealth in your life, you are more likely to attract prosperity if you blow cinnamon onto your door and sprinkle rue leaves outside of it.

Sage

Sage is another herb all African practitioners use. It is mainly known for its cleansing properties. For instance, Yoruba people and Hoodoos use sage smoke to cleanse their altars.

Sage is used to cleanse.
https://unsplash.com/photos/k44X7D5bpms

Haitian Voodooists use sage to cleanse themselves and their house. For example, let's say you had a guest in your house, and after they left, you felt the house's energy took a turn for the worst. In this scenario, the best thing to do is grab a sage bundle or sage leaves and burn them. Open a window so that the negative energy has a place to go, away from your house. Your house's energy will be replenished and renewed.

Sampson Snake Root

The Sampson snake root enhances male fertility and sexual performance. It is also used to gain power and respect in the community or workplace.

Practitioners usually soak the herb with whiskey and consume 1 tablespoon every day. Others prefer to make it into tea and drink it. Male practitioners wanting to perform better sexually wash their genitals with its water to get the full effect of this powerful root.

People who want to increase their male energy use this root. In other words, women can use this root, too. As people, we all have feminine and male energies, so people who want to connect with their male energies will benefit from using the Sampson Snake Root.

Saw Palmetto Berry

The Saw Palmetto Berry is mainly used by people practicing Santeria. People mix it with their alcohol and use it as an aphrodisiac. It is considered one of the main ingredients in love and lust spells. Practitioners also add honey to it to enhance its love-inducing powers.

During sex magic ceremonies, the saw palmetto berry is soaked with liquor and served to the participants. The drink prepares them for the energies and emotions they are about to experience.

Other practitioners use the berries as love charms and put them in their mojo bags or around the Voodoo doll to increase love and lust.

Sassafras

Sometimes practitioners find themselves targeted by other spellcasters. These practitioners could be victims of bad hexes or harmful entities. One way they protect themselves is by stuffing a mojo bag with sassafras leaves and leaving it near their bed or under their pillow.

The sassafras leaves are known for their protective properties. They mainly shield from evil entities and hexes or harmful spells. However, the sassafras leaves must be replaced with new ones every 2 days, depending on the entity you are dealing with. Change the mojo bag every 2 days to ensure your safety.

Solomon Seal Root

This root binds spirits, good and evil. Some practitioners use it to call on good spirits to protect themselves against evil entities targeting them. Others call on the spirits to get ahead in life or seek revenge on people who have wronged them.

Working with this root can be tricky and challenging. Novice practitioners are advised to avoid this root because it needs a lot of energy and experience they do not have. So, if you are not an advanced spellcaster, work with easier roots before using the Solomon seal root.

Quita Maldicion

The Quita Maldicion is a popular herb in Santeria. This plant is mostly known as the "curse remover" within the community. If you or someone you love is exhibiting symptoms of being cursed, it is best to burn quita maldicion around them. This herb also comes in handy when removing a hex or the evil eye from yourself or someone else. Remember, burning this herb removes curses, but they do not prevent them. So, the next time you are cleansing yourself from an evil eye or a curse, make sure to use herbs that also shield you from them. Moreover, do not use both herbs together. First, remove the curse, cleanse yourself with sage, and lastly, burn an herb to shield you from future harm.

Frescura Herb

The frescura herb is excellent for curing energy blockings. If you feel your house has lost its energy or has weird energy, then you need to burn this plant. You can also use it if your energy is blocked. How can you tell if your energy is blocked? Your intuition will not be as sharp, you may feel tired, and, most importantly, your spark will gradually fade away. Energy blockings are temporary, so you do not need to worry. Burn this plant to restore your energy and have it run smoothly through your body.

There are a plethora of herbs and plants to use on candles or bathe with. Moreover, other spells require ingesting certain plants but avoiding consuming any plant or root is best. However, if you are sure you will not suffer from a bad reaction, it is safe to ingest these ingredients. But, if you are unsure or have not consumed certain herbs before, it is best to avoid ingesting them. You can take allergy tests and always ask a health professional about the plants and roots you are curious about. Remember, not every spell here is for beginners, so if you are a novice, work with easier ingredients and spells that match your level. It is better to gain experience before working on challenging spells. Good luck, and be safe.

Chapter 8: Let's Talk about Altars and Shrines

Altars and shrines are considered highly delicate topics, as most African spiritual traditions require initiation. Therefore, you should always seek a priest's guidance and approval before you build your shrine and use it to work with your ancestors or the Orishas.

Altars and shrines are sacred in African spirituality practices.
Ji-Elle, CC BY-SA 4.0 <https://creativecommons.org/licenses/by-sa/4.0>, via Wikimedia Commons https://commons.wikimedia.org/wiki/File:La_Havane-Vente_d%27articles_religieux-Santer%C3%ADa_(4).jpg

At-home shrines and altars are relatively easy to set up. They're great because they can be adapted to a wide range of beliefs and faiths. A sacred spot for spiritual practices, rituals, and prayers helps strengthen your connection with the deities and the spirits and replenishes your faith. Regardless of your belief system, an altar can help you recharge and maintain your peace and inner comfort.

On reading this chapter, you'll understand the structure and general layout of altars in Yoruba, Santeria, Hoodoo, and Haitian Vodou. You learn about their differences and similarities and discover how each spiritual tradition sets up and works with Orisha and ancestor altars. Finally, we give you tips on how to build your own at-home altar.

Yoruba

Yoruba altars come in various sizes and appearances. A shrine's exact form differs from one practitioner's preferences and ideologies to the other. Yoruba shrines aren't typically ornate and humungous, and the best thing about them is they could be adapted to the space, monetary, and tool limitations of the average person. They are much like the characteristics the saint withholds.

Yorubas use shrines to communicate with the saints, so they're typically located on a higher level than the ground. A Yoruba altar is a sacred space where you can make offerings, perform sacrifices, pray, or partake in other spiritual activities. Your choice of practices and offerings mainly depends on whether you dedicate your altar to Orishas or ancestors. There's no need to worry if you want to worship Orishas and ancestors simultaneously because the Yoruba religion doesn't require altars to be immovable once set up.

On specific days of the year, such as October 4th and December 17th, Orula and San Lazaro days, respectively, practitioners build great altars and celebrate together. People also dedicate a large portion of their homes to making colorful altars with numerous symbols, representatives, and offerings.

Christian Yorubas often incorporate Catholic saints into their shrines. Most commonly include the Virgin of Rule, the Virgin of the Mercedes, Saint Barbara, and the Charity of the Copper, among other significant figures. They further decorate the shrines with fruits, candles, and flowers. The Yoruba Orishas are represented with ceramic, guira, porcelain, or clay soup containers in order of hierarchy.

Figures of the deities are placed on stones in the soup bowls and are typically adorned with rings, robes, and other symbols associated with the Orishas and the saints. These typically include food, drinks, flowers, fruit offerings, fans, toys, and tools. What you do to work with or honor an Orisha depends on its unique preferences and characteristics.

When preparing an ancestor shrine, you must seek a priest's help because you need to obtain 9 sticks from a specific tree and ritually prepare them before tying them together using a red cloth. This bundle of sticks is what you'll be making your offerings to. You also need an "Opa egun," any thick, straight, and tall wooden branch for your invocations. A male practitioner will use it to tap on the floor as you, or someone else, invoke the ancestors. Always offer them the first serving of any meal. Water or liquor is also typically offered.

Santeria

Like Yoruba, many major Orishas in Santeria have Catholic counterparts. You can build a shrine to honor the Orisha you wish to worship and honor using symbols and colors that represent them and make relevant offerings.

Yorubas and Santeria practitioners share the same belief regarding ancestors; they pass onto the invisible world to watch over their loved ones. However, only those who qualified to be honored through ancestor work can live up to their destiny. These are often people who lived honorable lives and contributed to their society. Those people should have also experienced long lives and natural deaths.

Some people dedicate a separate space or even a separate building for their altars. It depends on family traditions and personal preferences. Ancestor altars commonly include a white candle and cloth. Pictures or belongings of the ancestor, flowers, or three water glasses (you can use any odd number of water glasses) should also be added. Some people like to separate the male and female ancestors on the altar. Some people also separate different families, which would be a great idea for individuals who never get along well.

If you're setting up an Orisha altar., keep all the Orishas (except for the warrior deities) in ceramic tureens. The color and decoration of the tureen depend on the characteristics and symbols of the Orisha you're working with. These tureens hold the sacred stones of the Orishas, which is an extension of the Yoruba tradition of placing stones in bowls or pots.

If you're working with a warrior Orisha, avoid using tureens. Keep them in uncovered iron or clay pots. Use sealed containers with water for the water Orishas. Each Orisha accepts unique offerings, often left beside their tureen or another vessel. Some offerings, known as ebó, are considered sacrifices because they are either purchased, which is a financial sacrifice, or made, which is a sacrifice of time. Making a weekly ebó for the Orisha can keep it strong and pleased.

Hoodoo

Hoodoo practitioners prepare their altar by visiting their ancestors' graves with a small container. They introduce themselves and notify the ancestors of their intentions. They store a little dirt in the container, take it home, and use it to build a connection with the ancestor.

Hoodoo practitioners spoon the dirt into their containers by digging with coins near their ancestor's graves after pouring whiskey over the grave. When they get home, they empty the dirt into a nicer-looking container.

According to Hoodoo traditions, Saturday is ideal for working with the dead. They usually make food offerings of meat and potatoes and some dyed pale blue water. They set up a basic altar for their ancestors and create them weekly with music, food, or other offerings. You can also serve your ancestor's favorite dishes.

You can include several containers with grave dirt from different people's altars, with their pictures and a few of their belongings. Some practitioners include an empty picture frame as a symbol of the relatives and ancestors they don't know.

Haitian Vodou

Haitian Vodou shrines are known for their vibrant colors and magnificence. The Orishas are typically represented in their own spots. Haitian Vodou shrines incorporate several objects required by the deities, or Lwa, depending on who you're working with. Other tools, like decorated bottles, are considered offerings and serve a specific purpose.

Filled and empty bottles are usually ornamented with images and specific symbols. They are often covered with sequins or other colorful decorations. While dolls are used, they're not as terrifying as Voodoo dolls are thought to be. Many people believe practitioners stick pins in these dolls to cast harmful curses on others. However, they are used to honor certain deities. Some people employ dolls as messengers between the physical realm and the spirits. Herb-filled cloth packets are also popular altar decorations. The colors of the pieces of cloth and how they're decorated depend on the colors of the Lwas. These packets are believed to bring protection and stimulate healing. Interestingly, Haitian Vodou practitioners leave flags leaning against an altar as ritual objects that attract the Lwa to replenish its spiritual energy.

Building Your Altar

Decide Its Purpose

The first thing you must do before building your altar is to determine its purpose. Which spiritual path are you following? Do you intend to build an Orisha or ancestor altar? Do you have a specific deity you wish to honor? Will you use your altar for celebrations? Is your altar movable, or must it be fixed?

You need to ensure your altar offers a comfortable space, as you could use it to meditate, pray, communicate with your ancestors, make invocations, or conduct other rituals.

Decide Where to Place It

The location and size of your altar mainly depend on your needs, lifestyle, and preferences. Some people like to dedicate an entire room to their spiritual practices, while others believe their dresser or bookshelf would suffice. However, when setting up your altar, it should face a meaningful or pleasant direction. For instance, if you're building an ancestor altar, face it toward the direction of your ancestor's homeland.

It's best if you build your altar somewhere quiet and private. This way, you won't have to worry about someone knocking it over or interrupting your spiritual practices. You don't need to rush to find the right location. Some people are drawn toward a spot that just "feels right." Consider the energy this place gives off. Is it welcoming and bright? You can use smudging or other energy-cleansing techniques before you set up your space. It also helps if you do an energetic cleanse every once in a while.

Find Out Which Tools You Need

Even though there are some rules you must follow when setting up your altar, especially if you're working with specific Orishas, you'll often have to lean into your intuition. Pay attention to your cravings and signs to pick up on the offerings the Orishas wish to receive. Your gut may also signal certain objects to incorporate into your ancestor shrine. Unless you're going against instructions, there are no limits to what you're allowed to keep on your altar. However, always ask for your priest's opinion until you've gained enough confidence in your own knowledge.

Candles are very popular tools to add to your altar and are often required when working with certain Orishas. Be careful not to leave your burning candles unattended, and keep them away from flammable materials. Be extra careful if you have any children or pets at home.

Set Up Your Altar

Once you've cleaned your space energetically, think about how you'd like to arrange your tools and objects on your altar. Start with a few items to avoid feeling overwhelmed. As a rule of thumb, keep your altar symmetrical, with the tallest item in the middle. Cover your table or surface with a cloth if you wish to protect it from candle wax, ash, or other potentially damaging objects.

Maintain Your Efforts

You should aim to use your altar habitually. If it's too much pressure, start with a seasonal practice and build from there. For instance, if you practice Yoruba, set up an altar to commemorate notable celebrations. Once you feel ready, you can build an Orisha or ancestor altar and tend to it once a week. If working with an altar becomes a habit, you can easily incorporate it into your daily routine. Your day will eventually feel incomplete without the 10 or 15 minutes you spend at your altar daily.

Most importantly, your altar must always be clean and organized, no matter how often you use it. You should exude positive emotions each time you approach your altar; it should never feel like a chore. If you beat yourself up for not praying today, you'll eventually dread having to do it. Instead of being a peaceful space you can retreat in, it will feel heavy and suffocating. Refurbish your altar, remove items you no longer need, and introduce new ones every now and then. Clean the altar and everything on it often.

Your altar or shrine must be in a place where you won't be interrupted. You should dedicate the time to connecting with your ancestors for peace and guidance. Know your purpose for contacting them – have your questions prepared beforehand.

Now that you have read this chapter, you understand how different African spiritual traditions use altars and shrines. You are ready to build your ancestor or Orisha's altar with the guidance of an experienced priest. These spiritual traditions have been used for centuries, so they will work for you if you believe in the system.

Chapter 9: Mojo Bags and Gris-Gris

Mojo bags and gris-gris are typically mistaken as the same. However, both tools have significant differences. You must learn the distinctions between both instruments to guarantee a safe practice environment and experience.

This chapter delves deep into the differences between these talismans to identify the right one for you. You'll learn how mojo bags and gris-gris are created and how they're cleansed, consecrated, charged, stored, and safely used.

Mojo bag.
Teogomez, CC BY-SA 3.0 <http://creativecommons.org/licenses/by-sa/3.0/>, via Wikimedia Commons https://commons.wikimedia.org/wiki/File:Grisgristuareg.JPG

The History of Mojo Bags

Mojo bags were brought to America by enslaved Africans centuries ago. Making these mojo bags and carrying them around in their pockets was the only thing that kept them sane as they endured the terrors of the slave trade. Mojo bags were a lot more than talismans to enslaved Africans. They were a means of assurance and offered a sense of security in a highly cruel and uncertain environment. Soon, these small, good-luck charms were incorporated into Hoodoo, a traditional magical system.

The incredible thing about mojo bags and the entire practice of Hoodoo is they combine many African, Native American, and even European magical practices and traditions. Some people believe these talismans have a great number of similarities with medicine bags, which are indigenous to the Native Americans. Both magical tools incorporate several personal and natural items to induce a specific, powerful effect, and both are carried discreetly or kept in a safe place.

Mojo Bags

Mojo bags are created to attract certain things and energies into a person's life. Various mojo bags serve a wide array of purposes. For instance, you can create one to attract protection into your life and another to initiate love. Mojo bags come in different colors, depending on the energy and the results you wish to achieve.

A mojo bag contains various stones, herbs, and other trinkets that can help you manifest your desires. You must set a clear intention, name your mojo bag, and replenish it every now and then. A mojo bag must first be slept with to set its effects in motion. Keeping it under your pillow or bed or placing it beside you as you sleep allows you to bond with it. The main objective behind this practice is to amalgamate its essence with yours. Wear your mojo bag or keep it on you, but it should never be visible to others.

This talisman can transform or elevate several areas of your life. It can make you more successful, keep you in good health, protect you from potential harm, attract love and abundance into your life, and more. Think of it as an amulet charged with spells and magic. Many people regard mojo bags as mystical beings you must feed and properly care for, as it is the only way they will grow their powers and redirect their energies into their holders' lives.

Making and Using a Mojo Bag

Choose a cloth bag that aligns with your desire and intention. These pouches come in a wide array of colors and fabrics and are available at any craft store. Use the following list as a guide to help you choose the color that corresponds with your intention:

- Orange: success, stamina, endurance, and vitality.
- Purple: divination and spirituality. It's also used when overcoming and healing from karmic lessons.
- Red: protection, courage, and passion. Red could also be associated with marriage.
- Blue: wisdom and philosophy. Blue is considered the color of intellect.
- Black: protection and eliminating negativity. It is also related to discipline.
- Yellow: self-expression, happiness, and creativity.
- Pink: love, romance, and friendship. Pink also corresponds with art, emotional healing, and beauty.
- Grey: secrets and mysteries. It also represents neutrality.
- Green: wealth, abundance, and prosperity. Green is also associated with luck and employment.
- Silver: receptivity and meditation.
- White: peace and psychological healing. White is considered the color of angelic guidance.
- Gold: projectivity and prosperity.

After choosing a color that corresponds with what you want to manifest, you need to fill it with relevant symbols, herbs, and stones. While the possibilities are endless, here's a small list of items that correspond to certain purposes to get you started:

- Wealth: pyrite, emerald, bayberry, coins, and cinnamon
- Victory: nasturtium, High John the conqueror root, and carnelian
- Love: catnip, honey, rose, rose quartz, almond, and morganite
- Health: lobelia, hematite, clove, bloodstone, and orange peel

- Protection: salt, borage, black tourmaline, basil, morning glory

Consider hand-sewing your mojo bag instead of purchasing a ready-made one, as this helps amplify its effects. Here's how to do it:

1. Measure the width of your ribbon, and cut it at length 3 times as long. For instance, if you're using a 2-inch-wide ribbon, make it 6 inches long.
2. Fold it in half, ensuring both halves are perfectly aligned.
3. Sew the sides together, leaving around 1.25 inches unsewn at the end. The top must not be sewn, as this will be the mojo bag's opening.
4. Turn the ribbon inside out, hiding the stitching inside.
5. Fold the 1.25-inch flaps outside and down and make around 4 small cuts along both folds.
6. Unfold the flaps and thread a string through the cuts around the bag's circumference.
7. Fill your bag with your selected items and firmly tie the drawstrings into a knot.
8. To feed your mojo bag, anoint it with an essential oil or burn incense and pass it through the smoke. You should set a clear intention as you do this.

Keep the mojo bag in your pocket or underneath your pillow. If you feel comfortable with where you keep it, let it stay there. If not, try different locations until you find one that feels right. You should recharge your mojo bag regularly by feeding it. Most people do recharge it every full moon.

Gris-Gris

Many confuse mojo bags with gris-gris because the latter also serves as a talisman in a small satchel. However, the primary purpose of a gris-gris is to protect its holder from the evil eye and unwanted energies. The catch is that you must incorporate a body part of yours, or whoever wishes protection, into the satchel. This is how the holder connects with the gris-gris and becomes one with its essence.

Besides grisly ingredients like bones, hairs, and nails, this talisman also includes crystals, herbs, and other magical tools and ingredients. Unlike mojo bags, gris-gris is considered to be associated with black magic and darker arts.

A gris-gris creates a potent dark shield around its holder to keep negative and unwanted energy away. The talisman achieves this effect because it has to encounter heavier and darker magic at first.

Gris-gris is a Voodoo practice that can get very dangerous if not used mindfully. You need to be very careful with your intentions and what you're asking of this talisman. Also, you must put a lot of thought into the ingredients you use to make your gris-gris. Adding your body part can significantly amplify your connection with the talisman. Novices and anyone not ready for this bond won't handle its intensity and effects.

Making and Using a Gris-Gris

When creating a gris-gris, be very mindful of what you think and feel. You should only make or use a gris-gris whenever you're experiencing a positive state of mind. Direct all your attention with love and positivity toward your intention, whether you're making it for yourself or someone else. Be as specific as possible when expressing and wording your intention. Have unwavering faith in the talisman's ability to protect you from potential harm.

It's best to use a black pouch, as this is the color of protection and the banishing of negative energy. Also, use protective symbols, crystals, and herbs, such as salt, borage, black tourmaline, and basil. However, when creating a gris-gris, allow your instincts to take the lead.

You can include your desired number of items in the gris-gris as long as you end up with an odd number. Keep the number of items between 3 and 13, including your lock of hair or fingernail and the shells and charms. If you're making the gris-gris for someone else, ask them to add their hair or fingernails to the bag.

Cleanse and purify your space before you start making the gris-gris. If you have an altar, use it as a workstation. If not, find a place you typically associate with healing and positive energies. For example, dining tables are ideal because this is where warm family gatherings take place.

Wipe your surface clean and burn incense or sage. Many people prefer burning juniper leaves. When you're done, use cedar sticks to smudge the space or sweep the negative energy away with a ceremonial or old wooden broomstick. You don't need to sweep the floor. Just circle your broom around it. Lay your ingredients in front of you and light a candle in the center of your table. Say, "Bless this space and all power brought forth," as you light the candle. Ask for the universe's guidance and call upon a deity, an ancestor, spirit guides, or any higher power you wish to work with. Ask them to guide you throughout this endeavor.

If you're making a gris-gris for someone else, keep their picture in front of you or carve their name into the candle you use. Insert each item into the bag, thanking the stone, flower, or tree in the process. Be fully present and hold onto your intention throughout the process. Speak your desire for protection out loud. Once you tie your bag, thank the universe, your higher powers, and Mother Nature for their help, and then blow out the candle.

Recite your intention every night throughout the duration of each waning moon and until the new moon arrives.

Whenever you're creating a gris-gris, remember whatever thoughts, emotions, or intentions you send out to the universe will come back to you threefold. Therefore, always express your gratitude and be positive while creating the bag. If you're creating a gris-gris for someone else, ask their permission first. Avoid using gris-gris to influence other people's wills, and be very specific and mindful of your intentions.

Which Talisman Should I Go For?

If you're open to experimenting with different energies and magic, you probably feel conflicted about which talisman to use. Mojo bags are generally more versatile, which is why many people prefer using them. They can be adapted to your personal goals, intentions, and needs. Anyone who feels more comfortable using white or red magic spells should go for mojo bags.

Gris-gris is interesting to use. Some people enjoy the extra thought (and added risk) of creating and using this talisman. However, they're quite challenging and require a degree of knowledge and experience with black magic.

Mojo bags are great because they can be approached from a positive standpoint. When you feed it positive energy, expect it to send it back. Since mojo bags apply to a plethora of magic, they should be approached with love and an airy feel, which is very important in protecting yourself from negative energies surrounding you.

Some people don't feel comfortable incorporating parts of their bodies into magical practices. Your opinion regarding this matter makes you neither less nor more qualified to use talismans. It merely helps you determine which magic to use. Practitioners of dark arts lean toward using gris-gris, while green witches (they rely on essential oils, roots, herbs, and other natural ingredients) feel more at ease when using gris-gris.

If you're new to the world of magic or African spirituality, it could take some time to discover your scope and the areas you enjoy working in. Take your time to experiment and explore your inclinations, as long as you do it safely and under proper guidance.

Each person is different, so remember you're free to set the horizon and limits for your unique practice. Once you feel more confident in your ability to use talismans, you'll discover there's no right or wrong way to this practice. You'll lean into your intuition to determine the practices that you resonate with.

Chapter 10: Festivals and Ceremonies

Festivals are important in many religions and spiritual traditions. They're a time when communities and families can come together. Furthermore, celebrating religious festivals is a time when adherents can publicly express their beliefs and strengthen their bond with their deities. Religious festivals and celebrations are also a time when communities can create and disseminate religious narratives and stories, which are then passed down through generations.

Festivals and ceremonies celebrate spirituality.
https://unsplash.com/photos/tGfB7t4L1JY

The importance of these festivals and ceremonies is evident in religions and spiritual practices around the world, and African spiritual practices and traditions are no different. Each religion and spiritual practice promotes and celebrates a different set of holidays, which have spiritual importance in the specific tradition.

Kemeticism and Kemetic Orthodoxy

Kemetic Orthodoxy is an offshoot of traditional Kemeticism (known as Egyptian paganism) and features many holidays celebrating Kemetic deities. Some major holidays in Kemetic Orthodoxy include:

Beautiful Feast of the Valley

Also known as the Feast of the Beautiful Valley, the Beautiful Feast of the Valley is an ancient Kemetic holiday that celebrates the dead. In the modern calendar, it is celebrated around April 28th.

This festival involves remembering the dead and those gone before and was the major festival in Thebes. It had grand processions to temples and tombs, where families would hold feasts with their ancestors. It was also a time to celebrate the god Amun, whose figure led these processions.

In the modern day, this festival often coincides with the pagan festival of Beltane and is celebrated similarly. It involves creating altars for the ancestors and eating meals with friends, family, and other loved ones.

Opet Festival

Also known as the Beautiful Feast of Opet, the Opet Festival was one of the most prominent ancient Kemetic holidays. The festival celebrated the deities Amun, Mut, and Khonsu and took place over 24 days. It was the most prominent celebration in Luxor.

The festival was celebrated during the flooding of the Nile. Therefore, it also acted as a festival and celebration of fertility. In the modern calendar, this festival is celebrated in June and celebrates the deities Amun, Mut, and Khonsu. While modern festival celebrations do not last 24 days, many adherents of Kemeticism leave the altars up throughout June and make daily offerings to replicate the ancient celebration.

Aset Luminous

Aset is another name for the Egyptian mother goddess Isis. It is a festival of lights and commemorates Aset's (Isis's) search for her brother-husband Wesir (Osiris) after their brother Set (Seth) traps and kills Osiris in a wooden coffin.

In the story, Aset searches for her husband everywhere, including at night, by the light of her torch. Kemetic adherents light candles, lamps, and torches to aid her in her search. Additionally, they create paper boats with prayers written on them and containing a light source (like a tealight candle) and place them on a water source (like a river) so that the goddess has light available wherever she goes.

This festival is generally in early July, around July 2nd.

Wep Ronpet

Wep Ronpet is essentially the Kemetic New Year. The date of this festival varies every year, but it is generally celebrated at the end of July or the beginning of August. The specific date depends on when the star Sirius rises at the Tawy temple (the primary temple of Kemetic Orthodoxy, based in Illinois, United States).

Wep Ronpet is preceded by 5 days known as Epagomenal Days. These days are celebrated as the birthdays of the four or five children of Geb and Nut - in order:

- Osiris
- Horus - in some traditions (particularly later Greco-Egyptian), there are two deities known as Horus - Horus the Elder is a child of Geb and Nut, and Horus the Younger is the child of Isis and Osiris
- Set
- Isis
- Nephthys

During the Epagomenal Days, care is taken not to take too many risks, as these days are considered outside the traditional year. On each day, worship is given to the relevant god's birthday, including creating shrines for each god and making offerings.

On the day of Wep Ronpet, adherents celebrate the New Year by clearing out the old - usually by cleaning their homes or places of work and celebrating the day with family and friends. For magic practitioners, the day could include renewing wardings, performing cleansings, and doing other protective work in and around the home.

Wag Festival

The Wag Festival, or Festival of the Wag, occurs in late August and commemorates and celebrates the god Wesir (Osiris). It was essentially a festival of the dead and a day to celebrate and remember the souls who passed before, especially in the year that had just passed.

Wag Festival is one of the oldest known Kemetic festivals and has been celebrated since the days of the Old Kingdom. In ancient Egypt, people celebrated the festival by creating small papyrus boats decorated with prayers and sending them out on the East bank of the Nile. It was a way to commemorate the death of Osiris.

Other celebrations included visiting their ancestors' tombs with offerings for the dead to keep them satisfied in the afterlife.

Today, people celebrate the festival by creating paper boats and sending them floating on local bodies of water. It is a day to create altars for the ancestors and to place your offerings.

Sed Festival

The Sed festival, or the Feast of the Tail, is an ancient Kemetic festival commemorating the continued rule of the pharaoh.

In modern times, this festival is celebrated to honor Horus the Younger, who acts as the king of the living. It is also a chance to honor the memories of the deceased Egyptian pharaohs. Other deities honored during the festival include Sekhmet and Wepwawet. The festival is held on November 15th in the modern calendar.

These are only a few festivals followed in Kemeticism and Kemetic Orthodoxy. Hundreds of festivals are celebrated in ancient Kemeticism (in some calendars, there is nearly one celebration for each day of the year). Modern followers often choose prominent holidays or holidays that celebrate their preferred deities to celebrate.

Isese

Known as the Yoruba religion, Isese is followed by the Yoruba people in Africa, particularly present-day Nigeria. Some Isese festivals include:

Eyo Festival

The Eyo festival is primarily celebrated in Lagos and is known as the Adamu Orisha Play. This festival is traditionally held to escort the spirit of a deceased king or chief and help welcome his successor. The festival pays homage to the ruling Oba (king or ruler) of Lagos.

The festival takes place over 24 days and involves a well-known parade featuring performers dressed in white robes. The festival gets its name from these costumed dancers called "Eyo."

This festival is held when required and often to honor and commemorate prominent members of the Lagos Yoruba community and its chiefs and kings. However, this festival is also held more frequently as a tourist event and is a well-known source of tourism in Lagos.

Osun-Osogbo Festival

The Osun-Osogbo festival is celebrated in August every year at the sacred Osun-Osogbo grove located along the banks of the Osun River outside Osogbo city.

This festival is a celebration of the Orisha Osun (Oshun), the Orisha of love, beauty, freshwater, and wealth. The festival is at least seven centuries old and is a two-week celebration that includes the following:

- A traditional cleansing of Osogbo
- The lighting of the 500-year-old, sixteen-point lamp, the Ina Olojumerindinlogun
- The Iboriade, where the crowns of previous Osogbo rulers are gathered and blessed
- A large procession in front of the Osun-Osogbo shrine. This procession is a celebration featuring dancing, musical performances, praise, poetry, costumed revelers, and more. The procession is led by the sitting ruler of Osogbo, the Ataoja, the Arugba (calabash carrier), and a group of priestesses.

This festival replicates the meeting between Osun and a group of migrants fleeing from famine. The Orisha agreed to provide them with prosperity in exchange for an annual sacrifice, and the festival includes this annual sacrifice.

Like the Eyo Festival, the Osun-Osogbo festival helps promote tourism to the local area, besides being followed for religious and spiritual reasons.

Sango Festival

The Sango festival dates to over 1000 years ago and is held in August. It is celebrated to honor and commemorate Sango, the Orisha of thunder and fire. Sango is also considered the founding father of the Oyo people and is believed to have been the third Alaafin of Oyo, making him an ancestor to the current royals.

This festival is celebrated in Oyo state in Nigeria, and the primary celebrations are generally held in the palace of the current Alaafin of Oyo.

It is a 10-day festival celebrated by followers dressed in red or white. Some celebrations include an ayo competition (one of the oldest Yoruba games played using a wooden board and pebbles), cultural and traditional displays, and magic performances. Like the Osun-Osogbo festival, the Sango festival is a public spectacle celebrated communally.

Igogo Festival

The Igogo festival is held annually, celebrated in September in Owo. This festival celebrates the Orisha Queen Oronsen. Oronsen was Olowo Rerengejen's wife.

This festival has been celebrated for at least 600 years and is a 17-day affair beginning with a procession of Iloro chiefs. The Olowo of Owo and the high chiefs of the kingdom dress like women. The Olowo also celebrates the festival of new yams at the same time, as it is incorporated into the Igogo festival. During the festival, guns are forbidden to be fired, drums should not be beaten, and using caps and head ties is prohibited.

Olojo Festival

The Olojo festival is celebrated annually in October in Ife, Osun state. The festival is celebrated in honor of Ogun, the Orisha of Iron, who is believed to be the eldest son of the progenitor of the Yoruba people, Oduduwa. The festival is also a celebration of the creation of the world.

For seven days before the festival, the Ooni of Ife must be secluded, offering prayers for his people and communing with the ancestors. On the day of the festival, he emerges from his seclusion, wearing the Aare crown, believed to be the original crown of Oduduwa.

Along with a crowd of adherents, the Ooni visits several sacred shrines to offer prayers and perform rituals. The shrines visited include the Okemogun shrine and shrines of historical importance. The rituals performed include ones that ask for peace in all Yoruba lands.

Oro Festival

The Oro festival is an annual festival that occurs across Yoruba land and is celebrated by all towns and settlements of Yoruba origin. It is a highly specific festival only celebrated by men who are descendants through their paternal ancestors, native to each location.

During the festival, women and descendants of non-natives must always stay indoors. People often travel to their native places to celebrate this festival.

As its name implies, the Oro festival celebrates the Orisha Oro, the Orisha of bullroarers and justice. It is believed that Oro should not be seen by women and non-natives, so they are expected to stay indoors during the festival. If anyone not meant to celebrate the festival ventures outside and catches a glimpse of Oro, they will die.

The festival lasts several days, and specific celebrations vary from settlement to settlement. Since the festival is so exclusive in its celebrants, very little is known about how it is actually celebrated.

Vodoun

Vodoun is a West African religion, known as Voudou and Voodoo, practiced by Aja, Ewe, and Fon peoples.

Fête du Vodoun

Fête du Vodoun is a festival celebrated annually on January 10th in Benin. The festival is a celebration of all things Vodoun, and celebrations start with the slaughter and sacrifice of a goat.

Followers dress as gods and perform rituals, and one of the best-known parts of the festival involves people dressing as Zangbeto (traditional Voodoo guardians) and performing. People also dress as Egungun, and spectators should avoid these individuals, as it is believed that if one of the Egungun touches you, you could die.

Other parts of the festival include singing, dancing, and drinking. Besides being extremely popular among Vodoun adherents, the festival is a well-known tourist attraction. Tourists travel from all over the world to be part of the celebration.

Haitian Voodoo

Haitian Voodoo shares some elements with Vodoun, but it is a different religion and features different celebrations.

Fête Gede

Known as the Haitian Day of the Dead and the Festival of the Ancestors, Fête Gede is celebrated annually on the first two days of November.

This festival involves a public procession, and many of the participants dress up. People commune with their ancestors and travel to graveyards to offer their ancestors food and drinks. The festival also celebrates the Iwa of death and fertility and involves music, dancing, and feasting.

However, before adherents can travel to their ancestors' graves, they must first honor and make offerings at the grave of Papa Gede, the first man to die. For people who cannot travel to Haiti for the festival, offerings are made at their altars first.

The Festival of the Miraculous Virgin of Saut d'Eau

The festival of the Miraculous Virgin of Saut d'Eau is less of a festival and more of a pilgrimage. It is held every year from July 14th to 16th. The Miraculous Virgin of Saut d'Eau, known as Saint Anne and Little Saint Anne, is considered the Virgin Mary's mother. She is believed to bring luck in romance and finance.

This festival is a pilgrimage to the Saut d'Eau waterfall, located north of Port-au-Prince. At the waterfall, Voodoo followers conduct purification rituals known as "luck baths." It involves bathing under the waterfall, after which a calabash (water flask made from a gourd) is broken. Additionally, the person leaves their clothes in the waterfall and wears new clothes, symbolizing the removal of past bad luck and introducing new good luck.

While this pilgrimage is primarily performed in July, it can be performed at any time of the year. The July pilgrimage also attracts numerous tourists interested in watching the pilgrimage.

Plaine Du Nord Festival

Known as the Plen Dino Festival, the Plaine Du Nord Festival occurs annually over two days in July and is celebrated in Plaine-du-Nord in northern Haiti.

This festival celebrates the Haitian Revolution, believed to have been aided by the deities and spirits. The festival also celebrates the Orisha Ogun, the Orisha of metal, soldiers, and blacksmiths.

During the festival, believers make offerings at the church of St. James or Ogoun Feraille. They offer prayers to the Virgin Mary of Mount Caramel, associated with Erzulie Freda, the goddess of love. Pilgrims offer sacrifices to the gods, including animals slaughtered as offerings.

Additionally, adherents take a ritual mud bath at St. Jacques's Hole, a sacred mud pool. These ritual baths are helped by priests who pray with pilgrims, and the baths act as a rebirth and baptism. The festival is also celebrated by limiting food and drink (not a complete fast), allowing pilgrims to experience the deprivations warriors during the Haitian Revolution experienced.

Conclusion

The African continent is home to some of the oldest civilizations in the world and has a rich history of spiritual practices. Learning about these spiritual practices is a great way to understand the people who practice them and can be a great stepping stone if you want to explore these practices as part of your spiritual journey.

As you've learned from this book, African spiritual practices are many and varied and include practices such as Haitian Vodou, Hoodoo, Santeria, and Kemetic Orthodoxy. While these traditions are unique and disparate, they also share some similarities, such as primarily oral traditions, ancestor worship, and a belief in the spirit world and supernatural beings like Santeria saints, Vodou Lwa, and Yoruba Orishas.

Many Africans believe in newer religions like Christianity and Islam. However, traditional religions and spiritual practices are once more growing in popularity. The growth of syncretic religions and traditions like Kemetic Orthodoxy reflects this interest in the history of African traditional religions, and this book is an introduction to these traditions.

To master any subject, you must first understand its history and fundamental concepts; African spiritual practices are no different. Once you've learned the basics of each tradition, you can find the one that speaks to you the most and explore them further.

Once you've learned about these traditions, it's also essential to learn about some of their practices – specifically, the importance of ancestor veneration, building altars and shrines, and using gris-gris and mojo bags.

Ancestor veneration, in particular, is practiced by most traditional African spiritual practices and is a key pillar of the community on the continent.

Along with learning more about these practices, you should also focus on learning about the sacred herbs and plants of the African continent. These herbs and plants are key in many rituals and spells. They are often unfamiliar to non-African readers because of their traditional names or, in some cases, the difficulty of finding them outside Africa.

Similarly, it can be challenging to become familiar with many African spiritual practices because of unfamiliar terms and words. The glossary at the end of this book will help you, making it easier for you to understand the meaning of these words and how to pronounce them.

African spirituality is a rich, complex tapestry of traditions and practices often overlooked by the rest of the world. This book will help you understand the fundamentals of these beliefs and to get started on your journey to learning more about these fascinating traditions.

For many people, African spirituality is synonymous with evil and witchcraft. As you discovered from this book, this concept is far from the truth. These traditions are filled with deep emotions and rely on nature and gods.

Whether you're interested in this book as a guide to your spiritual journey or are merely looking to learn more about African spiritual practices, there's something in it for everyone. So, remember to keep this book by your side as you explore the world of African spirituality further. Good luck.

Glossary of Terms

African spiritual practices use plenty of foreign words and phrases that sound complicated and foreign to newcomers. While each term is thoroughly explained and discussed in the chapters, this chapter summarizes the difficult words used throughout the book. You can use it when looking up certain words while reading the book.

Commonly Used Terms in African Spiritual Practices

Ashe - the divine energy that can be obtained through African spiritual practices. Each Orisha has its distinct ache they offer for empowerment or blessing to devotees. Mentioned in chapter 1.

Akhu - known as akh, akhu are souls blessed after the death of their physical body because they survived this. These spirits emit a powerful (shining) energy, provide protection, and help find divine wisdom. Mentioned in chapter 2.

Ayo - is one of the oldest Yoruba games. It's played using a wooden board and pebbles during the Sango festival. Mentioned in chapter 10.

According to Kemetic Orthodox beliefs, Ba is the part of the soul that travels between the realms. Mentioned in chapter 2.

Baron Samedi - the most superior Lwa of the Ghede Lwa pantheon. He is the Lwa of death, and he greets the spirits of the dead and guides them on their journey to the other world. Mentioned in chapter 4.

Bondye - pronounced as "bohn-dyay,"- is a supreme being in Voodoo and Haitian Voodoo. He is the creator of the universe and the equivalent of Olodumare in the Yoruba religion. Mentioned in chapter 3.

Chango - known as Sango and Santa Barbara. Chango is the god of lightning and thunder, and he is associated with magic, masculinity, and sexuality. Mentioned in chapters 4 and 5.

Ebo - called ebbo. Ebo is a term used for offerings and sacrifices made to Orishas. Ebo can be presented in many forms, such as food, meals, objects, releasing live animals, etc. Mentioned in chapter 8.

Egun - these are the souls of deceased ancestors or spirits the practitioner feels close to. They are often blood relatives but can also be part of a person's religious family. Sometimes, spirit guides and even animal spirits are considered egun if honored, specifically in rites and ceremonies called toque de egun. Mentioned in chapter 6.

Egungun - evil ancestral spirits who should be avoided as they can hurt and kill people. Mentioned in chapter 10.

Elegba - known as Legba, elegba are the gatekeepers of the world. They safeguard the doorways between this world and the divine and spiritual realms. Elegba is derived from the name Eleggua (called St. Peter or St. Anthony), a powerful being who guards the crossroads all souls pass after departing. Mentioned in chapters 4 and 5.

Eyo festival - known as the Adamu Orisha Play. This festival is traditionally held to escort the spirit of a deceased king or chief and help welcome his successor. Mentioned in chapter 10.

Fet Gede - known as "Festival day of the dead," is a celebration in Haitian Voodoo. Mentioned in chapters 6 and 10.

Fête du Vodoun - a traditional Vodun festival where people dress up as evil spirits and guardians. Mentioned in chapter 10.

Ghede Lwa is one of the most significant Lwa families from West Africa. Mentioned in chapter 4.

Gris-gris - pronounced as "gree-gree," is an act of creating a powerful magical charm. Its creation typically requires combining white and black magic, and due to this, it is only recommended for experienced practitioners. Mentioned in chapter 9.

Haitian Voodoo - Similar to other African religions, Haitian Voodoo is a spiritual practice where the rituals involve foods, drinks, and herbs for healing and spiritual purposes. Mentioned in chapter 1.

Hoodoo - pronounced as "who-doo," is a magical practice incorporating folk traditions and herbal medicine. It also involves conjuring and other magical practices related to the similarly named Voodoo. Hoodoo combines African spiritual practice with European and Native American beliefs. Mentioned in chapter 1.

Ifa - the central dogma in the Yoruba religion. Mentioned in chapter 1.

Igogo festival - a celebration of the Orisha Oronsen and the yam harvest. Mentioned chapter 10.

Isfet - means disorder and stands in deep contrast to maat, which was created to abolish isfet. Mentioned in chapter 2.

Juju - pronounced as "joo-joo," is a Voodoo term for charms used for protection, healing, and other positive magical purposes.

Ka - this refers to one of the most fundamental parts of the soul as described in Kemetic traditions. Mentioned in chapter 2.

Kemetic Orthodoxy - an ancient Egyptian belief system, according to which the creators made the souls, and the deities guided them. Mentioned in chapter 1.

Lwa - known as loa, a lwa is a powerful spirit who, according to certain African spiritual traditions, governs the different realms of the natural world and can be asked for help, like saints and the Orishas in other religions. Mentioned in chapters 1 and 4.

Ma'at - also called Maat, signifies truth, order, justice, or balance. It represents a fundamental dogma in Kemetic beliefs and is linked to the deity of the same name. Mentioned in chapter 2.

Manman - a term of high respect used for female Lwas. It means mother and has the same bearing for the living elders. Mentioned in chapter 4.

Mojo - a Voodoo term used for charms to bring specific benefits, such as financial, protective, emotional, etc. Mentioned in chapter 9.

Mojo bag - for powerful spells, Voodoo practitioners use small bags filled with crystals, animal parts like fur, bones, feathers, and dried plants. These are called mojo bags and are used to harness or ward off the power. Mentioned in chapter 9.

Netjer - a Kemetic term for the source of divine forces. It is believed that all deities originate from Netjer. Mentioned in chapter 1

Olodumare - the Supreme Being and the creator of the universe according to the Yoruba religion. It's a being that only communicates with Orisha and can't be called on by people. Mentioned in chapters 1 and 3.

Opa egun - a thick, straight, and tall wooden branch. It's used to invoke Orishas. Mentioned in chapter 8.

Opet Festival - was one of the most prominent ancient Kemetic holidays. The festival celebrated the deities Amun, Mut, and Khonsu. Mentioned in chapter 10.

Oshun - the Orisha of the rivers, fertility, love, and marriage. Associated with Our Lady of Charity which is an aspect of the Virgin Mary. Mentioned in chapters 4 and 5.

Orisha - in Yoruba beliefs, the Orisha are spiritual beings that oversee other living creatures. They possess powers people can harness for success, spiritual growth, rites of passage, emotional and physical healing, divination, and more. The Orisha answer to the Supreme Being. Mentioned in chapter 1.

Orunmila or Ornula - is the Orisha of wisdom, knowledge, and divination. He is associated with St. Joseph, St. Philip, and St. Francis of Assisi in Christianity. Mentioned in chapters 4 and 5.

Papa - means father and is used for male Lwas. It denotes respect and honor for these powerful beings. Mentioned in chapter 4.

Petro Lwa - is one of the most significant Lwa families, originating from West Africa. Mentioned in chapter 4.

Polytheism - refers to the beliefs that acknowledge more than one deity (often a large number), as is the case in many African spiritual practices. Mentioned in chapter 1.

Ra - the sun god and the creator of the universe according to certain African religions. It's believed that Maat was made out of him. Mentioned in chapter 2.

Rada Lwa - one of the most significant Lwa families, originating from West Africa. Mentioned in chapter 4.

Rootworkers - a popular term for Hoodoo practitioners who use their wisdom to help others in different aspects of life. Mentioned in chapter 1.

Santeria - known as Lucumi in modern times, is a unique religion that incorporates African spiritual practice elements and Christian beliefs. Mentioned in chapters 1 and 5.

Sed festival - known as the Feast of the Tail, Sed is an ancient Kemetic festival commemorating the pharaoh's rule. More specifically, it honors Horus the Younger, the king of the living. Mentioned in chapter 10.

The Field of Reeds - the ancient Egyptians' equivalent to heaven. Mentioned in chapter 2.

The Weighing of the Hearts - is a trial and judgment every person must go through to determine where they would spend their afterlife depending on the life they've led. Mentioned in chapter 2.

Veve - symbols traced during rituals made for invoking and celebrating Lwas. Mentioned in chapter 4.

Voodoo - a magical practice combining rituals in Christian religious acts and African spirituality. Mentioned in chapter 4.

Wag Festival - a celebration commemorating the god Osiris, Mentioned in chapter 10.

Wep Ronpet - the Kemetic New Year, preceded by the 5 Epagomenal Days celebrating the birthdays of the children of Geb and Nut. Mentioned in chapter 10.

Yemaya - the protector of women and the Orisha of seas, mystery, and lakes. She resembles Our Lady of Regala. Mentioned in chapter 4.

Zangbeto - traditional Voodoo guardians that ward off evil influences. Mentioned in chapter 10.

Part 2: Isese

The Ultimate Guide to Ancestral Spiritual Tradition, Ifa Divination, Yoruba, Odu, Iwa, Asafo, and Orishas

Introduction

Do you want to learn more about Isese and its origins? Have you ever wondered how to follow its path? If so, this book is for you.

Isese is a set of practices that were traditionally used by the Yoruba people of Nigeria to maintain mental and physical health, as well as to cleanse the body and prepare it for special occasions. The word Isese means "purification," and these practices aim to purify the body and soul. Isese includes internal and external cleansing, dietary restrictions, meditation, and prayer. Many Yoruba people still use these practices today and believe they help bring physical, mental, and spiritual balance. In addition, Isese is often used as a form of preventative medicine, as it is believed to help ward off disease.

In this book, we will explore the history of the Isese and its significance in Yoruba culture. We will discuss the importance of honoring your ancestors and the role of orishas and Odu Ifa in Isese. We will also look at how to practice Isese divination and bring the practice into your everyday life. Finally, we will discuss the role of Iwa in Isese, which is a set of values people must adhere to maintain spiritual balance.

Isese is a traditional Nigerian religion that offers daily opportunities for Africans to connect with the spirit world. The practice of Isese involves communication with ancestors and other spirits through prayer, offerings, and divination. Followers of Isese believe that spirits can help them to navigate the challenges of everyday life.

Isese is usually practiced at home, often early in the morning or late at night. A typical session might involve lighting a candle and praying to one's ancestors. Many believers also keep a shrine for their ancestors in their homes, which might be decorated with photos, statues, or other symbols of respect. The practice of Isese can bring a sense of peace and connection to those who participate. It can also be a way to tap into wisdom from our ancestors that can help us make choices in our own lives. For many Africans, Isese is essential to their cultural heritage and identity.

Regardless of your background, this book will give you the tools and knowledge to live an authentic Isese lifestyle. By the end of this book, you will have a better understanding of Isese and its importance to the Yoruba people. You will also have gained insight into how to follow Isese in your own life, as well as how to use it to promote physical and spiritual balance. The path of Isese can be difficult and challenging at times, but the rewards are worth it in the end. So, if you are ready to begin your journey, come and join us as we explore the wonders of Isese.

Chapter 1: What Is Isese?

Isese is an ancient African spirituality and religion that has its roots in the Yoruba people of Nigeria and Benin. Over the centuries, it has evolved into a distinct belief system with unique practices. Isese is based on the worship of the Orisa, a pantheon of deities responsible for different aspects of human life. One of the most important aspects of Isese is the use of ritual and ceremony to honor the deities and ask for their guidance and protection. In recent years, there has been a resurgence of interest in Isese among the Yoruba people, and it is now practiced worldwide.

Isese has its roots in the Yoruba people.
Fastaschool, CC BY-SA 4.0 <https://creativecommons.org/licenses/by-sa/4.0/deed.en> via Wikimedia Commons
https://commons.wikimedia.org/wiki/File:The_Yoruba_Cultural_Group_Children_of_Fasta_International_School_-_Photo_Session.jpg

This chapter will introduce readers to the core concepts of Isese, provide an overview of its history and cultural context, and explore the structure and practice of Isese and the key figures and symbols associated with the religion. In addition, it will explain the differences between Isese and traditional African spirituality and outline the essential principles of Isese. Finally, readers will be provided with useful tips for pronouncing Yoruba and Isese terms.

The Origin of Isese

Isese (pronounced as "ee-SEH-shay") is believed to be thousands of years old and belonged to the ancient Yoruba culture, which flourished on the west coast of Africa in present-day Nigeria and Benin. This belief system developed from the indigenous people's traditional religions, a polytheistic faith that honored multiple deities and spirits.

Isese is based on the belief that the spirits of one's ancestors can help or hinder them in their life journey. If they are properly honored and respected, they will intercede on behalf of their living relatives. However, they may bring misfortune or even death if they are not honored. As a result, Isese practitioners put great emphasis on ancestor veneration. They build shrines for their ancestors and make offerings of food, drink, and other items. They also hold festivals and ceremonies in honor of their departed loved ones. By honoring their ancestors, they ensure that they will continue to receive their blessings.

Where Does Isese Come From?

The word "Isese" can also be translated to "divinity" or "deity," and practitioners believe in a pantheon of gods and goddesses who oversee different aspects of life. Isese is based on the worship of ancestors, and many ceremonies and rituals focus on honoring those who have passed away. Prayer, sacrifice, and divination are also key components of the religion. Isese has been passed down through generations for centuries, and it continues to play an essential role in the lives of its adherents. While the religion may be unfamiliar to some, its rich traditions and history offer a glimpse into the vibrant culture of the Yoruba people.

The History of Isese

Isese has its roots in the traditional beliefs of the Yoruba people of Nigeria and Dahomey (now Benin). Isese is based on the belief that there is a supreme creator god, Olorun, who is responsible for everything that exists. Olorun is served by a pantheon of lesser gods known as orishas. Each Orisha is associated with a particular aspect of human life, such as love, fertility, or war. Practitioners of Isese believe that it is possible to commune with the orishas and request their help in dealing with everyday problems.

Isese was brought to the Americas by Yoruba enslaved people who were taken to Brazil and Cuba during the Atlantic slave trade. In Cuba, the religion merged with Catholicism to create the popular Afro-Cuban religion of Santeria. In Brazil, Isese evolved into Candomblé, another Afro-Brazilian religion. Today, there are estimated to be over 100 million followers of Isese and its various offshoots around the world.

Cultural and Historical Context

Isese is about spirituality, community, and culture. Isese practitioners believe that everyone has two sides to their personality and that it is crucial to balance these two sides to lead a happy and healthy life. To achieve this balance, Isese practitioners use a variety of techniques, including trance rituals, singing, dancing, and drumming. Isese is often practiced within community events and ceremonies, as it is believed that the community can support and heal individuals. The practice has a long history within Yoruba culture and continues to be a vital aspect of Yoruba identity today.

Structure and Practice of Isese

The core tenets of Isese revolve around the worship of Olodumare, the supreme creator god, and the spirits known as Orisha. Adherents of Isese believe that Orisha occupies a realm between the human and divine worlds and serves as a mediator between Olodumare and humanity. Isese is typically practiced through communal rituals and ceremonies, often involving singing, dancing, and drumming. These activities promote a sense of community and unity amongst practitioners while also facilitating contact with the Orisha. Isese is a complex and dynamic belief system that millions of people have practiced for centuries.

Becoming a Babalawo

In the Yoruba religion, a Babalawo is a priest who serves as a mediator between the human world and the spirit world. The role of the Babalawo is to perform rituals and offer guidance to those who seek it. Becoming a Babalawo is not an easy task. It requires years of study and apprenticeship under an experienced Babalawo. The first step is to complete a course of study at a Yoruba divinity school. This typically takes four years. Once you have completed your studies, you will be apprenticed to an experienced Babalawo for two years. During this apprenticeship, you'll learn how to perform rituals and interpret omens. After completing your apprenticeship, you'll be ready to take on the role of Babalawo yourself.

Babalawo act as mediators between the human and spirit world.
Creator:Dierk Lange, CC BY-SA 2.5 <https://creativecommons.org/licenses/by-sa/2.5/deed.en>
via Wikimedia Commons
https://commons.wikimedia.org/wiki/File:Obatala_Priester_im_Tempel.jpg

Formal Initiation into Isese

Initiates into Isese undergo a rigorous process of study and training, which can last for many years. The final stage of initiation is a formal ceremony in which the initiate is formally recognized as a priest or priestess of the religion. The ceremony involves making offerings to the ancestors and nature spirits and is often followed by a feast. Initiates into Isese are expected to maintain a strict code of conduct, and they are required to wear special clothing and jewelry that signifies their status within the religion. Initiates into Isese often find themselves at the center of their community, serving as spiritual leaders and counselors.

Worship Practices of Isese

Isese practitioners believe in the power of ritual and ceremony to bring spiritual healing and balance. Here is a brief overview of the rituals and ceremonies that Isese practitioners typically perform:

1. Rites and Rituals

There are various rites and rituals associated with the religion of Yoruba. These are performed to promote balance and harmony in the world and honor the multiple deities of the religion. Some are performed communally, while others may be done individually. Common rites and rituals include offerings to the ancestors and nature spirits, chanting prayers, and making sacrifices. Many of these rites and rituals are still performed today and play an important role in the lives of those who practice Yoruba. From births and naming ceremonies to funerals and memorials, Isese helps Yoruba people to connect with their ancestors and the spirit world. It is a religion steeped in tradition and history, and its practices continue to provide comfort and strength to its followers.

2. Offerings and Sacrifices

The tradition of offering and sacrificing to the gods is an essential part of the Isese religion. Offerings can be anything from food and drink to candles and incense. Offerings are typically made in thanks for blessings or guidance, to seek protection from misfortune, and to honor the ancestors. Sacrifices, on the other hand, are usually more extreme. They may involve killing an animal. The purpose of a sacrifice is to show ultimate devotion to the gods and to receive their blessings. While some people may see these practices as barbaric, they are essential to the Isese religion.

3. Communing with Ancestors

Isese is based on the belief that the deceased continue to play an active role in the lives of their loved ones and that they can help to protect and guide them from the spirit world. Yoruba people often communicate with their ancestors through prayer, dance, and song. They also offer their ancestors food, water, and other items to honor them. In some cases, they will even ask their ancestors for advice or guidance on critical decisions. By maintaining a close connection with their ancestors, the Yoruba people can tap into a powerful source of wisdom and protection.

Key Figures and Symbols of Isese

Isese is an Afro-Brazilian religion that originates from the Yoruba people of West Africa. Many of the key figures and symbols in Isese come from Yoruba mythology. For example, the Orisha Oshun is associated with rivers and fertility and is often represented by a yellow butterfly. Similarly, the Orisha Obatala is associated with wisdom and purity and is often represented by a white dove. Other important symbols in Isese include beads, feathers, and shells, which are used in rituals and ceremonies. Together, these key figures and symbols play an essential role in the practice of Isese.

Isese vs. Traditional African Spirituality

Traditional African spirituality is based on the belief that everything in the universe is connected. This includes animals, plants, rocks, and even the spirits of the dead. God is seen as being present in all of creation, and humans are seen as part of this larger whole. As such, traditional African spirituality stresses the importance of living in harmony with the natural world. In contrast, Isese is a more individualistic religion that focuses on personal salvation and spiritual growth. While both religions have unique beliefs, they share a common goal: To help people lead fulfilled and meaningful lives. As such, they offer two different but equally valid paths to spiritual enlightenment.

Differences between Isese and Other African Traditions

Isese is an African tradition that is unique in many ways. For one, it is the only African tradition that focuses on the role of ancestors in the lives of the living. In addition, it is one of the few traditions that still rely heavily on oral storytelling. Isese also strongly focuses on community, which is evident in how families and clans are organized. Finally, Isese is distinguished by its use of symbols and rituals to communicate significant cultural values. While Isese shares some similarities with other African traditions, its distinctive features help it to stand out from the crowd.

Origin Stories and Practices

Many origin stories and practices are associated with the Isese tradition in Africa. In many other African traditions, ancestors are venerated and respected, but they are not necessarily seen as an integral part of everyday life. For the Isese people, however, ancestors are an essential part of their culture and play a role in everything from decision-making to healing. Another significant difference is the practice of divination. In Isese tradition, divination is used to communicate with spirits and seek guidance from them. This is a key part of their religious practice, and it is something that sets them apart from other African traditions.

Symbology and Practice Structures

The study of symbology is crucial to understanding both Isese and other religious traditions from around the world. Isese is often said to be a "symbolic" religion, meaning it uses symbols to represent ideas or realities. This use of symbols is one example of how Isese differs from other religious traditions. In contrast to Isese, many other religions focus on practices rather than symbols. For example, Hinduism has a complex system of puja, or worship, while Buddhism emphasizes meditation and the Noble Eightfold Path. This focus on practices rather than symbols means that Isese can be seen as a more "experiential" religion, while other religions are more "conceptual." While there are important differences between these two approaches to religion, both Isese and other religious traditions offer valuable insights into the human experience.

Essential Principles of Isese

The essential principles of Isese are based on the belief that humans can achieve spiritual growth and fulfillment through natural practices. This includes following a set of moral principles, such as respect for self and others, honoring ancestors, and living in harmony with the natural world. Here are some essential principles of Isese:

Duality

Isese is a principle of Yoruba cosmology that holds that everything in the universe is composed of both spirit and matter. This duality is reflected in the fact that all humans have an Egungun, or ancestral spirit, and an Orixa, or guardian spirit. These two spirits are believed to work together to guide and protect the individual. In addition to providing strength and guidance, Isese teaches that all humans are connected to the natural world. This interconnectedness is reflected in the fact that humans are born with a destiny, or Orunmila, determined by their past actions. By understanding and following the principle of Isese, individuals can live in harmony with the natural world and fulfill their destinies.

Ancestor Veneration

The practice of ancestor veneration is central to Isese, and it is thought to be one of the oldest religious traditions in the world. The Yoruba believe that the spirits of deceased ancestors continue to play an active role in the lives of their descendants. As such, they must be honored and respected through ritual offerings and prayers. In return, the ancestors bestow blessings upon their families and protect them from harm. This reciprocal relationship between the living and the dead is essential for maintaining balance and order in the universe. Without it, chaos would reign. Thus, ancestor veneration is a central principle of Isese and plays a vital role in upholding the cosmic order.

Nature Worship

Practitioners believe that the natural world is imbued with creative power and that working in harmony with this power can bring about personal and communal transformation. As such, they pay reverence to a pantheon of deities who oversee different aspects of nature, including earth, wind, fire, and water. Isese followers also believe that humans are an integral part of nature and should therefore strive to live in balance with their surroundings. This manifests in their practice of using natural materials in their rituals and ceremonies and their focus on sustainable living. By honoring the natural world and our place within it, Isese practitioners hope to create a more just and equitable society.

Divination and Healing

In the Yoruba tradition, there is a saying, "Ife ni mo pin, mo juba l'aiye," which means, "Ife is my tablet, I will erase it and start afresh in life." This saying encapsulates the essential principle of Isese, which is that through divination and healing, we can learn from our mistakes, make amends, and start afresh. The process of Isese helps us connect with our ancestors and the spirit world so that we can receive guidance and support on our journey. It is believed that when we let go of the past, we open ourselves up to new possibilities and potentials. Isese is, therefore, an essential principle for those who wish to create positive change in their lives.

Understanding and Acceptance of Natural Cycles

Isese describes the interconnectedness of all things and the natural cycles of life. For example, we rely on the cycle of seasons to provide us with food and water. The cycle of day and night gives us a regular rhythm in our lives. And the cycle of birth, death, and rebirth is a reminder that life is ever-changing and always unfolding. Understanding and accepting these natural cycles allows us to live in harmony with the world around us. This principle of Isese is essential for achieving balance and peace in our lives.

Commitment to Righteousness

Isese refers to the commitment to righteousness and truth and is often symbolized by the color white. To be pure in heart and mind is to be free from corruption and deceit, and those committed to Isese strive to live their lives by this principle. The pursuit of Isese is a lifelong journey, and it is believed that through Isese, one can attain spiritual enlightenment. In a world that is often filled with chaos and confusion, commitment to Isese can be a source of strength and guidance. For those who follow this path, Isese is more than just a religious practice; it is a way of life.

Recognizing the Power of Words

In the Yoruba tradition, it is said that "ese" (pronounced eh-shay) is the greatest of all powers. This is because our words can create and destroy. They can heal or hurt, build up or tear down. That is why it is critical to be mindful of our words. Every word we speak has energy and power behind it. This is why we must always choose our words carefully. When we speak words of love, peace, and happiness, we are helping to create a more positive world. On the other hand, when we use negative words engendered by hate, anger, and violence, we are contributing to the problems in our world. This is a fundamental principle of Isese, which means "respect for all things" in Yoruba. By respecting the power of our words, we can help to create a more positive world for all.

Tips for Pronouncing Yoruba Terms

Yoruba is a language spoken by the Yoruba people of West Africa. Here are a few tips for pronouncing some common Yoruba terms:

- Isese (pronounced: ee-shay-shay)
- Babalawo (pronounced: BAH-bah-lah-woh)
- Ifa (pronounced: ee-fah)
- Odu (pronounced: oh-doo)
- Orisha (pronounced: oh-REE-shah)

- Ebo (pronounced: eh-boh)
- Ase (pronounced: ah-shay)
- Iyanifa (pronounced: ee-yah-nee-fah)
- Iyanifara (pronounced: ee-yah-nee-fah-rah)

These are just a few examples of the many Yoruba terms you may encounter in this book. Learning to pronounce them correctly will help you understand the concepts presented in this book more accurately and fully.

As we have seen, Isese is an ancient tradition that provides us with a path to spiritual enlightenment. Through its core principles, we can live in harmony with the natural cycles of life, pursue righteousness and truth, and recognize the power of our words. By embracing Isese and employing its principles in our lives, we can create a more positive world for ourselves and for generations to come.

The next chapter will explore Olodumare, the Supreme Being, and other orishas in more detail. We will discuss their roles within the spiritual system of Isese and how practitioners worship them. We will also explore the creation story and examine this sacred divination system.

Chapter 2: Olodumare, the Cosmos, and You

Olodumare, the Supreme One, is a powerful and compassionate deity in the Yoruba religion. For millennia, Olodumare has been worshiped for his immense power and is believed to be the Creator of all that exists in the physical realm (Aye). In Yoruba cosmology, Olodumare is the source of all life and is seen as a benevolent force that guides and protects humanity.

Olodumare is the ruler of the universe.
https://unsplash.com/photos/Oze6U2m1oYU

This chapter will explore the importance of Olodumare in the Yoruba spiritual concepts and cosmology, how he is depicted in nature, mythology, religious beliefs, art, and music, his characteristics, his role in Yoruba society, and the teachings associated with him. We will also look at Olodumare's relationship and influence with Obatala, the Creator's agent and emissary, and how Olodumare influences the physical realm (Aye). Finally, we will discuss the importance of respecting and thanking Olodumare in everyday life. By understanding Olodumare and his role in Yoruba spirituality, we can better appreciate the power and beauty of this ancient religion. Olodumare is more than just a divine being; he is an integral part of Yoruba spirituality, cosmology, and culture.

Olodumare — The Supreme One

In the Yoruba religion, Olodumare is the Supreme One, the creator and ruler of the universe. Olodumare is often depicted as a young man, full of energy and life. He is said to be kind and loving but also just and fair. Olodumare is invoked in times of need, for example, when people seek guidance or strength. He is also associated with fertility and new beginnings. In many ways, Olodumare represents the best of what humanity can be: Creative, vibrant, and full of hope. Followers of the Yoruba religion believe that Olodumare is a guiding force in life, always there to provide guidance and protection.

Depictions of Olodumare

In Yoruba mythology, Olodumare is usually depicted as a young man with a long beard, wearing a linen cloth around his waist. He is sometimes shown with four arms, holding a staff and a sword. In some traditions, he is also associated with the Sun and the color white. Olodumare is usually portrayed as a benevolent god concerned with the well-being of humanity. He is invoked in prayers for healing and guidance and is believed to be the source of all abundance and prosperity. In many ways, he embodies the highest ideal of what it means to be divine.

A. In Nature

As mentioned, Olodumare is often depicted as the Sun, which makes sense given that he is the Yoruba god of creation. The Sun is a powerful symbol of life and growth, and it is easy to see how Olodumare might be associated with such an emblem. In some cultures, the Sun is also seen as a harbinger of death, so Olodumare's connection to it might be seen as a representation of the cyclical nature of life. Whatever the case, it's clear that Olodumare is a force to be reckoned with and that nature itself speaks to the power of this Yoruba deity.

Olodumare is depicted as the sun in nature.
https://unsplash.com/photos/obsBswnv7FI

B. In Mythology

In Yoruba mythology, Olodumare is responsible for the orderly functioning of the universe. He is often portrayed as a wise and benevolent father figure who dispenses justice fairly and evenly. Many myths associate Olodumare with the Sun, depicting him as dousing the world in light and warmth. While he is typically shown as being kind and just, Olodumare is also capable of great wrath, and those who anger him can expect to suffer severe consequences. Ultimately, Olodumare is a powerful and merciful god who ensures the world runs smoothly.

C. In Religious Beliefs

Olodumare is a supreme god in the Yoruba religion. He is depicted as the creator of the universe and the source of all life. Olodumare is also associated with rain and thunder. In some beliefs, he is said to live in the sky, while in others, he is seen as a more distant and mysterious figure. Regarded as a benevolent deity, he rewards those who follow his teachings and punishes those who go against him. His presence is often invoked in religious ceremonies and prayers, particularly when the Yoruba people seek guidance or strength.

D. In Art and Music

Olodumare is adorned with symbols of fertility. In music, Olodumare is represented by the drum, the instrument through which he communicates with the world. In art, Olodumare is portrayed as a peaceful and benevolent figure surrounded by animals and plants. In some artwork, he is shown as a powerful figure with four arms and a long beard. Olodumare's symbols of fertility and benevolence can be seen in many works of art throughout the Yoruban culture. For instance, some sculptures depict him as a guardian of nature and fertility, while others portray him as a wise and compassionate ruler.

Characteristics of Olodumare

In the Yoruba religion, Olodumare is a source of wisdom and knowledge, and he is always available to help humans when they need guidance. Olodumare is also known for his sense of humor, and he enjoys making people laugh. In addition to being the creator god, Olodumare is responsible for maintaining order in the universe. He does this by ensuring that all beings follow the natural laws he has set forth. Olodumare is a powerful and central figure in the Yoruba religion and is revered by all who believe in him. Here are some characteristics of Olodumare that are important to note:

A. Omnipotent

In the Yoruba religion, Olodumare is often described as omnipotent, meaning that he has the power to do anything. In addition to being all-powerful, Olodumare is all-knowing and all-seeing. He is the one who decides what happens in the world, and no one can escape his judgment. As the ultimate authority, Olodumare is invoked in times of trouble or danger. His power is absolute, and those who worship him believe he can protect them from harm. Whether you believe in Olodumare or not, there is no denying that he is a powerful force in Yoruba religion.

B. Omniscient

In Yoruba mythology, Olodumare is omniscient, meaning he knows everything that has happened, is happening, and all that will happen. He is believed to live in the sky and communicates with humans through oracles. If you want to ask Olodumare a question, you must first go to an oracle who will relay your question to Olodumare. In return, Olodumare will give the oracle a message to give to you. While Olodumare is kind and benevolent, he is also just and will not hesitate to punish those disobeying him. Followers believe that if they anger Olodumare, he may send thunder and lightning to destroy their crops or harm their livestock. For this reason, they always show respect for Olodumare and follow his commands.

C. All-Loving and All-Forgiving

Olodumare is an all-loving god because he loves all his children equally. He does not love one more than the other. He loves all his children with the same love. Olodumare is also all-forgiving. If his children make mistakes, he forgives them. He does not hold grudges against them and loves his children unconditionally. He does not love them because they are good or behave in a certain way. He loves them no matter what they do or how they behave. Olodumare is also all-merciful. If his children are in pain or suffering, he has mercy on them and helps them.

The Role of Olodumare in Yoruba Society

Olodumare is the creator god in the Yoruba religion who is responsible for everything that exists and controls the destiny of all humans. Olodumare is the source of all good things. In addition to being a powerful creator god, Olodumare is also seen as a guardian and protector. He watches over his people and is sometimes invoked in times of trouble or danger. Olodumare is a central figure in Yoruba society and plays an important role in the lives of all Yoruba people.

A. As a Source of Guidance and Support

Olodumare is responsible for the ordering of the universe and is the ultimate source of guidance and support for humans. In Yoruba society, Olodumare is often invoked during times of need, such as when someone is having difficulty conceiving a child or crop yields are low. He is also thought to be the protector of orphans and widows. Olodumare is typically portrayed as a kind and benevolent god, and his worshipers often pray to him for guidance, protection, and prosperity.

B. The Creator in Yoruba Religion and Cosmology

In Yoruba religion and cosmology, Olodumare is often called Olorun or Olofi. Olodumare is said to have created the world and everything in it, including humans, animals, plants, and the elements. He is also responsible for maintaining balance and harmony in the world. Olodumare is often portrayed as a kind and benevolent deity interested in the welfare of his creations. He is seen as a stern and just judge who punishes those who break the laws of nature. Regardless of how he is viewed, Olodumare is an important part of Yoruba religion and cosmology and plays a vital role in the lives of practitioners.

C. Olodumare's Role in the Creation Story

The creation story of Olodumare is an important part of Yoruba cosmology. According to the myth, Olodumare created the universe and all living things. He used his breath to bring life into existence and endowed each creature with special gifts and abilities. Olodumare gave humans the power of intelligence and creativity, and he tasked them with caring for the world and all it contains. Olodumare also gave humans free will to make their own choices about how they will live their lives. In the end, Olodumare is seen as the ultimate source of all life and all creation. He is responsible for everything that exists in the physical realm.

Olodumare and Obatala — The Creator and His Agent

Olodumare is the creator of all things, and Obatala is his agent. Olodumare is the source of all life, and Obatala is the one who brings it into being. Obatala shapes and molds the world, while Olodumare gives it form. Together, they are responsible for everything that exists. Olodumare is kind and loving, while Obatala is firm and just. They are both essential to the world and its inhabitants. We owe them both our thanks and our respect.

A. Obatala as Olodumare's Emissary

In Yoruba mythology, Obatala is the God of Creativity and Orisha of calm waters. He is also known as the father of all orishas, as he was the first to descend from Olodumare's heavens to the earth. Obatala is often depicted as a wise and peaceful elder, and he is associated with purity, chastity, and peace. As Olodumare's emissary, Obatala brings peace and order to the world. He is responsible for creating human beings and infusing them with his essence of calmness and peace. In many ways, Obatala embodies all that is good and holy in the world. He is a powerful force for good, and his presence is always a welcome addition to any situation.

B. The Significance of Obatala

Obatala is an important deity in the Yoruba religion. He is thought to be the patron of artists and healers, and his symbols include the colors white and silver. To many Yoruba people, Obatala is a powerful source of strength and inspiration. According to Yoruba belief, Obatala was the one who brought light and order to the world, and he is often invoked in prayers for peace and harmony. Obatala's role as Olodumare's emissary is important, and his presence in the world serves as a reminder of Olodumare's love and compassion for all living things.

C. The Relationship between Olodumare and Obatala

In the Yoruba religion, Obatala is one of Olodumare's chief subordinates. Although Obatala is subordinate to Olodumare, the two have a close relationship. Olodumare often consults with Obatala when making decisions about human affairs, and Obatala is said to be Olodumare's favorite child. In turn, Obatala is very loyal to Olodumare and always strives to please him. This close relationship between Olodumare and Obatala is reflected in the many stories and legends about them in Yoruba tradition.

One such story is the myth of how Obatala created the world. According to this myth, Olodumare gave Obatala a white palm nut and told him to create the world from it. Obatala accepted this challenge, and with his great intelligence and creativity, he created the earth, the sky, the seas, and all of the creatures that inhabit them. Obatala then presented his creation to Olodumare, who praised him for his work.

This myth illustrates the close bond between Olodumare and Obatala and their respective roles in the creation of the universe. It also shows that while Obatala is subordinate to Olodumare, he still plays an important role in the divine hierarchy. Obatala is a source of creativity and order and a reminder of Olodumare's love and benevolence.

Olodumare and the Physical Realm

Olodumare is a force of nature, and his energy can be seen in the ever-changing patterns of the world around us. Olodumare is responsible for guiding the destiny of humanity, and he is the source of all good and evil. While sometimes seen as a cruel god, he is also known to be just and fair, dispensing rewards and punishments according to our actions. In many ways, Olodumare represents the duality of life itself: He is both creator and destroyer, the giver and taker of life. It is through him that humans experience both joy and pain, success and failure. And it is only by understanding his will can humans can hope to achieve their goals in this world.

The Connection between Olodumare and Aye

Although Olodumare is often considered distant and removed from the day-to-day affairs of humans, he is still very much connected and involved in the physical realm (Aye). In Yoruba belief, Olodumare constantly communicates with humans through various means such as dreams, visions, divination, and sacrifice. Understanding these messages from Olodumare allows humans to gain insight into their past, present, and future. Olodumare is also thought to be involved in creating each individual's fate, and through his guidance, a person can understand the cosmic order of the universe.

Orishas as Emissaries of Olodumare

In addition to communicating with humans directly, Olodumare works through his emissaries, the orishas. The orishas are divine beings who act as intermediaries between Olodumare and humanity. Each orisha is associated with a specific area of life or energy and tasked with carrying out Olodumare's will in the physical realm. Through their guidance, humans can gain a better understanding of Olodumare's plans and have the opportunity to work toward their spiritual growth. The orishas act as divine guides, helping humans achieve harmony and balance in their lives.

Teachings Associated with Olodumare

The teachings associated with Olodumare are varied and complex; however, a few core beliefs remain consistent. First and foremost, Olodumare teaches that all things are connected and interdependent and that all life is sacred. This includes the physical realm (Aye) and the spiritual realm (Ire). Olodumare also teaches that all beings have a purpose in life, and each person must strive to fulfill their destiny. Here are some other teachings that are often associated with Olodumare:

A. The Need to Balance Opposites in Life

Olodumare teaches that to be successful, one must learn to balance the opposing forces of light and dark. This includes understanding how to constructively incorporate positive and negative energies into one's life . It also means recognizing the importance of order and chaos in the universe. With this understanding, one can strive to create a harmonious balance of energies in their life.

B. The Importance of Respect and Gratitude

Olodumare encourages us to show respect and gratitude to the physical and spiritual realms. This includes showing appreciation for the cycles of nature and divine guidance that comes through dreams, visions, and divination. By demonstrating respect and gratitude for the divine forces at work, humans can learn to create a more harmonious balance within themselves. The importance of this respect and gratitude to Olodumare extends to our relationships with other people, as it helps us build more meaningful connections.

C. The Power of Sacrifice

The Yoruba believe that Olodumare requires humans to make sacrifices to receive his divine guidance. Through sacrifice, humans exchange energy between the physical and spiritual realms. In this way, humans can understand the divine will of Olodumare and use it to improve their lives. The power of sacrifice brings a sense of gratitude and reverence that helps us connect with the divine. Sacrifices can be offered in the form of food, items, or even time and energy.

D. The Need for Compassion and Mercy

Olodumare teaches us to be compassionate and merciful in our dealings with others. This includes understanding that everyone has their struggles and that we must be willing to show mercy and kindness even when someone has hurt us. By doing this, we can create a strong sense of harmony in our lives and the world around us. This can be difficult to grasp, but it is a powerful tool for understanding and connecting with the divine.

E. The Role of Free Will and Responsibility

Olodumare believes that all humans have the power of free will; however, they must also take responsibility for their actions. This means recognizing the consequences of our choices and making the best decisions for ourselves and our communities. By exercising free will responsibly, we can move closer to achieving a spiritual balance in our lives and creating a more harmonious world.

Olodumare is the divine creator of the universe in the Yoruba religion. He is known as Olorun, Olofi, and Olofin. Olodumare is considered to be all-powerful, all-knowing, all-loving, and all-seeing. He is responsible for maintaining the balance of the universe and guiding the destiny of humanity. In addition to being the Supreme God, Olodumare is often associated with fertility and agriculture. Many of his worshippers offer prayers and sacrifices to him to ensure a good harvest.

Olodumare is sometimes invoked in healing rituals. He is believed to have the power to cure illness and restore health. Whether seeking guidance, protection, or healing, Olodumare is a powerful deity that can help you achieve your goals. The teachings of Olodumare provide an important foundation for understanding Yoruba spiritual beliefs and practices. These lessons are timeless, as they help us to connect with the divine, create meaningful relationships with others, and strive for a more balanced life.

By recognizing the power of sacrifice, respect, gratitude, compassion, mercy, free will, and responsibility, humans can strive to honor the divine.

Chapter 3: Odu Ifa, the Divine Scripture

Most organized religions revolve around a holy literary corpus that encapsulates the religion's wisdom and experience, and Isese is no different. Isese is an earth-centered religion that believes in the interconnectedness of all things. The Yoruba people of Nigeria, Benin, and Togo are the custodians of this religion, and it is often passed down through their families. The Isese literary corpus includes the Ifa Corpus, which is a collection of stories, proverbs, and songs that teach moral lessons; the Odu Ifa Corpus, a set of sixteen sacred texts that guide everything from birth to death; and the Ogbe Ifa Corpus, a set of verses that are used in divination practices. Together, these three bodies of work form the foundation of the Isese religion and provide its followers with a rich source of wisdom and advice.

This chapter will provide an overview of the Odu Ifa Corpus, discussing its structure and content. We will also explore the major themes in Odu Ifa literature, summarize the texts, and explain their cultural and historical significance. Finally, we will discuss how Olodumare is thought to have created the Odu Ifa and what is involved in becoming a Babalawo, a highly-trained priest specializing in divination. At the end of this chapter, we will present the Sixteen Principles of Ifa, each with a brief explanation of its relevance and how to incorporate it into your life.

Introduction and Overview of Odu Ifa

Odu Ifa is a Yoruba spiritual system used for divination and fortune-telling. The word "odu" means "sign" or "portent," and "ifa" means "Ifa Oracle." Odu Ifa is based on a body of sacred texts called the Ifa Corpus, which contains a wealth of information about the Yoruba people's history, cosmology, and mythology. Traditionally, Odu Ifa is encoded in a system of sixteen major signs, each corresponding to a different aspect of human life. The signs are often represented by cowrie shells, which are used in divination rituals. Odu Ifa is an essential part of Yoruba culture and plays a vital role in many people's lives in Nigeria and other countries with large Yoruba populations.

Cowrie Shells are used to represent the signs.
https://pixnio.com/miscellaneous/seashell-mollusk-conch-gastropod#

Structure of the Odu Ifa Corpus

The Odu Ifa Corpus is a collection of over 2,300 poems in the Ifa divination system. The Corpus is divided into sixteen major sections; each is subdivided into numerous smaller sections. The first section, the Odu Ifa, contains most of the poems and is used for divining purposes. The other fifteen sections, the Esoteric Odu, are used for different purposes, such as initiations, sacrificial rituals, and prayers. The Corpus is also divided into two parts: The Exoteric Odu, which is available to all practitioners, and the Esoteric Odu, which is only available to those who have undergone initiation.

A. Divination Verses

The Ifa literary Corpus is a collection of over 2,000 poems used in divination. The verses, known as Odu, are divided into sixteen main categories, each containing several sub-categories. There are 256 Odu used to interpret the signs and symbols that appear during a divination ceremony. While the Odu is primarily concerned with predicting the future, they also offer advice on everything from relationships to health and well-being. As such, they provide invaluable wisdom and guidance for those who consult the Ifa Oracle.

B. Commentaries on the Verses

The Odu Ifa Corpus contains commentaries on the verses. These commentaries, known as Esoteric Odu, are composed of longer passages that explain and elaborate on the meaning of the verses. They provide further insight and guidance for those who consult the Ifa Oracle and reveal a great deal about Yoruba cosmology, mythology, and culture. The Esoteric Odu is primarily intended for those who have undergone initiation and are thus considered adepts or experts in the Ifa tradition.

C. Other Texts

In addition to the Odu Ifa and Esoteric Odu, the Corpus also contains several other texts. These include hymns and prayers used in various rituals and stories about Yoruba gods, myths, and legends. The Corpus also includes information on the Yoruba people's history, customs, and beliefs. It is believed that Olodumare, the Creator God of the Yoruba people, created the Odu Ifa as a way for humans to understand the mysteries of life.

Major Themes in Odu Ifa Literature

Odu Ifa is a body of religious literature concerned with the worship of the orishas—deities that control various aspects of human life. The Odu Ifa corpus includes myths, stories, and songs used in ceremonies and rituals. Many of these texts focus on the idea of harmonious living, emphasizing the need for humans to live in balance with nature. Other major themes include the importance of ancestors, the role of women in society, and the need to maintain a healthy mind and body. While some of these themes may seem timeless, they remain relevant today. As we strive to create a more just and sustainable world, the wisdom of Odu Ifa can help to guide our steps.

A. Creation Stories

In the Odu Ifa texts, the Lord Ifa reveals himself as the creator of all things and speaks of his relationship with humanity. The Odu Ifa texts are divided into several categories: Creation stories, myths, folktales, and proverbs. Of these, the creation stories are perhaps the most important, as they offer insight into the Yoruba cosmology and worldview. In one popular creation story, the world is born from a cosmic egg hatched by a dove. From this egg emerge four beings, Obatala, Orisa-nla, Oduduwa, and Olorun. These beings go on to create everything else in the world, including humanity. While there are many versions of this story, all emphasize the importance of cooperation and interdependence in the world. As such, they provide an essential foundation for Yoruba culture and society.

B. Deities and Supernatural Beings

In the Odu Ifa literature, many deities and supernatural beings play important roles. For example, Orunmila is the god of wisdom and divination, while Obatala is the god of peace and purity. Many other gods and goddesses preside over different aspects of human life. In addition to the gods, a variety of spirits, including the orishas, are responsible for guiding humans on their path in life. The Odu Ifa literature provides a wealth of information on these different beings and their roles in human life. As such, it is an essential resource for anyone interested in understanding the beliefs and traditions of the Yoruba people.

C. Morality and Ethics

Odu Ifa contains a wealth of moral and ethical teachings. Traditionally recited by priests during religious ceremonies, these texts offer guidance on everything from the proper way to live one's life to the correct way to conduct business transactions. Many of the moral and ethical principles contained in Odu Ifa are still relevant today, and they offer a valuable perspective on how to live a virtuous life. The following are some of the most important moral and ethical teachings found in Odu Ifa:

- **Respecting Elders and Ancestors:** Odu Ifa teaches that respecting elders and ancestors is essential for maintaining social harmony. This principle is still relevant today, as respecting elders is important to maintaining a cohesive society.

- **Honesty and Integrity:** Odu Ifa contains numerous tales about the importance of honesty and maintaining integrity. This principle is as important today as in ancient times, as honesty and integrity are essential for maintaining trust in any relationship.
- **Compassion:** One of the most prevalent themes in Odu Ifa is the importance of compassion. This virtue is essential for living a moral and ethical life, as it helps us to see the humanity in others and to treat them with kindness and respect.

D. Rituals and Ceremonies

Many different types of rituals and ceremonies are described in the Odu Ifa literature. Some of these rituals are performed for particular purposes, such as healing the sick or asking for guidance from the spirits. Others are designed to be more general celebrations of life, love, and fertility. Regardless of their purpose, all of the rituals and ceremonies described in the Odu Ifa literature share a common goal: To bring people closer to the natural world and the gods living within it. By participating in these rituals, followers can learn to appreciate the rhythms of nature and better understand our place within the cosmos.

E. Social Structures

In the West, we often think of literature as telling of an individual hero's journey. Works like the *Odyssey* or *Beowulf* are stories of individuals who, through their actions, come to define themselves and their place in society. However, in Odu Ifa literature, much focus is on social structures. Accounts of heroes are often used to illustrate the importance of family, friends, and community in achieving success. This emphasis on social structures can be seen as a reflection of the collectivist values of many African cultures. It also highlights that, in many cultures, an individual's identity is not solely determined by their actions but by those around them. As such, Odu Ifa literature provides a valuable window into the values and beliefs of African cultures.

F. Proverbs, Wisdom, and Knowledge

Wisdom proverbs are an important part of Odu Ifa literature. These proverbs offer advice and guidance on various topics, from relationships to work to parenting. They are also often used to teach young people the significance of making good decisions. In addition to wisdom proverbs, Odu Ifa literature contains a wealth of knowledge about the natural world, including information on animal behavior, plant life, and the

Moon's cycles. This knowledge is essential for understanding the world and helping us make the best life choices.

How Olodumare Created the Odu Ifa Corpus

Olodumare (also known as Olofi and Olorun) is said to be the creator of all things and is therefore believed to have created the Odu Ifa corpus. According to this belief, Olodumare used the power of his wisdom and divinity to create the Odu Ifa texts, which contain the answers to all questions and the solutions to all problems. The Odu Ifa corpus was written by the sixteen orishas, or Gods of Ifa, sent by Olodumare to impart his wisdom and knowledge to the people. The Ifa texts are seen as a direct link to Olodumare, and those who study them can learn the secrets of life from the god himself.

Becoming a Babalawo and Learning the Texts

The Babalawo is the chief priest of Ifa and is responsible for interpreting the Odu Ifa, a sacred text that contains the wisdom of the Yoruba people. The Babalawo undergoes rigorous training to become qualified to interpret the Odu Ifa. After completing their training, Babalawos are considered experts in divination and Yoruba culture and play a crucial role in preserving traditional knowledge.

The Babalawo is trained rigorously to interpret the Odu Ifa.
Kehinde1234, CC BY-SA 4.0 <https://creativecommons.org/licenses/by-sa/4.0>, via Wikimedia Commons https://commons.wikimedia.org/wiki/File:Babalawo_Akinropo_(AKA._%E1%BB%8Cs%E1%BA%B9-tura_il%E1%BA%B9%CC%80_%C3%8Cb%C3%A0d%C3%A0n).jpg

A. Initiation and Training

Followers of the Yoruba religion believe that humans are born with a connection to the orishas and that this connection can be strengthened through worship and ritual. One of the most important roles in the religion is that of the Babalawo, or priest. Babalawos undergo a lengthy process of initiation and training to become priests. The first step is to complete an apprenticeship under a senior Babalawo. During this time, the apprentice learns about the history and mythology of the Yoruba people and the traditional methods of divination. This typically takes several years, during which time the apprentice learns about the history and mythology of the Yoruba religion and its various rituals and ceremonies.

Once the apprenticeship is complete, the Babalawo undergoes a series of initiations to join the ranks of the priesthood. These initiations are designed to teach the Babalawo about the universe's energies and how to use them for divination. These trials are known as the "egungun," which test their knowledge and skills. Those who complete the egungun are considered to be fully qualified Babalawos.

B. Learning the Verses and Commentaries

To become a Babalawo, one must first undergo extensive training in Ifa, the religion of the Yoruba people. This training typically takes place at an ile-Ifa, or house of Ifa, where a Babalawo-in-training will spend several years learning the verses and commentaries of Ifa. The Ifa corpus is vast and complex, and can take many years to master. However, the rewards of becoming a Babalawo are well worth the effort. As a Babalawo, a person can serve the community as a religious leader and counselor and have the opportunity to travel to Ifa shrines worldwide.

C. Orisha Initiation Ceremonies

The initiation process to become a Babalawo is long and arduous; however, it is essential to understand the role and responsibilities of this important figure within the Yoruba religion. There are three main stages to the initiation process. The first is the Iwori Meji, which involves undergoing physical and spiritual tests. The second stage, Ikini Meji, requires the initiate to perform a series of rituals to purify their mind and body. Finally, during the Ogun Meji stage, the initiate undergoes a series of initiations that end with their formal induction into the role of Babalawo. Each stage of the process is critical in helping the initiate to understand the complexities of their new role and develop the skills needed to serve their community effectively.

The Sixteen Principles of Ifa

At the root of the teachings and traditions of Ifa lies the Odu Ifa, a sacred text with over 256 verses that detail the laws of the universe and advice on how to live in harmony with God and creation. The Sixteen Principles of Ifa are fundamental principles derived from the Odu Ifa, which provide guidance and insight into Yoruban culture and religion. These principles are based on a deep understanding of how the universe works, and they can be used as a moral compass to help individuals strive for greater balance in their lives. The principles include:

1. **Omori** — Respect for the creator, Olodumare
2. **Iwa Pele** — The law of karma and balance
3. **Ore Oruko** — Respect for one's elders and ancestors
4. **Ebo Ri Aye** — Offerings in exchange for divine favor
5. **Ona Abiye** — Openness and honesty in dealing with others
6. **Oruko Akuko** — Honor for one's name and reputation
7. **Emi Ti Eja** — Care for the environment
8. **Se Iku Baba Wa** — Commitment to justice and fairness
9. **Onisowo Ni Iwa** — Respect for the rights of others
10. **Iwa Ni Ijinle** — Respect for tradition and knowledge
11. **Iwa Ni Imule Aye** — Respect for life
12. **Se Eru Igbeyawo** — Adherence to one's promises
13. **Omo Eniyan Lo Loju** — Kindness to others
14. **Iwa Ni Iwaju** — Respect for the law
15. **Se Ojuri Iwori** — Obedience to authority
16. **Alafia** — Peace, harmony, and well-being for all.

The Sixteen Principles of Ifa are essential teachings passed down through generations to uphold the sacred laws of Olodumare. These principles provide guidance and a code of conduct to live by and can be used as an ethical and moral compass to help individuals strive for greater balance in their lives. By following these principles, we can create more harmony, peace, and prosperity in our lives.

Summary and Content of the Odu Ifa Texts

The first section of the Odu Ifa texts, the Odu Ifa, contains the story of the world's creation and the first humans.

The second section, the Ose Otura, contains the story of the god Oturanoia and his battle with the demon Olokun.

The third section, the Ose Irete, contains the story of the goddess Irete and her marriage to the god Orunmila.

The fourth section, the Ose Meji, contains the story of the twins Meji and their battle with disease.

The fifth section, the Ose Odi, contains the story of Odiraa and her journey to find her lost husband.

The sixth section, the Ose Obara, contains the story of Obara and his quest for power.

The seventh section, the Ose Ogunda, contains the story of Ogunda and his battle with death.

The eighth section, the Ose Osa, contains the story of Osa and her fight against evil.

The ninth section, the Ose Oturu, contains the story of Oturu and his journey to find himself.

The tenth section, the Ose Irete Ketu, contains Ketu's search for his lost wife.

The eleventh section, known as "12 oko temi eru pele pele l'owo ni iku ni osun meje ati ni agbara ni olorun ni iretitated- ifa," says that there should be twelve markets in every town so that people can trade goods and services, including food, medicine, clothes, shelter, metal works, woodwork, artifacts, jewelry, and tools.

The twelfth section, the Ose Oyeku, contains the story of Oyeku and his wisdom in dealing with a dispute between two villages.

The thirteenth section, the Odu Itefa, contains verses about Ifa divination and its power to predict the future accurately.

The fourteenth section, the Ose Ifa, contains verses of praise and reverence for Olodumare and guidance on living in harmony with nature and one's fellow man.

The fifteenth section, the Ose Odi Meji, contains verses dealing with social justice and staying true to one's values in the face of adversity.

The sixteenth section, the Ose Irete Akuaro, contains verses of worship for Olodumare and guidance on how to lead a life of righteousness.

The Odu Ifa Corpus is an essential source of knowledge and guidance for all followers of the Isese tradition. It contains a wealth of wisdom and insight into living in harmony with nature, our fellow humans, and ultimately with Olodumare. The Odu Ifa teaches how to make ethical decisions, stay true to one's values, and practice the teachings of Ifa. To become a Babalawo, one must learn at least a few verses from each Odu Ifa to gain knowledge and insight into each principle. Individuals can strive for greater balance and harmony by incorporating these principles into daily life.

Chapter 4: Practicing Ifa Divination

The Odu Ifa, an ancient body of knowledge that contains all the secrets of life and holds extensive knowledge, is more than just a reference book. It is also the central element of the Ifa divination system. This Yoruba spiritual oracle helps individuals discover their destinies and plan their lives by these paths. It offers a practical way to help people who rely on natural laws, such as the law of cause and effect, achieve personal balance and wholeness. The Odu Ifa is not just a transactional tool; it can be seen as a manual for personal transformation!

Its documents provide useful insight into what makes us most true to ourselves, allowing us to embrace our greatness and foster purposeful relationships with ourselves, others, and nature to thrive. This chapter briefly introduces Ifa divination and its tools, symbols, and traditional practices. It also provides tips on interpreting these symbols and understanding the power of prayer. Finally, it includes information on how to access the guidance of Oracles and Babalawo.

Introduction to Ifa Divination

Ifa divination is a traditional African system of divination based on the belief that a cosmic order governs human affairs. This order is known as Ashe, and it is believed to manifest in the patterns of nature. To access the Ashe, practitioners of Ifa use various methods, including tossing cowrie shells or other objects, to create patterns known as Odu. The

Odu are then interpreted to gain insight into the past, present, and future.

Ifa divination is often used for guidance in matters such as marriage, childbirth, business ventures, and other important life decisions. It is also used for healing purposes, both physical and spiritual. In recent years, Ifa has gained popularity outside its traditional home in West Africa, with practitioners now found worldwide. Whether you are seeking guidance or simply curious about this ancient divination system, Ifa offers a unique and powerful way to connect with the deeper forces at work in your life.

A. History of Ifa Divination

The fascinating practice of Ifa divination has been a crucial part of African history for centuries. It is a form of divination using oracular chants and specific, sacred objects known as Opele. Many believe that these objects are used to divine the future. Practitioners all over Africa would use them and chants to attempt to answer all sorts of questions on behalf of their clients, from spiritual to personal matters. This holistic and compassionate practice has been adopted by many in recent years, primarily in Latin America and other regions with high populations of African descent. By furthering our understanding of Ifa divination's history, we can progress toward embracing its timeless wisdom.

B. How Does It Work?

Ifa divination is an ancient system of divine guidance originating from the Yoruba people of West Africa. It is traditionally practiced by Adhafa, Ifa Priestesses, and Priests, who can communicate with the Orisha—the deities and spirits that occupy their world. The divination process begins with a consultation between the practitioner and the client. During this session, questions are asked about the client's life to determine what deities or energies influence them and how best to seek guidance for their situation.

The practitioner then uses a variety of sacred objects and symbols, such as cowrie shells or palm kernels, which reveal messages from the spiritual realm and provide advice, warnings, and predictions for future events or experiences. With its focus on inner transformation through connecting with one's energies, Ifa divination provides unique insight that can help bring clarity to situations and make positive changes in people's lives.

C. Who Can Practice It

Practicing Ifa divination is an art form that can be studied and enhanced with dedication and the right guidance. Anyone open to learning the history and deep understanding of this African-based spiritual practice is capable of mastering it, regardless of gender, age, or cultural background. What sets Ifa divination apart from other forms of ancestral-based advice is its uniqueness in being a mental exercise—no tools are needed for practitioners to find answers and insight. With the proper respect and instruction from experienced teachers, all can become proficient in practicing Ifa divination.

Tools Used in Ifa Divination

Ifa divination utilizes tools and objects to uncover knowledge and secrets about past, present, and future events. These tools include sixteen palm nuts and a chain or kola nut with eight dried janus cowrie shells attached. A diviner uses these tools to cast, throwing them onto a "divining tray" while they listen intently to the interpretation of the patterns made by where they land. Through this process, Ifa practitioners gain insight into how best to bring stability and balance into current situations or lives. It is believed that if one aligns themselves spiritually with the "cosmic force," one finds a sense of peace in life's difficulties.

A. Divination Chain

The use of the Divination Chain (Opele) during Ifa divination is quite fascinating. This tool is composed of eight individually painted wooden blocks representing nature's forces and their influence on our lives. During a reading, they are cast onto an open palm or a conical diviner's tray to provide insight into difficult questions and situations. Each block within the divination chain is believed to carry a message from the Orisa, or spiritual realms, along with its associated energy. Through this divination process, we can gain clarity and guidance on all matters relating to our well-being and prosperity. It's no wonder that this ancient technique is so popular and potent today, as it has provided comfort and guidance for generations.

Opele.
Dornicke, CC BY-SA 4.0 <https://creativecommons.org/licenses/by-sa/4.0>, via Wikimedia Commons https://commons.wikimedia.org/wiki/File:Opele_ifá%C3%A1_MN_01.jpg

Opele is an important divination tool traditionally used to get answers to questions regarding a person's life, ranging from finding out why something is not working in their life to advice on upcoming business decisions. Opele consists of four sections, and Ifa priests or diviners perform the Opele divinations. As they divine, they make offerings and pray while shaking their Opele until it reveals their answer from the Orisha deities that provide guidance. Ultimately, it is believed that when asking Oshumare (meaning "divine messenger") for advice with this sacred tool, one can discover hidden truths about any given situation for greater understanding and progress.

B. Cowrie Shells

Cowrie shells have an incredibly rich historical past concerning spiritual and divination practices, particularly Ifa Divination. Native to the Mediterranean, Persian Gulf, and parts of India, cowrie shells have been used as a form of currency by many cultures for many centuries. According to Ifa practitioners, cowries are believed to be messengers from the gods, helping with spiritual guidance and revelation. While Ifa divination alters between eight and sixteen pieces of these exquisitely smooth shells, they often come adorned with symbols and markings that can offer insight into the reading being conducted. They are a helpful tool for accessing knowledge from our ancestors, with their utilization offering us a connection to the Divine that is otherwise inaccessible.

C. Palm Nut

The palm nut is an integral part of the Ifa Divination practice as it is a symbolic tool to communicate with and interpret the Orisa, spiritual energies. When performed, the Babalawo (divinity priest) will cast sixteen palm nuts in a traditional basket called ireke or ikin to receive messages from the divine. By deciphering how each nut has fallen, face down or upright, the Babalawo can determine which Orisha communicate through their blessings. And just like that, recommendations and advice will follow. This ancient tradition with an unbroken lineage of thousands of years is truly an incredible experience!

Palm Nut.

Edithobayaa1, CC BY-SA 4.0 <https://creativecommons.org/licenses/by-sa/4.0>, via Wikimedia Commons https://commons.wikimedia.org/wiki/File:Palm_nut_in_Ghana.jpg

D. Ewe

Ewe, an African plant fiber, is an intrinsic part of Ifa Divination, a system of consulting oracles for spiritual guidance. Ewe is made from the inner bark of select species of trees, dried in the sun, and then rolled into thin strips. These little strips are a significant aid to divination by serving as a visual representation of fate and how it can be influenced through human intervention. The Ewe also reminds people to be mindful of their thoughts and words to remain aligned with their intention and manifest their desired outcomes. The power of the Ewe comes from its direct connection to the divine, allowing us to gain insight and guidance for any aspect of life.

E. Ikin

Ikin is an ancient divination tool used in Ifa, a West African spiritual tradition. It is believed to connect people to the orishas, divine entities that can provide guidance and protection. Ikin is made of palm nuts, which are cast on a mat or sack to create patterns diviners interpret. The patterns created by the oracle give insight into current circumstances, obstacles, opportunities for the future, and advice on handling them. While knowledge of Ikin has become almost lost in recent years, it still offers an incredibly powerful way of gaining insight into our lives.

F. Iroke

Iroke is an important tool used in Ifa divination. Iroke is a type of small to medium-sized sea snail that produces white and cream-colored shells, which are harvested for commercial use. These shells are believed to contain the spiritual energy necessary for diviners to communicate with the Yoruba orishas or gods. Used by Ifa priests and priestesses along with various other objects during divination ceremonies, Iroke can answer questions about health, employment, relationships, and more. Divination is an ancient practice used to bring harmony into people's lives. Ifa practitioners continue this tradition using Iroke shells today as they work with their clients to help them understand their challenges and find solutions within themselves.

Odu Ifa Symbols

Odu Ifa symbols are an integral part of the Ifa religion, which is based on worshipping deities through encounters with divine messages or prophecies. These ancient symbols have been used for centuries and symbolize various aspects of Yoruba beliefs and traditions. Sixteen major Odu Ifa sacred symbols represent many destinies, good and bad luck, wisdom and knowledge, protection from harm, fertility, well-being, success, and personal progress. All these help shape character behaviors among people who practice the traditional Yoruba faith. Each symbol has a unique meaning and provides its followers with spiritual guidance in their daily lives. Divination can be found in every path we walk in life, as these powerful symbols remind us to follow our destiny no matter how unpredictable it may seem!

A. Meaning of Odu Ifa Symbols

Odu Ifa symbols are awe-inspiring relics of ancient African culture. Believed to be the narrations of millions of years ago, Odu Ifa is a sacred spiritual wisdom that provides insight into one's present and future. It is a corpus of symbolic verses culled from the timeless Orunmila, appointed by God as the custodian of knowledge, culture, and divination. Each symbol or Odu holds a unique meaning that can tell you about your destiny, relationships, guidance, and advice. There is power in knowing its secrets; it can help you make meaningful decisions and chart out a path for yourself in life. Unlocking these secrets is an exciting journey that offers untold wisdom.

Eji-Ogbe	Oyeku Meji	Iwori Meji	Odi Meji	Ogunda Meji	Osa Meji	Oturupon Meji	Ika Meji
Irosun Meji	Owonrin Meji	Obara Meji	Okanran Meji	Otura Meji	Irete Meji	Ose Meji	Ofun Meji

Odu Ifa symbols.

B. Major Divination Circles

Odu Ifa is an oracle and system of divination that has been used for centuries to gain insight into a person's situations, relationships, and fate. The symbols represent words of guidance revealed in sixteen basic archetypes, often symbolically drawn with cowrie shells, palm nuts, or stones. A skilled interpreter of the Odu will study a configuration of these symbols to identify the one oracle it represents and provide detailed guidance from its particular foundation principles. Each symbol contains a stories related to past wisdom, symbolic characters with powerful stories, lessons in morality and conduct, and universal spiritual laws on the basis of which our experiences are created. Those with proficiency in Odu Ifa can offer insightful knowledge to those who seek it!

C. Minor Divination Circles

Minor Divination Circles, or Odu Ifa Symbols, are essential to the African Yoruba culture. For centuries, they have been used to predict the future and offer advice on important life decisions. These symbols represent 256 different possible combinations or signposts that define the experiences of everyone's lives. They can be likened to GPS, guiding us down the paths we should take for the best outcomes. Every symbol has meaning, so those looking for insight into their present and future should familiarize themselves with them!

This form of divination originating in West Africa focuses on helping its patrons uncover deeper knowledge to understand the road ahead better. During this ritual, a recognized priest or initiate known as an Ifa Babalawo leads participants through a process that uses signs from shells or other objects to symbolize events and outcomes. Through this practice, individuals seeking guidance can gain direction on how to live their best lives and make informed decisions.

Traditional Practices in Ifa Divination

The interpretation of Ifa divination requires a spiritual connection with the forces of nature and a keen understanding of Yoruba culture, language, and symbolism. The Babalawo or initiate must be trained and initiated in the necessary procedures to provide accurate interpretation. It is also important for them to understand the history and culture of each Odu and the relevant proverbs attached to them.

The traditional practice of Ifa divination involves using cowrie shells, or Opele, representing the signs of the 256 Odu. The Babalawo will cast these shells to determine what sign or Odu has been revealed and then offer advice according to the appropriate proverb. Additionally, other traditional tools, such as palm nuts and stones, may be used.

While its traditional practice requires a certain level of expertise, Ifa divination can also be practiced on a more basic level. Various books, tutorials, and websites online can help guide someone through the process of understanding each Odu and its meaning.

A. The Written Word

The ancient practice of Ifa divination is based on the written word. As with many spiritual practices, a sacred language used in verbal and written readings establishes the foundation for divinatory wisdom. The written words used in Ifa divination are complex and in-depth, requiring special knowledge to interpret. Traditionally, an initiated priest or priestess partakes in the reading, often passing down the teachings to their apprentices over time. Today, online sources provide basic information to educate others on the foundational elements of this traditional method of divination. Although it is an ancient practice, it remains relevant today as a powerful spiritual guidance and transformation system.

B. Poetry and Song

Ifa divination is at the core of the traditional Yoruba religion, with poetry and song being a crucial part of its practice. Through specially crafted verses, shamans or priests involved in Ifa divination can receive clarifying instructions from their gods about how to best navigate a variety of life's choices. Interesting and unique, these practices demonstrate the importance of strong literary origins within this ancient tradition. As its followers rely on orishas or deities for guidance, divining by poetic structure is especially meaningful to those whose culture has endured many generations. By contemplating their spiritual connection through the potent words of these poetic messages, the Ifa devotees emphasize an important aspect of the ritual practice as it holds the power to shape those who follow it positively.

C. Oral Knowledge

While many practitioners today use written texts as aids, oral knowledge and traditional practices are still essential to this spiritual art. For example, every Ifa verse is chanted aloud to activate its power. It is a task that requires technical familiarity and emotional connection. Similarly, certain sacred songs accompanying divination readings must be sung in the original tonal language for the practice to be complete. This requires a skill that can only be acquired after dedicated study. As we seek new ways of understanding ourselves spiritually, it's essential not to underestimate the importance of traditional practices from cultures all over the world, such as those found within Ifa divination.

Consulting the Oracles

Practitioners of Ifa divination have access to deep insight and wisdom through the ancient practice of consulting oracles. At its core, Ifa divination is an African spiritual tradition that embodies guidance and a conscious connection to ancestors, wherein practitioners connect with the Yoruba spirit-deities known as orishas for guidance. After a thorough incantation, one of 256 verses from an oracle called "Odu" is prayed over to gain spiritual insight. Through this type of divination, it is not just the current life that practitioners receive guidance on but also all realms in between this life and the next, a marvelous blessing that only genuine seekers can gain access to. By consulting the divine oracles within Ifa Divination, we invite lineage-speaking truth into our lives, enabling us to deeply explore difficult topics with real understanding and compassion.

Tips for Interpreting Symbols

1. **Start with the basics:** Learn the meanings of each Odu and its corresponding symbols.
2. **Ask questions:** Contemplate what each symbol could mean about your current situation.
3. **Trust the process:** Follow your intuition and pay attention to signs that may provide further insight.
4. **Practice regularly:** Spend time exploring Ifa divination and its symbols to gain a deeper understanding of the practice.
5. **Seek guidance:** If you are serious about learning and practicing Ifa divination, seek assistance from a Babalawo or an initiated priest.
6. **Offering:** Before each reading, make an offering of thanks to the orishas for their help and guidance.
7. **Respect:** Approach each reading with respect and reverence, asking permission before attempting to interpret any symbols.
8. **Reflection:** After the reading is complete, reflect on what it could mean for your life.
9. **Gratitude:** Always thank the orishas and your ancestors for their guidance.
10. **Commitment:** Ifa divination is an ancient practice and should be approached with dedication.

Finding clarity through Ifa divination can give us deep insight into our lives and how to best move forward. Through the combination of written words, poetic songs, and traditional oral practices, the ancient art of Ifa divination offers powerful spiritual guidance for modern times. By educating ourselves and remaining open to the possibilities this practice offers, we can unlock a profound source of inner wisdom. With that, we can live our lives with greater understanding and joy.

Chapter 5: The Seven Great Orishas

The orishas are divine entities that are thought to inhabit the Earth. They were worshiped in Africa before being brought over as part of the slave trade to the Americas. In Santeria, they are believed to be intermediaries between human beings and the supreme divine being, Olodumare. Santeria is an African-based religion that combines elements of the Yoruba and Roman Catholic faiths and is practiced in many countries, particularly in Latin America. Out of the multitude of orishas—some say that there are "400+1"—seven of them stand out due to their influence, power, and general popularity. These orishas are Elegua, Obatala, Oggun, Chango, Yemaya, Oshun, and Orunmila.

In this chapter, we will explore the characteristics and personalities of each of these orishas. We will discuss their domains, manifestations, stories, and holidays associated with them, as well as other correspondences such as colors, their preferred offerings, animals, and how to know if an Orisha is calling to you. Let us begin with a brief overview of the seven orishas. Later on, we will dive deeper into each one of them. By understanding their personalities and correspondences, we can better understand their roles in our lives and how to work with them.

The Seven Orishas

The Yoruba religion of Nigeria is filled with many gods, goddesses, and other spiritual elements that make up its unique pantheon. Among the most important gods in this religion are the Seven Great Orishas, who serve as a foundation for many of the traditions and beliefs within Esese. These seven divine beings embody various aspects of the universe, such as air, storm, water, iron, fire, and fertility, granting their believers strength against misfortune. Adherents to Isese revere each of these orishas and often call upon them in times of need to intercede on their behalf. Through ceremonies and offerings to the orishas according to traditional customs and beliefs, practitioners can bring prosperity, luck, and protection into their lives.

A. Elegua

Elegua, the Great Orisha, is a significant deity in the Yoruba religion. This power-filled deity presides over the intersections between heaven and earth, playing a role in bringing humans closer to the divine. While some may see Elegua as a chaotic figure with a mischievous streak, his real function is to balance the two realms of existence, from providing individuals with divine guidance to granting permission for personal and spiritual growth by opening doorways to success. His powers contain universal knowledge and unspoken secrets that can help individuals uncover their true purpose and destiny. As such, those who offer homage or initiate ritualistic offerings in his name are sure to have their prayers answered.

Elegua.

Happycheetha32, CC BY-SA 4.0 <https://creativecommons.org/licenses/by-sa/4.0>, via Wikimedia Commons https://commons.wikimedia.org/wiki/File:Ellegua.jpg

B. Characteristics and Personality

Elegua is a powerful and unpredictable spirit. He is often depicted wearing red and black clothing, with his head covered by a hat or turban and a machete or staff in his hand. He is known for his sense of humor and being unafraid to speak his mind. He is also known to be a trickster and quite mischievous when it comes to getting what he wants; however, his intentions are usually good. He has a strong sense of justice and is a protector of the innocent, so he can be counted on to fight for those in need. Elegua is a strong believer in fate and destiny and works to ensure that everyone has their place on the path of life.

C. Domains

Elegua is the gatekeeper and guardian of thresholds, portals, and doorways. He is responsible for opening the path to spiritual growth and providing protection and guidance on life's journey. He is also a protector of children and a guardian of fate and destiny.

D. Manifestations

Elegua manifests in many forms, such as a small child, an old man, or a trickster. In his trickster form, he is often seen as a mischievous character who enjoys playing pranks on unsuspecting victims.

E. Stories

Elegua is said to have been born from the union of two powerful orishas, Obatala and Yemaya. He is also known as the "owner of roads and pathways" because he is said to have created them. He is associated with fate and destiny and is known to be a powerful protector of children. He opened the doorways between heaven and earth so mortals could access to the divine.

F. Associated Saint

The Catholic Saint of the Doorkeepers, Anthony of Padua, is often associated with Elegua. This connection is likely due to their shared role of opening pathways for spiritual growth. In some traditions, offerings to both Elegua and Saint Anthony are made to ensure spiritual protection.

G. Holidays

The anniversary of Elegua's birth, Iku Osogbo, is celebrated in April. Elaborate ceremonies, offerings to Elegua, and communal feasts mark the holiday. The feast day of St. Anthony is celebrated on June 13, and followers of the Yoruba religion often offer prayers to him and Elegua on this day.

H. Colors

Elegua is associated with red and black, representing his chaotic and unpredictable nature. He is also associated with white, symbolizing purity or innocence, and blue, representing the sea and his role as a guardian of portals between heaven and earth.

I. Offerings

Elegua enjoys offerings such as cigars, rum, palm oil, and coconut. He likes sweet foods such as candy or fruits. Red and black are his colors, so offerings should be wrapped in these colors when possible. He also enjoys being praised with songs and stories.

J. Animals

Animals associated with Elegua include monkeys, dogs, and roosters. These animals are seen as symbols of his mischievous nature and protectors of those who invoke his name. The rooster is a symbol of his connection to fate and destiny.

K. Knowing if Elegua Is Calling You

If you feel Elegua is calling out to you, he may be. Look for signs such as imagery of Elegua in unexpected places or a sudden desire to learn more about him. He may appear in your dreams, offering messages or advice. Pay attention to your surroundings and any coincidences that may have a deeper meaning. If you feel Elegua is trying to communicate with you, be sure to listen.

Elegua always looks out for the best interests of his believers. He will provide guidance and protection on life's journey and bring success when prayed to properly. He may be unpredictable, but his intentions are always pure, and he will remain a powerful and revered orisha in Isese for centuries to come.

Obatala

Obatala is one of the most important and powerful orishas in the Isese religion. Obatala is known as the Creator of Human Beings and the guardian of truth and justice. He carries a special machete to help him create humans from clay or cut away obstacles in our paths as we go about life. Obatala is associated with purity, light, white clothing, motherhood, and oysters. It is said that Obatala helped create Oyolu Meyi, charms worn for spiritual protection. We honor Obatala by celebrating the Obatala festival twice a year on December 22 and

January 1. On these special days, people gather together in joyful festivities to give thanks to this great orisha for bestowing us with his divine protection!

A. Characteristics and Personality

Obatala is known for his compassionate, wise, and just nature. He is a kind and loving orisha who values truth and justice. As the creator of human life, Obatala is deeply concerned with the welfare of humankind and will always be ready to offer guidance and protection. He's also known for his sense of justice and will always uphold fair judgment in any matter.

B. Symbolism

Obatala is often represented by a white rooster, which symbolizes his power of creation, and is associated with the color white, which signifies purity and innocence. His machete symbolizes his power to cut away obstacles and create paths for his believers.

C. Manifestations

Obatala is said to manifest himself as a white rooster or, in a dream, as an older man dressed in white. He is sometimes seen as a figure of light or an apparition of white smoke. Some may even hear his voice in their heads.

D. Stories

There are several stories about Obatala and his connection to human life. One of the most well-known is the story of how he created humans out of clay. According to this story, Obatala crafted seven human bodies, each one unique and special, and brought them to life with the help of his machete. Another popular story is how Obatala created the world with the help of Orunmila, another powerful orisha. Together they crafted a perfect world, but the mischief of other orishas soon ruined it. To save his creation, Obatala sacrificed himself and underwent a great transformation, emerging as a white rooster.

E. Associated Saint

Obatala is associated with Saint Michael, the Archangel. Both are protectors of justice and truth, and they carry a machete or sword as a symbol of their power. Obatala and Saint Michael are often invoked together in prayers to ensure protection and justice.

F. Holidays and Festivals

The Obatala festival is celebrated twice a year on December 22 and January 1. During this festival, people come together to give thanks and honor this great orisha. Offerings are made, and people dance in his honor. Prayers are said for good health, protection, and prosperity. This is a time of joyous celebration in reverence to Obatala.

G. Colors

The colors associated with Obatala are white and gold. White represents purity, innocence, and truth, while gold symbolizes wealth and prosperity. These colors are often seen in Obatala's clothing and decorations during festivals.

H. Offerings

Obatala enjoys offerings such as white flowers, white clothes, sweets, and fruits. He also loves to receive oysters and other seafood as offerings. It is crucial always to give thanks and show respect when offering to Obatala.

I. Animals

Obatala is associated with the white rooster, which symbolizes his power of creation. He is often seen riding a white horse in his chariot. He also has a special affinity for cats and is believed to look after them.

J. Knowing if Obatala Is Calling You

If you feel a deep connection to Obatala, he is likely calling out to you. You may experience a feeling of peace and joy when you pray to him or visit his shrine. A strong sense of justice, truth, and compassion may be signs that Obatala is trying to reach out to you. If Obatala has called upon you, it is vital to answer his call and begin connecting with him.

Obatala's message to the world is one of justice, truth, and compassion. He's a protector and guide who helps us find our true purpose in life. His teachings teach us to break down obstacles, create paths, and reach our highest potential. It's essential to recognize Obatala's presence in our lives and be thankful for all he provides.

Oggun

Oggun is a great power in Isese, the traditional spirituality of the Yoruba people's ethnicity and diaspora. Regarded as a maker of a brave and tempered character, wisdom, and strength, Oggun is one of the most popular orishas amongst those who practice Isese. Oggun is credited with giving success to human endeavors and providing magical protection for his devotees. He is an influential figure in ceremonies throughout Isese traditions, and his unique attributes cannot be overlooked by anyone who knows of him. Even if you have never encountered Oggun, there are many ways to learn more about him and connect with his teachings. For example, prayer or meditation can help you gain insight into this great orisha's strengths and potential. By understanding Ogun's mythology better and standing true to its teachings, you may find that encountering him can be an incredibly rewarding journey!

A. Characteristics and Personality

Oggun is a powerful and courageous orisha who stands as a protector of justice. He has an intense personality, often seen as impatient and irritable. Oggun is quick to anger and often speaks his mind without fear of consequences. He fights for what he believes in and is loyal to his loved ones. Despite his temperamental nature, Oggun is also an incredibly generous orisha who will always lend a helping hand if asked. He is honest and direct but also kind-hearted and forgiving.

B. Domain

Oggun is the orisha of war, labor, and iron. He works hard to ensure justice is served and that people are treated fairly. He is also the patron of artisans and blacksmiths, who are seen as his children. Oggun is often depicted carrying a machete, axe, or hammer. He is a master of all trades and can tackle any task put before him.

C. Manifestations

Oggun is often represented in cabildos, or spiritual assemblies, as an old man with a white beard wearing blue clothing. He is also seen as a blacksmith or warrior, wielding an axe or machete. He can manifest himself as a bull, symbolizing his strength and courage. In some traditions, Oggun is also known to manifest as a hunter or fisherman.

D. Stories

In Yoruba mythology, it is said that Oggun was born from the union of Obatala and Yemaya. His primary role was to protect humans from danger and conquer adversity. Oggun is a powerful warrior, fighting for justice and protecting the defenseless. In the famous story of Oggun and Osain, Oggun uses his machete to clear a path for an oppressed village to bring justice.

E. Associated Saint

Oggun is associated with Saint Peter, the apostle of Jesus. Just like Oggun, St Peter is seen as a brave warrior who is strong in his faith and willing to fight for what he believes in. He is also a patron saint of fishermen, making him a perfect fit for Oggun.

F. Holidays

Every year on June 29, devotees of Oggun celebrate his feast day with a great festival. The celebration usually includes an offering to Oggun and a ritual dance called the Opele. This day is seen as a time to honor Oggun and ask for his protection. Many regional traditions and festivals throughout the year celebrate different aspects of Oggun's power.

G. Colors

The colors associated with Oggun are blue and white. Blue symbolizes his strength, courage, and perseverance. White stands for justice and purity. Oggun's colors are often used in ceremonies, offerings, and devotional items to honor him.

H. Offerings

Regarding offerings, Oggun enjoys rum, cigars, and black coffee. He likes fruits, such as bananas and oranges, and offerings of iron and tools. Other items that can be used to honor Oggun include white candles, crosses, rosaries, and animal sacrifices. Any offerings made to Oggun must be done with the utmost respect and reverence.

I. Animals

The animals associated with Oggun are bulls and horses. Bulls symbolize his strength, courage, and perseverance. Horses represent freedom and swiftness. Animals can be sacrificed to Oggun or used in rituals to honor him and ask for his protection.

J. Knowing if Oggun Is Calling

When Oggun is calling, he will often manifest in dreams or visions. He can also be recognized by his colors, blue and white, or by the sound of a thunderclap. It is said that when he wants to communicate with his devotees, he will do so through metal objects such as nails, screws, or keys. If Oggun is calling, be respectful and answer his call with the appropriate offerings.

Oggun is a powerful and important Orisha who is worthy of respect. He works hard to uphold justice and protect the defenseless. Knowing more about Oggun and honoring him with offerings and rituals can help bring balance and harmony into our lives.

Chango

Chango is a beloved orisha, or deity, in the traditional Isese religion found in Nigeria and other parts of West Africa. He is praised for being strong, swift, and confident, attributes treasured in the culture. Chango's responsibilities include protection from harm and illness as well as guidance through difficult times. His appreciation is expressed through elaborate festivals wherein his followers offer sacrifices, music, and dance to show their devotion and admiration. He is especially fond of Yoruba drumming music, so naturally, these gatherings are loud, vibrant, and joyous occasions that leave all involved feeling blessed after honoring this important spirit.

A. Characteristics and Personality

Chango is often depicted as a male warrior with strong and muscular features. He is known for his strength, confidence, bravery, and battle and warfare skills. He's a passionate spirit who loves life, and his enthusiasm can be contagious. He's generous and compassionate, a natural leader who will stand up and fight for what is right. He has a temper, though, so it is best not to anger him.

B. Domain

Chango is the orisha of thunder and lightning, war, fire, and justice. He has dominion over the physical and spiritual realms, so his influence is far-reaching. He is a patron of music, dance, poetry, blacksmiths, and metalsmiths. His power is often expressed through thunderstorms, which signify his presence.

C. Manifestations

Chango manifests as a tall and powerful male figure dressed in red and crowned with an elaborate headdress of feathers. He is often seen carrying two swords, a machete, and an axe. A white dog or horse might also accompany him. When he is manifested in thunderstorms, he is accompanied by flashes of lightning and loud claps of thunder.

D. Stories

In Yoruba mythology, Chango is said to be the son of Obatala and Yemaya, two important orishas in the traditional Isese religion. He is often portrayed as a brave warrior who fought to protect his people from harm and injustice. He was a great leader and teacher, guiding his people with wisdom and strength. He was also a great lover, marrying many wives throughout his life.

E. Associated Saint

Chango is strongly associated with Saint Barbara, a Christian saint known for her faith and courage in the face of adversity. Her story serves as a reminder of Chango's power and protection, and she is often venerated alongside him in traditional ceremonies.

F. Holidays

Chango's festivals are usually held in the summer months, during the hottest days of the year. During these celebrations, his devotees dress in red, the color of passion and strength, and offer sacrifices to him. The festivities are marked by drumming, dancing, and feasting. At the end of the festivities, Chango is thanked and praised for his protection.

G. Colors

Chango's colors are red, white, and black. Red is a sign of his strength and courage, while white signifies purity and holiness. Black is associated with his power and ability to overcome adversity. These colors are often seen in Chango's traditional clothing and are used in offerings to him.

H. Offerings

Chango's traditional offerings include red wine, rum, cigars, and roasted corn. He loves music, so offerings of drums, flutes, and other instruments are often given in his honor. Offerings of food, especially roasted chickens, are also appreciated. Other items associated with Chango include weapons, tools, jewelry, and books.

I. Animals

Chango is associated with several animals, the most important being the white horse. This symbolizes courage and strength in battle and is used to honor Chango in ceremonies and festivals. The white dog is also associated with him, as it symbolizes loyalty and protection. Other animals include the cow, goat, and rooster.

J. Knowing if Chango is Calling

When Chango is calling, you may feel a sudden surge of energy or see flashes of lightning. You may also find yourself drawn to the color red or feel a strong connection to the thunder and lightning. If you are feeling inspired, creative, brave, or confident, it could be a sign that Chango is calling you. Additionally, if you feel a sudden urge to take action or speak up for what is right, it could indicate that Chango is trying to get your attention. In any case, if you feel the presence of Chango and wish to honor him, it is best to make an offering and thank him for his protection.

The power of Chango is immense and should be respected. He is a source of strength and courage, inspiring his followers to stand up for what is right and fight injustice. When called upon, Chango is a formidable ally and protector. Make sure to honor him with offerings and thank him for his protection.

Yemaya

Yemaya is a goddess within the ancient African religion of Isese. She is seen as the mother of all living things and governs acts of kindness, prosperity, and fertility. With her association with the Moon, Yemaya is known to be a kind spirit who provides positive balance in every situation. Legends say that no matter how bad the circumstance may be, she will always bring love and mercy. Many people invoke Yemaya to bring good fortune into their lives and increase their odds of success in all they do. Those who strongly believe in her powers are sure that wherever darkness may come, Yemaya will keep them safe and offer guidance during adversity. It is no wonder that she remains so beloved amongst her many devotees!

A. Characteristics and Personality

Yemaya is a goddess of love and mercy, and her presence is often felt in moments of need, joy, or sorrow. She embodies hope and comfort and is a protector of children and those in need. She will often lend her assistance to those who call upon her. A common theme in Yemaya's personality is that of abundance and fertility. She is associated with the ocean and has been known to bring wealth as well as fertility. Yemaya is believed to have a strong connection to the Moon, and her influence is often seen in matters of emotions, intuition, and spiritual development.

B. Domain

Yemaya is the ruler of the ocean and protector of all things that dwell within it. Her power can be felt on both land and sea, and she is known for protecting sailors, fishermen, and all who travel by water. The ocean also symbolizes fertility and abundance, and Yemaya is the perfect representation of this.

C. Manifestations

Yemaya is often depicted as a mermaid, and she can be seen wearing jewelry made of shells and pearls. Her colors are blue and white, which are also associated with water and the ocean. She is often depicted with seven orbs or stones in her hands, symbolizing wealth, fertility, and abundance.

D. Stories

One of the most famous stories about Yemaya is that she was born to Olokun, the father of all gods. It was said that Olokun had been looking out over the ocean one day when he saw a beautiful woman swimming in its depths. This woman was Yemaya, and she quickly became his favorite goddess. Yemaya was renowned for her kindness, generosity, and protection of those in need, and she always granted the wishes of her devotees. No matter how difficult the situation, Yemaya could be counted on for guidance and protection.

E. Associated Saint

Yemaya has been associated with Saint Barbara, a Christian martyr who was killed for her faith. She is often seen as a protector of those who need guidance and strength during difficult times. St Barbara is often depicted holding a tower, symbolizing the protection she offers, or with a crown of pearls, representing Yemaya's domain of the ocean.

F. Holidays

Many festivals celebrate Yemaya, but the most popular is the Yemaya Festival, which takes place on December 8. This festival is a time to give thanks to Yemaya for her protection and guidance and to ask for her assistance in the coming year. Yemaya devotees celebrate her birthday on August 15, known as "Yemaya Day."

G. Colors

The colors that are most associated with Yemaya are blue and white. These colors represent the ocean and water, which is her domain. She is also often associated with the colors green and gold, representing fertility and abundance. Symbols such as shells, pearls, and seven stones are also associated with Yemaya.

H. Offerings

Devotees of Yemaya often make offerings to her in the form of food, jewelry, or special items. These offerings are meant to show gratitude for her protection and guidance and can be placed on an altar dedicated to the goddess. Offerings can also be made during the Yemaya Festival or on any other special occasion which calls for thanks to be given to Yemaya.

I. Animals

The animals most associated with Yemaya are dolphins and fish. Dolphins are often seen as a symbol of protection, while fish represent abundance and fertility. Yemaya is also associated with birds, especially peacocks, seagulls, and sea turtles, representing freedom and new beginnings.

J. Knowing if Yemaya Is Calling

If you feel a strong connection to the ocean and if your intuition is particularly strong, or if you are seeking guidance for an important decision, Yemaya may be reaching out to you. Signs of her presence can include finding shells or dolphins as if by chance or even experiencing an unusual urge to take a boat ride. By paying attention to these signs and connecting with Yemaya, you can receive her gifts of guidance and protection.

The goddess Yemaya is a powerful and benevolent spirit of the sea. She is a protector and guide who offers strength and guidance to those in need. By understanding and connecting with Yemaya's energies, you can receive her gifts of protection, abundance, fertility, and freedom.

Oshun

Goddess Oshun is a great orisha in Isese. She is understood and corresponded with through her many attributes, such as fertility, joy, and sensuality. Oshun is seen as a compassionate and generous deity and represents the creative force of the universe, flowing like the rivers she is frequently associated with. Many worshippers believe that she helps to restore balance and peace when one has strayed from their purpose or destiny in life. As an influential figure in African diasporic religious practice, Oshun is celebrated amongst communities around the world for her wisdom, love, and grace.

A. Characteristics and Personality

Oshun is characterized as a powerful, loving, and nurturing mother figure. She is often seen as an embodiment of beauty, creativity, and fertility, a source of inspiration and hope, a powerful mediator between the spiritual and physical realms, and an essential protector of those she loves. This deity is known for her warm, inviting nature and often encourages people to embrace their vulnerabilities as a source of strength and power.

B. Domain

Oshun is associated with the elements of water and air. Her domain includes rivers, lakes, oceans, and other sources of water. She is a source of life-giving energy, and her presence can be felt in the changing of the seasons or the ebb and flow of a river or stream. She's also seen as a protector of travelers and explorers, ensuring they reach their destination safely.

C. Manifestations

Oshun is represented by a wide range of symbols and manifestations, including shells, fans, gold jewelry, peacock feathers, honey, and water lilies. She is often depicted with two or three strands of hair, wearing yellow or gold clothing, or with a crown of jewels. Her colors are typically bright and cheery, such as yellow and orange, and her number is five.

D. Stories

Oshun is featured in many stories and lore across West African religions. One such story tells of how Oshun used her power to bring the dead back to life. Another story tells of how Oshun saved a village from famine by using her power over the rivers and oceans to bring an abundance of fish. Oshun is also known for her temper and can be vengeful when those she loves are wronged.

E. Associated Saint

Saint Teresa of Ávila is often associated with Oshun due to her strong devotion to the Catholic faith and her love of nature. St. Teresa is a powerful and passionate advocate for the poor and vulnerable, and many believe she carries some of Oshun's energy. St. Teresa is also considered a patron saint of travel, as she often went on long journeys to preach and spread the faith.

F. Holidays

Many African diasporic communities celebrate the holiday of Oshun every year, usually around August. This celebration is meant to honor and recognize the powerful presence of this Orisha and to be thankful for her many gifts. During Oshun's holiday, people usually celebrate with dancing, singing, and offerings of food, flowers, and other items.

Additionally, many people will take a boat ride to connect with the spirit of Oshun and ask for her blessings.

G. Colors

The colors associated with Oshun are typically bright and cheerful, such as yellow and orange. These colors symbolize the energy of life and renewal that she brings, abundance, and joy. Gold and silver are also associated with Oshun, representing her power and wisdom. Additionally, Oshun is often depicted with a crown of jewels or other brightly colored items.

H. Offerings

Oshun is usually offered food, flowers, and other items to honor her presence. Honey and fruits, coins, and jewelry are popular offerings associated with Oshun. Some people leave her offerings of music or dance to show their appreciation for all she has done. Additionally, Oshun is offered prayers and petitions for her blessings and guidance.

I. Animals

The most common animals associated with Oshun are birds, particularly peacocks. Peacocks are seen as symbols of renewal and transformation, and they are often used to represent the energy of Oshun. Other animals associated with her include fish, frogs, and turtles, all of which symbolize abundance, protection, and fertility.

J. Knowing if Oshun Is Calling

One of the most common signs that Oshun is calling can be found in nature. If you find yourself being drawn to a certain body of water or the beauty of a flower or tree, this could be a sign that Oshun is reaching out to you. Additionally, if you feel overwhelming joy, love, or abundance, this could be a sign that Oshun is near. Finally, if you have a strong sense of intuition, this could indicate that Oshun is calling.

Orunmila

He is the all-knowing "Great Orisha," or spirit of divinity, in Isese. Orunmila is considered the true originator of the teachings of Ifa, which form the basis for morality within Yoruba spiritual belief. From these teachings, we learn how to live life in a balanced and harmonious manner and develop positive relationships with others and our natural environment. As such, Orunmila is often invoked during important ceremonies and rituals within West African society. He is also a great source of encouragement and solace during times of adversity by providing insight and guidance on creating a better future based on goodwill and hope. In this way, he has become an invaluable pillar of strength within Isese traditional culture and will never be forgotten or taken for granted!

A. Characteristics and Personality

Orunmila is an intelligent, wise, and compassionate spirit. He is known for his ability to foresee the future, provide guidance on navigating the intricacies of life, be fair and just, and deal out punishments and rewards with a balanced hand. Additionally, Orunmila is seen as a protector of the weak and vulnerable, coming to their aid in times of need.

B. Domain

Orunmila is closely associated with wisdom, knowledge, and understanding. He is often invoked for help in making important decisions or resolving disputes. Additionally, he's a great source of support and comfort in times of hardship and loss.

C. Manifestations

Orunmila is often depicted as a wise older man dressed in traditional West African garb. He is sometimes shown with four eyes to symbolize his all-seeing wisdom and knowledge and sometimes depicted with a staff in one hand, symbolizing his power and authority.

D. Stories

Orunmila is most commonly known as the storyteller who passes on the teachings of Ifa to others. He is also credited with the invention of the divination system, which is used to interpret messages from the gods and ancestors. Additionally, he's a great teacher and healer, using his wisdom to bring clarity and peace of mind to any situation. The symbol most associated with Orunmila is the staff, which he holds in his hand to signify his power and authority.

E. Associated Saint

Saint Vincent de Paul, an influential seventeenth-century French priest and theologian who dedicated his life to helping the poor and marginalized, is the Catholic saint associated with Orunmila. He was known for his compassion, humility, and wise counsel, traits that Orunmila also embodies. He is a powerful example of how we can use our skills, knowledge, and understanding to bring about positive change in the world.

F. Holidays

Orunmila is celebrated on the second day of the annual Ifa festival, which takes place in western Nigeria. On this day, people gather in public plazas to honor the spirit of Orunmila with songs, dances, and offerings. It is a day devoted to understanding and appreciating the teachings of Ifa and the power of knowledge.

G. Colors

The colors associated with Orunmila include blue and white, representing his power and authority. Additionally, he is often depicted wearing a long white robe, symbolizing his wisdom and understanding. The colors remind us that we should strive to learn and grow in knowledge, just as Orunmila did.

H. Offerings

Orunmila is often honored with offerings of sweet drinks, fruits, and other edible items. He accepts the offering of prayer and incense. Some people may give him a special gift or ritual object as a sign of their gratitude and appreciation for his wisdom and guidance.

I. Animals

Orunmila is closely associated with the bird, symbolizing joy, freedom, and heavenly power. The dove is also a popular choice as an animal offering to Orunmila because of its symbolic meaning. Others may honor him with other animals, such as a goat, sheep, or dog.

J. Knowing if Orunmila Is Calling

When Orunmila is calling, it can be a powerful experience. Signs that he may be calling you include feeling an inexplicable sense of peace and well-being, having strong dreams or visions, or hearing spiritual wisdom in your head. Additionally, it is said that when Orunmila calls a person, they will feel it in their heart. If these signs are present, it may be time to seek Orunmila's guidance.

Orunmila is an important figure in Yorùbá culture, as he is seen as a source of wisdom and guidance. His teachings, through the divination system, have helped many people make critical decisions or resolve conflicts. Additionally, his presence is felt in many West African countries, where he is celebrated for his powerful influence. By understanding the symbols associated with Orunmila, we can gain insight into his teachings and use them in our lives.

The Seven Great Orishas are essential figures in Yoruba culture. These spiritual leaders represent a variety of forces in nature, and each one brings its gifts to humanity. Elegua, Yemaya, Ogun, Oshun, Obatala, Shango, and Orunmila are all important figures in the Yoruba belief system, and understanding their symbols and stories can help us appreciate the power of their teachings.

By learning from these orishas, we can gain insight into how to live our lives with greater purpose, understanding, and respect for the world around us. We can also use their teachings to help guide our decisions and find balance in life. Understanding the symbols and stories associated with these orishas can be a powerful way to connect with their wisdom and guidance.

Chapter 6: Walk the Path of Your Ancestors

Ancestral veneration, known as Isese, is integral to the Yoruba tradition. The term Egungun is used to describe Yoruba ancestors, and it holds great significance in Isese. Egungun encompasses respect for those who have passed and is a way of connecting with the orishas or deities. Understanding the different categories of ancestors and how to identify them is essential to appreciate the concept of Egungun fully. This chapter will discuss the importance of Egungun in Isese culture by exploring its definition, necessary traits for veneration, and categories of ancestors. Tips and rituals to identify ancestors will be explored, and we will conclude with a summary of the concept and importance of Egungun.

The Concept of Egungun

Ancestors and ancestral veneration are two very important elements in the religion of Isese. Ancestors influence one's life and are seen as a bridge between humans and the orishas. It is customary for these ancestors to be written down on a patronage list. This list consists of names of deceased family members that were considered to have passed with good fortune and vitality. These ancestors are believed to be the gatekeepers into divine blessings from the orishas, so they need to be honored and respected through prayer and offerings.

In cases where a list cannot be created, Iyabó would serve as an ancestor, which is an individual divinity that looks out for the living but also remains connected in spirit to those who have died. Ultimately, paying homage to ancestral spirits can greatly help bring positive Gugbo (protection) over your living kin. A strong relationship between humans, deities, and those gone before us must constantly remain in balance so things go well here on Earth.

A. Definition

Egungun is an important concept in Isese spirituality, which refers to ancestral spirits. These spirits connect with their descendants, and many rituals and ceremonies are conducted to create this connection. Egungun ceremonies involve colorful costumes, music, dance, and offerings. Many believe that the energetic release of these festivities helps the living and the dead come together in a shared spiritual experience. Through the Egungun rituals, those who have passed on continue to shape and influence the lives of their descendants in a very meaningful way.

B. Respect and Veneration

These ancestors are revered for the good they have done, their strength, and the wisdom they provide to those still living. They are seen as gatekeepers who protect their living relatives from harm and guide them through difficult times. It is crucial to respect the wishes of these ancestors and pay homage to them to receive their blessings. The most meaningful way to show respect is by offering food and other items traditionally used in rituals during their lifetime.

C. Long and Moral Life

To be an appropriate ancestor for veneration and respect, one must have lived a long and moral life. This means they have led a life of good character and done many great things to benefit their descendants. Ancestors who have passed away with a legacy of wisdom, honor, and strength are most likely to be venerated. To be considered an ancestor, one must have left behind a meaningful impression in the hearts and minds of their descendants. With the help of the gods, these ancestors are believed to pass on their wisdom and strength from the afterlife.

D. Necessary Traits

The qualities of an ancestor are important to consider when determining who can be venerated. These traits include leadership, strength, humility, generosity, patience, understanding, and wisdom. Additionally, the ancestor must have passed away peacefully and not due to violence or accident. If these traits are met, the ancestor is believed to be a spiritual source of power and guidance for their descendants.

E. Significance of Ancestors

Ancestors are seen as a bridge between humans and the orishas. This is because they are believed to bring blessings and protection to their living descendants in the form of Gugbo. Ancestors are seen as spiritual guides who can help guide their living family members through difficult times. It is said that paying homage to them can help ensure a long and prosperous life for their descendants and a positive future for their family line. Ultimately, honoring and respecting these ancestors is essential to maintaining balance and harmony in the world.

Categories of Ancestors

Isese is built upon the family system with ancestors at its core. As part of the cultural heritage that ties individuals to their past and community, one must acknowledge several different categories of ancestors in Isese. These categories can be roughly divided into four main groups: Ase Afin (direct ancestors), Iyalode Alase (ancestral mothers), Ajala (civil chiefs), and Orisha (spirit protectors). Each category has distinct characteristics and importance in individual and communal religious practice. By recognizing each ancestor's role within Isese, individuals can form positive relationships and take on responsibilities between their past and present spiritual traditions.

A. Ase Afin

Ase Afin, or direct ancestors, are those who have recently passed away, typically within the last four to five generations. These ancestors are seen as guardians of the family line and are venerated for their wisdom and strength. This is the most commonly recognized type of ancestor, and individuals are expected to pay their respects regularly through offerings and rituals.

B. Iyalode Alase

Iyalode Alase, or ancestral mothers, are female ancestors venerated for their strength and courage. They are typically seen as the spiritual protectors of their descendants and their communities. Individuals are believed to receive guidance, protection, and blessings by honoring these female ancestors. As such, the veneration of ancestral mothers is essential for maintaining balance in the world.

C. Ajala

Ajala, or civil chiefs, are the ancestors who were leaders in the community during their lifetime. These ancestors are remembered for their leadership qualities and courage, as well as their commitment to justice and protecting the people of their community. Venerating these ancestors is seen as a way to ensure the prosperity and continuity of the community.

D. Orisha

Orishas, or spirit protectors, are supernatural entities with direct ties to the divine. It is said that these spirit protectors can act as intermediaries between the living and the divine and bring blessings to those who pay them homage. They are considered protectors of their descendants and the spiritual guardians of their family line.

Ultimately, honoring ancestors is an integral part of Isese. Through veneration and respect, individuals can ensure the spiritual protection of their family line and maintain balance in the world. This is done by offering prayers, making regular sacrifices, performing rituals, and showing respect to the ancestors. It's a way of showing reverence and gratitude for their wisdom and guidance, even in the face of adversity or hardship. By recognizing these ancestors and their distinct roles, individuals can find a deeper connection to the spiritual traditions of Isese and ensure the continuity of their family line.

Identifying Your Ancestor

Identifying and honoring one's ancestors is an essential part of Isese, as it allows individuals to form meaningful relationships with their past. To do this, individuals must first recognize which category of ancestor they are venerating. This can be done through various rituals and ceremonies, such as ancestor worship and libation. Once the individual has identified the type of ancestor they are venerating, they can pay their respects and form a connection with them.

Through ritualistic offerings and prayers, individuals can honor their ancestors and maintain a connection to the spiritual aspects of their Isese heritage. This section will provide tips and advice on how to honor and connect with one's ancestors. It will also discuss the various rituals and ceremonies that can help individuals form a meaningful bond with their ancestors.

A. Tips and Tricks

When honoring and connecting with one's ancestors, remember that the relationship should be a mutual exchange of respect. Individuals should pay homage to their ancestors through meaningful offerings and prayers while also listening for any messages or advice they might have.

In addition, remember that each ancestor should be respected in their own right. Different ancestors might require different offerings, prayers, and rituals to express one's gratitude. Here are some tips to keep in mind when honoring and connecting with one's ancestors:

- Offer up prayers to your ancestors. Prayers can be used as a form of honoring and expressing gratitude.
- Make offerings to the ancestors. This can be done through ritualistic activities such as libation, sacrifice, or ritual dance.
- Listen for any signs or messages from the ancestors. Many believe that the ancestors will send guidance and advice when needed.
- Show respect to the ancestors in your own way. Each ancestor is unique and deserves to be honored specially.
- Be open to the guidance and wisdom of your ancestors. They are a source of spiritual power and can provide great insight into life's challenges and struggles.

B. Rituals and Ceremonies

Isese has a variety of rituals and ceremonies for honoring ancestors. Practitioners believe that the souls of their ancestors continue to influence their daily lives. They offer food, clothing, and other things to their departed ancestors, who are seen as mediators between human beings and the divine. During festivals such as Egunitogun, practitioners bring offerings of flutes and drums to pay tribute to the dead and give thanks tenfold for what they have been provided. Daily events take place at shrines dedicated to particular ancestors, where family members will offer prayers and sacrifices for continued guidance. The services help create a powerful connection between past generations and those living today, one which is highly valued and respected within Isese tradition. Here are some of the rituals and ceremonies used to honor one's ancestors:

- **Libation:** A ritual in which oil, water, or alcohol is poured onto the ground or a sacred object as an offering to the ancestors.

- **Sacrifice:** A ritual in which something is offered up for spiritual purposes, such as animal or food offerings.
- **Egunitogun:** A yearly festival wherein the living pays homage to the dead by offering flutes and drums in celebration.
- **Shrine Visits:** Visiting a shrine dedicated to an ancestor is a way of honoring their memory and expressing gratitude.
- **Prayer:** Prayers can be used to give thanks and ask for guidance from the ancestors.
- **Dance:** Ritualistic dancing and drumming are powerful ways of connecting with the ancestors.

C. Connecting with Your Ancestor

Connecting with one's ancestors provides individuals with a deep connection to the spiritual traditions of their culture. It allows them to form meaningful relationships with their past and gain insight into their heritage. Through ritualistic offerings and prayers, individuals can honor their ancestors and maintain a strong connection to their spiritual roots.

The practices of honoring and connecting with one's ancestors are deeply ingrained in Isese culture. Here are some tips to help individuals connect with their ancestors:

- Keep an open mind and heart. Be open to whatever messages or advice the ancestors may offer.
- Meditate and practice mindfulness. This can help one become more aware of the subtle energies the ancestors may be trying to share.
- Create a sacred space for honoring the ancestors. This can be done by offering up prayers, offerings, and rituals to express gratitude and respect.
- Research one's ancestry and family history. Knowing more about the past can help bring the present into perspective and deepen one's understanding of their identity.
- Speak to a knowledgeable elder or spiritual leader about the customs and traditions practiced within Isese culture. This can provide deeper insight into the spiritual significance of connecting with the ancestors.

Honoring and connecting with one's ancestors is an important part of Isese culture. Through meaningful offerings and prayers, individuals can pay tribute to their ancestors and maintain a strong connection to their spiritual roots. Regularly engaging in rituals and ceremonies can help create a powerful bond between the living and past generations that can provide strength and guidance in times of need. In honoring our ancestors, we honor ourselves and the legacy they have left behind.

By following the tips and advice discussed in this chapter, individuals can form a meaningful bond with their ancestors and gain insight into the spiritual aspects of Isese culture.

Chapter 7: Honoring Your Ancestors

For generations, Isese people have held strong to the belief that their ancestors are still with them, watching and guiding them from beyond. This deep reverence for those who have come before carries through in many aspects of daily life in Isese villages, from offering prayers during meal times to celebrating events such as birth or marriage. As our ancestors carry us forward into tomorrow, we must never forget the ramifications and importance of honoring those who walked this path before us—something that the Isese people know only too well!

This reverence is an essential part of the spiritual, social, and cultural life of Isese. This chapter will provide a comprehensive guide on how to honor your ancestors in the Isese way. From offering Ebbo (sacrifices) to creating an ancestral shrine, we will cover all the main aspects of Isese ancestral veneration. You will learn what Ebbo is, the symbolism of Egungun (the Isese holiday for honoring ancestors), how to celebrate it, and the practice of ancestral meditation.

Ebbo

Ebbo holds a vital place in Isese culture. It is a series of rituals that honor the gods and spirits and mark special occasions in the community. Traditionally, it can involve everything from singing and dancing to offering food sacrifices. All these rituals are done with intention and deep reverence for the deities they seek to honor. To those unfamiliar with their traditions, Ebbo might seem strange or even outlandish; however, it has a long history of keeping communities connected and secure in their identity. This powerful practice continues to be an essential part of Isese culture today.

A. History of Ebbo

The Isese people, an ethnic group from West Africa, have a long and fascinating history with the Ebbo. This traditional religion dates back centuries and is still practiced today in Nigeria and other parts of West Africa. It centers around nature worship, ancestor veneration, rituals for sacrificing animals, moral values, and oracular consultations. Ebbo has changed over the years to accommodate modern technology, societal changes, and popular culture. Its symbols are worked into sculptures, paintings, jewelry, and theatrical performances. Even though it is not commonly known outside its origin countries, many Isese practitioners take great pride in their heritage and keep the faith alive by passing down stories from generation to generation.

B. How to Perform an Ancestral Offering/Sacrifice

Isese culture is the traditional way of life used by certain Yoruba-speaking cultures. It focuses on reverence for the ancestors and their continued influence over society. A ritual for honoring and connecting with our ancestors is known as an ancestral offering/sacrifice. An Isese practitioner must understand the right way to perform this ritual to invoke ancestral blessings. Preparation will involve assembling items, including a calabash, several kola nuts, efun (white chalk) powder, and an onion. Once everything is ready, the individual begins chanting prayers and salutations to their ancestors before breaking the kola nuts into pieces and scattering them around the shrine area or place of sacrifice. After completing some libations (pouring of wine or water), the ancestral offering/sacrifice is complete!

C. Symbolic Importance of Ebbo

Ebbo has many meanings and serves as a reminder of the people's heritage, faith, and beliefs. Ebbo is often used as a sign of spiritual protection, while other uses are more closely associated with promoting fertility. Ebbo can be used to honor ancestors and invoke their blessings and is seen as a source of strength, hope, and joy in everyday life, making it an integral part of Isese custom and tradition. The ritual of Ebbo is an essential part of Isese culture and a way to honor their ancestors.

Egungun

Celebrating the Egungun Festival is a great way to come together and pay homage to Yoruba ancestors in Nigeria. It is an incredible tradition passed down through the generations and still holds tremendous importance today. One of the unique aspects of this cultural practice is when dancers dressed as Eguns join in the celebration, helping people remember their rich history. Festivities include vibrant colors, deliciously prepared traditional cuisine, rhythmic music, and plenty of dancing. It's a joyous occasion that allows us to reflect on our heritage while connecting with friends and family in our local community. So, if you have the chance, be sure to experience the Egungun Festival for yourself. It's one of those rare moments that will leave lasting memories and unforgettable stories for years to come!

A. History of Egungun

Egungun is an age-old tradition of honoring ancestors in African Isese culture, believed to date back to the fifteenth century. Egungun festivals are typically filled with joyous and colorful dances, exquisite costumes, and commemorative speeches that honor and tell the stories of those who have passed before us. This tradition is rooted deeply in Isese society, provides a beautiful tribute to the deceased, and educates people about their culture and history. Each festival is unique, as each Egungun celebrates individual ancestry, allowing families and communities to come together to celebrate life from past to present.

B. Customs and Symbolism Associated with the Holiday

Egungun is an integral part of Isese culture, and many colorful customs and symbols are associated with it. Different colors have meanings and add to the festive atmosphere when Egungun festivals are celebrated. Red is associated with royalty and power, while white symbolizes purity and peace. A popular dance style associated with Egungun is the ogogo, where the dancer wears the Egungun mask, and energetic music plays as they whirl around, stomping their feet in a detailed series of steps often known as "throwback" moves. The Egungun carries objects such as coconuts, beads, and kola nuts to demonstrate wealth and abundance to onlookers. It is sure to be an exciting experience for anyone who attends!

C. Ideas for How to Celebrate Egungun

Isese culture celebrates Egungun through various festive activities. To properly celebrate the spirit, it is vital to honor those who have passed and show appreciation for their presence. One way to do this would be to carry out a special ceremony, full of drumming, song, and dance, in which members of the community follow steps traditional to Isese culture, such as wearing masks and colorful costumes. These costumes often feature intricate beadwork designs inspired by Yoruba art, adding beauty and bringing more joy into the atmosphere. Food is another integral part of every gathering, so a feast featuring different Nigerian dishes should be prepared so it can be shared with everyone. Finally, prayers can be offered throughout the day to honor their ancestors and thank them for their blessings. By participating in these meaningful ceremonies, people will better understand the importance of Egungun while still having fun and making lasting memories.

Creating an Ancestral Shrine

Isese culture celebrates ancestral shrines as a place of gathering and reverence. Family members come together to give offerings and reflect on the lessons their ancestors have taught them. They view the shrine as where, even in death, the deceased is still part of the community, watching over their loved ones and offering guidance and protection from beyond. It is a peaceful, reflective time for individuals to celebrate their deceased relatives and embrace their rich culture. By honoring this tradition, family members honor their ancestor's memory and create an atmosphere of goodwill among themselves that keeps generations unified in love.

This can be created by placing items such as pictures, jewelry, and other mementos of their loved ones on a table or altar in the home. Some families may even create a permanent shrine in their yard or garden.

A. Necessary Items for an Ancestral Shrine

When creating an ancestral shrine, a few items should be included. The first is a picture of the ancestor in question or a representation of them if one is unavailable. This will serve as the focal point for visitors and remind everyone of who their ancestor was. Other items that can be included are traditional Isese artifacts such as coins, jewelry, beads, ritual objects, and anything else that honors their memory. Finally, food offerings should be made to the deceased to thank them for watching over their descendants and offering love and guidance. By including these items, families can create a space of respect and love that will keep generations connected to their history.

B. Placement of Items

The placement of the items is also crucial when creating an ancestral shrine. It is best to have the picture or representation of the ancestor in the central position, surrounded by other items of significance. The food offerings should be placed on the right side of the shrine to honor those who have gone before, and the objects should be placed on the left side to remember their legacy. Once these items are in place, keep the shrine clean and tidy as a sign of reverence. The shrine should be a place of serenity and strength, reminding everyone that even though their ancestors are gone, they remain in spirit.

C. Rituals to Perform

Once the shrine is in place, it is time to perform rituals that honor their memory. Prayers and songs can be offered, along with incense burning to bring good energy into the home. Some families may perform traditional Isese dances or ceremonies to pay their respects. Lighting a candle can symbolize the deceased's presence in our lives and bring peace into the home. By participating in these rituals, family members will create a sense of unity and connection that will last for generations.

Ancestral Meditation

Ancestral meditation is a tradition that dates back thousands of years and can be used to relax and reconnect with the ancient energies of our ancestors. It is believed that when we take the time to practice ancestral meditation, we are helping bridge a connection between our present selves and those who have come before us. Our ancestors passed on their knowledge, strengths, and experiences to shape who we are today and help make our lives worthwhile. Taking time to meditate regularly on this connection helps us appreciate their influence and provides powerful healing effects. It also gives us gratitude for all those who have gone before us and is part of the fabric of us as individuals. Give it a try—you will be glad you did!

A. Purpose and Goal

Ancestral meditation practice is pursued to reconnect with one's family lineage and unlock the collective wisdom of ancestors. Developed by spiritual teachers, this form of guided meditation opens the door to deep spiritual awareness, healing, and transformation. Participants are brought back to their ancestral roots to explore their connection to an age-old lineage, bringing awareness to deeply held ancestral patterns, habits, and conditioning. As these anxieties and blocks are released, practitioners leave the experience feeling empowered and in harmony with the universe. With a wide range of techniques tailored to individual needs, ancestral meditation has become increasingly popular in exploring the personal and spiritual dimensions of existence.

B. Preparing for the Meditation Session

When embarking on a journey of ancestral meditation, prepare and understand the steps for the practice. Start by creating a sacred space to honor your ancestors, and make sure you design it accordingly and with intention. Clear your mind, ground yourself, set intentions, and be mindful of timing when performing any rituals. Creating a ritual makes the process more intentional: It can help break away from an anxious state of mind while honoring spiritual memories safely. Take the time to get to know each ancestor and show gratitude for their existence, reflecting on how they impacted your life and still influence you daily. Ancestral meditation is an extremely rewarding journey. With patience, commitment, and understanding, you will surely find great joy in this practice!

C. Steps for Ancestral Meditation Session

Bridging the gap between our current world and ancestors is easier than you might think with ancestral meditation. All it takes is a few simple steps to get started. First, you must find a quiet place and allow yourself to settle into a meditative state. Second, spend some time focusing on who your ancestors are or were and what values and views they may have held. Third, start developing a relationship by expressing gratitude for their presence in your life and moving on to ask for any guidance or wisdom they would be willing to share, anything from major life decisions to day-to-day challenges. And lastly, remember always to honor your ancestors as much as you can, keeping them close and in spirit all the time!

D. How to End the Session

Ending a session of ancestral meditation can be a tricky endeavor; however, there are simple steps that anyone can take to make sure that the ceremony concludes in good spirits and an atmosphere of positive energy. The first is to thank the ancestors who have been present during the meditation. This act of recognition honors their sacred space and shows gratitude for their presence. The second step is to call forth and invoke any deities or angels invoked during the session so they may offer blessings five-fold for yourselves, your families, your friends, your ancestors, and all others in need. Lastly, allow everyone to recognize their unique relationships with the ancestors by briefly offering personal words of appreciation at the end of the session. Completing these steps before closing the session ensures that it will end in tranquility and mutual respect between the mediator, ancestor, and descendant.

E. Benefits of Ancestral Meditation

Practicing ancestral meditation can bring about several important spiritual and personal benefits. These include improved self-awareness and emotional balance, increased understanding of one's spiritual lineage, and a closer connection with our ancestors. By aligning ourselves with the universal energies of our ancestors, we can access their wisdom and knowledge to help guide us in times of need. This meditation also gives us a greater appreciation for our family history, sense of identity, and the interconnectedness of all life.

Moreover, ancestral meditation can help us find meaning and purpose in our lives by uncovering our place in the grand scheme of things. Ultimately, this practice is a powerful way to bring us into harmony with our lives and those who have come before us. Through ancestral meditation, we can open ourselves up to a deeper understanding of our spiritual identity and gain greater insight into how we fit into the bigger picture. It is a practice that can profoundly affect our lives and relationships with those around us.

F. Ways to Increase the Effectiveness of Ancestral Meditation

The effectiveness of ancestral meditation can be greatly enhanced by taking certain steps, such as:

- Focusing on the positive rather than the negative.
- Letting go of any expectations when starting the session.

- Setting an intention for the session, such as connecting with your ancestors or learning something new.
- Allowing yourself to be open and receptive to whatever information comes in during the session.
- Taking time at the end of the session to reflect on what you have learned and feel gratitude for your ancestors.
- Practicing regularly since consistency is key to deepening your connection with the ancestors.

The Isese practice of ancestral meditation is an ancient one passed down through generations. It is a powerful way to reconnect with our spiritual heritage and access the wisdom and knowledge of our ancestors. By engaging in this practice, we can develop a greater sense of self-awareness, emotional balance, and understanding of our place in the world. However, ancestral meditation should always be approached with respect and reverence for those who have come before us. By taking the necessary steps to create a positive and safe environment for our meditation sessions, we can ensure that this practice remains powerful and meaningful.

Chapter 8: What Asafo Flags Can Teach

The Asafo flags of Ghana are a sight to behold! These vibrant pieces of art have been guiding communities along the coastal regions of the Fante people since the sixteenth century. Each flag is lovingly handmade, reflecting events that happened within each village and particular messages that need to be conveyed. Local chiefs can often be seen brandishing them during festivals and ceremonies as a sign of honor and respect. Through their intricate designs and bright colors, Asafo flags prominently stand as beacons of cultural identity within Ghana's historical landscape.

Asafo flag.

Brooklyn Museum, CC BY 3.0 <https://creativecommons.org/licenses/by/3.0>, via Wikimedia Commons https://commons.wikimedia.org/wiki/File:Brooklyn_Museum_2009.39.1_Asafo_Company_Flag_Frankaa.jpg

Asafo flags contain cultural meanings and narratives of the Fante people, located in the coastal regions of Ghana, and are commonly displayed at various social events, festivals (including Egungun), ceremonies, or even funerals. This chapter briefly explores the relevant cultural context of these flags. Then, we will discuss how people usually create them to transmit a message, parable, or moral. At the end of the chapter, you will find a few examples of flags with an interpretation of their meanings.

Cultural Context of Asafo Flags

Asafo flags are vibrant and intricate works of art created by the Asante people of Ghana. These flags are more than just art. They represent the rich cultural heritage, social identities, and distinct personalities of each flag group. Asafo flags include pictures and symbols that tell a story about each group's beliefs, values, alliances, histories, honors, and rites. They also reflect an essential part of the oral tradition in West African culture as they convey messages through symbolism related to proverbs, historical events, and experiences that have shaped the Asante people. The mass production of these flags has made them a symbol of resistance against oppression and a vehicle for cultural reinstatement within contemporary struggles for justice and rights. If you ever see one, take in all it has to offer—a glimpse into a culture filled with beauty and resilience!

A. Traditional Significance

Asafo Flags are traditionally used for various purposes, such as to mark the boundaries of a village, signal the location of an important meeting or event, or honor the dead. These flags serve as a reminder of traditional values and can be found at many festivals, funerals, weddings, and other special occasions. Asafo flags have also served as a form of protection from enemies, danger, or bad luck. The symbols on the flags are believed to have magical powers that can ward off evil spirits.

B. Symbolism

Asafo Flags contain symbols and images that convey a message or moral lesson. These flags often depict animals and other natural elements, such as the Sun, Moon, and stars. Symbols of unity, such as hands clasped together, two brothers embracing, and a single bird perched on a branch, are also commonly seen. Other symbols convey messages of honor, respect, peace, unity, courage, and strength.

C. Creation and Display

Asafo flags are usually created by the village chief or a group of elders and are handsewn with colorful cloth or fabric. They are then displayed at various events and hung in prominent places, such as on the walls of village homes or in front of public buildings. Asafo flags are usually proudly displayed at social events, such as funerals, weddings, and festivals. They often feature prominently in traditional processions or parades, signaling the start or end of a special event.

D. Modern Significance

Asafo flags are now widely recognized and celebrated in Ghana and beyond. These flags are seen as symbols of pride, cultural identity, and resilience in the face of adversity. They have come to represent a shared history, heritage, and culture that can be passed down from generation to generation. Asafo flags are also used in a variety of creative art forms, such as photography, fashion, and design.

Contemporary Relevance

Initially created by the Asante people of Ghana in the eighteenth century to display battle tactics during war times and unite multiple villages, their flags remain relevant today. Visitors to Ghana thoroughly enjoy seeing patterns, colors, and symbols that tell stories of family ancestry, history, and tradition on the Asafo flags. They also serve as a reminder of their many roots. These flying symbols have been used for political and cultural expression, inspiring communities and providing an important connection with the past. The narrative behind these flags is timeless. Various aspects of them are found in literature, poetry, film, music, and visual arts throughout the country. Asafo flags have truly stood the test of time!

A. Popularity and Recognition

Asafo flags have seen a massive surge in popularity and recognition over the past few years. Originating in Ghana, Asafo flags are an African textile art form traditionally used by warriors to rally troops and celebrate victories. Today, they can be found all around the world as symbols of positive energy, bravery, and strength. Asafo flags stand as beautiful reminders of African culture and traditions, beloved for their bright colors and creative designs. They make for great conversation pieces for homes and workspaces. Whether it is simply a way to spread positivity or to honor one's heritage, Asafo flags offer something special that captures imaginations everywhere.

B. Education and Cultural Preservation

Asafo flags are colorful traditional artifacts of the Akan people of Ghana. Although originally used in wars, today their significance has grown far beyond battle and spilled into contemporary life, playing a role in education and the preservation of cultural heritage. Asafo flags capture stories, symbols, and motifs that serve as both a documented history for subsequent generations and a visual reminder of past events. By displaying these artifacts to children, families can help to foster an understanding and knowledge of ancestry through educational dialogue and storytelling. Not only will this ultimately promote cultural engagement among Akan youth, but it also constitutes a lasting connection to their roots durably preserved in artwork unrestrained by written language. Undoubtedly, Asafo flags remain an integral part of cultural self-expression and identity that is essential to preserving the heritage alive.

C. Asafo Flag Art

Asafo flag art originated from the Akan people in Ghana and is still used today to represent the warrior spirit, community identity, and cultural nationalism of those from West Africa. The flags are created using brightly colored textiles, intricate patterns, and symbolic motifs with important meanings. Each symbol represents aspects of the group's social life, like bravery, courage, protection, values, and faith, all of which form an invaluable part of Akan culture. Asafo flag art may look stunningly simple on the surface; however, they carry hundreds of years of wisdom handed down through generations. Depending on whom you are talking to, these beautiful banners can tell many stories, whether it is a proud military display or a more ceremonial processional. They remind their observers of the power and beauty within West African communities and make for a delightfully positive reminder to cherish our cultures for years to come.

Process of Making Asafo Flags

For centuries, vibrant and intricate Asafo flags have been crafted in the Ghanaian village of Nkusukum. These flags are handmade with local materials such as raffia, cotton fabric, beads, and shells. While each is unique to its maker's village, all Asafo flags feature depictions of various animals to represent the beliefs and experiences of a particular community or organization. The process begins with sketching the artwork on graph paper and then transferring it onto the fabric using a tracing wheel before finally hand-stitching every detail onto visible pattern pieces. Once complete, the flag is ready to be used in special ceremonies made famous by Ghanaians everywhere.

A. Materials

Creating an Asafo flag is a unique and special process. From start to finish, each flag component carries its symbolism, importance, and history. To bring the project together, however, many materials are required. This includes fabric, brightly colored samples of Kente cloths, or plain pre-dyed cotton. Additionally, beads must be found or purchased to represent certain symbols or techniques used on the flags. Most importantly, the Ashanti knotting technique is necessary to tie all of these components together into something special. You can ensure your completed Asafo Flag captures its intended meaning with great care and attention to detail!

B. Design and Motifs

Design plays a major role in the process of making Asafo flags. From bold geometric shapes to intricate details, each flag is crafted with exceptional care. Colors often have symbolic meanings and illustrations representing a tribe's values or historical events. Inspiration for the designs comes from traditional African symbols such as Adinkra and Akan stamps, vibrant fabric cloths, and abstract representations of everyday life. The bold motifs are meant to be powerful declarations of pride for each tribe and honor their traditions. Crafting Asafo flags is an incredible art form that celebrates culture, creativity, and history.

C. Color Palettes

Asafo flags are important to Ghanaian culture and form part of the country's vibrant visual art scene. One of the key elements in their intricate beauty is the unique use of color palettes. The artists that create these stunning works of art stretch their imaginations to assemble striking combinations, which can incorporate several different shades to bring out a range of emotions. Given the traditional spiritual meaning behind each color, it makes sense why such time and effort are put into creating each flag. Therefore, when we view an Asafo flag, we do not just see something beautiful; we see a meaningful piece of art crafted with skillful precision and contemplation to honor its associated gods or community history.

Messages Transmitted through Asafo Flags

Asafo flags are brightly colored banners with distinctive patterns used to communicate messages in the Fante tradition of Ghana. Many of these symbols represent abstract concepts such as courage, strength, leadership, and unity, while others will announce a wedding or even advertise a local business. Every flag has a unique design and color combinations that were thoughtfully created to express each message, no matter the content. Asafo flags add vibrancy and culture to communities in West Africa, creating beautiful landmarks that remind us of the importance of heritage no matter where we originate.

A. Narrative Art

Asafo Flags have been around for centuries and convey messages through an artistic medium. Narrative art has captivated people of many different cultures throughout history. Asafo Flags, which originated in Ghana and Togo among the Akan people, are no exception. Through their vibrant colors and intricate designs, these flags tell vivid stories that encapsulate important values within their villages or regions. They may include symbols from their past, such as battles won or deities worshiped, reminding the viewer of how far their culture has come. The display of these flags is quite a spectacle. It is truly inspiring to witness the dynamic beauty of Asafo flags passing by in a parade!

B. Parables and Morals

Off the coast of Ghana, Asafo flags, also known as soldier's flags, are a feature of the culture in the Ga-Adangme region. They are beloved within their communities and crafted with beautiful fabrics. However, they're far more than objects of admiration. Each flag is said to carry with it a secret meaning. A moral is transmitted through symbols, patterns, and images on the flag. Much like a parable, this imagery conveys something greater than what can be seen. Each serves as an immortalized aid for local villagers to consider various life scenarios and ponder their inherent pros and cons. In this way, Asafo flags have been used for ages to commemorate bravery, express community values, and serve as additional subjects for conversation during social gatherings.

Examples of Asafo Flags

Asafo flags are made with brightly colored fabrics and filled with symbolic motifs. Depending on the context, they come in various shapes, sizes, and designs. Some flags are rectangular, while others feature the traditional triangular shape. Some have a combination of both shapes. The popular symbols on most flags include animals, gods, and symbols of courage or strength. Additionally, some Asafo flags are made with a specific meaning in mind, such as celebrating war victories or honoring the death of a leader. Here are some examples of Asafo flags:

- The Adomabenu Flag features an elephant on the red side, representing strength and courage.
- The Sankofana Flag features a black-and-white striped pattern with the image of a leopard to represent leadership.
- The Akosua Adwoa Flag features a combination of yellow and purple triangles, symbolizing unity and collaboration.
- The Denkyem Flag features the image of a crocodile on the blue side, representing wisdom and adaptability.
- The Nsoroma Flag features a combination of white and red rectangles, representing resilience and faith.

Asafo flags are a beautiful form of visual art and storytelling, with many symbols carrying significant cultural meaning. They provide a unique way of expressing the values of a certain region or village, and their beauty is undeniable. Seeing an Asafo flag parade is truly an amazing experience, and it is a great way to learn more about Akan culture and its many important values. Be sure to check out some of these unique flags the next time you are in West Africa!

Chapter 9: Iwa, or Building a Strong Character

Iwa Pele is an important concept in the Ifa tradition that focuses on a person's character or mental and moral qualities. Originating from the Yoruba people of Nigeria, Iwa Pele is a way to reinforce one's good character and work toward obtaining favor from the ancestors. It is a complex concept that has been passed down through generations and remains an integral part of the Ifa tradition today. This chapter will explain the origin and meaning of Iwa Pele, discuss its importance in the Ifa tradition, and outline the characteristics and benefits of a good character, as well as how one can attain this, according to Odu Ifa.

Definition of Iwa Pele

Iwa Pele is a term native to the Yoruba people of Nigeria. It is the idea that by doing the right thing, showing integrity in one's actions, and striving to be the best version of ourselves, we can attain a sense of peace and oneness with our higher power. Iwa Pele can apply to all aspects of life, including faith practices, relationships, careers, and more. No matter what or whom we interact with, it's thought that having respect and adhering to good morals will enhance our purpose as humans in this life.

Origin and Meaning

The phrase "Iwa Pele" has special significance in the Yoruba culture of Nigeria and translates to "good character" in the Yoruba language. The phrase reflects the collective elements that Yoruban people value as important traits: Honesty, humility, patience, respect, and strength. These values are ingrained in their everyday lives, aiming to foster strong relationships between individuals and create a harmonious environment within their community. Iwa Pele reminds people to strive for good character and behavior despite any difficult situations they might face. This notion helps instill resilience within each individual and recognizes the holistic importance of being well-rounded individuals contributing positively to society.

Significance in Ifa Tradition

The traditional Ifa faith is based on the idea of Iwa Pele, a phrase that means "the character of perfect behavior." In the Ifa faith, Iwa Pele refers to respect, honesty, and accountability in all aspects of life. It serves as a code of ethics that guides believers to make the right decisions in their lives. Furthermore, if one follows the teachings of Iwa Pele, they may gain access to divine help and support from Orunmila (the God of wisdom). Ultimately, Iwa Pele is an integral component of the Ifa tradition and serves as a moral compass for those adherents hoping to find spiritual enlightenment.

Characteristics of a Good Character According to Odu Ifa

According to Odu Ifa, a good character consists of several elements. These include respect for one's ancestors and humanity, the willingness to seek knowledge and wisdom, resilience in the face of adversity, and integrity through honesty and accountability. Additionally, a good character should have courage, patience, and dedication to doing what is right, no matter how difficult it may be. Lastly, Odu Ifa emphasizes being somebody with a kind heart that will never harm anyone, someone whose heart knows no boundaries or prejudices when it comes to loving others. With these qualities in our lives, we can certainly grow into true individuals respected among family, friends, and our community. Here are some ideas on how to develop and sustain a good character according to Odu Ifa:

A. Respect

Adopting an attitude of respect for the beliefs and opinions of others is essential to developing a strong moral character. Respecting people's boundaries is key when fostering healthy relationships and building trust. This idea is even more relevant when interacting with people from different backgrounds and cultures. We need to recognize our differences and embrace them instead of trying to ignore or devalue them.

B. Know Thyself

Self-awareness is essential if we are to grow into well-rounded individuals. Spend time reflecting and understanding your motivations, strengths, weaknesses, and values. Recognize the areas where you can grow and develop, and use this knowledge to better yourself. In the process, you will gain greater respect for yourself and those around you.

C. Live with Integrity

A strong moral code is rooted in upholding integrity. To live with integrity is to always act according to your values and beliefs, regardless of the situation you may be facing. This means living with honesty and accountability for your actions. Essentially, it is striving to be the best version of yourself in all aspects of life.

D. Persevere

Life can be full of obstacles, and many times it may seem easier to give up than push forward. However, having resilience and perseverance is key if we are to develop good character. Acknowledge the challenges that come your way as an opportunity for personal growth and development, and strive to take them on with strength and courage.

E. Compassion

Compassion is a powerful tool that should not be overlooked when striving to become a person of good character, and being compassionate means having empathy and understanding for those around you and being willing to forgive those who have wronged you. This is a crucial part of the Ifa tradition that should be remembered. Remember, kindness and love are the foundations of a strong moral character. With these values firmly in mind, we can strive to be our best selves and reach our highest potential.

Ultimately, developing a good character is an ongoing process that requires effort and commitment. By following the teachings of Odu Ifa, you can create a strong moral foundation that will guide you throughout life. Respect, self-awareness, integrity, and perseverance are integral components of a good character that will lead to spiritual growth and enlightenment.

Benefits of Having Good Character

Having a good character can result in truly amazing and positive outcomes. In terms of relationships, having a strong moral foundation and values can attract people who are similarly aligned and create more meaningful connections than those built on mutual convenience alone. This can lead to meaningful interactions with family, friends, coworkers, or significant others. On the professional front, having strong personal values, an honest work ethic, and reliable performance, can open up even more doors for success. People with good character will often be trusted by employers and given greater autonomy or responsibility within their position. Overall, having a good character is essential for creating meaningful connections in relationships and unlocking better opportunities for success in life.

1. Obtaining Favor from Ancestors

Having a good character is essential for attaining favor and blessings from our ancestors. Odu Ifa teaches that those who live with integrity and honor their ancestors will, in turn, be favored with spiritual protection and guidance from them. So, by living a life of good character, we can ensure that our ancestors are looking out for us and guiding us in the right direction.

2. Setting an Example

Having a good character means setting a good example for those around you. By living with strong values, treating others with respect, and having a moral code based on integrity, we can inspire those around us to do the same. This creates a ripple effect that can spread throughout society and lead to a better world for everyone. Our responsibility is to lead by example and create a legacy of good character that will last well beyond our lifetime.

3. Mental and Physical Well-Being

Having a good character is linked to better mental and physical health. Studies have shown that those with strong moral values experience less anxiety, stress, and depression. They also have higher self-esteem and overall better well-being than those who do not take the time to develop a strong character. Additionally, having a code of moral values can help keep us on the right path and make it easier to make decisions in our best interest.

4. Spiritual Fulfillment

Having good character is essential for finding spiritual fulfillment in life. By living a life of honesty, integrity, and respect for everything, we ensure that our actions align with the universe. This is essential for attaining spiritual enlightenment, as we need to ensure that our actions reflect the divine truth of the universe. We can strive toward a more connected and meaningful existence with these spiritual principles in mind.

5. Better Sense of Self

Most importantly, having good character can help us to understand ourselves better. By developing a strong moral foundation and following Odu Ifa's teachings, we can learn more about who we are, our true values, and beliefs. This can be very empowering, as it gives us the confidence to stay true to ourselves and follow our path in life. With a strong sense of self, we can make decisions that align with our values and morals, which can lead to even greater success in life.

How to Attain Good Character

Achieving a good character involves developing strong morals and self-discipline. To maintain these solid foundations of moral strength, starting with small changes you can make daily is critical. This could be something as small as always keeping your word or taking responsibility for your mistakes. However, these habits become invaluable over time since they help us build important qualities like honesty, courage, and respect. Additionally, taking action when facing difficult decisions and situations toughens our character further by allowing us to reach beyond our comfort zone. In the end, attaining good character comes down to slowly adding values such as trustworthiness and determination into our behavior while also gaining different knowledge from every new experience we encounter.

A. Education on Ifa Practices and Principles

One of the best ways to build a strong character is to educate oneself on Ifa practices and principles. Odu Ifa guides how to live an honorable and balanced life, which is essential for crafting good character. It also helps to develop respect toward the universe and all living beings, which is an incredibly important part of character building. Various resources are available to help us understand the teachings of Ifa and apply them to our daily lives.

B. Self-Mastery

Another important way to build good character is through self-mastery. This involves taking the time to assess our behavior and attitude and finding ways to improve them. Self-mastery is about understanding our strengths and weaknesses to make a conscious effort to improve ourselves. This process ultimately leads us to a better character, allowing us to take control of our actions and ensure they align with our values.

C. Prayers to Ancestors

One of the main ways to attain a good character is through prayers and offerings to our ancestors. Praying to our ancestors strengthens our spiritual connection and opens us to their wisdom and guidance. This helps us to stay on the path of virtue, which is essential for good character. Additionally, praying to our ancestors makes us feel more connected and grateful for their guidance.

D. Engaging in Traditional Rituals

Engaging in traditional rituals is another powerful way to build a good character. Traditional rituals are often steeped in culture and spiritual significance, making them incredibly powerful tools for self-reflection and personal growth. By engaging in traditional rituals, we can gain new insights into our behavior and attitudes, helping us to stay on the right path. These rituals can also help us better understand our underlying values and beliefs, which are key for attaining a good character.

E. Meditation and Reflection

Finally, meditation and reflection are important tools for attaining good character. Meditation helps to clear our minds and allows us to gain greater insight into our behavior and decisions. This is invaluable for character building since it gives us the clarity that we need to make wise choices in life. Additionally, through reflection, we can gain a deeper understanding of our values and what is truly important to us.

By applying these practices, we build our character gradually until it becomes solid and virtuous. Remember that character building takes time and effort; however, the rewards are worth it in the end. With a strong character, we can face any situation in life with confidence and grace.

Character building is an essential part of life that involves cultivating values such as trustworthiness, determination, respect, and self-mastery into our behavior. Educating ourselves on Ifa practices and principles, engaging in traditional rituals, praying to our ancestors, practicing self-mastery, and meditating and reflecting are all key ways to become the people we wish to be. By consistently following these practices, we can work toward attaining a good character that will serve us throughout our life.

Chapter 10: Practicing Isese Every Day

Isese is an ancient African spiritual tradition practiced for thousands of years. It embraces the interconnectedness of all life and teaches that the spiritual, physical, and mental realms should be in harmony to bring about true joy and contentment. Practicing Isese involves incorporating its wisdom and worldview into one's everyday life. In this chapter, we will discuss various daily, weekly, and yearly rituals as well as other practices that can help deepen one's spiritual connection and improve their life through Isese.

Daily Rituals

One of the most important aspects of Isese is that it encourages practitioners to be mindful in all they do. This includes taking time each day to gather one's thoughts and focus on the spiritual world. This can be done through prayer, mantras, chants, or other practices that help to quiet the mind and bring one closer to their spiritual self. Here are a few examples of daily rituals one may practice:

- **Meditation and reflection:** Take time each day to sit in stillness and reflect on the day's events. Think about how your actions have affected those around you and ask for guidance on how to serve better in the future.
- **Prayer:** Speak to your higher power and ask for guidance in all aspects of life. You can also ask for blessings for yourself and

those around you. If you need help with a particular problem, ask for assistance.

- **Chanting:** Chanting is a powerful tool to create positive vibrations that can help fill your entire being with peace and joy. You can chant your prayers or those of your ancestors.
- **Journaling:** Writing down your thoughts and experiences can help clarify what is on your mind. It is also a great way to express gratitude for all you have been blessed with. Write down your positive affirmations or any other words of encouragement that can help you stay on track.
- **Offerings:** Offerings are a way of giving back to the universe. By gifting small items, you show that you appreciate all that has been given to you. This can include food, flowers, incense, or any other items representing your gratitude.

Weekly Rituals

Most practitioners of Isese have weekly rituals they follow. These are usually centered around a particular theme or intention and involve activities such as singing, dancing, and chanting. Here are a few examples of weekly rituals one may choose to practice:

- **Singing and dancing:** Isese encourages the use of singing and dancing as a way to express joy and spirituality. Take some time each week to sing and dance in celebration of life.
- **Music circles:** Gather with friends and family to play instruments, chant, and share stories. This is a great way to strengthen bonds and connect with others.
- **Fire ceremonies:** Fire ceremonies are a powerful way to renew and cleanse the spirit. They can also be used to honor deceased ancestors and make offerings.
- **Baths:** Taking baths with herbs and oils is a way to relax the body and soul. It can also be used for spiritual cleansing and ritual purification.
- **Shrine tending:** Taking care of shrines or sacred places is a way to show respect for your ancestors and spiritual forces. This can involve cleaning, offering food, lighting candles, and more.
- **Celebrations:** Gather with friends and family to celebrate your ancestors, deities, and the cycles of life. This can involve

feasting, storytelling, and exchanging gifts.

Yearly Rituals

Yearly rituals are a great way to honor the cycles of life and connect with one's roots. These can include festivals, pilgrimages, and other events that celebrate the spirit of Isese. Here are a few examples of yearly rituals one may practice:

- **New Year Celebrations:** Gather with friends and family to celebrate the new year. This can involve feasting, storytelling, dancing, and more.
- **Odun Ifa:** This is one of the most important yearly festivals in Isese practice. It celebrates a new cycle of life and renewal. The event includes singing, dancing, and offerings.
- **Ugbodu:** This is a yearly ceremony that celebrates the ancestors. Offerings are made, and stories are told about the ancestors' deeds.
- **Iwure:** This is a yearly ritual of purification and cleansing. It is a way of thanking the gods and spirits for all that has been given.
- **Pilgrimages:** Take a pilgrimage to a sacred site to recharge your spirit and deepen your connection with the divine. This can be to a local sacred site or a long journey.
- **Ancestor Rituals:** Take some time each year to honor your ancestors and connect with the spirit of those who have gone before you. This can include offerings, rituals, and storytelling.
- **Harvest Celebrations:** Give thanks for the cycle of life and all that has been given. This can be done at home or in communal gatherings.
- **Solstice Celebrations:** Celebrate the changing of the seasons and the cycles of life. This can involve rituals, offerings, and time spent outdoors.

Regardless of the type of rituals one chooses to practice, the goal is always to create deeper connections with oneself and the divine. By engaging in these activities, one can find a sense of peace and fulfillment in life. Living an Isese life also involves making conscious choices that honor the spirit within. By living mindfully and with intention, one can find harmony and balance in all aspects of life. Remember that rituals are meant to bring joy and healing. Feel free to explore different types of rituals and find what works for you. With practice, your Isese rituals can become a place of peace, renewal, and connection.

Other Practices

Isese is a way of life that involves other practices such as eating right, exercising, and spending time in nature. Eating right can involve eating foods that are natural, organic, and locally sourced. Exercise can help keep the body in balance and lessen stress. Spending time in nature is a way to connect with the divine and find peace. Other practices may include prayer, meditation, chanting, and divination. Here are some ways to connect with the spirit and find balance in life.

Clothing

Wearing clothing that reflects your spiritual beliefs can help you stay in touch with the divine. This includes clothes made of natural fabrics and colors that connect you with the natural world. Symbols, such as ancestral marks and spiritual insignia, can be worn to honor your ancestors and spiritual forces. In Isese, it is also crucial to dress in a way that reflects humility and respect for the divine.

Intentional Living

Living with intention means making conscious choices that honor the spirit within. This can involve avoiding habits or activities that go against your spiritual beliefs and choosing to live in a way that aligns with your values. It can also involve participating in activities that bring you joy and helping others whenever possible.

Spiritual Practices

Engaging in various spiritual practices can help you stay connected to the divine. This can include praying, meditating, chanting, or engaging in divination. All these practices can help bring clarity and insight into your life and strengthen your connection with the divine. The Isese tradition also includes rituals celebrating life cycles, such as harvest festivals and solstice celebrations.

Foods/Dietary Guidelines

Eating natural, organic, and locally sourced foods can help keep your body in balance and bring you closer to the divine. Foods traditionally eaten in Isese culture include fruits, grains, legumes, nuts, and vegetables. Dairy products, eggs, fish, and poultry are also consumed in moderation. Eating eggs and poultry should be done respecting the animals, and the meat should be obtained ethically. Additionally, avoiding processed and unhealthy foods can help keep the body in balance.

Symbols and Objects of Power

Symbols and objects of power can be used to invoke the divine. These include talismans, amulets, crystals, sacred vessels, and other items. In Isese culture, these objects are used to honor the ancestors and invoke spiritual protection. They can also be used in rituals and ceremonies to honor the divine and recognize the power of the spirit. Additionally, these items can help bring clarity, insight, and guidance into one's life.

Connecting with Nature

Spending time in nature is a great way to connect with the divine and find peace. Walking in the woods, swimming in a lake, or sitting in your garden can help you find balance and appreciation for the world around you. Additionally, connecting with plants and animals can help you gain insight into the cycles of life. This can bring clarity and understanding to your spiritual journey.

Altars/Sacred Spaces

Creating an altar or sacred space in your home can help you stay connected with the divine. This could be where you pray, meditate, or perform rituals. Here, you can place symbols of your faith, photos of ancestors and spiritual guides, crystals, candles, and other items with special meaning. This sacred space can remind you of your spiritual journey and help to keep you in touch with the divine.

Drumming and Dancing

Drumming and dancing are important spiritual practices in Isese culture. They can invoke the divine, honor the ancestors, and celebrate life's cycles. They can also invoke healing energy and manifest positive change in the world around you. By engaging in these activities, you can connect with the divine and find joy in life.

Greeting the Dawn

Witnessing dawn is an important spiritual practice in Isese culture. It is believed that by greeting the dawn, you are acknowledging the power of the Sun and honoring your spirit. This practice can also be used to start each day with intention and gratitude, as well as give thanks for the blessings of the new day.

Journaling

Journaling is an excellent way to stay connected with the divine. Writing about your spiritual journey, reflecting on your experiences, and expressing gratitude for the blessings in your life can help you stay connected to the divine. Additionally, journaling can be a great way to gain insight and clarity on your spiritual path.

Community Practices

Participating in community practices is an important part of Isese spirituality. Gathering with others to celebrate festivals and holidays, performing rituals and ceremonies, and honoring the divine can help strengthen your spiritual connection. Additionally, gathering in the community brings a sense of belonging and unity that is essential for spiritual growth.

Listening

Finally, listening is an important spiritual practice in Isese culture. Learning to listen to your intuition, the wisdom of your ancestors, and the guidance of the divine can be an invaluable part of your spiritual journey. Listening to what is being said without judgment or expectation can help bring clarity and understanding into your life.

Healing and Divination Practices

Healing and divination practices are important spiritual traditions in Isese culture. Practices such as prayer, meditation, reiki, palmistry, and tarot can help bring healing and insight into your life. By engaging in these practices, you can gain clarity and understanding of your spiritual path while obtaining balance and harmony.

Connection with Ancestors

Connecting with ancestors is an essential part of Isese spirituality. Honoring ancestors through prayer, ritual, and storytelling can help bring their wisdom and guidance into your life. Additionally, connecting with ancestors can bring a deeper understanding of your spiritual path and create a powerful connection to the divine.

Other Practices Recommended by the Isese Tradition

The Isese tradition recommends other spiritual practices like fasting and vision quests. Fasting can be used to purify the body and is often used to honor the ancestors. Vision quests can be used to gain insight and clarity into life's purpose, challenges, and spiritual direction. By engaging in these practices, you can gain a deeper understanding of your spiritual path and connect with the divine.

The Isese tradition is rich with spiritual practices that can be used to deepen your connection with the divine. By engaging in these practices, you can find joy and healing in life and gain insight into your spiritual path. Additionally, these practices help bring balance and harmony to your life and manifest positive change in the world around you. By engaging in these spiritual practices, you can connect to the divine and embark on a powerful life journey.

Bonus: An Isese Glossary

Now that you have finished reading the book, you may be wondering about some of the more difficult Yoruba words and terminology used. Do not worry; you don't have to remember them all! Below is a comprehensive list of all the more difficult Yoruba words and terminology that appears throughout the book, as well as their phonetic spelling and the page in which they can be found being discussed more in-depth.

1. **Abiku (pronounced ah-bee-Koo):** In Yoruba culture, an Abiku is a child who dies young and continually returns to their family.
2. **Adura (pronounced ah-doo-rah):** In Yoruba culture, adura is the act of honoring the gods in ceremonies and rituals.
3. **Ase (pronounced ah-say):** Ase is an important concept in Yoruba religion, and it refers to the power of the gods that can be used for good or ill.
4. **Babalawo (pronounced bah-bah-lah-woh):** Babalawo is a Yoruba priest specializing in divination and healing.
5. **Chango (pronounced Shahn-go):** Chango is an orisha associated with family, strength, and justice.
6. **Egungun (pronounced eh-goong-goong):** Egungun is a masquerade festival where participants wear colorful costumes and masks to pay homage to their ancestors.
7. **Elegua (pronounced eh-lay-gwah):** Elegua is an orisha associated with communication and transitions.

8. **Esu (pronounced eh-soo):** Esu is an orisha associated with communication between the gods and humans, as well as luck and protection.
9. **Ibeji (pronounced ee-bay-jee):** In Yoruba culture, Ibeji are the twin spirit children of a family who have died young.
10. **Ifa (pronounced ee-fah):** Ifa is an oracle system used to communicate with the gods and is composed of a large corpus of Yoruba poetry.
11. **Itefa (pronounced ee-teh-fah):** In Yoruba culture, itefa is the act of an individual asking for divine guidance in making a decision.
12. **Iwa Pele (pronounced ee-wah-peh-lay):** In Yoruba culture, iwa pele is the concept of personal character and morality.
13. **Obatala (pronounced oh-bah-the-lah):** Obatala is an orisha associated with wisdom and purity.
14. **Oggun (pronounced oh-goohn):** Oggun is one of the most important gods in the Yoruba religion and is associated with war, ironworking, hunting, and farming.
15. **Oko (pronounced oh-koh):** In Yoruba culture, oko is the practice of using charms and incantations to bring good luck and fortune.
16. **Olodumare (pronounced oh-loh-doo-mah-ray):** Olodumare is the most powerful Yoruba god and is seen as the creator of all living things.
17. **Olokun (pronounced oh-loh-koon):** Olokun is an orisha associated with the sea, wealth, and fertility.
18. **Ori (pronounced oh-ree):** In Yoruba culture, Ori is the divine part of a person's soul that connects them to their fate.
19. **Orisha (pronounced oh-ree-sah):** In the Yoruba religion, the orishas are supernatural beings who possess powerful and mysterious forces.
20. **Orunmila (pronounced oh-roon-mee-lah):** Orunmila is an orisha associated with wisdom and divination.
21. **Ose (pronounced oh-say):** Ose is an orisha associated with healing and medicine.
22. **Oshun (pronounced oh-shoon):** Oshun is an orisha associated with love, beauty, and the river.

23. **Oya (pronounced oh-yah):** Oya is an orisha associated with wind, storms, and fertility.
24. **Sango (pronounced sahn-go):** Sango is an orisha associated with thunder and lightning.
25. **Yemaya (pronounced yay-mah-yah):** Yemaya is an orisha associated with the ocean and motherhood.

Conclusion

Isese is a spiritual practice with roots in Yorubaland, Nigeria. It is a way of life deeply connected to the worshipers' ancestors and the orishas or deities. For those who follow Isese, honoring this practice brings balance, knowledge, and understanding among various aspects of life. From honoring ancestral traditions to listening to the wisdom of one's elders, this spiritual practice links all generations, present and past, together as one.

The path to inner harmony with yourself and the divine is difficult but worth traveling. Isese can guide us on this journey, giving us the tools to connect with who we are and build relationships between ourselves, the orishas, and Olodumare. We also learn how to open our hearts to honor our ancestors, recognizing the legacy that connects us all. Through Isese's teachings of self-love, understanding, and compassion, we can discover lasting peace within ourselves and find comfort in embracing our cultural heritage.

The practice of Ifa divination is widely used in Isese. This tradition has been passed down for generations through oral teachings and written scriptures known as Odu Ifa. This form of divination is said to be the most ancient, as it predates all other forms of religion or spiritual practices. Through this practice, one can learn how to interpret their destiny, get answers to pressing questions, and develop a better understanding of the universe. Learning how to practice Ifa divination can help practitioners gain clarity, knowledge, and insight.

In Isese, the Seven Great Orishas are revered. These deities are seen as mediators between humankind and Olodumare, the Supreme Creator of all things in the universe. Each of these orishas has unique characteristics, symbols, rituals, and gifts to offer us. By showing them respect, we can receive guidance and strength from their presence in our lives.

Finally, Isese encourages practitioners to keep their ancestors close by honoring the path paved before us. This is done through various ceremonies and offerings, such as libations or commemorative feasts, which can bring a sense of peace and connection to our ancestors. By understanding the importance of their legacy, we can keep their memory alive and be guided by their wisdom.

This easy-to-read guide is an introduction to the practice of Isese, taking you on a step-by-step journey through various aspects such as Odu Ifa, the Seven Great Orishas, and honoring your ancestors. Topics also included Asafo flags, Iwa (building a strong character), and how to practice Isese daily. For further exploration, we added an Isese glossary for additional understanding of the terminology used throughout this guide.

We hope that by delving into Isese, you will have a greater appreciation and understanding of your cultural heritage and a deeper connection to the divine. With this knowledge, you can now make strides toward your spiritual journey, finding balance and inner peace. May Olodumare bless you on your way!

Part 3: Ori

The Ultimate Guide to Spiritual Intuition, Yoruba, Odu, Egbe, Orishas, and Ancestral Veneration

Introduction

At the start of this book, you'll be introduced to the fascinating background of the Yoruba religion. You'll learn how this belief system incorporates elements of art, religious and divinatory practices, and the myths and beliefs passed down through oral traditions. One of the fundamental beliefs of the Yoruba revolves around the concept of Ori. The term Ori is roughly translated to "destiny." However, as you'll learn later on, for the Yoruba, the meaning of Ori goes far beyond that. It's a means to spiritual elevation, a tool for developing one's intuition and using it to fulfill one's destiny - or change it if needed. That said, the concept of Ori contradicts another crucial element of the Yoruba beliefs, free will. To comprehend this conundrum, you'll need to understand how each component of Ori works together and how they relate to freedom of choice.

Through the intricate tales of the Yoruba, you'll learn how Ori was created and how Olodumare affects one's expression of it. As the supreme creator, Olodumare oversees all living beings and spirits, including the Orishas. The Yoruba venerate Orishas as deities and use them as spiritual messengers. Through spiritual communication, people can learn how to align their life and values with their Ori or intuition. It's believed that the Orishas can also contribute to how the Ori is expressed and how it affects one's life. According to a Yoruba myth, Ori can also be worshiped as an Orisha. As there are Orishas with different tastes, so there are different Oris that can be nurtured through a broad range of ways. Prayers, rituals, and offerings to one's spiritual intuition often go a long way toward healthy self-realization, which is sacred to the Yoruba.

Ancestral veneration is another practice that influences Yoruba beliefs and traditions. Ancestors play a crucial part in the life of the Yoruba. Their spirit can be evoked and asked for protection, guidance, and spiritual enlightenment through the wisdom the ancestors have gathered throughout their life. Consequently, the ancestors can help improve one's spiritual intuition and alignment with Ori. You'll also learn about another spiritual group that can assist you in this quest, the *Egbe Orun*. The Egbe are heavenly spirits who live in intricate societies and have their own characters and influences over human lives. Their impact results from their connection with the souls inhabiting the Earth.

Another way to ensure spiritual realizations is by living a righteous life. According to the Yoruba beliefs, this is only possible by following the *16 Truths of Ifa*, the decree created by Olodumare to help solve common issues people encounter throughout their lives. Last but not least, the book will remind you that the alignment of Ori depends mostly on you. While the spiritual entities mentioned in the previous chapters are certainly helpful to balance your Ori, in the end, it all comes down to your character. You'll be much closer to fulfilling your destiny or changing it by improving your character. This book will guide you through all the practices that contribute to self-realization through Ori. It provides a great stepping stone for those wanting to live a harmonious life by combining free will with fate. If you are ready to delve into the world of spiritual alignment through spirit guides and self-awareness, keep reading.

Chapter 1: Basic Spiritual Concepts of Yoruba

The Yoruba faith is one of the largest religions in West Africa, mainly Nigeria. It is estimated to be 5000 years old, making it one of the oldest religions in the world, even predating Christianity. Yoruba has a huge following, with about one hundred million believers in Africa and other countries worldwide. It is based on various African beliefs, songs, proverbs, myths, and legends. In the Yoruba religion, Olodumare is the supreme deity and the creator of the universe who doesn't have a specific gender and is referred to using the pronoun "they." They aren't involved in the matters of mankind, so they created the Orishas (spirits and demigods) to assist human beings in their affairs. The spirits of the ancestors also play a big role in the Yoruba faith. Worshipers believe that the spirits of their dead family members live on after death. The Orishas and the spirits of the ancestors are highly revered in the Yoruba religion. They provide assistance, are a source of inspiration, and protect people from evil.

Yoruba has over one million followers worldwide.
https://www.pexels.com/photo/photo-of-woman-lighting-the-candlesticks-6192006/

Like many other religions at the time, Yoruba was passed down orally from one generation to the next. In many ancient cultures, illiteracy was common, which is why they didn't have any written records. Many cultures wrote down and preserved their myths and legends when literacy began spreading. However, since these stories were passed down orally, many have drifted from the original source, and there can be more than one version of the same story. For instance, Olodumare goes by many names in different legends, like Olofin and Olodumare-Oloorun. Some stories paint Olodumare as an absent deity who isn't involved in mankind's affairs. They live far away in the heavens, unable to hear the people's prayers. While other stories claim that Olodumare is an all-knowing deity who knows everything that goes on in Heaven and on Earth.

In the Yoruba hierarchy, no one is more significant than Olodumare:
- Olodumare
- The Orishas and the Ajogun
- Mankind
- The spirits of the ancestors
- Animals and plants

The Ajogn are supernatural entities that share similarities with the concept of the Devil in Christianity. Just like evil spirits, these beings bring many misfortunes to human beings, like disease, accidents, and many other troubles. At the same time, they encourage mayhem and chaos like the devil. However, one can't label Ajogn evil or put them in the same category as demons. In the Yoruba religion, no human or supernatural being is considered all good or all evil. Good and bad exist in every creature, even the Ajogn. This applies to the Orishas as well, who can commit mischief. It is a fair and realistic conception of the world since nothing can be considered perfect or entirely flawed.

Interestingly, the spirits of the ancestors fall under human beings in the hierarchy, even though their influence is obvious in the Yoruba religion. However, these spirits can only exert their powers through human veneration and acknowledgment, which is probably why they fall under them. Last on the hierarchy are animals and plants. However, this doesn't make them any less significant than mankind or the spirits of the ancestors. All creatures possess the spirit of the divine, which makes them all of equal value and influence. Therefore, all human beings are also connected since they share the spirit of the divine. Neither people's skin color, culture, nor religion can set them apart. We all share a link with one another and all living things.

The Yoruba people believe in destiny or *Ori*, which each person must achieve before death. The Orishas and the spirits of the ancestors help people realize their destinies. However, if one dies before they fulfill their Ori, they can try again in the next life. Death is considered a happy occasion that people should celebrate. Reincarnation supports this belief as it is something people look forward to instead of dreading. The Yoruba people don't believe that death is the end. Reincarnation or Atunwa is a prominent concept in their faith. It is the belief that the spirit can continue its cycle even after the body dies by coming back in different physical forms. This concept exists in many religions, like Buddhism and Hinduism. However, it is different in Yoruba since it takes place within the family. For instance, a grandfather can come back as his grandson. However, gender doesn't play a role here. Male spirits can come back in female physical forms and vice versa. When the spirit is reborn, it carries with it the wisdom and knowledge of its ancestor.

Life and death aren't regarded as opposites or a beginning and end, but the spirit goes through an ongoing cycle from one physical form to another. Reincarnation is a gift that is bestowed on mankind. However, only the spirits of good people who lead an honorable life can experience rebirth. Cruel people who harm gods' creatures aren't given this gift. Living a good and happy life is an essential part of the Yoruba faith, unlike some religions where one must suffer in this life to get rewarded in the next.

Yoruba had found its way into many other countries and cultures worldwide during the time of enslavement when black people were brought to the Americas. Although they were pressured to convert to Catholicism privately, they held onto their beliefs and combined their Orishas with Catholic saints. Yoruba wasn't just a religion. It represented their identity that they weren't willing to compromise on. Holding on to it was an act of defiance against a new culture that wanted to erase its history and beliefs.

There are many festivals in the Yoruba religion that celebrate Olodumare, the Orishas, and the spirits of the ancestors. They present offerings and reenact some of their famous myths and legends. All worshipers must participate in these festivals, or it will be considered an insult to the Orishas, spirits, and gods.

Different tribes and people have their own ways of celebrating the Orishas.
https://www.pexels.com/photo/women-of-massai-tribe-11679893/

The priests and priestesses have a significant and influential role in the Yoruba faith. Priests are called Babalawo, which is a Yoruba word that translates to "father of the mysteries." They lead all the religious ceremonies. When invoking an Orisha during a ritual, the spirit usually mounts the priest or priestess. Mounting is a form of possession that isn't forceful or bad like demonic possession.

On the contrary, it is an honor for the host. Attendees can then ask the Orisha for guidance and enlightenment. Suppose an Orisha possesses someone who isn't a priest or priestess. In that case, it is a sign that this person should be initiated into the priesthood. The Babalawos also perform divination for the chiefs or kings of Yoruba and provide spiritual consultation.

A priest or priestess must first initiate people who want to practice this religion. After initiation, they must follow certain rules and guidelines, including venerating the Orishas and refraining from eating pork. During initiation, an Orisha chooses someone to guide and help fulfill their destiny.

The Yoruba guidelines are:

1. One can change their destiny except for the day they are born, and the day they will die.
2. Each person is a part of the universe (this isn't figurative but intended in the literal sense).
3. One must lead a successful, fulfilled, and happy life.
4. One should never harm nature.
5. One must acquire knowledge and wisdom throughout their life.
6. Each person is born with a destiny, and they must live through it.
7. One is born from their blood relatives.
8. One must never harm another person.
9. One must work with their worldly and spiritual self.
10. One must fear nothing.
11. Heaven is one's real home, while the physical world is the marketplace, and the human spirit is constantly journeying between the two.
12. There is no Devil.
13. The spirits of the ancestors must be revered.
14. The Orishas are a part of each person.
15. There is only one chief deity.

About 20% of the people of Yoruba practice the religion. Even those who converted to Christianity or Islam still hold on to some aspects of the Yoruba religion their ancestors practiced.

Santeria

Santeria is a religion that originated from Yoruba in South and Latin America and in parts of the United States. Santeria is a Spanish word that translates to *"the way of the saints."* The religion goes by other names as well, like La Religión Lucumí, which is Spanish for *"the order of Lucumí,"* and La Regla de Ocha, which is also Spanish and translates to *"the order of the Orishas."*

In the 19th century, Santeria made its way to Brazil, Cuba, Puerto Rico, Haiti, and Trinidad through the slave trade. The religion found its way to the U.S. in the 20th century. From 1959, after the Cuban revolution, and until the 21st century, about one million Cubans immigrated to the U.S. and other countries in South America, where they spread their religious practices. It wasn't just people of African descent who were interested in Santeria – but Latin and white Americans as well. Even those who didn't adopt the religion's traditions were still curious about the concept of the Orishas. It is believed that millions of people sought their help at one point in their lives.

However, before Santeria became widely accepted, worshippers practiced their faith in secret to avoid punishment. Therefore, people couldn't keep records of their faith for centuries and passed down all information orally from one generation to the next. Things changed after the Cuban revolution as the government openly acknowledged Santeria and its followers didn't need to hide. However, it still remains an oral tradition.

There were some concerns among the Cuban government that Santeria could be associated with witchcraft. However, this didn't stop people from showing interest in the religion. In the 1980s, many people were initiated into Santeria, and its popularity hasn't slowed since. About 80% of the Cuban people either follow Santeria or practice some of its traditions.

During enslavement, the African people found that they could only practice their religion by combining some of their Orishas with Catholic saints, hence the name Santeria. However, some disagree with the idea that both religions merged together. The Afro-Cuban people didn't find the need to blend the two but followed both religions simultaneously as they found many similarities between them. Many Santeria followers have converted and adapted to Catholicism. They baptize their children and go to church while still practicing Santeria tradition in their homes and temples. They don't feel the need to give up one faith to practice another as they see the parallelism between the two.

There aren't many differences between Yoruba and Santeria. In Santeria, Oldumare also created the universe, and the Orishas greatly influenced mankind and their daily lives. Santeria is based on the relationship devotees develop with the Orishas. It is a mutually beneficial relationship where worshipers venerate the Orishas and receive their blessings in return. The followers of Santeria also believe in the concept of Ori and that Olodumare grants every person a destiny they must fulfill.

Anyone can follow Santeria, no matter what their background or age. During initiation, people are asked to dress all in white. Those who want to follow Santeria must agree to live according to the way of the Orishas or *la regla de ocha*. There are certain rules that they must follow during the initiation process, which can last up to a year. For instance, they aren't allowed to leave the house at night for a whole year. They can't touch or let anyone touch them unless they are their partners or family members, and they should only wear white attire. All Santeria rituals, including initiation, take place in public or at home since there aren't any temples. Since it is an oral tradition, rites and ceremonies are a big part of the religion as it allows devotees to share and pass down the stories and practices.

Santeria has become a diverse religion, with people from different backgrounds and cultures practicing it. However, it is still identified as an Afro-Cuban religion.

Voodoo

Voodoo has always been associated with black magic, evil spirits, demons, and evil. This is an unfair representation of the faith that has been spread by pop culture. Like Yoruba and Santeria, Voodoo is a religious belief that isn't associated with witchcraft. This misconception stems from some misinterpretations linked to Voodoo for centuries. Hollywood has also played a part in creating a false image of the faith and associating it with cannibalism, torture, and devil worship. The misunderstandings began in the late 18th century when witnesses misinterpreted a Voodoo ritual and thought the people were making a deal with the devil.

Voodoo is one of the oldest religions in the world.
https://unsplash.com/photos/7PWISrkiPW4

Voodoo, also spelled Vodoun and Vodou, originated in Haiti and found its way to America through the slave trade. The followers of Voodoo are called Vodouisants, and many reside in New Orleans, Haiti, and different parts of the Caribbean. It is one of the oldest religions in the world, as it is believed to be 6000 years old. Modern Voodoo is different from its ancient practices as it has blended with African traditions, magic, and Catholicism. However, Voodoo is a dynamic religion that isn't governed by a set of rules. It is so flexible that two temples in the same town can practice completely different traditions.

There are common patterns among the traditions of Voodoo as the Yoruba religion heavily influenced it. For instance, Voodoo's followers venerate their ancestors' spirits and worship spirits similar to the Orishas called Lwas. Their rituals usually involve dancing and playing drums. Lwas serve the same purpose as the Orishas, acting as intermediaries between the Voodoo supreme deity Bondye and mankind. Humans present offerings to the Lwas, and they provide assistance in return. They exist with the spirits of the dead in a place called Vilokan. Voodoo is a monotheistic religion which is the belief in only one god, Bondye. The name is derived from two French words, *bon dieu*, which translates to "good god."

The Vodouisants use Voodoo dolls in their religious practices. However, they don't cause any harm. The dolls are mainly used to venerate Lwas. Voodoo also shares many similarities with Catholicism, like prayers and using candles.

Candomblé

Candomblé, originally called Batuque, is another religion borrowed from Catholicism and African traditions like Yoruba. The word Candomblé means *"dance in honor of the gods."* Over two million people from many countries, like Brazil, practice Candomblé. They believe that there are multiple deities, with each having its own responsibilities and powers. The concept of destiny is also prominent here, and the gods assist people in pursuing and fulfilling their destinies.

In the last few centuries, the religion has gained many followers in Brazil and other countries. However, Candomblé was outlawed for a very long time, and the Catholic Church prosecuted all its practitioners. The Church feared the growing popularity of Candomblé since it was associated with slave revolts and pagan practices. In the 1970s, things changed, and practicing Candomblé became legal again in Brazil.

Unlike the Abrahamic religions, Candomblé doesn't have sacred texts like the Bible or the Quran. It is an oral religion similar to other African-based beliefs. The followers of Candomblé, like Yoruba, believe in the supreme deity Olodumare and Orishas. However, Candomblé's beliefs differ from one region to another. Therefore, there are several variations of this religion.

Followers of Candomblé believe in reincarnation, which is why the bodies of their dead aren't allowed to be cremated. Although they believe in life after death, religion isn't concerned with the concept of the afterlife. Ori or destiny has a major role in the Candomblé faith, and each person must fulfill their own. Some destines are ethical, where the people lead an honorable life, while there are unethical destinies, where a person does harm to themselves and others. However, unethical actions have consequences. People learn about their destinies from the spirits of their ancestors. During a ritual, the spirit mounts (or possesses) the priest or priestess, and attendees can ask them about their destiny.

Priestesses play a bigger role in Candomblé than priests as they run Candomblé temples with the help of a priest. Priestesses are ialorixá - which means *"mothers of saints,"* and priests are called babalorixá -

which means *"fathers of saints."* Ialorixá also serve as healers and fortune tellers in their community. Followers of Candomblé can practice their religion at home or in temples. One must follow certain rules before entering a temple, like wearing clean clothes.

Umbanda

Umbanda is another Brazilian religion that is based on African beliefs. The religion was first practiced in Brazil in the 19th century. It spread to other countries in South America, like Uruguay and Argentina. It is estimated that half a million people practice Umbanda in Brazil. However, it is believed that the number could be much bigger as many people don't practice it in public. The Umbanda followers worship the supreme deity Olodumareb, but they refer to them as Zambia and highly revere the Orishas.

The Umbanda followers revere the spirits of their ancestors, who they call Preto Velho (the old black man) and Preta Velha (the old black woman). These are the spirits of the people who died during enslavement. These spirits are kind-hearted, compassionate, and forgiving. Baianos is another influential spirit. They are also the spirits of the ancestors, mainly of the dead Umbanda practitioners.

Umbanda rituals involve communicating with the spirits of the ancestors, dancing, chanting, and drumming. During rituals, all practitioners must wear white and be barefoot at all times. Shoes have no place in Umbanda rituals since they are unclean.

When slaves were brought from Africa to the new world, they couldn't bring many of their possessions with them. They lost their families, homes, and freedom. The only thing that no one could take away from them was their identity. The African religions represented who they were and what they believed in. For this reason, they brought their beliefs, stories, and songs with them. They were the only things that reminded them of home. Years later, these religions are still influential not only in the lives of the African people but on people from different cultures and backgrounds.

Chapter 2: What Is Ori?

In the Yoruba language, the word "Ori" means "head." However, the literal translation doesn't do justice to what this concept signifies. According to Yoruba cosmology, Ori represents human consciousness, a part of one's body and soul. And it connects the people to the supreme deity Olodumare. This connection is similar to the umbilical cord, which connects a mother with her child. Therefore, it is how one can connect and communicate with Olodumare. Since Olodumare is the creator of everything and exists in everyone, an Ori can be a symbol of the deity who breathed life into all living things.

Even though the literal translation of ori is 'head', it actually represents human consciousness.
Peter Rivera from Stamford, CT, USA, CC BY 2.0
<https://creativecommons.org/licenses/by/2.0>, via Wikimedia Commons
https://commons.wikimedia.org/wiki/File:African_mask_(3146098034).jpg

It is essential to note that Ori doesn't represent destiny itself but rather its structure. It is considered the arbiter of one's destiny. The concept of destiny, or Ayanmo, is one of the components of Ori. An Ori is a map that plans out the road each person will take in their life. The concept of Ori is connected to the idea of fate or destiny. It is the essence of each person, their true nature, and every individual has their own unique Ori.

Its association with the divine is what makes it sacred. It is more than just the physical head that contains one's brain. It's where the inner spiritual self exists. An Ori is also the essence of who you are. It is the personality that defines you and the main force behind all your actions. It is what drives your thoughts and emotions. If you want to learn about your true nature, understand your Ori. People who have an identity crisis or complain about not knowing who they are, need to dig deep within themselves, peel all the layers, and come face to face with their inner selves. The Yoruba people describe the Ori as a spirit, and its power lies between Olodumare and human beings. Hence, it can be its own entity, an Orisha.

Orishas are supernatural entities that were created by Olodumare. When they created the universe, they realized that the human brain was too simple to grasp the concept of such a powerful deity. Therefore, they would not be able to directly interact with human beings. They created the Orishas to assist in mankind's affairs. One of the Orishas' purposes is to help and guide mankind to realize their destiny. They can also bring balance and alignment between one's physical and spiritual aspects of self. Thus, achieving an alignment with one's Ori as well.

The Yoruba people believe that before each person is born, they choose their own destiny, like where they will live, who they will fall in love with, how many children they will have, and even how they will die. They describe it as each person kneeling in heaven in front of Orunmila, the Orisha of divinity, and choosing their destiny with Orunmila's approval. Olodumare then seals the chosen Oris, and they are kept away as no one is allowed to interfere or alter them. This means that every person chooses how they will live their life. However, when a person is born, they forget their Ori and spend their lives trying to remember it and fulfill it.

Since each person chooses their own destiny, they are responsible for the type of life they will lead. Choosing a good Ori guarantees one will live a happy and easy life where one can achieve all their goals. In other words, a good Ori is an equivalent of being "lucky," where someone can have everything they want. They marry their soulmate, have a fulfilling career, live in their dream homes, have good health and great kids, and become wealthy. Everything they touch turns to gold, and everything they want, they can have. The concept of the Ori explains why some people lead happy and successful lives while others struggle. All the big and influential events in a person's life, like having a special talent, becoming wealthy, or dying young, are all attributed to one's Ori.

Having bad or imperfect Oris will lead to a hard and unhappy life where one will only experience bad luck. They will struggle to achieve their goals and will suffer for most of their lives. However, one's Ori isn't fixed, and one can change things for themselves to repair their destiny. Whenever one feels down on their luck and nothing seems to go their way, or if one feels lost and is looking for answers as to what they should be doing with their lives, this means that their Ori requires appeasing. Certain rituals and sacrifices can bring a great transformation, alter one's destiny for the best, and bring balance and alignment to one's spiritual life. You will notice a change when you achieve alignment with your Ori. Positivity will replace the negativity in your life, you'll be satisfied, and you'll achieve fulfillment and inner peace.

This begs the question, do people choose bad Oris? If you control your destiny, how do so many people end up failing and suffering in life? Choosing a good Ori doesn't guarantee that you'll lead a happy life. How a person employs their Ori in both its meanings (head and destiny) is what determines if one fails or succeeds in life. For instance, if you choose an Ori to become a doctor but don't study medicine, you will not fulfill your destiny and may be unhappy as a result. Being a good person can also impact your Ori. Whether your Ori is perfect or flawed, you can never realize it without a good character.

"*Ori gbe eni naa*" is a very popular saying among the Yoruba people, and it translates to "*One's head can make him prosperous.*" While another proverb says, "*Ori eni naa gba'bode,*" which means "*One's head brought disappointment.*" The two sayings showcase the significance of one's Ori in determining what kind of life one will lead. According to the Yoruba people, those who fail to take advantage of their Ori are deemed fools.

Orunmila, the Orisha of wisdom and knowledge, can fix and change one's Ori. His influence in changing one's destiny was mentioned in Yoruba mythology. One of their prayer poems describes Orunmila as the savior of the less fortunate as he can change the Ori or the destiny of those who will die young. The poem mentions that he has the knowledge and wisdom to fix a bad Ori and change the course of people's lives.

Choosing your destiny proves that all these powerful beings like Olodumare and the Orishas have no control over one's destiny, indicating that the Yoruba people believe in free will. One's Ori can be interpreted as their own god who governs the person's life under the supervision of the divine, who doesn't control or meddle with mankind's destiny – but simply observes. Olodumare, with all their power, can't interfere and changes one's Ori. The deity's involvement in mankind's lives is non-existent. Although some stories describe Olodumare as a deity who is there for their creation, they still don't impact a person's Ori. Even Orunmila would not interfere in one's Ori unless he was invoked and asked to.

Each person must be born with an Ori. If a person doesn't have a destiny, there would be no point in their existence. They would have nothing to live for or achieve. When the Olodumare created mankind, they gave each person their own Ori so they could live the life they wanted and accomplish all their goals.

Since people forget their Oris after birth, they neglect the concept altogether and lose the connection they once shared with their destiny. *Your Ori isn't a stranger!* You made its acquaintance before you came out of your mother's womb or took your first breath. Reconnect with it once again by acknowledging it and showing it love and devotion. Ask it for blessings and good fortune, and pray that your Ori will give you a good day every morning. Make connecting with it a part of your daily routine to ensure an alignment with your destiny and a deeper understanding of yourself. Treat your Ori as a friend and talk to it whenever you feel alone. Open up to it, and don't be afraid to show it your most vulnerable self.

Obatala, the sky father and the Orisha who created human beings, molded the human head from clay. Thus, he was responsible for creating the human consciousness. Obatala didn't use magical powers to create the Oris. He molded each one by hand like an artist. Therefore, not all Oris look the same. Like any work of art, some will be perfect, while others can be flawed. In the myth of creation in Yoruba mythology, one time, when Obatala was molding human beings, he got drunk and ended up creating deformed people. Guilty and ashamed, Obalata vowed never to drink again, and he became the protector of the deformed.

When an individual chooses their Ori, they aren't just picking a destiny but also a specific pattern of energy to provide assistance and guidance to the consciousness during reincarnation. This energy pattern – which is also referred to as a spiritual force – helps the person's Ori or consciousness during reincarnation. This helpful spiritual force can also refer to one's personal Orisha since each person should have their own spirit to help them realize their Ori. In time, after the spirit experiences multiple reincarnations, the person's Ori or consciousness will expand due to the wisdom and knowledge they get with every reincarnation.

Ori Arena of Perception

The Yoruba people believe that four arenas of perception function as one's Ori. They are all governed by consciousness hence their association with the Ori.

- The first one is described as "identity emotions," which one uses to reflect on their internal experience when encountering a new one.
- Assess how a new experience can impact your relationship with others and your level of empathy toward them, as well
- Accessing one's memory to reminisce about similar past experiences
- Imagining the impact of the experience on the future

Throughout the day, one experiences these four modes. It is how the brain takes in and processes information. Whenever one encounters a new experience, one evaluates its impact on their emotions, which can bring up similar experiences and feelings from the past. Then they assess the impact the experience has on their current relationships and the consequences of this experience in the future. In Yoruba mythology, how a person perceives the information can heavily impact their personality. The Yoruba people have a saying that you leave your home as someone in the morning and come back at night as a different person.

Being connected with the spiritual aspect of one's self makes a person aware of how they process new information and experiences. By employing the Ori or consciousness, they can expand their perception of the world and how they live through their personal experiences.

Ori isn't only significant as one's destiny but also as their consciousness. Without Ori, you would be unable to interpret human experiences, understand, or process any new information.

Types of Ori

In Yoruba mythology, the human's head is the center of their divine power and was given to them by Olodumare. The head is considered the most significant part of the human body. Hence, it is the home of the Ori. There are three different types of Ori. It mainly consists of the physical and spiritual aspects of a person.

Ori Ode

The Ori Ode refers to the physical head. It isn't as significant as the Ori-inu. In fact, the value of the Ori-ode lies in its association with human beings and that it encompasses the spiritual head. Since the Ori-inu is invisible, the physical head symbolizes one's spiritual aspect and inner self.

Ori-Inu

Ori-inu is the spiritual head that exists within the Ori-ode, and they can't be separated from one another. It represents the connection between the physical and spiritual aspects of a person. They are intertwined, and together, they represent one's identity.

The Ori or consciousness is the mysterious aspect of one personality, while the spiritual aspect is shrouded in mystery. This makes the Ori-inu a mystery existing inside another mystery. The Yoruba people describe the Ori-inu in an interesting way as the inner self that dances and moves *"in front of the mat."* Mat here represents the unity of all the divine's creation.

The Ori-inu is complex and rich. Even when a person reaches to unlock their Ori-ode, they will find a much more intricate layer that is mysterious and elusive. Interestingly, this is the source of their knowledge, yet it's still unknown to the Ori. In many Yoruba rituals and ceremonies, practitioners seek the help of the Orishas to uncover the secrets of the Ori-inu and reveal them to the Ori.

In the Yoruba faith, the newly initiated are prohibited from looking into mirrors because they can lose a part of themselves in the mirror and won't get it back until they can access the Ori-inu.

Ori-Apere

The word Ori-Apere means patterns; in this case, it represents patterns of consciousness. In Yoruba mythology, energy patterns in every living being are referred to as "Odu." These patterns are repeated throughout creation. For instance, there are different types of fire, fire coming from an oven, the sun's fire, and fire from a match. They all share the same energy patterns but come from different sources. It's quite similar to the idea of reincarnation, where the spirit is reborn in different physical forms.

FAQs

Does everyone have an Ori?

Yes, everyone has an Ori. The concept of destiny has always been associated with mankind. Humanity would perish if one had nothing to look for or achieve. According to Yoruba mythology, each person must choose their own destiny.

Can Ori be bad?

Yes and no. This question is open to many interpretations. No one chooses a bad destiny on purpose. However, some aspects can interfere with your Ori and make it bad. For instance, if the Orishas are angry, you'll experience many unfortunate events until you appease them. If you don't take advantage of the wisdom and knowledge of Ori, it will become bad. A bad character can also impact an Ori.

Can I change my Ori?

Mythology varies here. Olodumare has the Oris of each person sealed and doesn't allow anyone to interfere with them. On the other hand, there are beliefs that you can improve your Ori and turn your luck around by connecting with your Ori and appeasing your Orisha. Ancient poems also tell of how Orunmila has changed the Ori of others. It is comforting to believe that one's destiny isn't fixed and can be changed,

Do all people fulfill their Ori?

According to the Yoruba belief, each person must fulfill their Oris. However, if they fail, they can try again in another life when reincarnated.

Can Olodumare or the Orishas alter my Ori or mess with it?

None of these beings can impact your Ori. A person's destiny is their choice, and no deity can change your chosen destiny, no matter how powerful. Only Orisha Orunmila has this power but will never interfere unless you invoke him.

Is my Ori attached to me or separated?

An Ori is attached to you. It is similar to the concept of the aura, something that is always there, but you can't see it nor separate yourself from it.

Will I discover my Ori?

Yes, but not right away. You will not discover your destiny as a whole. An Ori reveals itself little by little.

Do we remember our Oris?

We forget our Oris the moment we come to Earth. Life would be dull if everyone became aware of their destiny.

Does Ori mean that everything happens for a reason?

In Yoruba, there are no coincidences, and nothing is random. Everything is planned from the moment one chooses their Ori.

How can I fulfill my Ori?

You can fulfill their Ori by achieving wisdom through integrating your heart and mind or emotions and thoughts.

In life, there are many mysteries and unanswered questions. Although mysterious, the concept of the Ori can answer some of life's biggest questions, like why are we here? Simply, to fulfill our Ori. It sheds light and explains many mysteries in life. People always ask "why" questions whenever they encounter unfortunate events like Why me? Why now? Some religions teach their followers not to ask these questions, as everything happens for a reason or a part of God's plan. This answer isn't always satisfactory, and one may need more information.

The concept of Ori explains that everything is part of a plan, but it is *your plan*. Everything that happens to you is mainly to help you fulfill the destiny you have chosen for yourself. You don't need to ask yourself why? Because all answers lie in the destiny you chose for yourself. The closer you get to fulfilling it, the clearer things will become and the fewer questions you'll have.

Nothing has more influence or a bigger impact on every aspect of one's life than their Ori. A person's main purpose in life is to fulfill their destiny. Every action you take moves you closer to your Ori. It gives you purpose even when you aren't aware of it. Human beings are on this Earth with one purpose only, to discover and fulfill their Oris.

Ori is a universal concept that exists in all religions, not just African-based practices. It just has a different name, but no matter what you believe in, no one can deny or escape their destiny.

The concept of the Ori is as complex as it is fascinating. The idea of destiny exists in all religions and faiths. However, Yoruba portrays it differently by giving all the power to human beings rather than to the deity. This raises the question, does one operate on free will or destiny? The next chapter will answer this universal question that people have been pondering for centuries.

Chapter 3: Destiny vs. Free Will in Yoruba

In Yoruba, there is a long-standing debate between destiny and free will. This debate is deeply rooted in the traditional beliefs of the Yoruba people and has been echoed for centuries through their oral literature, religious practices, and philosophical traditions. On one side of this argument lies the belief that destiny or fate dictates the course of a person's life, and all outcomes are predetermined by a higher power. On the other side lies the belief that we have free will and that our actions directly influence our future. It is thought that within each of us waits a spark of divinity, which gives us the capability for free choice, no matter how small or insignificant it may be. Through examining the various perspectives of this debate, it is clear that Yoruba thought is far more nuanced and complex than what can be simplified into a binary choice. It exemplifies the complexities of human life as we continually search to make sense of our actions and place in the universe. Understanding both sides of this argument leads to an appreciation for all the possibilities our lives have to offer.

Free Will in Yoruba

In Yoruba culture, the concept of free will is integral to daily life in many ways. A core belief is that each individual has autonomy and control over their own destiny and that they have the power to shape their circumstances. This idea is reflected through various traditional customs, such as offering sacrifices to the gods or wearing certain charms to influence outcomes. It's also often seen in the importance placed on dialogue and debate - talking things out instead of submitting to a predetermined outcome is at the center of many Yoruba cultures. These beliefs often extend beyond individuals, too, as collective action and working together for change are both seen as powerful ways to assert one's will or bring about an intended result. As conceived by Yoruba culture, free will is about much more than having choice or agency - it's about recognizing how every effort we make impacts our destiny, whether individually or collectively. Thus, it encourages individuals to strive toward the desired outcome using all available tools. Ultimately, free will in Yoruba culture serves as a reminder that you have the agency to live life on your terms. It emphasizes the understanding that no matter what external forces are at play, individuals will always have the power of choice when taking action toward reaching their goals. This positive outlook can be embraced by people from all walks of life.

What Is Ori or Yoriba's Idea of Destiny?

In Yoruba culture, the concept of Ori is closely connected to destiny. At the time of a person's birth, it is believed that their Ori (or head) is joined with Olodumare, the supreme being of the universe. This connection allows people to access spiritual power, aligning them with their ultimate destiny. According to Yoruba tradition, this path must be followed during your life for you to fulfill your potential and achieve success. The Nollywood movie "Ori" (Head/Destiny), released in 1991-1992, addresses this idea uniquely and memorably. It follows three people struggling on various paths, trying to make sense of their fate and reach fulfillment and success. As they struggle through various challenges, they each come face-to-face with destiny as ordained by Olodumare - and ultimately reach a resolution. Much like in real life, it is only through embracing our Ori that we can take charge of our destiny and find our place in the world around us. As Yoruba philosopher Oduduwa once said: "If you want what you have never had, you'll have to do something you have never done before." It is up to us to listen to our Ori and step past fear or complacency, as only then will we be able to reach our full potential and achieve true success.

In the Yoruba people's belief system, Ori is a person's individual soul and inner being. It is seen as the part of oneself that determines destiny or the predetermined life path one should take. This idea stems from the idea that each person has a spiritual and physical guardian who helps guide them - called an Orisa - which is given at birth and remains with each individual for their entire life. Ori is believed to be connected to this Orisa and influences every aspect of your life in one way or another. The total of Ori's experiences determines an individual's future success, from health to wealth and even true love, making it a powerful force in dictating how life will play out for any given person. Believers strive to understand and align with their Ori to live prosperous lives. By meditating on the mystical connection between self and destiny, individuals can reach their highest potential while gaining clarity on their place in the world. According to traditional Yoruba beliefs, understanding your own Ori destiny is key to realizing fulfillment in life.

Beliefs surrounding Ori are vast and intertwined across many aspects of Yoruba culture and spirituality, giving rise to an important set of associated practices such as Ifa divination and maintaining spiritual order through ceremonial offerings for your Ori to remain balanced within. As a result, Ori has become firmly embedded as an integral part of history, tradition, ancestral reverence, moral righteousness, and personal identity within Yoruba culture - a testament perhaps to its important influence in revealing each individual's path toward thriving destiny outcomes in life. Whether you come from a place steeped in these traditions or have simply sought a greater understanding of Fate's influence over our life journey, grappling with Ori offers deep insights that may reveal your inner truth and connection with divinity more fully. Regardless of background or origin story, uncovering your Ori consciously helps orient you toward empowerment by revealing hidden gifts that help manifest personal growth milestones along life's spirit-led journey within intentions directed toward achieving freedom with grace!

How Do the Different Components of Ori Work Together?

Yoruba is a powerful way to understand the world and our place in it. At its core, Yoruba revolves around the idea of destiny – or Ori. According to Yoruba tradition, this destiny is informed by four key components: Iwa (Inherent Character), Arugba (Divine Guidance), Ebo (Exchange), and Ori Inu (Head Situation). When considered together, these elements provide a comprehensive explanation for how our destinies are formed.

Iwa is a person's inherent character or spiritual make-up, which shapes who they are at their core. Arguably the most important piece of your destiny, Iwa includes physical traits such as eye color and deeper qualities like your ability to create meaningful relationships. This element also helps explain why people may be inclined to repeat certain behaviors despite trying different approaches.

Arugba is similar to divine grace and relates more closely to external influences that come with being part of a larger collective. It relates to benefits individuals receive from their community, family, and ancestors and serves as an appreciation for links to the past and future, emphasizing interconnection with others.

Ebo focuses on exchanges between people and the universe, particularly actions that either increase or alter an individual's luck or fortune to help further develop their destiny. Ebo can include offerings, prayers, and sacrifices made for something positive to happen. It is also closely related to reciprocity between people exchanging items or favors that ultimately facilitate growth in each other's lives.

Finally, Ori Inu represents the power of the head – literally, a person's physical head but also figuratively their mind or thinking – and aims to remind people that they have control over themselves through thoughts and beliefs. This control can range from simple decisions on how we lead our lives right up to controlling our connection with unseen forces. In all cases, it helps define and refine the personal definition of self beyond biological limits so true destiny can be achieved. When combined, these elements offer unlimited potential for growth which fuels an individual's pursuit of a truly meaningful life based on destiny as defined by Ori in Yoruba culture. By understanding these components, we can learn how different aspects fit together, allowing us to effectively embrace our destinies. This understanding offers us deep insight into ourselves, further aiding us along our life path while showing us the significance behind meanings placed in every aspect around us. Together, these elements offer unlimited potential for growth which fuels an individual's pursuit of meaning based on destiny as defined by Ori culture. By embracing this unique system of beliefs, we can learn how all parts work jointly together, allowing access to understand ourselves more fully and to find paths toward satisfying life's meaningful existence.

How Can One Realign or Recreate Their Ori?

The concept of Ori or Head in Yoruba culture is deeply rooted in tradition and constantly evolving for each individual. It is a belief system that states that everyone carries their destiny within them - it works somewhat like a guiding force, balancing one's thoughts, emotions, and decisions. It cannot be created or changed entirely but can be aligned through rituals such as name-giving ceremonies, Ifa divination, and egungun masquerades. Generally speaking, changing one's Ori requires a consultation with an experienced Babalawo (diviner). This can help to realign your Ori if it has been disrupted by life events such as illness or a death in the family, and thus bring balance back into your life. As this consultative process unfolds, certain aspects of the Ori cannot be changed, no matter what. These sections are thought to represent parts of our collective identity, derived from our ancestry and handed down through generations of oral storytelling. However, many experts agree that you have control over those aspects of your Ori which relate to self-determination. This includes taking responsibility for decisions that impact the course of your life, including where or how you live, how you interact with people, what career paths you choose, and how you practice spirituality, etc. In essence, a person's Ori must be acknowledged as an integral part of their identity but also understood as something which can be affected by personal choices and decisions. Consequently, it becomes possible to adapt and modify one's journey over time without completely disregarding the foundations imposed by tradition or customs. At its core, the notion of an ancestral head serves as a constant reminder to reflect on the strength found in both dynamic change and deep-rooted acceptance within Yoruba culture.

To truly understand our Ori is to recognize the importance placed on honoring African heritage while recognizing our capacity for growth. Only then can individuals truly harness their ability to cultivate insight surrounding their destiny. According to Yoruba beliefs, when we live true to our authentic selves, we become spiritually connected with ourselves, family/community/ancestral bloodlines, etc., as well as with nature which surrounds us, ultimately understanding our Creator better to realize man's ultimate purpose on Earth is achieving peace and unity through love.

Ori-Apere and How It Can Change an Individual's Ori

In Yoruba culture, Ori-Apere is used to help a person achieve balance and harmony within themselves. It refers to the "personal force" or spiritual power that an individual has, which influences their behavior and their life trajectory. Ori-Apere acts as a compass, helping guide the individual through physical and emotional challenges. In traditional Yoruba beliefs, when someone's Ori-Apere becomes out of balance due to adversity or great life changes, it needs to be restored for them to reach their full potential. This can be achieved through prayer, meditation, and other forms of spiritual practice. The aim is to reawaken the power of one's original self and reconnect with their higher purpose. Ultimately, if individuals can realign their Ori-Apere, they will have access to new energy, which will help them move forward in their journey while staying true to who they are. By taking the time and effort to restore their force, they will become better equipped for life's challenges, whatever form they may take. Ultimately this helps a person tap into new sources of inner strength, and it acts as a pointer enabling them to move ahead while continuing to be true to themselves. That gives them strength regardless of the type of adversities they encounter on their path toward greatness. After all, personal alignment is key for individuals who want to realize their full potential. Consequently, imbalances between physical, emotional, and mental states will greatly decrease, which could stop you from reaching your goals.

Components of Ori-Apere

1. Ayanmo

Ayanmo is an integral component of Ori-Apere. It is one of the most important parts of Yoruba culture, which is closely associated with spiritual growth and personal harmony. Literally translated, Ayanmo means "*taking back the essence*" and refers to the process of getting back in touch with the divine source and restoring balance in both body and mind. This concept is based on the belief that every person has three souls. These are the physical (which resides in the body), the astral (which exists within and beyond space), and the spiritual (which is connected to a higher power).

Through meditation and introspection, an individual can develop their connection with these three souls, aligning themselves with their higher purpose. Taking part in these activities helps individuals understand what motivates them and guides them toward achieving greater self-awareness. By bringing balance to an individual's spiritual life, Ayanmo helps people live more harmoniously with themselves and their loved ones while fostering an unshakeable faith in divine order. Furthermore, it reaffirms that each person needs to be mindful of expressions from all three planes: physical, astral, and spiritual – for total fulfillment and enlightenment. Ayanmo is truly a foundational element for any who seeks deeper meaning in life or wishes to unlock greater inner potential in accordance with traditional Yoruba culture.

2. Akunleya

Found mainly in Nigeria, Akunleya is an important component of Yoruba culture. It is the concept of using respectful speech at all times, regardless of who we are speaking to and the situation; essentially, it refers to etiquette in conversation. Akunleya means politeness and refraining from talking about uncomfortable or controversial topics. This concept is based on respect for others as well as for ourselves. It plays an essential role in many aspects of life, from familial and communal relationships to business dealings. Proper use of Akunleya encourages a peaceful social environment. It allows people to problem-solve instead of clashing with one another.

Moreover, it fosters trust between individuals, helping them to build beneficial relationships based on mutual understanding and respect. Akunleya is part of Ori-Apere, which translates roughly to *"personal character"* or the practices a person should uphold if he wishes to be respected by his peers. The principle of Akunleya runs deep within the fabric of Yoruba culture, encouraging people toward empathetic conversations rather than heated disagreements. It serves as a reminder that polite speech should always be prioritized when interacting with one another.

3. Akunlegba

Akunlegba is more than just semantics; it carries a deep meaning for the Yoruba. In essence, this concept speaks to the physical, spiritual, and intellectual transformation that must take place in order for a person to be well-rounded. Physically, Akunlegba holds that we must work actively to develop and maintain a healthy lifestyle that can sustain life over time.

Those who adhere to these ideals seek physical strength and mental agility. Spiritually, Akunlegba emphasizes living a life with a mindset of understanding and respect for faith, taking responsibility for personal development, and outwardly practicing virtuous behavior through service to others. Intellectually, Akunlegba encourages individuals to hone their comprehension by engaging in analysis, critical thinking, and knowledgeable communication across cultures – basically mental transnationalism or education beyond one's individual faith system or culture. In summation, Akunlegba is a philosophical requirement essential to developing an authentic understanding of ourselves and our environment in the Yoruba context – both the tangible and the intangible aspects – serving as a guidepost for proper socialization throughout each person's life journey. By adhering to tenants like these within Ori-Apere, individuals holistically evolve into wise stewards who protect natural assets through sustainable practices while inspiring others to do the same.

Akunlegba is viewed as a gateway between heaven and earth, acting as a mediator between both realms. It involves rituals designed to open a connection between gods and spirits on the one hand and humans on the other. According to legend, man is said to descend from God through such gateways, encoded in various objects purchased by practitioners for use during spiritual cleansing or invocation ceremonies at altars. Those who partake in such festivities often receive guidance from godly energy forces or divinities that intermingle within these points of contact between heaven and Earth. Furthermore, it is also believed that utilizing Akunlegba's energies and aligning with divine powers through ancestral worship can reveal solutions to deal with unfavorable states and circumstances, keeping those relying on traditional methods of divination from achieving success and gaining purpose within life's journey toward destiny. Therefore, anyone seeking self-development or healing can explore this age-old practice as an effective solution to present predicaments. In conclusion, by utilizing this powerful component found within Ori-Apere, practitioners can utilize its wisdom, harnessed ages ago, to alter the destinies of individuals today to bring forth blessings and harmony in the mortal plain.

In conclusion, the debate between destiny and free will in Yoruba thought is a complex one that has been argued for centuries. It reflects the complexities of human life and encourages us to consider our actions carefully and make the choices that suit us best. It is up to each person to decide which side of the debate they believe in and how they will shape the course of their destiny. By understanding both sides of this argument, we can gain an appreciation for all that life has to offer.

Chapter 4: Olodumare and the Orishas

Aside from being described as a way of explaining someone's destiny and purpose, Ori is also often described as Olodumare's spark inside a person. It is a gift to humans and, therefore, can be understood better by understanding Olodumare and the Orishas.

This chapter will help you understand the importance of Olodumare to the Yoruba religion, explore the creation story in depth, and go over the concept of the Orishas. At the end of this chapter, you'll have a better understanding of Yoruba cosmology, and you'll be better able to understand the role of Ori in it.

Understanding Olodumare

Olodumare is one of the many names for the Yoruba supreme deity. Other names include Olorun and Olafin-Orun. Olodumare is the traditional name given to this supreme deity in the Yoruba language. The name "Olorun" has gained popularity due to the influence of other religions on Isese, including Christianity and Islam.

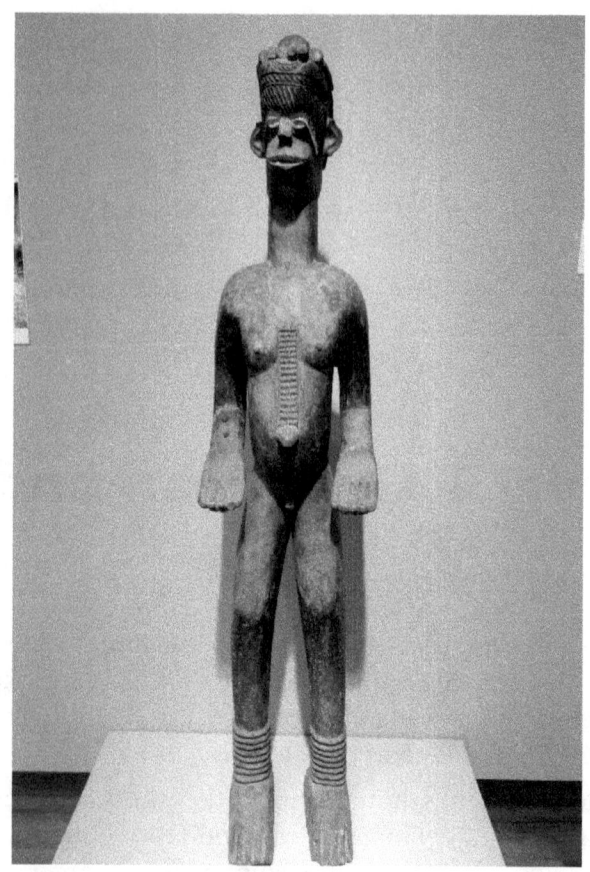

Olodumare is depicted in many ways in different cultures.
Daderot, CC0, via Wikimedia Commons
https://commons.wikimedia.org/wiki/File:Tutelary_Deity_or_Guardian_Figure_(alusi),_Nigeria,_Igbo_people,_c._1935,_wood,_paint_-_Chazen_Museum_of_Art_-_DSC01780.JPG

Olodumare is not only a sky and creator god; this deity is considered to be the "owner of life." In Yoruba, Olodumare is completely unique, and no other deity can come close. This uniqueness is reflected in the fact that, in the Yoruba language, Olodumare has no gender. Olodumare is purely a spiritual entity, unlike the Orishas.

As the owner of life, Olodumare is immortal, omnipotent, and omniscient. However, Olodumare is also aloof from humanity and communicates with the world through their helpers, the Orishas. For this reason, there is no image or shrine of Olodumare, nor are any sacrifices made directly to the creator deity. Very few Yoruba people worship Olodumare directly. Instead, they worship them through the agency and actions of the Orishas.

Olodumare is called to primarily when prayers to the other Orishas seem to go unanswered. This deity is not only immortal, omniscient, and omnipotent – they are also all-knowing and good and evil. Olodumare is, essentially, a representation of all the aspects of the universe.

The many names given to Olodumare reflect this deity's multiple roles as the head of the Yoruba pantheon. These names include:

- **Olofi:** The ruler of the Earth and the conduit between Orun (heaven) and Aye (Earth)
- **Olodumare:** The creator deity
- **Olorun:** The ruler of the heavens
- **Alaaye:** The living/everlasting one
- **Elemi:** The keeper/owner of life. As the keeper of life, Olodumare bestows "life breath" upon humans. When Olodumare withdraws this life breath, the person dies.
- **Olojo Oni:** Owner/controller of the day and daily happenings. This name implies that a person's destiny (Ori) is in the hands of Olodumare and their plan for humanity.

Because Olodumare is primarily distant from humanity, much of the connection between them and humanity is fostered by the creator's emissaries or helpers, the Orishas. The Yoruba creation myth is one of the most important stories to reflect this relationship.

The Yoruba Creation Myth

According to the Yoruba creation myth, in the beginning, the world consisted of nothing but the sky, the water, and the wild marshlands. Olodumare and the Orishas lived in the sky, above a young baobab tree, and descended and ascended to and from the marshlands below using a chain (or, in some versions of the story, a spider's web). During this time, there were no humans because there was no land for them to live on.

However, the Orisha Obatala was unsatisfied and, unlike the other Orishas, was not content to stay near the baobab tree and Olodumare. Instead, he was curious and would often look at the waters and wild marshlands below the sky. One day, when he was looking into the waters, he decided that the world needed more than that.

So, he traveled to Olodumare and asked the creator deity for permission to create solid land in the waters below. There, the Orishas and Olodumare could create beings who the Orishas could aid using their powers. Because of this, in one version of the story, Obatala is referred to as the Head of the White Cloth (that is, the Head of the fabric of creation).

Olodumare agreed to this request from Obatala. Having gained the permission he was seeking, Obatala then went to Orunmila, the Orisha of wisdom and divination, and asked him how he should prepare for his journey to the world below.

By reading the patterns of palm kernels and the powder of baobab roots, Orunmila told Obatala that he must create a chain of gold that he could use to travel to the world below. He would also have to gather sand, palm nuts, maize, plant seeds, a white hen, and have a black cat with him. Finally, he would have to carry the sacred egg, which contained the Orishas' personalities.

After hearing this, Obatala traveled from Orisha to Orisha, asking them to donate their gold. When he gathered gold from every Orisha, he had the goldsmith use it to create a chain. He also gathered all the sand in the sky and placed it in a snail shell, which he would use to carry it down to the waters with him. In the snail shell, he sprinkled some baobab powder. He gathered everything he needed, placed it in his pack, and carried the sacred egg close to his chest.

Once he had everything he needed, he hooked the golden chain to the sky and began climbing down to the waters below. For seven days, he traveled downwards until he reached the waters below.

When he reached the waters, he hung from the end of the chain and was confused, unsure of what he should do to create land. Seeing his confusion, Orunmila called to him, telling him to use the sand he had collected. He poured the sand into the waters and dropped the hen with it. The hen pecked at the sand, spreading it around, where it solidified and turned into land.

While Obatala was hanging from the end of the chain, his heart was pounding so much that it cracked the egg he was carrying close to his chest. From it emerged Sankofa, the sacred bird that carried the spirits of the Orishas. As Sankofa began to fly, it stirred up the sand and created a storm, blowing the sand here and there. This created hills, lowlands, dunes, and mountains, giving the land a unique character, just like each Orisha had a unique character.

Finally, Obatala let go of the chain, dropping onto the newly created land. He named this land "Ife," the place/land that divides the waters. Curious about this new land, he started walking around and exploring. As he walked, he planted the palm nuts he had carried with him, which sprouted into palm trees. He also scattered the other seeds he had in his pack, turning the barren land green with trees and plants.

The black cat he had carried from the heavens, Obatala, kept him company. However, he soon began to grow lonely – and thirsty. In his thirst, he stopped at the edge of a pond. However, before he could quench his thirst, his attention was grabbed by his own reflection in the pond. Seeing it, Obatala was pleased and decided to create beings like him to keep him company.

Using the dark earth clay at the pond's edge, Obatala began his task of forming these beings. However, he soon grew tired and even thirstier. He used juice from his newly planted palm trees to ferment into palm wine to satisfy his thirst. However, he soon grew intoxicated, and in his intoxication, he continued to create the clay figures.

However, unlike his initial figures, these figures were not perfect. Instead, they were misshapen, some without eyes, or with misshapen limbs, or many other imperfections. However, Obatala thought that these figures were beautiful, so he continued to create them.

While he was creating these figures, Olodumare sent down the Chameleon to check on Obatala's progress. The Chameleon reported back that Obatala had created figures with proper form but that he was disappointed in their lack of life.

In response, Olodumare gathered the gasses of the universe beyond the sky and sparked them into a fireball. He sent this fireball to Ife, where it dried the still-wet figures and baked them. The fireball also caused the earth to start spinning. Then, Olodumare blew across Ife, bestowing the figures with the gift of life and giving birth to the first people of Ife – and the first humans.

The next day, Obatala came to his senses and realized that, in his intoxication, he had brought deformity to the world. Regretting his actions, he vowed never to drink again and took the role of the protector of those born deformed.

Obatala's new people started to build huts and soon formed the first Yoruba village. Obatala returned to the heavens but split his time between Ife and the sky.

All the other Orishas were pleased with Obatala's work except Olokun. Olokun was the Orisha of the bottom of the ocean, and, as such, the waters below the world were part of her domain. Ife was created without her permission, and Obatala usurped much of her kingdom through his creation.

In her wrath, Olokun sent wave after wave from her oceans to destroy Obatala's creation and succeeded in destroying much of the kingdom. Obatala, who was visiting the sky at the time, was unaware of this until the survivors in Ife sent a message with Esu, the messenger Orisha, to Olodumare and Obatala, asking for help.

Upon hearing the news, Obatala climbed down to the Earth, which caused the waters to recede, ending the great flood. Worried that Olokun would cause another flood when he returned to the heavens, he challenged her to a weaving contest and sent Chameleon to Olokun to judge her skill. As Olokun wove, Chameleon changed color to mimic the fabric. Realizing that she couldn't beat Chameleon, Olokun accepted her defeat and agreed to stop her wrath. Thus, the people of Ife were free to live and reproduce.

It should be noted that this is only the best-known version of the Yoruba creation myth. In a variation of the myth, Obatala was not the Orisha who devised the idea of creating the land and humanity. Instead, it was the idea of Olodumare, and it was Olodumare who told Obatala to fulfill this mission. In this version of the story, every action that Obatala took was dictated by Olodumare and not Orunmila.

That said, regardless of the version, what is clear is that Olodumare remained one step removed from humanity. It was not the creator god who actually created humanity. It was Obatala who formed clay into the first humans. Olodumare was the deity who gave humanity life. Because of this, Olodumare is now worshiped as the aloof creator deity, while Obatala is venerated as the creator of humanity and the founder and first king of Ife.

The Orishas

Given that Olodumare is primarily aloof from humanity, their guidance must be carried out by their emissaries, the Orishas.

The Orishas are essentially the gods or deities of Yoruba belief. They are emanations/avatars of Olodumare, created to bring Olodumare's guidance to the universe. There are hundreds, even thousands of

Orishas, and it is most often described that there are "400 + 1" Orishas in the Yoruba pantheon: a way of saying that the Orishas are innumerable.

That said, while there are "400+1" Orishas, some are more prominent than others. It is primarily 20 or 30 Orishas who appear in the stories of the Yoruba pantheon. Of them, 7 are more prominent than the others: Esu, Ogun, Obatala, Yemaya, Oshun, Shango, and Oya.

The Orishas are meant to help humans achieve their Ori and self-actualize. However, they are not meant to be perfect deities and have their own personality and flaws. Because of this, they can occasionally get in the way of people achieving their Ori, whether purposefully or unknowingly. An Orisha may purposefully take steps to prevent a person from self-actualizing because the person has offended the Orisha and therefore has brought punishment upon themselves.

Seeing how Orishas are capable of weakness, pride, desire, spite, and arrogance, their relationship with Olodumare is complex and often hard to understand. In one well-known story, the Orishas tire of Olodumare's aloofness from humanity and the Orishas, and they plot to overthrow Olodumare as the supreme deity.

However, the Orishas forgot to include Esu in their plan. They plotted to scare Olodumare to death by inviting them to a hut and releasing mice inside, which the creator deity was terrified of. Esu, who was present in the doorway when the plot was being hatched, heard everything.

On the agreed-upon day, Olodumare arrived at the hut where the mice were hidden and crossed the threshold when the door was closed, and the mice were released. Olodumare was terrified and tried to run but could not. The door was closed. However, Esu appeared and ate the mice. He then pointed out the guilty Orishas to Olodumare, who punished them and rewarded Esu.

In another story, the Orishas once again attempted to overthrow Olodumare. After knowing their plan, Esu arrived at Olodumare's realm and let them know. In return, Olodumare stopped the rains from falling to the Earth. As a result, the waters of the Earth dried up, crops began to fail, and the Orishas repented their actions. However, the Orishas couldn't reach the palace of Olodumare to plead their case.

Finally, Oshun turned herself into a peacock and flew to Olodumare's palace. She lost most of her feathers during the journey and arrived exhausted and ill, having turned into a vulture. Taking pity on her state, Olodumare finally heard the Orishas' pleas and allowed the rains to fall on the Earth again. As a reward for her actions, Olodumare named Oshun the messenger of heaven, the only one who was granted leave to bring messages to Olodumare's palace.

Thus, though the Orishas are emanations and emissaries of Olodumare, they are not always aligned. However, in most cases, the Orishas attend to their duties, acting as the go-betweens between humanity and Olodumare. While every Orisha has a role to play, the seven most prominent Orishas are the ones who are best-known and most worshiped. These seven Orishas are most commonly referred to as gods and goddesses.

Esu

Trickster deities are common in many African belief systems, and Isese is no different. In the Yoruba religion, Esu serves as the trickster deity. However, he was not only a mischief-maker – but he was also the Orisha who brought balance to the world.

Esu is the Orisha of duality, balance, crossroads, beginnings, and orderliness. He was also the *messenger Orisha*, the one who ruled over travelers, chaos, death, and misfortune. He was a complex, dual-natured Orisha who now teaches believers that there are two or more sides to every issue and is also known as "A-bá-ni-wá-oràn-bá-ò-rí-dá" (He-who-creates-problems-for-the-innocent).

Even though he is an unpredictable Orisha, he is also necessary for order in life. Because of his importance, he is the only Orisha to be worshiped every day of the traditional four-day Yoruba week.

Ogun

Ogun is the Orisha of blacksmiths, craftsmen, metalworkers, iron, soldiers, and war. He is the owner of all technology, and as a warrior deity, all technology shares in his nature, and it is used first and foremost for war.

It is said that using his metal ax, Ogun clears the way for the other Orishas to enter the Earth. In the Yoruba creation myth, the gold chain that Obatala used to reach the waters is symbolic of Ogun and his role in clearing the way for the other Orishas.

It is said that Ogun was the first king of Ife as a human. After his death, he disappeared into the earth in the town of Ire-Ekiti, vowing to help those who called on him. The symbols of Ogun are the dog, the palm frond, and iron. He is often depicted with a spitting cobra and is recognized with the number seven and the colors black and green.

Obatala

Obatala is the sky father, the eldest of Olodumare's Orishas. He is the Orisha of creation, the sky, light, and morality.

In some stories, Obatala was also the founder and the first king of Ife-Ife. After his death, he was deified and merged with the Orisha Obatala.

He had 201 wives, with his principal wife being Yemaya. However, in some stories, his favorite wife was Yemowo. He is associated with the color white. White contains all the colors of the rainbow and therefore shows that Obatala opens different paths. Additionally, Obatala is the Head of the White Cloth. Thus, white is associated with him.

Yemaya

Also known as Yemoja, Yemaya was the Mother of All Water. She was the mother of all Orishas and was the Orisha of creation, water, motherhood, pregnant women, and all the waters on the Earth. She was also made the patron Orisha of the Ogun River.

She is often portrayed as a mermaid or dressed in seven skirts of blue and white. One of Yemaya's names means "Mother Whose Children are Fish," and she is mother to uncountable children – as many there are fish in the ocean. Yemaya is a gentle, caring Orisha who is slow to anger, but her wrath is destructive and violent when she is angered.

Oshun

Oshun is the Orisha of the sweet waters of the world and is also the Orisha of love, beauty, intimacy, diplomacy, and wealth. She is the patron deity of the Osun River and is honored during the two-week-long annual Osun-Osogbo festival that takes place in the city of Osogbo.

In one version of the Yoruba creation myth, it is said that Oshun, along with 16 other Orishas, was sent to create the world. Oshun was the youngest and only female, Orisha, and so she was ignored by the others. When the 16 male Orishas failed to create the world, they turned to Olodumare for help. Olodumare told them that creation could not happen without Oshun's help, so they returned and apologized to her. She accepted their apology and finished creating the world, bringing beauty, fertility, love, and sweetness to it.

While this is a less popular version of the Yoruba creation myth, it demonstrates the importance of Oshun in the Yoruba pantheon.

It is said that she was once mortal and, during her mortal life, attended a drum festival and fell in love with Shango, who made her his second wife. Despite not being his chief wife, she is his favorite. She is associated with the colors gold and yellow and the number five. In the traditional Yoruba creation myth, she is represented by the white hen, which was said to have five fingers.

Shango

Perhaps the most "popular" Orisha among worshippers, Shango is also the strongest Orisha in the Yoruba pantheon. He is the Orisha of lightning and thunder, fire, justice, dance, and virility, and is similar to storm gods in other pantheons.

A hot-blooded, strong-willed Orisha, he took the form of the third Alaafin of Oyo for a short period of time. In his time as mortal ruler, he was violent and bloodthirsty – but also one of the most powerful Yoruba rulers.

Shango was the husband of three wives – Oba, Oshun, and Oya. Of these, Oshun was his favorite. He is worshiped on the fifth day of the week, and foods consumed as part of his worship include bitter kola, guguru, amala, and gbegiri soup. He is associated with the color red and the numbers four and six and is represented by his powerful double-headed ax.

Oya

Oya is the third and youngest wife of Shango. She is the Orisha of storms, thunder and lightning, and the wind. She is also the guardian of the dead and the deity of transformation. She is also known as Oya-Ìyáńsàn-án (the mother of nine). This refers to the nine children she birthed, all of whom were stillborn.

She is the patron deity of the river Niger and is a warrior Orisha. It is said that she rides into war at the side of Shango and that she is unbeatable in battle. As a deity of change, she commands the essence of the constantly changing world around us and is the ruler of gifts like intuition and clairvoyance.

Chapter 5: Ori as an Orisha

By reading this chapter, you'll find out all about the different methods you can use to worship your Ori. You'll understand how to reach out to it as a single powerful entity and as an Orisha. Then, you'll find the basics of worshiping an Orisha.

Worshiping Ori

According to Yoruba, we all possess physical and spiritual self-healing powers that we can unlock by connecting with and worshiping the Orishas. Over time, this type of work can help us become more balanced, which allows us to align with our higher selves (Ori). Some practitioners suggest that one's Ori can be worshiped as an Orisha. After all, you can reach out to your divine self for guidance whenever you encounter a problem. You should also appease your Ori whenever things go wrong. Yoruba suggests that everything happening in your life is overseen by your Ori. Ori can be thought of as a spirit with an immense amount of power that lies between humans and God.

Everyone connects with their Ori in a unique way. Some people like to take simple approaches, while others believe that an Ori should be appeased like an Orisha. You can simply praise your Ori in the morning, express your love and appreciation toward it, and ask it for guidance or abundance. You can achieve an aligned and secure sense of self by regularly reaching out to your Ori. You'll eventually find yourself being naturally guided as if this sense of direction is coming from within. Others find it beneficial to have deep conversations with their Ori.

Those who prefer a more complete approach typically prefer rituals. While some rituals must be conducted by Orisha priests, there are others that you can try out if you believe you're qualified enough to do so. If you decide to do it yourself, you should ask an experienced practitioner to supervise the process until you get the hang of it.

Connecting with Your Ori

You have to explore your Ori and understand what it is to ensure that you're connecting with your Ori in the right way. If you don't have a background in astrology, you'll need to seek the guidance of a professional astrologer. You'll need to know more about what your birthdate entails, the areas in your life in which you're most aligned and abundant, and the aspects in which you're not.

To start connecting with your Ori, you must be living life in a way that's true to who you are. You'll never be able to align with your Ori if you don't embrace your true, authentic nature. The key is to be completely honest, not only with yourself but with others too.

If you wish to align with your Ori, you need to spend time with people you feel great around. Don't force yourself to fit into a social circle that has different values and beliefs you don't agree with, especially if you have to hide your own convictions and pretend to be someone you're not around them. Surrounding yourself with like-minded individuals encourages you to express yourself and feel at ease. It also makes it a lot easier for you to stay focused on things that matter and not lose sight of your goals.

Regularly surrounding yourself with nature can help you align with your divine self because it keeps you grounded, which can allow you to truly connect with your inner self. Spending time in nature is a great way to clear your mind and soothe your anxiety. Shutting down your intrusive and unnecessary thoughts allows you to pay more attention to your feelings, emotions, and true thoughts. Some practitioners believe that God manifests himself as the supreme deity through nature, which means that regularly spending time in nature can enrich your spiritual endeavors.

Surround yourself with nature to stay grounded and connect with the divine.
https://www.pexels.com/photo/photography-of-a-woman-meditating-906097/

Meditation is another great way to strengthen your connection with your Ori. One mantra that you can chant repetitively is the "Haaaaa." Take a deep breath and exhale while saying the mantra. You can also chant "O Ree Mo Pay Oh" three times, followed by "Or ree Sahn me" and "Or ree Sahn Ee get ee." Reciting this chant allows you to call to your divine self for guidance and support. Keep in mind that you may need to experiment with different techniques and chants until you find one that works for your Ori.

Exercising or doing Yoga can help you connect with your Ori because physical activities encourage your body to release the tension it's been storing. When you're exercising, pay attention to your breathing pattern. Yoga is great at helping you connect with your Ori because it teaches you to control and connect with your breath. This is why this mindfulness practice can help you regulate your thoughts and feelings, which leads to the overall peace of mind.

Ibori: Feed Your Ori

If you wish to take the other approach, you can conduct a very powerful yet relatively easy ritual. The Ori cleansing and feeding practices are known as Ibori. Remember that the following version of the ritual is the most basic. There's another much more complex practice. It must be conducted by an Orisha priest or an experienced Babalawo; hence the practice explained below will help you as a beginner.

To conduct this ritual, you must have some background in divinatory practices as you'll be determining when and if you need to perform an Ibori and which offerings you need to give to your divine self. You must also learn to tell whether your higher self has accepted your offering and if they're appeased. You'll benefit from using Opèle or Ikin and knowing the positions of the Odu IFA, as they can offer clear and distinct answers. Make sure you consult an Orisha priest to help you consecrate your IFA divination tools beforehand.

Choosing Your Offerings

Offerings can include many options.
https://pxhere.com/en/photo/1363848

Cast IFA to determine if your Ori currently needs to receive an offering and which offerings it wants. If you can't determine what to give to your Ori via divinatory practices, you can try a few of the following offerings:

- Meat is used to generate strength.
- Fruit attracts abundance and revitalizes your destiny
- Omiero is typically used in various rituals
- Dry gin can attract pleasure and resilience
- Native chalk is a popular ritual offering
- Honey can bring joy into one's life
- Shea butter is used for protection and calm
- Cool water is refreshing and soothing

- Coconut milk is known for being a cooling and calming agent
- Red palm oil is great for attracting abundance, ease, and sustenance
- Kola-nut is invigorating and vivacious. It can help you steer clear of challenges and roadkill and is good for fostering wisdom.
- Sugar cane can bring an element of agreeableness and pleasance into your life
- Bitter Kola is used to attract longevity and protection.

Preparing Omiero

While it's best if you ask a professional Babalawo to prepare Omiero for you, you can still do it yourself if you don't have access to an Orisha priest. Oftentimes, the liquid is made from water and a blend of specific herbs. Some Yorubas incorporate snail blood or blood from other animals into the solution. Omiero is believed to be Obatala's most preferred offering.

Omiero is used to wash one's head, the Ori, because it can attract good fortune, tranquility, and peace of mind. It also allows you to nourish your head with some elements of Orunmila and Obatala throughout the practice.

The best Omiero ingredients for Ibori are ewe ero, white native chalk, coconut water, shea butter, spring water, soft meat, and snail blood. You can add any amount of each ingredient to the blend but try to follow your intuition as you do so. You should be particular and clear about your intentions as you add each ingredient. Name the reason why you're adding each ingredient to the Omiero. When you've finished, you can bathe in it.

Note that you should be very careful about what you put on your Ori because it's really sensitive. While this blend is popularly used during Ibori rituals, each person's Ori requires unique offerings and responds differently. This is why you should determine which ingredients to use via divinatory practices or by consulting a Babalawo.

Getting Ready

You should try performing Ibori in the morning before interacting with anyone. However, many people don't like to do that because performing

Ibori requires you to stay at home for the rest of the day. If this isn't practical for you, you can perform the ritual in the evening when you're sure that you won't have to go out for the rest of the day. Your home – or at least room – should be free of disturbances during the entire ritual. Steer clear of anything that may hinder your peace of mind.

Take a bath or shower, and use consecrated black soap to wash your head before you present your offering. This allows you to wash away any negative energy you may have gathered. When you're in the shower, you should imagine that your spiritual, mental, and emotional dirt is being washed away. You can spend as much time as you want as long as you come out of the shower feeling relaxed and clean (physically, emotionally, mentally, and spiritually). Get dressed in all-white (or the next lightest color you have) clothes and undergarments. Avoid dark and bright clothes.

If you have an Igba'Ori, you should use it to perform your ritual. You can also perform your ceremony at an ancestral shrine if you have one set up. If not, choose a quiet and comfortable space to begin. The room should be clean, organized, and consecrated with Holy water. Conducting your preferred form of divination can also help you get rid of negative energy before you start the ritual.

Performing Ibori

1. Throw the cool water and earth around and call each of their names out. Call on the ancestors and Orunmila.
2. Use palm oil, kola, or power to anoint your tongue.
3. The tongue carries "ofo ase," which means the power of words. This is why you should say that the ase of the deities, or Orisha, is in your mouth as you do so.
4. Pay homage by chanting Iba and Oriki
5. Offer your chosen sacrifices to feed your Ori.

Start at the position of your third eye and move to the top of your head and down to the base of your skull. Do that with each offering and mention the reason why you're feeding your Ori this particular item. For example, you can say something like, *"Ori, please give me strength as I give you meat for resilience."*

Creamy and liquid offerings should be dabbed with the liquid middle finger and smudged between your eyes, around your eyebrows, and moving upward and down the base of your skull. Solid items should be presented to the forehead. Use the same finger to present your offerings to your navel and your index finger to present them to your right toe.

Secure all the offerings you've placed on your head using a special white cloth. You should keep wearing the white headscarf with the offerings underneath for the rest of the day, even after you've finished your ceremony. It helps deflect unwanted energies.

6. Cast IFA to determine whether your Ori has accepted your offerings.
7. Pay your homage by chanting Iba.

Closing the Ibori Ritual

Use Opèle or Ikin to determine whether your Ori wants another offering. In some cases, one's Ori may request an additional item in particular or ask you to repeat a certain chant or prayer. You shouldn't close your ceremony if you're not sure that your Ori is satisfied or has accepted all your offerings.

Try to maintain your peace of mind, avoid doing a lot of physical or mental work, and refrain from sexual activities for the rest of the day. Remove your offerings the following morning before you shower. Make sure you ask your Ori where they would like you to discard the items.

Worshiping the Orishas

You don't need to perform daily rituals in order to worship the Orishas. However, you should regularly recite your personal prayers and offer the appropriate sacrifices. The prayers and sacrifices you choose mainly depend on your divinatory revelations, your intuition, and the preferences of the Orisha that you're worshiping. Many people opt for fruit offerings, as they're generally favored among the deities and are associated with abundance.

Yorubas engage in communal celebrations during which they conduct drumming and dancing ceremonies as a form of prayer. These celebrations can also help induce a trance or altered state of consciousness, which can help practitioners connect with the spiritual world more effectively.

Each Orisha requires different objects to be placed on their altars. While some deities may prefer certain offerings, others may not accept them. This is why you should be very mindful about what you place on your shrine. Here are some examples of what you can place on the altars of a few Orishas:

Obatala
- Metal crown
- Bell with a dove-shaped handle
- White cloth (opt for a cotton material)
- White candle
- Statue or picture of Obatala
- Rice, cocoa butter, meringue, eggs, or other white offerings. Your offerings should be bland and not overwhelmingly flavorful. Avoid spicy foods, salt, and alcohol.

Shango
- Axe
- Sword
- Crown
- Wooden bowl with a cover
- Pedestal
- Wooden tools
- Drum
- Statue or picture of Shango
- Red or white candle
- Opt for spicy, red, and hot offerings

Yemaya
- Shells (preferably cowrie)
- Silver items
- Statues or pictures of dolphins, mermaids, fish, or other sea creatures
- Pearls
- Fans
- Blue or white candle
- Blue cloth
- Incense

- Blue or colorful lowers
- Your offerings should include seafood, fruits, lettuce, white wine, and coffee

Now that you have read this chapter, you understand how to worship your Ori as either a single powerful spirit or as an Orisha. You also understand the basics of worshiping Yoruba Orishas and know how to choose your offerings for both your Ori and the deity you're worshiping. If you wish to cultivate a strong connection with the Orishas, you must always start by aligning with your Ori.

Chapter 6: You and Your Ancestors

Ancestors are spiritual entities who can significantly influence your life in alignment with your Ori. After reading this chapter, you'll learn everything you need to know about the concept and importance of "Egungun." You'll also understand the types and levels of Yoruba ancestors and learn the basics of working with them. Finally, you'll find out how to reach out to your ancestors.

The Idea of Life and Death

Working with your ancestors is one of the best ways to overcome any challenges you face in life. They can provide you with the needed guidance and support. According to Yorubas, a person's connection with their ancestors must be held in the highest regard. It is considered a very intimate bond. Practitioners bury their loved ones at home instead of in the cemetery so they can wish them good morning and good night and share with them their joy and pain. Yoruba beliefs don't think of death as the end of existence, nor does it view death as a separation between those who are alive and those who have passed on. Yorubas simply think of death as a mode of transportation from one realm or state of existence to the other.

Yorubas use the word "Ódàbo" when communicating with their loved ancestors. This means that the person is looking forward to reuniting with their ancestor, whether literally, spiritually, via visualization practices, or in their dreams. Practitioners believe that they can reunite with their ancestors by worshiping them or allowing themselves to feel all the emotions and experience the necessary realizations associated with losing a loved one.

Yorubas think of death as a beginning and not an end. It doesn't suggest that something has ended. Instead, it indicates that new possibilities are coming to life. In Yoruba, a male ancestor is known as Egún (Egúngún is the plural form), and a female ancestor is known as Gelede. When practicing Yoruba, you must make peace with the idea of death. Otherwise, you'll never feel free and will think of death as something to be feared. It is then viewed as a danger that should be avoided instead of a passage to a new world. While Yorubas do grieve when they lose a loved one, they view death as a celebration for the most part. This view of life and death allows them to accept reality and the cycle of being.

Types and Levels of Yoruba Ancestors

Yorubas believe that there are two types of death. One is socially accepted, and the other isn't. The former refers to deaths occurring at a late stage in life, while the latter refers to deaths occurring earlier and unexpectedly. People who die young are called "Àbíkú," which is a term associated with premature death. Àbíkú is thought to be born only to die young. Yorubas believe that worshiping and working closely with their ancestors can help them steer clear of premature death and ensure that they experience their full fate.

Besides the types of ancestors and deaths, there are different levels of ancestors. Some people die honorably, while others are not fit to be regarded as honorable ancestors. Non-honorable ancestors are not eligible for worship after death. Those who are worshiped must have lived by certain standards and levels of existence in their lifetime. Honorable ancestors who make it past a certain level of living become disconnected from their loved ones once they die and become worshiped. These individuals are symbolic of the passage between the realms of the living and the dead. The behaviors, values, manners, and morals that a person exhibits during their lifetime are what determine their eligibility for veneration when they pass. If they prove to be respectable, an invocation is conducted upon their death, so their energy materializes. When this happens, the person becomes a messenger that all people, not just their friends and family, can worship.

This is why Yorubas strive to be and do good things and don't accept people who exhibit unwanted behavior. They understand that every moment in their lives counts when it comes to ensuring veneration after death. Ancestors are spiritual representations of important concepts, such as development, growth, creation, and community. They are also emblematic of harmony, balance, amity, and peace. We turn to our ancestors whenever we need guidance and seek a sense of direction in life. If you're close enough to your ancestor, you can encourage them to fight for you and direct you toward places and opportunities that are in your best interest. Yorubas believe that ancestors are powerful enough to shape our futures because they're the ones responsible for mapping out our fates. There is no better force to ask for orientation and attain a better sense of direction than our ancestors. Building a strong connection with them is a surefire way to easily overcome the obstacles we face.

Different Types of Egun

1. **Egun Iya or Egun Baba:** These ancestors are immediate family members.
2. **Egun Idile:** The souls of non-immediate family members. They are ancestors that we're related to or have a blood connection with.
3. **Eleye or Aje:** These are believed to be the souls of witches.
4. **Abiku:** The souls of children who either die young or during childbirth.
5. **Egun Ilu:** The ancestors who founded communities, cities, towns, tribes, clans, etc.
6. **Ebora:** The lava and fire spirits.
7. **Oso:** These ancestors were native medicine men and warlords during their lifetime.
8. **Egun Enia Sasa:** The ancestors who were once popular, renowned, or famous or served as priests or priestesses.
9. **Egun Igi:** The souls who live in trees.
10. **Egun Gun Olufe:** Ancestors who used to be Babalawos.

11. **Egun Eleko:** The spirits of the friends you made and acquaintances you met in your past lives.

The Basics of Working with Ancestors

To reach out to your ancestors, you must first say an oath for your well-being. Your undertaking can be recited in your own language and style; *however you like*. If you wish to make great transformations in your life, you need to seek the help of a professional Babalawo, as they are already aligned with this energy. In order to manifest the spirit of the ancestors, you must represent them through certain rituals and costumes. Priests and priestesses are typically the mediums used to invoke ancestors.

There is neither a right nor wrong time to worship your ancestors. You don't need to wait for calamities to happen to start working on building a connection with your ancestors. However, there are some signs that suggest that ancestor worship is long overdue. For instance, if you notice that there are unhealthy habits, such as smoking, drinking, or gambling, or certain illnesses and chronic diseases, like heart conditions, cancer, or even mental conditions running in the family, then it's time to reach out to your ancestors. Negative repetitive events and situations are also signs that you need to work with your ancestors. Worshiping them allows you to get rid of generational troubles and problems and can help you stop them from being passed down to future generations.

Some practitioners think that the experience that results from worshiping their ancestors is highly spiritual and that it transcends the worldly aspect of religion. There are two main ways in which one can worship the ancestors and appease them; making offerings of items that they enjoyed in their lifetime or cleaning their graves. Some people like to invite people over for dinner and dedicate the entire gathering to a deceased loved one. Regularly visiting your ancestors' graves and lighting up candles for them is also a highly appreciated act of worship.

How It Works

Yoruba beliefs distinguish between a person's biological genes and physical body and spiritual genes and astral body. When we are born into the world, we are granted our allotted physical body, and our genes are given to us by our parents. They are, however, not responsible for the astral aspects of our being. Our spiritual selves are influenced by our ancestors and are left behind in the spiritual realm even after our journey into the physical world begins. Our astral aspect stays behind because it keeps our physical bodies connected to the spiritual world and ensures that we don't get too involved in earthly matters. Our souls are supposed to remind us of the importance of partaking in spiritual activities, guiding us back whenever we want to visit the spirit world.

Since our souls, which are essentially linked to our ancestors, oversee our lives in the physical world, we can get rid of obstacles and achieve a more harmonious life by worshiping our ancestors. Another reason why Yorubas are attuned to their ancestors is they are constantly aware that the present moment is no more than a mere continuation of past events and that it is also an antecedent and a determinant of the future.

It's not a problem if your ancestors aren't buried anywhere near your home or even if you don't know where they're buried. What's more important than their physical location is recognizing that your body is a vessel of their biological and spiritual genetics and part of their physical and astral bodies. Our ancestors are always with us, no matter what we're doing and wherever we go, which is why you should let your intuition guide you when you're praying to your ancestors and working with them. When you pray to your ancestors, you're not only honoring them, but you're also asking them for things that you wish they could help you with. You can ask them for guidance, abundance, health, good fortune, and more. Open your prayers with something like,

> *"You, my ancestors, promised me a life of (abundance, good fortune, happiness, etc.), so bring the (abundance, good fortune, happiness, etc.) of this world into my life."*

Some practitioners prefer to pray to their ancestors at the place of worship to which they belong. Don't feel ashamed if you're reaching out to your ancestor to ask them for something. Recognizing their power and trusting that they can influence your life for the better is one of the best forms of veneration. The worst thing you can do is not remember them, recognize their power, or ask them for anything at all.

How to Reach Out to Your Ancestors

There are no guidelines you need to adhere to in order to successfully reach out to your ancestors. This is a very personal and intimate endeavor that should be guided by your relationship with your loved ones before they pass. Learn their preferences, know what your wishes are, and use your intuition. That said, it's normal if you don't know where to begin, which is why we are here to suggest a few things you can do to start building a connection with your ancestors.

Don't Hesitate to Talk to Them

If you wish to start working with your ancestors, you have to let go of any social constructs and worries that you have. This is about you and your relationship with your ancestor, which is why you should start clearing your mind and shifting your attention toward connecting with your deceased loved one. It's normal to feel awkward talking to the dead and working with them. If you decide to share your beliefs with anyone, you'll likely encounter people who think you're crazy, suggest that you're dabbling in demonic activities, or call you a witch. Release all your fears and understand that this is something that you have to do. You don't need to share your convictions with anyone unless you're ready to do so.

We all have masculine and feminine energies, and the parts of ourselves that can communicate with the dead happen to be feminine. This is because these energies are generally calmer, more receptive, and popular for their intuitiveness. Don't hesitate to lean into your feminine energy and listen to emotions like compassion and empathy. Learn to let go of unhealthy notions you may have, such as toxic masculinity.

If you're susceptible to reaching out to the dead, know that they will not harm you. You have nothing to worry about as long as you set strong and clear boundaries with your divine self and the spiritual realm and only reach out to the ones you're sure to have your best interest at heart. Consult a Babalawo or call on a protector guide before you begin. They can guide your prayers and rituals and ensure that you don't attract any low-vibrational or unwanted spirits into your life. Your protector guide can be any animal spirit guide or archangel that you're used to working with.

You have to accept that dark spirits exist and that not all of your ancestors have your best interest in mind. However, you shouldn't let this scare you away from connecting with souls who can guide you. You can transform your life by working with your ancestors if you take the right precautions and set clear boundaries.

Explore Family Traditions

Your journey will naturally be different from others because each person has unique family traditions. Working with your ancestors should be a personalized and unique process, which is why you shouldn't blindly copy what anyone else is doing, even if it feels safer. You must explore your cultural and family traditions to work with your ancestors. Your intuition is key, as well. You'll need all the help you can get at first, so you should try to speak to as many family members as possible. Talk to them about your ancestors, and if they're spiritual individuals, you can ask them if they have any rituals and prayers that they can pass on to you.

Learn about your ancestor's preferences, the activities they used to enjoy in their spare time, the food they liked to eat, what their spiritual beliefs were, what their veneration practices looked like, etc. Any information you get can help you strengthen your bond with your ancestors, understand how to reach out to them, and find out what your offerings should be. However, if you believe that they don't resonate with you and your intuition, you shouldn't force them into your practice. You won't succeed if you aren't fully convinced or don't feel comfortable with what you're doing. Remember that this is a shared bond between you and your ancestors.

Exploring your traditions and working your way up the family tree is an act of worship itself. You'll find it challenging to retrace your roots, especially if you encounter generational challenges and traumas in the process. Don't let this discourage you, and remind yourself that the process counts as an honorable intention. The more you familiarize yourself with your ancestors, the more easily you'll be able to call on their spirits and express your appreciation.

If you don't live in the land of your ancestors, you'll benefit significantly from going back to their homeland and learning about their cultural traditions. Get to know the elders who currently live there, as they'll be future ancestors. Find out about their rituals and veneration practices (if any), and ask them if they can pass on their traditions to you.

Pay Equal Attention to the Living Elders

You don't need to wait until members of your family move on to the spiritual realm so you can start working with them. You can still venerate living elders in your family and honor them. They are technically your ancestors too, which means that you're still doing spiritual work. Working with your ancestors during their lifetimes makes it easier to bond with them in the afterlife, as you've already established the basis of your connection.

Honoring your living elders is one way to honor the ancestors and to continue to bond with them after they pass.

https://unsplash.com/photos/uGDH9jS9bfo

You shouldn't hesitate to reach out to the ones you weren't close to in your lifetime. You should still give it a go even if you've never met them before. Worst case scenario, they won't respond to your efforts. This usually happens if the person never ever even made it to the other side, wasn't spiritual, or just didn't believe in these things. However, in most cases, they will. Even though you don't need to have a direct relationship with your elders to be able to connect with them after they die, it does help to have a pre-existing bond with them. This allows you to call them in, and you can align with their energy faster.

Besides, you can stimulate generational healing and diffuse years of traumas by working with your living elders. Have them tell you their stories and experiences- the good, bad, joyful, and painful. By doing so, you can help them relieve some of the burdens they carry before they pass onto the spiritual realm.

Call Their Spirits In

If you want to boost the effectiveness of your spiritual work, you should consider building an ancestral altar and consulting a Babalawo for specialized ritual work and prayers. Once you're ready, call your ancestors in by leaving them their preferred offerings on your shrine. These can include some of their possessions, favorite food, beverages they liked, and even promises. Your altar should be tailored to the needs and desires of the ancestor that you're working with, as this can help you strengthen your connection with your ancestors. Carefully selecting your offerings also shows them that you appreciate them and are determined to build a connection with them.

Besides praying to your ancestors, you should also call to your ancestors as you meditate. Meditation allows you to enter a trance or altered state of consciousness, making it easier to align with their energies and quickly feel their existence. You can spend as much time as you like (typically between 10 to 30 minutes) calling any ancestor you wish to work with. Work with ancestors to whom you feel most connected and build on your efforts from there. Lighting candles makes it a lot easier to interact with spirits, so choose candles in their favorite colors. Don't forget to celebrate their birthdays and other important events.

Now that you've read this chapter, you'll understand how to work with your ancestors and how this endeavor works. Read the following chapter to find out how you can enhance your Ori with the help of your deceased loved ones.

Chapter 7: Living with the Blessings of Ancestors

Improving your Ori and working with your ancestors is a two-way relationship. You need to strengthen your Ori and work with it before you can try to reach out to them. Worshiping your Ori can help you strengthen your intuition and enhance your connection with the spiritual realm, making it easier to enter a trance state of consciousness and communicate with your ancestors. You can ask them to help you improve your connection with your highest self or Ori. With their guidance and wisdom, you'll be able to grasp a deeper understanding of your authentic self and the purpose of your existence.

By reading this chapter, you'll learn how to build and work with an ancestor shrine. You'll also learn how to conduct ancestral visualization. Finally, you'll find out how ancestral meditation can help you understand the role that you play in the world.

Building an Ancestor Shrine

Ifa Yorubas believe that a person draws the power that allows them to invoke and work with spirits during the initiation ritual and the training period that follows. The only exception, however, is connecting with an ancestor spirit. According to this belief system, we all have the innate ability to bond with our blood relatives, even if they've passed onto the spiritual realm. It doesn't matter if we've been initiated into the practice or not, which just proves how intimate and powerful this connection is.

It is your birthright to get to know your ancestors and ask for their guidance and support.

Creating a shrine for your ancestors and placing offerings is important.
https://unsplash.com/photos/GRI_6wnQjjs

We bond with our ancestors every day without even noticing it. Cooking a recipe the way your great-grandmother made it or asking yourself what your grandfather would have done when you're at a crossroads in life are all examples of subtle ancestral communications. Direct interactions are also commonly made during dreams and when one participates in ancestor celebrations and festivals.

Since annual ancestor festivals are not prevalent in Western countries, many practitioners build altars and use them as the center of their spiritual activities. Building an Egun altar can get anywhere from very simple to highly intricate. Complex shrines, however, require extensive training to build and maintain. The most common traditional Yoruba ancestor shrine requires you to bury your ancestor under your home, so the tomb serves as the foundation. Since the chances are that you won't be able to do that, you can use basic traditional elements to construct your shrine.

Use the information you gathered about your ancestors, along with your intuition, to determine how you should go about the process. You can also incorporate spiritual items like an Opa Egun and an Egun pot to strengthen your efforts and improve your connection and ability to communicate with them. To do that, you'd have to consult a professional Orisha priest to find out which traditional items can be beneficial for your practice. You also need their guidance to prepare them correctly. Once you have all the basic elements put together, you can contact your ancestor to determine whether they would like you to add anything else to the shrine.

Basics of Setting Up an Ancestor or Egun Shrine

Prepare Your Space

Find a quiet and comfortable space to build your altar. Clean it thoroughly and organize the area around it. You should keep your altar as clean and tidy as possible after you build it because dirt and clutter can attract low-vibrational spirits. The environment around you mirrors your inner state of mind. Your home can either support your efforts toward change or hinder your journey toward growth. Ifa beliefs suggest that you should tidy your home up if you feel confused or overwhelmed. While this will not make all your problems disappear, it will give you some clarity about the situation.

Smudge your room after you've cleaned and organized it. A large seashell is typically used for this process. If you don't have one, you can light up some leaves in a clay pot or any other fireproof container. Make sure that the container you use is only used for the purpose of smudging. Use a feather or your hand to fan the smoke as you move and circulate the container around the room. Sage and cedar leaves are most popularly used for smudging traditions, as they're very aromatic and cleansing. You can use other types of leaves if those aren't available. Adding incense to the container can also boost the effectiveness of smudging.

Place your ingredients in a pile in the center of the fireproof container and say a prayer directly as you start to smudge the area) Be clear about your intentions of cleansing the room and dispersing any unwanted spirits. You can recite the prayer in any language you want. Start by paying your respects to the spirit of the ancestors, say your name and state your lineage, bless the spirit of the leaves, and then ask it to do something for you. You can ask it to attract good fortune, peace, stability, and wisdom. When you're ready, conclude your prayers by thanking the spirit of the leaves.

Use a match to light the smudge and wait for the flame to die down and leave a cloud of smoke behind. Move around the room, ensuring that the smoke spreads around. As you do that, focus on your intentions and smudge the rest of your home. Keep in mind that if you allow your mind to wander off and let intrusive thoughts take over, this will defeat the entire purpose of the process. After you've smudged your space, cleanse yourself with the smoke. Start at your feet and move up the front of your body. Cleanse your head and move down your back.

To keep the effects of the smudging practice, you need to seal the space. There are several types of seals that you can use. However, the easiest one, especially if you're uninitiated, involves water, fragrance, and body fluids. Fill up a bowl with water and add a few drops of a fragrance that you frequently wear. You should also add a small amount of urine or saliva to the mixture. This asserts to the ancestor spirits that you are in charge of any communications that take place.

Speak the names of the ancestors that you don't wish to communicate with – along with the reasons why you don't want them to participate – before you seal your space. If you don't know your ancestors by name, you can alternatively express the problems and behaviors that aren't welcome in your space. You should exclude ancestors who have committed suicide, died brutal or traumatic deaths, were physically abusive, engaged in sexual abuse, or suffered from addiction or substance abuse. Make sure to protect yourself from any potentially harmful influences and get rid of any possibilities before you seal the space.

Speak a prayer (similar to the one you made to the smudge) directly into the water. Then, sprinkle the water (using your left hand) all over the space that you cleaned using the smudge. Focus on your intention throughout the process.

Set Up and Use the Shrine

You're only ready to set up the shrine after you've cleaned and sealed it. Your altar should be a space of remembrance for your ancestors. Dedicate it to the elders who have added to your life and improved it through their wisdom and guidance. You can also use it to communicate with other deceased relatives or any popular figure or mentor who has inspired you, even if they aren't related to you.

Set up a table and place a white cover or cloth over it in your designated area. Decorate it with white candles, some of their possessions, items that they enjoyed in their lifetime, drawings or pictures of them, and a glass of water. The best thing about Ifa and Yoruba practices is that they welcome various spiritual and individual differences. Indigenous practitioners dedicate their altars to prophets and historical figures of different religions and backgrounds. For instance, if your ancestor was a devout Catholic, you can place a rosary or a Bible on the altar.

When everything's ready, light up one of the candles and stand in front of your shrine. Make a promise to your ancestors that you'll be using the shrine regularly for prayers, remembrance, and meditation. You should also provide offerings for them frequently. You don't need to promise to use it every day or three times a week if you know that you won't be able to live up to that type of commitment. However, if you agree to use it three times a month, you shouldn't break your promise. It's better to start slowly and steadily and work your way up than to make and break a promise that you can't handle. Otherwise, you'd be proving to your ancestors that you aren't serious about working with them and building a connection. While your ancestors will be happy to help you when you encounter challenges in your path, you should avoid turning to them only when you need them. This weakens the bond you have with them. It's a bit like only saying prayers when you want something.

Remember your ancestors and identify the ways in which they affected you and influenced your perceptions. Think of the influences you wish to keep and strengthen and the ones you want to eliminate. Meditate on all the positive characteristics that your deceased loved ones possessed. Were they helpful, wise, courageous, creative, strong, or honest? Which of their qualities do you want them to pass on to you? The stronger your connection with your ancestor grows, the easier you'll be able to call them into your day-to-day life whenever you need them to bless you with a specific quality. For example, when you don't know which decision to make, you can call on a certain ancestor because they're known for their wisdom. If a situation requires you to think outside of the box, you can call on the creative spirit. Every time you remember an ancestor and think about how they would have acted in a certain situation, you are communicating with them and engaging in the form of worship. When you've made your promise and meditated, end your session by thanking your ancestors for their wisdom and positive qualities.

Ancestral Visualization

Switch some soft lights on, light up a few candles, and sit by your altar. Make sure you have pictures of your ancestors put up, along with a few personal elements and cultural objects if you don't already. Burn incense, take a moment to express your gratitude, and gather all your attention toward this process. Thank your ancestors for granting you the opportunity to be in this world and honor their existence.

Draw in a deep breath and visualize all your thoughts evaporating from your mind. Once your mind is clear, start your ancestral visualization practice. Visualize yourself in a large, alluring field or any other place in nature. Allow yourself to feel safe in this space. It should be welcoming and familiar. Imagine all the details of the place, including how the grass or earth feels beneath your feet, the chilly breeze caressing your skin, and the smell of fresh air mixed with the subtle aroma of flowers. Try to make your imagination feel as real as possible. Once you feel like you're truly a part of your visualization, focus on your intention to meet an ancestor. Express the desire of wanting to connect with them. You can either choose a specific ancestor or open yourself to the collective and see who comes to you.

If you're struggling with making your visualization feel real, you can recognize it as a portion of your imagination and bring your consciousness into the process. That said, most people find the practice more effective when it feels real. The more you practice this visualization, the easier it will be to involve your senses and emotions.

When your ancestor shows up, start asking them questions. Allow your curiosity to take the lead, and don't worry too much about putting them on the stand or coming off as judgmental. Your ancestor is here to help and guide you. They will not necessarily tell you exactly what you need to do to fix a problem. However, they'll likely give you some advice or share a story that will help direct you toward the right path. Flexibility and openness are key here. Carefully listen and interpret their words as they speak. Once they've finished talking to you, thank them and take your time to exit the meditation and return to reality. You should regularly express your gratitude and pray to the ancestors that show up in your meditations because this helps you maintain a strong bond with them and shows them that you honor and appreciate their help.

Ancestral Meditation

Sit comfortably near your altar and draw in several deep breaths to clear your mind. This meditation is more effective when listened to because it guides your subconscious mind when you enter a trance state. You can ask someone you trust to read it to you. Alternatively, you can record your voice and play it to yourself whenever you read it. Either way, the words should be spoken softly, clearly, and slowly.

Relax your body and listen to the person guiding the meditation as they count down from 13. Don't imagine the numbers; just follow the voice of the guide. Start visualizing a giant tree. This tree is larger than anything you've ever seen. Tell yourself that this is the World Tree- the bridge between the realms of the physical and the spiritual. Think of the pictures in your mind as a portal that you can journey through. Bring yourself into the picture and imagine yourself passing through the doorway of your mind. Stand in front of the tree.

Listen to the sound of the leaves and the branches as the wind passes through them. Inhale the smell of the earth right after it has rained. Extend your arms and touch the monumental bark of the tree. With your hands there, focus strongly on the intention of calling on an ancestor spirit. Express your wish for them to help you bring balance and harmony to the world.

Move along the tree and keep observing its roots until you find an opening. Release all your fears and jump into the gap in the tree. You'll find a tunnel leading downward. Follow the spiral until you see a flickering light - much like a fire - at the end of the tunnel. Approach it.

The tunnel leads to a forest clearing with a huge fire in the center of it. The spirits of the ancestors are gathered around it. Some of them are dancing, while others are just observing it. Don't walk toward them. Stand by the trees at the edge and patiently wait for an ancestor to come to you. It may be someone you know well, a blood relative you heard or know of, or an ancestor of spirit that you don't know at all. If you don't know the spirit who approached you, simply introduce yourself to them.

Ask them about your purpose in the world and also ask for their guidance on how to make your world a better place. Try to learn more about what you need to do to make the world more harmonious and peaceful. Ask them for advice and wisdom you can live by and any other questions you have.

Your ancestor might offer you a gift that will put you on the right path. The purpose of the gift can also be to help you remember key aspects of your conversation. Take a moment of introspection to think of what you can offer them in return. Don't stress about it much but follow your intuition. When the conversation comes to an end, thank your ancestors for their guidance and step away.

Start searching for the tunnel and step through it. Follow the spiral as it spirals upward and leads you to the base of the tree. When you step out, rest your hand on the bark of the World Tree and thank it for making this journey possible. Step through the doorway of your mind and slowly shift your awareness to reality. The person guiding this meditation should signal that it's time to come back to the time and place of reality. Open your eyes whenever you're ready.

Now that you have read this chapter, you are ready to start living with the blessings of your ancestors. Read the following chapter to learn all about heavenly mates and how they can aid one's Ori.

Chapter 8: Egbe, Your Spiritual Family

This chapter is dedicated to a unique group of spirits called Egbe Orun. By reading it, you'll learn who these spirits are, their characteristics, and how to appease them through their preferred offerings. You'll understand how they influence your life and how they can help you with various aspects of spiritual communication, including your alignment with your Ori.

Who Are the Egbe Orun?

The Egbe Orun, also known as Alaragbo, Egberun, and simply Egbe, is a group of spirits who have served as companions for humans since the beginning of time. Their name is derived from the Yoruba word Egbe, which means *"heavenly spirit"* or *"astral mates."* According to the Yoruba people, every person on Earth has a comrade who lives in the heavenly realm. This belief is based on the idea that each soul comes from heaven and eventually returns there. People living on earth are the personification of their own spirit in a physical body. Olodumare created the souls, and Obatala molded a physical body for them. As Olodumare made the physical bodies come to life, he gave them two souls. One traveled back to the spiritual realm, while the other remained in the body.

People often see their spiritual counterpart in their dreams, whether it looks like them or someone else. Since both souls share a history, they know more about each other than unrelated souls. The two souls are identical and are able to find each other. However, Egbe are believed to be more powerful spirits than their earthly counterparts because they aren't polluted with the demands of the physical body.

According to Yoruba beliefs, one of the souls stays behind in the spiritual world to keep its twin tethered to it. This allows people to visit this realm whenever they wish to journey there or seek guidance from one of its inhabitants. Egbe also watches over their earthly counterpart, safeguarding them. Whenever an earthly soul veers off its path, its twin will remind them of its spiritual nature. Tapping into this unique bond with our heavenly mate is also a great reminder that our time in this realm is only temporary.

Because people have different characteristics, their connection with their twin souls also differs. This also affects their higher level of consciousness, which is reached through spiritual intuition. Those who have a strong bond with their Egbe are more frequently influenced by these spirits. They don't even need to put in much effort to reach the spiritual realm, yet their messages will be heard loud and clear. They allow themselves to be led by their spiritual intuition and communicate with Egbe, hoping to reach a spiritual awakening. The Egbe, in turn, send their messages back through dreams or visualization and divination practices. They can also cause objects to disappear from one's physical environment and others to appear. These are actions the Egbe uses to send specific messages which can only be understood by the twin soul. However, the Egbe will only provide their blessing, protection, and guidance if they're properly appeased. By learning to placate the Egbe and forming a bond with them, you'll be able to fulfill your soul's destiny.

Types of Egbe Orun

The ancient Yoruba people learned about the existence of heavenly mates through practices involving spiritual communication. As they started associating themselves with the spiritual world, they learned that the Egbe behave very similarly to humans. They live in communities organized based on beliefs, preferences, and characters. Some of the behavior displayed by these astral souls reminded the Yoruba of their own behavior from when they were children. It's believed that children still remember their twin souls but forget them as they become adults.

To this day, Yoruba practitioners actively communicate with the heavenly communities through different oracular practices and tools. They've identified different types of Egbe traits and societies, but there are many more that remain unknown. Below are some of the major groups of Egbe Orun.

Elééko

The Eléékò is a colorful group with many different types of personalities. Their moods are changeable, and they're often led by their desires. They're typically patient, but when angered, they show no mercy and are hard to appease. This contrasting behavior is very similar to that of Esu, a shapeshifting spirit and trickster deity known for his many mischiefs. Elééko is also intelligent and can be very creative, especially when it comes to sending messages and playing tricks. They can be sneaky, and their loyalty can shift very rapidly.

The Elééko are known to steal valuable belongings. This is a clear sign that they spend time around a person. However, they only steal from those who have more than enough or have disrespected them, the Egbe, or other inhabitants of the spiritual world. The Elééko will share their bounty with the less fortunate as a punishment or a lesson. Children of the Yoruba community who exhibit this behavior are thought to be members of the Elééko. Any child who is stubborn, steals, or is overly talkative has to undergo a specific ritual. Otherwise, they'll grow up to be just like Elééko.

Ìyálóde

The Ìyálóde is another large Egbe group. They are natural-born leaders and are often compared to leaders in society in the physical realm. While powerful, they're only considered leaders in the eyes of the souls living on the earth. Their society is named after Ìyálóde, a female leader who initially led the Yoruba to believe that the group has only female members. After further exploration, Yoruba practitioners learned that both men and women could be Ìyálóde.

Members of the Iyalode come in all shapes, sizes, and ages. They behave as leaders do. They're organized and motivated and can inspire others. They take care of themselves and dress nicely, which makes them easily noticeable. They like to show off even when sending messages, but they're also charitable. That said, it's not suggested that you anger them. Because they can be just as malicious with their punishment as they are generous with their blessings, the Ìyálóde are known to pay particular attention to children and do everything they can to protect them and their parents or guardians. Those who harm children have every reason to fear the Ìyálóde as their punishment is exceptionally harsh.

Baálè

Baálè is another talented group known to exhibit both the leadership skills of Ìyálóde and the colorful traits of Eléékò. Their name in Yoruba means "*the tribe's ruler.*" This name was given to them after the Yoruba discovered their qualities and virtues.

Their nature sets them apart from other Egbe groups, and they are often considered too domineering. Despite this, the Yoruba believe that the Baálè is one of the most straightforward Egbe groups. They often turn to them for divination or judgment. That said, one needs to be very careful when communicating with the Baálè as they are known to issue harsh punishment, especially when it comes to deviant behavior.

Asípa

The Asípa are another group that's very vocal in expressing their intentions and needs. As straightforward as they may seem, they aren't always truthful either. Sometimes, they hide their true intentions behind a grand display of false devotion and allegiance, which speaks about their disloyal nature. Not only that, but conveniently for them, they are often forgetful - especially when it comes to an untruth they've said. They can also cause temporary or permanent memory loss for earthly souls, which hinders their ability to fulfill their density.

Their influence on people makes them forget their encounter or talk so much they make a person dizzy. If one has a feeling that they've met the person they're talking to before - despite meeting them the first time they are likely a member of the Asípa society. You may also mistrust them instinctively without knowing why. The Asípa will often act against people who reject their fate or whose souls are meant to become Egbe but refused. The Yoruba believe that in addition to hindering people's destiny, the Asípa can also exchange people's fates. According to this idea, by appeasing this Egbe group, one can find a different, better path for themselves.

Jagun

Also known as Jagunjagun, Jagun is an Egbe society named after a warrior of the same name. Similar to their namesake, Jagun are known to be persistent and relentless in their pursuits. They're highly adaptable and accommodating and know what it takes to reach their goal. They don't like to waste their time on mindless activities or pleasantries, even to appease someone else.

Jagun are typically identified as children who exhibit very unusual behavior. Instead of acting infantile, these children are uptight and meticulous from an early age. This behavior is noticeable even in babies who don't cry much and patiently wait until the adults can tend to their needs. Adult Jagun can be promiscuous, but they're usually good at covering it up with seemingly model behavior.

Olúgbógeró

The Olúgbógeró is a group with a fluid nature, with its members having multifaceted personalities. They're free as the rivers and other flowing waters, and their characters can't be influenced. One behavior they can't be dissuaded from is carrying a piece of cloth on or near their body. Besides water, the Olúgbógeró are also associated with stillborn children. These are believed to be souls whose fate was influenced by malicious forces, such as curses. Consequently, they're left without the physical body they were meant to be born into.

Móohún

Móohún is a very defiant group of Egbe who don't care about following rules, helping others, or even making decisions. They also exhibit other childlike behavior like stubbornness and forgetfulness. Because of this, they were believed to be a group of children who couldn't be trusted with any critical task. They're unlikely to be relied on or help with any issue when called upon. The only thing they'll happily spend time on is making themselves look good.

Adétayànyá

Adétayànyá is a strange group consisting of children. They share similarities with Oro, Egunguns brother. Some even believe they are related to him. One of their most prominent characteristics is their reverence for refuse dumps. They either seek out even the most secluded dumps or greet the ones they pass on their travels. Adétayànyá spends a lot of their time at the dumpsites.

Honoring Egbe Orun

The Egbe is traditionally venerated through offerings, rites, and prayers, which are good ways to appease them. However, if angered, some Egbe will require spiritual sacrifices. For the Yoruba, the highest form of spiritual sacrifice is self-discipline. They use several self-discipline methods to build connections with their spiritual self and guides, including the Egbe. The Egbe, in turn, appreciate people's efforts to maintain their relationship with their heavenly mates and treasure their bond. If you wish to connect to an Egbe, you must prove to them that you are ready to form a strong bond with them and continue to reinforce it.

Building a shrine for an Egbe is a great way to honor them. Adorn it with a white cloth and red and white decorations. You'll be able to call on them to this sacred space, so make sure you set it up where you can work with them without interruptions. Egbe communicate through different means, including dreams and ocular prescriptions (causing visions). You'll also want to be able to hold bonfires near your sacred place or have a river or tree where you can leave your offerings. You can leave them organic foods like plantain, sugarcane, honey, shea butter, coconut, palm oil, kola nuts, as well as fresh water and alcohol. They also accept cheese, roasted or cooked groundnuts, a paste of yam, maize, or steamed white beans, sweet maize, beans, and yam.

Influence of Egbe Orun

Like human societies, the various Egbe groups have different influences over the spiritual realm and earthly souls. Those who carry bad news are considered taboos, which are traditionally carried down to generations within the same family, community, or society. These are thought to cause an imbalance in one's life, such as nightmares and other cognitive disturbances. Those who want to ascertain whether an Egbe is trying to communicate with them through nightmares will need to visit an oracle.

Other Egbe have very positive influences over their earthly counterparts. They forge a strong bond with them, allowing the person to rely on them as they navigate their way through life. Some feel the need to always consult their Egbe before making an important decision. Others will even form romantic relationships with their spiritual counterparts, which often causes them to remain alone in the physical world. Egbe can be very possessive and will try to keep away other potential partners, sometimes even by causing their death. According to Yoruba traditions, a human bride and groom must always confirm they have no arrangement with their heavenly mates before they marry. They will visit an oracle who can confirm this. The priests will conduct a rite that leads to the dissolution of the spiritual arrangement that has been previously made.

If contacted by their Egbe counterpart, one must ensure their twin doesn't have any harmful tendencies. Otherwise, they'll never be able to work in unison, and the Egbe will work against the person instead. If, after consulting an oracle, a person discovers that their heavenly twin is wicked, they are advised to sever this connection as soon as possible. Sometimes these influences aren't spotted or dealt with in time because they are taught to the infantile phase many children grow to. However, when influenced by a wicked Egbe, insolent children often become unruly adults. They will get into conflicts with their peers and will never trust others. The Egbe will continue to influence them by making valuable items disappear from their community, causing further issues between them and the rest of their community.

Never ignore the Egbe, not even the good-natured groups, as they can be angered. If they are, they'll block any blessings you may receive. If the Egbe is truly upset, they'll put obstacles onto your path, making it challenging for you to obtain your goals. Sometimes, a person ignores an Egbe because they aren't aware of their messages. If that happens, the Egbe will still punish them. Those who suffer an unexplained misfortune are advised to visit an oracle and see if their problems are caused by an upset Egbe.

Developing your spiritual intuition is a great way to ensure you'll never ignore their presence or messages. The more you communicate with the Egbe Orun, the stronger your relationships become, and the more heightened your intuition will be. Learning to ask your heavenly mate for guidance, protection, and spiritual healing can teach you how to use your Ori.

Chapter 9: Odu Ifa, a Guide to Righteous Living

Odu Ifa, the sacred scripture of the Yoruba, contains instructions for righteous living, which is one of the fundamental steps toward spiritual alignment. From this chapter, you'll learn how it was created and how it's structured, including its summary called the 16 Truths of Ifa. You'll also learn the underlying messages behind each truth and how to follow them to establish an honorable life for yourself.

Odu Ifa

As the number of people to whom Olodumare and Obatala gave life grew, the supreme creator realized that some common issues occur in human communities. The Orishas had given Olodumare reports about illnesses, losses of property and other money troubles, fears of impending death, and many other obstacles humans faced throughout their lives. In order to help counteract the negative influences that lead to these issues, Olodumare created a decree that contained all the problems and their solutions. Among the resolutions was cherishing what people have, including family, health and overcoming illnesses, life (especially those who live long lives), children, financial security, and creativity to prevent losses. The problems he found a resolution for were presented in a prophecy containing thousands of verses and organized into 256 sections. They were transcribed in a holy text, which, for the Yoruba, embodies the sacred essences of Ifa, including destiny, truth, life, and the ultimate destination of one's soul. The knowledge of the prophecy was first given to Orunmila, the Orisha with divinatory abilities, who also acted as the first Babalawo (priest) in Ife. At first, people came to Orunmila with their issues, as he was the only one who could look into their destiny. However, Olodumare and Orunmila believed this power shouldn't be left in the hands of one person, even one as powerful as the Orishas.

According to the lore, Orumnila learned to decipher the messages of the 16 Truths of Ifa after he married his second wife, Odu. His first wife, Egan, couldn't give him any children. He asked Olodmare what to do and was advised to marry Odu, so Egan would give him children. When Orunmila married Odu, Egan was able to bear 16 children, who are also considered to be the children of Odu. These children grew up to be the next generation of priests and priestesses, to whom Orumila passed down the prophecy of the 256 signatures. The 16 children of Orunmila used this knowledge to help people resolve common issues, lead a balanced life, and obtain spiritual enlightenment. They were often called upon by the King of Ife to resolve conflicts and other problems occurring in his dominion.

A story that illustrates how following the prophecy brings a happier life revolves around the youngest child of Orunmila, Eji-Ogbe. On one occasion, when the King of Ife asked for their assistance, his other siblings (led by Ofun-Meji) left Eji-Ogbe behind. When consulting the prophecy, he learned that he should go after his sibling. He was also warned not to overlook anyone asking for assistance along the way. The other siblings weren't aware of this prophecy. When they were asked for help by the King of the Forest, they declined, saying they needed to help the King of Ife first. However, when they asked for directions to the castle of the Ife King, they were given the wrong ones and got lost. Eji-Ogbe, on the other hand, helped the King of the Forest first, and as a reward, he was given the proper directions. He reached the King of Ife before his siblings, helped him, and was given a distinguished status. When they arrived and realized their mistake, his siblings were ashamed of overlooking both Eji-Ogbe and the King of the Forest.

The children of Orunmila also passed down the prophecy to the next generation of priests and priestesses of Ifa. To this day, fully initiated Yoruba priests and priestesses learn all 256 signatures of the script. The signatures serve as a divination system used every time a Yoruba turns to their priests or priestess with a physical or spiritual problem. The diviner looks into the prophecy and determines what the sufferer needs to do to resolve their issue. Those initiated as devotees don't need to learn 256 signatures, but they're advised to follow the 16 Truths of Ifa. Upon initiation, devotees become the children of Orunmila. They can call on him for spiritual guidance, alignment, and help to reach or change their destiny. If they follow the 16 Truths of Ifa, Orunmila will grant many blessings.

The 16 Truths of Ifa

Once the verses are transcribed, the knowledge from Odu Ifa can be summarized into 16 main points, called the 16 Truths of Ifa. According to another Yoruba tale, the truths were given to 16 priests who wanted to live forever. Orunmila decided to test them by telling them that if they followed the 16 Truths of Ifa, they'll live forever and become powerful spiritual leaders. However, the priests didn't follow the 16 truths and died soon after. The Yoruba believe that many of the issues the ancient people and Orishas encountered stem from not following the truths. Apart from the one example above, there are countless other tales about people facing problems due to disregarding dietary restrictions, disrespecting or overlooking others, and breaking taboos.

For thousands of years, the Yoruba have lived their lives following the 16 Truths of Ifa, which helped them gather an immense amount of collective spiritual wisdom. By consulting their ancestors, anyone can tap into this knowledge and gain spiritual awareness. By following these truths yourself, you can also learn how to stay true to positive spiritual values. These values are essential for finding your destiny, changing it, and aligning yourself with every part of your Ori.

The truths passed down through generations are as follows:

1. **There is only one supreme force:** Olodumare is the single being who created all things, including the universe. He was the one who provided essence to all living beings. Sealing an intention by asking for the assistance of Olodumare is the best way to ensure it takes effect.

2. **Our universe is good:** It was created by Olodumare, whose essence is entirely uncorrupted. Therefore, the universe can't be malicious. Knowing this allows people to access memories and information from the past, present, and future without fearing being misled.

3. **You should face life's obstacles head-on:** The Yoruba believe that the Orishas who faced hurdles without fear were rewarded with spiritual enlightenment, whereas those who lived in fear suffered. Consulting with spiritual helpers will enable you to conquer the toughest challenges.
4. **Evil doesn't come from one source:** For the Yoruba, the devil (as it's called in other religions) doesn't exist - and neither does its dominion (hell). Negative influences come from an infinite number of sources, and you should be prepared to ward them off at all times.
5. **You have the right to be cherished and reach fulfillment:** Don't believe anyone who tells you that you don't deserve love or to realize your dreams. Whatever experience you had in the past, accepting your rights brings you a step closer to spiritual alignment.
6. **People are in constant transition between two realms of existence:** The first one is heaven (our soul's home, according to Ifa), and the other one is called "the marketplace" (a transitional space for souls). Death is considered good because it ends the soul's suffering in an unhealthy body, and after reincarnation, it allows the soul to start anew in a healthy body.
7. **Every fiber of your being is part of the universe:** In spirit, you are one with the universe, including all of the other creations of Olodumare. Paying attention to the creations around you and honoring them through spiritual practices leads to higher self-awareness.
8. **A person's character and personality traits determine their fate:** How your character makes you think, feel, and actions will determine the ultimate course of your fate. Good character helps you fulfill your destiny (or change it), while a bad character will hinder you in this quest.
9. **Demonstrating superiority should be avoided:** Only Ifa and Olodumare can be superior to every other being in any realm. Among people, Babalawos, and Orishas, no one is superior, and no one is above making mistakes. Blaming your mistakes on others and complaining about them because you feel superior is a sign of evil influence.

10. **Don't hurt others in any way, even if they act maliciously:** Let their malicious nature consume them instead. Causing harm will only make you miss out on all the blessings you can get from the Olodumare and the Orishas for good behavior.
11. **Nourish your connection to the universe:** Every part of the universe is sacred and must be treated respectfully. You need to pay your respect to all its benevolent spirits to keep yourself in their good favor in case you need them.
12. **Don't discriminate against others:** Every person is valuable in their own way, regardless of their personality and appearance. Being ignorant of other people's values will prevent you from obtaining spiritual abundance, and you'll remain just as powerless as those you discriminate against.
13. **Diversity is a testimony to the infinite power of the creator:** It should be celebrated because it can bring all its creations together. In people, diversity manifests in the spectrum of potentials we all possess. This allows us to choose which one we want to see come true.
14. **You are free to determine the course of your fate and choose your guardians:** Whatever fate you pick for yourself depends on you alone. The same applies to the divine guardian you pick for guidance. Offering sacrifice to the Orishas, ancestors, and other spiritual guides is an excellent way to ensure you receive the assistance you need.
15. **Divinatory practices are an excellent way to find your path:** Whenever you need advice for fulfilling or changing your destiny or having a long and prosperous life, consult Ifa, and you'll have the answers.
16. **Have a goal to gather wisdom and spiritual growth:** These are required for spiritual alignment and a balanced Ori. Prayers and other forms of spiritual discipline are fundamental for spiritual growth and honing spiritual intuition.

Following the 16 Truths of Ifa

The truths are simple decrees anyone can follow in their daily life. Here is some advice on how to follow the 16 Truths of Ifa:

Don't Mislead People with False Knowledge

Don't talk about something without offering verifiable information. Thinking something is true doesn't make it the absolute truth unless you and others can verify it. Only talk about what you have knowledge of, and don't mislead people with your actions and words. Otherwise, you'll spread false information about your knowledge, thoughts, and behavior. Be transparent with your feelings, and always tell people what you expect from them and what they can expect in return. Practice open-mindedness when communicating with others, and listen to them - especially when they speak of things you aren't familiar with. The same applies to rituals and ceremonies you aren't familiar with. Only perform those you practiced before and have successful experiences following through.

Don't Pretend to Be Superior

No matter how much knowledge you've gathered throughout your life, you can always learn more. There will always be things you haven't learned yet, so don't pretend you are the source of all wisdom or that you're superior due to the knowledge you possess. Wise people never do that. Instead, they remain humble and continue learning because they are aware of the immense amount of wisdom they can still gather. They never let their egos get in their way, no matter how challenging this is at times. However, even if it feels unfair to deny satisfying your ego, you should look at this as another opportunity to learn and grow spiritually. By remaining humble, you have much better chances for self-realization.

Always Have Good Intentions and Respect

Bad intentions have a negative influence on your spiritual well-being. They can also prevent you from spiritual communication and hinder your ability to reach alignment with your Ori and improve it. This can also be challenging, especially if others don't have good intentions toward you or don't respect your opinions. However, by taking a positive approach, you'll be able to thrive despite their disrespectful and negative disposition. Respect other people's views and actions, even if they are different from yours. Pay particular attention not to disrespect your elders or those weaker than you (physically or mentally). Your elders are far wiser than you are, and you never know when you might need their assistance. Weaker people should also be respected because their weakness is not their fault. They can contribute just as much to the spiritual health of their community as any other member. Respect the taboos and prohibitions by not breaking them, ever. Otherwise, they'll have the same effect as malicious intentions.

Respect Your Friendships

You'll find that if you make yourself available for your friends when they need you the most, they'll respond accordingly. Don't disrespect them by gossiping about them behind their backs or sharing a secret entrusted to you. Honor their choices regarding their life, even if you disagree with them. Respect their loved ones, just as you would want them to honor yours. Try not to advise them against a decision too frequently, and let them make their own choices.

Always respect your friendships.
https://unsplash.com/photos/X1GZqv-F7Tw

Honor Your Sacred Space and Spiritual Tools

The Yoruba were always vocal about keeping their sacred places (where they perform rites and ceremonies clean). You should also ensure to keep your spiritual tools clean from negative influences. This applies to the shrine, symbols, and other items you use for spiritual communication and other spiritual practices. Your body, mind, and spirit are amongst these tools, too, so don't forget to cleanse them regularly. Taking cleansing baths and asking your spiritual helpers to purify you physically and mentally can go a long way to expel all the negative energy tainting your spiritual essence and hindering you from working on your Ori.

Adhere to All Laws

Adhering to moral and legal laws is another crucial aspect of the life of the Yoruba. Both make our communities safer, allowing everyone to live together peacefully. Good moral conduct enables you to stay true to your values and align your Ori with these as well. Remember that this is only possible if you cultivate values that adhere to commonly applied moral codes.

Chapter 10: Aligning with Your Ori

Even though your ancestors, the Egbe, the Orishas, and other spiritual helpers can pave the way to a balanced Ori, the only true way to accomplish this is through Iwa-pele, a good character. This chapter discusses what a good character is and why you should work on improving yours. You'll also learn how to identify a bad character, techniques to improve it, and live your life in a way that your character remains good at all times.

The Concept of Iwa-Pele

The teachings of Ifa all revolve around living an honorable life and being in good standing with other people in one's community. Iwa-pele is a concept that encompasses logical beliefs that help people live balanced lives. Essentially, according to Ifa, Iwa-pele is only an accurate description of how the world works. Unlike other belief systems, the religion of the Yoruba people has no myths and tales about miracles resolving people's problems. Instead, they have a concept that tells them how the Universe works and how they should act. It also teaches that when one behaves in alignment with the Universe, their life will be infinitely better. Olodumare created a Universe that has logical rules which keep it balanced and pure. While ebbos, sacrifices, prayers, and rites can help you manifest your intention, none will be enough if what you ask for goes against Iwa-pele.

Every person carries an essence that interacts with other people's energies. This interaction is present in every part of your life and is expressed through your behavior, speech, and thoughts. For example, if you were to steal a valuable item from someone else, they could do the same to you. Other people who see this can also steal from you, and soon none of your possessions would be safe. It's a logical chain of events caused by a force you launched by stealing. You also interact with other energies in your environment. Environmental pollution is a sign of many people being in misalignment with Iwa-pele - and one that often has dire consequences. If you don't respect natural forces, they will cause many disruptions in your life, including material losses and financial hardships. In both examples, your character sets the groundwork for the impending disaster, and it's on you to stop this from happening.

The ancient Yoruba people learned this partly from the Orishas and their own observations of how the world works. By applying common sense, they examined the negative occurrences. They concluded that Iwa-pele is a crucial tool for maintaining the balance of the Universe. According to the Yoruba, Iwa-pele does not require blind obedience to moral or legal rules. They believe that it requires spiritual intelligence, which they aim to nurture and cherish throughout their lives. Instead of obeying any divine rules, they organize their lives and act in a way that benefits them, their environment, and the Universe. It allows people to improve their lives and fulfill their destinies without hindering anyone else's.

Many of the spiritual practices of the Yoruba are based on Iwa-pele. They are designed to create unity, which further enforces people's will to behave according to the logical rules of the Universe. Most of the ceremonies require spiritual cleansing. The more people go through this in the community, the more members will start to feel closer to the Universe and each other. They become committed to demonstrating good character because they know it will improve their lives and, more importantly, do this without harming anyone else's. They know that by making choices that benefit others, they will be one step closer to spiritual fulfillment and self-realization. It's the highest blessing one can receive because it's something they've earned, and it wasn't bestowed on them by a deity or spiritual guard.

To this very day, the high priests and priestesses of Yoruba are encouraged to help anyone who asks for help. They are also taught to advise devotees to look out for people in their community and offer help whenever they can. During communal gatherings and festivities, priests and priestesses reinforce the need to spend time with family and friends and provide them with any type of support they need. They advise that you'll receive many blessings and grow personally when you demonstrate good character. Olodumare and Orunmila will grant any wishes made if these wishes are backed by a good character. If a person with good character finds themselves in trouble, they'll be more likely to receive help from others. This is probably because people with good character tend to share their good fortune with others.

Following the Yoruba example, you can also devote your time to your loved ones. You can spend quality time with them doing anything you all agree on. Sometimes just listening to each other is enough, especially if one or more of you is going through challenging times. If you can think of advice, you can offer it, but you don't need to. As long as you show unselfish interest in someone else's issue, your bond will deepen, and you'll be closer to your spiritual balance.

Good Character and Bad Character

The name of the Iwa-pele concept is rooted in the Yoruba word Iwa, which means "*character*." A person's character defines who they are, their essential qualities, and what makes them unique. A character can be both good and bad. Iwa-pele refers to good character. It's ascribed to a person with gentle and compassionate, and these are open-minded individuals. This is a person that respects everyone and everything in their environment. They never disrespect or overlook weaker individuals or their elders. They work with others to improve their community, which earns them great respect.

Bad character, or Iwa-buruki, on the other hand, represents the opposite of Iwa-pele. People with Iwa-buruki are disrespectful, reject other people's ideas, have a sense of superiority and don't work well with others. They often get into conflicts within their community and not only struggle to improve their lives but suffer losses and challenges in all areas of life.

The Yoruba have a fascinating tale of how good and bad characters can manifest one's destiny. In this story, Iwa is personified as a female character who became the wife of Orunmila. Before their marriage, Orunmila was advised that he would need to offer an ebbo. He was also told that he'd need to ensure Iwa remained happy after the marriage. After making the ebbo and marrying Iwa, he did as he was told, and he had every reason to be content with his life. He was successful in everything he did, and Iwa was happy. Unfortunately, Orunmila got so comfortable in his newfound happiness that he started to neglect Iwa. He began to complain about everything she did, and suddenly no meal she prepared or chore she did was good enough for him. One day, Iwa had had enough of his complaints and left him. After this, Orunmila began to suffer one loss after another. To find out why, he went to consult with Ifa. He was told that his bad luck persisted because he hurt someone in his life, and the only way to turn things around was to ask that person to forgive him. Orunmila made an ebbo and went on a journey to find his wife. On this journey, he encountered several people who had given him clues about Iwa's whereabouts until he finally found her. With the help of a few good souls who vouched for him, he convinced her to return to him. After this, Orunmila learned never to neglect Iwa again. He also remembered all the good people who helped him along the way and started to be gentle and understanding toward them, granting them many blessings.

The moral of this story is that even if you have a good character, by turning it into a bad one, you can lose all the blessings you received before. You shouldn't overlook your character and should always ensure it's good. Had Orunmila not neglected Iwa (the personified character), he wouldn't have lost everything he did when she went away. The Yoruba believe that those who receive many blessings must have a good character.

The Relationship between Iwa and Ori

According to the Yoruba, Iwa represents half of the personality. The other half is defined by Ori, which is the inner essence. Whereas Iwa is the outer manifestation of the personality. Iwa is what people see, and interact with, while Ori is the spiritual driving force behind the manifested behavior. When aligned with your values, Ori motivates you to display the character that protects you and carries you toward your destiny. In turn, a good character goes a long way in reinforcing an Ori with a positive disposition. Ise (skill) and Ogbon (wisdom) are two factors that affect Ori. By working on these, you can improve your Iwa. Apart from Ori, character improvement can also be inspired by Aiye (your environment) and the Orishas (through regular practice).

The Role of Iwa-Pele in Spiritual Alignment

According to the teaching of Ifa, everyone is capable of working along with the energies of the Universe. It's only a question of effort to make this happen. In addition, each person has the moral responsibility to improve their character. It's a requirement for having a balanced life, but it goes far beyond that. Just think about your loved ones. Wouldn't you want them to live in a safe world and find their own happiness?

Good character is the key to successfully reaching divine enlightenment and unification with the essence of Olodumare, the ultimate destination of every soul. In the meantime, good character acts as a shield and guide, similar to Ori. Ori and Iwa work together to guide the soul on its path to fulfill its destiny in each lifetime. By working on both, your efforts and practices devoted to self-realization and spiritual growth will be more fruitful. Soon, you'll be able to enjoy the success you deserve.

Signs of a Bad Character and How to Improve It

The ultimate goal of the Yoruba is to obtain Iwa-pele so they can reunite it with Ori and improve the latter. Both of these can be achieved by anyone. It only takes paying attention to certain actions and thoughts. This will enable you to start modifying them. You may be wondering how to tell if your character needs to improve. In order to answer this question, you'll need to look into your recent behavior. For example, if you're easily angered or provoked, you're quick to lose your temper and jump to conclusions without thinking things through, this indicates bad character.

Sometimes, bad character manifests in a way that makes you distance yourself from loved ones and the community. You can also feel the lack of inspiration to participate in spiritual gatherings and listen to your elders and spiritual leaders. You fail to devote time to prayers and other daily practices that promote a healthy spiritual life. If you're asked about this, you feel that you're being judged for not spending time cultivating your spiritual growth. You think that with so many things to do, it's not fair that you're being judged for missing a few prayers or rites. You can even start holding grudges against those who try to help you see the error of your ways. These will become triggers for sudden negative emotions.

There are also people with bad characters who feel trapped by unrealistic expectations or the need for dominance, limiting their own potential. When in fact, their options could be virtually limitless should they improve their personality.

You can also look into the character traits you have in your ancestral lineage. Sometimes, a bad character can be passed down in the family. This usually happens when one or more people fail to improve their personality, and the next generation learns their behavior. The bad character is repeated in the second or next generation, passed on to the third one, then the fourth, and so on.

Harboring negative thoughts about yourself can be another sign of bad character. While self-limiting and self-depriving thoughts can stem from traumatic experiences, cultivating them leads to even more misery down the line. Negative thoughts about others, including the feeling of superiority, also signify an unhealthy personality. Sometimes, people feel that they've reached a level of spiritual wisdom on which they can stop cultivating a positive character and start acting however they wish.

You can also experience losses, material, emotional and health-wise. Good luck will rarely be on your side if you're demonstrating bad behavior, but misfortune will definitely follow you.

If you've established that you need to improve your character, you can start working on this by learning about taboos and moral laws in your community. To further this development, look at moral expectations in broader society and learn how to respect them. Implementing certain acts of self-discipline is another way. For example, you can learn a few calming techniques if you have anger issues. These will teach you to think before you act or speak when you are angry, and you'll soon realize the benefits of not giving in to these disruptive emotions.

If your character issues are caused by unrealistic expectations (such as peer pressure and expectations from friends and family), the best way to tackle the problem is to counter them with positive affirmations. So, what if someone expects you to become someone you can't be? You've achieved many other things in life, so focus on these. If others can't see your success, this shouldn't be a problem for you. Remain gentle and kind to them. If their character is good, they will eventually understand. People with foul characters probably won't. However, since they have a negative influence on your spiritual energy, you should limit your interaction with them anyway.

Offering ebbos to Orishas and other spiritual leaders can also improve your character. You can ask your helpers for advice on removing negative influences from your life. Sometimes, appeasing a spiritual being alone motivates them to help you improve your character and Ori. Improving your character takes a lot of work. You'll need to arm yourself with patience while you're working on this. You'll need to be more tolerant of others and yourself too. You can ask your spiritual helpers for advice on practicing good behavior. This will enable you to become a valuable member of your community.

Bonus: Glossary of Terms

Many of the terms relating to Ori and other Yoruba practices can be overwhelming and quite difficult to understand for someone who is just starting out. This bonus chapter will go over the Yoruba terms used throughout this book and is meant to make it easier for you. You can refer to it whenever you feel like you're lost.

Ori (/ō.rí/): Ori is a Yoruba metaphysical concept. The word literally means "head" when used in common language. However, metaphysically, it refers to a person's divine self, destiny, and spiritual intuition. It is the spark of human consciousness found in a person. Ori is often worshiped as an Orisha in its own right. When a person has a balanced character, they can align with their Ori. If a person dies before they can do that, they are reborn in their next life to try again. Mentioned in Chapters 1-10.

Orisha (/ò.rì.ʃà/): Orishas are spirits or deities that are considered to be emanations and emissaries of Olodumare. They are meant to assist humanity in living a successful life on earth. They are essentially the "gods" of the Yoruba pantheon. Mentioned in Chapters 1 and 4.

Obatala (/ɔ.bà.tá.lá/): Obatala is the sky father and the Orisha who created human bodies. He is also the Orisha of purity and is considered to be the father of all Orishas. He is the oldest Orisha and was the first to be created by Olodumare. He is also known as Orisa Nla and Oxala. Mentioned in Chapter 4.

Esu (/è.ʃù/): Also known as Eshu, Esu is the Orisha of duality, balance, trickery, chance, and the essence of fate. He is the divine messenger of the Orishas and serves as an intermediary between humanity and the Orishas. Mentioned in Chapter 4.

Ogun (/ˈəʊɡən/): Also known as Ogum or Ogoun, Ogun is the Orisha of blacksmiths, craftsmen, metalworkers, metal, iron, soldiers, and war. He is often associated with justice. Mentioned in Chapter 4.

Yemaya (/jē.mɔ.dʒā/): Yemaya is the Orisha of childbirth and water. She is known as the Mother of All Water and is considered to be the mother of all Orishas. She is the patron of the Ogun River and is one of Obatala's wives.

Oshun (/ò.sǘ/): Oshun is the Orisha of sweet waters, love, and beauty, as well as diplomacy and wealth. In one version of the Yoruba creation myth, it is Oshun who completed the creation of the world. She is the wife of Shango. Mentioned in Chapter 4.

Shango (/ʃā.gó/): Shango is Orisha of thunder and lightning, fire, and justice. He is a storm deity and is the strongest Orisha in the Yoruba pantheon. His wives are Oshun, Oya, and Oba. Mentioned in Chapter 4.

Oya (/ɔ.jā/): Oya is the Orisha of transformation, storms, thunder and lightning, and the wind. She is also the guardian of the dead and is a warrior Orisha who is said to be unbeatable. She is one of the wives of Shango. Mentioned in Chapter 4.

Orunmila (/ɔ.rǔ.mɪ.là/): Orunmila is the Orisha of wisdom, knowledge, divination, and prophecy. It is believed that Olodumare placed Ori in him, and he is the Orisha who can most affect a person's reality. It is believed that he once walked the Earth as a mortal prophet. Mentioned in Chapter 2.

Ajogun (/ā.dzo.gũ/): Creatures that represent the negative forces of nature and are often associated with the Christian Devil. They bring misfortunes to people. However, they are not all evil and have some good in them. Mentioned in Chapter 1.

Santeria (/santeˈria/): Also known as la Regla de Ocha (the way/order of the Orishas), Regla Lucumí, or Lucumí, santeria is a religion that originated from Isese and developed in Cuba as a result of the slave trade. It is considered an African diasporic religion. Mentioned in Chapter 1.

Voodoo (/ˈvuːduː/): Also known as Vodoun and Vodou, Voodoo is a religion that developed in Haiti and traveled to the US as a result of the slave trade. It is a combination of several West and Central African religions, as well as Christianity. Mentioned in Chapter 1.

Lwa (/lwa/)**:** Also known as loa or loi, lwa are spirits worshipped in Voodoo. They are similar to the Orishas in Isese. Mentioned in Chapter 1.

Vilokan (/vilokan/)**:** Vilokan is the home of the lwas as well as the spirits of the dead. Mentioned in Chapter 1.

Bondye (/bondye)**:** The supreme deity in Voodoo. Mentioned in Chapter 1.

Candomblé (/kʊ.dõˈblɛ/)**:** Also known as Batuque, Candomblé is a religion that developed in Brazil but borrows heavily from Yoruba beliefs. It can literally be translated to "dance in the honor of the gods." Mentioned in Chapter 1.

Ialorixá and Babalorixá (/ˈiyə.lo.riˈʃa/ and /ˌba.ba.lo.riˈʃa/)**:** Priestesses and priests in Candomblé. Mentioned in Chapter 1.

Umbanda (/ũˈbʊdʊ/)**:** A religion that developed in Brazil and is based on a combination of several African religions, Roman Catholicism, and several other beliefs. Believers of Umbanda worship the supreme deity Olodumareb or Zambia and also revere the Orishas. Mentioned in Chapter 1.

Preto Velho and Preta Velha (/ˈpretʊ/ //ˈvɛ.ʎu/ and /ˈpre.tʊ/ /ˈvɛ.ʎʊ/)**:** Male and female spirits of the ancestors in Umbanda. Mentioned in Chapter 1.

Iwa-Pele (/ì.wà/ /kpɛ.lɛ/**:** The concept of having a good or gentle character. Mentioned in Chapter 10.

Ifa (/ì.fà/)**:** Both a Yoruba religion and a system of divination. Orunmila was considered the Grand Priest of Ifa. Mentioned in Chapter 9.

Odu Ifa (/ō.dù/ /ì.fà/)**:** Essentially a religious text comprised of 256 sections or odus. The knowledge of these sections can be transcribed into the 16 Truths of Ifa. Mentioned in Chapter 9.

Egbe Orun (/é.gbè/ /ɔ.rũ/)**:** Also known as "heavenly mates." These are spirits who live in the heavenly realm. Each person has a heavenly mate, and these spirits guide and protect their twin in the human realm. Mentioned in Chapter 8.

Eléékò (/eléékòò/): An Egbe group that is led by their desires and whose mood is easily changed. Mentioned in Chapter 8.

Ìyálóde (/Ìȉyálóde/): An Egbe group that are natural-born leaders. Mentioned in Chapter 8.

Baálè (/baálèè): An Egbe group that is a blend between Eléékò and Ìyálóde and has various personalities. Mentioned in Chapter 8.

Asípa (/asípa/): An Egbe group that is outspoken and vocal. They are often forgetful and disloyal. Mentioned in Chapter 8.

Jagun (/jagun/): An Egbe group that is highly adaptable and is identified with children who exhibit unusual behavior. Mentioned in Chapter 8.

Olúgbógeró (/olúgbógeróó): An Egbe group with a fluid nature and multifaceted personalities. Mentioned in Chapter 8.

Móohún (/móohún/): An Egbe group who are often childlike in their behavior and cannot be trusted with important tasks. Mentioned in Chapter 8.

Adétayànyá (/adétayànyáá): An Egbe group who revere refuse dumps. Mentioned in Chapter 8.

Ibori (/íbori/): A ritual that is practiced cleansing yourself and feed your Ori. Mentioned in Chapter 5.

Odun Egungun (/ɔ.du/ /ē.gũ.gũ/): Egungun are masked, costumed figures that represent the ancestors. Ofun Egungun are festivals that are held to celebrate the ancestors.

Gelede (/gelede/): A female masquerade held as part of Odun Egungun.

Oso Ijoba (/ɔ.ʃɔ/ /ì.dzo.bā/): A male masquerade held as part of Odun Egungun.

Omiero (/omiero/): Also known as purificacíon de santo. A sacred liquid that is used while conducting rituals. Mentioned in Chapter 5.

Igba'Ori (/ī.gbá/ /ō.rí/): A pot (sopera) that represents Ori. Mentioned in Chapter 5.

Opèle (/ɔ.kpɛ.lɛ/): A divination chain used in Ifa and Isese. Mentioned in Chapter 5.

Ikin (/ī.kɪ/): Sacred palm nuts that are used as divination tools. Mentioned in Chapter 5.

Ori-Apere (/ō.rí/ /apere/): Ori-Apere is a person's personal destiny. It also refers to a person's unique personal force or spiritual power and helps guide a person through physical and emotional challenges. Mentioned in Chapter 3.

Ayanmo (/ayanmo/): Ayanmo is a process by which people can get back in touch with the divine source and restore the balance of their body and mind. Mentioned in Chapter 2.

Akunleya (/akunleya/): Akunleya is the concept of being respectful while speaking, no matter who you are speaking to or what situation you are in. It is essentially speaking etiquette. Mentioned in Chapter 3.

Akunlegba (/akunlegba/): Akunlegba is the concept of transforming physically, spiritually, and intellectually to be well-rounded and develop a better understanding of oneself. Mentioned in Chapter 3.

Babalawo (/bā.bā.lá.wō/): Literally means "father of the mysteries." Babalawos are high priests of the Ifa oracle who perform various rituals and are believed to be able to tell the future of people who consult with them. Mentioned in Chapter 5.

Ebbo (/e.ˈbɔ/): Also known as ebo, these are sacrifices and offerings that are made to the Orishas, the ancestors, and other spirits. Mentioned in Chapter 10.

Ori Inu (/ō.rí/ /ˈi.nu/): The power of the mind, both physically and figuratively, in terms of power of thought and use of the mind. Mentioned in Chapter 3.

Arugba (/arugba/): Literally translates to "divine guidance." It is the external influences that benefit an individual – that is, the benefits they receive from being part of a community. Mentioned in Chapter 3.

Ebo (/e.ˈbɔ/): Literally translates to "exchange." It is the exchange between a person and the universe and refers to actions that affect a person's luck or fortune. Mentioned in Chapter 3.

Iwa (/ì.wà/): Literally translates to "character" in the Yoruba language. Mentioned in Chapters 3 and 10.

Olodumare (/ō.ló.⁺dù.mā.rè/): The Yoruba supreme deity. Olodumare is a genderless deity who is the creator of the world and the giver of the breath of life. They are also known as Olorun and Olofi. Mentioned in Chapters 2 and 4.

Iwa-Buruki (/ì.wà/ /buruki/): The concept of bad character. The opposite of Iwa-Pele. Mentioned in Chapter 10.

Ise (/ī.ʃɛ/): Literally means "skill" in the Yoruba language. Mentioned in Chapter 10.

Ogbon (/ɔ.gbɔ/): Literally means "wisdom" in the Yoruba language. Mentioned in Chapter 10.

Aiye (/aiye/): A person's environment or the world around him. The word is also used to reference the earth or the physical realm (as opposed to the heavenly/spiritual realm). Also known as Aye. Mentioned in Chapter 10.

Egan (/'iygən/): The first wife of Orunmila. Mentioned in Chapter 9.

Odu (/odu/): The second wife of Orunmila. Mentioned in Chapter 9.

Eji-Ogbe (/è.dzì ō.gbè/): The youngest child of Orunmila. Mentioned in Chapter 9.

Ife (/ī.fɛ/): The place where humanity was born. It is also an ancient Yoruba city located north of Lagos in modern Nigeria. Also known as Ife-Ife. Mentioned in Chapter 9.

Ofun-Meji (/ò.fű/ /médzì/): One of the children of Orunmila. Mentioned in Chapter 9.

Conclusion

The concept of Ori plays a central role in Yoruba beliefs and the practices of several other African Diaspora religions. Yoruba is a religion based on spirituality, where reverence for the soul is shown to both the living and the dead. According to them, the soul was given to living beings by Olodumare, which ensures its purity. Due to being preoccupied with mundane matters, spirits living on Earth have lost their connection to the divine essence they hail from.

Ori is a concept that encompasses the path to finding one's destiny and changing it if necessary. However, this is only possible if your values align with your Ori and if you have a sharp spiritual intuition. The concept of Ori is slightly controversial since it directly contradicts another fundamental Yoruba concept, the freedom of choice. However, Ori has several components and many forms, some of which make it possible to walk on the path of fate, all while maintaining and exercising free will.

The first step toward aligning with your Ori is to hone your spiritual intuition - as this is the part of you that lets you connect to the divine spirituality. One of the ways to do this is by calling on the Orishas, the divine messengers. The Yoruba believe that everyone has an "Orisha parent," but you can be guided by other Orishas too. In ancient times, people turned to Orunmila, a powerful Orisha and deity with divinatory powers. Nowadays, high priests and priestesses also perform prophecies to find a spiritual resolution to people's issues. Another reason venerating the Orishas can help you find your spiritual path is that Ori can also be viewed and honored as an Orisha.

Apart from honoring the Orishas and Olodumare, you can also work on your spiritual communication skills and awareness by remembering your ancestors. These wise spirits have a deep bond with you, which will come in handy if you struggle with awakening your spiritual intuition. If they see you have positive values that help continue their line, they will bestow many blessings upon you and your loved ones. Egbe Orun is another group of spirits you can turn to if you want to align yourself with your Ori. The Egbe has a tremendous influence over people's souls, but everyone should be careful when working with them. Some Egbe groups are easily angered and hard to placate. When crossed, they will retaliate by putting many obstacles in your path.

Odu Ifa, the ancient Yoruba prophecy, also plays a crucial part in spiritual fulfillment. It was created by Olodumare and given to the priests of Ife by Orunmila, who was entrusted with the resolution of conflicts and other issues among people. Since then, it has been passed down to the generations of high priests and priestesses of Yoruba, who learn to use its 256 signatures to guide, heal and support people in their communities. Odu Ifa can be summarized in the dogma named "The 16 Truths of Ifa." These truths serve as a guide to righteous living, which helps the Yoruba collect wisdom and reach spiritual enlightenment. Last but not least, you've learned that the ultimate role in improving and aligning your Ori depends on your personality. By improving your character, your values will become much closer to becoming an Ori representing that needed in order to live a fulfilled life.

Part 4: Egun

The Ultimate Guide to Ancestral Veneration, Spirit Guides, Odun Egungun, Reincarnation, and Yoruba Spirituality

Introduction

The Egun, spirits of the ancestors, play a huge role in the Yoruba religion and are highly revered among its people. Learning about these ancestors and their role will help you better understand your African roots. This book begins with an introduction to the history, culture, structure, and spiritual philosophy of the Yoruba religion. We also go into the world's creation - a significant part of any religion - and we explain the Yoruba creation myth and introduce you to the chief deity Olodumare who started it all. You will also learn about some of the core concepts in the religion, like reincarnation and the afterlife.

We then move on to explain the Orishas, who play a prominent role in the veneration of the ancestors. The second chapter will answer all your questions about these entities and clear up some of your misconceptions. We will also provide interesting stories about the most well-known Orishas to help you understand their personalities and powers. After learning about the Orishas and their purpose, the book will set out detailed information on how to venerate them and how to know if an Orisha is trying to communicate with you.

Another type of spirit is the Egbe, who can provide guidance and support. The book will explain the concept of the Egbe, its various types, and how it differs from the ancestors' spirits. You will also find out how these spirits can help you connect with your ancestors and what offerings will appease them.

The book will also answer the main questions you likely have in mind. Why are the ancestors so significant in the Yoruba religion? You will learn about the Egungun and what makes them highly revered. We will also include tips and tricks to help you identify your ancestors. The people of Yoruba show their love and respect for their ancestors by celebrating them in a festival dedicated to them. We will provide you with all the information related to this festival, including its origin and how you can celebrate it,

You will then learn the best methods to venerate the Eguns, like building an altar. You will find step-by-step instructions on how to build an altar and other relevant details like the best location for an altar and how to take care of it. The book will also introduce other methods, such as meditation and chanting.

Reincarnation is a popular concept in many cultures. However, the Yoruba people have a different understanding of this concept than that of Western cultures. We will explain its place in the Yoruba religion and how it relates to the spirits of the ancestors. The book's last chapter will cover ancestral curses, the reasons behind them, and how you can get rid of them.

The topic of ancestors' veneration can be complicated for beginners. We made sure to write the book using simple language to avoid confusing the reader and make it easy to grasp. The book also includes methods and step-by-step instructions, so you don't have to look elsewhere as you begin your journey of venerating your ancestors.

Step into the world of the ancient African ancestors and get acquainted with your roots.

Chapter 1: Yoruba Spirituality Basics

Egun (ancestral worship) is a fundamental concept in Yoruba. Before delving into the practice itself, you must familiarize yourself with this religion first. This chapter will introduce you to Yoruba's cultural and historical background, spiritual philosophy, and belief structure. Apart from the importance of Egun, you'll also be acquainted with other Yoruba practices, including their initiation process and how they honor their deities.

Yoruba dancers.
Ayo Adewunmi, CC BY-SA 4.0 <https://creativecommons.org/licenses/by-sa/4.0>, via Wikimedia Commons https://commons.wikimedia.org/wiki/File:Ayo_Adewunmi_-_Yoruba_Dancers.jpg

Yoruba Religion Background

Thousands of years ago, a unique belief system was developed in West Africa. Originating from a small ethnic group in Nigeria, Yoruba beliefs have become a set of highly spiritual concepts. Its followers believe that human souls pass through a cycle called Ayanmo, which determines their fate in the next life in their new physical body. Not only that, but according to the Yoruba, a person can choose their own destiny. They can control how their current life will flow and how their subsequent lives will evolve spiritually. In each life, the person can create every aspect of the future of their soul long before the soul is reborn in their new life. From the place they will live, through their purpose in life, to how they will die in their next life, everything can be predetermined by the decisions a person makes in their current life.

The ancient Yoruba traditions were passed down through oral traditions, which accounted for their change over time. They were also influenced by other religions and by migrations before the rule of the Egyptian dynasties and during the Transatlantic slave trade. Consequently, the ancient Yoruba beliefs have evolved into a widespread religious system. Today, people living in Tobago, Trinidad, the Dominican Republic, Brazil, Cuba, Puerto Rico, Venezuela – and even North America – actively practice the religion or are striving to return to their African roots and Explore Yoruba spirituality.

A broad range of aspects of Yoruba spiritual practices exist under different names. In Africa, some of these are still practiced in their purest form. Meanwhile, the diversity of cultural practices the African communities that moved to the New World brought with them all show slight differences from their parent religion. Some of these have even developed into new religions, such as Santeria and Candomble. In this religion, the divinities of the Yoruba pantheon are identified with Roman Catholic saints. However, as with the Yoruba, joining is only possible after a particular initiation period.

The Yoruba Creation Myth

The Yoruba have a unique and elaborate tale about the creation of life on Earth. According to ancient beliefs, it all began when Olodumare, the supreme God, was asked by Obatala (a noted Orisha) if he could create life on Earth. At that time, Earth was a barren land covered by water, making it impossible for any creature to live on it. Obatala wanted to create patches of dry land amid the water to change this. Curious about the unusual request, the supreme being allowed Obatala to take on this task. Before his journey, Obatala consulted with other Orishas and learned that he would need to gather a few things: a gold chain long enough to reach the water, sand, a black cat, a hen, nuts, seeds, and snail shells. After gathering everything except the chain, he fixed the chain in the heavy realm and started his descent. On his way down, he realized that the chain wasn't long enough to reach Earth safely. Thinking quickly during his climb, he released the sand from the bag, the seeds, and the hen. As the hen spread the seeds around, it created the mountains and the valleys of the newly formed dry land. On reaching the patch of land, Obatala named it Ife and began to make it his home. He planted the palm nut, which grew into a large tree with seeds.

Obatala used the new seedlings to make more palm trees for shelter and beverages like palm wine. He had a cat for company, but over time, he grew lonely. One day, while drinking wine, he had the idea of making clay figures. At first, he didn't know how to shape them, but after glimpsing his own face in a lake, he decided to make them into his own likeness. When he was done, he asked the supreme being to infuse the shapes with life. This is how people were created. The fact that the figures were made by hand explains the diversity of the human population. Later, the people were also infused with Ashe, the force that all living beings share. The other deities visited Obatala frequently, and while most were fascinated with his work, not everyone was happy with his creations. Olokun, the ruler of the water world, was particularly displeased by the new beings taking over her kingdom. One day, she waited until Obatala left Earth to visit the other Orishas and decided to end the budding civilization. She raised a wave so high that it washed away everything built by the people so far. The humans who survived asked the supreme being for help. Olodumare took mercy on them and ended the flood by making a new patch of land appear.

The Main Yoruba Beliefs

According to the Yoruba teachings born in Ife, every life and death are tiny elements of a continuous cycle. Through this cycle, human souls occupy different forms of physical bodies in each life. Meanwhile, living in each body and following the right path, one's spirit slowly evolves towards eternal transcendence.

Yoruba spirituality acknowledges that people learn their destiny through self-exploration and growth. It also proposes that when a soul is reborn into a new physical body, it doesn't consciously remember any plans for spiritual elevation from the previous life. However, according to Yoruba beliefs, this wisdom can be regained from the subconscious (where it's hidden) and added to the new knowledge the spirit gains in their current life. It takes effort, struggle, and learning to be successful in staying true to oneself. However, this is all done so the soul will remember its destiny. If a person regains wisdom and learns new truths, they can claim the future they desire to have.

Other beliefs of the people in Ife include divination, spirit possession, animal sacrifices, and initiation. These practices are prevalent in the lives of the followers of the Yoruba religion and its offspring.

Olodumare

Yoruba practitioners can take different approaches, including reaching out to Olodumare, the supreme God ruling over the skies and lands. Living in his faraway realm, Olodumare is the creator of the world. This is the being who accepts every deserving spirit back from where they've been. Olodumare transcends gender and is the ultimate source of divine energy, representing the power that can influence the destiny of every spirit. To achieve their carefully devised plans, a person must think, feel, and behave in a way that appears Olodumare. It takes a conscious act to anchor one's life to be the best person one can be and become worthy of the creator's acceptance. This has to continue through each life cycle, so spiritual growth can be achieved. Spiritual growth is required for everyone who wants to demonstrate that their soul deserves to be elevated to the next level and continue learning in their next life. After many cycles of life, death, and rebirth, human spirits are expected to become one with the spirit of the supreme God. This allows them to achieve transcendence and become immortal.

Through the different Yoruba traditions, Olodumare is also called Olorun, Oluwa, and Eleda. Whichever name this entity is known by, all are revered for the same unquestionable power and immortal status. None of these entities has a centralized place for worship but instead are honored in everyday actions and unique celebrations held by families and Yoruba communities. What all these forms of veneration have in common is that they all acknowledge Olodumare as the utmost authority in the world. According to the Yoruba, nothing happens without the creator's blessing, so if people or a person wants something, they must gain the creator's approval first. This is the primary reason the Yoruba people hold different ceremonies, especially daily ones.

The Orishas

Over time, more and more people in Ife found and started following this philosophy. Some even took it outside their birthplace when they moved away. And as the number of followers grew, the supreme being was called upon more and more. So, to facilitate communication between Olodumare and its loyal followers, new mediators were created. These entities are known as the Orishas, and they can greatly assist those wanting to reach divine consciousness. They have the same immortal quality as their creator, although they wield slightly less power. Some Orishas have been present since the beginning of time and hail directly from the line of Obatala. While others were once human souls and have successfully reached transcendence. Unlike their creator, the Orishas aren't perfect, and they all answer to Olodumare with their actions.

Ancestral Veneration

Another way to gain spiritual wisdom is by interacting with ancestral souls and other spirits of nature. Along with benevolent essences, the spirits of the ancestors are also believed to linger in this world. They watch over their family members and guide them through the hurdles in life up until they are ready to be rejuvenated again. The Yoruba believe that a spirit of an ancestor is reborn in a child in the same family, hence their traditional naming customs. These ancestors are always remembered and mentioned in everyday conversations in the same way as when they were alive.

Moreover, their living relations can even communicate with them, occasionally asking them to ward off dangerous situations and corrupt behavior. As an act of gratitude for their protection, ancestral spirits are honored through communal celebrations. Consulting their ancestry, a person can learn much about their own destiny. Ancestors can often provide clues about a soul's plans in their previous lives, helping to remember these.

Ajogun

Ajogun are beings that represent the negative forces of nature and can cause all kinds of mishaps in one's life. These demon-like creatures can be responsible for many hurdles, from accidents to illnesses and even issues with social connections. This is essentially how the Yoruba traditional religion describes almost every danger, illness, or mishap-afflicted person as either bewitched or possessed by an evil spirit. To be cured, these people visit a priest for divination rituals to learn why the Ajogun has attacked them. If possible, the priest or priestess will advise them on how to ward off anything troubling them.

Ashe

Ashe is an inner force possessed by humans, natural elements, Orishas, and deities. This force is similar to the natural form of energy called Qi (also known as chi) in Traditional Chinese medicine and other Eastern spiritual traditions. If one can reach it, this power can determine one's fate by occasionally pushing them either in the direction of good or bad. When contained in natural elements like lightning, rain, wind, or even blood, its character will be entirely determined by the supreme being. In humans, it can be influenced, which often begins right at birth, by giving a child a particular name. The Yoruba believe that Ashe can promote change, positive and negative, so it's paramount to start influencing it toward positive outcomes as early as possible.

Other Yoruba Beliefs

Apart from the veneration of deities, ancestors, and the divine spirit, the Yoruba have many other beliefs. Here are some of them:

Reincarnation

Aside from having a productive and generous existence for achieving personal goals in life, Yoruba spirituality also emphasizes the role of a higher spirit in reincarnation. This separates Yoruba from many other religions, where the emphasis is placed on salvation in the afterlife. According to Yoruba teachings, being a good person is necessary if one wants their soul to be reborn. As most followers look forward to earning the privilege of reincarnation, they will try to be compassionate and kind in their current life. They know that the souls of the deceitful will be denied transmutation and won't get the chance to come back in the next life. This applies to people who are unkind towards themselves and who self-harm too. The spirits who come back are reborn in the bodies of the children born in the same families. This concept of familial reincarnation is known as Atunwa and is the main reason Yoruba children are often given several names belonging to their ancestors at birth.

Mysterious Powers

Yoruba beliefs also point to mysterious forces associated with witchcraft, medicine, magic, sorcery, and foul magic. The powers associated with witchcraft are called osonga, eye, and aje. These are often viewed as negative forces. They, along with oso, oogun buburu, and oogun ika (the powers linked to sorcery), are used to harm someone or prevent them from reaching their goals. Whereas isegun, oogun, and egbogi (the forces associated with medicine and magic) are considered good influences. For the Yoruba, medicine and magic are interchangeable due to the numerous folk beliefs regarding nature's healing power.

Yoruba Spiritual Practices

Due to the incredible expansion of Yoruba spirituality and its frequent collusion with other religions, changes to its practices were inevitable. A small number of devotees in Nigeria still follow the traditional religion of their ancestors, which includes honoring the deities and the Orishas in everyday life and participating in rituals and festivities. Sacrifices are offered to the deities of the Yoruba pantheon, who are asked to influence natural elements, making them favorable for planting, hunting, and harvesting. Yoruba religious festivals often contain re-enactments of the ancient legends about the creation of life, ancestors' destinies, and spiritual journeys.

Reasons for Yoruba religious festivals and rituals include birth, marriages, and honoring their dead. Initiation into religion, cleansing, and other rites of passage are also common in the lives of Yorubans. They offer homage to their ancestors in body and spirit by participating in these ceremonies. During ancestral venerations, entire family lines can be celebrated by expressing the spiritual ideas and personality traits of the living and their ancestors. For most communal ceremonies, the Yoruba wear traditional dresses and dance to the music of drumming and chanting. Depending on the type of ritual or ceremony they're performing, the high priest or priestess often wears different clothing to distinguish themselves from the rest of the community. They often invoke the Orishas through trance. For this, they also wear protection made from natural (magically protective) materials like palm leaves and feathers. Yoruba religious traditions were partially created to promote spiritual connections within the entire community. It encourages families to help one another by providing food, clothes, and many other things to those in need.

One of the most well-known Yoruba rituals for honoring the deities is the celebration of the yam harvest. As an homage to Ifa, the God of wisdom and hard work, a sacrifice is made by cutting the new yam. This is followed by merriment and a large feast. At the end of each year, Yoruba people pray to Olodumare and the Orishas for protection in the coming year. At Ogun's annual festival, Yoruba priests vow to remain celibate, abstain from certain foods, and cease fighting to prove their worthiness to Ogun. On this festival, Yorubans also offer palm oil, kola nuts, and snails to appease Ogun and lure him to their side.

Divination

Yoruba priests and priestesses spend many years learning to communicate with the spiritual realm and harness its wisdom during divinatory practices. They learn to access information about past, present, and future influences and outcomes. The ones who can do this are called Iyalawo (translated as "mother of secrets") and Babalawo (meaning "father of secrets"). They can intercede between the rest of the community and the spirits and deities. By doing this, they become privy to secrets no one else in the community can reveal. They can answer questions about any aspect of life for themselves, their families, or anyone else in the community. It's said that other than being trained and wise, Yoruba diviners don't possess any extraordinary powers. They are merely people who can access prophecies and advise others on harnessing ashe. They reveal the information in several traditional prayers, spells, or poems, which they learn through their training.

Initiation, Devotion, and Training

To become a follower of the Yoruba religion, one must be initiated. In large communities, this is done by a member of the family. There are different ranks within each family, depending on experience levels. The lowest-ranking members are the yet-to-be-initiated, usually children below the age of five to seven. They are followed by the initiates, the devotees, and their godparents (a couple proposes a person's initiation and helps them through it). Then, there are the priests and priestesses, and finally, the high priests and priestesses. The latter can also perform initiation for people who aren't direct descendants of the family but have a connection to the Yoruba traditions. People who feel called on to follow ancestral beliefs by the spirit of Ifa can also be initiated.

Yoruba practices from all around the world have different rules for initiation. In Nigeria, the initiation lasts seven days and is followed by a year-long training period. At the start of the initiation process, the priest and priestess give the initiate a necklace made from dried herbs. This places the person under the protection of Ifa. It also helps evoke the spirit of Ifa to help the person through the rest of the process. After this, those involved in the ceremony will get the initiate into a trance state through drumming, chanting, and dancing, which lasts for several hours. This is repeated several times through the week-long initiation process, along with prayers and other communal functions. The person who went through the initiation is called aleyo. They've now gained the ability to access a higher level of consciousness and begin their journey to become one with Olodumare.

Apart from bringing the community together, the initiation rites and other Yoruba ceremonies have other social functions too. They promote traditional values to the youngest members and help preserve the culture for future generations. This is why those who move away and encounter other religions remain true to their Yoruba roots and peacefully coexist with the followers of other belief systems.

Chapter 2: The Orishas, Your Divine Spirit Guides

Discussing the Egun or the Yoruba religion without mentioning the Orishas is impossible. Orishas or Orisa play a huge role in the Yarouba faith as they act as intermediaries between Olodumare, the supreme deity, and mankind. The word "Orisha" comes from the Yoruba language, "ori" means a human's head. According to the Yoruba people, the "ori" acts as a vessel for another "ori," which is an invisible inner head or the human spirit that is the center of one's personality. The people of Yoruba believe that the human spirit comes from God, which influences one's personality and destiny.

Orishas are supernatural beings that have human characteristics.
Daderot, CC0, via Wikimedia Commons
https://commons.wikimedia.org/wiki/File:Pottery_shrine_piece,_Ibo_-_African_objects_in_the_American_Museum_of_Natural_History_-_DSC05998.JPG

Orishas are divine or supernatural beings. There is a misconception that the Orishas are gods, especially since the Yoruba people often refer to them as deities. Calling them gods isn't accurate, as these beings are far more complex. They are Olodumare's avatars, but the concept of an Orisha is more than that of a deity. The Orishas rule over nature, and you can only understand them by watching the forces of nature at work.

The Yoruba people believe that Olodumare created the Orishas because he couldn't interact directly with mankind. The human mind is so simple that it can't comprehend Olodumare or what he represents. Thus, he created the Orishas as parts of himself to act as his emissaries. He gave each Orisha power or influence and randomly distributed his powers among them by throwing them in the air, and whichever power an Orisha caught was theirs. However, the Orishas didn't want to use their powers to help Olodumare create the universe. Instead, they used them for their own personal gain. Only the Orisha Oduduwa helped Olodumare with creation, and he was the one who created the people of Yoruba. This makes Oduduwa one of the most significant Orishas. However, another version of the myth of creation tells how other Orishas assisted. Sixteen male Orishas and one female Orisha came down to finish what Olodumare had started.

Orishas are significant in the Yoruba religion, and they come second in the divine hierarchy, right after Olodumare. There are about 401 male and female Orishas altogether. Each is different, with its own interests, weaknesses, strengths, and unique personality. They have human characteristics and get angry, upset, happy, crave power, etc.

For this reason, mankind has always felt close to these entities as they can relate to them more than they can to gods. The Orishas are also involved in the day-to-day lives of mankind and provide assistance whenever needed. They are still revered to this day, and people invoke them in various rituals to provide guidance and enlightenment.

Although Orishas are meant to help people, they can unintentionally cause trouble. They are imperfect and flawed beings, just like mankind. Orishas face the same struggles as human beings. A part of them wants to do good and help others, while another part gives in to temptations. Like us, the Orishas have egos and weaknesses that stand between their sense of duty and personal desires.

Types of Orishas

Nigerian scholars have categorized the Orishas into three types, defied ancestors, forces of nature, and primordial divinities.

Defied Ancestors

The term *"defied ancestors"* refers to spirits who hugely impacted humanity when they were alive. These ancestors played significant roles in their society. They were brave soldiers, fair kings, heroes, and heroines whose names would live forever in Yoruba mythology. They established control over the forces of nature by making sacrifices and offerings and used its destructive power against their enemies while employing its benefits to help people. According to Yoruba beliefs, the ancestors ascended to the heavens or sunk into the ground and became Orishas.

Forces of Nature

The Yoruba people believe that any useful element of nature has its own spirit. The most powerful and distinguished of these spirits are the Orishas. The spirits of the lakes, mountains, rivers, winds, or trees are all Orishas. However, the Orishas don't represent the whole of the natural force. The Orishas are the spirits of the controllable and disciplined aspect that practitioners and people can use in their rituals.

Primordial Divinities

The Orishas of the primordial divinities are the oldest types of Orishas as they pre-existed creation itself. They emerged from the divine and came directly from heaven. Some inhabited the earth before mankind and have now become sacred beings.

There are a vast number of Orishas, and this chapter will focus on the most significant ones that impact the Yoruba religion.

Elegua

Elegua or Eshu is the Orisha of mischief and trickery, similar to Loki from Norse mythology and Marvel movies. He has a childlike nature and enjoys dancing and playing pranks on people. Unlike Loki, Elegua is a kind Orisha who provides protection rather than causing harm. He protects the homes of the people who present him with offerings by preventing forces of evil from entering. Elegua isn't an evil Orisha, but he craves attention. He punishes those who fail to notice his presence. He also shares similarities with the Greek god Hermes as both act as messengers between mankind and the other world (the world of the spirits, and in this case, Orishas). Although he is a trickster, Elegua is one of the most powerful Orishas. During any ritual or ceremony, his name is always invoked first. He is the gatekeeper of the Orishas, and his permission is required before you can communicate with them or the ancestors.

Elugua is the orisha of mischief and trickery.
Happycheetha32, CC BY-SA 4.0 <https://creativecommons.org/licenses/by-sa/4.0>, via Wikimedia Commons https://commons.wikimedia.org/wiki/File:Ellegua.jpg

He manifests as either an old man or a young child. This contradiction represents his association with the beginning and end of life. He is a protector and a warrior dressed in black and red, which is the image he often adopts to appear to. His favorite offerings are candy, straw hats, cigars, toys, silver coins, toasted corn, smoked fish, and coconut. He is associated with the number three and the colors black and red. The best time to present offerings to him is on Mondays. Elegua is associated with the Catholic priest Saint Anthony of Padua.

Elegua was one of Olodumare's favorite Orishas because he saved his life. As mentioned, Orishas had human-like qualities and succumbed to temptation. In one story, the Orishas, hungry for more power, decided that they should rule mankind instead of Olodumare, who was getting too old. They believed they were better fit to rule since they were already involved with humanity. Olodumare was terrified of mice, so the Orishas decided to scare him to death using his biggest fear. The Orishas planned for everything, but they forgot to tell Elegua. The trickster Orisha was aware of their intentions because he was the gatekeeper and standing at the doorway listening. However, he didn't inform Olodumare of the Orishas' treachery. Olodumare arrived at the Orishas' hut only to find hundreds of mice. He was terrified, but the Orishas locked the door, and there was no way out.

Elegua came to Olodumare's aid. He calmed the deity down and devoured all the mice. Olodumare was angry and disappointed and demanded to know who was behind this betrayal. Elegua gave him the names of all the Orishas involved, and they were all punished on the spot. Olodumare was grateful for Elegua's heroism and showed his appreciation by giving him the freedom to do whatever he wanted to whomever he wanted without suffering any consequences. This enabled him to perform all the mischief and trickery he desired - without answering to anyone.

Obatala

Obatala was the Orisha who assisted Olodumare with creating the universe as he created the earth and the human race and is the father of the Orishas and the sky. He was the first Orisha created by Olodumare, which makes him the oldest one. He is the Orisha of morality, light, and spiritual purity. Obatala appears in human form wearing white since he is associated with purity and is often referred to as the king of peace. He is responsible for everything that goes on in the human mind, including dreams and thoughts. He is associated with symbols of peace, like an olive branch, a white dove, and the color white. His favorite number is eight, and he is celebrated on September 24th. He is linked to the Catholic Virgin of Mercy. His favorite offerings include coca butter, marble eggs, cotton, black-eyed peas, white rice, rice pudding, white custard, sweet potatoes, pears, and pomegranates. Never include salt in any of his offerings. Obtala manifests in many forms, both male and female.

Obatala assisted with the creation of the universe.
Isha, CC BY 3.0 <https://creativecommons.org/licenses/by/3.0>, via Wikimedia Commons https://commons.wikimedia.org/wiki/File:Oxal%C3%A1.jpg

Olodumare sent Obatala to earth to be its king. Obatala was the right choice for the role because of his wise, calm, and understanding nature. He was a proper Orisha who despised obscenity and demanded respect. Obatala's followers should never appear naked, curse in his presence, or drink alcohol. People invoke Obatala to protect them from dementia, paralysis, and blindness. You will find him a very loving and patient Orisha if you respect and obey his rules.

One of Obatal's famous stories involved a fight between him and Elegua. One day, both Orishas had an intense argument about which one was the oldest Orisha of all time. The argument escalated into a physical fight. Obatala was stronger than Elegua and knocked him down several times, but Elegua was determined and kept getting back up each time. None of the Orishas used their magic. However, the people watching the fight were bewildered at how the Orisha of trickery never used his magic, so they suggested this to him since he was clearly at a disadvantage against the powerful Obatala. Elegua took their advice and used his magic. Elegua performed a trick that made Obatala's skin color disappear. He became an albino. However, Elegua's magic trick didn't help him as both Orishas kept fighting, and Obatala won in the end. This story also shows how Obatala became the protector of the albino people.

Ogun

Ogun is the Orisha of iron and war. He is a brave warrior, usually invoked by warriors, blacksmiths, and hunters. He is associated with mountains and weapons. Ogun is depicted as a blacksmith leading a solitary life in the forests. According to Yoruba myths, Ogun was Obatala's son and descended to earth with the rest of the Orishas. Each Orisha was given a task, and Ogun's task was to clear the forests using his machete. He is the patron of soldiers, surgeons, mechanics, and all people who work with metals. He can perform violent acts but also has a kind and tender side. Similar to Elegua, people invoke him to protect their homes from harm. He is associated with the numbers three and seven and is celebrated on June 29th. His favorite offerings include cigars, palm oil, roasted sweet potatoes, white beans, toasted corn, and smoked fish. He is associated with dogs and the colors black, red, and green. He is linked to the Catholic Saint Peter. As a result of his destructive nature, Ogun is feared by the Yoruba people. However, he only punishes the ones who break nature's rules, and he is very protective of his followers.

The reason behind Ogun's solitary existence was that he was in love with his mother, Yemu. Elegua always interfered to stop Ogun from giving in to his affection. When Obatala found out, he wanted to punish his son, but Ogun took matters into his own hands and cursed himself. He would live for eternity alone in the forests working all day. Ogun led a miserable existence as he was alone, and no one visited him except his brother Ochoshi. Ogun was consumed by his misery and heartbroken to spend eternity away from the woman he loved, so he decided the whole world should also live in misery. He spread a magical powder all over the earth to create pain and conflict. When Oshun, the Orisha of love, realized what Ogun was doing, she interfered. Oshun was a very beautiful Orisha, and she used her beauty to seduce Ogun. Her plan worked, and Ogun was no longer miserable. He was also married to Oya, the Orisha of the dead, for some time, but she cheated on him with Shango, the Orisha of thunder.

Chango

Chango or Shango is the Orisha of thunder and lighting, similar to the Norse god Thor. Chango was a king in his human form, which is why he was allowed to marry more than one Orisha since kings had this kind of liberty. He was married to three Orishas, Oba, Oya, and Oshun. Chango is the patron of dancing, drumming, and music. It is no wonder that Chango managed to make three Orishas fall in love with him, as he is a symbol of passion and male beauty. He is also charming and a womanizer. Chango is always a leader and doesn't like taking orders. He is also intelligent, brave, proud, fair, hard-working, and a fierce warrior. Just like other Orishas, Chango was flawed. He can be arrogant, a liar, domineering, violent, impulsive, and manipulative.

Chango is the orisha of thunder and lightning.
Cliff1066, CC BY 2.0 <https://creativecommons.org/licenses/by/2.0>, via Wikimedia Commons https://commons.wikimedia.org/wiki/File:Yoruba_Shango.jpg

Chango is associated with the colors white and red and the number six. He is linked to the Catholic Saint Barbara. He and Saint Barbara are both celebrated on December 4th. Chango's favorite offerings include okra, red palm oil, and bananas. He is depicted wearing a red shirt and red satin pants.

According to Yoruba legends, one day, Chango was so angry that he accidentally used his power over thunder and burned some of his wives and children. Heartbroken and regretful, Chango couldn't take the pain anymore and hung himself. His enemies took advantage of his death and wreaked havoc over his kingdom. However, his enemies were struck by lightning, which is how Chango became the lightning god.

Yemaya

Yemaya is the Orisha of seas and lakes. She is a female Orisha and is considered the mother of many Orishas. Like any mother, Yemaya is nurturing and maternal but can also be ruthless. She can inflict severe punishments when angered, yet she is quick to forgive. She is a fierce, brave, and intelligent warrior. Yemaya is the protector of fishermen, women, and children.

She is associated with the colors blue and white and the number seven, and she is also associated with peacocks, ducks, stars, and the full moon. She is celebrated on September 7th. She is depicted as a mermaid wearing a blue dress that symbolizes ocean waves. She is linked to the Catholic Virgin Mary. Her favorite offerings include anything from the ocean, like fish, seahorses, or seashells.

One day, Olokun, the Orisha of the bottom of the ocean, was angry at mankind because he felt he wasn't getting the respect and appreciation he deserved. He decided to end the human race by sending high and deadly waves to the land. Yemaya was concerned for humanity, so she interfered and calmed Olokun down. If it hadn't been for Yemaya, mankind would have perished.

Oshun

Oshun is the Orisha of fertility, love, and marriage. She is associated with fresh water and feminine beauty. Olodumare created her after he created the universe. As he was observing the world, he realized it was incomplete. Mankind would need something to live for and to bring them together. The world needed love, so he created Oshun and made her the Orisha of love. He sent her to Earth to spread love and all the other positive qualities associated with it. She is the most beautiful, sensual, and seductive of all Orishas.

Oshun is refreshing, vibrant, and full of life. She and Elgeua have a very close friendship. She is also the wife that Chango loves the most. Young, beautiful, and powerful, Oshun seems like she has it all. However, on the inside, she was miserable. Angering Oshun is a terrible idea because she is a very vindictive Orisha. She is depicted wearing a yellow dress.

The best offerings to give Oshun are jewelry, perfumes, mirrors, silk, fans, honey, shrimp, yellow rice, spinach, oranges, and sunflowers. She is associated with the number five and the colors yellow and gold and is celebrated on September 8th. She is linked to the Catholic Lady of Mercy. People invoke her when they require protection against certain diseases or suffer from fertility issues.

During one of the Orisha's rebellions against Olodumare, they decided to stop following his orders. They believed they knew enough about the world and mankind and didn't require Olodumare's advice. When Elegua found out about the rebellion, he told Olodumare, who punished them by stopping the rain, thus causing drought. The world was dying, and the Orishas regretted their actions and begged Olodumare for forgiveness. However, their voices and cries didn't reach him. Oshun transformed into a peacock and flew to Olodumare to inform him of the Orishas' repentance. However, she flew too close to the sun and damaged her wings, but she still managed to reach her destination and deliver the message. Olodumare admired Oshun's courage, brought back the rain, and healed her.

Orunmila

Ornumilla or Orula is the orisha of knowledge, destiny, and wisdom. He witnessed the creation of souls. Therefore, he knows the fate of every soul ever created. This makes Ornumilla one of the most powerful Orishas since he knows everyone's destiny and when they will die. His job is to ensure every person follows their destiny. He knows what makes each person happy, sad, and successful. Ornumilla is known for his healing abilities and protection from mental issues.

He is associated with the colors yellow and green. He is linked to the Catholic St. Francis of Assisi and is celebrated on October 4th. He is the only Orisha not to manifest through possession but through divination. His favorite offering includes red palm oil, candles, honey, and coconuts.

He is the brother of Elegua, Ogun, and Chango and the son of Obatala. When Obatala discovered that Ogun had feelings for his mother, Obatala sent all his elderly children away and killed the young ones. When Ornumilla was born, Obatala was going to have him killed the moment he discovered he was a boy. However, Elegua rushed to save his baby brother and took him away. He buried him under a tree and brought him food every day. One day, Obatala was infected with a very serious and incurable disease. Elegua asked Shango to come and help heal their father, and he obliged, and Obatala recovered. Elegua asked for a favor in return which was to pardon Ornumilla. Obata granted Elegua his request. Chango was happy that his brother was pardoned and celebrated the occasion by cutting down the tree under which he was buried, creating a wooden divination tray for his brother, and sharing the secrets of divination with him. This story reflects the close bond between the three brothers.

Orishas manifest themselves to human beings through possession or mounting. They possess a willing priest/priestess and interact with human beings during a ritual. All the Orishas mentioned here play a role in ancestors' veneration/reverence, which you will learn more about in the coming chapters.

Chapter 3: How to Venerate the Orishas

Now that you understand the Orishas, their personalities, and their significance in the Yoruba religion, you are ready to discover how to honor and get close to them. The relationship between these entities and human beings is a significant part of the Yoruba religion. The Yoruba people believe that the Orishas can provide enlightenment, protection, and support. However, certain rituals are required to appease the Orishas and help you reach out to them. One must honor the Orishas and acknowledge their existence to maintain a beneficial relationship with them.

This chapter covers the various methods to venerate Orishas and how to know if one is calling on you.

Altars

Altars can help you honor the Orishas and strengthen your relationship with them. The basic concept and layout of an altar are similar for all Orishas. You will need an empty space with a clear surface far away from any distractions. An altar is a sacred place designed for worship, so place it in a quiet spot so you can focus and feel the connection with the spirits. However, since each Orisha has a different personality, domain, colors, animals, etc., different items are required for each Orisha altar. One object can be offensive to an Orisha while sacred to another. Creating a proper altar is necessary to connect with your Orisha.

Altars are created to honor the Orishas.
Infrogmation of New Orleans, CC BY 3.0 <https://creativecommons.org/licenses/by/3.0>, via Wikimedia Commons
https://commons.wikimedia.org/wiki/File:BRStateMuseumJuly08VoodooAltar.jpg

How to Set Up an Orisha Altar

- Set an intention before you build your altar. Altars have various purposes like magic, worship, meditation, etc. Your intentions to build this altar to honor a specific Orisha must be clear. Set intentions by writing them down, saying them out loud, or whispering them under your breath. For instance, you can say, "I am building this altar to venerate Shango."

- Choose a proper place for your altar. Orishas don't require anything luxurious or over the top, so opt for a quiet, simple, and comfortable space. It can be a small space in your room or a shelf. Make sure it's in a private place, so no one disturbs your altar or interferes with your time of worship.
- Clean the space before you add any items.
- Choose the appropriate items for the Orisha you are honoring, like symbols or statues, to place on your altar. You can add as many items as you want. However, if this is your first altar, keep it small and simple at first to make it easy to maintain. After you get used to it, you can expand it and add more items. Make sure to first clean any items that you add.
- Now that you know which items to use, take each object and place it in an organized way. Some people prefer to put their items on a piece of cloth to protect the altar from damage. You can set the biggest object in the center and place the smaller ones around it.
- Setting up your altar isn't enough. You should honor your Orisha regularly and never abandon your altar.
- Keep your altar maintained. Ignoring it or leaving it covered in dust is a sign of disrespect.

Here are some of the main items required for the most prominent Orishas in the Yoruba religion.

Elegua

- Place a black or red piece of cloth on your altar since they are Elegua's colors
- Marbles, bells, and toys are perfect for the Orisha of trickery
- An incense powder for protection
- Sketches or portraits of crossroads
- Candles (red or black)
- An illustration of Elegua in any of his forms, whether as an old man or a child
- One or more statues of Elegua

Shango

- Candles
- Axes (single or double-headed)

- An illustration or statute of Shango
- One or more swords
- A bata drum
- A wooden bowl with a lid
- A pedestal to place the wooden bowl
- A set of wooden tools
- Thunderstones

Obatala
- An illustration, statue, or doll of Obatala
- A white piece of cloth to place under the items
- A sopera (soup bowl)
- A candle
- A metal crown
- A bell with a dove hand

Ogun
- A portrait or statue of Ogun
- An iron rooster
- Iron nails
- A cauldron
- A candle
- An iron object like an anvil

Yemaya
- An incense powder made to help with family issues
- Shells, preferably cowrie shells
- A candle to help with fertility or protection
- Fans
- A sopera (soup bowl)
- Objects made of silver
- An illustration or statue of Yemaya
- Pearls
- Silver or blue crown
- A piece of blue cloth

- Illustrations of the ocean or sea creatures like fish, dolphins, or mermaids

Oya
- An illustration or a statue of Oya
- Eggplants, preferably fresh
- A rainbow-colored candle
- Any piece of jewelry made of copper
- A sopera (soup bowl)
- Shea butter
- Red gourd
- A picture of a lightning bolt

Oshosi (Orisha of Hunting and Animals)
- An illustration or a statue of Oshosi
- A candle to provide strength and guidance
- Arrows and a bow
- Images of animals

Orunmila
- An illustration or a statue of Orunmila
- A candle to assist with spiritual growth
- A green or yellow piece of cloth to spread over your altar
- A bowl with a lid made of cedar wood
- Flowers, preferably yellow

Oshun
- Perfume
- An illustration or statue of Oshun
- Sunflowers
- A bowl
- White candle

Offerings (Ebbo)

Another method to venerate Orishas is making offerings. Each Orisha requires specific offerings. They can be food, drinks, or objects related to the Orisha and what it represents. In the Yoruba religion, there is a type of offering called "Ebbo." When worshipers present offerings, they say, "I am doing Ebbo." Worshipers "do Ebbo" to thank the Orishas for their help and guidance or to ask for a favor. However, Ebbo isn't a regular offering. It is a type of sacrifice that one makes to appease the Orishas. It is one of the oldest concepts in the Yoruba religion. Ebo is a must for every Orisha worshiper.

The word sacrifice can have a negative connotation as people often associate it with giving up something you love echoing when Abraham was asked to sacrifice his son in the Abrahamic religions or Jesus's sacrifice in Christianity. Sacrifice has always been associated with pain and suffering. In the Yoruba religion, this concept isn't always negative. The Yoruba people believe that to preserve life and all its beings. One must do favors to powerful entities who have the power to either destroy or protect life. Therefore, Ebbo guarantees the continuation of life and blessings in the physical world when you appease the Orishas and maintain a relationship with them. Another positive side of Ebbo is that it shows your gratitude for all the blessings you receive from the Orishas.

People often ask each other for favors or show gratitude by giving gifts. You choose gifts that you know the other person will appreciate. The same applies to giving offerings to the Orishas. Making an offering that appeals to your Orisha shows respect for them. However, doing Ebbo when you only need a favor shows a lack of gratitude. Therefore, one must keep giving offerings regularly to appease the Orishas. You should never make the Orishas feel ignored or abandoned, and Ebos show your acknowledgment and appreciation of these entities.

Ebbo is originally the child of Orunmila, the Orisha of knowledge and wisdom. He created Ebbo for the sake of mankind to provide them with an opportunity to make their lives easier. People don't just use Ebbo to ask for favors but to help prevent pain and suffering. When one makes an offering, Ebbo invites the messenger of the gods, Eshu, to descend and collect them as an initial payment for the Orishas. Eshu takes the offerings to the Orishas, so they would accept them and alleviate pain and suffering or grant a favor. People also do Ebbo to get blessings, love, and money or bring harm to their enemies. Both human beings and Orishas need Ebbos. Ebbos make people's life easier as it provides them with blessings and protections while the Orishas need them to survive. Offerings strengthen your relationships with the Orishas.

Ebbo exists in other cultures, such as Brazil, where it is more than just a practice but a tradition integrated into their beliefs.

Types of Offerings

Many people assume that offerings must involve animal sacrifice. However, other types are more appropriate for the modern age. For instance, if they grant you your favor, you can promise the Orishas to perform a certain action or abstain from a type of food or activities like drinking or sex. Plants and fruits also make great offerings to appease the Orishas. Any fire-related items like candles will help you get close to these spirits. They enjoy activities like drumming, dancing, and singing as well. You can also place an item on a shrine or altar as a gift for them. Make sure to choose offerings related to the chosen Orishas.

Talking and Praying

You can invoke Orishas by talking to them or praying for them. On the surface, talking to an Orisha sounds easier than abstaining from your favorite food or building an altar and making an offering. However, talking and praying can be a little complicated since they require you to connect with your spiritual side, which isn't always easy. Praying for any Orisha requires patience. Don't expect them to respond right away; be persistent and patient. You should also be respectful, clean, and wear nice clothes. Before asking them for a favor, show your appreciation and gratitude to Orisha first.

How to Talk to an Orisha

- Sit in a quiet place with no distractions
- Make sure to choose a clean spot in your home or outdoors
- If you want to be outdoors, choose a place in nature related to the Orisha. For instance, talk to Obatala near the mountains and Oshun near a river
- Calm your mind and quiet your thoughts
- Light a candle and pray. You can pray out loud, whisper your prayers, or pray in your mind.
- Tell the Orisha the problem that you want to solve or ask for a favor
- End by expressing gratitude to the Orisha

Make talking to your Orisha part of your daily routine. Even if you don't have a problem or a favor to ask for, talk about your day and open up to them in the same way you would to a friend.

Meditation is an effective method to communicate spiritually, so you can use it to reach out to the Orishas. Sit in a quiet spot and in a relaxing position, close your eyes, breathe slowly and deeply, free and relax your mind, and focus on the Orisha with whom you want to communicate.

Ceremonies

Throw a ceremony for the Orisha you want to venerate and invite them to attend. Orishas usually mount (possess) the priest or priestess leading the ceremony to communicate with the attendees. Possession here isn't harmful or forceful to the host as they are willing participants, and the attendees all have questions or favors to ask the Orisha.

Learn about Orishas

Nothing will show an Orisha that you highly revere them and are willing to communicate with them more than taking the time to learn about them. The more you learn about Orishas, the closer you will feel to them.

Finding Your Orisha

Now that you know how to honor and revere Orishas, you probably wonder which one is right for you to worship. According to the Yoruba religion, each person has an Orisha mother and father. Your Orisha parents protect you and guide you all your life. They are responsible for helping you reach your destiny. Finding your Orisha parents is key to choosing the right one to worship. It is a misconception that one shares the same Orishas with one's human parents. You can have a different Orisha mother and father than your parents, and they can come from different tribes. Ask your elders, like grandparents, to help you discover your Orisha parents. There are no better teachers than your elders, who have the knowledge and experience to guide you.

Your Orisha parents can also appear to you in your dreams. Pay attention to dreams, especially if you have been trying to get answers about Orishas, as this can be the only way they can reveal themselves to you. Talk or pray to the spirits and ask them to help you find your Orisha parents.

A Yoruba priest or priestess can also give you the answers you seek. They know the proper rituals to help you find your Orisha. The priest will ask you a few questions, including your date of birth, and after collecting the necessary information, they will provide you with an answer. After discovering your Orisha parents, learn everything about them, like their powers, colors, animals, stories, etc. Learning about the Orishas will help you establish a bond with them. Your Orisha parents will play a significant role in your life by providing guidance and protection and helping you reach your destiny.

When an Orisha Is Calling

Just as people invoke Orishas to communicate with them, Orishas can also reach out to you. Sometimes, you don't have to look for answers elsewhere. You can find out if an Orisha is calling on you deep inside. For instance, if you believe that a specific Orisha is calling on you, there is a high chance they are. You can also find Orisha's colors, symbols, illustrations, or animals in various unexpected places. An Orisha can also come to you in a dream when it wants to connect with you. A friend can mention a specific Orisha to you, or you randomly find information about them online. Respond to an Orisha's call by building an altar, praying for it, or giving offerings.

When Orishas reply to your call, they can also come to you in your dreams, or you can feel their blessings in different aspects of your life. If you invoke an Orisha to help you with a difficult situation, solutions will start appearing for your problem. You will know when an Orisha answers, and make sure to show your gratitude when they come through for you,

Although the Orishas are invisible spirits, treat them like they are physical beings. This can be easier when you learn about them and their personalities. Talk to them as if they are a close friend or family member. Learning about your Orisha parents is necessary as it will guide you toward the Orisha who will be by your side for the rest of your life. Never take the Orishas for granted or disrespect them. Remember that they are powerful entities, and you should never make them angry. Focus on appeasing them by providing offerings, Ebbo, prayer, ceremonies, and learning about them. Let your heart guide you on whether an Orisha is calling on you. Remain focused, and don't mistake a sign for coincidence. When it comes to Orishas, nothing is random, so keep your eye and heart open and be prepared to receive.

Chapter 4: Egbe, Your Spirit Companions

In reading this chapter, you'll learn everything that you need to know about Egbe Orun. You'll understand who this group is and how they can help you throughout your journey on Earth. You'll learn the characteristics that define each type of Egbe Orun and how you can please them. You'll also get to understand the influence and power that Egbe Orun can have over your life.

Your spirit companion is also known as your Egbe.
https://www.pexels.com/photo/silhouette-of-man-sitting-on-grass-field-at-daytime-775417/

What Are Egbe Orun?

Egbe can be roughly translated into "heavenly, spirit, or astral mates" or "comrades of heaven." This spiritual group of heavenly human companions is called Egbe Orun, Egberun, and Alaragbo.

According to Yoruba belief, each person has a special peer in the spiritual realm. This belief system suggests that we all come from heaven or Orun and that our physical bodies are mere personifications of our souls. The Orisa Obatala was the one who used clay to mold our heads, while Olodumare gave us life and created our souls. The soul flows freely in the spiritual realm before its physical body is created. It searches for its parents, the ones who eventually turn it into a human.

After Olodumare breathes life into the head, two souls emerge from it. One is transported to the physical realm when the physical form of the soul is created, and the other remains. The remaining spirit is then considered the human's heavenly comrade and is thought identical to its human counterpart. However, the spirit is believed to be much more powerful than its physical form.

In the spiritual realm, the soul stays connected to our physical selves. It is the version of ourselves that appears in our dreams, whether we dream of ourselves or someone else. Both versions are active in the spirit world and pass the time together until the corresponding human is born in the human realm.

The reason one version of the soul stays behind is to keep us connected to the spiritual realm and serve as a cord to guide us back if we ever wish to visit. They also watch over us, ensuring everything goes smoothly in the physical realm. Egbe Orun is meant to remind us of our spiritual nature, particularly when we get too caught up in Earthly matters. They help to remind us that our existence in the human plane is only temporary. The unique bond each person has with their spiritual counterpart is their only connection with higher levels of consciousness. We all have different bonds with our astral bodies. Some people have strong connections that allow Egbe to influence the person's experiences. For instance, someone with a very strong bond with their heavenly comrade may have items that disappear from their environment, be easily able to interact with the spiritual realm, or be particularly sensitive toward certain astral phenomena.

Practitioners aim to appease the Egbe Orun to thank them for their support, guidance, and protection, which can stimulate spiritual awakenings and personal development. If you know how to work with the Egbe Orun, you can have more fulfilling life experiences.

The Egbe Orun make their presence known by appearing in a person's dreams and divination practices, causing items to disappear, or delivering specific messages. In some cases, Egbe Orun may incarnate in masquerades – ceremonies conducted for ancestral protection.

Types of Egbe Orun

The Egbe live in societies like we do, and they organize themselves based on their interests, convictions, and commonalities. Traditionally, practitioners started associating the Egbe with certain astral communities by observing and taking note of the behavioral patterns that their physical counterparts displayed as children. Some Yorubas still practice these rites and confirm their revelations via oracular practices and tools and using professional practitioners. This means that the types of Egbe that we know of correspond with traits and characteristics that were traditionally identifiable. It should be noted that there are countless fraternities, or societies, into which Egbe Orun organize themselves. The following are some of the thought classifications:

Ìyálóde

Ìyálóde is characterized by the quality of leadership and, as such, is thought to be the society of leaders of Egbe in the physical realm. Since this group is named after Ìyálóde, the renowned female chieftain, many people mistakenly believe that only women can belong to it. However, this society accepts men and women, referred to as Ìyálóde.

According to IFA, the leadership power of this society is limited to only the terrestrial realm. One verse explains that Janjasa is the head of Egbe, who resides in heaven, while the head of Egbe, who resides on Earth, is Ìyálóde.

You could have come across numerous members of the Egbe Ìyálóde in your lifetime. They are believed to be well-dressed, neat, organized, inspirational, and motivational. They are often the center of attention in social gatherings. They enjoy partying and love to show off. But there is another side; Ìyálóde are charitable and mentally detached. They are very attentive to their children and do everything in their power to ensure they are protected, taken care of, safe, and successful.

While they are quite generous, no one should attempt to offend an Ìyálóde. They are capable of sending their offender all types of evil.

Eléékò

This group is rather difficult to understand, as its members are characterized by their personalities. So, depending on the circumstances, Egbo Eléékò can be patient or impatient, merciless or merciful. Their moods swing easily depending on their momentous desires.

The behavioral patterns of the Eléékò are usually comparable to those of Esu, who take on different forms. Many practitioners suggest that the Eléékò are the Esu of the Egbe. Like Esu, who is known as the trickster deity, Eléékò is believed to be very mischievous. They're both intelligent, creative, and crafty, as well.

Members of the Eléékò can also be disloyal and very sneaky. They steal from those who are more fortunate to give to the poor. If you notice valuable belongings and money disappearing, it is often a sign that the Eléékò is stealing from you. When a person wrongs or disrespects Egbe, Eléékò may also steal from them as a form of punishment. Often, this group haunts or controls disrespectful individuals.

Traditionally, children who steal, talk a lot, are sly or stubborn, or are highly ambitious, are considered members of the Eléékò. A child will continue having no regard for others and grow up to do only what they want if the appropriate rites and rituals aren't performed.

Asípa

Members of the Egbe, Asípa are characterized by their inability to express themselves clearly. They are vocal and mysterious. Asípa are difficult to understand, have a sense of grandiosity, and are not loyal.

Forgetfulness is also a common influence of Asípa. They also induce a sense of disorientation in people, which is why many associate the Asípa with the Idaako deity Oyo. If you often feel like you've previously met people you're meeting for the first time, you could well be a member of this Egbe society.

Members of this Egbe may experience temporary and even extended memory loss. They may sometimes have this effect on others too. This happens particularly to individuals who reject their faith or need to be pulled into piety. Forgetfulness can also affect people who are meant to join Egbe but are very stubborn. Many practitioners say that Asípa can trade the destiny of a person for another.

Jagun - Jagunjagun

Due to its relentlessness and persistence, this fraternity earns itself the name *warrior*, or Jagun. Members of this group are known for their benevolence and adaptability. While they are highly accommodating, they know better than to make every moment count. They don't let their leisure time go to waste.

A child can be identified as Jagun immediately after birth. However, they may not show all the qualities and power of the Jagun until they've grown up a little. Children who belong to this society are unlike others. They don't get the urge to steal things or tell lies. They are meticulous, uptight, and strict, which isn't typical juvenile behavior. Older Jagun members can be rather promiscuous.

Baálè

Baálè is often regarded as a blend between the Ìyálóde and Eléékò as it is characterized by their leadership skills and tendency to exhibit various personalities. You can set a Baálè apart by their countless talents. Even though they can get quite domineering, members of this Egbe are very honest and have fair judgment.

The term Baálè could be translated as "village's ruler." While this isn't necessarily the role of Baálè members, there are many qualities and virtues in common between this Egbe group and the typical village ruler. Like all the other groups, Baálè has its downsides. The punishment of deviant children is often incredibly harsh.

Olúgbógeró

Many people associate the Olúgbógeró with free-flowing waters or rivers. Traditionally, Abiku or stillborn children are thought to be related to the Olúgbógeró. This is another Egbe group that has a variety of personalities. For some reason, regardless of how well-dressed they are, it is found that these individuals have a piece of cloth wrapped around some part of their bodies. They may even keep the piece of cloth inside their purses.

Adétayànyá

Adétayànyá children are mysteriously attracted to refuse dumps. They don't care how dark, secluded, or far away a dump is; they will manage to find it and stay there. These children seldom pass by dumpsites without greeting them. Sharing similarities with Egungun's brother Oro, Adétayànyá is believed to be related to him.

Móohún

Children who belong to this Egbe society are often very hesitant to do chores or run errands. They come across as lazy and can be very reluctant when making decisions. Members of Móohún are quite stubborn and forgetful, which is why they rarely get any of their tasks done. That said, Móohún members are pristine and well-put-together. They don't mind spending the extra time and effort to look good.

Appeasing Egbe Orun

Egbe Orun can be honored and pleased through various offerings, prayers, and rites. They also accept sacrifices and specific forms of personal discipline. They appreciate those who spend time and effort building connections with them and maintaining, treasuring, and caring for these relationships. Suppose you wish to work with Egbe Orun. In that case, you must show that you cherish the relationship and continuously reinforce the bond you've managed to build with them. Egbe communications take different forms. However, the most popular ones happen via ocular predictions. You can also ask them to send you direct messages through your dreams.

You can keep an Egbe shrine either inside or outside your home. You must be mindful of where you decide to build it because they are believed to reside or show up in specific areas when summoned. These places include areas where bonfires are held, river banks, and certain trees. Egbe Orun prefers offerings like cheese, roasted or cooked groundnuts, a paste of yam, maize, or steamed white beans, fruit assortments, or yam (either pounded or in the form of porridge). You can also express your appreciation by pounding sweet maize and mixing it with sugar and palm oil or pounding beans and frying them in palm oil. They also accept offerings of plantain, sugarcane, honey, shea butter, coconut, palm oil, and kola nuts. Make sure to serve food alongside fresh water or alcohol. You may offer animal sacrifices on certain occasions. You can include red and white decorations on your shrine, as these colors are associated with Egbe Orun.

Influence of Egbe Orun

Each class or type of Egbe comes with its own prohibitions and taboos. Like modern-day human societies, these differ from one family, region, society, and community to the other. Unfortunately, Egbe is not always a bearer of good news or protection and may sometimes manifest as imbalances in one's life. For instance, during pregnancy or birth rites, an oracle may reveal that the child is a member of the Olúgbógeró, meaning they are an Abiku or stillborn child. In other words, they were "born to die." These messages suggest that the spiritual counterpart of the human has a strong influence on them, which will result in premature death, whether through a miscarriage or during infancy. The concept of Abiku in Yoruba refers to the disruption of the natural cycle of life when a person, regardless of age, dies before their parents.

Egbe can also induce nightmares in the targeted person's sleep to call their attention. If someone thinks that an Egbe influences their nightmares, they can confirm their suspicion by consulting oracles. It is generally believed that dreams that include sexual intercourse are also related to the influence of the Egbe.

Some people make agreements with their astral mates before they make their way to the physical realm. Some of them will even find spiritual spouses in the astral realm. Those individuals are bound to experience numerous challenges regarding love and marriage on Earth. Egbe influence may go as far as causing the death of the person's partner. This is why practitioners conduct oracle consultations to confirm whether the bride and groom have made any agreements in the spiritual realm before a traditional marriage is conducted. In the case of a covenant, spiritual rites must be conducted to ensure a healthy and successful marriage.

Egbe can sometimes be notorious, so individuals must ensure that their spiritual mate has no evil, harmful, or toxic tendencies. Wicked Egbe won't work in the interest of their physical counterpart, and if that's the case, this bond must be cut so that the person can experience healthy growth and development in life.

Egbe's influence can sometimes be spotted by observing the behavioral patterns of children. These behaviors typically include stubbornness and insolence. Egbe influence may also cause the child to run away or feel the overpowering urge to steal items that they don't need.

Egbe Orun may give rise to problems and conflict between individuals by causing them to be suspicious of each other. They will often steal items and cause them to disappear, so the intended humans clash with one another.

A person's astral counterpart can intentionally trouble them by calling out their name at night. If you ignore Egbe, they'll likely block all abundance and blessings from entering your life. You'll encounter various obstacles, problems, challenges, setbacks, and even disasters in your life. Someone who keeps turning a blind eye to Egbe will always be haunted by misfortune. When people suspect that Egbe influences their lack of fortune, they should seek oracular confirmation. If their suspicions prove to be founded, they should appease their astral mate to restore balance to their life. There are specific rituals, known as Igba Didi, which can help remedy a broken or blocked connection with Egbe Orun. In severe cases, however, rites and sacrifices won't be enough. A person must conduct Irari Egbe, an initiatory rite, to form a covenant with their astral counterpart. You should never attempt to conduct these rituals and rites on your own without the guidance of an expert.

Now that you have read this chapter, you know everything there is to know about Egbe Orun. You are ready to start working on building a better connection with your heavenly comrade so you can obtain their guidance, protection, and support. Read on to learn about ancestral veneration and why it's an important concept in Yoruba.

Chapter 5: The Importance of Ancestors in Yoruba

The Yoruba religion and its attendant mythologies are one of the spiritual pillars of West Africa, particularly Nigeria, and it is difficult to understand that part of the world without fully appreciating the religion's intricacies. The fact that Yoruba is the origin of most New World religions also means that it informs many practices we recognize in the West today, and getting to grips with Yoruba is one way we can avoid simplistic and ill-informed approaches to newer forms of spirituality. As previously covered in the book, the Yorubas possess several deities they believe serve as intermediaries between the world, themselves, and the supreme god. And the legacies of these deities are deeply tied to the ancestors.

Honoring the ancestors is extremely important in Yoruba.
https://www.pexels.com/photo/people-celebrating-at-a-traditional-festival-5377719/

Ancestral veneration is extremely important in Yoruba for reasons which will be laid out in simple terms in this chapter. In essence, the ancestors symbolize community, development, peace, and harmony. They are invoked as a way to understand our life path, which is essential to achieving a high level of spirituality in Yoruba. Given the divergent paths of the African Diaspora, feeling connected to a shared sense of history is more important than ever.

The Concept of Egungun

The term used for ancestors in Yorubian is Egungun, a core concept to master while becoming familiar with the religion. There has been a long-standing, incorrect assumption about Egungun, usually connected to a sense of fear. For some, seeing an Egungun is akin to seeing a ghost, whose discontent with the present should make you run for the hills. There is even a common proverb that when you see an Egungun, you should either run as fast as you can or stay in place till the spirit passes. What gave birth to this misconception? For one, it is an extension of how the concept of Egungun has evolved in Yoruba culture over time. They are a part of ancestral veneration, contributing to the sense that something has gone amiss. But what if there's a cryptic message we are missing and unable to receive?

The role of Egungun in Yoruba culture also moves beyond the realm of the spiritual. Their role combines ancestral protection and theatrical performances, which usually take place in the streets. Historically, they were summoned for military-oriented exercises in pre-colonial times. Their presence was used to remind people of important familial and social bonds to preserve cultural heritage, all through a colorful mix of costume and ritual.

What makes an ancestor someone we look up to, revere and respect, sometimes even fear? It boils down to them living a long and moral life, proving themselves to be positive examples to their communities. The Egungun are the spirits of these departed ancestors, who could be related to us either by blood or religious lineage. Honoring them through rituals or metaphysical terms is possible, whether through prayer or colorful dress.

Put another way, the basis of Yoruba is the idea of paying tribute to those who have transitioned into the ancestor realm and officially entered ancestor hood. In Yoruba, it is believed that when an individual is born, their soul takes on a form within a physical body. Furthermore, that very soul is thought to be connected to the family line, taking form in the body of someone they were connected to in a previous existence. This is one of the hardest aspects of Yoruba to disentangle since it's a broad idea, but when it comes down to it, what it means is that all family lines return to the same people, given that familiar energies tend to stay together. So, while the soul spends time in this earthly realm, it gathers the necessary wisdom through life so that when the individual dies, the spirit then reincarnates again and joins a constellation of energies, waiting again for reincarnation.

Healing and Ancestry

The ancestors are important because they anchor us on this earth and keep us grounded as we try to carve our own paths in life. Paying homage to the ancestors helps give you the strength necessary to face life's problems. Since they are forging new connections in the present without denying the pain of what occurred in the past, they also help heal the spirits of the ancestors.

In the Yoruba religion, it is felt that ancestors are at a disadvantage of sorts since they have the wisdom to make things better yet no longer possess the body they need to make the positive change they would like. The flip side is that we have a body but don't yet have the hard-earned wisdom that the ancestors have. Therefore, in terms of spiritual practice, Yoruba underscores the importance of having the spirit work through us since the body is the perfect vehicle to manifest positive things. When you feel disconnected or lost, these feelings can be repaired by reviving your connections with your ancestors.

The ancestors, however, are not a nebulous indistinct entity. They have different categories, each with distinct qualities and purposes. The next section of this chapter will illuminate these categories. Understanding them better will underscore how we can pay tribute to them and incorporate this new understanding into our daily lives.

Spiritual Forces

In Yoruba, there are three ancestor groups: Sango, Orisa-Oko, and Aykela. The first, Sango, has roots in history since he is considered to be the royal ancestor of the Yoruba. He can manifest in different ways, from aira, agodo, lubé, and so on, which are a constellation of different spiritual entities that fall under one ancestor.

Sango's main symbol is the double ax, and he is revered as the most powerful ruler the lands of Yoruba have ever produced.

The spiritual entities that fall under Sango:

- Aira represents the spirits of young children who live short lives between reincarnations. They are also known as the Spirits of the North.
- Agodo represents the destructive spirits that bring about death and poverty, and they are associated with other spirits, such as Esu, who is the Spirit of the Divine Messenger, and are a crucial aspect in balancing the dynamism in nature.
- Egun is the spirit of the deceased, who speaks at their own funeral through a medium.
- Agbasa represents the Spirits of sacred stones.
- Lubé is the spirit of the dead.

Defining characteristics of Sango include the colors red and white, and he is represented by thunder, lightning, and fire. Furthermore, common instruments are not just the double ax but also the bangles, brass crowns, thunder stones, and any object struck by lightning. When it comes to popular rituals paying tribute to Sango, special food, costumes, jewelry, and dances particular to him are used to respect his spirit. Animals sacrificed and cooked to honor Sango can include a male goat, duck, or freshwater turtle. A food usually served in these ceremonies is amalá, a fragrant stew of okra with shrimp, often cooked in palm oil.

In terms of clothing, a red cloth with printed white squares is often donned to signify Sango's spirit, and necklaces made with red and white beads are also worn. The archetypes of power and dominance most represent Sango, and tribal dances such as alujá, the roda de Xangô are performed to discuss his achievements in battle and governance.

Next up is Orisa-Oko, the ancestor representing farming, fertility, and the cycle of life and death in nature. Paying tribute to this ancestor is believed to impart a sense of health, stability, and vitality. The entire myth of Orisa-Oko is centered on the cycles of nature, and according to mythology, he is married to the Orisha of the sea, Yemanja. Their union symbolizes balance and a sense of unity between the elements. In the Yoruba religion, he is seen as a fighter against sorcery and is associated with the annual new harvest of the white African yam. Since he is so tied to agricultural activities, bees are usually considered messengers of Orisa-Oko.

In terms of physical manifestations of his character, he is also identified with the colors red and white, although pink and light blue can also make an appearance. Compared to Sango, he is not often revered in the same way in public ceremonies, but if his spirit is called for, a wooden staff and a flute made of bones is meant to denote the physical manifestation. Followers of the religion who wish to connect with him or ask for assistance will often give him offerings of root vegetables and hearty dishes made of small animals like quail or rabbit.

Aykela, also known as Bablu-Aye or Sopona, is one of the spirits manifested as the Earth and is strongly associated with infectious diseases and healing. Aykela is thought to help promote cures for various illnesses and is close to Iku, a spiritual force thought to be responsible for taking life. Followers of Yoruba will pay tribute to him in an attempt to promote healing for those suffering from physical ailments or who may be close to death.

It is thought that this spiritual ancestor possesses dominion over the Earth and the disease of smallpox. Because Aykela is identified with death, followers of Yoruba know that he demands respect, and even gratitude, when he claims another life, and they pay tribute to him accordingly.

Regarding spiritual manifestations, Aykela is linked to the earth and, given its historical roots, is considered the god of smallpox. Aykela is thought to punish people with illness and reward them with health, so followers looking to recover and feel better make ritualistic prayers to him, imploring for their safety and that of their loved ones. He is also connected with the twin concepts of secrecy and revelation, silence and speech, darkness and light, exile and movement, and death and resurrection. This is not entirely surprising given that healthy bodily functions, negative manifestations, illness, and so on are tied to the understanding of Aykela and how the spiritual ancestor moved throughout the world.

Outside of public celebrations of the ancestors, devoted followers of Yoruba can pay tribute to the deities in different ways. A simple shrine of two main components is often used. Firstly, a bundle of nine sticks tied together by a red cloth. The branches must be taken from an appropriate tree identifiable by priests fluent in the rites of Egungun. The next component is often referred to as the "opa egun," a walking stick or a regular branch that is thick and long and used during an invocation. One person taps the floor with the staff as another works to invoke the ancestors. The slow tapping is used to get the ancestor's attention so that they can hear the prayers of the descendants clearly. The tapping of the floor is crucial to the rite because you are clearly signaling to the ground where the ancestors are buried. After this, a basic offering is made to the ancestors, such as water, wine, a bit of palm oil, smoked fish, or other smaller food offerings.

If you're interested in becoming even closer to your ancestors in Yoruba, this is just one way of doing so. Other key rituals can be employed to help you connect to your ancient ancestors with relative ease.

Identifying Your Ancestors

Most people come from mixed ancestry, and our lineage represents a complex range of religious and spiritual influences. You might want to represent some of these influences in various ways. For example, it's pretty standard to bring copies of the Bible, Qu'ran, or I Ching when building a shrine at home to signal your attempt to get to know the ancestors. A big part of following Yoruba is acknowledging the universal nature of the spiritual principles as expressed through the ancestors since they can manifest in various forms throughout history, utilizing various cultural activities.

To construct the shrine, remember to keep things simple. Place a table in the space in which you intend to perform regular rituals. Then, cover it with a white cloth, placing a glass of water and a candle on it. These represent the basic elements needed to create human beings: earth, air, fire, and water. On the wall above the shrine, hang pictures of your relatives, as they are one vital way of connecting with your spiritual ancestors.

Next, stand in front of the shrine, light the candle, and state aloud your commitment to regular use of the shine for meditation and prayer. This way, you are making your intentions and desire for connection loud and clear. Certainly, the extent to which you intend to use the shrine is not as important as committing to doing your best and feeling open to expanding your spiritual practice. So long as the ancestors know that you are attempting to establish a connection with them, the lines of communication won't be blocked. In fact, the combination of white cloth and the elements you placed upon it are thought to draw spirits to the shrine. Just don't make the mistake of turning to your shrine only in moments of crisis since that will dilute the powers quite a bit. If you keep the lines of communication open regularly, the spiritual connection between you and the ancestors will remain dynamic and accessible.

The next step you can take in invoking the ancestors is to make a food offering to your shrine. This is thought to be a show of reciprocity since you are actively engaged with the spirits, and they are responding to your request for connection in their own way. Therefore, the act of offering food is not at all meant to be literally feeding the spirit. It's a genuine gesture honoring the memory of those who once sat in your company and ate with you.

In some traditions, the food is offered on the floor by the shrine, but it's also common to simply place the plate on the table. For practitioners of Yoruba in the diaspora, the offering is usually placed on a cracked plate, which symbolizes how the body is discarded when the soul is elevated and makes its way to the next realm. In terms of the food itself, small cooked animals or smoked fish can suffice, as explained earlier in this chapter. The food is also typically accompanied by something to drink. The offerings can range from cups of coffee, tea, or alcohol placed next to your plate. If it is an alcoholic drink, it is customary to hold the bottle with your left hand and cover the spout with your thumb, sprinkling a few drops on the floor.

Flowers are another common way of paying tribute to the ancestors at your shrine. Some people can even use cigars since smoke is used as a cleansing method, similar to smudge sticks. The ancestors will make specific requests for all kinds of offerings, and it is expected that you do your best to comply with said requests to refine the quality of communication.

Keeping Traditions Alive

Yoruba has gained more recognition in the West during the past few decades because it provides a vital way for members of the African Diaspora to feel connected to their ancestors and each other. It has also become ever clearer just how widely New Religions have their roots in Yoruba and the religions of West Africa. It is a vital way of understanding our shared past and honoring our ancestors. Paying tribute to them is a special way of giving thanks and feeling grounded in the present. Especially for those who are part of the diaspora, feelings of disconnect and alienation can be hard to avoid. Recounting the stories of ancient spirits and building shrines to communicate with them is an emotional way of remembering one's roots and our shared histories.

Chapter 6: The Odun Egungun

In most cultures, death is seen as a time of transition and rebirth rather than an end. In Nigeria, the Yoruba people have a festival called Odun Egungun, which celebrates the ancestors and honors their continued presence in the lives of their descendants. The Yoruba Egungun, meaning "honor or respect one who is dead," is also used to describe the annual Masquerade festival. Followers dress up in costumes and paint their faces to look like the dead, and ancestors are honored through song, dance, and food. The festival is also a time for families to reconnect with their ancestors and ask for guidance. The Egungun masquerade is a colorful and vibrant tradition that has been passed down for generations. It is a time when the spirits of the dead come back to Earth to celebrate life, death, and the spirit world.

Odun Egungun is a festival that honors the dead.
DEGAN Gabin, CC BY-SA 4.0 <https://creativecommons.org/licenses/by-sa/4.0>, via Wikimedia Commons
https://commons.wikimedia.org/wiki/File:The_resplendent_colors_of_the_Egun-guns.jpg

Origins

During the Egungun masquerade festival, participants dress up in colorful and elaborate costumes to honor their ancestors. The costumes often include large headdresses, beaded necklaces, and billowing skirts. The masquerade is lively, with dancers moving to the rhythms of traditional drums. The Egungun masquerade festival is thought to date back to the 16th century when European explorers first observed it. Since then, it has become an important part of Yoruba culture and is now enjoyed by people of all ages. The festival is held during the dry season, from January to March. Egunguns are also thought to bring good luck and prosperity, so they are often seen as positive symbols of change.

The Egungun are usually spirits of the dead that come back to visit the living. There are different types of Egungun, each with its own unique costume and dance. The masquerades are a big part of Yoruba culture and play an important role in religious ceremonies. The most common type of Egungun is the Ogun, which is a spirit of a warrior who comes back to bring peace and protection. The Ogun is usually represented by a man dressed in red with a mask that has horns.

The Egungun is a masked character that is popular in Nigerian culture. The word "Egungun" translates to "reincarnated spirit." The Egungun Masquerade is a way for individuals to communicate with these spirits. The costume comprises brightly colored fabric, feathers, and beads. The Egungun often wears a veil over their face, which makes it difficult to see their features. Members of the Egungun family will often wear similar costumes to identify them as members of the same group. The Egungun Masquerade is typically performed during festivals and ceremonies. It is believed that the Egungun brings good luck and prosperity to those who witness the performance.

Classification of Egungun

Every ethnic group in Nigeria has its own traditional masquerade festival. While some of these are more subdued affairs, others are exuberant spectacles featuring colorful costumes, music, and dance. The Egungun is one of the most popular masquerade traditions in Nigeria, and it is also one of the most varied. Depending on the region, the Egungun can take on many different forms.

One of the most common types of Egungun is the Oso Ijoba, which is found in the Yoruba-speaking regions of southwestern Nigeria. The Oso Ijoba is traditionally a male masquerade and is often associated with death and fertility. During festivals, groups of Oso Ijoba masqueraders will parade through the streets, stopping to perform for onlookers. Another popular type of Egungun is the Gelede, which is found in parts of southwestern Nigeria. The Gelede is a female masquerade, and it is associated with maternal power and protection. Unlike the Oso Ijoba, the Gelede does not usually travel in groups. Instead, individual Gelede masqueraders will visit homes in their community, entertaining the residents with song and dance.

The Egungun tradition is just one of many fascinating aspects of Nigerian culture. If you ever have the chance to see an Egungun masquerade festival, you will be impressed by the variety and ingenuity of the costumes on display.

Role of the Family

The role of the family is central to the Odun Egungun festival. This annual event also celebrates the ancestors and honors their spirits. During the festival, family members will dress up in colorful costumes and paint their faces to resemble the spirits of their ancestors. They will also offer prayers and sacrifices to honor the dead. The festival is presided over by an elder known as the Alagba. The Alagba is responsible for invoking the ancestors and for leading the community in ancestral rites. They may also be responsible for ensuring that the deceased are properly buried and their spirits are at peace. During the Egungun festival, families will often offer food and drink to the ancestors as a way of honoring them. Families come together to prepare for the festivities, which include traditional music, dance, and food and remember their loved ones who have passed on. It is also an opportunity to celebrate life and create new memories.

- **Women**

The role of the family is essential in the Odun Egungun festival. Women were once in control of Egungun, but their men tricked them and took away their power. The ritual originates from women's religious experience in Yoruba. The Odu Irantegbe chapter of the Ifa corpus claims that women were in control of the Egungun cult. However, they were tricked by men and lost control. Despite this, women still play a vital role in the Odun Egungun festival. They help to prepare the food and decorations for the event. They also dance and sing songs performed during the festival. They offer prayers and sacrifices to ensure that their ancestors continue to watch over them from the other world. Without women, the Odun Egungun festival would not be possible.

- **Men**

One important part of this festival is the role of the Egungun man. The Egungun man is a masked dancer who embodies the spirits of the deceased. He is responsible for leading spirits in their procession through the streets and for communicating their messages to the living. In addition, he often provides guidance and advice to those who are grieving. To become an Egungun, a man must undergo extensive training, during which he will learn about the history and traditions of his people, as well as the proper way to honor and respect the Egungun. He will also undergo physical training to endure the long hours of dancing and drumming required during a masquerade. Man's role in Odun Egungun is to provide a link between the world of the living and the world of the dead. By honoring their ancestors this way, they ensure their lives will be blessed with good fortune.

Egungun Ensembles

The Egungun Festival is an important annual event in Nigeria, during which Egungun ensembles perform to honor the ancestors. The festival lasts several days and includes food, drink, and dancing. On the festival's final day, a grand procession is convened in which all of the Egungun ensembles participate. The procession is led by the most senior member of the group, who carries a staff adorned with feathers. The Egungun Festival is a time of joy and celebration to honor those who have passed away and remember their lives.

The Egungun is a masquerade costume worn by men in many parts of Yoruba land. It is often brightly colored and festive and is made up of a variety of different fabrics. The Egungun covers his entire body with a large headdress and long, flowing sleeves. The costume is usually completed with a staff or sword, which the Egungun will use to perform dances and other movements.

The ensemble is made up of five or more performers, who each wear a different piece of the costume. The headdresses and staffs are often decorated with colorful feathers, beads, and other materials. The Egungun will also often wear face paint or masks, which help to create a more fearsome appearance. When the ensemble is complete, the Egungun looks like a giant, colorful bird. The ensemble typically consists of a lead singer accompanied by a drummer and a dancer. The lead singer wears a mask and costume representing the deceased, while the drummer and dancer wear brightly colored clothing. Egungun music is often upbeat and lively, meant to encourage participants to dance and celebrate the deceased's life.

The Egungun ensemble performs a variety of functions within Yoruba society. During religious ceremonies, the Egungun is said to represent the spirits of the dead and come to earth to partake in the festivities. The costume is also worn during funerals and other important life events. In addition, the Egungun is sometimes used in political processions or as a symbol of royal authority. Regardless of its specific function, the Egungun always brings a sense of pageantry and joy to any event at which it appears.

Types of Masks Worn by Odun Egungun
1. Akinlari Mask
Akinlari is one of the most popular types of masks worn by Odun Egungun dancers. The name "Akinlari" means "one who cannot be seen" in Yoruba, and the masks are used in ceremonies and rituals designed to protect the wearer from evil spirits. They are usually made of wood or fabric and cover the entire face. In some cases, the mask also covers the body and can be decorated with feathers, beads, or other materials. The exact appearance of the mask depends on its purpose and the region in which it is made. For example, a mask used for healing rituals might have a different design than a mask used for mourning ceremonies. However, regardless of their specific purpose, all Akinlari masks share one common goal: to help their owners avoid harmful spirits and lead happy, healthy lives. These masks represent the heads of birds and are often brightly colored. The significance of Akinlari masks is that they represent the spirits of ancestors who have come to visit the living. By wearing these masks, dancers are able to commune with their ancestors and receive their guidance and wisdom. Akinlari masks are also believed to bring good luck and prosperous tidings to those who wear them. As such, they are highly revered by the Yoruba people.

When selecting an Akinlari mask, it is important to choose one that resonates with you on a spiritual level. This will ensure that you are able to connect with your ancestors and receive their blessing.

2. Igun Mask

The Igun people of Nigeria wear Igun masks. These masks take the form of crocodile heads and are made from wood or fiber. The masks are used in ceremonies and are believed to possess magical powers. The Igun people believe that the crocodile is a powerful creature that can protect them from harm. The masks are also used to communicate with the spirits of their ancestors. When an Igun man wears an Igun mask, he is transformed into a crocodile spirit and can communicate with his ancestors' spirits. The Igun mask is a prominent part of the culture of the Igun people and is revered for its power and beauty. The significance of the Igun mask is in its ability to protect the wearer from harm. Crocodiles are feared, and by wearing an Igun mask, the wearer can channel the creature's power. This makes the mask a powerful tool for those who wear it and is often used in ceremonies and rituals. The Igun mask is just one example of the important role that masks can play in African culture.

3. Ata Mask

The Ata mask is a traditional mask worn by the Yoruba people of West Africa. The masks represent the heads of humans and are often very detailed and life-like. They are used in religious ceremonies to honor the dead and also play a large role in social and political events. The masks are usually brightly colored and decorated with a variety of materials, including feathers, sequins, and beads. The Ata mask is a highly revered object within Yoruba culture and is often passed down from generation to generation.

The Ata mask is a type of wood carving that is native to the Yoruba tribe. They are oval and feature intricate designs. The Ata people believe they have supernatural powers. The masks are also thought to represent the spirits of deceased ancestors. Ata masks are made from softwood, such as cedar. The wood is first carved into the desired shape and then decorated with materials such as feathers, paint, and beads. The finished product is then polished to a high shine. Ata masks are usually only worn by tribal chiefs or other important community members. The Ata mask is a beautiful and unique piece of artwork that is steeped in tradition and meaning. If you ever have the chance to see one of these masks, you will be truly amazed by its beauty.

4. Aso Oke Mask

Aso Oke is a traditional Nigerian fabric often used for special occasions, such as weddings. The fabric is made from cotton or wool and woven into a variety of colors and patterns. Aso Oke is also commonly used to make masks worn during festivals and ceremonies by the Yoruba. The masks are made of cloth and usually have two eye holes and a mouth slit. The masks represent different animals or ancestors. The most common animals are lions, elephants, and monkeys. The masks are also sometimes decorated with beads, feathers, and shells. Aso Oke masks hold important cultural significance in honoring ancestors. They are used to communicating with spirits and teaching lessons about morality. In addition, wearing an Aso Oke mask is thought to bring good luck. These masks are usually brightly colored and adorned with intricate designs and are believed to possess magical powers. They are often used to protect the wearer from evil spirits. In some cultures, the masks are also thought to bring good luck. Aso Oke masks are always handmade and can be passed down from generation to generation. Whether you are looking for a unique gift or a special piece of art, an Aso Oke mask is sure to add beauty and excitement to any collection.

5. Iya Oke Mask

The Iya Oke mask is another type of mask worn by men and is associated with fertility and virility. The mask is traditionally made of wood and is usually decorated with animal skins and hair. The name "Iya Oke" means "mother of the forest." This masquerade is usually associated with fertility and childbirth. The Iya Oke mask represents the head of a mythical creature known as the Iya, which is said to be a cross between a human and an antelope. The Iya is considered a symbol of strength and power, and it is believed that the Iya's spirit can help protect crops from pests and disease. Iya Oke masks are made of wood and cloth and are often decorated with beads and cowrie shells. The masks typically have large eyes and mouths, and they are worn by men who dance and sing while carrying them. Iya Oke is believed to represent the earth goddess, Obatala. She is considered to be the protector of mothers and children and is also thought to bring good luck during childbirth. Iya Oke masks are often seen during celebrations such as weddings, funerals, and traditional healing ceremonies. The Iya Oke mask is worn during special ceremonies and festivals and is often mentioned in folktales and stories as a representation of virility and power.

Chapter 7: Creating an Egun Altar or Shrine

We briefly touched on how to create a shrine to pay tribute to the ancestors earlier in this book. However, creating an Egun altar or shrine can be a bit more complicated, with different details incorporated according to the discretion of the worshiper. There are also very specific ways in which you are expected to care for the altar, ensuring it continues to nourish your relationship with your ancestors. Getting deep into the details of creating a shrine or altar is a crucial element that cannot be ignored for those who are just beginning to learn about this important spiritual practice.

Egun altars are detailed and have several components.
Susanne Bollinger, CC BY-SA 4.0 <https://creativecommons.org/licenses/by-sa/4.0>, via Wikimedia Commons
https://commons.wikimedia.org/wiki/File:SB090_Santer%C3%ADa_altar.JPG

Location

The location is the first element to establish as you consider putting together a shrine. One rule of thumb is that if you want a space that is hard to ignore, you need a place that calls to you. Praying or paying tribute to the ancestors just once a month does not help nurture an effective spiritual connection to them. It is something that must be cultivated continuously.

Once you have found an appropriate space in your home, clean the area and ensure it's neat and organized. A lot of clutter is disrespectful and can add to any negative energies you're trying to dispel. Using smudge sticks made of sage or rosemary is also helpful to clear out unwanted spirits or negative thought patterns. Smudge sticks can be used in two different ways. One way is to simply light the bundle of dried leaves you have in hand and wave it around the room for a few minutes, allowing the smoke to infiltrate and create a blank canvas of positive energy for you.

The second way to use a smudge stick is to place the bunch of herbs or leaves in a bowl, light it, and leave it as is for a few minutes, waving the smoke with a feather. Do this till the smudge stick has been burned away, and the smoke works its magic within the space. Suppose you're not exactly sure which kind of leaves to use. In that case, you can follow this simple rule: cedar and sage are extra pungent, and their aroma will allow for deeper cleansing. If there was a lot of clutter in your space and it required a deep cleaning, you might as well finish the job with a strongly scented smudge stick. Rosemary is gentler and works just as well if you feel your space does not require much work. It is also a good stick to set alight if you've recently lost a loved one and want to commemorate their memory. Rosemary smudge sticks are often used to acknowledge our grief, and they work well as you set up a space to ask the ancestors for guidance during an exceptionally difficult time.

Some people choose to say a prayer to the Egun as they use the smudge stick, hoping that the spirits can hear their call for help and connection. Different prayers can be used to establish clear lines of communication. It helps to start by thanking the ancestors and then making your intention of paying tribute to them clear. Do this till the smoke dissipates, and you're left with a deep sense of clarity.

These measures will act as a safety valve of sorts and will provide extra insurance in your efforts to build a healthy relationship with the ancestors. A newly transformed physical environment is the first positive step to help you feel better as you start preparing the shrine or altar you are about to build, so don't skip this.

Now that you have established a clean slate for the invocation of the ancestral spirits you're trying to connect with, you're ready to carry out the next few steps.

Assembling the Shrine

Once you've cleaned the space and said your initial prayers, begin to assemble the shrine. This step can be as complicated or as simple as you'd like it to be, although you will need a few basic items.

- **Book of Wisdom**

This isn't in reference to a specific Yorubian text to purchase and keep in the home. Rather, the book is used as something to help you reflect and add meaning to the realities of every day. A book of proverbs and meditations steeped in the traditions of Yoruba is preferable and can be used to great effect in this case. But if you can't get such a book, any book of wisdom will help you mentally and spiritually transcend the present while gaining a crucial perspective that can be applied to your spiritual practice.

- **Small Statue or Image of a Deity**

While using figures is less necessary in Yoruba than in other religions, it's still helpful to have something to look at while you pray at the shrine. It could be a painting or a small figurine of a spiritual symbol or deity whose example means a great deal to you and whom you'd like to emulate. Feel free to choose any figure that helps provide you with a sense of peace, calm, and stability.

- **Candles**

Like smoke and smudge sticks, the presence of fire at the altar will help enliven the area and provide a spark of positive energy. Plain white, unscented candles work well enough, although you can consider getting candles with colors that match the deity or symbol in which you are interested. For example, Oshun is often associated with yellow, whereas the colors red and gold are associated with Lakshmi.

- **Natural Elements**

No altar is complete without a few elements representing nature. Place a small bowl, preferably one made of crystal, and fill it with water. You can also place a few other gemstones on the altar, raw crystals such as amethyst, rose quartz, amber, and so on. Each emits specific kinds of energies, and they can be helpful towards your hopes of pursuing the sort of spiritual work you'd like to accomplish on a daily basis. Try researching the uses of different kinds of crystals before placing them on the altar. Dried flowers and other natural elements provide the perfect touch and will allow you to feel rejuvenated and at peace in your sacred space.

- **Oil Burners or Incense**

Incense or oils give us a feeling of calm and can open the door to helpful meditative practices. This is why they have been used in different religions worldwide for thousands of years. As you prepare to sit before your altar or shrine for a short while, it helps to burn a stick of incense and allow a sense of peace to overcome you as you get to feel more settled. Trying to calm your anxiety and frayed nerves is an important step before submitting your prayers to the Egun, and incense is a good way of helping you to do just that.

- **Table and Cloth**

Lastly are the two main elements on which all of this will be spread: a table and a cloth. A small table that isn't too high is key since you need it to be low enough for you to kneel in front of it. Glass or wood are recommended; plastic – *not so much*, but it will do in a pinch. Then, a clean piece of cloth should be placed on top. There is no preferred color, although you will find that many will use a simple white material made of cotton or some other woven fabric.

- **Optional: Music**

This is not essential, but some people find that adding calm, ambient music can help set the scene for them to pray to the spirits. Much like using incense or oils, the music can help set the mood, clear your mind, and allow you to be rid of any sense of anxiety. Songs accompanied by traditional instruments are helpful, although you can opt for soundscapes, meditative sounds such as rainfall, or mantras set to relaxing music. Do whatever you find helpful, although many individuals feel that silence allows for a deeper, meditative experience.

Offerings

One major part of keeping an Egun altar or shrine is the offerings. The Egun are sometimes looked on with a sense of fear and awe, as they do effectively represent the dead, and we are sometimes unsure of what they need from us. Offerings help temper the hustle and bustle of daily life and, since they signal love and respect, as opposed to fear, are very useful. Offerings can take different forms, although the most recommended way of going about this is to prepare special foods the ancestors may like and place them on plates around the shrine. You can also offer them different beverages, such as coffee, tea, wine, rum, and the like. Some people even go as far as to offer things that seem more contemporary, like soda. Although this stems from the belief that someone to whom they were close and who has recently passed is the reincarnated version of one of the ancestors.

It is customary to offer the food on a chipped or cracked plate since this signals the practice of smashing plates on the ground in the event that a priest dies. Harking back to customs that occurred when the ancestors were alive is a nice touch and shows that you are keenly aware of how they lived their lives.

As you set down your offerings on the shrine, be sure to light a white candle in a symbolic offering of clear light to Egun. And, you don't always have to give food and drink. Some people may even want to light a cigar in an attempt to give their ancestors tobacco smoke, a much-loved pastime. A fresh bouquet of flowers in a vase on or near the shrine is another lovely offering to the spirits and signals your care for them since flowers have traditionally been used to honor the dead. However, this depends on the kinds of spirits you're honoring. Flowers are considered improper if you wish to pray to the Orishas since, according to Yoruba, they are not dead.

While most offerings are made during a ceremony, such as Oriate, that is not always the case. Again, you are expected to use the shrine to cultivate your relationship with the Egun, so waiting for a particular occasion may not be looked upon very kindly by the spirits. You can make offerings at the pace you choose, although it is recommended that you keep up the ritual and do it at least once a week. Some can perform this tradition on a nightly basis, whereas others make their food offerings as often as three times a day. Every time they are about to eat with their family, they place a small plate for the spirits as well. Find the rhythm that makes the most sense for you, but generally, when you place offerings at the shrine, you can leave them till they start to go a little bad or are ready to be thrown away. In some practices, it isn't uncommon for the food and drink to be left till they start to attract mold. While this may seem odd, it signals the nature of death and thus serves another spiritual function that a priest may want to signal every so often during their sermons.

However, since your shrine or altar will be at home, it makes sense to attend to it at least once a week and not leave things hanging about for too long. The ancestors will be aware of your attempts to reach out to them and foster a healthy spiritual relationship through your daily meditative practice, and that is an important step to take as you continue to delve deeper into the religion.

So, you're probably wondering about what not to include. This varies according to the kind of ancestor you're trying to connect to, but the general rule is to avoid the use of live or dead animals. For example, animal parts, insects, and taxidermied birds are also frowned upon. Flowers that have spoiled or decayed are also unwanted, as is blood, and most amulets are also unnecessary. Don't include rosaries, necklaces, or sticks of any kind - regardless of their use - which are larger than a standard pencil, as these are not considered part of the traditional offerings to an altar. Also, while we mentioned that some could leave food offerings until they become a bit moldy, note that this is a fairly contentious issue, and it's best to avoid doing this whenever possible!

Frequently Asked Questions

So, you've learned the basics of creating an altar or shrine, but you probably still have a few lingering questions. The following are a few of the most commonly asked questions about setting up a shrine, and hopefully, you will find the answers helpful.

1. Can I dedicate an altar to more than one ancestor?

The short answer is yes. The main thing to be on the lookout for is that not all spirits enjoy the same offerings as others, so make sure to study each of their defining characteristics and construct your shrine accordingly.

2. How is the Egun altar different from other ancestor altars, like those based in Western traditions?

An Egun altar is mostly paying tribute to ancestors based in Yoruba traditions. However, you can also include images of your immediate ancestors, those whom you've lost recently, and pay tribute to their spirits as well. In most cases, there is no separation between what we consider to be our immediate ancestors and the Egun, and how we would like to pay tribute to them can be similar.

In Western traditions, a shrine is usually dedicated solely to the religious figurehead at the helm of everyday spiritual life, and it is rare for those representing our recent history of merging with figures considered to be ancient. For example, in Christianity, the shrine will mostly be dedicated to Jesus Christ and sometimes to the Virgin Mary. You won't really find the image of a recently deceased loved one kept in the same shrine.

3. Can I - or should I - keep more than one altar in a house?

This is a complicated one. While you can keep more than one altar in the home in theory, in practice, this can be hard to keep up. And you don't want to risk angering the Egun by neglecting one group or creating so much spiritual work in the home that you inadvertently invite more spirits than necessary. Balance is key as you work to establish an equilibrium with the ancestors and become more familiar with Yoruba's intricacies, which can be hard to do if you have more than one shrine in the home.

A Wave of Remembrance

As you set up your shrine and prepare for prayer, light the candle and kneel before it. Close your eyes, remember your loved ones, imagine connecting with the ancients, and be receptive to the messages they send your way. Begin to identify the qualities that mean a great deal to you and the things you hope to emulate, such as courage, generosity, kindness, and creativity. Imagine manifesting those characteristics within yourself and praying to the ancestors for guidance. As you work to develop this connection with them spiritually, be sure to continue to call on them throughout the day to find clarity and feel a sense of belonging.

The shrine or altar is one way of connecting with Egun, but it's only a starting point. You should work throughout the day to find small moments for prayer and remembrance so that your spiritual practice becomes deeper over time. There are many books of prayers based in the Yoruba religion that you can look to for further guidance, which can be used to help you pray at the altar. In the end, remember that an altar is your very own personal space, and the set-up should grow with you as your spirituality grows over time.

Chapter 8: More Ways to Venerate Your Ancestors

Now that you know how to set up an ancestral altar, it's time for you to learn a few other ways to venerate your ancestors. From meditation to chanting and oriki to leading an honorable life by following Odu Ifa, this chapter brings you several beginner-friendly ways to honor your lineage. Depending on what feels right to you or how your altar is set up, you can venerate your ancestors either at or near your altar or shrine.

Ancestral Meditation

One of the best ways to honor and connect with any spirit is through meditation, and ancestral souls are no exception. Meditate with your ancestors at your altar to facilitate communication, and focus on visualizing them while doing so. If you don't have a shrine or altar, you can meditate in front of an open window. Before you start, place a candle on your altar (or windowsill) next to the picture of your ancestors. You can also meditate in front of something associated with or symbolizing your ancestral home. As you light the candle, express your gratitude to the ancestors for getting in touch with you and sharing the wisdom they acquired throughout their lives. Thanking your ancestors for their help, apart from being good manners, is always a polite thing to do and will be appreciated. Just taking a few minutes a day to think of them will be greatly appreciated, and your ancestors will be more inclined to help you when you need them.

Meditation allows you to connect with your spirits.
https://www.pexels.com/photo/woman-meditating-in-the-outdoors-2908175/

Work out what you want to ask them. Do you need to ask them for guidance, healing, prophecies, or help to resolve any issues that you think their wisdom can solve? If you don't have a specific intention in mind (whether because you don't need help with anything or because your only purpose is to deepen your bond with the ancestors), ask the ancestors if they have any messages for you. Sometimes, they'll have powerful messages to share but are waiting for you to ask them.

Settle in front of your altar or window. Clear your mind of everything except your intention. Take a few deep breaths to calm your mind and body. . . and then focus. After doing this for a couple of minutes, close your eyes and visualize a natural scene familiar to you. Imagine yourself standing in the middle of it and taking in all its details. This will make the experience feel more authentic and facilitate the rest of the process. Try grounding yourself in this serene space, then call on the ancestors you want to meet. You can call on one soul or your entire lineage. The former approach is recommended for beginners still learning the basics of spiritual communication. If you're calling on more than one soul, be open to whoever shows up. Sometimes they'll surprise you, and you'll receive messages from someone you don't expect to be helpful.

Once the ancestral souls have materialized in front of your eyes, feel free to ask them any question. Be polite, but open about your needs. Your ancestors have access to much wisdom, and they're ready to share it with you and won't judge you for wanting help. In most cases, they'll listen and offer advice on how to proceed. That said, when you're speaking with them through mediation, they'll only grant a piece of wisdom, but they won't tell you exactly what to do. Listen carefully to whatever story they tell you and the images they show you. Keep your mind open to any other messages as well.

When you're done receiving ancestral messages, let the image of the ancestors and the natural scene fade away while whispering a soft thank you. Open your eyes, snuff out the candle, and let your mind return to its daily preoccupations.

Leading a Righteous Life

Leading an honorable life is a fundamental part of Yoruba traditions. Your ancestors gathered all their wisdom because they stayed true to positive spiritual values. These were always passed down to the next generation, so they would also be able to live an honorable and spiritually fulfilled life. Some of these stem from the Ifa Oracle, a Yoruba divination system. The divine messages received through this system are decoded by Babalawos and Iyanifas. Among the information translated thousands of years ago were 16 core principles, which form the basis of Odu Ife, a collection of truths righteous people should live by. According to the lore, 16 Babalawos visited Ile Ife, hoping to obtain eternal life. They were granted their wish, with the condition that they'll have to follow the 16 truths of Ifa.

The truths are as follows:

1. There is only one creator. Olodumare is the single being who made all things come to life, including the universe. Sealing an intention in the name of the supreme creator is a sure way to ensure it manifests.
2. Our universe is benevolent. The universe was created by Olodumare, whose power is pure; therefore, its creation can't be tainted. This allows people to access memories and information from the past, present, and future.
3. Don't be afraid to face the challenges. The Orishas who faced life's hurdles were rewarded for their effort, while those who lived in fear suffered. Consulting with ancestral lines can help you gather the courage to face the toughest challenges.
4. There is no one powerful evil force. The devil, as it's called in other cultures, does not exist, and neither does hell. However, the possibilities of negative influences are limitless.

5. You have the right to be loved and successful. Never believe that you don't deserve love or to achieve your goals and dreams. Accepting your birthright brings you a step closer to spiritual growth.
6. We are in constant transition between two places, one is heaven (our soul's true home), and the other one is called "the marketplace" (a transitional space for souls). Death ends many bad things and allows the soul to start anew.
7. Every part of you is part of the universe. In spirit, you are one with the universe, including all of the other creations of Olodumare. Paying attention to what is around you can help you learn about yourself.
8. Your character and personality traits determine your fate. Whatever way your character makes you think, feel, and act will determine your destiny. Good characters help you fulfill your destiny.
9. Showing superiority is a sign of evil influence. Only Ifa can be superior to every other being. Even the Babalawos and the Orishas can't be superior to each other. No one is superior, and no one is above making mistakes. Complaining about other people's mistakes and disregarding yours is a sign of false superiority.
10. Never inflict harm on others, even if they are wicked. Let their wickedness consume them instead. Being good will attract many blessings from the ancestors, the deities, and Olodumare, while causing harm will make you miss out on these.
11. Don't harm the universe. Every part is sacred and must be treated respectfully. You need to pay your respect to the spirits to keep yourself in their good favor in case you need them.
12. Don't discriminate against others. Every person has their own value, regardless of their appearance or personality. The biggest hindrance in this is ignorance. This negative trait can also prevent you from obtaining abundance, and you'll remain just as powerless as those against whom you discriminate.
13. Olodumare created diversity for a reason, and it should be celebrated because it can bring people and other beings together. People are born with an entire spectrum of potentials, allowing you to choose which one to manifest.

14. You can choose your fate and your guardians. Whichever path you set for yourself and the Orisha you pick for guidance on this path depends only on you. Offering sacrifice to the Orishas is an excellent way to ensure you receive the assistance you need.
15. Practicing divination is a great way to find your path. Whenever you need advice on how to fulfill your destiny, consult Ifa. It will guarantee a long and prosperous life.
16. Your goals should be to gather wisdom and grow personally. These are required for spiritual growth and a balanced life, which most people desire. Prayers and other forms of spiritual discipline are key to spiritual growth.

According to the Yoruba, the Babalawo didn't follow the 16 truths and consequently died. However, all the ancestors did, which allowed their souls to move on and go through several life cycles to gather all the wisdom they could. The truths are simple decrees anyone can follow daily, and doing so is one of the best ways to pay homage to your ancestors.

Following the 16 Truths of Ifa

Here are a few pieces of advice on how to follow the 16 truths of Ifa:

Talk Only about What You Know

Don't talk about something of which you have no knowledge. – Just because you think something is true doesn't mean that it is unless you verify it. Only talk about topics you have knowledge of. Be ready to listen to others who speak about things unfamiliar to you. The same applies to rituals and ceremonies. Only perform those you have practiced before and have been successful in.

Don't Mislead People

Don't be deceitful in your actions or words. This could mislead people into thinking you think or feel something you don't. Try leading them on the right path instead of always being transparent. Be open about what you're offering and what you expect from them. In the same way, you need to be open-minded when communicating with your ancestors. You'll also need to be open when communicating with other people.

Don't Pretend to Be Wise

Remember, no matter how much wisdom you've gathered throughout your life or having it given to you from the ancestors and Orishas. You can always learn more. There will always be things you don't know, so don't pretend you are the source of all wisdom. Wise people never do that. Instead, they continue learning because they are aware of the immense amount of knowledge they can still gather.

Be Humble

Wise people are humble and never let their egos get in their way. Sometimes, putting the ego aside is challenging, and it feels unfair to deny yourself something. However, this can be another learning opportunity for you and a great way to strengthen your character, which leads to fulfilling your destiny.

Always Have Good Intentions

Bad intentions have a negative influence on your spiritual well-being. They can also prevent you from spiritual communication, honoring your ancestors, and fulfilling your destiny. This can also be challenging, especially if others don't have good intentions toward you. However, by taking a positive approach, you'll be able to thrive despite their malicious intentions. The same applies to taboos and prohibitions. These should never be broken or disrespected, and otherwise, they'll have the same effect as foul intentions.

Honor Your Tools and Sacred Space

A great way to venerate your ancestors is to keep whatever tools you use to communicate with them clean from negative energies. This applies to the symbols, pictures, and other items you use for your ancestral veneration practices, including your altar. Your body and mind are also essential tools, and you'll need to cleanse these regularly as well. Taking cleansing baths and asking the Orishas to help purify your body and mind through the bath is a great way to expel all the negative energy that is potentially in you.

Respect Others

You should always respect other people's views and actions, whether you agree with them or not. Pay particular attention not to disrespect your elders or those weaker than you. The elders are wiser than you, and you never know when you might need their help. Weaker people (including people with disabilities) should also be respected because their weakness is not their fault. Besides, they can spiritually contribute just as much to the community as any other person without weakness or disability.

Respect the Law

This applies to both moral laws and legal ones. Both exist for a reason: to make human communities a place where everyone can coexist peacefully. Following legal laws can make your life much easier because you can avoid penalties. Following moral codes of conduct gives you even more than that. Providing that your values align with the moral laws, staying true to your values can give you peace of mind. Make sure you cultivate values that adhere to the most common unspoken moral codes, and you'll have no problem respecting the latter.

Cultivate Your Friendships

Be available for your friends when they need you, and they'll do the same for you. Never betray them by revealing their secrets or gossiping about them behind their back. Respect their loved ones, just as you would want them to respect yours. Honor the choices they make, even if you don't agree with them. If you wish to advise them against a decision, do it carefully. Never tell them why you think they shouldn't do something.

Chanting and Praying

Chanting and praying are two methods that help you liberate yourself from the material world and are excellent tools for connecting to your ancestors. Chanting means offering prayers, affirmations, and other spoken words, such as poems or songs. You can pray to your ancestors in a traditional way or chant the prayers while communicating with them. There are several forms of prayers you can offer, all of which are wonderful reminders of your power as well as the power of your ancestors.

Praises

Praising the ancestors is a great way to maintain the communication between you and your ancestral line. Here is a praise verse you can offer to your ancestors while sitting at your altar:

> "*I praise the universe and its creator Olodumare.*
>
> *I praise nature and all of its inhabitants.*
>
> *I praise my spirit guides, but most of all,*
>
> *I praise my ancestors.*

I praise those who came before me

I praise those who struggled, just like I do."

Gratitude

Chants and praises can also be about expressing gratitude. Here is a prayer to express your appreciation of the ancestors:

"I thank you for helping me to wake up this morning with a positive attitude.

I thank you for helping me through my journey

and for those you sent to accompany me along the way.

I thank you for being part of my family and community

and for providing me with the support I need."

Forgiveness

Sometimes, you'll need to be humble and simply ask for forgiveness. Here is an example of how to ask your ancestry to forgive you:

"I ask for forgiveness for not following your advice.

Forgive me for offending you with my ignorance of your wisdom.

Forgive me for the harm this caused to my family and me.

Forgive all of us, your living descendants, for hurting each other when we do."

Asking for Blessing and Protection

Prayers and chants can also serve as a communication tool when you want to ask your ancestors for protection or blessing:

"My ancestors, I ask you to protect me (or us if you're asking for other people too)

From losses, illness, and death.

I also ask you to protect me from conflicts and the hands of my enemies.

Please help me have a long life and good health.

Help me remain calm, strong, and resilient when facing challenges.

Help me see things clearly, and be courageous and loving."

Creating a Family Oriki

The Yoruba are known for having a unique form of praise poem or chant called oriki. They have orikis for the Orishas, spiritual guides, the ancestors, and the living. The latter is given their oriki in childhood, but you can also write praise poems for adults. In children, orikis praise the positive characters the adults want them to cultivate. Whereas the orikis made for adults are not always flattering. Families have their orikis, too, which are passed down the male line. While children can learn the oriki of their mother's family, this isn't used later on. Brides-to-be are required to memorize the family oriki of their future husbands before their wedding.

Creating an oriki for your family is a way of acknowledging your ancestral lineage and your identity. It'll also allow you to discover what each member has in common, which can come in handy when you need additional help with a specific issue. You will have more souls to turn to and better chances of finding a resolution.

To write your family oriki, you'll need to research the individual members' achievements, beliefs, trade, typical behavior, strengths, and weaknesses. You can also look into what they found challenging and their aspirations. Once you've gathered all this information, you can start adding them besides the names of the family members. For the male members, write short phrases that describe their strengths and how they overcome challenges. For the female members, the lines should illustrate how they supported their families and what they loved to do.

Chapter 9: Reincarnation in Yoruba

In Yoruba culture, the concept of reincarnation is central to beliefs about the afterlife. According to tradition, the spirit of a dead person will be reborn into another body, and this cycle will continue until the spirit reaches a state of spiritual perfection. This belief helps to explain why many Yoruba people place such importance on ancestor worship; they believe that their ancestors' spirits are still present in the world and can influence their lives. It also helps to explain why certain families produce many children. They believe each child represents another chance for the family's ancestors to achieve spiritual perfection. Ultimately, the belief in reincarnation is just one of many ways that the Yoruba people attempt to make sense of the cycle of life and death.

There are several reasons someone may be reincarnated, including unfinished business or unresolved problems from their previous life. It is believed that the Yetunde must complete whatever task they were unable to in their previous life to move on to the next level of existence. This cycle of birth and death is known as "samsara."

Death in Yoruba

In Yoruba culture, death is not seen as the end of life but rather as a transition to another realm. The soul is believed to leave the body at the time of death and enter the spirit world, where it will spend eternity. If the soul cannot find its way to the spirit world, it may remain earthbound and become a ghost. Belief in ghosts is very strong in Yoruba culture, and it is said that they can cause great harm to the living if they are not properly respected. The deceased's spirit is believed to continue living on in the world of the ancestors, and they can still influence events in the lives of their relatives. As such, it is important to maintain a good relationship with one's ancestors, as they can provide guidance and protection. When someone dies, their spirit is said to go to the "land of the living dead," where Olodumare, the creator god, will judge them. If they have lived a good life, they will be allowed to enter heaven. If not, they will be sent back to earth to live out their lives in suffering. In either case, it is believed that the ancestors can still interact with the living, so it is important to honor them through prayer and offerings.

Death is, therefore, a very serious matter; great care is taken to ensure that the dead are properly memorialized, and their spirits are allowed to move on. In Yoruba culture, death is not seen as the end of life but as a transition to another realm.

Immortality in Yoruba Culture

In Yoruba culture, immortality is a key concept. The ultimate goal is to achieve immortality, which can be done in several ways. One is to achieve physical immortality, which means that the body does not age or decay. This can be done through magical rituals and spells. Another way is to achieve spiritual immortality, which means that the soul does not perish after death. This can be done by reaching a high level of spiritual development and enlightenment. Finally, one can achieve immortal remembrance, meaning one's name and accomplishments will be remembered long after death. This can be done by achieving great things in life and Leaving a lasting legacy. In Yoruba culture, there are many ways to achieve immortality, and each individual must choose their own path.

Reincarnation or Atunwa in Yoruba Culture

In Yoruba culture, there is a belief that the soul never dies. Instead, it is reborn into another member of the family. This belief is called Atunwa. According to Atunwa, at death, the soul leaves the body and enters a state of limbo. It remains there until it is reincarnated into another member of the family. The cycle of life and death is continuous, and the soul is constantly being reborn into new bodies. This belief helps to explain why many Yoruba people are so attached to their families. They see their loved ones as individuals and reincarnations of previous ancestors. In this way, Atunwa provides a sense of continuity and connection between the living and the dead. It also helps to explain why many Yoruba people take great care in burial rituals. They believe the soul must be properly prepared for its journey into the afterlife, and those proper burial rites will ensure that the soul is reborn into a good home.

In Yoruba culture, the concept of familial or lineal rebirth is vividly illustrated through four important figures: Babatunde, Yetunde, Babatunji, and Sotunde. Each figure offers a unique perspective on familial rebirth in Yoruba culture. Combined, they provide a comprehensive picture of this important concept.

- **Babatunde**

Babatunde is a concept in the Yoruba culture that explains how a father can return to his family through reincarnation. According to the Yoruba people's beliefs, a deceased father's soul can be reborn into a new body, and this new child will inherit the father's name and position within the family. In Yoruba culture, a father returning home is cause for great celebration. Babatunde, or "father returns," is a special occasion when the head of the household comes back to his family after being away for an extended period. The event is celebrated with music, dancing, and feasting, and all community members are welcome to join in the festivities. The father's return is seen as a symbol of hope and renewal, and it is believed that his presence will bring peace and prosperity to the household. On this day, families reconnect and reaffirm their bonds of love and respect. The return of the father is a time of joyous reunion and celebration in Yoruba culture.

While some cultures may see this as a form of reincarnation, the Yoruba believe it is more than just a simple transfer of the soul. Instead, they see it as a way for the deceased father to maintain his connection to his family and continue to play an important role in their lives.

Babatunde is a name of Yoruba origin given to males. It is closely associated with the belief in reincarnation within the culture. The name is given to a child believed to be the reincarnated spirit of a relative or ancestor. The name may also be given to a child born into a family with a strong tradition of spirituality and mysticism. Babatunde is also a popular name in Nigeria and among the Yoruba diaspora. The name was borne by several notable individuals, including a 16th-century Nigerian king, an 18th-century West African warrior queen, and a 20th-century Nigerian writer and politician. The name has recently been gaining popularity in the United States.

While the concept of Babatunde may seem strange to some, it is an important part of the Yoruba culture and helps to explain their beliefs about the afterlife. For many people, the idea of their father returning to them after death is a comfort, giving them a sense of continuity between this life and the next. Whether or not you believe in reincarnation, the concept of Babatunde is an interesting glimpse into another culture's belief system.

- **Yetunde**

In Yoruba culture, the belief in reincarnation extends to the idea of Yetunde, which is the concept of a mother returning to her children in a new life. According to this belief, a mother's love is strong enough to last through multiple lifetimes. Furthermore, it is said that the soul of a child who dies young will be reincarnated into the body of another child who is born soon afterward. This cycle of reincarnation ensures that the bond between mother and child is never broken. Yetunde is an important part of Yoruba culture and belief system. It is a reflection of the deep respect and love that Yoruba people have for their mothers. It also highlights the importance of family bonds and how they can span beyond just one lifetime. In some cases, the Yetunde may not remember their previous life or only have vague memories. However, they believe they will still be drawn to certain people and places they were connected to in their past lives.

- **Sotunde**

Sotunde was a young man who died suddenly. When he arrived in the afterlife, he was surprised to find that he could still see and hear what was happening on Earth. He asked the spirits why, and they told him it was because he had not yet been reincarnated. They said that he could choose to return to Earth and live again if he wanted to, but warned him that he would forget everything about his previous life. Sotunde thought about this for a while and decided that he wanted to return to Earth.

When Sotunde woke up, he found himself in a baby's body. He didn't remember anything about his previous life, but he could still hear the spirits' voices sometimes. They would tell him things about his past life and what he needed to do in his new life. Sotunde took their advice and lived a good life. When he died again, he was reborn as an elephant. And so it goes on throughout eternity: The spirit of Sotunde being reborn repeatedly, each time learning more and becoming wiser until eventually, they achieve enlightenment. This story illustrates the Yoruba belief that we are all immortal souls who are constantly being reborn into different bodies. Sotunde represents the wise man who returns. He embodies the importance of knowledge and understanding in the family. It also shows that our actions in one life can affect our experiences in future lives.

In the Yoruba culture, reincarnation is a belief that after a person dies, their soul is reborn into another person or animal. This belief is based on the idea that an immortal part of the human soul lives on after death. The concept of reincarnation is also found in other cultures worldwide, including Hinduism and Buddhism. In the Yoruba culture, it is believed that a person's actions in their previous life determine what they will be reborn as in their next life. For example, if a person was evil in their previous life, they might be reborn as a snake or a rat in their next life. Conversely, if a person was good in their previous life, they might be reborn as a human or an elephant in their next life. The story of Sotunde is a popular Yoruba folktale that illustrates this belief.

- **Babatunji**

In Yoruba culture, Babatunji is the name of the father who wakes once again. The concept of Babatunji is based on the belief that the dead can be reborn and awaken into a new life. This rebirth can take place either in the form of a new baby or through the reincarnation of an older person. The Yoruba believe that when one dies, their spirit will come back in another life, and so they continue to honor the values and teachings passed down from their fathers even after they have gone.

The importance of this concept is highlighted through various cultural practices, including naming ceremonies, initiation rites, and rituals surrounding death. In naming ceremonies, parents may look back at their own families to find inspiration for meaningful names or bring positive energy into their child's life. Initiation rites are also known to be held in honor of the father. During these initiation rites, teachings and examples from the father's life are shared among those present.

When a death occurs, Babatunji is often celebrated by Yoruba people as it symbolizes that one's father has left this world but that their spirit will remain alive through them and their children. They may express grief over the loss of their loved one yet also take comfort in knowing that he will live on through them. This belief helps to bring peace and healing when dealing with difficult circumstances such as illness or death. Babatunji is an important concept for many Yoruba communities and is used to remind people of the values they should uphold in their lives. Babatunji is a way to honor and remember the fathers who have passed on yet live on through their children. Through this concept, Yoruba people keep the memory and teachings of their father alive for generations to come.

Types of Reincarnation in Yoruba Cosmology

In Yoruba cosmology, there are three main types of reincarnation: àtúnlé, òrìṣà, and egbé. Of these, àtúnlé is the most common and refers to the rebirth of the human soul into a new human body. This can happen immediately after the previous body's death or many years later. Atúnlé is usually seen as a positive thing, representing the continuation of the soul's journey through life. Each life is believed to be like a step on a staircase, leading closer and closer to Òrúnmìlà, the creator god.

In some cases, àtúnlé can be seen as a negative thing. Suppose someone dies in a particularly violent or tragic way, for example. In that case, their soul may be reborn into a difficult life to work through their karma. However, even in such cases, it is believed that eventually, the soul will be released from the cycle of rebirth and attain salvation.

The latter is often seen as more desirable, allowing the soul to rest and rejuvenate before taking on a new physical form. Orìṣà reincarnation occurs when the human soul is reborn into an animal body. This is generally seen as a punishment for bad deeds in a previous life and is therefore considered to be relatively rare. Finally, egbé reincarnation refers to the rebirth of the human soul into an inanimate object, such as a rock or a tree. This is extremely rare and is usually only seen in cases where the soul has committed a very serious offense in its previous life.

How Ancestral Veneration Is Possible, Despite Atunwaye

Atunwaye is the belief that everything in the universe is connected and that all human beings are descended from a common ancestor. This belief is at the heart of ancestral veneration, which is the practice of honoring one's ancestors. It is based on the idea that our ancestors are with us even after death and that they can help us achieve our goals in life. While atunwaye may seem like a strange concept to some, it is actually very widespread. In many cultures, ancestor worship is an essential part of life. In China, for example, it is believed that one's ancestors can help to bring good fortune and protect against misfortune. As a result, Chinese families often make offerings to their ancestors, such as food and incense. In Japan, ancestor worship is known as ubasoku and is considered a deeply spiritual practice. Families often visit their ancestors' grave sites to pay their respects, and they may also offer prayers or perform traditional dances in their honor. While atunwaye may seem like a foreign concept to some, it is actually quite common. In many cultures worldwide, ancestor worship is an important part of life.

Which Souls Reincarnate in Yoruba Culture's Concept of Atunwa?

According to Yoruba culture, there are two types of soul: the ori, which is the individual's spiritual essence, and the ayanmo, which is the part of the soul that joins with others after death to form an ancestral spirit. The ayanmo is what reincarnates, and it is believed that each person has multiple ayanmo. When a person dies, their ayanmo goes to the spirit world, where it waits for a new body to be born. The ayanmo can choose to incarnate as any living creature, including humans, animals, and plants. It is also believed that the ayanmo can influence the events of its life and that it is possible for the same ayanmo to reincarnate multiple times. Consequently, everyone has the potential to be related to everyone else through their ayanmo.

What happens if you venerate an ancestor who might have reincarnated?

It's believed that when a person dies, their soul is reborn into another person or animal. As a result, it is possible that someone you are venerating as an ancestor may have actually been reborn into someone else. If this happens, there is no need to worry. It is still possible to honor and respect the memory of your ancestor by making offerings to their spirit, telling stories about them, and keeping their memory alive in your heart. Ultimately, whether or not your ancestor has reincarnated, they will always be with you in spirit. And as long as you remember them and keep them in your heart, they will never truly be gone.

What do spirits reincarnate in (only humans, animals, insects, etc.)?

There are many different belief systems around the world when it comes to what happens to our spirits after we die. Some believe that we are reincarnated into another human, some believe we become animals, and others become plants or insects. In Yoruba culture, there is a belief that our spirits can rebirth into any form depending on how we lived our previous life. If we led a good life and were kind and generous, then we would be reincarnated into a higher form. However, if we lead a bad life full of selfishness and greed, then we will be reincarnated into a lower form. This is based on the idea that our deeds in this life determine our station in the next. As such, it is important to live a good life and treat others with respect if we want to achieve a higher level of existence in the next.

Difference between the Western Concept of Reincarnation and Yoruba Reincarnation

There are many different beliefs about reincarnation, and it can be a complex subject to understand. The Yoruba concept of reincarnation differs from the Western view of the afterlife. In Yoruba culture, the soul is believed to remain in the physical world after death and can be reborn into another human or animal form. In general, the western concept of reincarnation is based on the belief that the soul is reborn into another body after death. In contrast, the Yoruba concept of reincarnation is based on the belief that the individual's spirit remains in the world after death and can be reincarnated into any number of different forms. There is no concept of heaven or hell, and the focus is on living a good life in order to achieve a positive afterlife. The Western view of reincarnation is often more focused on the spiritual realm, and the idea that the soul may be reborn into another human or animal form is not always emphasized. Yorubas also believe in heaven and hell, and a person's afterlife depends on their deeds in this life. As a result, the two concepts of reincarnation are quite different.

Difference between the Buddhist Concept of Reincarnation and Yoruba Reincarnation

In Yoruba belief, reincarnation is a continuous cycle in which the soul is reborn into different bodies. There is no set number of times a person can be reborn, and there is no final goal or destination. In Yoruba, reincarnation is the belief that a person's spirit can be reborn into another person or animal after they die. The soul simply continues to recycle through different lives, learning and growing with each new experience. This belief contrasts sharply with the Buddhist concept of reincarnation, which sees it as a process of progression toward Nirvana. In Buddhism, the soul is born into different forms based on its karma and will continue to be reborn until it reaches a state of perfection. At that point, it will be released from the cycle of rebirth and will attain Nirvana. For Buddhists, reincarnation is not an endless cycle but a journey with a specific goal. This is different from the Buddhist concept of reincarnation, which holds that a person's spirit is reborn into another person or animal after they die. In Yoruba, it is believed that a person's spirit can be reborn into another person or animal after they die. This is because the spirit is believed to be eternal and immutable. Consequently, the spirit can exist in multiple forms over time.

On the other hand, the Buddhist concept of reincarnation holds that a person's spirit is reborn into another person or animal after they die. This is because the spirit is considered impermanent and subject to change. Consequently, the spirit can only exist in one form at a time. While both concepts of reincarnation differ in their beliefs about the nature of the human soul, they both share the belief that the soul survives death and can be reborn into another body.

Difference between the Hindu Concept of Reincarnation and Yoruba Reincarnation

In both Hinduism and Yoruba, the concept of reincarnation is central to the religion. However, there are some key ways in which the two belief systems differ regarding this principle. For one, the Yoruba believe that a person can be born again as either a human or an animal, while Hindus generally believe that a person is reborn as another human. In addition, the Yoruba believe that a person's fate in their next life is determined by their actions in this one, while Hindus believe that karma determines what form a person will take in their next life. In Yoruba cosmology, reincarnation is a continuous cycle in which the human soul is reborn into different bodies. This cycle is known as "àyànjú." Unlike in Hinduism, where the soul is believed to be reborn into a higher or lower form based on their karma, in Yoruba cosmology, the soul is believed to be reborn into different forms to gain new experiences and learn new lessons. This means that the soul does not necessarily progress or regress in each life but simply moves through different forms to grow and develop. As a result, these different beliefs can lead to very different worldviews and approaches to religious practice.

Chapter 10: Ancestral Curses and How to Break Them

When someone utters the phrase "ancestral curse," you might think that they are being figurative. In reality, an ancestral curse is, unfortunately, a real problem that a lot of families face.

The African community explains that ancestral curses are cast on a single family member. The curse begins to spread to others through the cursed member. The cursed person passes it to their children then the children pass it on. Slowly but surely, the whole family becomes carriers of this misfortune.

Casting and breaking an ancestral curse is risky. Even if someone has expertise in witchcraft, it does not mean that they should be working with this kind of energy. The amount of energy that it takes to curse a whole family is unfathomable, and interfering with it is dangerous for both the spellcaster and the individuals involved. The same logic applies to spellcasters who are trying to break the curse. Why is that? The amount of energy it takes to curse a whole family is the same amount it takes to heal them from their misfortune.

This chapter will cover elements regarding the topic. It is better to be curious and wary than try to take on the responsibility of dealing with this type of magic. Ultimately, dealing with this kind of energy can result in consequences that you did not anticipate.

Types of Curses

Everyone experiences misfortunes now and then, but how can you tell the difference between random bouts of bad luck and a generational curse? The answer is both simple and complicated.

The simple answer is that if you have observed that you and your family have been suffering from the same problem or that a pattern is damaging your loved ones, then your family is probably cursed.

However, if you want to know whether you are a victim of a generational curse, you must first know what you are dealing with. There are many types of curses, and each one manifests differently. One curse might affect a family in one way, and another might affect them completely differently. You need to learn about different curses and how they affect people, and this will tell you whether you are suffering from bad mojo or not.

The Red Thighs

The red thighs curse refers to women who have been cursed with husbands who don't live long. This means that a woman with this curse will constantly be stuck in a cycle of grief, and she will be continuously grieving her dead husband.

Women with red thighs are not the only victims, unfortunately. Their daughters and husbands are too. The husbands will die shortly after marrying the woman. On the other hand, the daughters will inherit the curse from the mothers. This means that the daughters will be widowers who might also pass the same curse to their daughters.

It does not end here, though; it gets worse. Women with this curse are not just widowers; they are also face discrimination from their community. It is difficult to keep this a secret; eventually, society will notice the many deaths of men who married the same woman, and once it becomes evident, the cursed woman will have fewer and fewer friends. She will, most likely, spend her whole life without a mate because men will fear for their lives.

Bad Omen

Men are usually the targets of the bad omen. It is said that when a man is cursed with being the carrier of a bad omen, he disrupts and destroys anything he sets his gaze on. For instance, if a cursed man touches a child, the child might get sick. If the man plays with an animal, the animal might get sick or die. The curse also disrupts the man's sexual relations with his wife or other women. This makes it uncomfortable and unpleasant to enjoy his sexual life.

The curse also ruins his relationships and connections with others. This man will most likely unconsciously offend someone or find himself in a heated argument because of something he said.

In short, the bad omen curse is not deadly, but it makes life incredibly challenging and stifling. It is said that men with this curse are most likely to die because of the horrible situations in which they find themselves because of the curse. So far, there have not been any accounts of any men dying early because of this curse.

There are, of course, other types of curses, but these target certain people. For instance, any man or woman who desecrates nature or a sacred tree will be cursed. They may be shunned from the community or forbidden from receiving guidance regarding witchcraft. Men who rape or practice incest are also said to be cursed. These curses manifest differently because the spellcaster decides how they are going to punish an individual. One spellcaster might harm a man's land, and another might make a man infertile.

The Delicate Nature of Ancestral Curses

There are many beliefs surrounding the nature of ancestral curses. Some practitioners believe that it can only be broken through spellcasting. Other witches believe that breaking generational curses are more about personal beliefs. In other words, one does not have to resort to casting spells to separate themselves from the pain that has been haunting their family.

To know how to rid yourself of curses, you must first understand how they work. Yorubas believe the curse loses some of its power when the spellcaster dies, but it will still haunt the family.

New-age spiritualists believe that when a witch casts a curse on a person, they live their whole lives dedicating some of their energy to this curse. When they die, the curse dies with them. However, when the cursed family begins to talk about it, they give it power. In a way, the curse lives on through their words and beliefs. The more one addresses it, the more control it has over their life. In other words, the cursed family becomes the same person who has cursed them because now they are giving it energy.

How to Break Generational Curses

Modern-day practitioners have come up with a few solutions that could sever individuals from their curse. First, they say that if you have begun to believe that you can break a negative pattern, you have already started to weaken its effects.

Secondly, breaking a generational curse can be done through means that do not involve casting a spell to counteract the original spell. Combating a spell with this amount of energy can be dangerous to everyone involved. If you would like to know more about breaking a curse through safe means, then you will find a few safe options below.

The Power of Thoughts and Beliefs

This is a universal truth; your thoughts and words have power. Whatever you believe in has tremendous influence over you and your life. This might sound like magical thinking, but it really is not. How you perceive your life and the set of beliefs that you have, shape your life, whether you see it or not.

Once you believe that your thoughts, beliefs, and words have power, you can begin to weaken the curse's effects. By doing this, you give yourself control over the curse. You can do this by simply poking holes at the curse and its effects. Begin asking questions about the nature of the curse. Distance yourself from the idea of the curse as much as possible.

Write down a list of affirmations that deflect the power of the curse and empower yourself through them as much as possible. Try to repeat these affirmations as frequently as you can. Avoid associating it with the curse when something bad happens to you. Whatever misfortune has reached you could have been caused by a million other factors that are not the curse. Also, remember bad things happen to everyone all the time. It does not mean that they are cursed, and neither are you.

The More, The Merrier

The faster you recognize that there is power in numbers, the faster you will rid yourself of your generational curse. Now, how does this work? Well, it is really simple. If one man's thoughts are powerful enough to change the course of his life, then imagine if it were a group of people moving toward the same target. What do you think will happen?

All you need to do is gather your family members. Address the problem head-on and suggest you all gather together and affirm your affirmations. Send them out to the universe. Pray to the ancestors and ask them to help you reach your goal. Affirm to yourselves and others that this curse has no power over you.

One activity you can do as a family is praying to the ancestors at an altar. Pray together as one. Ask the ancestors to help remove the negativity surrounding you. When you are done, imagine the ancestors removing the curse from you and begging to celebrate. You can celebrate by offering food and drinks to the ancestors to show gratitude. Then begin dancing and chanting. This sends a message to you and the universe that the curse has been lifted from you. The more you do this, the less you will feel the curse's effects. Eventually, it will be completely powerless, and you will finally be free.

Affirmation rituals are also powerful. They let you affirm to one another that the curse has no power over you. It would be best if you give each other logical reasons why you are not cursed. When should you do this? Every time you or a family member thinks the curse caused a certain event, gather around and loudly say that you are not cursed. Tell the universe that you and your family are blessed. Assure one another that the ancestors are protecting you and shielding you from harm's way.

Forgiving the original spellcaster is one final solution you can resort to as a family. This, of course, can be a challenging task to complete. However, if you see this act as a way to empower you and your family, it might become a bit easier.

You can discuss the positive outcomes you will gain as a family when you forgive the spellcaster. Then work your way up to forgiving them. Try to understand why they cast the curse. Whatever their reasoning was, maybe it was not their right to take matters into their own hands. By forgiving them, you release yourself from their negative energy toward you.

Cleansing Rituals

If your energy has been tainted with negativity, then it must be spiritually cleansed. The beautiful thing about spiritual cleansing is that anyone can do it. You do not have to be well-versed in the realm of magic to uplift your energy. The process is simple, and the results are profound.

To get started with a cleansing ritual, you need to know a few things. Firstly, you need to be introduced to the concept of energy cleansing. Secondly, you should know which ingredients to use. Thirdly, pick a few cleansing rituals to do alone or with your family.

1. Energy Cleansing

Energy cleansing basically means replacing negative energy that has attached itself to you with a positive one. You cannot uplift your energy with neutral energy or by simply ridding yourself of negativity. Negative energies must be replaced with more positive ones.

Ingredients and rituals will help you gain more positive energy. However, if you keep negative beliefs about yourself, then you won't get anywhere. Remember to empower yourself with positive thoughts as you use sacred ingredients that will remove any negativity surrounding you.

2. Ingredients

In the realm of spirituality, there are various ingredients that you can use to have more positive energy around you, especially if you are pushing away unwanted energy from your life.

The most powerful ingredients that you can use are:

- Sage
- Rosemary
- Sea salt
- Salt
- Holy water
- Basil

3. Cleansing Rituals

There are different cleansing rituals that you can practice. Let's start with the simple ones. One thing you can do is cleanse your house and altar with sacred ingredients.

First of all, declutter. Remove anything that you do not need or brings you unhappiness. Secondly, if you have received any object from the spellcaster who cursed your family, get rid of it. If you have gifts from witches whom you do not trust, then get rid of their gifts.

Thirdly, add sea salt to the cleaning detergent you use to clean the floor. Scrub the floor with water that is mixed with sea salt. As you do so, picture the negativity evaporating from your house.

Fourthly, burn sage in your house. Open the windows before you burn the sage, then start moving around from one room to another with the burning sage. As you do so, envision the sage's smoke cleansing the house's energy. You can add rosemary and basil to the mix as well.

Next, clean your altar. A clean altar tells the ancestors that you respect them and appreciate their protection. When you are done, pray that they shield you from any unwanted energy.

Lastly, do a cleansing ritual for yourself. Dress in white and surround yourself with sage smoke. Then fill your bathtub with water and add sea salt to it. Add a few drops of rosemary essential oil to it, but only if you are not allergic to it. Soak in the water and feel the negativity leaving your body and being replaced with more positive energy.

Ancestral curses are a great misfortune to carry, but you do not have to succumb to their power. Recognize the amount of power that you and your family have. Once you do, the curse will have less and less power over you. You do not need to resort to dangerous methods to rid yourself of this. You can try different things, and the best part is that these methods have worked for others, so why wouldn't they work for you too?

To summarize, believe in yourself and your power. Once you believe that the curse has no control over your life and your start living according to this belief, your life will begin to change. Do not shy away from having tough family discussions regarding the curse. Yes, it may be challenging or embarrassing to address. However, it must be talked about so that you and your family lead a better life. There are various activities that you and your family can do together to get rid of this negativity. Think about this thoroughly and believe that you have the power to change the negative chain of events.

Conclusion

African spirituality mainly revolves around family, bloodlines, history, and the land. This is why Yoruba is fixated on concepts like reincarnation, ancestral veneration, and connecting with the Orishas.

Looking closely at Yoruba practices, you will find that its belief system is built on Nigerian history. Nigerians have immense gratitude for their families, which is why they honor them even after death. Building altars and shrines to honor and communicate with them is their way of remembering and keeping them close to their hearts.

The Yorubas believe that there is life after earthly death. The spirit continues to live on in another realm. When the soul separates from its fleshy body, it enters a greater state of consciousness. This elevated state provides spirits with great wisdom and powers that they lacked when they were human. The soul does not forget who it loved and was connected to when it was on earth. This is why Yorubas know that when their family members die, they become spiritual ancestors who look out for them.

When Yorubas maintain their ancestors' shrines and pray to them, the ancestors see that they are being appreciated and remembered. In return, the ancestors hear their humans' calls and answers in their unique way.

Death does not separate Yorubas from their loved ones. In one way, the ancestors are with them in spirit, and in another, their loved ones can be reincarnated as another life. They might not see their families in the way they are used to, but they know in their hearts that their loved ones are alive in the universe somewhere.

Offerings, prayer, worship, and witchcraft play an important role in Yoruba. First of all, offerings and prayer are how one can communicate with the Orishas and ancestors. When practitioners need divine help with their lives, they humbly ask their spirit guides and ancestors to help them. Often, the Orishas call out to the practitioners themselves. To keep this line of communication open, one needs to be connected with one's spiritual life; otherwise, you will not hear or feel your spirit guides.

Secondly, witchcraft opens a direct doorway between the practitioner, their ancestors, and Orishas. Of course, this divine art can be complicated to navigate, but Yoruba provides enough knowledge for everyone. Priests help other practitioners find their way around sacred ingredients and powerful prayers. It is not recommended that beginners dabble with complicated spells. On the other hand, novices can still practice this divine art when provided with guidance and supervision.

Aside from shrines and prayers, the Odun Egungun is a powerful tool to connect to the spirits as well. This festival is a gathering of human and divine energy on the same day during the same time. When humans dedicate their energies to their ancestors, something extraordinary always occurs. This is why multiple stories about spirits reveal themselves during this day. Honoring the ancestors privately is worship, but collectively honoring the ancestors is a divine act that is much greater than one person. The Odun Egungun reminds Yorubas that they will always be connected to one another and their ancestors.

Glossary of Yoruba Terms

Yoruba practices often use many unfamiliar words and terms that may sound foreign to beginners. This chapter summarizes all the Yoruba terms to help you navigate through the book. You can use it as a reminder when you want to look up certain words as you continue reading.

Commonly Used Yoruba Terms

- **Adétayànyá:** An Egbe group comprised of children who are mysteriously attracted to refuse dumps and will do everything to find these and stay near them. Mentioned in Chapter 4.
- **Abiku:** Also known as stillborn children. In Yoruba, this term refers to the interruption of the natural cycle of life when a person, regardless of age, dies before their parents. Mentioned in Chapter 4.
- **Ashe:** The divine energy each spirit possesses or has the ability to harness for empowerment. It can be obtained through different Yoruba practices, including ancestral veneration. Mentioned in Chapter 1.
- **Aje:** Known as the other mothers, Aje are wise women with extraordinary powers. They help conduct ceremonies, perform divination, and make people both fear and revere them. Mentioned in Chapter 1.

- **Ajogun:** Creatures representing negative forces of nature, and they can cause all kinds of mishaps in one's life. Mentioned in Chapter 1.
- **Akinori:** One of the most popular types of masks worn by Odun Egungun dancers. "Akinlari" means "one who cannot be seen" in Yoruba. These masks are used in ceremonies and rituals conducted to protect the wearer from evil spirits. Mentioned in Chapter 6.
- **Asipa:** A group of Egbe characterized by their ability to express themselves clearly. They are vocal and mysterious. Asípa are challenging to understand, have a sense of grandiosity, and aren't loyal. Mentioned in Chapter 4.
- **Ayanmo:** The cycle of life each soul passes through, according to the Yoruba people. Mentioned in Chapter 9.
- **Ayala, also known as Bablu-Aye or Sopona:** The third ancestral line named after one of the spirits manifested as the Earth and is strongly associated with infectious diseases and healing. Mentioned in Chapter 5.
- **Baálè:** An Egbe group often regarded as a blend between the Ìyálóde and Elééko as it is characterized by their leadership skills and tendency to exhibit various personalities. They stand out due to their numerous talents. Mentioned in Chapter 4.
- **Babalawo:** High priests of the Yoruba, who perform various ceremonies, including rites of passage and ancestral veneration. Their name is translated as "the father of the secrets," as they can harness divine wisdom no one else can access. Mentioned in Chapter 1.
- **Chango, also known as Shango, or Xango:** The god of storm and lighting and the brother of Ogun. It is said that he was a famous Yoruba warrior who ascended to the status of Orisha through spiritual enlightenment. Mentioned in Chapter 2.
- **Ebo, also known as ebbo:** A term used for sacrifices and offerings made to deities, ancestors, and other spirits. It can be presented in many ways, including by placing food, drinks, objects, and decorations on one's altar or releasing live animals. Mentioned in Chapter 3.

- **Egbe Orun, also known as "heavenly mates":** Egbe Orun are spirits that provide assistance, guidance, and protection during spiritual communication. Mentioned in Chapter 4.
- **Egun:** The souls of deceased ancestors or spirits you feel drawn towards. They can be blood relatives or part of your religious family. Spirit guides and animal spirits are considered egun and are honored specifically in rites and ceremonies. Mentioned in Chapter 9.
- **Eleggua:** Eleggua, Èṣù-Ẹlegbára, or Elegua, is the guardian of the crossroads of life. According to the Yoruba, he is the Orisha of new opportunities and can help carry messages to the spiritual realm. However, he's prone to mischief, trickery, and mayhem. Mentioned in Chapter 2.
- **Eléékò:** An Egbe group with members whose mood is easily swayed by overwhelming desires. Mentioned in Chapter 4.
- **Gelede:** A female masquerade held for Odun Egungun. It's associated with maternal power and protection. Mentioned in Chapter 6.
- **Igba Didi:** A specific ritual conducted to help remedy a connection with Egbe Orun. Often used together with Irari Egbe. Mentioned in Chapter 4.
- **Irari Egbe:** An initiation rite to form a covenant with a person's astral counterpart to help establish a connection with Egbe Orun. Mentioned in Chapter 4.
- **Ìyálóde:** The society of leaders of Egbe in the physical realm. Characterized by the quality of leadership. Mentioned in Chapter 4.
- **Iyalawo:** The female counterparts of Babalawo. Iyalawo are Yoruba priestesses that perform ceremonies, rituals, and prayer sessions, officiate ceremonies and are held in the highest esteem by their families. Mentioned in Chapter 1.
- **Jagun:** An Egbe fraternity whose name means warrior due to its relentlessness and persistence. Members of this group are known for their benevolence, adaptability, and ability to accommodate others. Mentioned in Chapter 4.
- **Móohún:** An Egbe group of Children who are often very hesitant to do chores or run errands. They come across as lazy

and can be very reluctant when making decisions. Mentioned in Chapter 4.

- **Obatalá:** The creator of living beings and the Yoruba God of purity. Also known as Obàtálá, Orisha-Popo, Olufon, Orisanla, Orisala Orisha-Nla, Oshanla, and Orishala, he was given the task of inhabiting the Earth by Olodumare. He is associated with fortune, fertility, and childbirth. Mentioned in Chapters 1 and 2.
- **Odun Egungun**: a celebration of the ancestors and a way to honor their continued presence in the lives of future generations. Mentioned in Chapter 5.
- **Ogun:** The Yoruba god of weapons and warfare. Ogun is the patron of metalworkers, blacksmiths, and hunters. His followers are called Abogun. He also created weapons using iron and other metals and is often associated with justice. Mentioned in Chapter 2.
- **Olodumare:** The supreme God, Olodumare or Olorun, is the creator of the world. A genderless being that lives in the heavenly realm, overseeing peace, justice, and spiritual ways. Mentioned in Chapter 1.
- **Olokun:** The Yoruba god of the sea and the husband of Elusu, Olokun is associated with the ocean, rivers, and the sea. He is quick to anger and must be kept appeased with frequent offerings. Mentioned in Chapter 1.
- **Olúgbógeró:** An Egbe group associated with free-flowing waters or rivers. Traditionally, Abiku, or stillborn children, are thought to be related to the Olúgbógeró. Mentioned in Chapter 4.
- **Oogun:** Along with isegun, and egbogi, oogun represents a trio of mysterious powers associated with medicine and magic. All three can facilitate spiritual communication and ancestral worship. Mentioned in Chapter 1.
- **Ori:** A Yoruba word for a person's head. The ori acts as a vessel for another ori, which is an invisible "inner" head. The latter refers to the human spirit that is the center of one's personality. Mentioned in Chapter 2.

- **Oriki:** A praise poem often used to venerate ancestors, Orishas, or other spirits. It describes their characters, their most memorable deeds, and whatever contribution they made to their family and community. Mentioned in Chapter 8.
- **Orisha:** Spiritual beings that oversee other living creatures and answer Olodumare. They possess powers people can harness for success, spiritual growth, communication, rites of passage, divination, healing, and more. Mentioned in Chapter 2.
- **Orisa-Oko:** The ancestral line representing farming, fertility, and the cyclical nature of life and death. Mentioned in Chapter 5.
- **Orunmila:** The Yoruba deity of wisdom and prophecy is known to lend a helping hand to those seeking spiritual knowledge. Whether you're seeking to obtain spiritual wisdom through divinities, ancestors, or other spirits, Orunmila can show you the way. Mentioned in Chapter 2.
- **Oso:** Along with oogun buburu and oogun ika, oso is a power linked to sorcery. It's often used to cause harm or prevent spiritual communication and growth. Often the result of an ancestral curse. Mentioned in Chapter 1.
- **Osonga:** Along with eye and aje, osonga is a mysterious force associated with witchcraft. Similarly to sorcery, witchcraft has negative connotations as it is often linked to curses and other malicious acts. Mentioned in Chapter 1.
- **Oso Ijoba:** Traditionally, a male masquerade held for Odun Egungun. It is often associated with death and fertility. Mentioned in Chapter 6.
- **Oshun:** The Yoruba Goddess of love, Oshun governs love, sensuality, and creativity. She also protects the river Oshun and facilitates intimacy and love in relationships. Mentioned in Chapter 2.
- **The 16 truths of Ifa:** A list of recommendations to follow if you want to lead a righteous life and obtain spiritual enlightenment. It is also a form of ancestral veneration, as mentioned in Chapter 8.
- **Tunde:** Refers to spiritual rebirth, which allows the soul to gather more spiritual wisdom. It can also signify the symbolic

rebirth after the initiation into the Yoruba religion. Mentioned in Chapter 9.

- **Sango:** A Yoruba ancestral group hailing from the royal ancestor of the Yoruba. He can manifest in different ways, including aira, agodo, and lubé. Mentioned in Chapter 5.
- **Yemaya:** The Yoruba Goddess of childbirth and water. According to the Yoruba, she has a fluent personality that changes with the phases of the moon. She is the wife of Obatala and is known by the names of Iamanjie, Yemanja, Yembo, Yemonja, Yemoja, and Yemowo. Mentioned in Chapter 2.

Part 5: Ogun

The Ultimate Guide to an Orisha and Loa of Yoruba, Santería, and Haitian Voodoo

Introduction

Have you ever wondered what secrets lay within the ancient religion of Yoruba? Do you want to uncover the mysteries of Ogun, the God of Iron? In this book, you'll explore the secrets of Ogun's divine power and learn how to incorporate Ogun's teachings into your everyday life.

For centuries, the Yoruba people of West Africa have celebrated Ogun, a deity revered for his life-giving and transformative energy. He is cited as the ancestor of warriors, hunters, artisans, and those who brought culture and technologies (like ironworking) to the area. This incredible technology transformed the region's culture by easing laborious tasks with tools made out of iron. The region was strengthened through cultural exchanges, such as ivory carving, metalworking, and furniture making.

In honor of Ogun's transformative energy, devotees still celebrate him at the annual Ogun festival in Nigeria. During the festivities, reverential monks invite blessings from the god and offer magical objects in exchange for blessings. They are hopeful that these rituals will bring great fertility to their crops and ensure protection against any untoward situations in their lives and community. This book will explore various aspects of Ogun's worship, including his symbols and offerings, rituals and spells, holy days and festivals, and daily rituals to celebrate him.

Ogun is an amazing figure who has been worshipped worldwide since ancient times. He is known for his strength and power, and those qualities are evident in his presence across the continents. Many cultures have embraced him as a god of protection or a patron of metalwork, such as that performed by blacksmiths or warriors. Through this incredible reach, Ogun has shared his power with people from all walks of life, allowing them to embrace his awesome strength daily!

This book explores the depths of Ogun's power, and readers will learn how to invite his divine gifts into their lives. It will also uncover the secrets of his symbols and offerings, delve into rituals and spells, and discover how to celebrate his festivals and holy days. At the same time, it explores why Ogun is still relevant today and what he can teach followers about the power of strength and courage.

Ogun, the fourth king of Ife and the Yoruba people, was a warrior and protector god who brought multiple blessings to the kingdom. His worship is still alive amongst many who strive to honor him with small festivals, music, and offerings. The secrets of Ogun's worship, which hew to ancient traditions, are carefully guarded. However, it's possible to pay homage to this fascinating deity and learn more about his past through this book. Readers will gain invaluable insight into the power and mystery of Ogun and how to make the most of his gifts. Happy exploring!

Chapter 1: Who Is Ogun?

Yoruba and Haitian Voodoo are two spiritual traditions with powerful histories passed down through the generations over centuries. It's incredible to think about how long these two practices have existed. The concept of a shared cultural identity between African people is inspiring, as it shows that regardless of where people come from, everyone can still be connected by their roots. While the two practices may seem different on the surface, they have many core values, symbols, and practices in common. This is an example of the strong spirit of unity that transcends time and place.

Yoruba and Haitian voodoo have a powerful history within many communities.
Calvin Hennick, for WBUR Boston, CC BY 3.0 <https://creativecommons.org/licenses/by/3.0>, via Wikimedia Commons
https://commons.wikimedia.org/wiki/File:Haitian_vodou_altar_to_Petwo,_Rada,_and_Gede_spirits;_November_5,_2010..jpg

Ogun, an illustrious figure in the Yoruba religion and Haitian Voodoo faith, is among the most revered figures in these two sacred traditions. Ogun is worshipped as a warrior god and guardian of iron. He is seen as a protector who can fight off evil forces. On either side of the Atlantic, believers seek his strength and guidance for protection in times of need. Whether found on the African continent or the Caribbean island of Haiti, it's easy to see why Ogun is such a significant part of both civilizations' spiritual life!

This chapter will explore the concept and significance of Ogun in the Yoruba and Haitian Voodoo religions. It will discuss the characteristics, spellings, rituals, offerings, and associations in each tradition, as well as their differences and similarities. It will also show how Ogun is viewed in both cultures and how he is connected to his other identities. By the end of this chapter, you should better understand Ogun's importance and relevance in the Yoruba and Haitian Voodoo religious beliefs.

Overview of the Yoruba and Haitian Voodoo Religions

The Yoruba and Haitian Voodoo religions have a long and fascinating past, stretching back hundreds and hundreds of years. Both religions are tied to the African diaspora, tracing their origins back to West Africa. They each offer insight into the spiritual practices of the people who created them and have impacted many other cultures worldwide. While their customs, beliefs, and traditions may differ significantly, their common ancestry still connects these faiths profoundly. It's incredible to think that they remain so influential despite having such distant points of origin!

Originating from African cultures, these faith systems were brought to the Caribbean by enslaved African people during the diaspora. Both are unique religions steeped in rituals and practices used for divination, healing, and prayer for protection. All of these practices involve elements of nature, such as magical charms, ancestral spirits, and sacred objects. The Yoruba spread to other parts of Africa and the Americas, while Haitian Voodoo mixed with Catholicism over time. These religions emphasize living harmoniously with one's environment, which is very relevant in the modern world. By understanding the foundation and tenets of both Yoruba and Haitian Voodoo, you can learn more about each other's cultures and healing practices and how you can better honor this shared planet.

Ogun across Yoruba and Haitian Voodoo Religions

Ogun is a prominent god in Yoruba and Haitian Voodoo religions and African Diaspora spiritual systems. He is known as the Orisha of metal, strength, war, and protection, among other things. In the Yoruba religion, he is one of the most powerful spirits, charged with leading other spirits in times of crisis. In Haitian Voodoo, Ogun's special focus is to bring luck to his devotees along their journey in life. The rhythmic chants used to honor him emphasize his importance and power. Across these two religions and even beyond Africa, people who revere Ogun honor him in different ways. Some pray while others perform rituals such as dancing accompanied by drums or banging tools relating to his affinity with metalwork.

Ogun in the Yoruba Religion

Ogun holds a lot of significance for those who follow the Yoruba faith. His importance lies not only in providing protection and guidance, but his biggest impact is on the culture itself. Ogun teaches humility, respect, justice, courage, and industry. He is credited with enforcing laws and creating avenues for artistic expression through song, dance, poetry, and sculpture. As one of the most powerful gods of Yoruba mythology, Ogun inspires generations with his strength, devotion, and love for the Yoruba people.

Ogun is considered the god of ironwork and war and is celebrated by one of the biggest religious festivals in Nigeria, a weeklong event during which people come from all over to pay homage to Ogun. Worshipers offer him yams and other foods as he is known for providing abundance when prayers for success are answered. Ogun appeals to all classes, embodying hard labor and courage as he pushes through obstacles and finds solutions to any challenge.

A. Characteristics

Ogun is an Orisha warrior god with incredible symbolic potential. He is associated with the metal-smithing trade and represents the strength and power of iron. His presence is strongly felt whenever people are busy constructing things from metal or otherwise manipulating its form.

He's seen as a beloved protector who watches over warring parties to help bring about peace and a kind-hearted figure who provides advice and assistance to mortals in times of need.

Ogun possesses unique characteristics that give him unquestionable authority and immense wisdom, making him highly respected among his followers. Regardless of the task at hand, when Ogun's guidance is sought after, he never fails to bring about positive results for those who call upon him, making himself irreplaceable in Yoruba religious practices.

B. Symbolism

Symbolically, Ogun is associated with strength, justice, and being a protector of the people. He is often depicted as a warrior, representing his willingness to physically fight for what he believes in. Additionally, it is said that Ogun created tools and imbued traditional medicines such as herbs or protective charms with his powers and which are used for healing and protection. In other words, Ogun's symbolism represents not only the battle but also accomplishment and construction.

The machete is another significant symbol associated with Ogun, as it represents the physical strength of warriors and is also a tool used to cut through any obstacles that may be standing in the way. Other symbols include fire, swords, and horses, all meant to represent Ogun's readiness to fight for what is right. The colors red, black, and white symbolize Ogun as they represent the element fire, which manifests his power.

C. Rituals

The Yoruba religion has many unique practices, including the ritualistic worship of Ogun. Derived from their ancient African folklore, this deity stands for strength, courage, and determination. It holds a vital place as a spirit guide who helps lost souls find their way back to safety. Although his presence can be overwhelming at times when it comes to combat, he ultimately serves to protect those in need.

His rituals are often incorporated into ceremonies like birth rites and fertility celebrations as a symbol of progress and security in the community. Some of the rituals and festivals dedicated to Ogun involve offerings of food, drink, and in some cases, sacrifices. It's interesting to consider how traditional practices such as these have been able to endure throughout time and remain influential in modern society today!

D. Offerings

Ogun is seen as a powerful ally with the ability to protect and give guidance throughout life's struggles. His offerings are believed to be highly beneficial for those looking to improve their physical and spiritual health. It's not uncommon for offerings of food, specially prepared meals, or even metal tools or statues of Ogun himself to be placed at his altars to honor his presence.

Offering tribute to the influential Ogun of Yoruba faiths is a meaningful way to express gratitude and respect for his many blessings. Tributes demonstrate appreciation and maintain a positive relationship with this powerful figure. Whether it's in the form of daily prayers, artwork, jewelry, or other offerings, being mindful of worshiping Ogun through tributes can profoundly impact your life. It's one small step that can reap big rewards.

E. Association with Other Gods

Ogun is an openly revered god in the Yoruba religion, along with Obatala and Ile. He is a symbol of strength and courage, offering protection to those who call upon him. Ogun is also associated with ironworking and new beginnings, so he holds a special place in marriages and initiations into adulthood. People who follow the Yoruba faith will often leave offerings for him at crossroads to mend any grievances that may have arisen. He brings life-sustaining elements like rain, the wind, and fire which are necessary for everyday life. In short, Ogun is an important part of the Yoruba religion and is highly regarded as a protector and foundation of well-being amongst followers of the faith.

Ogun in the Haitian Voodoo Religion

Ogun is an influential lwa in the Haitian Voodoo religion. He's frequently depicted as a soldier dressed in either red or white, holding a machete and smoking a cigar. As in the Yoruba religion, Ogun is the lwa of metal, iron, and weapons, making him the protector of people who labor for their living using such tools. He's also deeply associated with technology since he guards and controls the machines humans use to perform physical tasks, making him an essential deity in contemporary Haitian culture, where many inhabitants integrate technology into their lives.

Ogun, the powerful son of Yemaya, is great to have on your side. His passion for justice and his fierce wrath towards evil have earned him a place in the pantheon of many African tribes. Yet Ogun also shows a sweet reverence towards those who pay respect to him by honoring and understanding his power. If an offering is made with proper respect and admiration, he will offer protection and blessing to whoever requests it. His presence brings strength, courage, and true healing to those within his realm.

A. Origin of the Loa

Ogun is an essential figure within Haitian Voodoo and plays a big role as the Warrior God or Lord of Iron. He is considered to be a guardian of travelers and a protector from danger. On top of this, he symbolizes strength, courage, assertiveness, creativity, and fertility, the attributes that many venerate in their daily lives. Ogun was first introduced to Haitians with the arrival of African slaves in the 18th century. Before then, worship of the Loa was unknown.

The slaves adopted Afro-Caribbean spiritual traditions such as Vodou, integrating them into their belief systems while keeping ancient secrets alive throughout generations. This explains why Ogun remains so important to Haitian people today. He has roots deep within the country's history and continues to promote resilience among its citizens.

B. Role in Haitian Voodoo

Ogun is an essential figure in the Haitian Voodoo religion, a major African-Caribbean faith. Ogun, sometimes referred to as the "Warrior God," represents a powerful spirit associated with control and protection. Those who worship Ogun will often pray for his assistance during difficult times of struggle and unrest. He is seen as the guardian of justice and protector of all living things. His skill at protecting from enemies and misfortune is renowned throughout the religion and by anyone engaging in Voodoo practices or seeking guidance on a spiritual journey.

Worshipers are encouraged to always show their utmost respect for Ogun, offering various types of offerings, such as sacrificial animals that represent peace and prosperity. Beyond this, Ogun has become increasingly popular even in non-Voodoo circles. Travelers, adventurers, business professionals, students, athletes, and others also seek out his guidance and protection when embarking on life-changing events or projects.

C. Characteristics

Ogun is seen as fierce, powerful, and unyielding. He's a necessary figure for times when his followers feel overwhelmed and must draw on power from within themselves. He is known to be passionate about justice and economic success and can provide both protection and guidance. He is often imagined as dressed in red with a machete in hand. He is associated with fire, steam, or smoke rising from the fire used in ancestral ceremonies. He provides strength and integrity to those who venerate him. Worshipping Ogun enables Haitians to feel empowered regardless of their circumstances, something that has been particularly valuable throughout Haiti's long history of oppression and upheaval.

D. Connections to Other Loas

Holding a place of prominence in the Haitian voodoo religion, Ogun is often referred to as the god of iron and war, but his impact on religion goes far beyond that, representing technology and progress. Ogun has many connections to other Loas in this religion, like Baron Samedi and Damballah. For instance, like Baron Samedi, Ogun connects with leadership and guidance. Like Damballah, who represents communication and emotions of connection with oneself during difficult times, Ogun is a loa who takes on the role of protector of those who are at their most vulnerable. All these shared connections make him an important part of the Haitian Voodoo religion's tradition and practice.

E. Offerings

People honor Ogun by having rituals set around iron implements and giving offerings such as four-sided nails or blades. It is said that if respected, Ogun has the power to make unimaginable changes in an individual's life. As a representation of strength, protection, justice, and growth, offerings are made to Ogun on specific days in the hopes of receiving his goodwill and blessings. Offerings such as tobacco are also given to keep Ogun appeased. It is believed that those who have called on Ogun's blessing can receive immense power over their destinies if they follow their dedication through. Ogun is truly a unique symbol of power and resilience from the Haitian Voodoo religion.

Comparing Yoruba and Haitian Voodoo

Yoruba and Haitian Voodoo have many similarities and differences, making them both unique and fascinating. Yoruba is distinct in its roots, which go back to traditional African beliefs, while Haitian Voodoo has kept its iconic voodoo dolls around for centuries-long. Both practices put faith in deities, sacrificial offerings through ritual ceremonies, consulting with spirits or gods to receive advice or blessings, and use talismans for protection.

Nigerian practitioners embrace a more communal approach to the practice, usually gathering together in groups during ceremony time, and are mostly centered on family lineage, whereas practitioners of Haitian Voodoo seek out solitary rituals, take their solo path outside the prescribed ceremony setting, and ask help from powerful Loa spirits. All in all, Yoruba and Haitian Voodoo remain fundamentally different yet similar in many ways.

In Yoruba tradition, Ogun is also called Ogou, Ògún Lákáayé, or Ogúm depending on the individual worshipper's affiliations and preferred dialect. His power over human existence through creativity and production has meant that even today, adherents will seek out his assistance when working with iron or undertaking political actions. Whether pacifistic or fierce, Ogun offers guidance to those dedicated to the transmission of knowledge across time and space.

However, Ogun is known as a Loa (spirit) in Haitian Voodoo. His presence holds a similar importance in Haiti's religious traditions as he is an intermediary between the spirit world and humanity. Ogun is a champion of justice, a creator of order, and a defender of those who have been wronged. He is often seen with an axe in hand, a symbol of his ability to clear the way for spiritual communication and connection.

Ogun's dual roles in Yoruba and Haitian Voodoo offer a fascinating insight into the differences between these two religions. While both traditions honor him as a spirit of strength and protection, how he is venerated differs. In Yoruba, Ogun is seen as an Orisha, who is worshiped and celebrated through rituals and sacrifices, whereas in Haitian Voodoo, he is seen as a Loa, or one who an individual can summon for direct communication and help. This illustrates the central difference between these two religions. Yoruba worships and appeases Orishas and other powerful spirits with ritual ceremonies. Haitian Voodoo places a greater emphasis on the autonomy of individuals, meaning that people are free to choose what they do. With the help of devotees, individuals can gain a deeper comprehension of a Loa's power and use it to their advantage.

A. Commonalities

Yoruba and Haitian Voodoo are fascinating forms of spirituality with incredible similarities. Although they may have originated in other parts of the world, both share common African roots. Both practice similar concepts, such as ancestor veneration, encouraging resilience from believers, and teaching them how to live purposeful lives. Even though traditional creeds differ in practices and foundational beliefs, the power structure and relationship between humans and gods are shared. Thus, the spirit of universality within both religions continues to unite diverse peoples who practice different faiths in respectful discourse and understanding.

B. Differences

The topics of Haitian Voodoo and Yoruba are a great way to learn about the distinctions between different cultures. Both faiths have been practiced for centuries throughout the same geographical region, yet distinct differences make each one unique. While both traditions rely heavily on spirit attachments, Yoruba focuses more on appeasing these spirits with ritual ceremonies, while Haitian Voodoo places a greater emphasis on the autonomy of individuals with activities like possessing worshippers and controlling their behavior. Haitian Voodoo also allows for the possibility of even creating new gods. All in all, studying the disparities between Yoruba and Haitian Voodoo opens one's eyes to how two divergent cultures can take fundamentally similar approaches yet still yield two drastically different results.

Ogun's Other Identities

Ogun is associated with metalworking, war, and other titles such as the God of Blacksmiths and Warrior Deity. While Ogun is famously known for his warrior spirit, he's also revered as a god of creativity, technology, and growth, offering divine inspiration to those who work with their hands to make things in life. His metalworking abilities allowed him to shape symbols of power, weapons that could both protect and harm if necessary. He has historically been seen as the patron saint of protection in times of war while providing guidance and strength during peaceful times.

Ogun, regarded as the patron of ironworkers, is one of the African religions' most powerful and widely-revered deities. Ogun's domain extends across all aspects of life, playing a part in procreation, marriage, birth, and death rituals. For example, traditionally, couples about to get married invoke his name while asking for a happy marriage. His influence is also extended beyond the realm of human activity. Ogun is often asked to protect fields from damage by animals or inclement weather. As an orisha (deity), Ogun plays an integral role in the local culture. His presence permeates many Nigerian traditions, both collectively and individually.

In Yoruba and Haitian Voodoo, Ogun is revered as a strong, powerful, and reliable spirit. He offers protection, guidance, justice, and strength in times of hardship. His roles as a deity of creativity, metalworking, and warfare make him one of the most popular Orishas/Loa in African religions. Despite his different names, titles, and roles, Ogun remains a powerful and influential spirit for people of both religions. He embodies strength, courage, and resilience in difficult times. Followers of Ogun are compelled to use his courage and strength in times of uncertainty, knowing that he will never abandon them regardless of what happens in their lives!

Chapter 2: Ogun as a Saint

Santeria, also known as La Regla Lucumi, is an Afro-Caribbean religion that blends elements of Yoruba and Haitian Vodou traditions with Roman Catholicism. It is especially popular in Cuba, but there are also a large number of followers in the United States as well. While Santeria honors both ancestral gods and those of African diaspora religions, the primary belief system is based on the veneration of Catholic saints and Jesus Christ himself.

Santeria is a religion that blends Vodou traditions with Catholicism.
Nheyob, CC BY-SA 4.0 <https://creativecommons.org/licenses/by-sa/4.0>, via Wikimedia Commons https://commons.wikimedia.org/wiki/File:Saint_Luke_Catholic_Church_(Danville,_Ohio)_-_stained_glass,_Saints_Teresa_of_Avila,_Clare_of_Assisi,_Monica,_and_the_Immaculate_Conception.JPG

The ritual practices associated with these saints give devotees a way to connect their spiritual beliefs with their everyday realities. Different levels of complex initiation rites must be completed before someone can become a part of the religion, though many devotees tell stories of receiving guidance through visions or dreams. All in all, Santeria encourages its followers to live harmonious lives with other cultures and religious systems.

This chapter will explore the role of Ogun in Santeria and how he is syncretized with various saints. It also discusses his protective capabilities and the offerings made to him. By the end of this chapter, you'll have a deeper understanding of how Ogun is venerated in Santeria. You'll also have a better appreciation for the spiritual power of Ogun and understand how his influence can be used to protect both individuals and their communities.

Introduction to Santeria

Santeria is a vibrant and colorful religious tradition that originates from the Caribbean islands. It is a polytheistic religion rooted in West African spiritual traditions, particularly its core beliefs and rituals. Santeria has grown in popularity since it arrived in the U.S., especially due to its eclectic syncretism, which melds African spiritual elements with other world religions such as Christianity and Indigenous American faiths. Santeria recognizes various deities called Orishas, who reflect forces of nature and represent moral values and ethical principles to inspire believers on their journey through life. Practitioners of this vibrant faith seek to create harmony between their visible world and unseen forces while gaining strength, power, courage, and knowledge through each interaction.

Santeria Differs from Yoruba and Haitian Voodoo

Santeria is an intriguing religion where ancient influences meet modern life. It is rooted in the beliefs of the indigenous people of Nigeria and Benin but has been recognized as distinct from both Yoruba and Haitian Voodoo. The primary difference lies in their approaches to magical practices. For example, Santeria seeks to not only present offerings to gods to have one's life changed but also seeks advice from oracular divination, whereas Yoruba and Haitian Voodoo practices focus more on the use of talismans and supernatural powers such as shape-shifters or zombies to respond directly to individual needs. Although it takes elements from all three religious traditions, Santeria is unique in its elements and meanings. Those practicing it believe nothing can happen until the ancestral gods are consulted. It is a process steeped in altruism rather than self-interest, emphasizing responsibility toward community harmony more than personal gain.

Ogun in Santeria

Ogun is a powerful god in the Santeria religion and is seen as a kind and protective deity who gives guidance to passionate individuals who ask for direction. He represents power, strength, and courage while embodying traits like intimacy, fervor, and enthusiasm. He is also known as the deity of war, ironworks, creativity, and hunting. Ogun is often associated with tools used by blacksmiths, such as anvils, hammers, and axes. This makes him one of the most significant deities to pray to for success if you are looking to start your own business or seek luck in any entrepreneurial endeavor.

The Role of Ogun in Santeria

Ogun is Santeria's African Orisha spirit of iron, fire, and war. He is an incredibly powerful Orisha who helps his followers better themselves to gain strength and courage. Ogun teaches that not all journeys have a single path and that he will bring you the power and insight needed to face any challenge, regardless of the difficulty. His signature color is red, and things like tools, weapons, and military equipment represent him as these are the things most associated with his domain. Ogun bestows upon his followers' great courage to deal with misfortune in life and heal their minds and hearts of sadness or sorrow so they can move forward in life, overcoming all obstacles. One thing followers of Ogun must remember is that power isn't just given but must be taken. He will mentor you on the journey with courage while you face the fear of taking action!

The Attributes of Ogun

In Santeria, Ogun is commonly referenced as the "father of all Orishas." He's known for being a warrior spirit and, as you know, is represented by iron and other metals. Ogun is the patron of technology, politics, jobs, and justice. His attributes include intelligence and knowledge, strength, inventiveness, and creativity. These traits symbolize how he can bring prosperity. Worshippers often offer him iron tools so that he can help them with their endeavors. Ogun's colors are green, black, and red, representing his strong connections to the Earth and protection from negative energy. He's also known for his passion and loyalty to those who serve him faithfully. All in all, Ogun is an incredibly important figure in Santeria and should not be overlooked when studying its belief system.

How to Invoke Ogun in Santeria

Santeria is a diverse religion, and many people have been learning its traditions for centuries. Ogun is one of the deities most commonly venerated in this belief system. If you are interested in some ritual practices to invoke Ogun, begin by investing in items that represent Ogun, such as tools or weapons of iron or a red candle. Ensure that you create an altar devoted to him and lay out your goods on it before lighting those candles and presenting offerings like fruit or other foods. As you do, keep petitioning the deity and explain what it is that you need help with, whether it's money, family matters, or education. When ready, close off the prayer with offerings of thanks and slowly finish off the ritual by blowing out each candle with a few words of gratitude directed towards Ogun for hearing your prayer.

Ogun's Syncretism with Saints

Ogun, the powerful Yoruba deity of Iron and War, is one of the most beloved figures in African diasporic religions worldwide. Ogun is celebrated among diverse cultures, which honor him for his multifaceted roles, from work and industry to protection and justice. Interestingly, Ogun has been syncretized with various saints in some folk religious cultures, connecting this powerful West African spirit to Roman Catholic figures like St. George and St. Jerome. By doing so, practitioners can connect with both religious legacies in unique ways and emphasize the shared values of strength, courage, tenacity, and nobility believed to be common between Ogun and such venerated saints. This syncretism highlights how connected everyone is on a spiritual level across time as well as space.

A. Saint Paul

The syncretism between the pre-colonial deity Ogun and St. Paul is interesting. Ogun was widely worshipped across West Africa as a spirit of iron and war, while Saint Paul is widely known today as an early Christian scholar and missionary. This syncretic link between the two faiths provides an opportunity to bridge traditional African religions and Christianity meaningfully. What's more, examining this history of religious mixing can even open up choices for Africans today on how they may pursue conformity (or not) with incumbent views on faith. From the outset, it appears that both beliefs can coexist peaceably in addition to fueling each other's growth – which makes for interesting reading!

B. John the Baptist

Ogun, an important deity worshipped in West Africa, holds a special place in the religious beliefs of Yoruba-speaking peoples. His ties to Christianity are especially noteworthy since he has been syncretized with John the Baptist, who enjoys particular significance in Christian scripture. This represents a blending between two belief systems and speaks volumes about the welcoming and tolerant values of the people of West Africa, who embrace many faiths and create open spaces where all cultures and religions can mix harmoniously. The connection between Ogun and John the Baptist is also interesting from a historical perspective, as it gives you a glimpse into the spiritual changes that have occurred over time.

C. Saint Jacob

Ogun is often syncretized with Saint Jacob in many parts of the world. This unique and fascinating phenomenon mirrors aspects of syncretism found in different belief systems throughout history. Ogun is known for being a formidable fighter, a great predictor of success, and a provider of strength for his followers. The character traits Ogun and Saint Jacob share include compassion, determination, and undying commitment to those they serve. It's no surprise then that so many cultures have found similarities between these two figures, illustrating how traditions around the globe are connected despite the geographical distance.

D. Saint Barbara

Ogun is widely regarded as a saint-like figure in the Yoruba religion. Still, it turns out that his syncretism reaches further than simply being Yoruban. Ogun's source of adoration has been linked to Saint Barbara in both Catholic and Orthodox Christian traditions. A strong connection between the two exists because they are so similar. Both are considered guardians who protect against political strife and other forms of chaos while also watching over crossroads, travel, and justice. The syncretism of Ogun with Saint Barbara appears to be less a combination of figures and more of a recognition of each other's virtues. Celebrating them together is just one way West Africans recognize their connectedness with the rest of the world!

E. Saint Peter

The Catholic Saint Peter is yet another example of syncretism with Ogun. It was believed that Ogun's power and strength could be called on through prayer to Saint Peter, showing how the two stories were interwoven. This is a powerful example of syncretism, blending two seemingly disparate entities and finding a culture, tradition, and power in their unity. Syncretism formed much of the basis for religious traditions for African Americans during the times of slavery – and carried forward even after emancipation; Ogun-Saint Peter is just one of many examples that continue to exist today.

By looking at these synergies, you can learn more about African cultures and the religious beliefs that have been shaped in the diaspora. Syncretism has enabled people of faith to build a bridge between disparate belief systems, creating a link between the divine and mortal world as well as creating a powerful way to express values and honor ancestral figures. Through the syncretism of Ogun with various saints, you better understand how West African spiritual traditions have evolved and why certain deities have become so important to people living in today's world.

Ogun as a Protective Force

In Santeria, he is considered a powerful protective force, a warrior, and a crusader, ready to leap into action to safeguard his people. Worshipping Ogun enables Santeria followers to feel protected within their community. It is believed that Ogun can provide strength when confronted with physical or spiritual obstacles. He also promises security against evil spirits and vigilante justice against any harm that may come to his devotees. Even in difficult times, having faith in Ogun ensures that his followers will not wander unprotected through the world. If you show respect to him, he will reward you with his protection, so it's crucial to honor him however you can.

A. Protection from Evil Spirits and Negative Energy

Thought of as a protective force against any dark forces that seek to harm, Ogun is honored by many practitioners of Santeria, who look to him for protection from evil spirits, negative energy, and generational trauma. He is seen as an extremely powerful weapon to be wielded against the darkness, a shield that will ward away anything with evil intentions. When you call on Ogun's strength and courage, you can feel empowered knowing you have a powerful ally behind you.

B. Uplifting Those in Need

In the Santeria tradition, the African god Ogun is viewed as a powerful force of protection and creation. Ogun is also considered a deity of war in the pantheon of Yoruban gods, but in Santeria, he is seen as more than just that. He is a deity who protects those in need, encourages creativity and changes through innovative thinking, and guards against anything threatening safety or well-being. Those who call on him for help often experience greater clarity in their lives and find the strength to take bold steps forward on their paths. In emphasizing love, peace, and compassion for all living things, Ogun serves as an uplifting force in the lives of those he helps.

C. Physical Protection

Ogun is an immensely influential Santerian figure. He is a powerful warrior, protector of the family, community, and home, and a defender of justice and retribution against oppressors; because of these strong associations with protection, many Santerians will call on him to offer physical safety from harm and maliciousness. Ogun offers a benevolent strength that ensures harmony and balance between the human realm and divine forces. There is something comforting about knowing that you have a powerful figure watching out for you when no one else can protect you. With his help, your well-being can be better secured and maintained.

D. Protection from Harmful Intentions

In Santeria, Ogun is a spiritual force of protection and defense. He guards people against harmful intentions and provides divine assistance to ensure that one is safe from danger. He is believed to be an immensely powerful deity, equipped with supernatural strength, and can overpower any enemy attempting to enter his domain. Ogun is also seen as a symbol of justice and retribution. In some traditions, he represents the fight for power or dominance over injustice, which makes him an effective source of protection for those in need. Through his strong presence, he brings about aid in difficult times and offers safety by deflecting harm away from those under his watchful eye, making him an invaluable asset in Santeria's pursuit of safe havens against dark forces.

E. Protection of the Home

Santeria is a faith practiced by millions of people, and at its center are powerful spirits called orishas. Ogun has long been associated with protection, especially when it comes to guarding homes. Ogun is considered a strong defender who stands ready to ward off evil forces should they ever attempt to cause harm to the inhabitants of the house. He helps not only to protect those within the house but also serves to purify the home and those who inhabit them. Ogun devotees give thanks to this spirit for his watchful presence and pray that his power will always work together with their energy and efforts to provide total safety and security in every home regarded as sacred by Santeria.

Ogun and His Offerings

A much-revered god in the practice of Santeria, Ogun is a powerful spirit and the orisha of war, labor, justice, and iron tools. He has many different facets to his identity, including a warrior spirit who fights for justice as well as a protector of riches and material wealth. Devotees to Ogun give offerings to show respect and appreciation, ranging from cigars or rum to coins or knives, depending on the individual looking for divine aid. People seeking fortune in their work may offer shiny coins, while someone looking for courage may present the orisha with a blade. No matter what the offering, Ogun is honored, usually with fire, and these offerings will be faithfully received.

A. Ebo for Ogun

Santeria is a powerful African-diasporic faith tradition with a strong connection to nature, as seen in the veneration of the Orisha Ogun. Ebo for Ogun honors and reinforces this connection by providing offerings of fruit and vegetables, along with items made from iron and other natural materials. The offering is a way for followers to give back to nature and revere Ogun, the most significant Santerian Orisha. Through these offerings, worshippers can honor his power to shape the physical world while affirming future success and peace. Furthermore, these practices carry symbolic meaning, which opens spiritual connections between humankind and the spirit or divine forces influencing everyday life.

B. Sacrifices to Ogun

The offering of sacrifices to Ogun is considered a form of honoring and offering respect. These sacrifices may include goats, roosters, yams, or other produce native to the region. In many cases, it is believed that sacrificing one's possessions pays greater homage than sacrificing an animal because the personal bond between practitioner and offer is stronger. Regardless of what a Santeria adherent chooses to offer as a sacrifice to Ogun, it should be conducted with love and respect for this generous spirit who so willingly gives his presence within rituals honoring him.

C. Offerings and Appeasement to Ogun

In Santeria, Ogun requires offerings and appeasement to grant his followers protection and abundance. Offerings for Ogun typically involve metals such as iron or copper, even gunpowder. Other sacrificial items, including food, alcohol, cigars, or smoke, may also be used to appease him if desired. If Ogun is invited into a ceremony, he will command attention. It is said that when he speaks, no other voice can compete! It is clear how his presence alone generates immense respect within the Santeria tradition.

Ogun has such great influence in Santeria, and he has many different aspects to his identity, often invoked by followers seeking protection, prosperity, courage, and justice. Offerings made to Ogun can include food, cigars, rum, coins, knives, or animal sacrifices, depending on what the devotee seeks from the spirit. When appeasing Ogun, it is necessary to do so with love and respect for the orisha to grant one's wishes. Ogun can also be syncretized with various saints, such as Saint Paul, John the Baptist, and Saint Jacob.

Each saint brings unique characteristics that make them a suitable companion for Ogun, such as Paul's strength and courage or John the Baptist's devotion and piety. Through these practices, Santeria adherents honor Ogun in a way that is meaningful to their faith and seek divine guidance from a spirit that will always be loyal. Ultimately, what one offers to Ogun is up to individual interpretation and depends on the devotee's desired outcome. Ogun is a powerful spirit who will always answer those who call upon him with love, honor, and respect.

Chapter 3: Are You a Child of Ogun?

African spirituality experts posit that every person has two Orishas or spiritual parents. To epitomize this belief, one of the two is always considered the head of their relationship. In other words, it is thought that your life is not just determined by a single force but rather by a team effort on behalf of your spiritual parents. This double representation gives you the understanding that your life is in no way predetermined and instead is equipped with all the support needed to make the decisions that await you. It is an amazingly empowering concept and further exemplifies the beauty of African spiritual practices and beliefs.

This chapter will explore this concept in more depth and discuss how to identify the Orishas that are your divine "parents" and which one is the head of the relationship. To do so, a simple quiz has been added, which will help you to answer the question posed in the title of this chapter. This quiz lets you check whether your preferences, lifestyle, or personality traits can be associated with Ogun. By doing so, you'll closely examine Ogun's personality traits and characteristics.

Introduction to Divine Parentage

African spirituality is characterized by rich traditions and beliefs that are often steeped in elements of divine parentage. This concept relates to the belief that a higher being created the universe, served as its commander, and is essentially its parent. African cultures understand this power from many perspectives, with names such as Olodumare in the Yoruba culture, Ngai among the Kikuyu people, and Qamata among the Xhosa people. Beliefs about divine parentage generally tie into broader principles of belonging, servitude, order, and respect for synergy across all living beings in their environment and ancestries. Worship around divine parentage is part of celebrating African identity, integrity, and a sense of responsibility. It reminds Africans of their connectedness to something larger than themselves as they strive to be stewards in honoring resiliency through spirit.

Identifying Your "Parent" Orisha

Identifying your "parent," Orisha, is an amazing and important journey. It goes far beyond any test results as it requires knowledge, intent, and respect for the process. In traditional Yoruba religion, every person has a "parent," Orisha, who is their spiritual guardian and offers guidance on their life's journey. Knowing your parent Orisha can open up a world of potential to understanding yourself spiritually. This helps you answer who you are meant to be, what kind of work you should pursue, and the goals best suited to finding happiness. Do some research, speak with elders in the Yoruba tradition, and take time to quieten your mind. With persistence, you can tap into extraordinary levels of insight and clarity that will shape your decisions as you move through life.

The Quiz

Ogun is a powerful Orisha in the Yoruba pantheon and is considered the god of iron and fire. He is associated with strength, power, action, and innovation. Think about the following questions to determine if Ogun is your divine parent:

Do you like a challenge?

Ask yourself if you prefer to take on tasks that require hard work, dedication, and skill. Do you enjoy the feeling of accomplishment after a difficult task is completed?

Are you resilient in the face of adversity?

The path of life often presents many obstacles, but do you approach them with determination and a positive attitude? Are you willing to pick yourself up after a setback and try again?

Do you enjoy taking risks?

Do you often make bold moves to reach your goals? Do you like pushing yourself out of your comfort zone to see what's possible?

Do you prefer to take the lead?

In any situation, do you like to take charge and direct the flow of things? Do you often prefer to be the one making decisions and leading others? Do you have an innate ability to inspire those around you to achieve greatness?

Do you tackle obstacles head-on?

Facing problems can be intimidating, but do you choose to confront them directly? Do you think the best way to overcome an obstacle is to tackle it head-on?

Are you confident in yourself and your decisions?

It's often easy to doubt yourself, but do you stand strong in the face of uncertainty? Do you have faith in your abilities and trust yourself to make the right decisions? Do you think that self-assurance is essential for success?

Do you take charge and take control?

A true leader can take charge and lead. Do you have the ability to make decisions quickly to get things done? Do you have confidence in your judgment and take charge of the situation?

Are you competitive?

While competition should not be taken to extremes, do you strive to be the best? Do you take pride in your accomplishments and want to do better than before?

Do you tend to be assertive and focused?

Getting tasks done requires an assertive attitude and focus. Can you remain calm and composed under pressure? Do you think that success requires unwavering concentration?

Do you look for solutions rather than problems?

Having a problem-solving mentality is essential. Do you look for creative ways to approach situations? Are you willing to think outside the box to find the best solution?

Answer these questions honestly to find out if Ogun is your divine parent. Whatever the answer, use this knowledge to deepen your understanding of Yoruba spirituality and build meaningful connections with your divine parent. Speaking with an elder or spiritual practitioner in the Yoruba tradition may also be useful to gain insight into your divine parent. With knowledge and understanding, you can tap into extraordinary levels of personal power and spiritual growth.

Key to the Quiz

Now that you've taken the quiz, it's time to see if Ogun is your divine parent. If you answered yes to most of the questions, Ogun will likely be your divine parent. He is a strong leader who embodies strength, courage, action, and innovation. He encourages you to take risks, be resilient in the face of adversity, and take charge of your life. You can use the power of Ogun to reach your goals and achieve greatness.

On the other hand, if you answered no to most of the questions, then Ogun is not likely to be your divine parent. However, that doesn't mean he isn't part of your spiritual journey. Ogun's energy can be called upon to help you overcome obstacles, find solutions, and become a leader in your own life. Even if he is not your divine parent, understanding Ogun's energy can still be beneficial in guiding you on the right path. Here's a deeper look at what Ogun represents, so you can use his energy to your advantage.

1. Challenges

Ogun is not one to shy away from a challenge. He's willing to take risks, often finding himself in tight spots with no clear solution in sight. But that's exactly why Ogun takes on such tasks. He loves the thrill and adrenaline of pushing the limits and pressing beyond his boundaries. In the end, it only enhances his growth as both an individual and a leader, giving him greater insight, stronger skills, and more resolve. As someone who is always looking to better himself, Ogun embraces these challenging situations with confidence and optimism.

2. Resilience

Ogun, the god of both war and creation, epitomizes resilience in many ways. He was born of thunder and then forged his path through battle. This example of determination to never give up is something everyone can strive for. Sometimes failure is inevitable, and getting back up and fighting can be difficult after you fall short. But with a bit of Ogun's spirit, hope, determination, and action-oriented progress, you can all build your path to success and develop an unwavering sense of resilience. After all, Ogun was full of knowledge, courage, and strength, something you can tap into as well when times get tough!

3. Risk Taking

Ogun is a real go-getter who's always looking out for new opportunities and embracing risks when they come his way. This can-do attitude has helped him succeed in his career, relationships, and hobbies. Whether it's building a business, learning something new, or pursuing a romantic interest, he won't be intimidated by obstacles or the possibility of failure. His ability to recognize the potential outcomes of his decisions and choose the paths with more worthy rewards has opened many doors for him and will surely continue leading him to greater accomplishments. He's an inspiration for everyone!

4. Leadership

Ogun is an inspirational leader who confidently guides his team toward success. He understands that a strong, confident presence is key to motivating and encouraging others, and he applies this to his leadership style. Ogun also understands that trust must be part of any successful team dynamic and works hard to ensure everyone feels comfortable enough to voice ideas and opinions. He leads with integrity, fairness, and wisdom, demonstrating how those qualities are essential components of good leadership. Ultimately, he is someone that you can look up to as an example of what true leadership should be.

5. Conflict

Ogun always hits the bull's eye when it comes to dealing with conflicts, showing his honest and direct approach. He's not one for beating around the bush and prefers to navigate these kinds of situations head-on in a friendly manner. This can often lead to a surprisingly peaceful outcome as he has an incredible knack for understanding both sides of the argument and finding common ground that everybody can agree on. Ogun is highly valued by those around him thanks to his diplomatic conflict resolution style, which almost always ends in a win-win scenario for everyone.

6. Confidence

Ogun is one inspiring god! He consistently sets goals for himself and has all the confidence he needs to accomplish them. Ogun's self-belief gives him the strength to face any challenge head-on, and he doesn't take no for an answer. That's why you can always count on him when times are difficult. His unwavering assurance in himself and positive attitude keep him going no matter what. He is someone to look up to in terms of confidence and perseverance, and he demonstrates that anything is indeed possible with enough drive and passion.

7. Control

Ogun is known for being a take-charge kind of god. If there's ever a difficult situation, he'll always do his best to be the one in control. His determination and resourcefulness make him an excellent leader who can find order even in the most chaotic moments. He has the confidence to make tough decisions and inspires those around him to keep pushing forward no matter what they face. You're lucky to have someone like Ogun to pray to. His composure and resilience help you out of tricky spots time and time again!

8. Competition

Ogun is the epitome of a modern, successful individual. He always aims high and gives his all in every endeavor, striving to reach goals with genuine ambition. However, what truly sets him apart is his unique ability to know when it's time for competition to give way to collaboration. He understands the importance of teamwork among peers and when tackling larger initiatives. Not only does it make things easier for everyone involved, but it also encourages others to step up and be part of the whole process. When Ogun puts aside individual pride and instead focuses on a collective end goal, amazing things often happen, which just goes to show how powerful working together can be!

9. Assertiveness

Ogun is a strongly assertive god who knows how to prioritize what matters most. He is adept at tackling tasks with a clear focus, getting in the right mindset, and never wavering until completion. His approach toward projects fosters a sense of efficiency as well as a great teamwork spirit. His no-nonsense attitude combined with a friendly demeanor helps him remain calm and composed while still efficiently making his voice heard among the team. Ogun's assertiveness is something that should be admired and thought of fondly, providing a much-needed dose of enthusiasm for people to bond over.

10. Solutions

Ogun takes a unique approach when it comes to problem-solving, always looking for solutions instead of dwelling on the negative. By taking this optimistic outlook, Ogun often stumbles on great opportunities that otherwise wouldn't have been noticed. Adopting the same perspective can make all the difference in terms of creating positive change in any situation and can often yield much more than expected results. You could take a page out of Ogun's book and take a shot at problem-solving with an optimistic attitude!

Deepening Your Understanding of Ogun

Delving deeper into Ogun can be a powerful way to connect with your sense of identity and spirituality. Whether you're seeking to learn more about the Yoruba culture in which he originates or is looking to channel his energies as part of your spiritual practice, studying Ogun can lead to a wealth of new knowledge and wisdom. As an Orisha and quintessential warrior, devotees worldwide have found power from connecting with his presence during times of transformation or upheaval. With research, rituals, and dedication, understanding Ogun can be hugely rewarding and enriching for anyone looking for a glimpse into the depths of African spirituality.

A. Ogun's Relationship with Change

Ogun is a fascinating African deity, often associated with a change in the Igbo tradition. He symbolizes both a beneficial and powerful force of growth, embracing transformations and helping humans to break through obstacles. Ogun can also provide protection during times of turmoil and stress, offering wisdom on tackling life's biggest challenges. This makes him a valuable figure for those looking to adjust their lives for the better or overcome difficult transitions. He may not be the most recognizable or popular deity, but this allows followers to truly appreciate his unique perspective and learn from his experiences of living through major shifts in understanding.

B. Ogun and Adaptability

Ogun embodies adaptability and resilience, two traits we all could use more of during these uncertain times. Ogun teaches us to look past the surface level of things and see the potential future waiting to be unlocked through creative solutions. This could mean altering your approach or viewpoints, finding new ways to interact with the world around you, and letting go of the status quo. With Ogun's guidance, you can better navigate these ever-changing tides in life and become empowered agents of change within yourself, your communities, and your environment alike.

C. Ogun and Taking Action

Ogun, the great Yoruba god of iron and war, reminds us to take action. It's easy to get stuck in the same routine, feeling like you are on a hamster wheel where day after day can blur into one long slog. But Ogun is here to tell you that just because something has been done before does not mean it cannot be improved. This can apply to any part of your life, from making small changes to spark joy in your everyday life to standing up and speaking out against injustice whenever possible. Making an effort to take action each day gives us a sense of accomplishment while helping us reach our goals and improve the world around us. By embracing Ogun's energy, you can work together toward improving yourself and your community with passion and determination.

D. Ogun and Courage

Ogun, the noble orisha of Yoruba mythology, is known as a brave warrior. He symbolizes strength and valor in the face of adversity, being a pillar of strength to whom we turn in moments of despair. Ogun gives you courage and fortitude to trudge through difficult times. He's a symbol of protection, too. His presence can be felt all around you every time you go on a difficult journey, every time you strive for success against great odds, and even when something appears impossible, but you still summon the inner strength to try, nonetheless. You should always remember Ogun, the brave spirit who embodies courage within everyone.

E. Ogun and Overcoming Adversity

Adversity comes in all shapes and sizes, and it can be daunting to face it. However, the Yoruba deity Ogun provides hope to those struggling against it. The god of iron, warfare, and labor champions those who strive to overcome their difficulties despite the odds. As long as you stay strong and persevere, Ogun will help you reach your goals. Whether it's conquering a battle or completing a project, this spirit offers unwavering strength and courage to reach peace and success. So, if you are facing an obstacle or have recently gone through a tribulation, remember that with Ogun supporting you, better days lie ahead!

How to Identify Your Divine Parent

Knowing which divine parent you are blessed with is an astonishing feeling. It helps shape who you are, giving you insight into what makes your character unique. Identifying your divine parent is easier than you might think. All it takes is a little honest introspection and being open to the answers that come. Start by thinking about what wisdom and skills come naturally to you. What do you feel passionate about or have an exceptional understanding of? Also, consider how your relationships have formed. Are there any particular gods or goddesses that always seem to attract your attention or influence in your life? Once these questions have been answered, doing some research into the gods presented can give more clarity on whether they could be your divine parent. Ultimately, no one can tell you who your divine parent is. You can take this extraordinary journey only by connecting to yourself and trusting in yourself.

This chapter discussed the concept of divine parenting in African spirituality and how Ogun, the great Yoruba god of iron and war, embodies courage and strength in difficult times. The quiz is provided as a tool to help you zero in on Ogun's personality traits and characteristics, as well as how to identify your divine parent. Hopefully, this chapter has provided insight and clarity into the power of divine parenting and explained how to connect with Ogun. Ultimately, it is up to you to connect with yourself and discover who holds this special place in your life. People should all strive to embrace Ogun's energy and work together towards a more peaceful, prosperous world.

Chapter 4: Ogun in Myths and Legends

Ogun is an influential Orisha, esteemed in the Yoruba religious tradition. Ogun has no single form or appearance. Instead, the deity encompasses a complex and multifaceted range of characteristics. The powerful and multifaceted deity is known as a warrior and protector and is associated with justice and loyalty. In addition to these roles, Ogun also governs conflict, purity, blacksmithing, metalworking, hunting, and agriculture, among other areas. His spirit embodies courage, strength, and transformation.

Ogun is associated with many forms, including a warrior and protector.
Wood, J. G. (John George), CC BY-SA 4.0 <https://creativecommons.org/licenses/by-sa/4.0>, via Wikimedia Commons https://commons.wikimedia.org/wiki/File:African_Warriors_Skirmish.jpg

Considering all his many responsibilities and abilities, it's not surprising that devotees give thanks to Ogun for providing them with protection in this life. This chapter will overview Ogun's origin, his paths, and the different legends and stories that portray him as a powerful being. It will also explore his relationship with Olodumare, the Supreme Being in the Yoruba pantheon. By the end of this chapter, you should have a better understanding of Ogun and the role he plays in Yoruba culture.

Overview of Ogun

Ogun is a fascinating deity who is said to have been the first Orisha to come from heaven. He descended with his machete and forged a path through the wilderness for humans to follow, thus allowing humankind's progress. Ogun developed tools and weapons out of metal, tamed the wilderness, and gave people access to knowledge that allowed them to prosper. Ogun is revered as the god of metal and is often associated with blacksmithing, war, hunting, and labor.

The Origin Story of Ogun

Ogun is the chief Yoruba deity of iron and warfare, a powerful figure of ingenuity and invention. He is often seen as a messenger, liaising between the gods and humans, as he is connected to mankind and the gods. Ogun's origin story goes back to ancient times when he emerged from a calabash planted on the bank of the northern Niger River. He is said to be small inside the calabash but powerful, representing hope and prosperity of becoming something greater. Ogun's message is still honored today, and his mythology remains integral to Yoruba folklore, inspiring their people even centuries later.

Paths of Ogun

The Paths of Ogun, an African symbol of power and strength, have long been a key source of inspiration for many. Imbued with perseverance and determination, the powerful spirit of Ogun has been a beacon that beckons us forward on life's journey. In some traditions, Ogun is also associated with justice and insightfulness, thus a pillar of support when facing difficult decisions. At their core, the Paths of Ogun show followers that though life may have its twists and turns, they always have their inner guide to return to in times of strife. So, if you ever need inspiration along your path, take comfort in knowing the Paths of Ogun are ever-present to light your way in times of darkness.

Ogun worshipers sure know how to honor their deities! By singing Ogun's oríkì (a powerful greeting in hymns/mantras, etc.), worshippers proclaim their appreciation for this powerful Yoruba god. One line that carries so much weight is: "Ògún ó tí bá rè sílé síle" which translates to "Ògún is in seven paths." This term reflects an understanding of the god as a pathfinder or one with unrivaled access to all routes. Essentially, it reminds followers that Ogun is everywhere, heading up growth and progress with each step he makes across the seven paths!

1. Oggun Alagbo

The paths of Ogun Meji comprise many ancient rituals and traditions unique to the religion, originating from Ifá, a traditional Yoruba divination system. Oggun Alagbo is a powerful deity highly respected by those in the blacksmith profession. Known as the patron of blacksmiths, he exemplifies hard work and dedication, toiling endlessly from night to day. He may come across as harsh and fearful at times, but this strong personality has helped forge Oggun into a symbol of strength for those in his field. Worshipped alongside Yemaya Okute, his wife, Oggun's presence can be seen throughout smithing communities who recognize him according to various names such as Alaguede, Alagbo, and Alagbede.

2. Oggun Onile

Oggun Onile is a fascinating spirit renowned for its connection to the realm of land and exploration. This spirit brings with it feelings of comfort and security when connected to the home, but it also holds the promise of unveiling vast discoveries. Oggun Onile's wisdom can be seen in his ability to recognize the potential in unmapped regions, allowing him to traverse the land like no other. It is no surprise why this spirit is so beloved. From his ability to provide a stable foundation to inviting encouragement for growth, Oggun Onile celebrates stability and potential. Whether through physical travel or inner self-reflection, this spirit takes great delight in your open spirit of discovery and gives you the courage to take on life's challenges with boldness and assurance.

3. Oggun Meji

Oggun Meji represents strength and communication within oneself and the community, an understanding that strife can occur without balance within our communities and us. This path focuses on sacrifices given to balance the needs of humans and nature, allowing them to live in harmony. The practice of meditation helps humans to understand how they exist in the world. It helps them see their place among others and also understand themselves better by listening carefully and responding thoughtfully. By paying close attention to Oggun Meji's teachings, anyone can find a sense of peace and connection with themselves as well as the world around them.

4. Oggun Oloyon

Oggun Oloyon is the most well-known of all Ogun's paths because it is here that the story of how he became the god of metal originated. It tells of how a farmer was having trouble clearing his land, as every time he tried to do so, his tools kept breaking. In frustration, he made a plea to the gods, and Ogun answered his call. Ogun used his tools to clear the land in mere moments, thus earning him the title of "the god of metal."

5. Oggun Irumole

Oggun Irumole is a powerful spirit who embodies protection and guidance. He can be seen as the guardian of travelers on a journey, helping them to stay safe and find their way home. This spirit also works to protect individuals from evil influences and negative energies while guarding homes against robbery and burglary. Ogun Irumole also lends a hand in matters of love, such as helping heal broken hearts and opening up communication channels between two people.

6. Oggun Oyeku Meji

Oggun Oyeku Meji is the spirit of war, conflict, and courage. This path emphasizes the importance of standing up for justice when needed and having the courage to face one's fears and fight for something one believes in. Oggun Oyeku Meji teaches followers that victory comes through hard work and perseverance, reminding them to never give up on their dreams no matter how difficult the path ahead may be. He also reminds them of the necessity of protecting those who are weaker and standing up for what is right.

7. Oggun Akomi

The Ogun Akomi path embodies the spirit of healing and creativity. This spirit works to inspire individuals to practice their unique gifts and express themselves creatively, helping them appreciate the beauty in every aspect of life. He encourages followers to have faith in their abilities and push beyond any boundaries that may prevent them from achieving greatness. Additionally, Ogun Akomi is a symbol of hope, offering comfort in times of difficulty and reminding followers to always look toward the future with optimism.

Legends and Stories about Ogun

Legends and stories about the God Ogun are plentiful in West African culture. This deity of metalworking, war, and hunting is believed to have many facets, including the ability to bring fortune, create powerful tools for those with the skill to wield them, and protect those who honor him. In some versions of the mythologies surrounding Ogun, he is portrayed as a trickster who uses his knowledge of powers to outwit his opponents or even fellow Gods. Because of this, these stories are just as much about ethical dilemmas as they are about wisdom found through his teachings. Legends about Ogun make for fascinating tales that may illustrate lessons on bravery, strength, and justice that can still be embraced today.

1. Ogun and Yemaya

Ogun and Yemaya are very prominent deities in Yoruba culture. Ogun is the god of iron, warriors, and hunters and is said to be ever-present in times of warfare and death. Yemaya is the great mothering spirit, often shown with a crown of shells on her head, who provides guidance and protection to those seeking it. Both of these deities have fascinating stories associated with them. From tales about how Ogun created the world to festivals sponsored by Yemaya for her followers, these legends are timeless reminders of these figures' central role in Yoruba mythology. Whether you're looking for guidance on your spiritual journey or just curious about the legends that make up this cultural tradition, learning more about Ogun and Yemaya can be an enlightening adventure!

2. The Story of the Talking Stone

Many stories and legends exist about Ogun, the Yoruba God of Iron and War. One of the most popular is that of the talking stone. According to legend, when Ogun seeks to hear words of counsel on a particular issue, he visits a talking stone found in the Ira forest. When he arrives at the forest and kneels before the stone, it begins to speak with divine knowledge, offering advice on his journey. This story's variations span West Africa and even beyond geographical borders, proving how this cherished tale has ingrained itself into the culture. Even today, communities continue to be charmed by the story of Ogun and his magical talking stone!

3. The Suitors Tale

Ogun is a god of many stories and legends, especially concerning his relationship with the suitors who pursue him. According to one tale, Ogun had no home long ago and was looking for a place to stay. Every evening he would arrive in a new village hoping to find kindness and shelter. Instead, he would be met with disdain and rejection. One night, despite being turned away from three consecutive households, Ogun found comfort when an anonymous benefactor opened their door and welcomed him in for restful sleep. Whether this legend was based on fact or fiction remains unknown to us today. However, it serves as an example of how much the people of ancient times admired Ogun's resilience and bravery against adversity.

4. Ogun and Osun

Ogun and Osun are two fascinating gods from the Yoruba religion of Nigeria. Ogun's stories tell of a powerful, brave warrior figure who could also be extremely creative. The most popular story tells the tale of how he discovered ironworking to help his people build tools, weapons, and other important items in their daily lives. Osun, on the other hand, is the goddess of beauty and feminine love. According to legend, she brings abundance and fertility to people's lives. She uses her beauty as a source of inspiration for many art forms, including painting, poetry, music, and dance. Stories around Osun often revolve around romance between people or between different gods or goddesses. Regardless of the story type, Ogun and Osun play an important role in Yoruba culture.

5. Ogun and the Forest of Truth

Ogun is a powerful figure in West African folklore, often depicted as a warrior and blacksmith. He is broadly associated with justice, truth, and protection, the three values that were highly prized during the period in which the myth of Ogun originated. Ogun's most prominent story takes place in the Forest of Truth, where he embarks on an epic journey to receive guidance from his ancestors. As Anansi, the spider, says: "Ogun is no ordinary feat. He marched through woods unknown, searching for his father's lore, and left with a knowledge greater than before." This classic story serves as an ode to the pursuit of resilience, strength, and understanding. These are values followers can all take away from when exploring stories centered on Ogun.

6. Ogun and Eleggua

Ogun and Eleggua are revered figures in African folklore, with countless legends and stories devoted to them. Ogun is associated with war and skillful weapon smithing, while Eleggua's purpose was to serve as a messenger between the spiritual realm and humankind. Together they were regarded as two of the most influential gods of old African cultures, with celebrated stories detailing their fascinating adventures.

Tales of mighty battles between Ogun and the trickster deity Eshu offer insights into how African societies viewed victory and defeat. Furthermore, the characteristics associated with Eleggua of mischievousness, cunningness, and cleverness have been celebrated for generations in African story-telling. If you're looking for exciting tales to bring history to life, look no further than the legends of Ogun and Eleggua.

7. The Battle of the Beavers

Legends and stories about Ogun and the battle of the Beavers are part of many cultures, but most commonly those originating from Western Africa. Ogun is credited with fighting off the beavers who were trying to take over the forests. The legend usually goes that he leads his troops into battle against the beavers and eventually defeats them. The stories vary slightly depending on the culture, but generally, it is held up as an example of courage and perseverance in making sure that humans retain control over their environment. It's a cautionary tale against greed and lust for power, urging followers not to let their desires take away their resources or burden them with too much work. In that sense, this legend has left a lasting impression on humankind throughout the ages.

8. Ogun and the Seven Leaf Clover

Ogun is an influential figure in many African religious traditions, and one of the most iconic symbols associated with him is the seven-leaf clover. These seven leaves are meant to represent the seven paths of life that Ogun laid out, and each has its own story attached to it. Legends tell of Ogun traveling around his kingdom, teaching people about these paths and about how precious freedom was. Other stories center on Ogun as a powerful warrior who won battles with superhuman strength. While the truth of these stories may be up for debate, they show us how deeply Ogun has been a part of African culture throughout history – and why his symbol of the seven-leaf clover continues to be held in high regard today.

9. Ogun and the White Robe

Ogun is one of the most beloved characters in African folklore. One of his many stories involves a mighty battle with a spirit wearing a white robe. Ogun had to accomplish two tasks before being crowned king: 1) taking possession of the white robe and 2) beating the spirit. His courage, intelligence, and strength helped him succeed, setting an example for future generations. Ogun is also well-known for his role as the god of war, iron, and technology, so it's no wonder he has become such an influential figure throughout history. Today, he is remembered as a powerful hero who challenges injustice and evil wherever they may be found. Although his stories are rooted in legend, his qualities remain timeless and can inspire everyone!

10. The Legend of Oshun River

The legend of the Oshun River is full of deep mystique and exciting stories and tales. In the mythology of the Ogun people, stories are handed down through generations to explain why things occur in nature. It is believed that Oshun River has been blessed by the God Ogun, who resides atop its banks and looks out for his people. Ogun is considered to be an ironsmith who creates tools for warriors to use in battle, but he also serves as a protector who generously showers his followers with blessings. He is famous for challenging death, rescuing innocent souls from harm's way, and helping bring justice whenever injustice was found. Followers believe that anyone who respects Ogun properly will be rewarded with protection and good fortune. These legends offer a unique insight into the Oshun River's history and its inhabitants' culture while captivating listeners with incredible stories.

It is believed that the Oshun River is blessed by Ogun.
https://www.pexels.com/photo/body-of-water-between-green-leaf-trees-709552/

Ogun and Olodumare

Ogun and Olodumare are two of the most important deities of Yoruba culture. Ogun is revered as a great spirit of knowledge and strength, while Olodumare is seen as the highest deity, having created all things and whose power surpasses any other spirits or forces. This relationship between Ogun and Olodumare is fundamental in the practice of Yoruba spiritualism as they are thought to be inseparable energies that work within your life. They are understood to often have complementary roles, balancing your spiritual experience. It's incredible to reflect upon how these powerful gods remain relevant today!

Significance of Ogun's Relationship with Olodumare

Yoruba mythology tells a fascinating story of the relationship between Ogun and Olodumare. Deeply intertwined in the stories about creation and the order of life is an understanding of how the two worked together to bring about powerful change for those who believed in them. As a powerful elemental god, Ogun ensured Olodumare's creations were developed by his plan. Ogun is said to be a skilled metalworker who taught humans how to work with iron and smelt it into weapons and tools. His teachings were essential to help humans decimate the Earth's resources while ensuring they could build civilizations from scratch. Many followers of Yoruba mythology will point out that Olodumare would have been lost without Ogun's influence over human development. The world's modern advances owe much to this duo's partnership!

Olodumare's Role in Ogun's Legend

In the legend of Ogun and Olodumare, Olodumare plays a critical role in delivering a valuable lesson. Ogun, the warrior-king, ventures out on a quest to find solace after losing his wife and children. His journey leads him to meet Olodumare, the All-Pervading One. Through this divine encounter, Ogun grows spiritually as he learns humility and faith, and surrenders to the will of Olodumare. This powerful lesson encourages followers to be steadfast in their belief that justice and mercy come from our Creator above all else. Ultimately, Ogun's story proves that when you give everything to Olodumare, his grace will produce positive life-changing results.

Symbolic Meaning of Ogun's Connection to Olodumare

Ogun, a force that works to make change and progress, is also closely connected to Olodumare, the supreme creative being in the universe. While Ogun's might and strength are meant to stand out and make an impact, it is only through his relationship with Olodumare that he can fulfill that purpose.

Symbolically, the connection indicates the importance of understanding where your power comes from and keeping it grounded in something greater. If it is not underpinned by your connection to your deity and their cosmic plan, then there can be no true transformation or growth. Understanding this partnership between Ogun and Olodumare shines great insight into our own lived experience. You may have strength, but if you're not present with your spiritual connection and have layer upon layer of self-reflection, you'll never truly reach your highest potential.

Ogun in Other Worlds and Religions

Ogun is often seen as a heroic figure in religious and mythical stories, ranging from West African folktales to Russian epics and beyond. Represented through different symbolisms depending on the origin story, Ogun is revered across the world for his strength and determination. Like many gods of power, he is often associated with weapons such as swords or spears. In addition, he stands out from other gods worldwide because of his ability to teach people skills in craftsmanship and blacksmithing, an essential skill in societies throughout time. Overall, it's awe-inspiring how Ogun's presence has been preserved and celebrated through the ages!

Significance of Ogun in Afro-Cuban Spirituality

Ogun is also a significant Afro-Cuban spiritual figure representing strength and passion. He is honored as one of the most powerful armed warriors and is believed to open any door that has been closed. Ogun is seen as a patron for those seeking their freedom, whether physical or spiritual. He encourages Cubans to move forward with courage, allowing them to develop connections between their past and the present. For this reason, many devout people continue to pay homage to him today by lighting candles in his honor or reciting prayers in the name of Ogun on special occasions.

Ogun is among the most timeless and highly celebrated deities in many different cultures worldwide. As a god of strength, courage, and passion, he is often seen as the forerunner of progress and change. His connection to Olodumare reinforces the importance of understanding where true power comes from and how your spiritual practices can be used to reach a higher potential. His heroic deeds continue to inspire people worldwide, as his stories remain part of the collective history and culture. Through this shared understanding, you can honor Ogun in all his greatness!

Chapter 5: What Ogun Teaches His Followers

Ogun is an influential figure for many, both spiritually and historically. If you take the time to learn, his experiences are filled with valuable lessons showing you how to live in the world. Ogun's life taught him to adapt and embrace change with courage and strength. He also embodied kindness towards others, especially those who were as displaced as he was. Every attempt at reinvention requires resilience, but when you look at it through the lens of someone like Ogun, it also carries promise and possibility. The spiritual legacy of Ogun gives followers hope that even when faced with such uncertainty, there is beauty in reimagining what your life can become.

Embarking on a journey through the paths of Ogun, the Yoruba god of iron and technology, can be intimidating, exciting, and ultimately enlightening. Each step you take will help you discover your unique place in the world, whether that is understanding your creative skills, exploring career paths, or learning to overcome personal challenges. You can also gather the experiences necessary to break down barriers and build bridges between people and communities by pushing through difficult terrain. The search for identity is a crucial quest for many people, but Ogun's path may offer you something even greater, a gateway to creating your future.

This chapter will explore the eight Paths of Ogun further and how we can use them as inspiration to guide us on our paths. It will discuss the importance of the preservation of knowledge, traveling and movement, strength, communication, helping others, spiritual awakening, courage, and finally, healing and creativity. By the end of this chapter, you'll better understand each path and how it can be applied in our everyday lives.

Oggun Alagbo - The Path of Elderly Wisdom

Oggun Alagbo is the path that celebrates the value of wisdom through age. It encourages you to step into your role as an elder, leader, and teacher with clarity and conviction, and it highlights the necessity of relying on years of experience to guide you through life's complex challenges. Oggun Alagbo reminds people that if they embrace their human history without fear or apprehension, accepting who they were in the past while embracing their future with open arms, they can rise above any obstacle. This ancient path sheds light on how you can use knowledge learned over a lifetime to leave a lasting mark on the world.

Oggun Alagbo encourages the value of wisdom through experience and age.
https://www.pexels.com/photo/two-woman-looking-on-persons-bracelet-667203/

A. The Importance of Preservation of Knowledge

Preserving knowledge and wisdom is something that many cultures have done through the years, and one good example of this is Oggun

Alagbo, or "the path of elderly wisdom." This Nigerian tradition emphasizes the wisdom of respecting and seeking out the advice and knowledge of elders in our communities. It serves as a reminder to all that knowledge never becomes obsolete. Regardless of how experienced or well-educated somebody may be, there is always something else to learn from those with greater understanding, life experience, and knowledge than them. Keeping these traditions alive ensures that generations before you are remembered and celebrated for their contributions to your shared human experience.

B. Finding Your Own Path with Oggun Alagbo

Oggun Alagbo is an amazing opportunity to find your path and learn from the insights of experienced, wise elders. Learning from those who have come before us and understanding their perspective gives us a much clearer look at our paths and guidance that sometimes only the wisdom acquired over time can provide. Through the inspirational teachings of Oggun Alagbo, you can recognize your destiny and take steps towards achieving it with newfound clarity. Embark on this journey and embrace the growth and enlightenment this process can bring.

C. Appreciating the Power of Elders

Appreciating the power of elders is both a humbling and enlightening experience. Oggun Alagbo, which translates to The Path of Elderly Wisdom in West African Yoruba, shines a unique light on the motivations behind this appreciation. It suggests that ancient wisdom often gives us perspective, regardless of how turbulent or unclear our world may seem. This wisdom may be attained by seeking out elders in their community who share their stories and experiences to gain knowledge and insights into facing life's most trying times with grace and strength.

Embracing the power of elders can help us expand our horizons beyond what we thought possible while holding fast to the traditions passed down from generation to generation. By paying homage to those that have gone before, you are gifted with an invaluable resource for growth in both your personal and professional life.

Oggun Onile - The Path of Traveling and Movement

Oggun Onile, or the Yoruba path of traveling and movement, has been around for centuries. It is a fascinating exploration into the spiritual aspects of movement and how different cultures from around the world approach human interactions on the go. In Yoruba culture specifically, Oggun Onile is a belief system that centers on ensuring one's safety while traveling and emphasizes the importance of clear communication in interpersonal relationships.

It also focuses on building harmony between those with varying superstitions. Oggun Onile practices often involve revealing physical symbols to signify safe passage while traveling and an openness to discuss any pressing issues respectfully. This ancient belief system provides insight into how different societies have coped with what could have been very difficult journeys like traveling long distances on foot or at sea.

A. Embracing Adaptability with Oggun Onile

Oggun Onile is a unique path of traveling and movement embraced by the Yoruba people that focuses on adaptability. This philosophy involves understanding your environment, using it to your advantage, and staying fluid to move in the best direction for your growth. Practicing this method can give you real benefits, such as improved navigation and navigation-based problem-solving skills. On top of that, developing an appreciation for how environments can affect your life fosters a more dynamic mindset and allow you to prepare yourself better when faced with change or challenges. Learning to embrace adaptability through Oggun Onile may be just what you need to get ahead in life.

B. Going Out into the World to Seek Opportunity

For anyone interested in seeking opportunity, the Yoruba path of traveling and movement, Oggun Onile, is a great way to embark on the journey of discovering what lies beyond. This practice can provide insight into the challenges which may come up while stepping out into the world, along with how to work through them. It involves having faith in oneself and one's journey, creating a system of support among close family and friends as one embarks on different life experiences, and realizing that no matter what challenges arise, one will navigate them skillfully. In times when it may not seem easy, listening to the voice of intuition within oneself can make all the difference.

C. Utilizing Self-Reliance to Forge Your Path

Oggun Onile is an ancient and powerful philosophy. In essence, it is a path of self-reliance that encourages individuals to take charge of their lives, forge their paths and break away from conventional thinking. Oggun Onile urges its adherents to seek deeper understanding and insight into life by becoming better communicators, establishing greater connections with their environment, and mastering the creative self-expression necessary for personal growth.

By learning this ancient wisdom, each person has the potential to bring peace and harmony into their lives, as well as enhance their health and well-being. Embracing Oggun Onile grants you greater freedom when deciding how you'll approach your travels through life and create your unique path with courage, confidence, and strength.

Oggun Meji - The Path of Strength and Communication

Oggun Meji is a powerful path originating among the Yoruba people, who worship deities representing different forces of nature. Along this path, individuals explore strength and communication through metaphysical practices deeply embedded in their ancestral roots. Oggun Meji instills meaningful insight into life's daily struggles and encourages adherents to strive for inner peace and balance.

Through spiritual rituals, including medicine circles, drumming sessions, and offerings to pot shamanism, one can develop a stronger sense of self, open communication channels within their community, and cultivate greater awareness about their environment. By cultivating inner strength through Oggun Meji, you can establish effective healing relationships with fellow humans and deepen your connection to the surrounding world.

A. Taking Action to Better Yourself with Oggun Meji

Oggun Meji is a powerful Yoruba path of strength and communication that can help you better yourself in many different areas. This ancient practice holds the secrets to unlocking what's holding you back and equipping you with the strength, courage, and wisdom to take action at any time. Within this path lies powerful rituals, affirmations, and meditations to help guide you on your spiritual journey and manifest your desired life. These teachings will help support your spiritual goals and provide practical advice on how to recognize and push through any obstacles preventing personal growth.

B. Understanding the Power of Words and Expression

Oggun Meji provides insight into the power of words and how they can be used both positively and negatively to shape our lives, relationships, and circumstances. Oggun Meji teaches us how to use our communicative abilities strategically to effectively share our thoughts and feelings better while avoiding misunderstandings. Through this traditional practice, you learn how to exercise good judgment during important conversations and begin to repair damaged bonds by using sincere words with love, sincerity, respect, and understanding. By speaking directly from the heart to those you care about most, you can reach a level of mutual understanding which will benefit all sides long-term.

C. Learning to Harness the Strength within You

Oggun Meji teaches you to recognize and access your power within, allowing you to navigate through life's challenges with clarity and grace. Oggun Meji's guiding principles include introspection and self-reflection, embracing innate strengths, accepting the truth, and recognizing boundaries. Through these practices, you can harness the force of your inner voice, allowing it to guide you through difficult situations while maintaining peace of mind in both success and failure. As you become more attuned to this path of strength and communication, you can become your own most authentic self with greater ease.

Oggun Oloyon - The Path of Helping Others

Oggun Oloyon is a Yoruba path that encourages us to help others above all else. Genuine service is paramount, whether it's with tangible items, advice, or support. It resonates with a strong sense of community where everyone works together to preserve harmony in their families and neighborhoods. Oggun Oloyon allows you to practice being selfless even if there may be no immediate reward, as it's been said that "helping people in need makes all your actions more meaningful." Although this may be an ancient tradition, you can adopt and apply it in your daily life for its timelessness and relevance.

A. The Value of Compassion with Oggun Oloyon

Oggun Oloyon is an ancient Yoruba tradition that values compassion and helping others as an integral part of a meaningful life. This path recognizes your interdependence with each other, encourages you to be helpful and generous, and allows you to form meaningful connections both within your community and beyond. Oggun Oloyon is rooted in the belief that there is fulfillment in giving rather than taking or accumulating material possessions. By engaging in acts of care and generosity, you can experience greater joy in your life, feel connected to others, and bring about positive change. Practicing compassion makes you a healthier individual, builds stronger communities, and, ultimately a better world for everyone.

B. Understanding the Power of Kindness

Oggun Oloyon, or the Path of Helping Others, is an ancient philosophy of kindness that connects to the spirit of humanity and its importance in personal development. Oggun Oloyon comprises the idea that your spirituality and well-being will flourish if you strive to understand those around you and empathize with their struggles. Invoking this concept means it is your responsibility to care for others through material items or financial support and acts of love and compassion.

For example, think about a time when you shared a comforting conversation with someone who felt alone. That's a powerful act of kindness with deep spiritual significance for both of you. By recognizing your interconnectedness with each other and understanding how impactful careless gestures can be, you can start leveraging the power of Oggun Oloyon in your everyday life to spread more healing energy.

C. Utilizing Your Resources to Help Others

Oggun Oloyon, the Yoruba spiritual path of helping others, can be a powerful and rewarding way to aid those in need. It encourages you to use all physical and mental resources to extend assistance. From giving basic physical items, possessions, or money, to providing emotional support or caring services, it is possible to make a positive difference in everyone's lives. Understanding the importance of relationships and mutual interdependence makes it possible to serve with sincerity, patience, and humility while elevating our spiritual growth – and that of others.

Oggun Irumole - The Path of Spiritual Awakening

Oggun Irumole, the Yoruba spiritual path of awakening and transcendence, is an ancient practice that remains a powerful force today. It emphasizes developing a strong connection to the divine forces of nature while elevating spirituality through music, movement, prayer, and hieroglyphs. To stay true to its core values of knowledge, understanding, and respect for others, followers must abide by certain principles like the discipline of the mind and body, seeking inner peace, and understanding one's place in the universe.

Oggun Irumole teaches you how to access spiritual guidance from your ancestors and divine forces that lead you to open up new paths of self-transformation. Its long-lasting tradition of cultivating strong bonds between people from different cultures and backgrounds nurtures personal growth, which can only have positive consequences for present and future generations.

A. Growing with Oggun Irumole

Through Oggun Irumole's teachings, practitioners gain a new understanding of the basic principles of spirituality and learn how to wake up their own power. As part of this process, you are taught that knowledge is only partially found in books but must also come from experience for it to be truly meaningful. By learning more about this traditional practice and using it as guidance for spiritual growth, practitioners will discover a path to greater knowledge, intuition, and peace of mind.

B. Encouraging Self-Reflection and Improvement

Oggun Irumole is a practice that provides inspiring and meaningful encouragement to practice self-reflection and improvement. Through various techniques and rituals, this Yoruba spiritual path takes a holistic approach, helping practitioners to become more mindful of their thoughts, feelings, and behavior. It also helps you to better understand your strengths and weaknesses while developing inner peace, clarity, purpose, and motivation.

With its transformative potential, Oggun Irumole can be a powerful tool for those on the journey to self-improvement. Plus, the supportive community that often forms around this practice adds vital support from those with expert knowledge and experiences in the way of life. As a bonus, Oggun Irumole is highly adaptable, offering flexibility for individual or specific needs, so anyone can benefit from it regardless of what stage they're at in their lives.

C. Seeking Out Spiritual Growth

Oggun Irumole, the Yoruba path of spiritual awakening, offers a unique opportunity to seekers of spiritual growth. It is a deeply enriching experience that provides teachings to open your mind and soul and exercises the body through energetic rituals. Through this powerful practice of self-reflection, understanding one's inner truth and life purpose are revealed. And while there may be challenges on this journey of exploration and growth, the experiences gained from doing this work will guide you throughout life. Connect with Oggun Irumole today and witness how it can open up new pathways for enlightenment and give you a new perspective on life!

Oggun Oyeku Meji - The Path of Courage

Oggun Oyeku Meji is a powerful practice within the Yoruba tradition. Oggun Oyeku Meji is the path of courage and strength that comes from inner knowledge. It encourages individuals to be brave in overcoming fear and difficult emotions and find strength in their spiritual journeys. People who practice Oggun Oyeku Meji strive to have faith in themselves and trust themselves, even in seemingly impossible situations.

This ancient set of principles can bring courage and mental clarity to anyone who puts effort into understanding it properly. With greater self-awareness comes better decision-making, greater compassion for others, and a renewed spirit of fortitude. As you endure different challenges, Oggun Oyeku Meji can offer insight into how best to manage them while remaining connected with your inner resolve.

A. Embracing Change with Oggun Oyeku Meji

Embracing change can be challenging, especially when we aren't sure of the outcome. But embracing change with Oggun Oyeku Meji, a set of philosophical and spiritual principles, can help you work your way through change with courage and the belief that the result will be better than before. Oggun Oyeku Meji helps you push beyond your physical and mental boundaries and recognize that taking risks is okay while staying focused on your purpose. With this philosophy, change can be embraced and bring out the best in you as you step into new opportunities and face your fears head-on.

B. Learning to Overcome Fear

Ogun Oyeku Meji, or the Path of Courage, is an ancient meditation and visualization practice that helps you improve your courage and overcome fear. Positive affirmations make you feel strong, empowered, and confident in this practice. You learn to ground yourself in the present moment, let go of worry and anxiety, and find inner peace through intentional focus and relaxation techniques. With regular repetition, the ability to access your inner strength builds up so you can face fearful situations with greater resilience and poise. Through Ogun Oyeku Meji, you discover how easily your fears can be allayed as you align more with your highest potential for success.

C. Encouraging Self-Confidence and Determination

Oggun Oyeku Meji is an ancient practice that originated within the Yoruba culture, and its primary purpose is to give individuals the courage to increase their self-confidence and determination. This belief system combines purposeful movements, special mantras, proverbs, meditation, rhythmical clapping of hands, and visualizations. The idea behind this tradition is to reunite oneself with the higher power to strengthen self-identity in life's experiences and trials.

Those who practice Oggun Oyeku Meji believe it can provide resilience and emotional balance when facing difficult times by deepening people's connection with their spiritual essence. This practice has proven successful for generations of followers, invoking positive changes in behavior and beliefs regarding life's challenging moments. As a result of its spiritual support, Oggun Oyeku Meji leaves practitioners feeling empowered and ready to face any adversity head-on.

Oggun Akomi - The Path of Healing and Creativity

Oggun Akomi is a unique system of healing and creativity developed by the Yoruba people. While traditional Western medicine focuses on treating symptoms, this holistic approach sees health as an interconnected combination of mind, body, and spirit that must all be in balance to achieve optimal well-being. Combining traditional methods such as herbal remedies with activities such as singing, dancing, art therapy, storytelling, and divination, Oggun Akomi helps individuals identify and release physical, emotional, and spiritual blockages to achieve a deeper sense of connection with themselves.

Through its focus on creativity and self-expression, this practice offers communities a powerful tool for connecting with their ancestry while addressing present-day burdens. Oggun Akomi is transforming how you think about healing in a way that prioritizes growth over suffering, making it an invaluable pathway to discover a healthier, more vibrant life.

A. Appreciating the Power of Healing with Oggun Akomi

Oggun Akomi is an amazing practice that has been used for centuries to help its practitioners find peace and clarity. Through their combination of art, music, prayer, and reverence for ancestors and the divine spirit, Oggun Akomi creates a powerful healing journey of self-discovery. When embraced with an open heart and mind, this path of creativity and spiritual connection can bring about profound changes in one's life, from finding inner strength to unlocking untapped potential.

Oggun Akomi invites you to be present in the moment, appreciate your higher power, recognize the beauty that lies within yourself and create your own story through meaningful ritual practices. Its power lies in its ancient traditions and its ability to transform you by connecting you deeply with who you are at your core. There truly is nothing like it.

B. Learning How to Deal with Loss and Grief

Grief and loss can be incredibly painful to manage. But there's hope. The ancient practice of Oggun Akomi, based on the Yoruba understanding of healing and creativity, offers a unique approach to dealing with these complex emotions. It includes effective methods of managing the energy that comes along with grief and loss while honoring the individual's spirituality and values.

This path of healing takes into consideration an individual's unique background, view on life, and relationship with others while finding creative ways to manage strong feelings to avoid becoming overwhelmed by them. Anyone looking for an alternative way of managing grief or loss should consider exploring Oggun Akomi. It could offer clarity, direction, and peace through a traditional process meant for healing and creating lasting change in all aspects of life.

C. Using Creativity to Overcome Challenges

Oggun Akomi is a Yoruba path of healing and creativity that encourages individuals to solve their challenges creatively. Through this practice, you can identify the constructive power of your imagination, develop greater self-awareness, and learn to manage difficult moments. This involves learning the art of transforming raw thoughts into achievable goals while recognizing potential risks and threats to prevent future consequences.

Through Oggun Akomi, individuals gain the confidence they need to move forward and discover new ways to nurture their creativity and use it as a tool for problem-solving. With dedication and proper guidance, practitioners can practice Oggun Akomi to unlock their full potential, overcome obstacles with grace, and create a supportive environment for themselves along their journey toward healing and mental well-being.

Invoking Ogun in Everyday Life

Ogun is an incredibly powerful figure in the Yoruba pantheon, and his presence can be felt everywhere. In everyday life, you may invoke Ogun for any number of reasons, from protection to healing to insight, using traditional prayer and honorifics. This can be done at home at any time, although many adherents like to hold ceremonies before important events or transitions. It is said that Ogun can bring courage and strength to those he watches over while banishing obstacles out of their way. You can ask him to support and guide us through difficult journeys by calling upon his name with respect and reverence.

Here is a list of tips and tricks for invoking Ogun in everyday life:

- Offer prayers and honorifics to Ogun before important events or transitions
- Connect with the spirit of Ogun by calling him in moments of need - be it protection, healing, insight, or courage
- Stick to traditional prayer and honorifics when invoking the power of Ogun
- Spend time meditating on his role in your life and the lessons he teaches.
- Seek out guidance and support from experienced priests and priestesses when in doubt

- Remember to always show respect to Ogun and thank him for his guidance
- Find ways to express your gratitude for Ogun's help in your life

By following these simple tips and tricks, you can invite the spirit of Ogun into your life and benefit from his wisdom.

This chapter has presented Ogun's teachings through the paths of Akomi and Onile. Through Ogun's example, you can learn to show courage in the face of adversity and use your creativity to overcome any challenge. With respect and reverence, you can also invoke the power of Ogun to bring courage, strength, and guidance into your life. By following the tips and tricks mentioned here, you can benefit from Ogun's wisdom and experience growth through healing, creativity, and spiritual understanding.

Chapter 6: Ogun's Symbols and Offerings

Ogun, the Orisha of iron and labor, is seen as a major deity across many parts of the world. He is known for his strength and unyielding determination; these traits were so honored that he was presented with the title "Ender of Difficulties." Ogun leads by example, inspiring those who revere him to work hard to meet their goals. An inventive god, he influences progress and encourages posterity. All who look toward Ogun for guidance can be sure that success will follow if they strive for excellence. He is an invaluable source of comfort and power during times of hardship, ever encouraging you to rise above your struggles.

Ogun is a complex deity with many facets, reflecting deep history and resonance in the African diaspora. He is associated with a wide variety of colors, animals, plants, crystals, symbols, and veves. Each has a distinct meaning that identifies the kind of energy Ogun wields. From the vibrant shades of crimson and maroon to powerful animals like the ram and rooster, each forms a connection between Ogun and the people who revere him. The plants representing his strength, solutions from crystals for protection from negative energy, and symbols of power carved into wood or painted with brightly colored dye on canvas are used as offerings in rituals or placed around your environment as reminders of light and beauty in dark times.

This chapter will explore Ogun's characteristics and traits, diving into the colors, chakras, animals, plants, crystals, symbols, and veves associated with him. It will also include information on what offerings and meals he prefers to receive. By understanding his energies and how to use them, you can appreciate the strength that Ogun offers you in greater depth. The more you understand Ogun, the better you can use his power in your everyday life.

Going Deeper into Ogun

In the Yoruba religion, Ogun is a symbol of strength and skill, represented not just by symbols but also colors, animals, and plants. The veve pattern is believed to be a way to direct energy in rituals to connect with the spirit of Ogun. Additionally, his red color often represents battle, leadership, and authority. It is believed that wearing red clothing during rituals helps to show respect for this complex Orisha.

The veve of Ogun (or Ogoun).
https://commons.wikimedia.org/wiki/File:VeveOgoun.svg

Ogun is also associated with animals, such as goats and dogs, which are said to have been his companions during trading journeys. These animals are sacrificed during celebrations in honor of Ogun. Lastly, many plants are seen as his companions, including melegueta pepper (grains of paradise), used for seasoning food, symbolic of opening the door for communication between oneself and the divine realm. So, through him, you can see how different symbols unite to honor this powerful deity. While these are just some of the symbols associated with

Ogun, it's worth diving deeper into the specifics and learning what they mean.

Ogun's Colors

Ogun is the Yoruba god of metalworking, war, and the hunt; he is represented in many cultures across the African continent. And if there's anything he's a master of, it's his signature red hues! Maroon, rust, and crimson are all divinely associated with Ogun; with them come power, authority, battle, and courage. Red is symbolic of the strength of this powerful deity. Red and all its dynamic tints and tones also signify the strength of will and spiritual power he gives his followers.

Ogun's Chakras

Ogun's primary chakra is powerfully associated with *the root chakra*, which symbolizes grounding and stability in difficult times. Those called to work with Ogun are guided by his presence and strength to stay rooted in their purpose during challenging moments of life. He helps you take action toward your goals, provides protection, facilitates courage and stability, and boosts creativity in problem-solving. Whether you are just learning about him or are an experienced devotee, you'll likely find comfort in his colorful chakra energy as he helps manage chaos with wisdom, balance, and strength.

Ogun is associated with the root chakra.
https://pixabay.com/es/illustrations/chakra-centros-energ%c3%a9ticos-cuerpo-3131630/

Ogun's Animal

Ogun is an incredibly powerful god, and it's no surprise that rams and roosters are associated with him. Rams represent strength and vitality in life, while roosters symbolize energetic positivity. In Yoruba culture, Ogun is honored through sacrificial offerings of these two animals to show reverence for his power. This connection between rams, roosters, and Ogun has been upheld since ancient times, a testament to God's importance within this cultural tradition.

Ogun's Plants

The mysterious and powerful Ogun has been associated with several plants and herbs, including melegueta pepper (grains of paradise). Not only is this herb very distinctively tasty in so many dishes, but it's also believed to open the doors of communication between the divine realm and oneself. Imagine what life could be like if you had direct access and understanding from the divine realm. Other plants associated with Ogun are agbo, calabash, and natal plums. The calabash tree is said to have been where Ogun first brewed his signature beverage of strength and courage, while the natal plums represent prosperity. Agbo is a Yoruba aphrodisiac, reinforcing Ogun's connection with fertility and creativity.

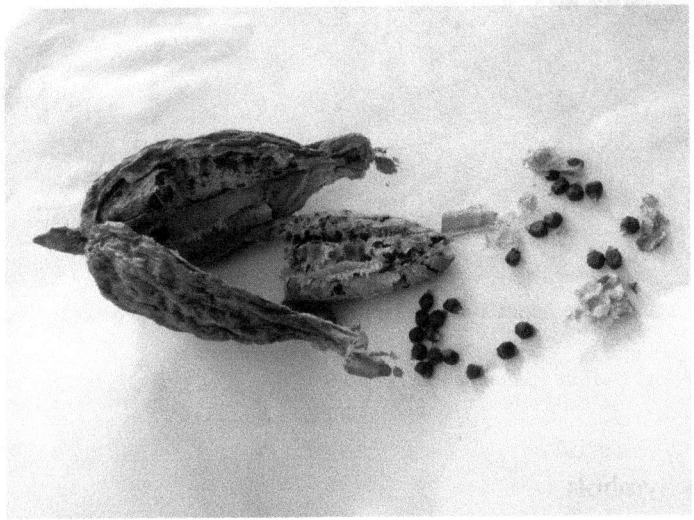

Ogun is associated with the melegueta pepper.
Adoscam, CC BY-SA 4.0 <https://creativecommons.org/licenses/by-sa/4.0>, via Wikimedia Commons
https://commons.wikimedia.org/wiki/File:Graines_d%C3%A9cortiqu%C3%A9es_de_gousse_de_poivre_de_Guin%C3%A9e_ou_de_maniguette_ou_de_graine_de_paradis_ou_(ou_encore_ata_koun_au_B%C3%A9nin).jpg

Ogun's Crystals

Ogun, the powerful Orisha of Nigeria and Benin, is associated with a few crystals that have certain unique benefits. Black tourmaline shields its holder from negative energy and provides strength and courage in difficult situations. Red jasper, a beautiful stone with a red tinge to it, restores balance and can bring peace amidst chaos. Lastly, the tiger's eye, and its seemingly endless depths, help you to understand yourself and create strong boundaries with the people around you. These powerful crystals associated with Ogun help promote positivity in your life.

Red jasper is one of the stones associated with Ogun, as it symbolizes restoring peace among chaos.
あおもりくま, *Aomorikuma, CC BY-SA 4.0 <https://creativecommons.org/licenses/by-sa/4.0>, via Wikimedia Commons*
https://commons.wikimedia.org/wiki/File:Red_Jasper_Tugaru_Nishikiishi_Japan_IMG_8854.jpg

Ogun's Symbols

Ogun is known as a spirit of great strength, associated with both war and peace. As such, his symbols are diverse but also quite powerful. Ogun's symbols are made up of a machete, an axe, a chain or manacles, and a rum bottle or gin. All because these items represent the presence of strength that Ogun embodies. They indicate Ogun's capacity to unite multiple ideas and concepts into one powerful force. His overall power is often touted in many spiritual circles as being simply invincible!

While Ogun's symbols are powerful, they also represent a variety of meanings. Here is a breakdown of what each symbol stands for:

Ogun's Machete

A Machete is one of the most powerful symbols of Ogun, the god of iron in Yoruba mythology. It represents strength, power, and vitality that are essential for a successful life. Ogun is also believed to be the ancestor of blacksmiths who forged iron tools like machetes with skills and wisdom passed down from generation to generation. The machete was used not only for its practical uses, like clearing foliage during farming and harvesting crops, but also to indicate authority because of its power. The machete represents the strength and courage that come with an indomitable spirit and winning battles against adversity. It serves as a reminder that anything can be achieved through perseverance and discipline.

The machete represents courage and strength.
https://pixabay.com/es/photos/machete-tronco-naturaleza-campo-4528976/

Ogun's Axe

The Axe is an iconic symbol amongst many traditional African communities. It's associated with Ogun, the Yoruba warrior-creator God of Iron. The axe stands for courage and determination to grind through obstacles you may face in life. The symbolism of the tool reflects Ogun's ability to protect and guide his people. It also demonstrates that strength comes from persevering regardless of the situation. For many, an axe is a reminder to stay strong in hard times or when dealing with challenging situations. With the axe as a symbolic representation, followers are inspired to keep moving forward and achieve their goals despite any difficulties thrust upon them.

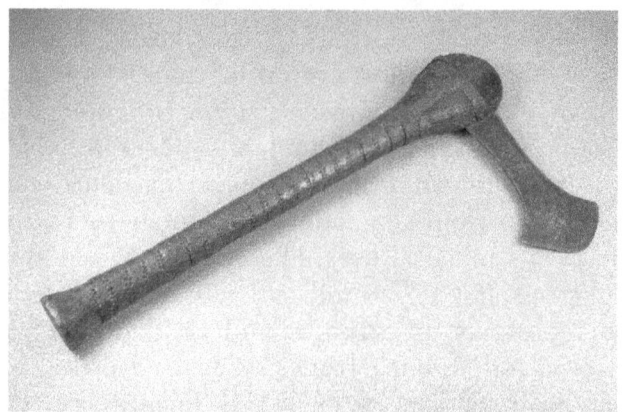

The axe represents the determination to push through any obstacle.
Brooklyn Museum, CC BY 3.0 <https://creativecommons.org/licenses/by/3.0>, via Wikimedia Commons
https://commons.wikimedia.org/wiki/File:Brooklyn_Museum_22.578_Axe_with_Handle_and_Blade.jpg

Ogun's Chain or Manacles

Ogun has long been associated with chains or manacles as symbols of his power to bind and control. While these objects can be seen as a form of restriction, they offer the promise of protection and strength when called on correctly. This can be seen in how Ogun's story is told across many parts of Africa. He saves warriors from enemies, helps craft tools for success, and forges paths for others to find freedom. Chains or manacles can also symbolize empowering the results that come from hard work and dedication, something befitting an ironworker like Ogun. At its core, this powerful symbol represents the strength that comes from facing challenges and staying committed!

Ogun's chain is a symbol of his ability to control and bind power.
https://unsplash.com/photos/2zGTh-S5moM

Rum Bottle or Gin

Ogun is often represented by a bottle of rum or gin. When these symbols are seen, they represent joy, celebration, and merrymaking. They also express strength and resiliency, both qualities that Ogun exemplifies and encourages in his worshipers. For many, these symbols are a reminder of Ogun's support and strength when times become difficult. Embracing these symbols is essential to honoring Ogun and the values he represents. Regardless of the situation, raising a toast with a glass of rum or gin reminds you that there can be joy in any circumstance.

The bottle represents celebration and joy.
https://www.pexels.com/photo/a-dark-brown-liquor-in-a-decanter-7253927/

Ogun's Veves

Ogun's veves are vibrant symbols found among a variety of African-based religions and cultures. These symbols typically include a cross and a circle inside which the figure of Ogun can be seen. Veves are used in spiritual ceremonies and signify an offering to Ogun, the spirit associated with strength, fertility, fire, and ironworking. He is both a protector of justice and capable of imparting good fortune. A veve then acts as an invocation to Ogun so that his energies may be summoned into existence and provide protection or blessing before beginning a ritual or undertaking an important task. Here's a deeper look into some of the most popular veves associated with Ogun.

- **The Veve of Earth:** This veve is represented by a small circle with a larger circle around it, symbolizing the cycle of death and renewal. This veve is used to invoke Ogun's protection and strength in times of difficulty or strife.
- **The Veve of Water:** This veve comprises two concentric circles, with an open eye in the middle. It is believed to offer protection from emotional and physical harm, as well as bring an abundance of luck and prosperity.
- **The Veve of Fire:** This symbol is often used to invoke Ogun's presence and power. It's formed by a circle with a triangle in the center, symbolizing Ogun's ability to bring transformation and protection. The triangle is also a reminder of Ogun's brave spirit.
- **The Veve of Air:** This veve is characterized by four circles connected in the center by a small line, symbolizing the four directions of the wind. This veve is used to invoke Ogun's wisdom and insight, as well as offer protection from harm.

Offerings and Meals for Ogun

Regarding offerings and meals for Ogun, the Yoruba people offer a wide variety of traditional meals and special items. Cooked food like jollof rice, roasted plantains, beef stews, and various other meals are regularly cooked to honor the spirit of Ogun. Additionally, items usually put out are fruits such as oranges, limes, and olives, together with other objects used in sacrifices such as candles, rum, and cigars. For more specific religious ceremonies involving Ogun, there are stronger offerings that include cocks and other animals sacrificed on his altar. These rituals involve prepared chants accompanied by special percussion instruments that reflect his presence as an Orisha or God in the Yoruba religion.

Here are some recipes which can be used to honor Ogun:

Jollof Rice

Ingredients:
- 2 cups of long-grain rice
- 2 tablespoons of vegetable oil
- 1 onion, finely chopped
- 2 cloves garlic, minced
- 1 teaspoon ginger, grated
- 1 teaspoon curry powder
- 1 teaspoon chili powder
- ½ teaspoon ground cumin
- 2 tablespoons tomato paste
- 2 cups chicken broth
- 1 can diced tomatoes
- Salt and pepper to taste

Instructions:
1. Heat oil in a large skillet over medium heat.
2. Add onions, garlic, ginger, and spices and cook until fragrant and the onions are translucent, about 5 minutes.
3. Add tomato paste and stir for 1 minute.
4. Add rice, chicken broth, and diced tomatoes, and season with salt and pepper.
5. Bring to a boil, reduce heat to low, and simmer covered for 20 minutes.
6. Remove the lid and fluff with a fork before serving.

Using this recipe to honor Ogun will bring good fortune and protection from harm. It can also be used in special religious ceremonies where Ogun is invoked to bring transformation and protection.

Roasted Plantains

Ingredients:
- 2 ripe plantains, sliced into 1-inch thick rounds
- 2 tablespoons olive oil
- Salt and pepper to taste

Instructions:
1. Preheat oven to 350°F.
2. Grease a baking sheet with olive oil.
3. Arrange the plantain slices in an even layer on the baking sheet.
4. Sprinkle with salt and pepper to taste.
5. Bake for 20 minutes, flipping halfway through until plantains are golden brown.

Serving roasted plantains as an offering to Ogun is a traditional way of honoring him and asking for protection and strength. Additionally, plantains are believed to bring good luck and prosperity in times of difficulty or strife.

Beef Stew

Ingredients:
- 2 tablespoons vegetable oil
- 1 onion, diced
- 1 pound beef stew meat, cubed
- 2 cloves garlic, minced
- 2 carrots, peeled and diced
- 1 celery stalk, diced
- 1 teaspoon ground cumin
- 1 teaspoon paprika
- ½ teaspoon dried oregano
- 2 tablespoons tomato paste
- 2 cups beef broth
- 2 cups potatoes, diced
- Salt and pepper to taste

Instructions:
1. Heat oil in a large skillet over medium heat.
2. Add onions and beef and cook until lightly browned, 8-10 minutes.
3. Add garlic, carrots, and celery, and cook for an additional 5 minutes.
4. Add cumin, paprika, oregano, and tomato paste and stir to coat the beef and vegetables.
5. Add the beef broth and potatoes and bring to a boil.
6. Cover, reduce heat to low, and simmer for 1 hour.
7. Remove the lid and season with salt and pepper before serving.

Serving a beef stew around a sacred fire is believed to show respect to Ogun and can bring positive energy in the form of protection, strength, and courage. The beef stew is a symbol of sustenance and nourishment, which are important elements when honoring Ogun.

Ogun is a hugely influential and powerful deity in the Yoruba religion. He is associated with strength, courage, and protection from harm. Symbols such as a machete, hammer, and veves can be used to call down his spirit and bring positive energy. His colors are red, black, and blue, his chakra is the first or root chakra, his animal is a ram, and his plant is cotton. His crystal is jasper, and his symbols are the machete, hammer, and veves. He is often called down with a specific veve, believed to bring forth his spirit and protection. Offering him rum, cigars, incense, and traditional meals such as beef stew or roasted plantains is a good way to honor him.

Furthermore, Ogun likes to receive a variety of foods and drinks as offerings, including rum, cigars, and traditional meals such as beef stew or roasted plantains. Eating these meals can bring good fortune and protection from harm – while invoking Ogun through symbols and veves can bring transformation and protection. Therefore, by honoring Ogun in these ways, one can bring positive energy into their life.

Chapter 7: Making a Sacred Altar

Dedicating a shrine to Ogun can be an awesome experience full of significance and an invaluable way to honor the Orisha. Not only is it beautiful and captivating to create a space that captures your vibrant interpretations of Ogun, but it also serves to deepen and enrich your spiritual journey with him. A creative offering of visual expressions, such as art pieces and even scents, can be put together in a way that makes you feel deeply connected with Ogun. With time and practice, shrines can become powerful spiritual tools used to petition Ogun's guidance, protection, strength, and blessings on your life.

Ogun altar.
https://commons.wikimedia.org/wiki/File:Acentamento_de_Ogum,_Orossi.,JPG

This chapter discusses the benefits of building a shrine to Ogun, where to create it, what to place on it and how to take care of it, how to give offerings through it, and when to clear the gifts. It will also provide examples of traditional shrines and offerings. By the end of this chapter, you'll have a better understanding of how to create and maintain your own Ogun altar. The knowledge shared here will help you to make your spiritual journey with Ogun more meaningful and powerful.

Benefits of Building a Shrine to Ogun

The African deity Ogun brings immense good fortune and strength to those who worship him. Building a shrine can be an excellent way to honor Ogun and take advantage of the blessings he bestows on those who pay tribute to him. According to legend, having a shrine can protect against misfortune, promote prosperity, and even create opportunities for advancement. It can also serve as a reminder of one's spiritual beliefs and keep them close to the heart, especially in difficult times. It also offers a central location for rituals or ceremonies held in honor of Ogun, ensuring his legendary power remains ever-present. Ultimately, building a shrine to Ogun is a powerful spiritual practice that not only honors the deity but could potentially lead an individual or community toward the path of success.

A. Respecting and Honoring Ogun

Building a shrine to honor and respect Ogun can bring immense blessings into your life. Not only will you be in Oguns' favor and protected by his presence, but you may also find yourself gifted with increased creativity, freedom of expression, and enriched physical well-being. By creating an altar or shrine dedicated to Ogun, you are inviting his potent energies into your life and allowing him to bring abundance to new areas of your existence. Showing reverence, respect, and care for this great deity can lead to blessings far greater than you could ever imagine!

B. Strengthening the Connection with Ogun

Building a shrine to Ogun is said to be the best way to strengthen your connection with this powerful and respected Orisha. Adding an altar in your home or community serves as an essential reminder of his blessings and helps create a spiritual atmosphere in which to receive divine guidance. Regular sacrifices and offerings at the shrine will generate positive manifestations such as improved health, enhanced focus and productivity, increased wealth and prosperity, and secure protection from enemies, both seen and unseen. As your connection deepens over time with Ogun, through contemplation and reverence before the altar, you may experience an even more profound transformation within yourself.

C. A Place of Emotional Support and Comfort

Building a shrine to Ogun bring with it many benefits, and one of the most significant is providing emotional support and comfort. By gathering with other followers to honor and celebrate Ogun, participants experience a sense of connection that can help reduce feelings of isolation. Offerings made at these shrines are also a great source of solace. For example, small items such as food or drink are given in appreciation for Ogun's guidance, providing physical nourishment and spiritual renewal. Ultimately, when you take time to unite and venerate, your actions will positively strengthen you emotionally and spiritually.

D. A Place for Ogun to Grant Blessings

Building a shrine to Ogun comes with so many benefits and can be a great way to practice your faith. As a sacred place to come to pray and bask in the presence of the gods, it's also an opportunity to experience the prosperity and peace that Ogun can grant an individual. When you place your faith in Ogun, this deity provides safety and protection, financial security, and general guidance throughout everyday life. Furthermore, having a designated place to recharge spiritually from daily stress brings more balance into your life, leaving you more energized and motivated. A shrine to Ogun is good for individuals and families wishing to keep the ancient traditions alive, blessing themselves with strong community support. With all these amazing benefits, building a shrine to Ogun is worth every second of the time and effort you put into it.

E. A Place to Share Blessings with Others

Building a shrine to the Yoruba god Ogun is a meaningful and interesting way to share blessings with others. It's an incredibly powerful way to connect with the energetic forces of Orisha and tap into his potential to help improve your life and the lives of those around you. It's also a great way to honor Ogun and embrace his attributes, such as knowledge, innovation, courage, strength, protection, and more.

Building a shrine embodying these core values is honoring Ogun and reminding yourself why he is necessary to your spiritual journey. And for those who have already established a connection with the Orisha, it's an opportunity to show devotion in a tangible form through artwork or decoration on the shrine. By creating this sacred space dedicated to him and sharing joy with others, you can ensure your blessings are being passed along in an abundant flow.

Where to Create an Ogun Altar

Ogun is an important deity in many African traditions, and having a personal altar dedicated to him is a deeply spiritual veneration of this powerful god. When creating an Ogun altar, it is critical to think carefully about how and where to set it up. An ideal place for such an altar would be somewhere outdoors, like a backyard or natural area that feels connected to the Earth. This will help you feel at one with the environment, much like the spirit of Ogun.

However, sometimes it's not feasible or convenient for everyone to have an outdoor altar. In these cases, setting up your altar indoors can also be meaningful if done thoughtfully. The key is finding a comfortable and private space to focus on worshipping Ogun without any distractions. Ultimately, you should create a space that reflects your relationship with Ogun and makes you feel connected to him on a deeper level.

A. Indoors or Outdoors

When it comes to creating an Ogun altar, the choice between indoors and outdoors can be difficult. While an outdoor altar is sure to capture attention and create an impressive sight, some worries about safety and security may become an issue. An indoor alternative may provide more privacy but require a more creative and thoughtful setup. Before picking a location for your altar, consider both options carefully so that you can create the atmosphere you want, whether it be mystical and comforting or awe-inspiring and powerful. Ultimately, the decision of where you choose to create your Ogun altar should depend on what works best for your goals.

B. Location and Direction

When creating an Ogun altar, it is vital to choose the right location. Ogun's power lies in the depths of metals, and it is believed that his altars should be mounted on an open rock in a public area. An ideal location would be a mountaintop or a crossroads, as these areas are symbols of transformation and justice, which are also principles deeply rooted within this tradition. This ensures that you are aligning yourself with the energies of Ogun while allowing it to reach its full potential, bringing strength, perception, and determination into your life.

C. Size and Design of the Shrine

When creating an Ogun altar, think carefully about size and design. If the space is large, the larger the shrine can be and more elaborate in terms of decorations. But a modest altar can still attract positive energy if only a smaller area is available. When selecting adornments or materials for the altar, choose items that speak to your spirituality as well as Ogun's principles. These can be anything from beads and fabric to feathers or jewelry. Consider your color scheme carefully. Most altars use red, black, and white with touches of green or blue to represent the four cardinal directions. Above all else, when choosing where to create an Ogun altar, ensure it is a spot where you feel comfortable and safe. Its purpose is to energize you spiritually and connect you with this powerful deity!

What to Place on an Ogun Altar

Making an altar to Ogun is a great way to honor and show your devotion to the Yoruba deity. Though many materials can be placed on an Ogun altar, some of the most common include wooden and metal elements, such as knives or axes, which symbolize his power over iron tools. You'll also want to add drinking and cooking items, like a pot or traditional gourd cleaners or "Osun," which symbolize his help with cooking up delicious food for the family.

Red cloth is also commonly used since it is intended as a reminder of Ogun's ability to break through any obstacle and clear the way ahead. Finally, you should consider adding stones from around your home or nearby riverbeds since nature-based elements have always been important in African religions. With these meaningful additions to your altar, you can demonstrate your appreciation for Ogun's role in the spiritual world!

A. Traditional Offerings

The Ogun altar is a sacred space honoring the Yoruba Orisha, Ogun. It is traditional to leave offerings on the altar to honor and give respect to the Orisha, who is known as the patron of technology, blacksmiths, war, and hunting. Common offerings include cowrie shells, red and white cloths, kola nuts, palm oil, yams or potatoes, coins, rum or gin, cigars, or cigarettes. In addition to these offerings, it's also customary for devotees of Ogun to create items for his altar that are built out of metal, such as scissors and other tools which can symbolically connect him with our creative and technological endeavors. By leaving items on his altar that are meaningful to you, you aim to reaffirm your relationship with the spirit realm and honor your connection with the divine through honoring Ogun.

B. Symbols of Protection and Strength

Ogun altars are a great way to embrace the power and protection of the Ogun spirit. To create an altar, start by gathering symbolic items connected to strength and safety. Some good choices could include a bright red piece of fabric or cloth, useful tools such as hammers and tongs for demonstration of strength or protection, dried or fresh herbs which visually evoke protection like rosemary, salt for cleansing and protection against evil, stones or shells for grounding energy, candles to lead the way, incense-like camphor, or copal to purify the space and enhance your spiritual connection with Ogun, and perhaps an image of Ogun himself. With each item placed on the altar, ask Ogun to infuse it with his energy. Focusing on your intentions can help you enjoy the power of your altar to its fullest extent.

C. A Statue of Ogun

Ogun, the Yoruba Orisha of iron and war, is honored with a statue or altar. Whether you are a Yoruba devotee of Ogun or greatly appreciate Yoruba culture, creating an Ogun altar can be a wonderful way to pay tribute to this powerful deity. An altar should include things such as stones, coins, dried herbs, and leaves from plants representing protection and prosperity, like Olugbo leaf and bitter kola, vegetable oils for illumination, prayer beads and bells for spiritual cleansing, and brass tools representing power. If you already have an Ogun statue, candles could be lit in front of it as expressions of respect and as an offering of thanks. Whatever objects are included on your altar will be unique to your connection to the Orisha deity honoring him in all his glory.

D. Candles

If you are making or setting up an altar to the Orisha Ogun, you may be wondering what candles to use. Candles are a simple but powerful way to call upon and pay tribute to this powerful God of iron and forge. Consider black, red, and white candles for your altar when working with Ogun's energy. Black candles are great for protection and material success, red for joy, strength, vitality, and power, and white for devotion and spiritual growth. You can also combine all three colors in one large candle or place them side-by-side around your altar. Adding coins from different countries is another powerful way to show appreciation to Ogun, as coins represent wealth in all forms, such as currency, knowledge, and wealth of energy. Lastly, adding an offering of assorted fresh fruit (such as apples or oranges) or a strong drink, such as a glass of whisky, on top of the altar will please him greatly, ensuring his blessings are reaped again and again.

E. Incense and Other Scents

Incense and other scents are also great for setting the atmosphere around an Ogun altar. Ogun is known as the warrior of change, so many people use this deity to honor their bravery and transition in life. Incense is often used on an Ogun altar because it is believed to open up portals between worlds, enabling communication between humans and spirits. People may also consider placing aromatic herbs like Hops, Rosemary, Vervain, Angelica root, and Sarsaparilla as offerings in their Ogun altar. Each herb has its own special properties that work together with the energies within nature or even within yourself to create powerful changes. Heavily scented oils such as sandalwood or patchouli can also be used to help bring good luck and success during times of upheaval or transition.

How to Take Care of the Altar

Taking care of your altar is essential to honoring and connecting with this beloved spirit. We suggest you regularly give offerings and sacrifices on your altar to show respect and gratitude, especially when you have asked for specific things from the deity. You should also cleanse your shrine around once a week by burning incense; you might try a leathery scent used traditionally in Orisha worship. Make sure the altar is well-lit and free from any clutter or dust. Filling it with fresh fruit, flowers, or other natural offerings is a great idea too! Overall, taking care of an Ogun altar requires consistent commitment, but the rewards in your spiritual experience can be immeasurable.

How to Give Offerings through an Ogun Altar

Ogun, who is one of the oldest deities in Yoruba mythology, can be honored at an altar with offerings. It's a great way to show your respect for Ogun and maintain a connection with him. To make your offering, start by cleaning your hands and preparing the space where you intend to honor Ogun. Make sure it is neat and inviting so that you can focus on offering your reverence. Then, choose a gift appropriate to the occasion and align it with Ogun's values. Think along the lines of farm tools, machetes, or any type of iron items for strength. Place these in front of the altar as if welcoming him into your home and express gratitude for his presence in your life. Finally, spend some time in meditation before dispersing energies with gratitude and light humming sounds. This is a great way to establish a strong relationship with Ogun's energy!

When to Clear Offerings from an Ogun Altar

Clearing offerings from an Ogun altar is an important practice for anyone honoring the deity. The methods used to clear these offerings depend on individual preference and may range from physical disposal and/or burning of offerings. The frequency of clearing should respond to signs that appear when it is time to remove offerings, such as shifts in energy or feelings of heaviness. Reaching out and paying attention to the spirit realm can provide clues that it is time to clear the altar and ensure your Ogun altar is regularly refreshed with the intention and presence of honor, respect, and adoration.

Examples of Ogun Shrines and Offerings

Ogun, the Yoruba god of iron and war, is honored with shrines throughout Africa and countries in the African diaspora. The celebration varies from region to region, but all celebrations involve offerings placed at the shrine. Depending on the area, these offerings can include the sacrifice of chickens or goats, palming coins, pouring libations of palm wine or rum, burning paper money or items symbolic of Ogun's power, and iron tools such as machetes, hatchets, and hoes, and by leaving alcohol for him to drink. More modern forms of celebrating Ogun include cultural performances such as drumming, dancing, and singing songs dedicated to him. All of these offerings are made with the understanding that although Ogun can be a destructive force when he needs to be in wartime, he is also generous to his followers, who honor him faithfully with devotion.

Honoring Ogun with an altar is a great way to connect and show your appreciation for this powerful spirit. Creating an altar involves setting up a clean and inviting space, offering items or sacrifices specific to Ogun's values, and regularly clearing away these offerings. With consistent commitment and effort, connecting to Ogun through an altar can be a rewarding part of your spiritual practice. It is also vital to remember that although Ogun can be a destructive force in wartime, when necessary, he is also generous to his followers, who honor him faithfully. One way of showing your respect is by connecting to Ogun through an altar, offering appropriate items and sacrifices, regularly clearing these away as instructed, and always showing sincere devotion. A connection and relationship with Ogun can be achieved with dedication and effort.

Chapter 8: Useful Rituals and Spells

Ogun, the highly respected warrior spirit, can bestow great power of protection, strength, and clarity on his followers. His presence increases your self-confidence by guiding you through paths of obstacles and conflict and helping elicit creative solutions to problems, increase productivity, help with troubleshooting, and overcome blocks. His presence also guides physical traveling or journeying on a spiritual level. By completing rituals or offerings for Ogun, you open yourself up to receive his blessings in these areas. All it takes is an open heart, faith, and trust for him to come and guide you whenever you need it.

This chapter outlines recipes for spells, rituals, and prayers dedicated to Ogun. All the necessary ingredients are listed with steps to take for protection, self-confidence, creativity, productivity, and traveling. By following these with reverence, respect, and mindfulness, you can invoke the power of Ogun to help manifest your intentions. Remember that any spell or ritual should be done with a clear and pure intention, as Ogun's power can be destructive and productive depending on one's intention.

Protection

Ogun, also known as the Dauntless Warrior and Master of Iron, is an influential deity in the Yoruba pantheon. Those looking for protection can find strength and guidance through rituals, spells, and offerings to Ogun. Many of these offer recognition and respect to this great god while helping proprietors build a spiritual connection with him. Inciting Ogun's protection can be done through ancestral offerings such as animal sacrifices or honey libations. Other protective symbols, such as iron nails or four-pointed stars, are also appreciated by Ogun.

Spells invoking Ogun tend to involve singing, dancing, drums, and sharing stories of courage and bravery, the qualities held in high esteem by the deity himself. In addition to speaking prayers of protection in the direction of an iron shrine dedicated to Ogun, other rituals like meditation are also useful for reaching out to the Dauntless Warrior for help. Of course, not all fear can be blocked with spells or formulas. Sometimes courage has to come from within, and with a little help from your deities, you'll find a path through any darkness.

Ritual to Protect Your Home from Unwanted Influences

Creating a safe, peaceful home can be tricky. Ogun is an incredibly powerful energy we can call on when we're looking for extra protection. From simple sprinkling of salt and bay leaves to offerings and more involved rituals, there are also plenty of spells using Ogun's energy to protect your home from outside influences. Whether you are looking for his power to guard your physical dwelling or metaphorical home against darkness, the strength of Ogun gives us the potential to keep our cherished places of peace safe for ourselves and those we love.

The Sprinkle Salt and Bay Leaves ritual requires only a few ingredients and is effective for many kinds of protection. Here's a detailed recipe:

Ingredients:
- 1 white candle
- 1 black candle
- 2 tablespoons of sandalwood incense
- Salt
- Bay leaves

Instructions:
1. Start by creating a sacred space in your home by lighting the white candle and the black candle.

2. Chant a prayer or invocation to Ogun and ask for protection from all that is negative, unwanted, and harmful.
3. Take the salt and bay leaves in your hands and sprinkle them around the perimeter of your home, starting at the front door. Visualize a protective barrier surrounding your home to give you strength and courage.
4. Finally, light the sandalwood incense and walk around the house, allowing the smoke to purify and cleanse all rooms.
5. Allow the candles to burn out naturally, and use this time for meditation and reflection on the protection that Ogun brings.

Ritual for Protection against Negative Thought Patterns

Practicing rituals to protect against negative thoughts establishes healthy practices that balance our mental health and well-being. Ogun, the Yoruba spirit of iron, is one powerful figure who many turn to for protection from negative thoughts or unwanted energies. There are a variety of useful chants, invocations, and spells related to Ogun, which can be used depending on what you need. Grounding meditations and visualization exercises can further empower a person seeking protection from negative mental cycles. Connecting with the strength of Ogun through these practices can help you find greater resilience in times of difficulty and trust in your innate power.

Rituals to Combat Bullying

Ogun embodies strength, craftsmanship, and war and is an important figure in many rituals. If you've experienced bullying or know someone who has, Ogun can provide powerful protection. Incorporating Ogun into your rituals to combat bullying could bring about comfort and a sense of security. He can provide the timely boost of courage and assurance that, so often, what is needed in the face of bullying. With his protection, you can find resilience no matter the situation. In ceremonies involving Ogun, powerful trinkets such as iron, black textile, honeycomb, and healing stones are used as offerings to invoke his presence. These meaningful rituals could be especially beneficial to those who have gone through extreme bouts of bullying, providing solace where none seemed possible before.

Self-Confidence

Ogun is connected to many different skills and passions. One of these is self-confidence, which can be built through a variety of different rituals and spells. Ogun's powerful spirit can help you grow and develop your self-assurance through certain offerings and recitations. However, remember that you are the main driver of your self-confidence. All Ogun can do is provide an extra bit of support on your journey toward feeling comfortable in your skin.

Spells and Rituals to Help with Low Self-Esteem

One of the most empowering practices for anyone struggling with low self-esteem is to turn to Ogun. Spells and rituals devoted to him can be immensely helpful in helping you reclaim your true identity and power. The aim is to fill yourself with courage, strength, and resilience to bravely confront any obstacles life may bring.

When you feel unworthy or defenseless against life's difficulties, calling on Ogun can provide courage through his strong nature. Similarly, symbols related to Ogun can be used as reminders of strength and be placed around the home as talismans of security. Through spell casting, offerings, and daily affirmations, you may find yourself becoming more vibrant in both the physical and spiritual spaces. By strengthening yourself internally, facing your fears or anxieties head-on may become easier so that paths to empowerment can truly start leading you down a new path.

Spell work to Boost Self-Confidence and Courage

Ogun is the traditional Orisha of strength and courage, providing faith and protection to African people for centuries. He is undoubtedly a powerful ally, especially when it comes to modern-day struggles with self-confidence, fear, and anxiety. If you're looking to gently remove obstacles, reaching out to Ogun may be just the thing you need.

Whether through ritual or spell work, Ogun can help guide you on the path toward new levels of self-acceptance and fearlessness. Amongst other activities, such as creating affirmations or speaking incantations relevant to your goals, one basic ritual is as follows:

Ingredients:
- Honeycomb
- Iron trinkets/nails/rings
- Candles (preferably black or blue)
- Stones of your choice

Instructions:
1. Place the iron trinkets, honeycomb, and stones on an altar or any other sacred space of your choice.
2. Light the candles, and begin to focus all of your energy on the items in front of you.
3. Speak out loud your intention for the spell, or recite a prayer or incantation dedicated to Ogun (see below for one example).
4. Leave the items and candles on the altar until they have burned out, then discard them safely and respectfully.

Prayer to Ogun

"Ogun, sacred spirit of strength, courage, and power, I ask you to grant me divine protection so that I may have the strength and courage to face my fears. Fill me with infinite peace, clarity, and understanding so that I may be free from worry and anxiety. Protect me from the forces of darkness, and guide me to new heights of self-confidence and power. I offer my humble gratitude and devotion at this moment. May it be returned tenfold. Amen."

Once the spell is completed, and the prayer said, keep your energies high by following up with affirmations or activities that help you stay focused on your goals. With Ogun's help, the path to self-empowerment should become clearer and more attainable.

Meditations for Overcoming Fear

When it comes to overcoming fear, there might not be a better tool than Ogun. He is a powerful protector and warrior who comes to the aid of those who need it most. Through meditations and rituals in the Yoruba tradition, you can tap into the power of Ogun to help you move through fear and into courage and action. There are a wide variety of rituals for accessing Ogun's help, depending on what you need, from personal protection spells to rituals for banishing anxiety. Whether you're feeling overwhelmed or looking for an empowering boost, connecting with Ogun can be an invaluable resource on your journey toward conquering your fears.

Here are a few exercises to consider:
- Visualize yourself facing and conquering your fears by calling on Ogun's power. Imagine his fiery energy providing you with strength, protection, and courage.
- Recite a prayer or incantation to Ogun that reflects your current goals (see above for an example).
- Create a physical altar or offering to Ogun with items of your choosing.
- Engage in active visualization. Imagine a protective shield around yourself, empowered by Ogun's energy.
- Participate in meditation-focused rituals such as "shaking out" negative energy (this involves physically shaking your body as if you are shaking out old, stagnant energy).
- Spend time in nature and take a moment to appreciate the power of Ogun and the protective energy he provides.

Creativity

Ogun is a powerful spirit associated with creativity and transformation, particularly relating to new beginnings. Many wonderful rituals and spells are available to honor this spirit to embody his transformative energy in your life. One popular practice that helps to unleash creativity is ancestor reverence which means relating stories of your ancestors, honoring them through offerings such as candles or fruit, and weaving their lessons into your life.

Incorporating drumming or chants related to Ogun can also create a much-needed path for creative flow while allowing you to connect deeply with this powerful force. Whatever ritual you choose, remembering to be mindful of the vibrant energy it brings to your creative endeavors can make all the difference in unlocking Ogun's transformative power within you!

Rituals to Unblock Creativity

There are many rituals and spells to unleash creativity that involve calling upon the energy of Ogun. When beginning a creative process, it can be helpful to call on Ogun's energy asking for guidance to overcome any blocks or inhibitions. Here are a few rituals to reignite the creative process:

- **Burning Offerings** - Light a candle or incense to symbolize your offering of gratitude and respect to Ogun.
- **Drumming** - Use a drum or other percussion instrument to create energy and open up the creative path.
- **Dancing** - Find a rhythm and allow yourself to move freely as you invoke Ogun's energy.
- **Prayer** - Recite a prayer or chant to Ogun, expressing your gratitude and asking for guidance in overcoming creative blocks.
- **Ancestor Veneration** - Spend time in conversation or offer an offering to your ancestors and ask for their guidance on your creative path.
- **Nature walks** - Spend time in nature, reflecting on the power of Ogun and asking for guidance.

Ritual for Abundance and Opportunity

Ogun can also be a powerful ally to manifest abundance and create opportunities for success. When working with Ogun's energy, it can be helpful to focus on taking action, as his energy is associated with assertive force and strength. Here are rituals to help bring abundance and opportunity into your life:

Ingredients:
- White or brown candle
- Seven coins (or another offering to Ogun)
- Fire-safe container

Steps:
1. Place the candle in your fire-safe container and light it.
2. Call upon Ogun, asking for his assistance in manifesting abundance and creating opportunities for success.

3. Place the coins in a circle around the candle.
4. Visualize the energy of abundance and opportunity radiating out from the candle in a circular pattern.
5. Speak your intentions aloud for what you want to attract into your life.
6. When finished, allow the candle to burn out safely in the fire-safe container.
7. Offer your gratitude to Ogun for his assistance.

You can also connect with Ogun's energy by reciting this prayer:

"Ogun, mighty warrior and protector, I come to you seeking your guidance. Help me to forge a path of abundance and opportunity. Help me to be brave in the pursuit of my goals. I thank you for your strength and protection on my journey."

By using these rituals and prayers, you can draw upon Ogun's energy to help manifest abundance and create opportunities for success in your life.

Cleansing Ritual

Ogun's energy can be used to cleanse and clear away any obstacles in your life, opening up avenues for new possibilities and beginnings. Practicing rituals or ceremonies involving taking advantage of Ogun's energy can be beneficial, such as lighting candles to help you meditate and focus on his power. As you tap into his strengths, they can become your own, helping to clear out any negative feelings or clutter that may have been blocking the way forward. Once freed from these restrictions, you'll find yourself more open than ever before to new opportunities and possibilities.

Here is a cleansing ritual that can be used to clear the way for new beginnings:

Ingredients:
- White candle
- Garlic
- Frankincense
- A bowl of water
- Salt

Steps:
1. Begin by carving your name into the candle. Place the garlic and frankincense around the candle.
2. Light the candle and pray to Ogun for protection, cleansing, and any new opportunities you wish to manifest in your life.
3. Sprinkle a pinch of salt into the bowl of water and stir with your fingers as you focus on your intent for the ritual.
4. Dip your fingers into the water and sprinkle it around the room you're in as an offering to Ogun.
5. Allow the candle to burn completely, and give thanks to Ogun for his guidance and protection.

Ogun Prayer:

"Ogun, Ogun. I ask for protection, cleansing, and blessings upon me. Guide me through my journey and open the paths that are meant for me. I thank you for your blessings and trust in your divine guidance. Amen."

For centuries, Ogun has been revered for his power and strength. He is still a great source of protection, cleansing, and the opening of paths for those who seek it. Through the use of rituals and prayers, Ogun helps people manifest their desires into reality. This chapter has outlined some rituals and prayers that can be used to draw on Ogun's energy and help bring abundance, opportunity, protection, and cleansing into your life. May you find success in all of your endeavors with his blessings!

Chapter 9: Ogun's Festivals and Holy Days

Each year, the Yoruba people of Nigeria and other West African countries celebrate the Ogun festival with joy and exuberance, honoring Ogun. He is a powerful archetype revered for his enduring strength in navigating challenging circumstances, qualities the Yoruba people continue to embody today. The celebration itself lasts for days, at times featuring parades and sacrifices in addition to performances from religious dance troupes.

Many West African countries celebrate the Ogun festival every year.
South African Tourism from South Africa, CC BY 2.0 <https://creativecommons.org/licenses/by/2.0>, via Wikimedia Commons https://commons.wikimedia.org/wiki/File:Zulu_Culture,_KwaZulu-Natal,_South_Africa_(20325264550).jpg

While the rituals may differ across different regions, it's certain that wherever it's celebrated, Ogun's festival serves as an integral part of cultures that have survived and grown through time and never lost sight of the traditions that underpin them. This chapter explores the origins of Ogun's festival, how it's celebrated today, and why, as well as tips for honoring the deity in our daily lives. The chapter also dives into Ogun's feast day (which coincides with Saint Peter's Day) and the days associated with Ogun to provide a holistic overview of this important festival and its relevance in modern-day Yoruba culture.

Ogun's Festival

This traditional Yoruba festival honors Ogun, the god of iron and war. Thousands of devotees congregate to pray, sing, dance, and make offerings to show their reverence for Ogun's power and strength. Celebrations can last anywhere from three days to several weeks and are held to honor Ogun and all the gods associated with him. Daytime activities consist of parades featuring colorful costumes and ornately decorated pieces made from metal and iron, including swords and farm tools. In the evening, there are sacred ceremonies of prayers, music, and special meals created using ingredients believed to bring God's blessings. If you have a chance to witness or participate in such an event firsthand, don't hesitate, it will be a memorable experience!

Origins of the Festival

Ogun's festival is an annual celebration held in Nigeria and other West African countries. Its origin dates far back in ancient history when warriors used iron on their weapons for protection. Ogun was thought to be so powerful that an entire festival was created in his honor. Every year thousands of attendees gather to participate in rituals that include drumming and dancing, believed to be a grand show of respect for Ogun's strength and power. People dress up in traditional clothing and enjoy a variety of food made especially for a holiday. Ogun's Festival continues to live on today in traditional societies that want to pay tribute to their ancestral roots by honoring this remarkable deity.

Celebrations and Rituals

Ogun's Festival, also known as Oguinha, is a spectacular and vibrant celebration of the Yoruba religion. Colorful costumes, elaborate masquerade dances, drumming music, and lively parades fill the streets to honor Ogun by offering ceremonies at sacred sites. Families come together to share traditional dishes and exchange blessings while worshiping Ogun. This special period allows families to strengthen the bonds in their relationships and appreciate each other on a much deeper level. The energy of this joyous event is truly infectious. Even those who are not religious can join in on the festivities as long as they respect the culture's customs.

Ogun's Pilgrimage

Ogun's Pilgrimage is an annual celebration of the Yoruba god of iron, metallurgy, and hunting in parts of southwestern Nigeria. This spiritual pilgrimage has been traditionally celebrated for centuries and continues to be celebrated today. Every year, people dress in all-white garments to symbolize spiritual purity and ritual cleanliness. Led by senior members of Ogun, devotees march around the sacred space dedicated to Ogun to access blessings.

During this time, beautiful displays of vibrant energy accompanied by instrumental music and rhythmic dancing bring celebrations alive. There are also traditional offerings made in honor of Ogun, such as kola nuts and palm wine presented by devotees honoring Ogun's power over growth and sustenance, which he provides. This historical event is alive with energy and devotion as Yoruba people come together to seek spiritual guidance from their beloved Ogun. It's truly an awesome experience worth seeing if you get given the opportunity.

Feasting and Dancing

Celebrated from August through September, Ogun's Festival is known for its feasting and dancing. Feasting and large communal meals are shared among community members and speak to the importance of social bonds in Yoruba culture. Additionally, energetic dancing is a mainstay of the celebrations. It engages and energizes community members, showcasing their creativity and rich culture. All festival attendees dress in their finery as they come together to honor Ogun while engaging with one another. The colorful costumes and lively music create a vibrant atmosphere.

Processions and Parades

Each year, processions and parades are held where community members carry colorful umbrellas along with implements made of iron, such as spears or tools used to cut metal, while they march around various parts of Yoruba land. It is a ritualistic tradition with inspirational, joyous music, culminating in a grand feast given by the host village. It doesn't matter where you are from. If you're looking for an exciting cultural experience, be sure to get out to participate in these boisterous festivals!

Contemporary Significance in Yoruba Culture

To this day, this festival remains an important date in the Yoruba cultural calendar. Traditionally, it is acknowledged through rituals, feasting, and offering sacrifices. Nowadays, the festival embodies Yoruba values that transcend societal structures, focusing on justice, equal access to opportunities, and collective progress. It provides an opportunity for family members and friends to come together as one to live life in balance.

Ogun's Festival reinforces our shared understanding that we should continue to move forward as a collective, both spiritually and economically. This shared value system reinforces beliefs about accountability for positive communal action at the end of each season's festival period. People pray for another year filled with an increased understanding of the world and treasure what it means to live as stewards of this beautiful earth as our ancestors intended.

How to Celebrate Ogun's Festival

The Ogun Festival is such an exciting time, and there are so many ways that people can come together to celebrate it. Taking part in traditional ceremonies is one way to honor the spirit of Ogun. The festival is a time of joyous celebration, filled with the sounds of laughter and merriment. So having a parade around your community with drums, flutes, and whatever instruments you can get your hands on would be sure to make an impression. If you're looking for a more mellow approach, cooking up some tasty dishes like cassava bread or plantain pottage are all fun ways to celebrate. And don't forget that part of Ogun's strength and power comes from being able to help others; making donations to a local charity or offering assistance in some form would also be an excellent way to pay homage this season. Have fun celebrating!

Ogun's Feast Day

Ogun's Feast Day is a celebration of the fearsome god from Yoruban mythology, who is the leader of all warriors. By honoring him on his feast day, devotees pray for protection and hope for their enemies to be vanquished. In most celebrations, offerings traditionally consist of food, drink, and drums. As people gather together to mark this special day, it's also an opportunity to connect and continue to share stories of Ogun's heroic deeds while enjoying the company of family and friends. The reverence of Ogun is intended to unite all people rather than divide them, making his feast day a beautiful reminder that no matter our differences, we still have much in common.

When Is It Celebrated?

Ogun's Feast Day is a much-anticipated celebration for the Yoruba people every year. Taking place over three days, starting from the first to the third day of the fourth month of their calendar. People participate in many cultural activities and traditional prayers as they thank Ogun, their god of iron and technology. Activities may include singing, dancing, and feasting exquisite delicacies prepared specially for the festival. As well as being an important spiritual event in honor of Ogun, the feast day is also a great opportunity for families and friends to come together in celebration.

Celebrations in Different Regions

Across West Africa, members of the Yoruba diaspora gather to honor Ogun and show their appreciation for his protection. An intricately planned ceremony featuring music, singing, dancing, and unique local dishes is the climax of a month-long celebration. During this time of gratitude, celebrants donate money to those in need and distribute food to honor Ogun's generosity. Participants in the festival often leave offerings at shrines that are erected during the event to thank their deities for protecting them from harm over the past year. All who take part leave feeling inspired by Ogun's graciousness, forming memories that last far beyond the festival's end.

Offerings and Activities

During this annual celebration, all kinds of offerings and activities take place in honor of Ogun, from homemade metal implements to sacrificing animals. Many people also enjoy taking part in drum circles, feasts featuring traditional Nigerian dishes, and lively dancing from different parts of the country. Everyone is welcome to join the festivities or simply observe as they happen. However you choose to participate, Ogun's feast day is sure to be an amazing experience!

Days Associated with Ogun

Ogun, an ancient god of the Yoruba pantheon, represents virility and power. He is strong and brave, able to forge his path. This spirit of strength and determination is why many cultures across the continent honor Ogun on special days. Tuesdays are especially associated with him, as they are seen as days of courage and strength that break through any obstacles encountered in a person's journey. Wednesdays also represent Ogun's steadiness and resilience, a day named to remind you that you can hold firm to your dreams regardless of what life throws your way. Lastly, Ogun is honored on the fourth day of every month. This special remembrance serves as an opportunity to reflect on the past and call on his energy so that you can strive for greatness in your present endeavors. Celebrations dedicated to Ogun remind everyone to remain determined in pursuit of their goals!

How to Honor Ogun during These Days

Ogun has many qualities, such as strength and bravery, a strong sense of justice, as well as benevolence, and healing. Consider visiting a local temple or shrine dedicated to Ogun and sharing your offerings of candles or alcohol. You can also take time to reflect on the symbolization of Ogun, with offerings of black and red cloth to represent its colors in syncretism. Remember that if you are observing the day for the first time, it's okay for your devotion not to be perfect, but it can still be a meaningful ritual, nonetheless.

Here are some more tips for celebrating Ogun's festival, whether you are alone or with friends:

- Spend time meditating and reflecting on the qualities of Ogun and why they are important.
- Create a personal altar to show your devotion - gather items that symbolize Ogun's strength and fortitude.
- Spend some time journaling - write down your gratitude for Ogun's protection or any challenges you have faced over the past year and how his presence has helped you overcome them.
- Hold a ceremony with friends or family to honor Ogun: dress in red and black, light candles, and read prayers or poems dedicated to the Orisha.

- Share stories of Ogun's many feats or of how his presence has impacted your life.
- Finally, enjoy a traditional Nigerian feast to honor the Orisha - you can make this meal yourself or order delivery from a local Nigerian restaurant.

Ogun's festival is an incredible event that celebrates the strength and resilience of its namesake. By taking part in the festivities, you can connect with him and receive his protection during your journey. Through thoughtful reflection, meaningful ceremonies, and delicious meals, you can honor the Orisha and continue to remain determined in pursuit of your goals. So, gather your friends or find a quiet spot to reflect; it's time to celebrate Ogun!

Chapter 10: Daily Rituals to Celebrate Ogun

Ogun, the African Orisha of Iron, is a deity with a passionate spirit who can bring a blessing or curse upon people. Aligning with this singular warrior's energy daily is incredibly rewarding for those brave enough to do so. This can be accomplished through offering prayers, performing rituals, and engaging in activities that acknowledge and honor his empowering presence. Those who align with Ogun's strength experience great protection, stamina, and resourcefulness while they walk their life paths.

For those looking for a deeper connection to Ogun, take the time to honor him daily and watches your life transform. This chapter explains how to venerate him and align with Ogun's energy daily. It provides ideas and rituals, prayers, spiritual baths, and activities one can do each day of the week. Each activity holds a blessing, from protection against negative thought patterns to working towards a goal or deepening your connection to the divine. By engaging in each of these daily activities, you'll move closer to Ogun and experience a deeper connection with him.

Prayers to Ogun

Invoking Ogun through prayer is a powerful way to honor the Yoruba deity of metallurgy and physical power. Ogun is known and respected across many African cultures, including Nigeria and Benin. In Yoruba tradition, special rituals and prayers to Ogun have been practiced for centuries. Often these include burning cigars or incense, which is said to help communicate with the spirit world. To receive the blessings of Ogun, it is essential to pay respect and reverence by engaging in sacred prayers. Worshippers may find their spirits filled with power and strength when they connect with Ogun through prayer.

Rituals for Aligning with Ogun

Taking part in rituals that call upon Ogun can be a powerful and meaningful way to align oneself with his spirit. Often, these rituals involve offering prayers and songs while garbed in colors such as red, white, or black. Other offerings for Ogun might include tools such as axes and hammers, money, or other metal items that symbolically represent strength or fortitude. During the ritual, take some moments to set intentions of what you hope to gain by uniting with this mighty Orisha. Connecting with Ogun often leads to more clarity of purpose and brings strong spiritual and physical protection. Whether you are exploring a self-directed ritual ceremony or joining an established one, be sure to keep your eyes open and all your senses alert. You never know when help from Spirit will show up along the way!

Daily Activities That Honor Ogun

Every day, you can take part in activities that honor Ogun. From offering special drinks to the mischievous and powerful deity to telling stories of his strength, you can do your part in venerating him. Every morning pay homage to Ogun with a prayer. Every night, leave offerings out for the Orishas. Additionally, for more permanent gestures of appreciation and respect, people may create physical shrines or alter rooms in their homes solely dedicated to this popular god. Regardless of how you choose to honor him daily, you should remember that by participating in these activities, you are paying tribute to the creativity and power of Ogun.

Monday

The start of a new week can bring both excitement and anxiety. On Mondays, take the time to honor Ogun with the following rituals and activities.

1. Ritual: Protection against Negative Thought Patterns

Mondays can be rough, and it's easy to think negatively about what is traditionally the first day of the work week. By honoring Ogun, the god of power and strength, you can use rituals as protection against those negative cycles and have a great start to start. To begin, gather a few tools or items that represent Ogun's strength and power: such as an axe, hammer, knife, or other metal tools. Anoint yourself with oils dedicated to Ogun, such as frankincense or myrrh. Light a candle and say a prayer or mantra.

2. Activity: Learning a Craft

Mondays can become the start of a new beginning. Why not use it to learn something new? This is a great way to honor Ogun, the Yoruba spirit of iron and war. An activity such as candle- or soap-making works with Ogun's element of fire, and learning how to fabricate metal tools can be very fulfilling. Learning a craft also encourages strength of mind, body, and soul, which is needed to face life's challenges. It teaches you that hard work will lead to joy in the end.

3. Meditation: Connecting to Nature

Start your Monday with activities that bring clarity and focus to your mind, body, and spirit, such as taking a walk outdoors, doing deep breathing exercises, or writing in a gratitude journal. If you're creative, you could even make a physical representation of Ogun on the day. Draw or craft something that speaks to his power and place it where you'll see it often.

Tuesday

Fear and doubt can often creep up towards the middle of the week. Tuesday is a day to shed your worries and doubts, so you can keep marching forward confidently. On Tuesdays, use the following activities to align with Ogun and his energy:

1. Ritual: Protect Your Home from Unwanted Influences

Since Tuesdays are the day that honors Ogun, it is the perfect time to perform a ritual for protection. Begin by purifying your home and yourself with smoke from herbs such as sage or frankincense. Call upon Ogun to protect your home from any unwanted energies, negative entities, or evil influences. Gather metal tools and items that represent his strength, such as hammers, axes, knives, and swords. Place them all around your home to symbolize Ogun's protection.

2. Activity: Working with Metal Tools

On Tuesdays, it is especially fitting to do something that involves metal tools since this is Ogun's element. Try your hand at making tools out of metal, or find a class where you can learn to work with metal tools. Working with these materials will help you form a connection with Ogun and his power.

3. Meditation: Overcoming Fear

Take some time out of your day to meditate on overcoming fear. Fear can paralyze us and make it hard to move forward. By calling upon Ogun's power and strength, we can invoke the courage to overcome fear and make progress. Visualize yourself surrounded by a circle of metal tools, representing Ogun's protection. As you take deep breaths, imagine the fear dissipating and being replaced by steely courage and strength.

Wednesday

Negativity can be hard to shake, but on Wednesdays, you can use the following ideas to align with Ogun and his energy.

1. Ritual: Protection against Negative Thought Patterns

Wednesdays can be especially draining, and protecting yourself from negative energy is crucial. Begin the ritual by gathering items representative of Ogun's strength and power, such as an axe, hammer, knife, or other metal tools. Anoint yourself with the oils dedicated to Ogun. Visualize a bright white light surrounding you and say a prayer or mantra for protection.

2. Activity: Inventing Something New

Wednesdays are perfect for honoring Ogun by challenging yourself and pushing your creative boundaries. Spend some time inventing something new, whether it be a recipe, craft, or tool. Ogun is the spirit of creation and innovation. Celebrate his energy by coming up with something unique.

3. Meditation: Purification

Meditate on purifying your thoughts and emotions. During this meditation, visualize yourself surrounded by a bright white light of protection. Imagine the light entering your mind and body, purifying, and pushing out all negative thoughts, emotions, and energies. Call upon Ogun to help you stay focused on positive thoughts and maintain your strength against any negativity that may come your way.

Thursday

Cleansing and purifying are essential steps to take on Thursdays. Use the following ideas to honor Ogun and bring his energy into your life.

1. Ritual: Clearing Out Old Energy

Thursdays are a great day to honor Ogun and clear out any old energy that may be weighing you down. Begin by cleansing your home and yourself with smoke from herbs such as sage or frankincense. Then, take a spiritual bath to further purify your energy. As you bathe, call upon Ogun to help you clear out any old patterns and make room for new beginnings.

2. Activity: Taking a Spiritual Bath

You can use herbs such as lavender, rosemary, or eucalyptus to cleanse your aura of any stagnant energy. Begin the day by taking an herbal cleansing bath to purify your body and spirit. You can also create an herbal smudging stick using sage or lavender. As you do this, call upon Ogun for strength and protection.

3. Meditation: Letting Go of Attachments

Take some time to meditate on releasing any attachments that may be holding you back. It can be difficult to move forward when we cling too tightly to things or people. Visualize yourself surrounded by a circle of metal tools, representing Ogun's strength and guidance. As you take deep breaths, imagine the attachments being cut loose and fading away. Repeat a mantra such as "I let go of all that no longer serves me, in strength and courage."

Friday

Friday is the day to take the time to focus on your goals and ambitions. Here are some rituals and activities you can do to align yourself with Ogun

1. Ritual: Connecting to Your Path

Fridays are for focusing on connecting to your spiritual path. Start by lighting a white candle and calling upon Ogun for protection and guidance. Then, take a few moments to reflect on the goals you have set for yourself and how you can use Ogun's strength and courage to help you reach them.

2. Activity: Working towards a Goal

Take some time to focus on working towards a goal that you have set for yourself. Ogun is the spirit of progress, so use this day to tap into his energy and make strides toward achieving your goals. Whether it means taking classes, doing research, or reaching out for resources, take action to keep moving forward.

3. Meditation: Facing Difficult Tasks

Meditate and visualize yourself surrounded by Ogun's strength and protection in the face of difficult tasks. Call on Ogun's courage and strength to keep you motivated to get through the toughest of times. Focusing your energy in a positive direction will help you overcome any challenge that lies in your way.

Saturday

Being creative and inventive is key on Saturdays. Here are some rituals and activities you can do to align yourself with Ogun.

1. Ritual: Rituals to Unblock Creativity

Saturdays are a great day to focus on unblocking any creative energy that may be stuck. Begin by lighting a green candle and calling upon Ogun for creative inspiration. Then, spend some time engaging in rituals such as writing a poem or painting to help you reconnect with your inner artist.

2. Activity: Exploring the Unknown

Ogun is a spirit of exploration, so use this day to explore the unknown. Take time to wander through nature and see what new adventures present themselves. Get out of your comfort zone and try something new, such as a new craft or skill.

3. Meditation: Honoring Ancestors

Take some time to honor your ancestors and call upon Ogun to guide you on your journey. Imagine yourself surrounded by a circle of metal tools, representing the strength and protection of your ancestors. Close your eyes and reflect on the stories, wisdom, and knowledge that have been passed down to you from your ancestors.

Sunday

Hope and faith are the themes of Sundays. Here are some rituals and activities you can do to align yourself with Ogun

1. Ritual: Abundance and Opportunity

Sundays are a great day to focus on creating abundance and opportunity. Begin by lighting a yellow candle and calling upon Ogun to open the doors of abundance. Take some time to focus on manifesting the life that you want and creating a plan for achieving your goals.

2. Activity: Visiting a Shrine or Sanctuary

A great way to honor Ogun is to visit a shrine or sanctuary dedicated to him. Connect with his energy and offer prayers and gifts. You can also create your shrine in your home to keep Ogun's spirit close by.

3. Meditation: Deepening Your Connection

Take some time to meditate and deepen your connection with Ogun. Imagine yourself surrounded by a circle of metal tools, representing his strength and guidance. Visualize yourself embracing his energy and using it to empower you in your daily life.

These are just some ideas that can help you align with Ogun's energy on a day-to-day basis. Feel free to get creative and explore other rituals, activities, and meditations to help you connect to him more deeply. Remember, Ogun is the spirit of progress and transformation, so use his energy as your guide on your journey.

Extra: Glossary of Terms

This extra chapter provides a comprehensive glossary of terms to help you navigate the book more easily. Below, you'll find an alphabetical list of foreign words and their definitions, accompanied by pronunciation and phonetics.

Baron Samedi (bah-RAWN sah-MEH-dee): Baron Samedi is a deity of the dead in Haitian Vodou.

Damballah (dahm-buh-LAH): The great serpent spirit of the heavens, also known as a "great sky father."

Obatala (oh-bah-TAH-lah): The Orisha of peace, justice

Ifa (ee-fah): A spiritual or divinatory system that is the foundation of Yoruba religion.

Loa (low-ah): A spirit in Haitian Vodou.

Obatala (oh-bah-tuh-lah): The Orisha of creation, peace, and purity. Obatala loves harmony and justice in all things.

Ogun (Oh-goon): The Orisha of iron, war, and labor. He is known to resolve difficult situations and protect or defend his devotees.

Oggun Akomi (Oh-goon ah-KOH-mee): One of the seven paths of Ogun, also known as the path of healing and creativity.

Oggun Alagbo (Oh-goon ah-lah-GOH-bo): One of the seven paths of Ogun, also known as the path of wisdom and knowledge.

Oggun Irumole (Oh-goon eer-oo-MOH-lee): One of the seven paths of Ogun, also known as the path of spiritual awakening.

Oggun Meji (Oh-goon meh-jee): One of the seven paths of Ogun, also known as the path of communication and strength.

Oggun Onile (Oh-goon oh-NEE-lee): One of the seven paths of Ogun, also known as the path of movement and traveling.

Oggun Oloyon (Oh-goon oh-low-YOHN): One of the seven paths of Ogun, also known as the path of helping others.

Oggun Oyeku Meji (Oh-goon oh-yay-koo meh-jee): One of the seven paths of Ogun, also known as the path of courage.

Orisa (or-ee-sah): Deities or divine beings in the Yoruba pantheon, venerated in both Africa and the African diaspora.

Yemeya (yay-may-yah): The Orisha of the sea, ruler over storms and shipwrecks. She is often invoked to protect sailors and travelers.

Yoruba (Yoh-roo-bah): The language spoken by the Yoruba people of Nigeria in West Africa.

Conclusion

Ogun is a fascinating deity who forms an important part of the belief system of the Yoruba people. He had a long and complicated history for hundreds of years before becoming firmly entrenched in Yoruba mythology and culture as the god of ironwork and war. Ogun is called on by his followers to remove obstacles, allowing them to overcome challenges and create their own destinies. Today, he is still worshipped by many adherents of traditional Yoruba beliefs throughout Nigeria.

Ogun, the god of knowledge, power, and creativity, is a source of great strength and guidance. His continuous presence is comforting to those looking for help in times of need. While Ogun is primarily associated with ironwork and war, he also has strong connections to protection, justice, trustworthiness, and the spirit of progress. He is also considered to be both a saint and a warrior.

Whether it is his powerful grace that protects us from harm or his creative genius that helps us find solutions when all else fails, Ogun finds a way to give meaning to life and restore balance in the universe. He knows no boundaries and will always be there for you, no matter the situation. To seek counsel from Ogun is to tap into an infinite source of wisdom and protection, delivering clarity in times of distress.

Ogun has been a legendary figure for centuries. He is credited for having inspired many aspects of the Yoruba people's vibrant culture. For example, he has been invoked in various literary and artistic works as a symbol of strength. He also is given immense respect due to his representation of life-sustaining powers like creativity and productivity.

His influence extends to different realms, such as spiritual, political, economic, and social. It continues to shape how the Yoruba people identify and live today. Regardless of their specific faith, it is impossible to deny Ogun's monumental effects on Yoruba cultural identity throughout history.

This guide provided a comprehensive overview of Ogun, focusing on the history and mythology surrounding his cultic following, how to identify as a child of Ogun, and the rituals, symbols, and festivals associated with him. It also includes information on setting up a sacred altar, performing useful rituals and spells, and celebrating Ogun through daily practices. Finally, a glossary of relevant terms and phrases is included for easy reference.

Through this guide, we hope you gained a deeper understanding of Ogun and will come to appreciate his power and presence in your life. By following his teachings, you can make significant progress on the path of life and achieve your goals. Ogun is always with you, helping you to create a brighter future.

Part 6: Oshun

The Ultimate Guide to an Orisha of Yoruba and Santería, the Divine Feminine, and Ifa

Introduction

Oshun is among the most powerful female deities in Yoruba, Santeria, and Ifa. She is one of the 401 Orishas created by the supreme deity Oludumare, and she acts as a messenger between this powerful being and people. Often called the *divine feminine,* Oshun is a benevolent goddess who looks out for those under her patronage. Even though it's mainly women who tend to adopt her as their patron, she can be revered by anyone who wishes to form a connection with her. Her main powers include bringing love and prosperity to her followers, and she is also associated with running water and fertility. At the beginning of this book, you'll learn about her different aspects as viewed by the ancient Yoruba religion, *Ifa,* and the African Diaspora religion, *Santeria.*

According to Yoruba lore, all people hail from the Orishas. Bearing this in mind, everyone has at least one parent, Orisha. In this book, you'll learn to identify your parent Orisha and discover whether you're Oshun's child. After that, you'll be introduced to the colorful legends, myths, and stories (*patakis*) connected to Oshun, including her ever-popular love story with Shango and stories involving her mother, Yemaya, and son, Eshu. Learning about her interactions with the other Orishas and humans will help you understand how to connect to her divine feminine essence. While she is only the archetype of this power, her stories have much to tell about the connection between the divine feminine and the divine masculine.

The subsequent chapters will be a comprehensive guide to Oshun's symbolism. You'll be introduced to her favorite plants, offerings, and the associations you can use to honor her, connect with her, and ask her for favors and blessings. One of the best ways to celebrate her is to visit her favorite places. These are rivers, waterfalls, and other sources of sweet water. Another excellent way to venerate any deity, including Oshun, is to build an altar. The book will give you all the information you need to create and dedicate this sacred space to the goddess. While having a dedicated altar is unnecessary, it can do wonders for building your spiritual connection with her, especially if you're her child.

Once you've learned about her association, you'll be ready to expand your knowledge of the spells and rituals you can perform to honor her. You'll also be able to use these to communicate with her and use her ashe in order to better your life. The relevant chapter offers plenty of spells and rituals and spells for love, beauty, abundance, and prosperity, along with beginner-friendly instructions for each work. You'll be able to perform these on her holy days and festivals.

Lastly, you'll learn that you don't have to wait for a momentous occasion to venerate Oshun. The little tips and tricks provided in the last chapter can help you align with her energy on a day-to-day basis, allowing you to form a much deeper bond with her. You'll find beginner-friendly guides for meditating, crafting, and other activities. Just practicing self-love will help you connect to this divine feminine. If you're ready to embark on this journey and start celebrating Oshun, all you need to do is keep reading.

Chapter 1: Oshun - Spirit, Saint, Orisha

Oshun is among the most significant and influential Orishas in the Yoruba, Santeria, and Ifa religions. These religions originated in Africa but have managed to spread to different countries around the world. This chapter will introduce these three religions, the concept of the Orishas, Oshun, and her role in them.

An artistic depiction of the birth of Oshun.
Tmanner38, CC BY-SA 4.0 <https://creativecommons.org/licenses/by-sa/4.0>, via Wikimedia Commons https://commons.wikimedia.org/wiki/File:Birth_of_Oshun_HR.JPG.jpg

Oshun in Yoruba

The Yoruba Religion

The Yoruba religion originated in Western Africa, particularly in West Nigeria. The Yoruba people consist of various ethnic groups, and they reside in the southern Sahara desert. It is one of the oldest religions in the world, even predating Christianity. They have their own set of beliefs and traditions, which they have been practicing for years. Their religious customs are based on their culture and history, and they influenced their literature, arts, and lives, creating fascinating and rich mythology, songs, and proverbs. The Yoruba people passed down their traditions orally from one generation to the next. Therefore, one myth can have several different versions.

People from all over the world practice Yoruba – even in the U.S.; the religion found its way to the new world during the slave trade. The African people were forced to convert to Catholicism and prohibited from practicing their own beliefs. However, they still held on to their religious traditions and practiced them in private.

Olodumare is the supreme deity of the Yoruba religion and the creator of the universe. In different myths, he goes by the name Olofin or Olodumare-Olorun. Olodumare doesn't have a gender and is usually referred to as "they" because they are all things and can't be categorized into one gender. In the religious hierarchy system, Olodumare sits at the top. There is no one above the deity who existed before the universe itself.

- Olodumare
- Orishas
- Mankind
- Ancestors
- Plants and animals

The Yoruba religion doesn't have the concept of the angel or devil because they believe nothing is all good or all bad. Everything has a positive and negative side. However, there are similar beings to demons who are known as Ajoguns. They are trickster beings who, unlike the Orishas, bring misfortune to mankind.

The spirits of the ancestors also play a big role in the Yoruba religion. They are individuals who had an influence on mankind when they were alive, like brave warriors or kings. After they die, the living keep their memories alive by honoring and making offerings to them when they need their guidance.

On the bottom of the hierarchy are plants and animals. Although they don't have the same power as other beings, they are no less significant.

Ayanmo, or fate, is a main concept in Yoruba. According to its cosmology, when all humans were created, they chose their destiny, where they would be born, who they would marry, how many children they had, what they would do with their lives, and even how they would die. However, when they come to Earth, they forget their destiny and spend their lives trying to remember and achieve it. Each human being is assigned an Orisha who helps them realize their Ayanmo.

In some cases, a person can die before they achieve their destiny, but they are usually given a second chance through reincarnation. Reincarnation in the Yoruba religion is often regarded as a positive experience. It is a reward for the people who lead an honorable and virtuous life.

In the Yoruba religion, it is also believed that the soul continues to live on after death. The soul is then reincarnated into another body, where it can continue its journey toward fulfilling its destiny. This process is seen as a natural cycle of life and death, and it is believed that the soul can be reborn multiple times until it achieves its true purpose. The Yoruba people also believe that reincarnation is a way for the soul to learn valuable lessons and gain wisdom, which will help it to achieve its destiny in the next life. Ultimately, reincarnation is viewed as a journey toward spiritual enlightenment and ultimate liberation from the cycle of birth and death.

Orishas

Right after Olodumare comes the Orishas, who are the most significant beings in the Yoruba religion. Orishas or Orisas are supernatural entities and are different aspects of Olodumare. They are often described as deities, demigods, or spirits. Olodumare created the Orishas before creating the universe. The deity breathed life into all mankind which makes all humans connected to one another.

The concept of the supreme deity is too complicated for the simple human brain to comprehend, so Olodumare couldn't directly communicate with the people. The deity also lives in the heavens, far away from Earth, so they are unable to listen to people's prayers and are usually unaware of the affairs of mankind. For this reason, Olodumare created the Orishas to act as intermediaries between them and humans. The deity randomly gave each Orisha a domain of influence where they would watch and protect mankind and report to Olodumare. There is an Orisha for everything like thunder, agriculture, water, rivers, iron, hunting, and love.

However, some historians don't agree that Olodumare was a distant and unaware deity. They state that some stories portrayed Olodumare as an attentive god who was involved in the lives of mankind and heard their prayers.

Orishas are highly revered among the Yoruba people because they greatly impact their daily affairs. They interfere in every aspect of human life but only when needed. The relationship between mankind and Orishas is mutually beneficial as both cannot survive without the other. The people venerate the Orishas and present them with offerings while the Orishas, in turn, provide their assistance.

Although one can seek the help of any Orisha, modern practitioners prefer "The Seven African Powers." These seven are considered the most powerful and influential out of all these Orishas.

1. Oshun, the Orisha of love and fertility.
2. Shango, the Orisha of thunder and lighting.
3. Yemaya, the Earth mother and the mother of Orishas.
4. Esu, the messenger between the Orishas and mankind and is the trickster Orisha.
5. Obatala, the sky Orisha and creator of mankind.
6. Oya, the Orisha of death and rebirth.
7. Ogun, the Orisha of iron and metal.

Orishas aren't perfect beings. They have many human qualities, have made mistakes, and caused trouble to the supreme deity. In one story, they tried to kill Olodumare and take his place because the god was getting old. They believed that they should rule alone since they were more involved in people's lives and didn't need the deity's permission or supervision. Many stories show the Orishas as imperfect beings with egos – who are sometimes weak when faced with their desires. However, they are still responsible beings and always come through when people call for them.

Therefore, one can't describe the Orishas as gods. They have human weaknesses, and their powers are still limited since they can't do anything without Olodumare's permission. For instance, in the creation myth, when Obatala wanted to create dry land and mankind, he first had to go to Olodumare for permission. However, they still share similarities with gods as they have powers, can hear prayers, and can help humans.

No one has ever seen an Orisha. They are depicted in several paintings based on their description in mythology and using known characteristics. Even when you invoke them, they won't appear to you. They possess a willing person, usually a priest or priestess, during certain rituals.

Orishas can sometimes cause problems for people instead of helping them. They don't do this intentionally, but they are flawed and have goals that can influence their actions. Like human beings, they struggle between their duty and their personal desires.

Oshun

After Olodumare created the universe, he felt that it was missing something. It needed love, romance, beauty, and sweetness, so he created Oshun. Oshun, which is also spelled Ochun, Osun, or Oxum, is pronounced as "O-shan," and she is the Orisha of love, beauty, freshwater, purity, sensuality, and fertility. She is described as a goddess and spirit and is the youngest of all Orishas. Some legends mention that Yemaya was her mother, while others state that she was her younger sister. Oshun is Olodumare's favorite, and she is one of the few allowed to communicate directly with the supreme deity and deliver messages to him from the Orishas.

Oshun played a huge role in creating the universe, and various myths mention how she helped save the world too. She is extremely powerful and can be either a force of destruction or a force of creativity. She is fair and doesn't enjoy the extreme actions she sometimes has to take, but she only punishes those who deserve it, like when someone disrespects nature or the divine, offends her, or shows cruelty toward other humans or creatures. She can bring drought by withholding the rain or causing floods. You should never cross Oshun as she is vindictive, and her sweet nature can instantaneously change to reveal a terrifying Orisha.

Her anger is merely a response to sinners and doesn't reflect her true character. Oshun is described as loving, kind-hearted, generous, noble, merciful, and warm. She is a symbol of feminine beauty and has domain over all types of relationships. She protects, guides, heals, and provides fertility for those who respect her and repent for their mistakes. Never has Oshun broken a promise, and she expects her followers to keep their word as well. She rewards their loyalty by always answering when they call on her.

Oshun is always there for her people and shows sympathy to those struggling or experiencing big changes in their lives and heading toward new beginnings. When someone loses a loved one and is dealing with grief, Oshun helps them deal with their pain.

Oshun has the same qualities as the rivers she rules over. She is charming and charismatic, *and many male Orishas find her irresistible*. On the outside, Oshun seems like a happy Orisha who lights every room she walks into with her beauty and positive attitude. However, deep down, she suffers and struggles with loneliness, sadness, and heartache. As the Orisha of love, she often gives her heart to those she cares about. However, no one has ever shown her the same amount of passion, love, and devotion, which is why she always ends up disappointed.

Oshun is a beautiful, sensual, seductive Orisha with a lovely feminine figure. She is depicted wearing a golden dress decorated with beautiful jewels. She often holds a mirror in her hand to marvel at her own beauty, showcasing her vanity.

Human beings first encountered Oshun in Nigeria in a town called Osogbo. To this day, the people of Yoruba consider it a sacred place. They live under her protection, and, in return, they venerate her and present offerings.

Just like all Orishas, Oshun is flawed and has human qualities and weaknesses. She was Shango's second wife. He was also married to Oba, the Orisha of time and rivers. She was jealous of Oba and played tricks to make Shango hate her. In most legends, Oshun is portrayed in a heroic light by always doing the right thing. However, the stories that show her humane and weak side makes her relatable. People identify with her as they see her as an imperfect being who also makes mistakes.

Oshun is associated with magic and is often called "the queen of witches." She teaches her followers spells and mysticism. Oshun enjoys watching people fall in love and will cast spells that bring lovers together.

People invoke Oshun when they're in need of prosperity, good luck, change, health, and strength. Although she is an Orisha for all people, she pays extra attention to women. She helps those who are looking for love or who want to get pregnant.

Oshun and the Myth of Creation

In Yoruba mythology, the Orisha Obatala played a huge role in creating the universe. When Olodumare first created the world, there was only sky and water. Obatala felt that the world was lacking, so he asked for Olodumare's permission to build and create lands which he agreed to. With the help of Orunmila and other Orishas, Obatala descended to Earth and began creating dry land. After Obatala finished, he spent some time on Earth enjoying his creation. However, he felt lonely and desired company. He asked Olodumare's permission to create human beings, and again, he obliged. However, Obatala was drunk during the creation process and ended up making deformed people. Before realizing his mistake, he asked Olodumare to breathe life into them. When Obatala woke up, he realized what he had done and was horrified. He vowed to never drink again and became the protector of the disabled.

Obatala played a huge role in creating the universe.
fenixcs, *ATTRIBUTION-NONCOMMERCIAL-NODERIVS 2.0 GENERIC, CC BY-NC-ND 2.0*, <https://creativecommons.org/licenses/by-nc-nd/2.0/>
https://www.flickr.com/photos/fenixcsmar/34206000186

Now that the universe was created, Olodumare sent some of his Orishas to Earth to complete the process. There were sixteen male Orishas and one female, Oshun. Oshun had many ideas on how she wanted to spread beauty and love in the universe. However, because she was young and female, the other Orishas didn't listen to any of her ideas. She was offended and left. They continued their work, but without Oshun's guidance, they failed. They didn't know what to do and had no choice but to go to Olodumare and tell them that they couldn't complete their mission. Olodumare was bewildered that Oshun wasn't with them and asked about her. They told them what had happened. Olodumare was rightfully angry. Not only did they fail their mission and ignore Olodumare's orders, but they also disrespected the deity's favorite Orisha. He told them that for this mission to work, they must listen to Oshun. The male Orishas put their egos aside and apologized to Oshun. She accepted their apology and accompanied them once again to Earth. She blessed the world with love, beauty, and fertility.

Oshun in Santeria

The Santeria Religion

The Santeria religion is also called "La Religión Lucumí" which is Spanish for "The Order of Lucumí," and "La Regla de Ocha," which means "The Order of the Orishas." The word "Santeria" means saints or the way of the saints. The religion's practitioners often describe the Orishas as saints. When the Afro-Cubans arrived in the new world, they were forced to convert to Christianity. Since they wanted to keep practicing their own religious beliefs, they found a parallelism between Santeria and Catholicism, giving them a chance to practice both religions. They found that the Catholic saints and the Orishas had many things in common as they both acted as intermediaries between God and the people. They assigned Catholic saints to their Orishas, so they could appear to practice Catholicism when they were, in fact, practicing their own religion. This connection added to the complexity of Santeria. In this context, Oshun was linked to Our Lady of Mercy.

There is a misconception that the Afro-Cubans merged Santeria with Catholicism. However, it was more of a parallelism based on the similarities between the two religions. To this day, there are people who practice both religions as they don't find any contradictions between them. For instance, someone can go to church while still practicing

Santeria at their home or decorate their homes with Orisha pictures *and* statues of Catholic saints.

The Afro-Cubans practiced Santeria in secret for hundreds of years. After the Cuban revolution, the government acknowledged and accepted Santeria, and the people were allowed to freely practice their religious beliefs. However, there were still some concerns about the religion because of its association with witchcraft.

The religion originated in West Africa and was brought to countries like Brazil, Cuba, Puerto Rico, Haiti, and the U.S.A. during the slave trade. It is a diverse faith combining different beliefs from many cultures and religions, like the Yoruba religion, Catholicism, and Caribbean traditions.

Orishas

Orishas play a similar role in Santeria. They watch over mankind, report to Olodumare and assist the people when they need help. Invoking an Orisha requires rituals or divination. A priest or priestess leads a ritual and invites an Orisha to possess them. The attendees then ask for advice and guidance. Some Santeria practitioners even invoke Orishas to help them with their magical practices.

There are many similarities between Santeria and Yoruba. In both religions, Olodumare created the universe and left it to the Orishas to watch over it and provide assistance to the people. In Santeria, Orishas are also extremely powerful and can do the impossible, which is why people call on them when they are helpless. However, they also have the power to bring misfortune to mankind. When a person experiences bad luck, it usually means they have been neglecting their Orisha. Building an altar, praying, or presenting offerings can get you back on their good side. When Orisha is happy with you, you will feel better and notice an improvement in all areas of your life.

Orishas aren't immortal, and without the people's acknowledgment and offerings, they can't survive.

Oshun

Love is what makes life worth living. Olodumare realized this fact after creating the universe. The only thing that can guarantee this new world's survival is for people to experience love. Olodumare created Oshun (also spelled Ochún's) and sent her to Earth to spread love and joy among the people. Oshun is very close and devoted to her mother (or elder sister), Yemaya, and they both work together very well. Yemaya as Orisha's mother, and Oshun, as her love. Orishas help people with issues concerning love, motherhood, and marriage.

Oshun seduces men with her dancing, charming laugh, and full hips. Many Orishas and people consider Oshun to be inexperienced because of her young age. However, on more than one occasion, she has proven herself to be smarter and more capable than other Orishas. She is very good friends with Orisha's messenger Esu. She was married to multiple Orishas like Shango, Ogun, Orúnmila (the Orisha of wisdom and divination), and Ochosi (the Orisha of hunting.) She is the daughter of the creator Orisha Obatala and sister of Oya and Oba (the river Orisha). She learned a lot from her husband, Orúnmila, and became a very talented diviner as well. Although she had many husbands, she never loved anyone as much as Shango. From the moment she met him, she fell for him. However, Shango was a womanizer and broke her heart many times. Yet, he remained her greatest love.

Although she is a powerful Orisha, Oshun can act like a spoiled child and get very angry when people ignore her or don't meet her demands. She has saved human beings and other Orishas on more than one occasion. She has a domain on all types of freshwater, like ponds and lakes. All the elements necessary for life on Earth, like love, water, and prosperity, are under her control.

Oshun in Ifa

Ifa is a religion that is based on divination. It originated in Yoruba from the Olori family and is heavily influenced by magic. Ifa also focuses on venerating the spirits of the ancestors and healing. Similar to the Abrahamic religions, Ifa followers worship only one god, Olodumare.

Orishas play a prominent role in the Ifa religion, and each one of them is associated with an element of nature. Practitioners seek the Orisha's help through divination, incantation, and prayers. They can appear to people in their dreams to give advice or answer their questions.

Oshun's role in Ifa is similar to her role in Yoruba and Santeria. She provides guidance and assistance but must be respected, or she will exert vengeance on those who offend her. As an expert diviner, Oshun greatly impacts the Ifa religion.

Yoruba, Santeria, and Ifa share many things in common. One of the basics of these religions is Orishas. The people depend on them in every aspect of their lives. When the Afro-Cubans came to the new world, they brought their Orishas with them for support and protection during these tough times. This led to the spread of these beliefs to various places around the world.

Many people found it easy to accept the Orishas. They related to them and their struggles. The people sympathized with the Orishas because they shared similar experiences and were often led by their emotions. Oshun isn't seen as different from any other human. When someone insults her, her ego gets the best of her, and she can be angry and vindictive. She can drown cities to punish sinners. Beautiful and seductive, Oshun is obsessed with her looks. She is aware of her beauty and the impact she has on men. The mirror she carries with her reflects this vanity.

Still, Oshun has a big heart and has often come through to human beings and other Orishas. She is the equivalent of Aphrodite and Venus in Greek and Roman mythology. Her main purpose is to spread love and beauty. She cares for women and their struggles and protects them and their children. There isn't a problem that Oshun can't fix. In most cases, she doesn't resort to violence. She uses her seductive dance moves, beauty, and charm to help her people. It is impossible to deny Oshun's role in mankind. Not only has she assisted with the creation of the universe, but she is the heroine of many legends where she saved the Orishas or mankind using her wit, kind heart, or by sacrificing something. The more you learn about Oshun, the more you will understand why she is significant in these religions and why you need her in your life.

Chapter 2: Are You a Child of Oshun?

Determining who your Orisha is can be a very tricky task. You may feel lost as to where to begin – especially if you're new to the African Traditional faith. In this chapter, you'll learn everything you need to know about mother and father Orishas and head Orishas. You'll find out the difference between them, how to determine who they are, and understand when is the best time to embark on this journey. Finally, you'll understand what it means to be a child of Oshun and find a quiz that will help you determine if you are one.

Mother and Father Orishas

According to the Traditional African faiths, everyone is assigned a biological mother and father and spiritual Orisha mother and father figures upon birth. The Orisha mother ensures your safety, well-being, and protection throughout your life. Your Orisha parents are the ones who guide you, help you when you run into challenges, and look after your happiness. You can only unlock your destiny when you work with your mother and father Orishas, and accept their guidance.

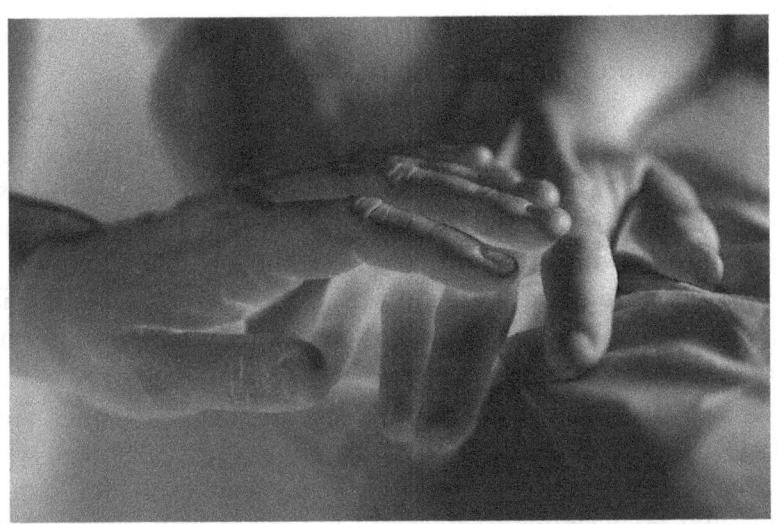
According to African traditions, everyone is assigned spiritual mothers and fathers upon birth.
https://unsplash.com/photos/r6_xcsNg0kw

Each Orisha embodies one of Olodumare's archetypes to serve as an intermediate between worshippers and the Supreme God. There are 4oo+1 Orishas, each of whom rules over a certain aspect of life. This numeric representation shows how limitless the pantheon is. While there isn't an infinite number of Orishas, the "+1" suggests that you can never name all 400, even if you know them all. You will always likely miss at least 1.

There are specific Orishas for everything, from wisdom to healing. Since each person faces the most difficulties in a certain aspect of their life, they are given a personal Orisha at birth – one who is considered to be the person's destined helper. That said, you can still invoke *any Orisha* when you're facing certain troubles in your life. For example, someone who always ends up in toxic romantic relationships should consider working with Oshun. A person who's embarking on a healing journey will need the assistance of Obatala.

If you wish to learn more about your parent Orishas, you must first release any expectations you may have. Your Orishas are seldom who you think they are, so any previous attachments may affect your ability to determine who your parent Orishas are. Also, your Orishas are not necessarily the same as your parents. If your elders follow the African Traditional faith, you should consider talking to them; they are the best teachers you can turn to. Not only do your elders know you since birth, but they are also very wise and experienced and have likely been working with the Orishas for a long time now. They can give you insight and clarity into who your Orisha mother and father are.

If your elders have different spiritual beliefs or it's not possible to contact them directly, you can look at your dreams. Dreams can give you a lot of information and clues into who your Orishas are. Deconstruct the message and, if needed, consult a Babalawo. If all else fails or you're still uncertain, you can ask the Orishas themselves and work with them with the help of a priest or priestess. A specialized Babalawo may even be able to help you out right away based on your answer to certain questions.

Once you determine who your Orisha mother and father are, you need to learn more about them. Read all about their traditions, symbols, preferences, and traditions. Build them an altar and find out which elements and associations to decorate the space with. Find out which offerings they enjoy and make sure you leave gifts for them, and pray to them regularly. Keep the space clean and well-organized, and always approach it with positivity and respect. You should consciously and actively make an effort to connect to your parent Orishas on a deeper level because they're vital figures in your life. Show them that you're committed to working with them so they can offer you the guidance you need.

Head Orisha

Head Orishas are commonly known as tutelary Orishas in African Traditional Religions. Several traditions believe that you can either have two parent Orishas or a single head Orisha or Ori Orisha. Head Orishas act as balancing and guiding entities like mother and father guardians. You don't get to choose your head Orisha, as it is associated with your destiny. This Orisha is the source of spiritual energy a person needs to lead a harmonious life.

You can know who your head Orisha is by undergoing a specialized ceremony. This ritual, however, can only be conducted once in a person's lifetime. Once you know who your head Orisha is, they hold a place in your spirit and soul. You must be aware that you will be committed to your tutelary (custodial) Orisha once you find out who they are. This is why you must be certain you're ready for initiation and this lifelong undertaking. Many practitioners believe that a person becomes a "prisoner" of their chosen faith once the head Orisha settles in. When you dedicate yourself to this spiritual system, you are expected to undergo a series of appropriate initiations, which are often costly. Your head Orisha expects you to be fully brought into the belief system.

If you talk to your elders or other practitioners of the faith, they'll likely tell you to take your time before you learn about your head Orisha, especially if you're still unsure about the spiritual direction you wish to take. If you're interested in the African Traditional Religion but aren't sure whether you're ready to commit, you should consider putting off the tutelary Orisha revelation process. Get to know all the aspects of the religion and learn as much information as you can about the Orishas. Avoid getting too attached to a single one, and make sure that you have a good relationship with the entire pantheon. The Orishas feel jealous when a person favors one over the other or pays them more attention. They may also feel confused about who your tutelary guide is. Only when you're ready to get initiated and undergo Ocha should you consider finding out who your head Orisha is.

You're probably wondering how you can possibly build positive relationships with 401 Orishas. One thing you need to know is that not all Orishas are of equal power and abilities. Only a few of them can seize control of a person's mind. The tutelary Orishas may differ from one faith to another. However, according to the Santería Lukumi religion, the Orishas with this capability are Oshun, Obatala, Elegguá, Shango, Oya, Orunmila, Yemaya, Ochosi, and Ogún. All of these, except for Orunmila (who is initiated through Ifá), become an individual's tutelary spirits through Kariocha.

What Does It Mean to Be a Child of Oshun?

Oshun is the goddess of fertility, love, prosperity, and beauty. It would make sense for the children of Oshun to reflect her qualities and embody her energy. The children of a specific Orisha are expected to paint the lives of other people with the blessings of their deities. You would also be accountable for keeping the spirit of Oshun alive in the minds and hearts of other practitioners.

Quiz: Am I the Child of Oshun?

This quiz is not meant to replace the formal and traditional process of uncovering one's parent or head Orisha. This quiz, however, can help you gain insight into who your Orisha might (or might not) be. It can also allow you to confirm your suspicions and the validity of past evidence that you may be the child of Oshun.

Mark the statements that apply:

1. You enjoy living in luxury and constantly pursue a wealthy lifestyle.
2. You find that wealth and money are very important aspects of life.
3. You enjoy showing off your expensive possessions to others.
4. You wear designer clothes and love to accessorize.
5. You invest in technologies that make your life easier and more comfortable.
6. Some people believe that you're hopeless when it comes to managing your finances.
7. Gold is your favorite color.
8. You like working with gemstones like Carnelian, Agate, Brown Jasper, and Blue Calcite.
9. You care a lot about the opinions of others.
10. You worry about what other people say and think about you.
11. You care a lot about your appearance and reputation.
12. You consider yourself a highly determined individual.
13. You're always driven by your goals and believe you have a greater purpose in life.
14. You plan strategically and never give up on your goals.
15. You are ready to fight for the things you want, even if it means that you need to manipulate others in the process.
16. You enjoy positions that allow you to influence others.
17. You are a natural-born entrepreneur.
18. You don't thrive in commercial or corporate environments.
19. You are a competent and dedicated employee.
20. Your sex life is interesting and intense.
21. Many people claim that you're very flirtatious.
22. You lead by your emotions.
23. You are highly sensitive and responsive to the needs of others.
24. You have a tendency to gain weight.
25. You are very charismatic, loving, and welcoming.

26. If you have children, you're often praised for how you care for them.
27. While you don't like to force your opinions on others, you don't like it when others contradict you.
28. You don't get angry easily, but when you do, it is intense.
29. You are highly affectionate and compassionate.
30. You easily get jealous in romantic relationships, and you have possessive tendencies.
31. Love can make you blind.
32. You like to do everything with your partner, but you realize self-love is more important.
33. You are fair and honest.

Answers Analysis

You are likely a child of Oshun if most of the statements above apply to you.

Oshun is usually depicted as a beautiful woman with charisma, playfulness, and charm. Her clothes are gold and very luxurious, and she's often portrayed wearing expensive jewelry. Oshun enjoys showcasing her breathtaking possessions. Some depictions of Oshun show her holding a mirror, causing her to appear vain. The children of Oshun are expected to have similar expensive tastes, justifying the first 8 statements.

Oshun is known to worry a lot about what other people think and say, which is why her children are also expected to worry about public opinion (statements 9 and 10). She is highly fixated on maintaining a beautiful appearance and an esteemed reputation. She steers clear of scandals and anything that may slightly tarnish her image (statement 11).

Oshun is an archetype of strategic thinking and planning. Her kind and beautiful exterior manipulate and trick others into thinking she doesn't have what it takes to get whatever she wants. Little do they know, however, that she's highly determined and desires social influence and affluence (statements 12 through 19).

Oshun is often portrayed with a honeypot wrapped around her waist. This is a symbol of male sexual pleasure, pregnancy, and fertility. Oshun's children are expected to embody her sensual, seductive, and charming energy (statements 20 and 21).

Oshun is popularly known for being the most sensitive and emotional of all the Orishas in the pantheon. She is even thought to be whiny and reserved at times. Her sensitivity, however, is what makes her attentive to the needs and well-being of others. She is believed to be the protector of the sick and poor and is associated with healing and prosperity. She brings abundance into the lives of others. Even though she's very kind and giving, she can get really angry when someone steps on her toes. She's understanding and tolerant but doesn't like it when someone disagrees with her. Oshun knows when giving becomes too much, as she always prioritizes her well-being. She loves others, but she loves herself more. The children of Oshun are never sheepish when it comes to giving love and showing care, but they know better than to compromise their own needs and welfare. They are affectionate with their partners, friends, and family (statements 22 through 32).

Even though she can get manipulative, if need be, Oshun likes to do things the right way. She is righteous and values qualities like honesty and fairness, especially when dealing with people who deserve this treatment (statement 33).

Now that you know everything you need about mother, father, and head Orishas, you can determine if you're ready to know who they are. You must remember that finding your head Orisha is a lifelong commitment. You must be completely ready to undergo the initiation process.

Chapter 3: Oshun in Myths and Legends

Oshun is among the most prominent figures in Yoruba, Santeria, and Ifa. She plays a role in many stories in African mythology, either as the main character or featured in a supporting role that impacts the story's events.

This chapter will cover myths and legends about Oshun. These will reflect her significance, true character, and relationship with other Orishas.

Oshun has many myths and legends associated with her.
fenixcs, ATTRIBUTION-NONCOMMERCIAL-NODERIVS 2.0 GENERIC, CC BY-NC-ND 2.0 <https://creativecommons.org/licenses/by-nc-nd/2.0/>
https://www.flickr.com/photos/fenixcsmar/33227614663

Betrayal

One day, the Orishas met to discuss their place in the hierarchy. They were displeased that Olodumare had all the power and that they had to consult him before making any decision. The Orishas were very involved in the affairs of mankind and were doing all the work. Not only was Olodumare a distant deity, but he was also getting old and didn't have any direct influence on people. The Orishas thought that if anyone should be in charge, it should be them.

They decided to rebel against Olodumare. They would no longer follow the deity's orders and would run the universe on their own terms. Eshu (also spelled Esu and Eschu and referred to as Elegba in Santeria) was the Orisha of trickery, similar to Loki from Norse mythology, and was the messenger between the Orishas and mankind. He was a devoted and good friend to Oshun. Eshu was also the Orisha of crossroads. He stood at the doorway, so he heard their rebellious plan.

Eshu ran to Olodumare to tell them about the Orishas' treachery. Olodumare was furious and felt betrayed. The deity had always trusted the Orishas and held them in high regard, which made their actions unjustified and hurtful. Olodumare decided to punish the Orishas by preventing rainfall which then caused a drought. This was the high price paid by the Orishas and mankind alike. The rivers and lakes dried up, plants died, crops failed, humans suffered, and the Earth was perishing. Everything the Orishas created and built was dying. Humans were crying and begging for their help. They thought they had done something to anger the Orishas and asked for forgiveness. However, the Orishas knew that it was all their fault and not the fault of mankind.

The Orishas repented for their actions, cried, and wailed for Olodumare to forgive them. However, Olodumare lived far away in heaven and couldn't hear them. The only solution was for the Orisha to travel to Olodumare and beg for his forgiveness. However, many tried and failed.

Oshun offered to make the journey for the sake of mankind and the universe. However, the Orishas mocked her because she was young and small in size, and she wouldn't be able to succeed, especially when other elder Orishas had failed. They made fun of her vanity and told her to just focus on looking pretty. However, Oshun was much stronger than she looked, and she persisted. The Orishas were desperate and had no other choice. They figured there was no harm in letting her try. However, they all expected her to fail.

She transformed into a peacock and flew away. It was a very long road and close to the sun. Oshun lost her wing feathers and was extremely exhausted, yet she kept flying because she was determined to reach Olodumare. She fell very ill, but nothing could stop her.

Oshun finally made it to Olodumare, but she was so sick she couldn't speak. She fainted in his arms. She was no longer a beautiful peacock but a worn-out vulture. The deity looked after her until she was able to speak. Oshun explained that the Orishas were remorseful and begged for the deity's forgiveness. Olodumare was impressed by Oshun's sacrifice and determination and accepted her apology. The deity explained that her bravery warmed his heart. Olodumare brought back the rain, and all was well again.

Olodumare didn't forget about Oshun's heroic actions. He healed her wings and bestowed on her a huge honor. She became Olodumare's messenger and the only Orisha the deity would communicate with and allow in his realm. Oshun flew back to the Orishas in her vulture form. She had saved the world, and everyone was grateful for her heroism.

Oshun, the River Orisha

Oshun wasn't originally the Orisha of the river. It was Yemaya, the mother of all Orishas and Orisha of the water. Some legends describe her as Oshun's mother, while others say she was her elder sister. All the main Orishas were older than her and had their own realms. Since she didn't have a palace to reside in, Oshun lived a carefree life traveling the world. One day, as she was wandering around, she encountered Ogun. Ogun was a warrior and the Orisha of iron known for his strength and intelligence. When he saw Oshun, he was mesmerized by her beauty.

Ogun wanted Oshun and chased her across the land. She wasn't interested and ran away from him. However, she had nowhere to hide and, as she was running, she fell into the river. The river was dragging her away. When Yemaya saw Oshun, she ran to her rescue. Yemaya realized her daughter needed protection and must have her own realm. Hence, she gave her domain over the rivers and fresh waters.

Oshun and Shango Love Story

One day, Oshun was attending a drumming festival. There was a very handsome man dancing like no one she had ever seen before. Oshun, who had many admirers, felt enamored by him. This man was Shango, the Orisha of lightning and thunder, the equivalent of Thor in Norse mythology. When Shango laid eyes on Oshun, he was taken in by her beauty. No man could ever resist Oshun, and Shango was no different. He was already married to Oba, the Orisha of time and the river Oba. She was also Yemaya's daughter and Oshun's sister.

Shango was a womanizer and desired Oshun, and the feeling was mutual. He and Oshun got married. Although Shango later took a third wife, Oshun remained his favorite. She was a very skilled cook and managed to please Shango with her delicious meals.

Jealousy

Shango was madly in love with Oshun, and he never stopped desiring her, even after they were married. He never got enough of her or her delicious cooking. This broke Oba's heart, who felt that Oshun was taking her place. Oba wanted Shango to desire her in the same way, so she sought her sister's help. She asked her for the secret that made her food irresistible.

Oshun was jealous of Oba and her relationship with Shango. Although Shango truly loved Oshun, Oba had a very special place in his heart which was very hard for her to accept. Oshun decided to cause a rift between them. She told Oba if she wanted Shango to enjoy her cooking and be drawn to her, she should cut off her ear and add it to the food. At first, Oba wasn't convinced and thought her sister may have lied to her. Oshun decided to play a trick on her to make her lie more believable.

Oshun prepared a dish for Shango, added a type of mushroom resembling an ear, and wore a scarf. Shango ate the food and was very pleased. When Oba saw what she thought was the truth, she cut off her ear and used it to prepare a dish for Shango.

Shango ate the meal and enjoyed it. When Oba found her husband loved her food, she decided to tell him the truth so he would know how much she loved him and sacrificed for him. Oba took off her scarf, revealing her missing ear. When Shango found out what she did, he was enraged and disgusted. He couldn't look at Oba's face as she was mutilated. He kicked her out and went to live with Oshun, who was very pleased with herself. Not only did she humiliate Oba, but she also got rid of her.

Oba was heartbroken because she truly loved Shango. She kept weeping and wailing until she turned into the Oba River.

In another version of the myth, Oshun was jealous of Oba because her children would inherit Shango's kingdom one day. When Oba asked for her help, Oshun told her that she had once cut off a piece of her ear and added it to a dish she was making for Shango. Ever since he ate it, she became his favorite wife. Oba couldn't believe that her sister was so gullible to trust her with this secret. She decided to outdo her and cut off her whole ear.

Shango discovered the ear while he was eating. He was furious and felt betrayed because he thought Oba was trying to poison him. His anger was so out of control that he caused thunder to hit his home. Oba and Oshun were terrified and tried to escape, but both women fell and turned into rivers that bore their names.

Oshun's Sacrifice

Yemaya was married to Arganyu, who was one of the eldest Orishas. Some legends say he was Shango's father, while others called him his brother. Yemaya and Arganyu were madly in love. They stayed married for a very long time, and their union benefited mankind. However, Yemaya felt that this relationship had to end. She wanted to spend her life serving the world, but her marriage to Arganyu was holding her back. She wasn't learning anything new and wanted to do more and make a real difference. Yemaya decided to separate from her husband. However, she loved him deeply and didn't want to leave him alone. She wanted Arganyu to be with someone who would take care of him, fulfill his needs, and help him get over her. She knew there was no one better suited for the job than her favorite daughter, Oshun. She wasn't only the Orisha of love but also very beautiful, and no man could resist her. She could also use enchantments and magic on Arganyu so he could forget about Yemaya.

Yemaya headed to her daughter's house to talk to her. Oshun loved her mother so much and was very happy to see her. However, she felt that something was wrong since Yemaya rarely visited anyone, and she also had a concerned look on her face. Oshun fell at Yemaya's feet to show her respect and devotion. She told her that she would do whatever she asked of her. Yemaya held her daughter and was touched by her loyalty. She looked at her face and couldn't help but admire her beauty. She knew that Oshun was the only person who could make Arganyu happy.

Yemaya opened her heart to Oshun and explained her desire. Oshun was shocked as she didn't expect her mother to ask something like that of her. She felt she had spoken too soon by agreeing to the request before knowing what it was. Oshun found herself in a terrible position. She didn't want to go back on her word, but she also couldn't marry a man she didn't love. Yemaya explained her plan to her daughter. She would bring Arganyu here and then make an excuse and leave. Oshun should then start flirting with Arganyu and have sex with him.

After Yemaya left, Oshun pondered what her mother had asked of her. She was still in shock at the request. How could she marry a man she didn't love? There was no denying that Arganyu was good-looking, but she didn't have any feelings for him. However, her mother had told her this was for the greater good, and Oshun loved and respected her mother so much that she couldn't say no.

Oshun couldn't sleep. She knew that her life would never be the same again. She was worried about how Arganyu would react. She loved her mother so much and couldn't get angry or be unkind to her. She decided to accept her mother's request and fell asleep ready to prepare for the big day.

The next morning, Yemaya took Arganyu to Oshun. They didn't speak much on the journey as her mind was preoccupied. She was going to abandon the man she loved forever. Oshun prepared herself and made sure to look her best. Yemaya and Arganyu arrived and saw Oshun; she had never looked more beautiful. After some time, Yemaya excused herself while giving her daughter a look that she should execute the plan. Oshun nodded to reassure her mother. Yemaya embraced her husband, and he knew then that he would never see her again. He felt that his heart was breaking as he saw her walking away.

There was a very long silence before Arganyu began speaking. He wasn't as angry as Oshun had feared. Arganyu was calm and spoke in a soft voice. He told her she didn't need to do that, he would be fine, and she didn't have to displease her mother. Oshun stared at Arganyu without saying a word. She thought about what would happen next and realized that the situation wasn't as horrible as she initially thought. Both agreed to stay together. Arganyu found Oshun beautiful and wanted to keep her word to her mother.

Arganyu was the first man she had ever been with, as this story took place before she met Shango. Although they were never in love, Arganyu was very special to Oshun because he made her feel like a woman. They lived together for a long time in peace and harmony.

Oshun and Ogun

As the Orisha of iron, Ogun worked as a blacksmith. The other Orishas and all of mankind benefited from his work. However, he was tired and wanted to retreat to the forest, where he felt happiest. He knew no one could stop him because he was strong and powerful. One day, he decided to leave and went to live in the forest. However, his absence was noticed. The universe needed a blacksmith to make tools and build things. The Orishas agreed to go to the woods and convince Ogun to come back. None of them were successful. Ogun chased any Orisha who came to visit him out and was adamant about remaining in his new life.

Oshun was the only Orisha who had never tried her luck with Ogun. One day, she went to the other Orishas and asked permission to speak with Ogun. Again, the Orishas underestimated her because of her young age and lack of experience. They were also worried because she was small, and Ogun was very strong and unpredictable. However, Oshun was determined and asked them to give her a chance. She explained that she was stronger than she looked and that she knew exactly how to bring him back. No one took her seriously. They all underestimated her because of her age and naivety.

Obatala, the sky father, creator of mankind, and the father of all Orishas, including Oshun, was present. After a while, he signaled with his hand for everyone to stop talking. Silence filled the room. He said that since all Orishas failed to bring Ogun back, there was no harm in giving Oshun a chance. Obatala knew Oshun was desirable and could entice Ogun and bring him back.

Oshun headed to the forest, ready to execute her plan. She stood in the middle of the forest and started dancing. She wasn't wearing anything but five transparent scarves. Ogun was taking a walk, and when Oshun saw him, she started dancing in a seductive way. She pretended she didn't see Ogun and started singing. He heard her voice and approached to see where it was coming from. Oshun noticed and adjusted the scarves to reveal parts of her body. When she saw Ogun, she approached him slowly and cast a spell by applying honey to his lips.

He was mesmerized by her and fell into a trance. Oshun continued pretending that she didn't see him. She kept moving away from the forest and toward the town and applying honey to his lips to prevent the spell from wearing off and keep him entranced. Suddenly, Ogun regained consciousness to find himself in the city surrounded by all of the Orishas. They were so happy to see him and cheered Oshun for successfully returning him. Ogun decided to stay to make it seem that he returned willingly and that he wasn't fooled. From that day, everyone saw Oshun as a capable and powerful Orisha.

Cheating Death

A beloved king was lying on his deathbed. He was very sick, and Iku, the god of death, was preparing to take his soul. His people were heartbroken and weren't ready to see their king go. They sought the help of an oracle who told them that Oshun could drive Iku away, but they needed to present a great offering. Oshun felt sorry for the people and was impressed by their devotion to their king. She accepted their offering and went to see Iku, who was at the king's house. She firmly told him to leave the king, but he wouldn't accept.

Oshun told him she wouldn't give up until he left. Iku tried to scare her, but Oshun was brave and wouldn't back down. She got closer to him and touched him in a sensual way. He was confused, and before he realized what was happening, Oshun stole his talisman of power. Iku now had no power and was ashamed that Oshun could trick him. She told him he would only get his talisman back if he agreed to leave. Iku left, and the king lived. Oshun was the only Orisha who was able to cheat death.

Seducing a Ghost

Oya, the Orisha of rebirth and death, was Oshun's sister and Shango's third wife. She was jealous that Shango favored Oshun and only paid attention to her. She played a trick to keep her husband near and prevent him from seeing Oshun. Using her power over the dead, Oya summoned ghosts and made them surround the house so Shango couldn't leave. She knew that he couldn't tolerate the dead, so he wouldn't try to challenge them.

Shango was trapped. Days passed, and Oshun started to worry. Shango never stayed that long without seeing her, so she knew something was wrong. She went to see him, and he told her what Oya had done. Oshun went outside and met with the leader of the ghosts. She did everything she could to make him leave. She flirted with him, offered him rum, and seduced him with her beauty. The ghost caved in and walked away. Shango was able to leave and be with Oshun.

It is very clear from all these legends that Oshun was a strong, determined, brave, confident, and clever woman. People would mock and underestimate her, but she defied all odds, believed in herself and proved everyone wrong. She was courageous and always volunteered to help. Selfless and caring, she didn't gain anything from her actions; she just wanted to do well for the sake of mankind and the Orishas.

In many cases, Oshun used her sexuality to resolve issues. It wasn't only one of her powers and a peaceful way to get things done. However, Oshun made it clear that she was more than just a beautiful woman. Her real powers lay in her personality. You cannot help admiring her.

There are many lessons to learn from these stories, but the most significant is believing in yourself even when no one else does. When someone says you can't do something, tell them to watch while you do it. That was Oshun's attitude, and she always showed the other Orishas how capable she was.

Chapter 4: Connecting to the Divine Feminine

The universe is one gigantic being made of endless energy. It constantly creates and is continuously being created at the same time. Its energy is restless, always buzzing and multiplying, but never diminished or destroyed.

The divine feminine is an energy form that is always present.
https://pxhere.com/en/photo/247503

The universe is also governed by its own set of laws. There are twelve laws. One is the law of polarity, and the other is the law of gender. The law of polarity states that everything exists within a binary dynamic.

Basically, this law states that if there is light, there must also be darkness, and if there is warmth, then there is cold, etc. This contrast did not exist by chance; it was by design. This duality creates harmony and balance; without it, everything would devolve into chaos and destruction.

The law of gender is another vital law. It states that every being exists with its counterpart. It is very similar to the law of polarity but does not serve the same purposes. This law also creates balance and harmony between every energetic being.

Now, you may wonder, how are these universal laws related to the divine feminine? Simply put, the divine feminine could not have come into existence if these two laws did not govern the world. This chapter will give you an in-depth understanding of the divine feminine and its role in the Yoruba tradition.

What Is the Divine Feminine?

A divine feminine is an energy form that takes place in almost everything around you. For example, Mother Earth is the divine feminine. The water, moon, and humans have the divine feminine in them. This energy does not exist in one place or in one creature; it exists anywhere and everywhere.

To understand the divine feminine, its qualities must first be understood. How can you distinguish this energy?

1. Creativity

The divine feminine is full of creative energy. It always creates, and its creations are seen as sacred, beautiful, and unique. Think of the Earth and think of all of its creations. Trees that reach the heavens, delicate flowers drawn with intricate details, or lands that are home to millions of living beings. Think of birds that sing, wolves that howl at the moon, roosters that crow at sunrise, creatures that fly between the clouds, and others that live in the ocean's depths. Mother Nature is in a constant state of creation, and its creativity displays its divine feminine energy.

2. Intuition

Intuition is a powerful sensation exercised by both humans and nature. People are inclined to believe that intuition is a tool humans use, but that is far from the truth. Intuition is an energetic force that can exist anywhere and in anything. For instance, the moon is linked to intuition. Various spiritual faiths and cultures believe that the moon strengthens your intuition. It is believed that it elevates your intuitive abilities. This is why the moon is seen as a divine feminine and is often associated with several goddesses in various cultures.

3. Innate Wisdom and Regeneration

Spirituality links the serpent with divine femininity. Several centuries-old cultures used the snake as a symbol of wisdom and transformation. These two qualities are part of the divine feminine archetype. Humans connected to this energy tend to understand themselves through self-reflection. The act of seeking knowledge from within allows people to access their innate wisdom, eventually leading to a transformative cycle. The snake sheds its skin and becomes a new and enhanced version of itself. The divine feminine also knows when it is time to shed their skin and become an advanced version of who they are.

4. The Giver

The divine feminine is a giver by nature. When people tap into this energy, they become givers too. This means a person is generous with time, love, and effort. They are forgiving and empathetic toward themselves and others. This is reflected in nature too. The best way to understand the giving nature of the divine feminine is to compare it with trees. Trees are givers. They provide shade, fruit, and cleaner air, and they are relaxing to look at. They are home to many animals, and their very existence is a gift for every living creature. Like the tree, the divine feminine is naturally giving. However, because the divine feminine is intuitive and wise, it knows when its generosity is being abused, meaning you do not have to be endlessly giving. However, you will find that you are more generous when you are in tune with your divine femininity.

The Divine Feminine and Its Counterpart

To fully comprehend the divine feminine, you need to understand what exists on the other side of it. The laws of polarity and gender state that everything must exist with its counterpart. This means that the divine feminine is one side of the coin. It does not exist on its own. So, what is on the other side of this sacred coin? The divine masculine. The divine feminine and masculine exist in harmony. Together, these two energies create a necessary equilibrium. Too much of anything can and will create chaos. This is why the divine feminine exists alongside the divine masculine.

This is not to say that one is incomplete without the other. On the contrary, both of these energies are perfect the way they are. However, they each add qualities that the other lacks. For instance, the law of polarity says that everything and its opposite co-exist together, right? So, for instance, the divine feminine is more reflective and seeks wisdom from within. On the other hand, the divine masculine seeks wisdom from the outside or through others.

Of course, this does not mean that one way is better than the other. However, it would not be wise to only seek wisdom from within and to just depend on the outside for insight. This is why it is best to rely on either strategy occasionally.

Now, you must remember that the divine feminine and masculine are energy forces. What does this mean? Simply put, both energies are frequencies anyone can tap into. For instance, it is natural to assume that women are naturally connected to the divine feminine and men tap into the divine masculine, right? Not exactly.

To understand this, you need to look deeper into the components of a human. People physically exist in an earthly plane and spiritually exist in a spiritual realm. The way people understand gender on Earth only works for the physical realm. However, gender does not work the same way in the spiritual world. Why is that? Because spirituality states that gender in the spiritual form is nothing more than energy. What is energy in the spiritual world? In its simplest form, it is a frequency. This means anyone can naturally tap into a certain frequency or consciously switch from one energy to another.

In clearer words, both women and men can tap into either energy. Women can be connected to their divine masculine, and men can act from their divine feminine energy. Humans can also switch between these two energies at any time they want.

Now that you have a good grasp on the divine feminine qualities, it is time to familiarize yourself with the divine masculine so that you can understand the workings of the divine feminine.

The divine masculine is a chaser, meaning it is active and assertive. It is not known for deep self-reflection because it is more focused on setting goals and following through with plans. This energy is more decisive and logical. This does not mean that people who are in tune with their divine masculine are emotionless. On the contrary, they feel their emotions, but they act on their logical side. The divine masculine is naturally protective and has a good sense of leadership.

One can find a good balance between both energies – meaning you can be more in tune with your divine feminine and connected to your divine masculine a second later. You can easily do this when you have good discernment between both and know how you feel when connected to either of them.

The Oshun Archetype and the Divine Feminine

The divine feminine concept is universal. This means various cultures with different backgrounds recognize these sacred energies. Of course, the term "divine feminine" is more westernized. The Yoruba people believe in the divine feminine energy, and they know it as Oshun. Who is Oshun?

Oshun is a Nigerian goddess. She rules the rivers, water, love, sensuality, fertility, and purity. She is portrayed as a gentle and kind goddess, but she is also known for her fiercely protective nature. She is known to take her vengeance on anyone who dares cross her.

The goddess is named after the Osun River in Nigeria. The goddess of the Oceans, Yemaya, and Olofin, king of the skies, were in a union and gave birth to Oshun. The goddess is more in tune with her divine femininity, but she also displays minor divine masculine qualities. This makes her perfectly balanced.

How does the goddess balance both energies? To answer this question, you must first familiarize yourself with Oshun.

Oshun was the only female sent to Earth, along with 16 other male gods. These divine beings were sent to Earth to populate it and create life. The gods attempted to create life, but they failed. Oshun was the only goddess who successfully created life.

Does this remind you of the divine feminine qualities? Oshun used her creativity, inner wisdom, intuition, and fertility to create life. Oshun brought water to the earth, creating and giving life to everything around her. The goddess's impact on Earth was so strong that the Yoruba people believed that humanity would not have existed had Oshun not helped in any way.

The Yoruba people pray to the goddess to help them with their fertility. This shows the goddesses' generosity and love for her devotees. Oshun uses her powers and helps her worshippers by allowing them to create like her. The goddess is pleased when she sees her devotees create and endlessly give and love their creations.

She is a clear example of the divine feminine, but she also connects to her divine masculine when needed. For instance, she protects her creations and children. She is also known to show her wrath when angered. For instance, one myth describes violent floods and heavy rains that destroyed the people who wronged the goddess. These stories display how the goddess is naturally in tune with her divine femininity. Still, she also has the power to connect to her divine masculinity when needed.

Divine Feminine Lore and Proverbs

The Yoruba tradition has several stories of Oshun which display her divine femininity. For instance, one myth describes Oshun as a clever goddess who could cheat death. It was known that certain gods and goddesses could not reach the heavens by themselves. However, Oshun wanted to challenge the Orishas and reach the heavens. The Orishas laughed at the goddess and did not believe she could reach the skies.

Oshun was adamant about reaching the heavens, so she turned herself into a beautiful peacock with colorful feathers. She successfully flew to the sky, but the sun began to burn her feathers away. The sun started eating at her skin, but the goddess continued flying higher. Oshun finally reached the creator, Olodumare. She collapsed in his arms and turned into a vulture. The creator admired her dedication and bravery and nursed the goddess back to health. Olodumare honored Oshun's dedication by only communicating through her.

Since then, the peacock and the vulture became symbols of Oshun's transformation, regeneration, courage, and dedication.

Another myth displays Oshun's intelligence and sensuality. The story begins with Oya, Oshun's sister, and Shango's third wife. Oya was jealous because Shango favored Oshun over her. One day, she summoned a ghost and demanded that it surround the house. Oya knew that Shango did not dare challenge the undead. The ghost haunted their house, per Oya's request, and Shango could not escape the house.

Meanwhile, Oshun was worried because she knew that nothing could keep her husband away from her. She visited the house and found the ghost that Oya had summoned. Oshun tried to make the ghost leave by offering it rum, but the ghost did not leave the house. The goddess then used her sensuality to seduce the ghost into leaving the house. The ghost eventually got scared of Oshun's attempts and left. Once the ghost left the house, Oshun and Shango were reunited.

What do these stories display? They showcase Oshun's divine femininity. As a human, you do not have to use your divine femininity similarly. Through these stories, Oshun shows how anyone can manipulate their divine femininity and use it as a powerful tool to achieve anything their heart desires.

How Can You Connect to the Divine Feminine?

If you want to be in tune with your divine feminine, you must familiarize yourself with its qualities. Now that you know what qualities you must work on, you need to have self-reflection sessions with yourself.

Ask yourself, "What is my relationship with my intuition? Do I listen to my intuition? Do I follow my inner wisdom? Or do I discredit it?" Your relationship with your intuition here is key to connecting with the divine feminine.

Get used to having self-reflection sessions with yourself; if it feels foreign to you, then this is a sign that you must practice self-reflection. That will help you be more in tune with your body and spirit. The more you do this, the more your intuition will be in a smooth flow state.

Remember that the divine feminine is known for its creativity. This does not mean that you need to give birth physically. It simply means that you need to allow yourself to be in a creative flow. Once you allow your creativity to flow through your body, allow yourself to create. Your creations can take on any form: pottery, a piece of fiction, an artistic piece, etc.

The divine feminine is also a giver. Now, ask yourself how I can be more giving. Your generosity should begin with yourself first. This means you must be generous, gracious, and forgiving of yourself first. The more you practice being generous with yourself, the more you will find yourself naturally generous with others.

This may sound daunting at first. Do not worry; there are rituals that you can try to help you connect with your divine femininity.

Self-Love Ritual

Ingredients:
- 1 large white candle
- 5 sunflowers
- 1 teaspoon of cinnamon
- 1 teaspoon of honey
- 1 bowl
- Your signature perfume
- An Oshun statue

Instructions:
1. In a safe space, light a candle for five days in front of the Oshun statue.
2. Place the candle in the center of the bowl.
3. Dress the bowl and candle with cinnamon, honey, and sunflowers.
4. Converse with Oshun during the five days and ask her to help you find your sensuality or to help you fall in love with yourself.
5. On the fifth day, blow out the candle.
6. Remove the candle and any leftover wax. Take the bowl with its ingredients and fill it with warm water.
7. Step into the shower.
8. As you pour the water, pray to the goddess.

Fertility Ritual

Ingredients:
- 1 large yellow candle
- 1 teaspoon of honey
- 1 pumpkin

- 1 pencil
- An Oshun statue
- 1 brown paper bag

Instructions:
1. Light the candle.
2. Leave it in a safe space.
3. Light it for five days.
4. Pray to the goddess and share your wishes with her.
5. Create a large opening on top of the pumpkin.
6. Cut out a piece of paper from the brown paper bag.
7. Use your pencil and write your wishes on it.
8. Place the paper in the pumpkin.
9. Seal the pumpkin with candle wax.
10. Place the sealed pumpkin on top of your stomach so that you can conceive.
11. Place the pumpkin and leave it next to a river as an offering for the goddess.

To summarize, the divine feminine is an energetic force. It is a state of mind that anyone can tap into. You do not need to be a man or a woman to be connected with their divine femininity. Remember that you can shift between the divine feminine and masculine whenever you want to. Most importantly, remember that balance is key between both energies. You can be naturally more in tune with your divine femininity, but remember to connect with your divine masculine as well. Whenever you need to connect with the sacred feminine energy, pray to Oshun or read stories about her and let her inspire your divine feminine.

Chapter 5: Plants, Symbols, and Offerings

Now that you know how to connect to the divine feminine, you're ready to learn what offerings to place on your altar or in any other of her favorite places. By reading this chapter, you'll uncover what the goddess of love and prosperity prefers to receive as offerings and what symbols or objects you can use to invoke her powers. It lists Oshun's associated plants, animals, symbols, flowers, fruit, meals, and so on - including the reasons they relate to the goddess. You'll also find a few recipes for meal offerings you can prepare on any day you wish to honor Oshun.

Plants Associated with Oshun

Like all other Orishas, Oshun also has her representation in herbs and healing plants containing her energy. By using them in spells and rituals devoted to the goddess, you can obtain her ashe and use it to empower yourself in love and other endeavors and acquire success. Below are the most common plants associated with Oshun.

Different herbs and plants are associated with Oshun.
https://unsplash.com/photos/6LTAljmu2cY

Cinnamon

The cinnamon bush is a plant highly associated with Oshun, mainly because it goes well with the sweet recipes the goddess of love prefers. It particularly pairs well with honey, another one of Oshuns natural symbols. Followers of Oshun believe that cinnamon attracts love and good fortune. Apart from offerings, they often use this herb in cleansing rituals before performing a spell or rite for the goddess.

Cinnamon also has medicinal properties and is known to aid digestion, regulate blood sugar levels and boost immunity. Healers often use it in syrups to treat colds and respiratory infections. One of the best ways to honor Oshun is by taking care of your health - and this herb is one of the best tools for that. Being in better shape helps you take better advantage of the blessings the goddess provides.

Cloves

Cloves appeal to Oshun for several reasons. They're associated with protection and empower the practitioner during their work. They also help cleanse the spirit from negative influences, creating space for the goddess's ashe. Cloves embody fertility and can help connect with the goddess when asking for her assistance to make any aspect of life more fertile.

Calendula

Also known as tufted marigold, calendula is a plant infused with incredibly potent energy emanating from the goddess. It has purifying properties, which come in handy for cleansing rituals and prayers you can use to invoke and honor Oshun. It's said to cleanse one's energy and dispel negative influences. All of this is essential for communicating with the goddess.

Calendula infusion treats ear and gum infections, relieves toothache and skin irritations, and regulates the menstrual cycle. Due to the latter effect, the plant contributes to fertility - the primary reason it's linked to Oshun.

Sunflower

The sacred plant of Oshun, the sunflower, has many uses in a wide range of Orisha-related rituals. Its healing properties include relieving symptoms of respiratory infections, fever, colds, nosebleeds, and gastrointestinal conditions. This plant is also effective against kidney infections, kidney stones, and infections of the lower urogenital tract. Because of the latter effect, it has a positive impact on fertility. It enables women who want to conceive to take advantage of Oshun's blessings.

The sunflower is the sacred plant of Oshun.
https://unsplash.com/photos/oO62CP-g1EA

The sunflower is also the symbol of good luck and the beneficial effect of water on nature. Due to Oshun's association with the waters, it's easy to see why she prefers this plant to be given as an offering. Besides water, the sunflower is also known to constantly look for sunlight, attracting good energy to its flowers. You can use it to attract positive energy and empower any spell or ritual you perform in the goddess's name.

Pumpkin

According to the Yoruba lore, Oshun carved the first lamp out of a pumpkin and used it to dance beside. It's also believed that the goddess keeps her riches in pumpkins. These gifts can be accessed with the invisible spells she stores in the rivers, so pumpkins are typically offered to her near running water.

In some traditions, pumpkins cannot be consumed or sold for eating, while other practices use them for their healing properties. It treats digestive issues, burns, and skin inflammation. It can also be used in purification and beauty rituals associated with Oshun. It makes the skin, hair, and nails look healthier, specifically when used with Oshun's blessing. Other uses for pumpkin include spells promoting fertility, brightening one's life, reigniting old relationships, personal growth, success, and more.

Melon

Traditionally, Castille melon is used for this purpose (it's the sweetest one, and Oshun likes things sweet), but any kind of melon will do. Similarly to the pumpkin, melon is offered at the riverbanks or near large bodies of water as this is the best place to reach out to the goddess. If you don't have rivers near you, you can prepare the melon for a spell, ritual, or as a meal offering and serve it at your altar along with saying a prayer to the goddess. Melon is often offered alongside honey and cinnamon, which enhance its powers. The plant has similar properties as pumpkins and is often associated with fertility. It's used in rituals invoking the goddess to make any area of life more fertile.

Yams

Yams have been a staple food in African cultures for centuries. Besides the great flavor that allows them to be incorporated into a variety of meals, yams are also highly fruitful plants. Because of this, they're often associated with fertility. Yams are often used in offerings for this cause or simply because the goddess favors them. They are typically offered alongside honey or incorporated into a honey-sweetened meal.

Oranges

Oranges are also sweet fruits Oshun loves to receive in offerings. Orange seeds appeal to her even more as they're associated with fertility and new life. Place the seeds on your altar in a small bowl of honey after removing them from an orange you've eaten. Say a prayer to the goddess, and she will grant your wishes regarding fertility. Oranges are also packed with vitamins you can use to boost your immunity and prepare yourself for the blessing you're about to receive.

River Flax

If you live near a river, you'll come across river flax, a type of grass favored by Oshun in rituals and offerings. One of the common ways river flax is used to obtain the goddess's favor is a five-day ritual performed at a riverbank. On the first day, a stone symbolizing Oshun is put in honey, after which she is offered her favorite animals (nowadays only symbolically). On the second day, the honey is removed from the stone, and the stone is covered with a yellow linen sheet. On the third day, the person performing the ritual fans themselves five times (traditionally with five different fans, but you can use one). On the fourth day, Oshun is offered five different natural sweets. Until this time, everything is done at an altar. On the fifth day, the stone is carried to the river and placed in a basket together with a piece of gold. The basket is traditionally sent toward the middle of the water for the river to carry it away. You can also leave it at the riverbank while dedicating a prayer to the goddess, asking her for her blessings.

Hawksbill

According to Yoruba beliefs, Oshun requires the hawksbill plant when she is asked for a more extensive favor. It's her way of ensuring the requester is empowered through the plant and is ready to receive the goddess's ashe. It's typically used as a seat (put under) for shells containing spiritual water. At other times, the plant is infused to create the spiritual herbal water needed for spells, rituals, and offerings.

Freshness

This unique herb grows in humid soil, such as that found near rivers and other bodies of water - hence why the goddess prefers it. It's believed that it attracts good fortune and wards off evil spirits. It's often used for the cleansing rituals enacted for homes and to help the soul prepare for the goddess's blessings. It can also be infused into water, which is used to clean the floors. Another way to use freshness-infused water is to drink it. It improves kidney function, which further purifies the body from negative influences. You can leave it on your altar for a day and ask the goddess to bless it, then drink it or use it for its intended purpose.

Macaw

In South America, Oshun is often offered yellow macaw. The roots, leaves, and stems have medicinal properties. These can treat digestive issues, regulate the metabolism, and relieve chronic pain. However, Oshun prefers the flowers of this plant in offerings because they help cleanse the spirit from harmful energies. You can ask the goddess to bless the flowers on your altar and use them in a cleansing bath. This way, you'll be ready for Oshun's blessings.

Parsley

Parsley is commonly used in food. It is also another one of Oshun's favorites. It has many uses in folk medicine due to its antioxidant, immune-boosting, anti-inflammatory, and cleansing properties. You can offer parsley as part of any meal offerings you prepare for Oshun, in teas, or as a part of a cleansing ritual. Depending on how you use it, parsley can purity the body, mind, and spirit. All this is essential for receiving blessings - whether you ask for fidelity, love, or prosperity.

Oshun's Animals and Other Symbols

Besides plants, Oshun is also associated with several animals and other symbols.

Sacred Birds

Oshun's sacred animals are clever birds, such as vultures and peacocks. According to Yoruba lore, when some of the Orishas rebelled against the supreme rule of Olodumare, Oshun summoned her sacred birds for protection against the creator's wrath. Her sacred birds helped protect Oshun and the rest of the Orishas, for which she will always cherish them and prefer their symbolism in offerings. These sacred birds symbolize Oshun's courage and ability to stand up for herself and others and persevere. Because they prefer to live near water, these birds are associated with the goddess. For the same reason, they're also linked to healing and life. It's believed the Oshun sacred birds can carry on their healing powers through the water and grant assistance in fertility, cleansing, and love spells and rituals. You can use symbols or images of these birds or feathers if you can obtain them. Place these on your altar when invoking the goddess for a protection spell or ritual.

The peacock is one of the sacred birds due to their intelligence.
https://unsplash.com/photos/_7S3tOs424o

Honey

Oshun is often portrayed with a honeypot at her waist. According to ancient beliefs, honey symbolizes fertility and sexual pleasure, which, in turn, is often linked to pregnancy. It's said that women who want to conceive should offer honey to Oshun, asking her to bless them with a child. As another form of honoring Oshun as the fertility goddess and depicting her powers of femininity and sensuality, women often carry honey cakes with them or wear honey (or golden) colored beads and belts around their waist.

Another way to use honey when asking for Oshun's blessings is in spells and rituals. Like all sweet things associated with the goddess, honey can also help you attract good luck, wealth, and prosperity. You can incorporate this into any work you perform for this purpose, ask the goddess for assistance, and you'll receive what you desire in abundance. Oshun will particularly appreciate it if you taste the honey before incorporating it into your work.

Essential Oils

Oshun prefers essential oils extracted from her favorite plants, herbs, and spices. However, you can use your favorite oils, even if they aren't on her preferred list. The goddess is guaranteed to like them as long as they're colorful, fragrant, and have an air of sensuality. The best way to incorporate essential oils into spells, rituals, and offerings made for

Oshun is to pair them with cinnamon, cloves, and other dry spices she likes.

Running Waters

As the goddess of rivers, Oshun prefers her offerings to be left near running water, such as rivers and waterfalls. If you don't have a running or sweet water source nearby, you can use their symbols at your altar. For example, you can use the picture of a waterfall when you ask for purification, healing, or warding off hostile influences. If you have these sources nearby but can't (or prefer not to) leave offerings out in nature, you can take some from the source of that water. Bring it home and place it on your altar next to the other offerings you've prepared for the goddess.

Items of Value

While Oshun is traditionally associated with the color gold and gold items, other items of value also appeal to her. When followers ask for significant favors, including fertility and financial prosperity, they typically offer gold coins or objects. Brass and copper are also great alternatives to gold items.

Incense

Due to its light sweet aroma, Oshun particularly loves sandalwood incense. It's associated with protection and will help you evoke the goddess's protective powers. However, once again, you can use any sweet incense you prefer during your work. Oshun can infuse her powers into anything sweet; incense makes this even easier as it permeates your senses. It envelops your body and spirit and wards off any negative energies which threaten to disrupt your work.

Cowrie Shells

According to ancient lore, Obatala passed on his divinatory powers to Oshun with the help of cowrie shells. When Obatala needed to retrieve his belongings from Elegba, he asked Oshun to do it for her and, in turn, taught her how to use the shells for divination. As she was about to complete her task, she was instructed by Elegeba to train the other Orishas to divine using cowrie shells. The Orishas, in turn, taught the humans this art. These shells then became associated with prophecy and Oshun. They're used in rituals, spells, and offerings made in her honor. Cowrie shells can evoke her and ask her for guidance regarding success or spiritual growth. Cowrie shells also symbolize waters and water creatures Oshun rules over. Anytime you need cleansing or to evoke the power of water and its creatures, you can incorporate cowrie shells (or any other shells you can find) into your work with the goddess.

Drinks

Oshun loves sweet drinks, typically made from fruit. Orange juice is one of her favorites, but chamomile tea appeals to her also, especially if it's sweetened with honey. The goddess also likes sweet white wines as an offering - particularly if they are accompanied by one of her favorite meals.

Femininity Symbols

Oshun is one of the most empowering female deities, but even she loves to be reminded of her femininity. Using femininity symbols is also great for female followers as it helps them embrace their feminine side without having to compromise other aspects of life. You can offer the goddess makeup, perfume, brushes, and other products associated with feminine beauty - even if you don't use them yourself every day. Alternatively, you can recite a prayer to the goddess after a cleansing and pampering ritual or while looking at your own image in the mirror. The latter is an incredibly empowering experience for those looking to enhance some parts of themselves to attract love.

Recipes for Honoring Oshun

While she loves fruit and drinks more, Oshun won't turn her back on some of the following meal offerings either.

Oshun's Butternut Squash Soup

This soup can be offered alongside spells and small rituals for love or prosperity. As the goddess who is always willing to embrace her feminine powers, Oshun is ready to show her talents in the kitchen too. According to lore, her favorite foods were pumpkins and melons. Therefore, this butternut squash recipe is one of the best ways to honor her in your meal offerings. Serve on the altar or a table covered with gold or yellow cloth to represent Oshun's traditional colors. The recipe is enough for at least four people, so feel free to share it with your friends or loved ones.

Ingredients:
- 2 cups of chicken broth
- 3 cups of butternut of cleaned squash cubes
- 2 tablespoons of butter
- Half an onion
- 1/4 cup of applesauce
- ½ teaspoon of dried parsley
- ¼ teaspoon of ground sage plus more for garnish
- ½ teaspoon of onion powder (optional for added flavor)
- Pinch of ground nutmeg
- Pinch of ground cinnamon
- ¼ cup of cooking cream
- Sunflower or dried pumpkin seeds (optional for garnish)

Instructions:
1. In a large saucepan, melt the butter on low heat. While it melts, mince the onion.
2. Transfer the onion to the pan and cook until it becomes translucent.
3. In another pan, add the squash and cover it with water. Bring to a boil and simmer until it becomes tender when pierced with a fork.
4. When the squash is cooked, drain it, mash it, and transfer it into the pan with the onion.
5. Add applesauce, spices, and chicken broth, and mix until well combined.
6. Bring to a boil again, and cook for 10 minutes on low heat while stirring frequently.
7. Remove from the heat, and add salt, pepper, and cream. Serve with sage and, eventually, sunflower or pumpkin seeds for a garnish.

Oshun's Honey Yams

This recipe is perfect for celebrating the goddess on her feast day. However, you can also prepare it whenever you need empowerment from her or want to celebrate your connection. She is extremely fond of yams and honey - and this recipe is another of her favorites. She'll grant your wishes if you seek her help with fertility, wealth, or anything else she has power over. The recipe only has a few ingredients and takes no time at all to prepare, so you'll have plenty of time to prepare other meals and offerings to celebrate the goddess. You can place a plate of yams for her on your altar or a table covered with golden or yellow cloth and eat one yourself while celebrating Oshun.

Ingredients:
- 2 - 3 yams (if you're eating alongside Oshun, you'll need 3)
- 2 teaspoons of dried chamomile flowers
- 3 tablespoons of raw honey
- 2 cinnamon sticks

Instructions:
1. Pour water into a medium pot and bring it to a boil.
2. Break the cinnamon sticks in half and add them to the water along with the dried chamomile.
3. Add the yams to the pot, and bring them to a boil once again. Cook until the yams become tender.
4. Once the yams become as soft as you prefer them, remove the pot from the heat, drain the water, and peel the yams. (You can peel them before boiling, but it's easier to remove their skin when they're cooked).
5. Mash the yams or cut them into bite-sized pieces depending on your preferences. Add a little ground cinnamon and honey on top, and the goddess won't be able to resist it - and neither will you.

Chapter 6: Creating an Altar for the Goddess

Although not all devotees see creating an altar as a compulsory part of their practice, those who do agree that having a dedicated spiritual center for any purpose has many advantages. Regarding Oshun, having a place where you can connect with her through daily rituals is particularly beneficial for your health and spiritual growth. Reading this chapter, you will learn about the additional benefits of creating an altar for Oshun in or near your home and using this space to celebrate the goddess and the divine feminine within you. You will be provided with plenty of user-friendly tips for fashioning a shrine to Oshun, learning how to care for it, and how to use it to make offerings to this Orisha. That said, the advice from this chapter should only serve as a starting point. Some elements in a shrine are necessary to venerate the goddess of love and prosperity. That said, feel free to add personal touches to your creation to empower your sacred spiritual space completely. Not only will this enable you to form an unbreakable bond with Oshun, but it will allow you to strengthen yourself spiritually.

Make sure your altar represents aspects to help you celebrate Oshun.
https://www.rawpixel.com/image/5943767/free-public-domain-cc0-photo

The Benefits of Creating an Altar for Oshun

A sacred place for one's spiritual practice is vital to many belief systems, including the Yoruba, Ifa, and Santeria. Many followers of these religions believe that having a holy place dedicated to your practice has benefits for your spirit and your connection with your guides and the Orishas you worship. Below are a few of the greatest gifts you can attain by creating an altar for the goddess Oshun.

Gaining a Space for Invoking the Goddess

Oshun's favorite places to hang around? Rivers! However, if you don't have those nearby, the next best place to invite her is a sacred space dedicated to her. Each item you place on the altar connects to your soul and the spirit of the goddess you want to evoke. The items you use to decorate your Oshun altar represent emotions and intentions. They also denote symbols that can help you grow spirituality, find love (including self-love), achieve prosperity, and more. You will have a straightforward way to communicate with Oshun through the shrine you've erected and maintained in her honor. The more you use this place to call on her, the more power (ashe) you can harness throughout your spiritual practice. From the elements representing Oshun to your offerings for her, the items you place on the goddess's altar will help you become more confident in your goals - just as Oshun was always in hers.

Whether you're a child of Oshun or a simple devotee, building a relationship with her involves using a dedicated space for several days. Not only that, but you'll be required to place new symbols on the altar each day. Whether you exchange the existing ones or add new items depends on the objective of your spiritual work. Either way, using an altar will empower you spiritually and deepen your connection to this Orisha. You can also share the space with others who want to connect to the divine feminine. It's a wonderful way for devotees to find common ground and empower each other's sensuality and self-confidence through mutual practice.

Focusing on Your Intentions

Whether you communicate with Oshun daily or only during the days associated with her and festivals, having a space dedicated to this can help you focus on your intention every time. As you decorate the altar, you will already start focusing on your purpose of reaching out to the goddess. As you place her correspondences in front of you, you leave ordinary thoughts and worries behind. Your mind is slowly shifting into a calmer plane, where there is only you, your intention, Oshun, and the tools which help you form a connection with her. For example, if you wake up feeling negative energies lurking around you, your intention could be to ask the goddess to help you dispel them. You can ponder on this while you set up the altar. By the time you've finished and have invited her, she will know how to help you.

Garnering Positive Vibes

There is no better way to celebrate Oshun than to empower yourself with positive energy. Feeling positive gives you confidence and allows you to cultivate self-love - both of which will please the goddess. After all, she is a woman who knows her value and expects her devotees to have the same approach to life. An altar can also be a valuable tool for inviting and retaining her loving energy into your home for an extended period. This is especially helpful if you've been struggling with a lack of confidence and positive thoughts lately. Setting up an altar for the love goddess and caring for it will ensure positive energy continues flowing through your space.

Negative experiences and influences can hinder your ability to grow spiritually, be productive and cultivate self-love. If you've felt their effects, building a shrine to Oshun is the first step toward breaking away from negativity. By making an altar for Oshun, you'll have a space for addressing and counteracting negative influences, regardless of their origins. Whether it comes from malicious spirits or envious living, having a space dedicated to the love goddess will empower you to dispel the negativity from your life and replace it with positive influences.

Learning Oshun's Correspondence

While this book enlists Oshun's correspondences, you, as a novice, aren't expected to learn all of them right away. Building an altar to this goddess can be a wonderful learning experience. During this, you can learn to understand what you should display and why. After visiting this sacred space regularly, you'll know instinctively which color to use and what offerings she prefers. Learning the correspondences of Oshun will let you see firsthand how they work best. This will also help you understand what she dislikes and what to avoid when making offerings for her.

Discovering Your Creative Side

Decorating an altar is an excellent way to express your creativity - even if you didn't think you had one. While there are certain objects you'll need to use, figuring out how to place them requires some creative thought. You'll be surprised to discover how resourceful you can be during this process. It allows you to create something unique and express your thoughts and emotions through your handy work. Whether you revere Oshun as an Orisha, the archetype of the divine feminine, the patron of sweet water, or any of her other aspects, you will always have several options for celebrating her and communicating with her. Whichever your goal is for calling on her, there is a way to express it creatively through the adornments you use for the altar.

Creating a Space for Yourself

By bringing together the right combination of elements, you can create a space to pamper yourself whenever you feel the need to do this. Whether you do this through a spell, ritual, prayer, meditation, or any other means, you can use the altar to invoke Oshun's spirit. As her divine essence permeates your senses, your body and mind relax, and your spiritual experience becomes deeper. After this, you can make an inquiry - using incense and other tools that help you focus on the specific intention you have in mind. Choose the ones that feel right to use in the current situation. Another option is to empower yourself by grounding your mind and body by meditating in front of the offerings dedicated to Oshun. The goddess will show you how to use nature's power to nourish your self-confidence and love so you can achieve your goals. Or, you can pray to Oshun and do other self-empowering exercises, such as saying positive affirmations or praising yourself while looking at yourself in the mirror. Anything you do to elevate your spirit will appeal to the goddess, as she is known to do that for herself too.

Connecting with Nature

Anytime you work with an Orisha, you're getting closer to nature, and forming a connection to Oshun is no exception. This goddess favors natural elements such as herbs, bird feathers, water, and delicious fruit and vegetables. Whether you can grow and harvest these yourself is irrelevant. As long as you express your gratitude for them when placing them on your altar, the goddess will know you respect them just as much as she does. Some of these can be perfect for offerings. In contrast, others can be used in spells and rituals to encourage Oshun to help you gain insight or do any other work which aligns with your traditions and culture. You will leave most of Oshun's correspondences and offerings on the altar for several days (or at least half a day). This is plenty of time for her to notice their presence. Once she does, she will bestow many blessings in return.

How to Build an Altar for the Goddess

From where you place it to the items you put on it, many details go into creating an altar. Here are a few tips for making a shrine for Oshun in or near your home.

Altar Placement

Before you start adorning the altar, you must choose a fitting place for it, ideally in a quiet space in your home. If you live near a river or another freshwater source, you can also set it up near the house and as close to the water as possible. As a general rule of thumb, the altar should always be placed away from high-traffic areas. Otherwise, you won't be able to calm your mind and body, rendering you unable to focus on your intention during your work. It's also a good idea to place the altar in a south-facing room, so you can have as much sunlight as possible. Sunlight is essential for working with Oshun, as it's associated with one of her favorite flowers, the sunflower, which uses sunlight to attract positive energy. Having a sacred place in your bedroom would facilitate morning and evening prayers to the goddess, which are recommended for building a strong bond with her.

If you don't have space for a full table to serve as an altar, you can always set up a smaller area on your dresser, vanity table, or inside your closet. Alternatively, you can set up a small altar on the windowsill. This way, you can leave the window open and bask in the sunlight (unless it's too hot outside) during your work. If you plan to practice meditation or similar self-empowering exercises, set up the altar in a space that can accommodate these activities.

What to Put on the Altar

Creating an altar requires using all the items associated with this goddess:

- A yellow piece of cloth, or several of them, depending on how big your altar is
- Yellow and orange crystals - use real stones, if possible
- Cowrie shells, or, if you can't find these, you can use any variety of shells, or symbols of water creatures
- A small statue or picture of Oshun
- A white plate
- A glass of water (river water works best, but you can also use tap water)
- A glass of white wine (or a bottle if you plan to toast her and drink in her honor)
- A small dish with honey
- Gold coins or jewelry
- 5 pieces of fruit (or whole fruit if you're using smaller yellow or orange fruit)
- Beauty products such as perfume, makeup, and a mirror
- Sunflowers (preferably fresh, but you can also use dry or artificial if they aren't in season)
- Feathers
- 2 Yellow candles
- Sweet incense (or one you prefer)
- A cup of chamomile tea with cinnamon (or just a cinnamon stick)
- Yellow clothes (optional)

- Prepared meals you plan to offer (or raw yams, pumpkins, or other produce she favors)

Healing herbs After gathering your tools and ingredients, you can start setting up the altar:

1. Begin by draping the yellow cloth over the surface of the altar.
2. Place the representation of Oshun in the center and the white plate in front of it. Fill the latter with the offerings.
3. Put one of the candles on the left side of the symbol and the other one on the right-hand side.
4. Place the cup of water next to the left candle, the cup of wine next to the right-hand candle, and the dish with the honey somewhere between the two candles (behind the goddess symbol).
5. After placing the fruit where you have larger bits of space, scatter all the small items that symbolize Oshun.
6. Scatter the sunflowers and the healing herbs between the other items.
7. Take the clothes and leave them on the far left side of the altar.
8. Place the incense on the left. Light it just before you start your work, along with the candles.

How to Make Offerings and Clear Them

Before using the shrine, don't forget to bless the shrine by dedicating a short prayer to the goddess before using it. It's also a good idea to cleanse your space and yourself with smudging and even by taking a cleansing bath before you start working. The latter will put you in a better mood, facilitating your communication with the goddess. Alternatively, you can ground yourself and cleanse yourself through nature's power.

After this, you can start presenting the offerings. If you're working with the goddess daily, be generous, and leave a small item every day. Say a prayer or do a quick meditation every time you do. Don't leave out food items for more than two or three days. If the food is cooked, remove it within eight hours. The sunflowers will also wilt, so you'll need to replace them. Non-perishable items can remain for as long as you need them or until you decide to replace them with other ones.

Apart from the tools listed above, you can also adorn your altar with items that reflect your current needs and wants. The number of smaller objects should be five, the goddess's sacred number. If you think that your altar is getting too crowded, feel free to remove some items. As you continue your daily communication with the goddess, you will soon start adding new ones.

Besides daily veneration and honoring her on her holy days, you can also leave offerings to Oshun when you wish to connect to the divine feminine, re-discover your sensuality, or need a helping hand to find love or the key to prosperity in any area of life.

How to Care for the Altar

For new devotees, having only a small altar in your home is generally recommended - so you can concentrate your power. It will also make it easier to nurture it with positive energy, which you'll receive back with the help of Oshun. Remember to keep your altar clean, both physically and spiritually. The easiest way to do both is to cover it with a large piece of yellow cloth when you aren't using it. Occasionally, you can remove everything, clean the dust and other debris from the surface, and put everything back on the altar. Make sure you cleanse it regularly with incense or smudging to dispel negative influences, as these can interfere when it comes time to communicate with Oshun. Pay attention to the goddess's clues regarding the offerings she wants to receive. Sometimes, she will tell you exactly what to prepare next or what tools to use.

Chapter 7: Spells and Rituals for Love and Beauty

Now that you've learned about Oshun correspondences, you'll be ready to try them out in spells and rites dedicated to the goddess. This chapter is about love chants, baths, rituals, and other work that can enhance your natural beauty by healing you from the inside out. Using Oshun's correspondences, you can attract new love, strengthen the love you already have, and empower yourself with confidence and strength.

It's important to focus on love and beauty when creating these rituals.
https://unsplash.com/photos/1H973Qz0Iy4

Oshun's Self-Care Ritual

Oshun is known for her benevolent and caring nature, and she can inspire you to take better care of yourself. The colors of the tools used in the ritual, including the sunflower, pumpkin, and honey, are all associated with the power of the love goddess, which you can harness through this ritual.

Ingredients:
- A statute or picture of Oshun
- Sunflower petals (Fresh - or dried if they aren't in season.)
- 1 pumpkin
- 1 large yellow candle
- 1 piece of a brown paper bag (Or any brown, yellow, or gold recycled material.)
- 1 pen
- A few drops of honey
- Yellow, gold, or copper jewelry
- Yellow fruits if they're in season; if not, orange ones work as well

Instructions:
1. Place the yellow candle in front of the statue or picture of Oshun on your altar and light it.
2. Close your eyes, take a deep breath to calm your mind, and concentrate on your intention. Repeat it in your mind a couple of times and, if needed, say it out loud to solidify it.
3. Pour a few drops of honey into a container you've placed beside the candle. Arrange the yellow fruit and jewelry around the candle, honey, and representation to make the offering.
4. Open your eyes, set the pumpkin in front of you, and make a round opening on its top.
5. On the piece of paper, write your intention down. Fold the paper and place it inside the pumpkin.
6. Take the candle, tip it, and pour the wax on top of the paper. The wax will seal the opening in the pumpkin too.
7. Repeat your intention before putting out the candle.

8. If you can, take the pumpkin to the nearest river or sweet water source and offer it to Oshun.

If you need to reiterate your intention or require more time to get empowered through Oshun, you can relight the candle and repeat your intent any time you want during the following five days.

Sour Bath to Empower Yourself Mentally

The purpose of this bath is to acknowledge that while negative energies are currently affecting you, positive influences are just waiting for you to invite them. Immersing yourself in this sour bath made from bitter herbs will help you deal with the negativity in and around you and dispel it, all while boosting your mood.

Ingredients:
- A cup
- 7 drops of ammonia
- A few tea light candles
- 1/2 cup of vinegar
- Sunflowers and other yellow, orange, and white flowers
- Fresh or dried bitter herbs, such as dandelion, yarrow, horehound, wormwood, and stinging nettle

Instructions:
1. Start this ritual before sunset by filling up your bathtub with hot water. Adjust the temperature to how you usually like it.
2. Carefully arrange and light the tea light candles around the bathtub's rim. Leave enough room between at least two of the candles. You'll need this space to safely enter and exit the tub.
3. When the water in the tub has reached the desired level, turn off the artificial lights in your bathroom.
4. Toss the rest of the ingredients into the bathwater, then enter the tub between two candles.
5. As you immerse yourself in the water and inhale the bitter scent of the herbs, focus on the different aspects of your life to see if there is hidden negativity in any of them.
6. If you require additional guidance, you can ask Oshun to help you overcome any bitter experiences.

7. Aim to spend a total of seven minutes immersed in the water, so make sure you dip your head into the water from time to time.
8. Once your bathwater starts to cool, exit the tub through the same gap between the same candles you entered through.
9. Scoop some of your bathwater into the cup - along with the ingredients.
10. Drain the tub while you let yourself dry naturally so the beneficial effects of the herbs can soak into your skin.
11. Put on dark clothes, and take the cup with the bathwater outside.
12. Face east, hold the cup over your head, and chant:

   "I have now handed the goddess her due.

   I now ask her to hold onto me.

   With this water, I cast out all the negative energies from my life. Ashé, ashé!"
13. Toss out the water from the cup, return to your home, and reflect on your strengths.
14. Drink lots of room-temperature water after the bath to replenish the fluids you lost while soaking.

You can include this bath in your regular pampering and healthcare practice. Apply Shea butter or other natural moisturizing agents afterward so the herbs can take a better effect. Instead of using electronics right after your bath, spend your time doing mindfulness exercises instead.

Bath for Attracting Positive Energy

Once you've dispelled the negative influences from your life, you'll need to replace them with positive energy. This will help you find the love (starting from self-love), confidence, and strength you need. Take this bath at sunrise to cleanse and revitalize your body. The ingredients, like milk, eggs, and honey, are Oshun's favorite - and they will nourish your body and invigorate your mind anytime you need some pampering.

Ingredients:
- A few tea light candles
- A few drops of honey

- 3 cups of milk
- 1 teaspoon of ground cinnamon
- 1 teaspoon of ground nutmeg
- Flowers with all-white petals, such as roses, lilies, white chrysanthemums, and daisies
- Sunflowers
- Five different fresh or dried herbs with invigorating effects, such as angelica, hyssop, allspice, and comfrey
- Cocoa or Shea butter (optional)
- 1 raw egg
- 1 cup
- Your favorite perfume

Instructions:
1. Shortly before sunrise, fill your bathtub with hot water.
2. Carefully arrange the tea light candles around the tub's rim as instructed in the previous recipe and light them.
3. When the bathtub is full enough, turn off the water and all the other lights in the bathroom.
4. Crack the egg and toss it into the water. It may start to cook a little bit, but this is normal.
5. Throw in the flowers, herbs, and cinnamon, followed by the nutmeg, milk, and honey.
6. Add a few drops of your favorite perfume, and gently stir the water to evenly distribute all the ingredients.
7. Enter the tub through the gap between two candles.
8. When you enter the water, focus on the positive aspects of your life. Consider all the good experiences you had on that day.
9. It's a good idea to express your gratitude to Oshun for all the blessings you've received so far.
10. Aim to spend 7 minutes completely immersed in the water, so make sure you dip your head under the water from time to time.
11. Once the water starts to cool, exit the tub through the same gap you entered through.

12. Scoop some of your bathwater into the cup along with the ingredients.
13. Drain your tub while you let yourself dry naturally instead of using a towel so the effect of the herbs can soak into your skin.
14. Put on light-colored clothes, and take the cup with the bathwater outside.
15. Face east, hold the cup over your head, and recite:

    "I welcome all the positive energies into my life that await me on my path!

    As I toss this water where it's needed the most,

    I ask the goddess Oshun to bless me with health, love, and happiness! Ashé, ashé!"
16. Toss out the water, go back inside, and get ready to welcome the blessings you've invoked.

Like in the previous bath, you can incorporate this bath into your regular beauty and healthcare routine. Aim to meditate, journey, or perform any other form of self-care after bathing and heading out for the day. However, if you don't have time for these, don't worry. Avoiding using electronics and having calm thoughts right after your bath can still help you remain positive throughout the day and attract more positive energy.

Ritual Love Bath

Since Oshun is the patroness of love, she can make your wishes come true regarding matters of the heart. Instead of using a yellow candle, this rite uses a white candle. This ensures that you can see clearly and don't overlook the person intended for you. Using your favorite perfume will attract them to your side.

Ingredients:
- 5 sunflower petals
- 1 large bowl
- 1 white candle
- A few drops of honey
- A statute or symbol of Oshun
- A pinch of ground cinnamon

- Your favorite perfume

Instructions:
1. Place the white candle in front of the representation of the goddess on your altar and light it.
2. Tell Oshun about your desire to attract love into your life. If possible, say it out loud.
3. Place the sunflower petals in a bowl, drizzle them with honey, and sprinkle cinnamon on top. Lastly, add a few spritzes of your favorite perfume.
4. Cover the ingredients with water and let them soak for a few minutes.
5. Take a shower or a bath, and slowly pour the contents of the bowl over your body. Start at your neck and slowly move toward your feet.
6. Close your eyes and repeat your intention once again silently.

The candle should be only lit when you have time to supervise it. You can ignite it any time during the following 5 consecutive days. The bath, on the other hand, should only be repeated once every 2-3 weeks to leave enough time for love to find its way into your life.

Spell to Strengthen Your Love

This spell is perfect for strengthening love and waking up passion in a romantic relationship. The spell should be enacted on Oshun's sacred day, Friday, for the best effects. It's an incredibly popular spell among Santeria practitioners.

Ingredients:
- 5 different types of alcoholic beverages
- 1 coconut
- 1 tablespoon of molasses
- 1 tablespoon of honey
- 1 tablespoon of brown sugar
- 1 tablespoon of white sugar
- 1 yellow candle
- 1 yellow ribbon

Instructions:
1. Break the coconut down the middle, remove half the water, and put that aside.
2. Add a tablespoon of each beverage and the rest of the ingredients, then pour the other half of the water back into the coconut.
3. Close the two halves of the coconut by pressing them together and tying them with the yellow ribbon.
4. Place the coconut in front of the candle on your altar.
5. Light the candle and ask Oshun to help you strengthen the love in your relationship.
6. Repeat the last step for 5 nights, lighting the candle each time. Leave it lit while making your inquiry and saying a quick prayer of gratitude.

Love Potion with Jasmine, Rose, and Cinnamon

By using this love potion, you can improve your relationship and boost your mood. Due to its blood-regulating properties, cinnamon increases passion and lets you enjoy your relationship even more. Jasmine and rose are both associated with sensuality. They also cause euphoria and reduce anxiety which would hinder the development of your relationship.

Ingredients:
- 1 tablespoon of dried rose petals
- 2 tablespoons of dried jasmine flowers
- ¼ teaspoon of vanilla extract
- 1 cup of fresh water
- 2 cinnamon sticks

Instructions:
1. Pour a cup of water into a pot. You can use more for a stronger effect or less for a softer potion.
2. Add the remaining ingredients to the water and stir until well combined.
3. Bring the mixture to a boil and simmer for 2-3 minutes.

4. Remove the mixture from the heat.
5. Let the potion cool, then consume as needed. Drink with a little sparkling water whenever you feel stuck in your relationship or need to stir up passion.
6. You can leave the mixture in the fridge in an airtight container for 5-7 days.

Spell for Enhancing Your Beauty

If you would like to enhance your attractiveness and gain a little more confidence, this spell will be the perfect tool for it. You can use it alongside any ritual you do to communicate with Oshun, including meditation, or even when saying a simple prayer of gratitude for her blessings.

Ingredients:
- 5 yellow candles (or 3 yellow and 2 white ones)
- A few drops of rose essential oil
- 1 piece of yellow tape or thread
- Offerings for the goddess
- Representations of Oshun (status and common symbols such as gold coins, shells, feathers, etc.)
- Sunflower petals, your favorite incense, music, or anything else that can put you in a good mood

Instructions:
1. Prepare all the ingredients and place them in front of you on your altar or sacred place.
2. This is optional, but if you want to, you can take a soothing bath beforehand (you can take one of the baths described above) to ensure your body and mind will be relaxed enough to focus on the spell.
3. Make sure you don't get distracted, and set the room temperature to slightly warm. Feel free to put on sensual clothes or, if you prefer, anything you feel the most comfortable wearing.
4. Get into a comfortable position in front of your sacred space.
5. Place the candles on the edges of the altar and light them. Scatter the sunflower petals and the representation of the

goddess around the candles.

6. Place the symbol of Oshun in front of the offerings you've prepared.
7. Take a few relaxing breaths and start focusing on your intention. Exclude anything else from your mind.
8. Take the piece of yellow thread and start rolling it around the index finger of your dominant hand. While you're doing this, recite the following:

    "I see myself as a vision of beauty as I am now full of confidence.

    I'm filled with love, passion, and warmth, and my face is ever-graceful.

    Everyone will notice how attractive I am now, inside and out.

    And I will soon find someone who appreciates what lies beyond my beauty."

9. Close your eyes and repeat the chant in your head. Keep twisting the thread around your finger until you're ready to open your eyes.
10. Tie the thread to the base of one of the candles but remain in the same position. Visualize your newfound attractiveness and being full of confidence and inner strength.
11. Look into the candlelight, and let it fill you with all the self-confidence, energy, and grace you need to find the happiness you deserve.
12. Focus on this intention as long as possible. When you feel ready, eat and drink from the offerings you've prepared for the goddess. Sharing the meal with her symbolically will prompt her to help you faster.
13. When you're ready to finish, blow out the candles and take the thread with you. You can put it into your pocket or bag or wear it as a reminder of your intention and attractiveness.

Spell to Sweeten Your Relationships

With this simple spell, you can sweeten any relationship in your life. You can make anyone from your partner to your boss more receptive to your needs and become more caring toward you. It uses the sweetness of honey, although you can substitute it with sugar if you're in a hurry to get positive attention.

Ingredients:
- A bottle or a jar you don't mind discarding
- Honey, as needed
- Tap water
- Pen and paper

Instructions:
1. Add water and honey to the bottle and shake it to combine.
2. Using the paper and the pen, write the name of the person you want to sweeten toward you.
3. Place the bottle on the altar until your intention has been realized. After that, you can discard the bottle. Alternatively, you can pour the contents out and use them as sweet incense.

Chapter 8: Spells and Rituals Abundance and Prosperity

Besides love and beauty, Oshun can also help obtain prosperity and abundance in several aspects of life. Whether you wish to grow spiritually, are dealing with fertility issues, or want financial security for yourself and your loved ones, obtaining Oshun's blessings can be the key to a better life. This chapter enlists several spells and rituals designed for abundance, fertility, and even the protection of those who wish for these gifts. With the help of these tools and by building a powerful connection with the goddess, you can make your dreams come true.

Abundance and prosperity come from giving an offering to Oshun.
https://unsplash.com/photos/K0E6E0a0R3A

Prosperity Offering

Oshun is one of the best choices as an Orisha associated with prosperity. While she is often associated with abundance in relationships and spiritual wealth, you can also invoke her regarding any other area of life you want to improve. With the right combination of tools, you can have Oshun grant you material wealth and financial security.

Ingredients:
- 5 oranges
- 1 yellow candle
- 1 white plate
- Cinnamon
- Honey
- A representation of Oshun

Instructions:
1. Place the yellow candle in front of the representation of Oshun on your altar and light it.
2. Recite your intention out loud to make sure Oshun can hear you.
3. Put the oranges on a white plate and drizzle them with honey.
4. Sprinkle some cinnamon on top of the oranges as well.
5. Leave the oranges and the topping in front of the Orisha beside the candle for five days.
6. When the five days are up, you can put away the candle and dispose of the offering too.

The candle shouldn't be left burning continuously for 5 days. Ensure you snuff it out anytime you can't attend to it and light it again when you can supervise it. Also, use fresh oranges to stay safely at room temperature until the ritual is completed.

Offering for Professional Growth

The best time to make this offering to Oshun is when you're seeking a promotion or a new job. However, you can also present this at any other time throughout the year if you require her protection or guidance. Doing it at a riverbank will let Oshun know she is needed much faster.

That said, you can do it through an open window if you don't have a river or other freshwater source nearby.

Ingredients:
- A statue or picture of Oshun
- A coin or money bill
- A piece of yellow cloth
- Oshun incense powder
- Cowrie shells (these are associated with divination, so you can foretell whether you're getting the new job)
- Fruit, veggies, or other offerings of your choice
- A basket

Instructions:
1. Spread the piece of cloth onto your altar and place the representation of Oshun on top of it in the center of the altar.
2. Place the money into a small bowl and pour some incense powder into another one.
3. Light the incense powder and place the shells in the basket.
4. Place all your offerings around the basket as well.
5. Light the candle and say the following prayer to Oshun:

    "I celebrate you, Oshun, the goddess of sweet waters.

    I will praise and serve you as long your waters nourish the Earth.

    Let your waters be calm - so they bring me my job.

    And I'll forever hold you in my heart. Ashé, ashé. "

6. Calm your thoughts by focusing on the flame of the candle. You can also close your eyes and meditate for a couple of minutes if you find it easier to relax your mind this way.
7. Work on manifesting your intention until the incense burns out, then express your gratitude to Oshun for the blessing she may bestow on you.

The Oshun incense powder can be substituted with another of your choice.

Oshun's Ritual for Creativity and Prosperity

You can achieve spiritual prosperity by engaging in new creative activities. If you don't know where to start your creative journey, you can ask Oshun for guidance using this ritual. Besides showing you how to express your creativity, she can also help you release all the burdens hindering you from reaching your full spiritual potential. Like many other rituals for Oshun, performing this near a river is recommended. If you don't have access to one, you can do it at the altar and symbolically send your worries downriver.

Ingredients:
- A piece of yellow or gold cloth to represent Oshun
- A jar of honey
- Spring water in a large container (if you're doing this at an inside altar inside rather than near a water source)
- A piece of sweet fruit (seasonal)
- Seeds you would plant in the spring (preferably pumpkin, sunflower, squash, or any other of Oshun's favorites
- Fresh flowers - yellow, white, and orange
- Pen and paper
- A bell
- A small basket
- Glitter and other craft material

Instructions:
1. Spread the cloth on your altar or the ground if you do this in the open.
2. Write your intention on a piece of paper, fold it, and place it into the basket.
3. While focusing on your intention, start decorating the basket with glitter and other crafting materials.
4. When you've finished, place the fruit and seeds into the basket, sprinkle them with honey and flowers, and place it into the river (or water container).
5. Ring the bell to call on Oshun's attention and say a prayer of gratitude for her blessings.

Fertility Ritual

This traditional Yoruba ritual has been used by young women who want to conceive a child. Apart from this, Oshun may grant you fertility in many other aspects of life, such as art, work, and even cultivating relationships. The colors and seeds of the pumpkin symbolize the power of nature's fertility.

Ingredients:
- 1 melon
- 1 yellow candle
- Paper and pen
- A representation of the goddess

Instructions:
1. Place the yellow candle in front of the representation of Oshun on your altar and light it.
2. Close your eyes and focus on manifesting your wishes. Saying them out loud often helps.
3. Open your eyes, take the pen, and write your wishes down on the paper.
4. Place the piece of paper on top of the melon. Then, hold it on your stomach (if you want to conceive), in front of your heart (if you want fertility in your relationships, or on your head (for productivity in work, hobbies, or art).
5. Repeat your wishes and ask the goddess to help you realize them.
6. When you feel your wishes have been heard, take the melon to the nearest water source and offer it to Oshun. Alternatively, you can bury it in your garden or eat it within a day or two.

You may leave the candle burning briefly after the ritual is completed. Still, if you are likely to leave it unattended, it's best to snuff it out. You can relight the candle any time you wish during the next five days.

5-Day Candle Ritual for Oshun

Calling on Oshun can be helpful when you need to eliminate bad luck from your life and replace it with good fortune. A large yellow candle will ensure you acquire the abundance you desire. The addition of the yellow food will appease Oshun, so she lends you the ashe you need to obtain your goals.

Using a large, yellow candle brings abundance.
https://unsplash.com/photos/66qsl7ia2cE

Ingredients:

- A piece of yellow cotton yarn or thread
- Yellow and white flowers - fresh or dry
- Sweet potatoes
- Coconut shavings
- Honey
- Pumpkin seeds
- A large yellow candle
- A representation of Oshun

Instructions:

1. Organize your altar or sacred space by clearing up anything you won't need for this ritual.
2. Place the yellow candle and the symbol representing Oshun in the middle of your altar.
3. Prepare the sweet potatoes, pumpkin seeds, coconut shavings, and honey in separate bowls and place those on the altar.
4. If you're using chopped dry flowers, sprinkle them around the candle and tie the yellow yarn or thread around the bottom of the candle.

5. If you're using fresh or whole dried flowers, tie them in a bunch with the yarn or thread.
6. When you are ready, light the candle, close your eyes and prepare to call on Oshun.

   Then, recite the following chant:

   "Oh, powerful Oshun, please lend me your strength,

   Send me luck and fortune.

   May I be strong and wise,

   So, I can obtain prosperity.

   Help me stay loving and caring,

   And keep treating others with the same integrity."

Traditionally, the candle was intended to be left burning 5 days and nights after saying the prayer. However, this is generally not recommended due to safety concerns. Not to mention that, like many other spells, this one works only as long as you maintain a fierce focus on your intention. No matter how eager you are to obtain prosperity, you'll only be able to concentrate on this for a short period of time. Because of this, it's better to burn the candle for several minutes over 5 days. Whenever you have time during the day, light the candle, and recite the spell. When you've finished, snuff it out and go about your day. When you can, relight it once again until it burns out. The food is supposed to be served raw, but Oshun will also accept your offering if you prepare a dish from the above-mentioned food sources - especially if you eat alongside her.

Ritual for Fertility and Protection

This ritual can serve as both a tool for resolving fertility issues and protecting expectant mothers and their families. It uses Oshun's ultimate fertility symbol, the pumpkin, along with plenty of her other associations. They can help you ward off the negative influences causing fertility issues or threatening the safety of a pregnant mother, their baby, and their family. This ritual can be performed by pregnant women, their female family members, friends, or even the unborn child's father. You can combine this rite with other purification or protection rituals, including cleansing baths and self-care routines.

Ingredients:
- 1 medium-sized pumpkin
- 1 white plate
- A handful of patchouli roots
- Sunflowers and other yellow flowers (Life Everlasting is particularly recommended for this purpose)
- Honey, as needed
- Orange essential oil, as needed
- 1 yellow candle
- A few drops of your favorite lotion or soap
- A statue or picture of the goddess, Orisha, or saint (depending on how you wish to celebrate her)
- A bell
- A beaded necklace or bracelet in Oshun's colors
- 5 gold coins (regular coins work too if you can't find gold ones)
- Yellow and gold glitter to represent the goddess, as these are her favorites
- Silver and white glitter for stability
- Blue glitter for harmony
- Red glitter for passion and success for the mother and the child
- 1 Glass of water (river or tap water)
- 1 Glass of white wine or champagne (optional)

Instructions:
1. Place the white plate in the middle of your altar, right in front of the representation of Oshun.
2. Sprinkle some dried patchouli and flower petals on the plate, and place your pumpkin on top. If you wish (and if you're the one who is expecting or wanting to conceive), you can hold the pumpkin in front of your heart or stomach and quickly say your intention before placing the pumpkin on the plate.
3. Place the yellow candle on the right of the plate, and light it. You can anoint it beforehand with orange essential oil.
4. Put the cup of water or wine on the left side of the plate, next to the bell.

5. Pour some lotion, orange essential oil, and honey on the top of the pumpkin. Use your hands to cover the entire pumpkin generously with these wonderful liquids. While you do, say your intention, and ask for Oshun's blessings.
6. Use the bell to get Oshun's attention before moving on to the next step.
7. Once you've got her attention, you can retain it by sprinkling the glitters on the top of the pumpkin.
8. After anointing it with the liquids, place the necklace or bracelet on top of the pumpkin.
9. Place the 5 coins on the plate around the pumpkin. If your pumpkin is large and you don't have much space around it, you can place the coins on top of it, around its stem.
10. Raise your glass in the name of Oshun as you recite a prayer of gratitude for the blessings you're about to receive.

Suppose you're working in a closed space. In that case, you can leave everything on the altar (after snuffing out the candle, of course) for 1-2 days, depending on the room's temperature. After that, remove the plate with the pumpkin, but you can leave the rest. Gently wash the bracelet and place it on the representation of Oshun. Say a prayer to it every day while you wait for the blessings.

Oshun Protection and Luck Spell

If you feel down on your luck, this spell can manifest Oshun's blessings. They can come in the form of good luck, an abundance of fortune, or simply having better experiences in life. The spell will also provide you with the protection you need from those who will envy your success once luck returns to your side. You can combine it with other prosperity rituals and prayers.

Ingredients:
- 1 yellow candle
- Your favorite incense
- Honey, as needed
- A piece of parchment paper
- Money (paper bill)

- Natural soap (with honey, sugar, honeysuckle, or other sweet natural ingredients)
- A few drops of magnet oil (optional, you can use a magnet instead) to attract fortune
- 1 black crystal (for example, jet) for luck, protection, and money
- A skipping river rock (or another representation of a river)
- A picture or statute of Oshun
- 1 small red candle for making the intention into reality as soon as possible
- 1 small gold candle for success
- 1 small yellow candle to help communicate your wishes
- 1 bell
- A pinch of dried chrysanthemum, marigold, and rose petals to keep things going once you've got your luck
- Bee pollen, as needed

Instructions:

1. Start by writing your request on parchment paper and join the paper with the money bill.
2. In your hands, mix a few drops of soap and magnet oil. Gently cover the paper and the money with the mixture.
3. Place the paper and the money on the altar, and put the river rock and black crystal on top of it or next to it, depending on how the rocks are shaped. If they're too large and round, you can place them next to the paper to prevent them from rolling off.
4. Tell Oshun what you wish for and say a prayer of gratitude. You can use the bell to get her attention.
5. Place the large yellow candle next to the paper and money and light it.
6. Sprinkle some chrysanthemums, marigolds, and roses around the candle and put a little aside for a bath.
7. Sprinkle a little bee pollen around the candle. Alternatively, you can also anoint the candle with honey.

8. Prepare your bathwater with honey, bee pollen, herbs, and natural soap. While preparing your bath, write an intention for each small candle.

9. After taking your bath, return to your altar and light the smaller candles while making your intention known for one final time.

10. Take the skipping rock or other representation of a river to your nearest water source, along with some honey, and say a prayer of gratitude for the blessing you'll receive. Keep the black stone with you as a talisman or reminder of your intention.

If needed, you can recite your intention several times. You don't need to take the cleansing bath every time, but you can call Oshun with the bell to remind her of your wishes. Alternatively, you can use 3 small candles of the same color if you have a specific request to reinforce. For safety reasons, snuff out the large candle while you're taking a bath, and relight it along with smaller ones once you've returned to the altar.

Chapter 9: Holy Days and Festivals

The celebrations of Oshun, known as Holy Days and Festivals, are an essential aspect of honoring the Goddess. However, many devotees may be uncertain about what these celebrations entail, when to observe them, and how to properly honor Oshun during these events. Therefore, educating oneself on Oshun's traditional ceremonies, rituals, and practices is crucial. By gaining knowledge of the origins and cultural background of each Festival, practitioners can deepen their understanding of Oshun's power and her role in everyday life. Continue reading to learn more about the Festivals related to Oshun and the best ways to celebrate them with respect and reverence for the Goddess.

Festivals allow people to celebrate and praise Oshun.
Image by Sylwia Głowska from Pixabay https://pixabay.com/photos/africa-the-festival-man-piece-3644226/

Osun-Osogbo Festival

The Osun-Osogbo Festival is a highly popular and significant traditional festival celebrated in Osogbo, the capital of Osun State, Nigeria. It has been held annually for centuries by the people of Osun State. The festival is dedicated to the goddess Osun, who is believed by the people of this area to be responsible for fertility and prosperity.

The celebration begins around August 1 to 29th each year and features a variety of events such as parades, music and dance performances, masquerading rituals, and spiritual invocations. The highlight of the festival is when devotees visit the riverbank shrine of Osoogun, located along the River Osun, to make sacrifices to their ancestors and seek blessings from the River Goddess.

Oshun is an Orisha, or goddess associated with love, fertility, beauty, gold, abundance, and diplomacy. This Yoruba deity is revered in many religions as a bringer of peace and prosperity to her devotees. During the Osun-Osogbo Festival, people gather to honor Oshun through celebration and prayer.

In Nigeria, one of the largest celebrations occurs in Osogbo city, where thousands of people come together to participate in processions often accompanied by music. People decorate their homes with colorful fabrics, ornaments, and banners to mark the occasion. During the processions, people pray and make offerings in honor of Oshun.

In Ghana, the festival is commonly known as Osun Festival. It is celebrated in the same way as it is in Nigeria, but with a greater emphasis on traditional activities such as drumming, dancing, and storytelling. These activities are believed to unite the community and are an important part of the celebration. The festival is also a time for families to come together and give thanks for the blessings that Oshun has bestowed upon them.

In Benin, the festival is known as the Igue Festival. It is celebrated similarly to Nigeria, focusing on traditional activities such as dancing and drumming. The festival is also a time for the community to come together and give thanks to Oshun for her blessings.

In Latin America, the festival is celebrated in honor of Yemaya – the equivalent of Oshun in the Yoruba religion. The celebrations tend to focus more on water rituals such as bathing in rivers or seas to cleanse oneself of any spiritual impurities. This is believed to bring balance and harmony to the individual and their community and is seen as an important aspect of the celebration.

Overall, the Igue Festival is an important celebration deeply rooted in the history and culture of Benin and celebrated in other African countries and Latin America. It is a time for the community to come together and give thanks.

The festival culminates on August 31st with the traditional Osun-Osogbo procession. This procession is an important ritual in which worshippers walk from the sacred grove of Osoogun to Osogbo town, carrying a statue of their goddess and singing her praises. In the evening, a grand finale is held at the palace of the Ataoja (king), where all those who participated in the procession are honored.

The best way to celebrate an Oshun Festival at home is by creating a sacred space dedicated to honoring her. This could include setting up an altar and decorating it with offerings like fruits or coins. Other activities include singing traditional songs in her honor and performing special dances or rituals that celebrate her divine presence. You can also get creative and make your own festivities by organizing a potluck dinner or gathering of friends where you can share stories about Oshun and exchange tokens of appreciation for her blessings.

No matter where you are in the world, the Osun-Osogbo Festival is a great reminder to appreciate the beauty and power of nature. By celebrating this festival, people honor their ancestors and their shared humanity.

Oshun River Festival

The Oshun River Festival is a vibrant celebration of the Yoruba goddess Oshun, held annually in Osogbo, Nigeria. The festival, which typically takes place over three days in September, is a time for devotees to pay homage to Oshun through traditional worship practices, music, and dance performances.

At the heart of the festival is the main event, which takes place at a shrine located near the banks of the Osun River, dedicated to Oshun. Here, devotees gather to offer prayers, make offerings of food, flowers, and other items, and participate in rituals for blessings from the goddess. After these ceremonies, the festivities begin with lively drumming and dancing around bonfires, celebrating Oshun's presence.

The festival's second day is dedicated to traditional worship practices, including ceremonies for cleansing the body and spirit. These activities occur in shrines and sacred spaces throughout Osogbo, such as Olumo Rock and Opa Oranmiyan Shrine. Parades also feature colorful floats, musicians playing traditional African instruments, and people dressed in vibrant ceremonial costumes singing and dancing in praise of Oshun.

On the final day of celebrations, processions lead people through different parts of the town to visit sites associated with Oshun's history before returning to the main shrine to present offerings and give thanks to the goddess. The festivities continue late into the night, with food being shared among families and friends as they exchange stories about past festivals.

The Oshun River Festival is a time of joyous celebration, recognizing the connection between humanity and divinity. It provides an opportunity for participants to express gratitude and connect with their goddess through devotional acts in her honor.

Igue Festival

The Igue Festival is an annual five-day celebration occurring in Uselu, Benin City, Nigeria, from October 28th to November 2nd. It is a time of great joy and celebration for worshippers of the Yoruba goddess Oshun as they gather to honor and pay homage to her. The festival is deeply rooted in the history and culture of Benin and has been celebrated for centuries.

On the festival's first day, participants gather at the shrine of Oshun to decorate it with flowers and white cloths, make offerings of thanksgiving, and petition for blessings. Traditional music and dancing then begin as people give thanks and praise to Oshun. Throughout the five days of celebrations, there are parties, parades, performances by dancers and masqueraders, feasts of delicious foods, singing competitions between groups or villages, traditional ceremonies such as blessing children with water from Oshun's sacred river Obo Osebo, storytelling sessions by elders sharing ancient stories about Oshun's power over life on earth, and cultural art displays including weaving baskets with natural dyes.

At night during the festival, special rituals are held under the moonlight to bring about luck for individuals or families who have made offerings to Oshun. These rituals can include pouring specially prepared water over pieces of cloth laid out around shrines, representing different types of fortune or wishes that may be granted by Oshun, such as health or prosperity.

For those unable to attend the Igue Festival in Uselu, there are still ways to participate in the celebration from home. One popular method is dedicating a day or two to prayer, specifically honoring Oshun and her power over life on Earth. One could also incorporate herbs associated with Oshun, such as rosemary or basil, into meals while offering silent prayers of thanksgiving for all that Oshun has done in their lives. This allows for a personal and spiritual connection to the festival, even if physically absent from the celebrations.

The Igue Festival is integral to Benin City culture, passed down through generations since ancient times. It provides a unique opportunity to connect with history and celebrate one's faith in a vibrant atmosphere. Each year in October and November, thousands gather in Uselu, regardless of religious differences, to honor Oshun.

During the festival, devotees participate in various rituals and ceremonies steeped in tradition and symbolism. They make offerings to Oshun, such as fruits, sweets, and flowers, to show their gratitude for her blessings. They also participate in traditional dances and drumming to invoke the goddess' presence and connect with her energy. Many people also visit the various shrines and sacred sites in the area dedicated to Oshun, where they can give thanks and seek her guidance. Overall, the Igue Festival serves as an important reminder of Oshun's enduring power and the Yoruba people's deep cultural roots.

Oshala Festival

The Oshala Festival is an annual celebration occurring in December, honoring the Yoruba river goddess Oshun. It is a time of prayer and thanksgiving, where devotees offer sacrifices and offerings to Oshun to obtain healing and protection. The festival is celebrated at various locations throughout Nigeria, typically near rivers or other sources of water. The dates of the festival vary each year based on the lunar cycle but generally fall within a two-week period leading up to December 31st. In some areas, celebrations may last up to three weeks, beginning on the full moon closest to December 21st.

It is particularly renowned in riverside communities such as Osogbo, Ijebu-Ode, and Ilesa. During the festival, participants make offerings of fruits, grains, and other ceremonial items at shrines near water sources to ensure that Oshun's blessings reach them in abundance. They also offer prayers for healing from physical and emotional distress and protection from danger and hardship.

In addition to these traditional practices, modern-day devotees can celebrate the Oshala Festival by participating in activities such as drumming circles and dancing around sacred fires lit in honor of Oshun's spirit. Special songs are sung in her praise, and delicate gifts are presented at her shrine as tokens of respect and appreciation for all that she has done for them.

For those who cannot attend the local festivities, it is still possible to honor Oshun's spirit at home by adorning living spaces with yellow cloths (representative of Oshun's color) or making small offerings at an altar dedicated specifically to her divinity. Candles and incense can also be lit, symbolizing the connection between humanity and nature to ensure that blessings reach those who are far away from any celebration site.

The Oshala Festival is a time-honored tradition celebrated in Nigeria for centuries. It is an annual two-week celebration, usually leading up to New Year's Eve, during which devotees of the Yoruba river goddess Oshun come together to express their gratitude and honor her divine grace. This festival is deeply rooted in the cultural and spiritual heritage of the Yoruba people. It is a celebration not just of the goddess but also of the devotion and dedication of those who have honored her for generations. The festival is marked by elaborate ceremonies, traditional music and dancing, offerings, and feasts, all in honor of Oshun and her powerful presence in the lives of her followers.

Elegba Festival

Elegba Festival is an annual celebration that honors the powerful Orisha Elegba and the Yoruba deity Oshun in Nigeria. Held every February at the Ile-Ife Palace in Osun state, the festival is a time for offering prayers and offerings to Oshun, the goddess associated with love, fertility, beauty, wealth, and prosperity. The festival includes offerings of food, drink, flowers, and other items to Oshun, as well as traditional Yoruba music and dance performances.

The festival typically takes place in February, with the dates varying from year to year. The event begins with a procession carrying offerings to Orisha Elegba, followed by a series of rituals and ceremonies honoring Oshun. Traditional music and dance performances pay homage to both Orisha Elegba and Oshun during this time.

At the Ile-Ife Palace, people gather to celebrate and offer their prayers and offerings to Oshun in an atmosphere of joyous singing, dancing, and feasting. Local markets are also present, where people can buy gifts for friends or loved ones or simply participate in the vibrant atmosphere permeating the palace grounds during the festival.

The celebrations don't end at the Ile-Ife Palace, as many communities across Nigeria have their own celebrations that honor Orisha Elegba, featuring colorful parades with dancers costumed as animals and wearing elaborate masks depicting different gods or goddesses such as Oshun. Traditional drumming and acrobatics also add an extra layer of enjoyment to these festivities.

Those who cannot attend the festival in person can still participate by offering prayers or burning incense to honor Orisha Elegba and Oshun before images representing them both. Special meals or drinks can also be prepared in their honor, allowing you to be a part of this sacred annual tradition even from a distance.

Ultimately, Elegba Festival provides an opportunity for people to come together in celebration while also honoring one of the most important deities in Yoruba culture, Oshun. The festival brings people together spiritually, and whether they are participating in large parades or intimate home gatherings, it is sure to bring people closer together no matter where they are

Holy days

Osunseya or Ironmole Day

Osunseya, or Ironmole Day, is an annual celebration honoring the Yoruba goddess of love and fertility, Oshun. Held on the last Saturday of August, devotees celebrate the festival both in Nigeria and other parts of West Africa. The day is dedicated to Oshun's power to bring people abundance, prosperity, and fertility. It is a time for reflection on the goddess's message of love and harmony.

The celebrations usually occur in riverside villages, where devotees gather by candlelight around a shrine devoted to Oshun. They offer prayers and sacrifices, such as honey, eggs, fruits, jewelry, and animals. Many wear yellow clothing, said to please Oshun more than any other color. Traditional dances and cultural activities are also a part of the festivities.

At sunset, small boats filled with candles are lit and released into the water to symbolize hope for good fortune in the coming year. Afterward, a bonfire is lit, which is said to connect humanity directly with divinity through its flames. Families enjoy a feast as a thanksgiving offering to their protective deity.

Osunseya, or Ironmole Day, is an important annual celebration among followers of Yoruba mythology and an opportunity to renew their commitment to living better lives rooted in spirituality, kindness, love, and respect towards nature. The festival is a time for coming together to honor Oshun and a reminder of the timeless messages of love and harmony that the goddess represents.

Fridays

Every Friday, the Yoruba religion of Nigeria celebrates Oshun, a beloved deity known for her vibrant energy, creativity, and kindness. Devotees pay homage to the goddess through rituals that involve offerings of food, drink, and other gifts, dressed in yellow and white clothes to represent the sun and purity.

The celebration begins with prayer and singing at sacred sites or shrines dedicated to Oshun. Offerings of fruits, eggs, cornmeal, milk, honey, and sugar are presented to the goddess as a way of expressing gratitude and asking for blessings. After invoking the goddess's presence, devotees proceed to dance around bonfires while holding on to a white cloth, symbolizing their faith in Oshun.

For those who cannot attend the physical celebrations, it is still possible to honor Oshun at home by setting up an altar dedicated to the goddess. This can include items such as flowers, yellow candles, and river stones as offerings, along with foods associated with Oshun, such as honey cakes, mangoes, or millet porridge.

The celebration is also an opportunity for reflection and introspection, not only on one's personal life but also on the interconnectedness of all things. By embracing these beliefs and values, followers can create a harmonious space within their homes and ultimately lead themselves toward freedom from suffering and experience true bliss.

Oshun's Birthday

Oshun's Birthday is a revered and highly-anticipated annual celebration in the Yoruba religion, marking the birthday of Oshun, the goddess of love, pleasure, and fertility. This sacred day is celebrated on the 5th of April. It is steeped in tradition and historical significance, having been observed for thousands of years.

Devotees honor Oshun on her special day by performing rituals and ceremonies that involve making offerings and giving thanks for her blessings. These offerings may include flowers, sweet treats, or even animal sacrifices to express gratitude for the goddess's divine gifts and seek her protection and guidance.

In addition to traditional rituals, many followers also celebrate Oshun's Birthday in the comfort of their own homes with their loved ones. This may include hosting small gatherings where they give thanks to the goddess, enjoying sweet treats and traditional foods prepared in her honor, and dressing up in traditional clothing or adorning themselves with jewelry associated with Oshun.

It is believed that those who properly observe Oshun's Birthday will be blessed with good health, prosperity, love, joy, and harmony in life. Therefore, this special day is an essential opportunity to connect with the goddess and bring spiritual balance to one's life. Whether through traditional rituals or personal celebrations, honoring Oshun on her birthday is a powerful and meaningful way to show devotion and seek blessings.

Chapter 10: Daily Rituals to Honor Oshun

Honoring the Yoruba goddess Oshun is a wonderful way to show appreciation for her blessings. To make this daily ritual meaningful, connecting with Oshun through simple acts of kindness and generosity can be rewarding. While she is the African goddess of love, beauty, and sensuality, Oshun is also associated with fertility, abundance, and fresh water. How can one honor her in a meaningful way? This chapter will explore some creative daily rituals. From cleansing baths to affirmations of love, these rituals can promote healing and renewal. By committing to a regular practice, you are honoring her and inviting more of the supportive energy of this benevolent deity into your life.

Daily Rituals

1. Offerings

Honoring Oshun through daily offerings is important to building a relationship with the goddess and receiving her favor. These offerings are a way to show your gratitude and appreciation for all that she has done for those who love her and to ask for her blessings and guidance in your daily life.

Traditional offerings to Oshun include honey, yellow flowers, and yellow cornmeal, which are believed to have special significance for the goddess. Honey symbolizes sweetness and prosperity and is often associated with the goddess's ability to bring abundance to life. Yellow flowers, such as marigolds and sunflowers, are believed to represent joy and sunshine and are often used to invoke the goddess's blessings of happiness and positivity. Yellow cornmeal is a staple food in many African countries, is believed to represent nourishment and sustenance, and is often used to ask the goddess for her blessings of health and well-being.

Cooked rice sweetened with honey or sugar is also a common offering. Fruits such as apples, oranges, mangoes, and coconuts can also be offered, each representing different qualities associated with the goddess. For example, oranges are believed to represent joy and fertility, while coconuts are believed to represent nourishment and protection.

Yellow and gold flowers are popular choices for offerings to Oshun, as they correspond with the goddess's color associations. Still, any type of flower can be used depending on the intent of the offering. For example, tulips are believed to symbolize prosperity, while roses symbolize love and gratitude. Incense, such as cinnamon and jasmine, are also great ways to honor Oshun, as they have deep spiritual connections to her energy. They can be used to create a calming and meditative atmosphere and to invoke the goddess's presence.

Finally, simple offerings such as a glass of water or honey can also be made to show respect and ask for her blessings and guidance. These offerings can be placed on an altar dedicated to Oshun and can be accompanied by prayers or chants. By making daily offerings to Oshun, devotees can deepen their connection to the goddess and receive her blessings in their lives.

2. Meditation

Self-reflection and meditation are important aspects of honoring the goddess, Oshun. By clearing your mind and focusing on connecting with divine energy, you can deepen your connection to the goddess and receive her blessings.

When meditating in honor of Oshun, focus on visualizing her golden light within you and surrounding you, bringing balance and harmony into your life. Oshun is a powerful African goddess of love, beauty, and fertility; meditating in her honor can be a transformative experience.

To set up your daily meditation for Oshun, find a peaceful location near the water or create an artificial body of water by filling a shallow bowl with fresh spring water. Place the bowl before you and light white candles on either side. You can set up a small altar for Oshun in the area where you meditate. Place items representing her, such as gold jewelry, coins, flowers, or food offerings, such as oranges and honey. If you can burn incense, use scents like jasmine and orange blossom, which are associated with Oshun's energy.

Sit comfortably on a chair with your back straight, feet flat on the ground, hands resting palms-up on your knees, and eyes closed. Take several deep breaths as you relax into the moment. Visualize yourself opening up to receive unconditional love from the goddess Oshun. Imagine her light radiating from her heart and entering yours, opening it up even further. Notice how her light brings warmth into your body. As you continue to breathe deeply, consider any areas in your life where you feel limited or restricted. Affirm aloud that these areas are now open for transformation and growth through the power and grace of Oshun as you continue to breathe deeply in this sacred space dedicated to her energy.

When you are ready, focus on your breath and repeat mantras in honor of Oshun, such as "may I be connected to the source" or "may I have abundance in my life." Chant whatever resonates most deeply within you, such as "Oshun protect me" or "all power belongs to Oshun."

As your meditation continues, take time to visualize the blessings you want from Oshun. It could be guidance or inner peace in times of difficulty or creativity when feeling blocked. Whatever form these blessings may come in, commit them wholeheartedly to Oshun in the hope that she will hear them. After visualizing these blessings for several minutes, open your eyes and end your meditation practice with a prayer of thanksgiving for her presence in your life. Offer gratitude for all that Oshun has brought into your life so far, such as love, beauty, and fertility. Thank her for existing and being a source of nurturing energy in the universe. Express gratitude for the opportunity to receive her gifts daily if you accept them with open arms while remaining aware of personal boundaries. Allow yourself a few more moments before gently returning to physical reality, taking all the healing energy she has blessed you with today.

Once finished with your meditation practice, spend some time expressing gratitude towards Oshun for listening to your prayers and dedicating this special time to her spirit each day. Thank her for all the love, protection, and guidance that she offers to you and everyone around the world who calls upon her.

Meditating near water while honoring Oshun through mantras and prayers is a powerful way to tap into her divine energy and gain insight into your life. Oshun, the African goddess of love, beauty, and fertility, offers a wealth of knowledge, abundance, and protection to those who honor her. This daily practice helps you connect to the divine feminine energy flow and allows you to honor those who have come before you throughout history. By meditating in her honor each day, you can deepen your connection with Oshun and receive her blessings in your life.

3. Music and Dance

Music and dance are powerful ways to honor the Yoruba goddess Oshun. Oshun is a goddess of love, beauty, and fertility; music and dance are powerful expressions of these qualities. The Yoruba people have long used music and dance as a way to honor their gods, including Oshun. Traditional Yoruba songs dedicated to Oshun often include prayers of gratitude or requests for blessings and are accompanied by rhythms created with drums and other percussion instruments. The dances performed for Oshun use symbolic movements to express admiration and respect for her. One such dance, "Oshoaluwo," involves stamping feet on the ground in patterns representing the goddess's power and influence over nature.

Another traditional dance that honors Oshun is the "Ebora" dance. It is a celebratory dance performed in honor of the goddess and her powers of fertility. It is usually performed by women and involves sensual, fluid movements meant to emulate the flow of water, which is closely associated with Oshun.

The "Osun Osogbo" dance is another traditional dance performed in honor of the goddess Oshun. This dance is performed during the annual Osun Osogbo Festival in Nigeria, dedicated to the goddess. The dancers wear brightly colored clothes and headdresses adorned with beads and other ornaments. They carry staffs and swords as they perform the dance. The dance combines rhythmic movements and choreography to represent the goddess's power and influence over the natural world.

In addition to these traditional dances, there are also modern interpretations of Oshun-inspired dance. For example, the "Brown Skin Girl" music video by Beyoncé, which was shot on location in Nigeria and featured traditional African clothing and cultural elements, has been seen as a modern interpretation of an Oshun-inspired dance. The video's use of movement, costuming, and imagery has been interpreted as a way of expressing admiration and respect for the goddess and her influence on women of color.

Music and dance are integral parts of Yoruba culture – and powerful ways to honor the goddess, Oshun. They serve as a means of expressing gratitude and admiration for the goddess while also connecting with her energy and power physically and spiritually.

4. Prayers and Blessings

Prayer is a meaningful way to honor the goddess Oshun and connect with her powerful energy. It can bring balance, peace, and joy into your life. To make the most of your prayers, try to recite them at sunrise or sunset, when the day and night transition, as it is a special time to thank all the gods, including Oshun, for their blessings, guidance, protection, and love. You can recite traditional prayers such as "Omi Tutu," meaning "Mother River," as one of Oshun's domains is rivers. Alternatively, you can create your own prayers from the heart, whatever feels most authentic. It is important to focus on the intention of your prayer and speak from the heart to connect with Oshun's energy.

Honoring the goddess Oshun through prayer is an important aspect of spiritual practice. Here are a few suggestions for incorporating daily prayers and blessings into your routine:

Start each day with a prayer of gratitude to Oshun. Thank her for her guidance and blessings, and take a moment to appreciate and be grateful for all the positive things in your life. Expressing gratitude helps you to stay positive and open to receiving more blessings.

Before setting out for the day, offer a morning blessing to Oshun, asking for her protection and guidance throughout the day and for success in all your endeavors. This is also a great opportunity to set an intention or goal for the day.

At the end of each day, take some time to reflect on what has transpired during the day and offer an evening blessing to Oshun. You can use this moment to thank her for her guidance and protection and ask for her protection while you sleep.

Expressing creativity is another way to honor Oshun, as it involves opening yourself up emotionally, spiritually, and physically. When you feel inspired, create something unique, such as a painting, dance, or song, in honor of her presence in your life.

Lighting candles is an ancient practice used as a symbol of hope, faith, and guidance across many cultures, including the Yoruba people, who revere Oshun as one of their main deities. Sit quietly before lighting a candle dedicated solely to Oshun. Take a moment to breathe deeply and concentrate on her energy, letting go of any worries or troubles from the day. This can help to balance your emotions and bring inner peace and positive energy back into your life.

5. Spiritual Baths

A spiritual bath is a powerful and meaningful way to honor Oshun, the revered Orisha of beauty, love, and fertility. In the Yoruba tradition, taking a special bath with herbs and other natural ingredients is believed to purify the body and soul, honor Oshun, and attract her protection, blessings, and love into your life.

To truly connect with Oshun through a spiritual bath, it is important to engage all five senses: sight, smell, taste, touch, and sound. Start by setting an intention or prayer that acknowledges why you are connecting with her. Gather natural ingredients that have a symbolic meaning connected with Oshun, such as honey or cornmeal, which are known as "Sacred Waters" in Yoruba culture. Additionally, use herbs that correspond with Oshun, such as rose petals or lavender buds, to bring forth her soothing energy when ceremonially added to your water basin or tub.

If possible, take your spiritual bath near bodies of water, such as rivers, as water is closely tied to divinity in traditional African religions like Yoruba. Being in nature while taking your bath enhances the power of the cleansing ritual. Light candles around your bathroom basin or tub before beginning your ritual if this isn't possible. Singing is also a powerful addition; traditional Yoruba songs called Oriki that praise the Orishas can be used.

During the bath, focus on visualization and imagine yourself being surrounded by golden light, the color associated with Oshun, as it cleanses away any negative energy from your body and spirit. Once the bath is complete, reflect and allow the positive effects to sink deeply into your soul. As an offering, leave out a small token such as flowers or food outside near where you took a bath, giving back energy to nature.

6. Creativity

Honoring the Yoruba goddess Oshun through daily rituals and practices can bring peace, joy, and abundance into our lives. One powerful way to connect with Oshun is through prayer or meditation, where we offer gratitude and appreciation for her blessings and guidance.

Another way to honor Oshun is through creative expressions, such as painting, drawing, sculpting, or writing. Creating something to offer to Oshun can help focus your energy and provide a tangible representation of her presence in your life. Incorporating colors and symbols associated with Oshun, such as yellow, gold, orange, and symbols of water or rivers can further strengthen the connection with her energy.

Poetry is another way to honor Oshun daily. Writing about her attributes in poetic form can help bring her power into your own words and thoughts while focusing on specific areas that she governs, such as love or abundance, which can add even more meaning to your devotions.

Crafting candles, particularly yellow beeswax candles, can also be a powerful way to connect with Oshun. These candles can be used during prayer and meditation in her name and can also serve as an offering when accompanied by seeking blessings. Performance art, such as traditional African drumming, dancing, and singing, can also be used to honor Oshun, as it can elicit powerful responses from both the audience and the deity.

7. Practicing Self Love

Honoring Oshun, the Yoruba goddess of love, beauty, fertility, and abundance, can be done through daily practices which promote self-love and care. Here are some suggestions for how to honor Oshun in your daily life:

Speak kindly to yourself – As a goddess of love and compassion, Oshun wants you to treat yourself kindly. Speak words of encouragement and positivity to yourself each day to honor Oshun's nurturing nature. This will help you to cultivate greater self-esteem and confidence in yourself.

Take time for self-care – Taking time for yourself is a great way to honor Oshun and her divine femininity. Spend some time each day doing something pleasurable, such as reading a book or taking a warm bath. Doing something nice for yourself will help you feel better mentally and physically, allowing you to replenish your energy reserves so that you can be your best self for others throughout the day.

Avoid negative influences– Negative influences such as gossiping or judgmental people do not honor the spirit of Oshun's loving nature, so it is important to avoid them as much as possible to keep your energy positive. If you find yourself in situations where other people are being unkind or negative, take some deep breaths to ground yourself before you walk away from the situation to remain centered amidst any chaos around you.

Exercise mindfully – Practicing yoga, or another form of mindful movement, helps you to become aware of your body in space and helps you move past physical limitations you may have set upon yourself without even knowing it. Moving your body mindfully helps bring greater awareness into your life, which honors Oshun's devotion to beauty and artistry through movement.

Practice gratitude – Taking time daily to practice gratitude shifts your perspective from lack to abundance, which honors Oshun's symbolism for plenty. Keep a journal where you write down three things from your day that you are grateful for every night before bed.

Give back – One way to honor Oshun, the Yoruba goddess of love, beauty, fertility, and abundance, is through acts of generosity and giving back to others. By volunteering your time or resources to support a local non-profit organization or cause that aligns with your values, you can acknowledge and appreciate the abundance in your life and contribute to creating a more equitable and just world for all. This act of service not only honors Oshun's principles of compassion and generosity but also demonstrates your commitment to being a responsible steward of the blessings and resources you have been given.

Extra: Glossary of Terms

If you're new to African Traditional Religions, you've likely encountered several unfamiliar terms in this book. Use this glossary as your go-to guide if you need help understanding or remembering what any of the following terms mean.

Ajogun

The Ajogun is the personified form of evil forces. This personification manifests itself as 601 warriors who pursue warfare and battles to destroy humanity. There are 8 leaders of Ajogun: Ikú, the governor of death, Egbà, the embodiment of paralysis; Òfò, the manifestation of loss; Èṣe, the essence of affliction; Ewon, the embodiment of imprisonment, Àrùn, the symbol of disease, Oràn, the personified form of problems, and Èpè the symbol of curses.

Learn more about Ajogun in chapter 1.

Ashe

Ashe is a term that can reference three very important concepts in the Yoruba tradition. For one, it is used as an affirmation following a prayer. It is considered the equivalent of "Amen," and translates to "yes!" or "that's right!" Many natives even use it in informal contexts during their everyday lives. If you say something or share an idea with someone and they shout "Ashe," know that you said something they really like or agree with. This word is considered very affirming and expressive.

This word can also be used to refer to life energy or force. If you're interested in Indian or Chinese Traditional Medicine, you may find that the word "Ashe" is the equivalent of "Prana" or "Qi." People were all born with a specific amount of life force. Your experiences and choices in life, however, can either contribute to this amount or take away from it. Harmful, negative thoughts and toxic companies can decrease your life force, and the opposite is true. Yoruba practitioners believe that your Egún, or ancestors, are the ones who bless you with Ashe. They have created a certain grandeur and left it behind, so it becomes your Ashe. Yorubas also believe that descendants can contribute to your Ashe. Giving birth to them allows you to extend your bloodlines, which further expands your influence during your lifetime.

The last definition of Ashe is considered the most important and builds on the previous life force definition. It refers to the power that your words carry. Every word you speak carries the essence of Ashe since it's your life force. This is why Yorubas tie significant importance to and are very mindful of everything they say. They believe that you need to be very intentional about your words because you can manifest anything you say out loud. You want to be careful of what you attach your life force to.

When you hear something you deeply agree with, think about the role that your energy and existence play in the world or want to manifest an affirmation. End your sentence with "Ashe." Speak it with every bit of essence and life force energy you have.

Alternative spellings: Asé, Axé

Ashe is referenced in chapter 6.

Ataoja

Yoruba practitioners use the term Ataoja to refer to spiritual leaders or rulers. The term translates to "the person who can drink water from a fish's mouth." Being a spiritual leader, the Ataoja is expected to offer blessings to the public and practice spiritual healing. Some people believe that the Ataoja garners their strength from the river and uses this power to help their people during times of need.

Ataoja is mentioned in chapter 9.

Ayanmo

Ayanmo, which means destiny or fate, is a very important concept in African Traditional Religions. This term describes a person's spiritual intentions or will, the future, and the force that controls all events. According to Yoruba beliefs, a person's environment, date of birth, and the present moment all shape their Ayanmo. It is also believed that a person chooses their Ayanmo upon their birth.

Learn more about Ayanmo in chapter 1.

Babalawo

The term Babalawo, also known as Babaaláwo, translates to "the father of hidden secrets/mysteries." This highly esteemed title describes the Ifá oracle's high priest.

Babalawo is mentioned in chapter 2.

Ifá

Ifá is a divination system that represents the teachings of the Òrìṣà Ọrunmila, the Òrìṣà of Wisdom, who in turn serves as the oracular representative of Olodumare.

Learn more about Ifá in chapter 1.

Ile Ife

According to Yorubas, Ile Ife is where their civilization first came to life. They also believe that the gods stayed in this city when they traveled to Earth. The city's name translates to "place or location of dispersion." They say that the Orishas Obatala and Oduduwa were the ones who founded this city when they were creating the world. The Yoruba tradition suggests that Oduduwa appointed himself as the first Yoruban king, while Oduduwa created the world's first citizens using clay.

However, historically speaking, the Igbo people were already inhabitants of the area that later became known as Yorubaland when Oduduwa arrived. His army approached the city's northern borders, pushing the Igbos out and to the east. When Oduduwa died, his descendants started expanding Yorubaland and founded new cities surrounding Ile Ife. It was not long before Yoruba became one of the largest ethnic groups on the continent.

Find out more about the celebrations that take place in Ile Ife in chapter 9.

Kariocha

Kariocha, otherwise known as "making ocha," is the initiation process of a new priest or priestess that is a part of the Santería Lukumi African Traditional Religion. During this week-long ceremony, a person's tutelary, Orisha, is crowned on their head. The initiate then enters a year and 7 days long period known as Iyaworaje, during which they experience purification, rebirth, and transformation and expand their knowledge.

Kariocha and making ocha are mentioned in chapter 2.

Omi Tutu

Prayers and offering liberations are two crucial aspects of Ifá Orisha rituals. Practitioners are expected to do both regardless of how simple and intricate the ritual they're conducting is. Libations are completed in the form of Oriki - the act of praise. Performing Oriki is a means of acknowledging the energy of the Orisha while asking them for their guidance and blessings. According to practitioners, these prayers and rituals promote the opening of the consciousness of those who perform them. This can be valuable in any ceremony, ritual, or other spiritual endeavors because it aids in aligning their consciousness with that of the divine forces, making it easier to contact them.

Omi Tutu is a traditional prayer that practitioners use to invoke divine forces to bring cooling energy to the practitioner. It's also used as an enhancement prayer - practitioners use it to manifest anything they want through ancestral intervention. Omi Tutu is usually recited at the beginning of any ritual before partaking in any spiritual practices. A cool water libation is often offered to the Orisha when reciting the prayer. This prayer is also popularly used in spiritual cleansing rituals because it removes negative energy and makes the practitioner more receptive to the guidance of Orisha.

Learn more about prayers and when to use Omi Tutu in chapter 10.

Ori

The Ori is an African traditional metaphysical idea. The word literally translates to "head" but often points at an individual's Ayanmo (destiny) and intuition. The Ori is the embodiment of the human consciousness, which is why several belief systems regard it as an Orisha on its own. Some practitioners worship their Ori, appease it through offerings, and pray to it just as they would for any other Orisha. It's believed that working with your Ori can help you lead a more harmonious life and enhance your character. Practitioners often ask Ori for guidance whenever they're experiencing challenges because they believe that Ori is responsible for everything that happens in a person's life - it determines one's destiny.

Mentioned in chapter 2.

Orisha

An Orisha is one of the deities (plural: Orishas) in the pantheon worshipped by several African peoples - most notably, the Yorubas of southwestern Nigeria. The Ewe peoples of Benin, Ghana, and Togo, the Edo peoples of southeastern Nigeria, and the Fon of Benin also venerate the Orishas. While the myths and rituals associated with the Orishas might differ from place to place, the underlying spiritual concepts of all Traditional African Religions are relatively similar. Some people claim that the definition of "deity" doesn't capture the real essence of the Orisha and suggest that it is an intricate, multidimensional unifying force.

Alternative spellings: orixa, orisa

Tutelary Orisha

Every person has a tutelary or head Orisha. This entity is also popularly known as a guardian Orisha because they serve as your spiritual guides and for balancing life forces. They are called head Orishas because they claim the individual's head once they are acknowledged. Knowing and working with your tutelary Orisha is a lifelong commitment. Practitioners don't get to choose their head Orishas - they're determined by a person's destiny at birth. You can only attain your Ayanmo if you follow the guidance of this force. According to the Santería Lukumi belief system, only 9 Orishas can serve as tutelary Orishas.

See chapter 2 to learn more about tutelary Orishas.

Conclusion

Oshun is the youngest of the Orishas and is often considered the gentlest one. She is the patron of the rivers, love, and sensuality. She is also associated with fertility and new beginnings. However, despite her seemingly serene and benevolent nature, she is one of the most empowering female forces you can seek out. She is patient and not easily angered, but like all Yoruba deities, she has negative aspects too. Oshun is known to be a vain creature, often displaying jealousy and acting in spite. Ruling over rivers, she can easily take away the life her waters gave by flooding the fruitful lands.

Oshun is central to the ancient Yoruba religion, and Santeria and Ifa - and each of these belief systems have tales and myths associated with her. One of the most famous ones revolves around Oshun's contribution to the population of Earth - only rivaled by her love story with Shango, the mighty thunder god. According to the Yoruba myths, humanity only exists because of Oshun, the goddess of love and fertility. She is the mother of many; if you're attracted to her power, she may be your Orisha parent too. If this is the case, the information you've gained by reading this book will be an excellent stepping stone for building a substantial relationship with her.

The goddess Oshun is the universal archetype of the divine feminine, an incredibly potent and spiritually uplifting source of female power. Connecting with this aspect of Oshun (as well as with any other ones) is only possible after learning correspondence and favorite offerings. For example, knowing that she prefers to receive offerings and be addressed near running or sweet waters can help you appease her and ask for her favors and blessings. Similarly, representing her with the colors gold and yellow and the multitude of natural elements linked to her will allow you to form a powerful bond with her.

Oshun is often called on by women who struggle with infertility, but she can also bring productivity into any area of your life. You can also request her assistance when struggling financially or when you wish to empower yourself through sensuality. You can work with her at her favorite places or dedicate an altar to her. The latter is particularly beneficial for daily practices and for many other reasons related to spirituality, magic, and self-empowerment. Besides working with her, the spells and rituals contained in this book will aid your spiritual growth and help you become a more confident and self-loving version of yourself.

Oshun is typically venerated on Fridays, as this is her favorite day. She is also celebrated through several festivals held by the devotees of Yoruba and African Diaspora religions. One of the most popular events is the Osun Osogbo festival, held during the last week of August. This momentous event celebrates several other Yoruba deities, culminating with elaborate rituals held in Oshun's honor. Another great way to honor the goddess of love is through daily self-care rituals, such as meditation, journaling, singing, baths, and more. You can use the ones referenced in this book or devise a pampering ritual of your own. Either way, the goal is to become empowered and ready to take on any challenge in love or any other aspect of your life.

Part 7: Yemaya

The Ultimate Guide to the Mother of All Orishas in Yoruba and Santería

Introduction

Human beings often tend to give identities, names, and faces to any natural and supernatural forces they encounter to better understand them and to make them more relatable. In Yoruba tradition, these forces or spirits are known as Orishas. While some people confuse Orishas with gods, they should more likely be considered spirits or deities. They are supposed to be the intermediaries between mankind and the celestial forces of the universe.

According to Yorubaland myths, Orishas were brought into this world by Oludumare. Most myths surrounding Orishas and Yoruba history take place in a region of West Africa that encompasses many rivers. The names of these rivers resemble those of the Orishas, which is why many Orisha deities originate from these rivers as guiding river spirits. One of these river spirits, if not the most crucial, is called Yemaya, also known as the Orisha of the sea.

While each Orisha is deemed equally important and is worshiped and celebrated by many people from Yoruba culture, Yemaya (or Yemoja) is one of the most worshiped Orishas in Yoruba culture. This book will thus go into great detail about Yemaya, mother of all and queen of the sea. To fully understand a deity, you need to learn the various practices and rituals associated with them. However, before you can go on to practice the various rituals associated with an Orisha, you must learn about the myths associated with them.

Particularly when it comes to Yemaya, there are innumerable stories and legends which have been passed down in Yoruba and Santeria families for centuries. Each of these stories has spiritual lessons that will make you feel closer to the wondrous goddess and help you learn valuable life lessons. Many people compare the goddess Yemoja with the Virgin Mary, which can be observed by several arguments.

There is limited literature that details the history, mythology, practices, rituals, offerings, and charms associated with each Orisha, especially Yemaya. Unlike other books about the Orisha, this book will include not only the interesting stories associated with Yemaya but also her likes and dislikes, charms, offerings, and specific prayers. To truly call upon the power of Yemoja, you'd need to fully appreciate her many aspects and create a unique relationship with her. To do this, you need to equip yourself with every bit of information about the goddess of the sea.

Overall, the devotees and initiates of Yemoja often consider her to be a compassionate, gentle deity. However, there are so many more aspects to her which should be recognized by her followers to truly connect with her divineness. As you will see in the upcoming chapters, there are many layers to the goddess of the sea. You'll also be able to learn about the various offerings you can present her with and how you can properly pay homage to her legendary existence. You don't have to practice every ritual provided in the book, only the ones that resonate with you and allow you to feel Yemaya's divine presence.

Chapter 1: Who Is Yemaya?

Yemaya is a significant Orisha, venerated in several religions such as Yoruba, Santeria, Candomblé, Umbanda, and Haitian Vodou. She is the daughter of Olodumare, the creator of the universe and the chief god of the Yoruba and Santeria religions. Yemaya is the Orisha of motherhood and sea and the mother of all Orishas. Followers of Yoruba and Santeria believe that she is responsible for all life on Earth since she is the Orisha of seas, and water is what sustains and nourishes all living creatures.

Yemaya is the Orisha of motherhood.
This file is licensed under the Creative Commons Attribution-Share Alike 2.5 Generic
https://creativecommons.org/licenses/by-sa/2.5/deed.en
https://upload.wikimedia.org/wikipedia/commons/9/9d/Yemaya-NewOrleans.jpg

Although Yemaya is highly revered in many religions, this chapter will focus on her role in the Yoruba and Santeria religions.

The Yoruba Religion

The Yoruba religion originates from West Africa, mainly Nigeria. According to their mythology, Olodumare (or *Olorun*) is the chief deity and the creator of the universe. This deity doesn't conform to a specific gender and is referred to using the pronoun "they." After they created the universe and the Orisha, there was only water and the sky. Obatala, the sky father, felt that the universe was lacking, so he asked Olodumare for permission to create dry land. They granted Obtala his request, and with the help of other Orishas, Obatala gathered the required tools and descended to Earth. He created hills and valleys and planted palm trees. Obatala spent his time on Earth enjoying the world he built, but after some time, he became lonely and required company. He asked permission to build human beings and for Olodumare to breathe life into them, which they obliged. However, Obatala was drunk when making mankind, and his creation was extremely flawed. When he woke up the next day and discovered what he had made, he was consumed with regret and vowed never to drink again.

Spiritual concepts and traditional practices govern this religion, such as Fate or Ayanmo. The Yoruba people believe that mankind must experience their destiny. Part of each person's "Ayanmo" is to become one with the divine since he is the creator of the universe and, thus, the source of all energy. This unity is referred to as "Olodumare." Before birth, every spirit chooses its destiny, who it will fall in love with, where it will be born, its career, and how its life will end. However, when a person is born, they forget everything they planned for themselves and spend their lives trying to find and achieve their forgotten destiny. Everything one thinks, says, or does, and all our interactions with one another, have one purpose; to meet and achieve one's spiritual destiny.

Another concept is the Ajogun, which is similar to the idea of the devil or a demon in the west. They are responsible for all misfortunes that befall mankind, such as diseases or accidents. One should never try to communicate with Ajogun, as they should be avoided at all costs. The Yoruba people don't believe in the devil. The concept of good vs. evil doesn't exist in their religion. No one can be all evil or all good. Human beings and morals are more complicated than that. Ashe is another concept that refers to a force that exists in all human beings, deities, nature, and even names and blood. It resembles the concept of chakras or Chi.

The Yoruba people don't consider death the end of the soul's journey. They believe in a concept similar to reincarnation, where the spirit experiences a rebirth in various physical forms. Unlike other religions, reincarnation is a positive experience that rewards good people. Bad individuals who cause harm and suffering aren't reincarnated.

The Orishas in the Yoruba Religion

Olodumare is the most powerful being in Yoruba, but they aren't involved in the lives of mankind and can't hear their prayers. They created the Orishas, who are second in the religious hierarchy after Olodumare. They are supernatural entities who act as intermediaries between the deity and mankind. They are involved in people's lives and assist them in their daily tasks by providing guidance and enlightenment. There is a misconception that the Orishas are deities. There are different types of Orishas. Some of them are demigods who were created before mankind and assisted Olodumare in the creation of the universe. They can also be the spirits of the ancestors who had an impact on the world with their good deeds and heroic actions.

There are about 401 Orishas in the Yoruba religion. Each is associated with specific powers, colors, animals, and offerings. The Orishas and mankind have a mutually beneficial relationship where human beings present offerings to appease them and ask for favors and protection. At the same time, the Orishas accept these offerings and bestow blessings in return. Both need each other to survive. People still worship and invoke these spirits to ask for their assistance. If one wants to communicate with an Orisha, they require Eshu's permission first, who stands guard at their doorway. These spirits take the form of various elements of nature, such as trees and rivers. The Yoruba people believe that whenever a misfortune befalls someone, an Orisha is angry with them and must be appeased.

The Orishas have human-like qualities. They feel happy, sad, envious, and angry. According to mythology, they rebelled against Olodumare and tried to kill him. They believed that he was getting old and they were more worthy to rule the universe since they were more involved in mankind's affairs. However, Olodumare found out and punished them.

There are seven Orishas who are referred to as "The Seven African Powers." They have the biggest number of devotees and are the most involved in people's lives.

1. Yemaya, the Orisha of the sea and motherhood, and the mother of all Orishas.
2. Obatala, the sky, Orisha, and the protector of the disabled.
3. Eshu, the Orisha of trickery and the messengers between the Orishas and mankind.
4. Shango, the Orisha of thunder, lighting, and war.
5. Ogun, the Orisha of healing and strength.
6. Oya, the Orisha of rebirth and transformation and the guardian of the dead.
7. Oshun, the Orisha of love and fertility.

Yemaya in the Yoruba Religion

Yemaya is also spelled Yemaja, Yemoja, Yemonja, and Yemalla and is referred to as "the Queen of the Sea." Her name means "*the mother whose children are fish,*" which can imply that she either has many children (like fish) or many worshipers due to her generosity. She is the Orisha of rivers, oceans, and seas and one of the most powerful spirits in the Yoruba religion. Yemaya is among the oldest children of Olodumare. She is married to her brother Aganyu, the Orisha of volcanoes, while different legends mention that she was married to other Orishas like Obatala, Ernile, and Okere. She is the mother of the Orishas Shango, Oya, Ogin, and Oshun. However, some people believe that she never had children of her own but raised many Orishas like Dana and Shango. She resides in the sea. According to the Yoruba religion, life began from her because she is water. Yemaya is the secret behind existence; without her, all life on Earth would perish.

For a long time, Yemaya was only the Orisha of the river. Her association with the ocean came later when enslaved people came from Africa to the new world. She couldn't leave her people alone, so she came with them, thus becoming the Orisha of the ocean. Yemaya is very popular among the people of Yoruba and the most beloved among the Seven African Powers. She loves all her worshipers dearly, and most of them are females. Hence, she has become the protector of all women. She represents a motherly figure with whom many of her devotees associate and form a close connection. However, just like all Orishas, she can get in the way of her followers. Invoking Yemaya at sea can be dangerous. She is a good Orisha who would never harm anyone on purpose. However, she wants to keep everything and everyone dear to her at sea. She can forget that her followers need to live on land, and she takes them when they approach her domain.

As the Orisha of motherhood, Yemaya is the most nurturing Orisha. She always comes through for her people as she cares for and protects all of them. She shares the same personality as that of her domain, the sea. She is generous and giving but can be ruthless when angry, just like the sea. When someone disrespects her or brings harm to any of her children, Yemaya brings floods and tidal waves. Beyond that, she is usually calm and patient and rarely gets angry.

She is depicted as a good-looking young woman in a blue dress with seven skirts, each one representing the seven seas. Or as a very beautiful mermaid. She wears jewelry from the sea, like pearls, crystals, and corals. She puts tiny bells on her clothes and hair that make noise whenever she moves. Yemaya causes waves by simply walking and swaying her hips. She is associated with the number seven, which represents the seven seas. She is drawn to the colors white and blue, and her favorite animal is the peacock. Everything that exists in the sea is associated with her, like shells and fish. Legends say she has long breasts because she has nursed many children. Other Orishas mocked her appearance, which affected her self-esteem. She even transformed into a river to escape their judgment.

People invoke Yemaya when they are suffering or experiencing grief, as she can cleanse their pain with her motherly love. Women struggling with infertility issues also seek her help since she has the power to heal them. Yemaya is sympathetic, listens to all her devotees when they are struggling, and comes to their aid. Women suffering from self-esteem issues invoke Yemaya as well to help them love themselves. Whatever issues women face, such as pregnancy issues, parenting problems, or when their children are in danger, they always go to their protector Orisha for help.

As the oldest Orisha, people have been worshiping Yemaya for centuries. When enslaved Africans came to the new world, more people became aware of the Orisha in North and South America.

Santeria

Santeria is a Spanish word that translates to *"devotion of the saints."* It is also called *La Religión Lucumí,* which is Spanish for "The order of Lucumí," and *La Regla de Ocha,* which means "The order of the Orishas." These names are more popular among practitioners than the name Santeria. It is often considered an Afro-Cuban religion that reached countries like the U.S., Cuba, Haiti, Brazil, and Puerto Rico through the slave trade. When Africans arrived in the Americas, they weren't free to practice their religious beliefs, as most people were Catholics. However, Africans held onto their faith to preserve their identity and as a form of rebellion. They practiced their religion in private. They passed down their traditions orally from one generation to the next. After the Cuban revolution, people wanted to be free to practice Santeria, but the Cuban government didn't trust this religion and accused its followers of practicing witchcraft. It was outlawed for a very long time, but it has recently been acknowledged, and people can now legally practice it.

Even when it was illegal, Santeria was very popular and spread all over Cuba. About 80% of Cubans follow the religion or practice some of its traditions. It is believed that Cuban's former president Fidel Castro was a Santeria follower.

Many people think that Africans and Cubans combined Santeria with Catholicism to become one faith, but this is a common misconception. The Afro-Cubans practice both religions due to the similarities between them. Some of them practice Catholicism and go to church while also practicing Santeria and going to temples. They also link the Orishas to Catholic saints. Santeria came to be from the combination of the Yoruba religion and Catholicism. Although they are different, they found similarities in their stories or personalities. For instance, Yemaya is associated with the Virgin Mary, Ogun is associated with Saint Peter, and Shango is associated with Saint Barbara. The origin of this association goes back to the time of slavery when enslaved Africans were punished for practicing their faith, so they pretended to honor Catholic saints instead. This resulted in the overlapping between the two religions and the association between the Orishas and the saints. This adds to the complexity of Santeria.

Santeria has borrowed from various cultures and religions worldwide, like Yoruba, Catholicism, and Caribbean tradition. Many of these beliefs and traditions contradict each other. Yet, the Afro-Cubans have found elements they can incorporate into their beliefs.

The followers of Santeria also believed in the supreme deity Olodumare and that he was the creator of the universe. They also believe that there is good and evil in each person and Orisha. By doing good things, you ensure your actions align with your destiny. Ashe also exists in Santeria. The followers believe that Ashe comes from Olodumare and exists in all beings and aspects of nature. Thus, Ashe is sacred, and nature is revered.

The Orishas in the Santeria Religion

Santeria, similar to Yoruba, mainly focuses on the relationships between people and the Orishas. Worshipers connect with the spirits through mediumship, sacrifice, divination, and initiation. The Orishas provide them with guidance, wisdom, success, and protection. Santeria devotees appease the spirits by presenting offerings and carrying out rituals like drumming and dancing in the hope the Orishas will assist them in achieving their destiny. They also act as messengers between the supreme deity and mankind. Only priests (babalawos) and priestesses can communicate with the Orishas through rituals, divination, and possession. Possession in Santeria (also called *mounting*) isn't a negative or forceful experience like demonic possession. When Orishas are called on during ceremonies, they mount a willing attendee, which is usually the priest or priestess leading the ritual. People can interact with the Orishas and ask them for help or advice. The Orishas also help followers of Santeria with their magic practice.

Good deeds and bad luck are associated with Orishas. Devotees believe that the Orishas are so powerful that they can perform miracles, but when they are angry with someone, they will suffer from bad luck and must acknowledge the Orishas by presenting offerings to appease them. Orishas and human beings need each other. Although they are demigods, Orishas are mortals and could die without people's offerings, sacrifices, and devotion.

The Orishas' mythology is referred to as Patakis. The Santeria practitioners are aware that these legends aren't based on facts. However, the lessons behind these stories and personal interpretations make these myths significant.

Santeria followers worship all 401 Orishas, but only a handful play a big role in the religion.
- Chango, the Orisha of sexuality and masculine energy
- Elegua (Eshu) is the messenger between Orishas and mankind
- Oya, Orisha of the dead and a warrior
- Babalu Aye, the Orisha of healing and referred to as the father of the world
- Yemaya, the Orisha of motherhood

Yemaya in the Santeria Religion

Yemaya's role in Santeria is similar to that of Yoruba. She is the Orisha of the seas and is responsible for maintaining life on Earth. She isn't the Orisha of the whole sea or ocean but only the parts known and accessible to mankind, where there are fish, plants, etc. The deeper parts of the oceans and seas belong to the Orisha Olokun. Yemaya is also associated with motherhood. Her worshipers know they should avoid angering her at all costs because her punishments can be severe. However, she quickly forgives once a person repents for their mistakes. She is a very smart Orisha and is known for her courage. She never shies away from a battle. As a protective mother, she would go to war in her children's place with a machete and defeat all her enemies.

She is often depicted wearing a long blue dress with white and blue ruffles and a belt. The color and design of the dress symbolize the waves. Her necklace is made of transparent crystal and blue beads in a pattern of her favorite number, seven. Her favorite scent is verbena, and she is associated with Saturday. Yemaya has all the qualities of a loving mother, including virtue and wisdom. However, she has a fun side as well and enjoys dancing. Her dance moves are choreographed as she starts with graceful and slow moves and then swirls while moving her skirt.

Yemaya is an expert in divination, which she learned from her husband, Orula. Back then, women weren't allowed to practice divination, so Yemaya had to spy on her husband to learn. She was so talented and a fast learner that he helped her to practice using cowrie shells. Nowadays, priests and priestesses of Santeria perform divination using the same shells as well.

Yoruba and Santeria share more similarities than differences. Both religions center on the worship of the Orishas. These entities are responsible for everything on Earth, and mankind would be lost without their constant guidance and protection. People don't only worship the Orishas because they want something. In fact, it is a sign of disrespect to only go to them to ask for a favor. Devotees should regularly express their gratitude to the Orishas for all the blessings they bestow upon them. Each person also identifies with one or more Orishas since they have human qualities which make it easy to sympathize with them and relate to their struggles.

The role and impact of Yemaya are the same in both religions. She is highly revered and loved among all her devotees. She is a nurturing mother who one can go to with any problem, and she will meet them with love and affection. There is still more to learn about Yemaya. This chapter is only the beginning. In the next chapter, we will focus on all the interesting stories that feature the Orisha of the sea.

Chapter 2: The Mother's Wisdom in Myth and Lore

There is a popular saying in Africa that *God created man because he likes stories*. Indeed, mythology has always been the cornerstone of many religions. These stories aren't just for entertainment. They explain various practices and traditions so you can better understand your faith. Stories about Yemaya showcase her personality and shed light on why she is one of the most worshiped Orishas. Wise and nurturing, there is so much one can learn from the myth and lore about Yemaya.

Stories passed down through generations allow us to understand more about Yemaya.
https://unsplash.com/photos/6jYoil2GhVk

The Birth

Santeria and Yoruba followers passed down their myths and legends orally. Therefore, there can be contradictions or different interpretations of the same stories. One version of the myth of creation shows Yemaya's role in birthing the first human. She was pregnant, and one day her water broke. Since she was one of the most powerful Orishas in the world, this event brought one of the greatest floods the universe had ever witnessed. It resulted in the creation of rivers and streams. Afterward, she gave birth to the first human. The proud mother gave her first human child a very special and personal gift. It was a seashell that carried her voice so the child could always hear its mother.

Yemaya gifted her first human child a seashell that carried her voice.
https://unsplash.com/photos/cNtMy74-mnI

Yemaya's voice still echoes to this day. When you hold a seashell to your ear, it isn't the sound of the ocean that you hear. Yemaya's voice provides her children with serenity and reminds them that their mother is always there.

A different version of this creation myth involves Orungan, Yemaya's son, with her husband, Aganju. Orungan was an aggressive, angry, and rebellious teenager. He developed feelings for his mother, which drove him to try and kill his father. Yemaya was so broken-hearted by her son's dangerous and unstable behavior that she hid on a mountaintop.

She was consumed with pain and anger, and since she was known to be ruthless when her temper flared, she constantly cursed her son. One day, her cursing worked, and Orungan died.

No mother can ever tolerate the pain of losing a child, even if she is furious or disheartened with him. Yemaya's heart was so full of regret and grief that she could not handle the sorrow and died. After her death, fourteen Orishas came out of her body. Holy water was released from her womb, creating the first water on Earth, the seven seas.

Moral Lesson

Whether Yemaya gave birth to the first human or not, she was still the bringer of life on Earth by creating water. Yemaya's giving nature is also apparent in this story, as even in death, her blessings never ceased. This story showcases Yemaya's motherly, caring, loving side. Although her son committed horrendous acts and tried to kill his father, she still couldn't live without him. Just like any mother, she could never hate her son.

All mothers can learn from Yemaya's loving nature. She could have given her child gold or any expensive gift fit for a demigoddess. However, she chose something that reflects her love for her child. Who wouldn't want to hear their mother's soothing sound whenever they are hurting or struggling? Some parents can be obsessed with the material aspect of life and forget that their children could be struggling, and all they need is their soothing voice reassuring them that everything will be okay.

The Tidal Waves

Olokun is the Orisha of great wealth. He is very powerful and worthy of great admiration and reverence. However, Olokun felt that he wasn't getting the respect he deserved. This hurt his ego, and he was adamant about punishing humans to teach them a lesson. He ordered the water to send powerful tidal waves to drown everything on Earth. The ocean obliged and sent large waves to invade the lands. The people were terrified as they saw the enormous waves approaching and ran for cover.

The Orishas weren't happy with Olokun's actions – as he was destroying mankind and Olodumare's creation. They were put on this Earth to protect and assist mankind, not to cause havoc. The Orishas agreed that they must interfere and end Olokun's reckless and dangerous behavior. They went to Orunmila, the Orisha of wisdom and knowledge, to help them devise a plan. He suggested that they seek the help of Ogun, the Orisha of metal and iron, who was also a fierce warrior. Ogun told them he would design a long metal chain they could use against Olokun.

Meanwhile, the people sought the help of their protective mother, Yemaya, since she was the Orisha of the upper level of the ocean while Olokun was the Orisha of its lower level. They asked her to intervene and save them from imminent doom. Yemaya didn't hesitate and immediately took action to help her children. Before she headed to Olokun, she went to Ogun and took the chain. Standing tall like the fierce mother she was with the metal chain in her hand, Yemaya prevented the ocean waves from reaching her children.

Olokun went to meet Yemaya when he learned that she was waiting for him. Using her wise and caring nature, she calmed Olokun down, and he ordered the ocean to retreat. When the water receded, it left behind many treasures like corals and pearls as gifts for the people. Yemaya saved mankind.

Moral Lesson

There are various ways Yemaya could have handled this situation. For instance, she could have used her powers and attacked Olokun to teach him a lesson. However, Yemaya decided to use her wisdom and soothing nature to end this attack. This story teaches us that violence should never be the answer. One must always use their heart and mind. Thinking of positive solutions and approaching the situation with understanding and compassion can change its outcome.

The Slap

Yemaya was one of the most beautiful Orishas, but she had one flaw which affected her self-esteem: Yemaya only had one breast (in other legends, she had two very long breasts). She was only focused on this flaw, which made her very insecure about her looks. Yemaya believed that she would never find someone to love her. She gave up on romance and marriage. Ogun was madly in love with her, and in his eyes, she was perfect. He wanted to make her happy and prove his feelings for her. Ogun decided to impress her with his cooking skills and make her favorite dish. As he was preparing the meal, Ogun accidentally broke one of Yemaya's pots. She was furious, and they ended up having a serious confrontation. Ogun was angry at Yemaya's reaction, and he lost his temper and slapped her. She was shocked and furious, and she disappeared without giving him a chance to say or do anything else. However, Yemaya wasn't going to let him get away with his aggressive behavior without punishment. Before disappearing, she took a piece of his power, leaving him fuming angrily.

Moral Lesson

This is a story about domestic violence. Even though Yemaya suffered from self-esteem issues and believed she was unlovable, she didn't tolerate this behavior, allow Ogun to lie, or make up an excuse for his inexcusable actions. Yemaya also showed courage by taking a piece of Ogun's power. She didn't allow this abuse to go unpunished.

Yemaya's devotees usually seek her advice on domestic violence issues because she gives women the courage to handle abusive husbands. Every domestic violence victim can learn from Yemaya's story. The best reaction to physical abuse is walking away because no explanation or excuse can make this behavior acceptable. Her reaction inspires all women who look up to her and invoke her for protection and strength.

The Marriage of Shango

Shango was having an affair with Oya, who was his sister and his brother Ogun's wife. This created discord between the two brothers. Their father, Obatala, was displeased by their situation and worried their conflict would impact the kingdom. He advised Shango to get married and settle down. Shango was a womanizer, and Obatala wanted him to focus on his work and mend his relationship with his brother. Obatala suggested Shango marry his sister Oba, who was in love with him, and Shango obliged because he believed this was the only way to protect their kingdom. When Shango saw Oba, he was smitten by her beauty and kindness and found her to be the perfect match for him. They wed, and Oba proved herself to be perfect for her new role as a queen. However, there was a green-eyed monster lurking from behind.

Shango's first lover Oya was jealous and adamant about getting him back. Even though Oya loved her sister and saw how happy she was with Shango, she wasn't backing down. She was consumed with anger and wanted to unleash her wind to destroy the kingdom. However, her love and respect for her father, Obatala, prevented her. She was hurt and lonely, so she turned to the one person she trusted the most, her mother, Yemaya.

She confided in her mother about her feelings and asked for help. Oya suggested they use their powers of wind and water to destroy the marriage. Yemaya calmly and patiently listened to her daughter express her feelings. However, she was shocked to see her daughter in this condition, angry and jealous. She couldn't believe that Oya wanted to destroy her sister and the man she claimed to love. Yemaya was a strong woman and a feminist, even before the concept existed, so she was also bewildered at her daughter's willingness to start a war over a man.

Yemaya refused to be a part of this plan. Shango was her favorite son. She would never harm him or destroy his marriage. Yet, she sympathized with Oya and was sorry to see her in pain. She tried talking to her and helping her see that this wasn't the solution. Yemaya wanted her daughter to be reasonable, accept that Shango was married, and move on. She was hoping that Oya would listen to her as she always did. Both mother and daughter had a close bond, and Oya respected her mother and always sought her guidance. However, things were different this time, and nothing would be the same from then on.

Oya wouldn't be reasoned with, and for the first time in her life, she didn't take her mother's advice. Yemaya told Oya that she would protect her children against anyone who wanted to harm them. Oya made it clear to her mother that she was prepared to fight to win her lover back. From that day on, they grew apart, and their relationship never recovered. Yemaya loved her daughter very much, and it pained her that their relationship had fallen apart. However, she was still a mother, and her duty was to protect all her children, so she decided that she must stop Oya. Yemaya is an Orisha who protects and creates. She could never tolerate chaos and destruction, especially to any of her Orishas. After Oya calmed down, she realized that going into battle with her sister would make her mother angry – and Yemaya could be unstoppable when she lost her temper. She decided that the only way to win Shango back was by befriending the enemy, her once beloved sister Oba.

Moral Lessons

Yemaya's wisdom is apparent in this story. She handled her daughter's wrath with compassion and reason instead of being cruel and heartless. Yemaya was unyielding, refusing to hurt one child to please another. Oya thought her mother took Shango's side over hers, which could seem like that to some since Shango was her favorite child. However, a different interpretation of this story would suggest that she was protecting Oya from herself. She didn't want her daughter to give in to her jealousy and do something she would later regret. One should always follow Yemaya's footsteps when dealing with tough decisions, especially with family. Being calm and collected while not giving in to your feelings can be the best approach in these situations.

Duty Over Love

Yemaya fell in love with Arganyu, and they got married. They were together for many years, and their union benefited the Earth and mankind. Yemaya felt there was still more she could do to benefit the world. Still, she couldn't achieve anything new while married to Arganyu. However, she couldn't just abandon the man she loved dearly. She decided to find someone to fulfill his sexual needs and help him forget about her. No one was more perfect for this role than her daughter Oshun, the beautiful Orisha of love.

Yemaya visited Oshun, who was very happy to see her mother. However, she had a bad feeling since her mother rarely visited anyone and looked sad and anxious. Oshun knew Yemaya would ask her something, and before she could speak, her faithful daughter fell on her knees as a sign of her respect. She told her that she accepted whatever her mother asked of her. Yemaya was proud of her daughter's loyalty. She kept looking at her beautiful face and thinking she had made the right choice. Yemaya told Oshun her proposal, and her daughter was shocked.

Oshun never imagined her mother would ask her to marry her husband. She found herself in a tough position after she had already agreed to her mother's request. Oshun didn't want to disrespect her mother by refusing. Yemaya, happy that her daughter was on board, made a plan for Oshun to seduce Arganyu.

Yemaya prepared to execute her plan. She took Arganyu to Oshun's home, pretending it was a regular visit. Oshun was dressed for the role. She was so mesmerizing that Arganyu could not take his eyes off her. Yemaya signaled to her daughter that she would leave them alone to carry out the rest of the plan. Before she left, Yemaya hugged her husband tightly. Arganyu knew something was wrong, and he understood that his wife was saying goodbye. Yemaya always favored her duty and the kingdom above everything else, and he had always admired this about her. Both lovers parted ways. With every step she took away from him, he could feel his heart breaking little by little. Yemaya was devastated to leave the man she loved, but for the sake of the Orishas and the kingdom, she had to give him up.

Moral Lesson

It's a tale as old as time, sacrificing love for the greater good. Yemaya loved Arganyu, but she had to leave him to focus on the kingdom and her Orishas. She could have explained to him that she couldn't abandon her duties and must leave. However, she opted for a less cruel option by finding him someone to love so he wouldn't be alone. Giving up love for duty is one of the hardest choices anyone could ever make. Yemaya made it without hesitation, even when her heart was breaking, which shows her brave and selfless nature.

Oshun's reaction to her mother's request reflects how Yemaya was loved and highly revered among all her children.

The Road to Divination

Yemaya needed some time to be alone to recover from the pain of giving up the man she loved. As she pondered her decision, she heard a voice speaking to her. She followed the voice, and it led her to a very large tree. She found a man sitting by the tree. It was the master of divination, Orula, who asked her to be his wife. Yemaya felt bad for him. He seemed lonely and wanted to be loved. She realized that marrying could benefit them both. She would provide him with company while he taught her about divination.

They got married, but it didn't last long. She wasn't in love with him, and she still couldn't forget Arganyu. She learned so much from her new husband that she began practicing divination herself. Orula never taught her anything, but she watched him practice and was able to learn fast due to her intelligence. She was practicing in private without her husband's knowledge. People would go to her everywhere to tell them about their future. They were impressed by her talent and would talk about this great diviner until the news reached Orula.

Unaware that it was his wife, Orula was curious about this new diviner. He asked around until he found her. Yemaya was doing her readings at the tree where they first met. She was surprised to see Orula, who felt hurt and betrayed. He ended their marriage on the spot. She was grateful for her time with him and the things she had learned. This time, Yemaya wasn't heartbroken because she was not in love with

Orula. Arganyu was still in her heart, lingering on her every thought.

Moral Lesson

Marrying Orula out of pity shows how kind-hearted Yemaya was. She didn't want to see a poor soul alone and suffering. Her purpose wasn't only to learn from him and change his life for the better. This story also shows how big her sacrifice was, as she still couldn't forget about the man she loved. Her intelligence also came through here in how she didn't require someone to explain to her how divination worked. She learned everything just by observing and became one of the greatest diviners of all time.

Yemaya was brave, intelligent, selfless, loving, caring, wise, strong, and a mother. Her stories help us understand her not only as a supernatural being but as a woman, a human who loves and feels pain. They are filled with lessons one can learn from and incorporate into daily life. Yemaya is worthy of being an idol to all women. The mother, lover, protector, and feminist, Orisha is an admirable character that is worthy of being highly revered.

Her actions also teach us that change is necessary and nothing stays the same. You can grow and transform when you welcome change with love and compassion. Yemaya is the protective mother who exists in all her children. One should always turn inward and seek her protective spirit and endless love.

Chapter 3: Yemaya and Virgin Mary

In several African Diaspora religions, Yemaya is syncretized with the Virgin Mary, the Catholic saint with similar characteristics. She is also known as the Virgin of Regla and Our Lady of the Sea – a portrayal that's more accurate to Yemaya's divine nature than the spirit of a saint. This dedicated chapter discusses the connection between Yemaya and the Virgin Mary and how this syncretism came to be. You will learn how Yemaya is worshiped as a saint and how the depiction of the Virgin Mary relates to the portrayal of Yemaya as a Yoruba Orisha.

The Virgin of Regla.
Christian Pirkl, CC BY-SA 4.0 <https://creativecommons.org/licenses/by-sa/4.0>, via Wikimedia Commons https://upload.wikimedia.org/wikipedia/commons/e/e7/Virgin_de_Regla_Cuba_001.jpg

What Is Syncretism?

In order to comprehend how the image of Yemaya became associated with the Virgin Mary, you must first understand what syncretism is and why it happens. The term syncretism depicts the fusion of religious ideas rooted in two or more different belief systems. Religious beliefs can only be accepted if they are based on thoughts people are familiar with. Consequently, it can be concluded that all religions have syncretism. For example, the idea of the creator or God (or gods) was only accepted because it helped explain events people already considered as deeds of a higher power. Once a religious thought becomes a belief, it can be interpreted in many ways. How these sentiments are interpreted and diversified over time shapes the cultural and traditional evolution of the different belief systems. Sometimes, syncretism only causes religious systems to adopt new ideas. On other occasions, it leads to the formation of new belief systems. A classic example of the latter is Santeria, the African Diaspora religion which syncretizes African deities with Catholic saints.

During the Transatlantic slave trade, thousands of Africans were brought to the New World, where they were forced to convert to Christianity. Their indigenous pagan practices were banned, and they were expected to be devoted to saints instead of deities. However, followers of the Yoruba religion soon realized that saints had much in common with the gods and goddesses of the Yoruba pantheon (the Orishas). This made it easier for them to accept saints as patrons but also allowed them to keep venerating the Orishas. They renamed the Orishas to the names of the saints with similar characteristics and started worshiping them as saints. Some consider this false syncretism since the Orishas were only masked with the name of the saints. In some religions, like in Santeria, this can be true. After all, the practitioners of Santeria didn't fully convert to Christianity; they just pretended that they did. Then again, in countries like Cuba, Yoruba deities are worshiped as Orishas and saints, which alludes to at least partial acceptance of Catholic beliefs.

Other fully-syncretic religions contain elements that come from contradictory sources. Voodoo and Hoodoo, for example, incorporate segments of Christian beliefs, African spirituality, and African folk magic practices. Magic and Christian beliefs couldn't be further from each other, yet these religions make them work together naturally. Religions such as Judaism, Islam, or Christianity aren't considered syncretic – although historically, they have been known to draw elements from each other.

The Connection between Yemaya and Virgin Mary

Now that you've learned what syncretism entails, you can explore why Yemaya has been syncretized with the Virgin Mary and not any other Christian saint. In Yoruba, Yemaya is viewed as the Orisha of the seas and a warrior goddess. She is also the divine mother to the human race, embodying the most powerful feminine force in the universe. She is the champion of defenseless children and mothers, empowering them. Yemaya nurtures maternal values and promotes love and peace amongst humans - in their personal life and in their communities. She can also contribute to the balance of the family by keeping children safe and ensuring the family's economic well-being is secured so the children can thrive.

As one of the most prevalent figures in Christianity, Mary is viewed very similarly to Yemaya. She is a symbol of purity and motherhood. Not only is she the mother of a son who had a tremendous role in shaping the belief system, but Mary is also the motherly figure of all human beings. She is known for having a loving and nurturing nature, both towards her son and the rest of humanity. Always ready to help those in need, the Virgin Mary is a source of spiritual empowerment and the patron saint of mothers, children, and families.

While Yemaya is known for her fluid nature (she is a water goddess, after all), she is a generally good-natured Orisha. She can be angered, especially if someone disrespects her or her protegees. However, she can be easily appeased with offerings and other acts in her favor. Mary is always depicted as a serene woman who calmly expresses her faith in her son and the rest of humanity. She is more of a silent protector than Yemaya, who isn't afraid to voice her opinion as needed. Their syncretization in Santeria and other diasporic religions helped reconcile the differences between these feminine divine aspects. Mary became stronger while staying true to her calm protective nature. In contrast, Yemaya remained the fierce patron of mothers and families while gaining the ability to resolve situations more calmly.

Yemaya and the Virgin Mary teach their followers to believe in themselves and live purposefully. They intercede on behalf of mothers and children. They also help those who struggle to keep their families happy, healthy, and secure. This is particularly true for Yemaya because, as an Orisha, she can relay messages people can't convey otherwise. She carries these messages to Olodumare, the supreme creator and spiritual guide. While Mary's interference is more subtle, she still provides strength for overcoming obstacles. In some religions, Oludumare is called Olofi and is syncretized with the Holy Spirit in Christianity. The Virgin Mary is associated with the Holy Trinity, which also connects her to the Christian version of Olofi. In syncretized religions, Olofi is the patron of worldly affairs and communicates with Orishas/saints. Depending on the specific interpretation, Olofi/the Holy Spirit can also be addressed by people.

How Is Yemaya Worshiped as a Saint?

Yemaya has a rich history of being worshiped as an Orisha, as known from the rich oral history of the Yoruba. Her actions are immortalized in the repositories of the wisdom collected by the Yoruba ancestors. These vessels of knowledge can be accessed by modern generations, and this is how present-day practitioners have found their connection to the Yoruba deities, including Yemaya. The beliefs surrounding Virgin Mary have a similarly long history. While she is rarely mentioned in the New Testament, she is referenced several times in the Old Testament. African Diaspora religions have a much shorter past. Still, the element of Yemaya's syncretization as a saint has left its mark on the cultural background of these religions and their devotees. Just like the Yoruba offered prayers, rituals, and personal sacrifices to Yemaya, so do the practitioners of African Diaspora religions with her person as a saint.

Amongst the Cuban practitioners of Santeria, Yemaya is known as the Virgin of Regla (or Our Lady of Regla), a black saint capable of materializing divine empowerment into people's lives. She is often asked to change people's disposition, allowing them to reach spiritual enlightenment and have a balanced life. She can also help dispel negative influences and transform one's life by encouraging them to take a positive approach. Yemaya - as a saint - can be asked these favors by individual people who make small offerings and prayers to the saint regularly. When the inquiry is more significant, it requires a ritual performed by a priest or priestess, just as it's done in the parental religion. However, unlike in Yoruba, Yemaya - as a saint does - not need to provide her ashe (spiritual essence) to the devotees. She bestows her blessing, provides guidance, and does whatever she is asked for without any spiritual possession.

The Virgin Mary has several forms, including Mary, Star of the Sea, and Our Lady of Rule. In Santeria, Yemaya (again, as a saint) is associated with both. She is revered as Our Lady of Rule (Virgin of Regla) for her identity as the Mother goddess. Santeria's followers give her just as much prominence as the Catholic Church. She is offered prayers on Saturdays, observed in visions during meditation, and is expected to perform miracles when invoked. Mary, Star of the Sea, represents the ultimate fusion of Yemaya and saint. She possesses both the Sea goddess's power and the Virgin Mary's nurturing nature. She is also honored on Saturdays. Expecting mothers pray to her for safe delivery and healthy children, while those wanting children ask her to bestow the gift of fertility. Those wanting a safe journey overseas will also pray to her before departure.

Lone practitioners and people who want to keep a strong connection to this saint pray to her daily. Here is a typical prayer that followers of syncretic religions offer to Yemaya as a saint. It's known as the Pagan Hail Mary. It is recited by facing a large body of water (sea or ocean) or at the altar while looking at a small bowl filled with saltwater. It goes like this:

> *"Hail Mary, the embodiment of grace,*
> *You are enlightened.*
> *You are blessed among women,*
> *and so is the fruit of your womb.*
> *Hail Mary, mother to us all,*
> *Bless your children now and throughout their lives."*

Santeria practitioners often use a rosary as well when praying to Yemaya/Mary. If you are comfortable with this, you can also try repeating several Hail Marys while going through the beads. Start with a few and slowly expand your focus until you can recite an entire rosary of prayers. The prayer can also be said before meditation and other practices dedicated to Yemaya.

When they're finished with the prayers, followers typically ask the saint for guidance or any other form of intercession they need from her.

This works if Yemaya knows what your problem is. If you're asking her a favor, provide a clear description of your issue.

Celebrating the Virgin of Regla

Santeria and other syncretized religions aren't centralized, nor do they have assigned places for worship. Rituals in the name of Mary and other saints are held at the home of the high priests and priestesses. Eventually, they can be hosted at a place of importance for the local community. A great example of this is the procession of the Virgin of Regla. It celebrates Mary in her aspects as Our Lady of Regla. The procession is held every September seventh between the docks of Regla (entry point for Havana) and the Church of Our Lady of Regla, located nearby. Worshippers gather near the church to venerate the saint patron of Havana and the sea. They wear layered dresses in colors of the sea – blue, azure, turquoise, and white – and carry white flowers. They also wear colorful necklaces made of flowers and beads.

Priests and priestesses express their devotion by carrying white candles and holding traditional beaded bracelets. Apart from these devotees who worship Yemaya as an Orisha (masked as a saint), some venerate her as a saint, holding the symbol of the Virgen de la Regla and crucifixes. Some (typically the latest generations) try to respect both sides by exhibiting symbolic behavior. As they walk toward the church, they cross themselves in the name of Mary (a Catholic tradition) and offer coins to Yemaya (a Yoruba custom). Around them, dancers are moving in a floating motion. They wear a blue skirt made of several layers (seven is the traditional number after the number of seas governed by Yemaya) and a white blouse. As they dance, they simulate the movement of the sea, accentuated by the color of their clothing, which makes them look like they're foaming waves.

Until recently, they danced to the traditional Yoruba drum rhythms called bata. Due to the overlapping motives in the different faith systems, the traditional drummers quit supporting the procession of saints. Now, the dancers and the devotees are accompanied by simple, newer forms of music authentic to Cuba.

When they enter the church, devotees of the Virgin make their way to the large statute elevated in honor of the saint. There, they lay flowers and say a quick prayer to her, expressing their gratitude and wishes. Some wish to spend a few private moments with the Virgin. After everyone has paid their respect to the Virgin, a traditional Catholic mass is held. Then, everyone leaves the church, carrying the statue with them. They walk towards the dock, crossing seven "windows" made of a wooden construction adorned with flowers and icons of the Virgin. The dock of Regla has a symbolic significance for many devotees. It opens to a waterway that connects Cuba to Florida and the Atlantic Ocean. It was also the first place the freshly enslaved Africans set foot in the New World during the transatlantic slave trade. At this place, devotees feel a deeper connection to their roots and ask the Virgin to help them keep these memories alive. After this, they sing a few traditional songs devoted to Mary. They turn the statute towards the water, so she can admire her kingdom, then say goodbye to her. The statue is then carried back to the sanctuary, where worshipers can visit her, offering prayers and asking for guidance.

Devotees who also celebrate Mary as Yemaya hold a different ceremony in the evening of the same day. They use drumming and chanting, calling on the Orisha. Those devoted to the combined version of her aspects will hold séances called *misas espirituales*. As their name implies, these spiritual masses have the purpose of communicating with the saint on a spiritual level. It's also customary for the hosts to contact the souls of ancestors and spiritual guides. The souls of former slaves who, in their time, also venerated Yemaya or the Virgen de la Regla are also called upon.

The Depiction of Virgin Mary

In art, Virgin Mary is depicted very similarly to Yemaya. She's wearing a serene expression while sitting or standing in her kingdom. However, there are several distinctions between the portrayals of Yemaya and the Virgin Mary. Notably, the saint is surrounded by clouds, watching over her children. Meanwhile, Yemaya is often depicted as standing in or over water, overseeing her kingdom and making it safe for travelers. Another difference is that while Yemaya is typically dressed in blue, Mary is seen wearing a white dress and a blue cloak or veil. Her white dress reflects her virginal status, which is in stark contrast to Yemaya's passionate nature. With the blue veil, Mary retained some of Yemaya's symbolism, which alludes to her status as a patron of the seas. It also gives her an allure of purity, as water is considered one of the most powerful cleansing agents.

Mary wearing blue isn't present only in the new, syncretized religions. It's referenced in the Old Testament, where Mary is compared to the Ark of the Covenant, a sacred relic protected by a blue cloth. This reference stems from the description of Mary carrying her son shrouded in Heavenly protection. In Christianity, the color blue is the symbol of the sky. When used in clothing (especially a piece reflecting modesty like a veil or cloak), the color blue means the person is protected by the Heavens. Mary (with her blue veil) is blessed for her devotion to all her children. It shows that she is a radiating female force who uses her power subtly and only when asked to do so.

Mary's blue veils also give her a distinguished status. Historically, blue and purple have always been associated with royalty and other people in good material standing. Until the invention of artificial dyes, clothes were colored with natural agents. This made blue fabric extremely hard to create and so expensive that only the richest members of society could afford them. Mary is always depicted as a modest woman. However, her blue veil indicates that she wasn't lacking anything (at least not in what's truly valuable, such as moral riches). That said, unlike Yemaya, who is typically portrayed with a large, floating skirt made of seven layers, Mary's clothes are more modest. Her dress is long but has a simple design.

Other depictions show her as the Queen of Heavens, with a blue veil denoting her divine status. In Santeria's religious art and symbolism, she is dressed in elaborate clothes, wearing blue and white, even when referred to as Yemaya. Mary is depicted as a young white woman, just like in Christian art. Yemaya, the saint, is notably black, sometimes with water droplets shining on her skin as she has risen from the sea. In rituals, people wear both blue and white as colors of Yemaya, using these as a connection to her grace and nurturing wisdom.

Sometimes, Mary is depicted wearing all blue clothes, standing over a snake. This image symbolizes her powerful nature and refers to her defeating the snake (the devil) by crushing its head.

Chapter 4: How to Connect to Yemaya

Whether you're already familiar with Yoruba practices and traditions or just getting introduced to them for the first time, connecting with Yemaya shouldn't be seen as something very hard to achieve. The best approach to this is to properly understand the goddess's origin and the cultures, traditions, and religions she comes from. You cannot truly connect with the goddess until you've learned all about the heritage she comes from – this is essential, even when praying to the goddess, as it will convey your respect for her and the cultural practices associated with her. Moreover, the practices associated with Yemaya's worship vary widely due to unique origin points, so it's vital to learn about each religion and culture.

Connecting with Yemaya is a spiritual experience.
https://unsplash.com/photos/0chVl3b15MQ

Although connecting with Yemaya shouldn't be intimidating, it does require you to put in some effort. Like many religions, the true secrets and rituals needed to fully connect with the goddess are only revealed to the initiated. So, it's preferred that you get properly trained within one or all of the religions associated with her. Suppose you're not well-informed about the rituals that you attempt to practice. In that case, you'll only end up with an ineffective spell at best and may even risk offending Yemaya. It's also disrespectful to Yoruba practitioners and Yemaya devotees when you perform their rituals without any prior training or knowledge. Therefore, it's critical that you always approach these rituals and traditions with respect and honor. This chapter will serve as a proper guide to connecting with Yemaya and explain how you can worship her respectfully.

Connecting with Yemaya: The Basics

Let's start with the basics of incorporating various practices into your life, which will make you feel more connected to the mother goddess, Yemoja. These simple gestures and daily rituals will greatly affect your spirituality and allow you to understand your favorite Orisha more deeply. Here are a few ideas on how to incorporate the magic of Yemoja into your daily life and rituals:

- Incorporate blue and white-themed clothes and charms into your life. This way, whenever you wear the sea Orisha's colors, you'll be reminded of her.
- If you're fond of long, flowing skirts, try an outfit with some white skirts to be reminded of Yemoja.
- Yemoja devotees wear seven silver bracelets on one arm to portray their allegiance to the sea goddess.
- Practice ocean or water magic when visiting the beach, river, or lake.
- Jot down your wishes, spells, and prayers to Yemaya on a blue or white paper boat, and float it out to the sea.
- Drink more water throughout the day.
- Spend time looking at the fish at an aquarium, river, or beach.
- Do some water activities like sailing, boating, or cruising to feel the sweeping power of the ocean.

- If you've been praying to have children, include Yemaya in your fertility rituals and spells.

Symbols, Magical Attributes, and Offering

In addition to common practices used when invoking Yemaya, you can also include some symbols, charms, and magical offerings into your practices to have a better chance of forming a bond with the goddess. You can use these items on your altar or in daily rituals to attract Yemaya's energy.

- Dry sand from a beach
- Fresh water from a beach, river, or lake
- Pearls, fish, rocks, and shells found on a beach
- Fish nets
- Fountains
- Small paper or wooden boats
- White flowers
- White or blue ceramic dishes that carry fresh water from the sea or river
- Blue and white-themed charms
- The number 7
- 7 cowrie shells, 7 pennies, or 7 white roses

Most people associate Yemaya with fertility and other feminine aspects in life. However, she has much more depth than is usually observed. True devotees of the goddess know her actual value. Every Orisha she came into contact with developed their potential when she came into her full form. Yemaya shouldn't only be invoked when trying to perform fertility rituals but, most importantly, when you're planning to nurture your goals and manifest your true purpose. If you want to bring their ideas to life, Yemaya's energy will be extremely beneficial for you.

Altar for Yemaya

An altar for Yemaya can be created similar to how you'd design an altar for the element of water. For this purpose, you can choose a smaller-sized altar that you dedicate to the sole purpose of praying to the sea goddess. Before you can start practicing rituals or praying to Yemaya, you will need to cleanse this altar and bless it with positive energy.

This altar will act as a proper channel through which you can connect to the goddess and should therefore be free from any negative energy. Take a few minutes out of each day to pray to the goddess using this altar and make regular offerings in her name. Meditate on her presence at this unique altar you've created just for her (more about meditating later). When you meditate with the altar right in front of you, imagine yourself being surrounded by the goddess's pure white energy and her element of clear, blue water. Either chant to her, pray to her or play songs that remind you of her or the ocean.

While there will be a proper guide to creating an altar for Yemaya's worship later in the book, ensure you follow a blue and white theme to adorn the altar. Use sea shells, models of fish and other sea creatures, and even pictures depicting the sea goddess. Use white candles to create a luminist scene at the altar while adding some flowers as well.

Other Ways to Connect with Yemaya

As discussed before, Yemaya is frequently associated with the moon, and many of her worship rituals involve the moon cycle alignments. Therefore, a good way to connect with her would be to incorporate the moon and symbols associated with the moon into your worshiping practices and any other rituals. Secondly, Yemaya is also often associated with the number seven. She's depicted wearing seven skirts which basically represent the seven seas. Therefore, the number seven should also be included in your practices in whichever way you see fit. For instance, you could light seven white candles on your altar or arrange seven cowrie shells while you're meditating. There should be no limits to your creativity when invoking Yemaya. She is a creative spirit herself and greatly appreciates any kind of innovation and creative spirit. For instance, some people make offerings to Yemaya for seven consecutive days.

Many ancient drawings and paintings also often depict her wearing bells in her hair and clothes. Therefore, the sound and use of bells can also be associated with the goddess and incorporated into ritual practice. Another common symbol linked to the sea goddess is the peacock. So, try using peacock symbols or peacock feathers as charms on your altar. Yemaya quite often responds positively to spells or rituals done in the name of healing, protection, creativity, and self-love. However, you should avoid asking for favors if you're not leaving enough offerings for the goddess because, with Yemoja, it is a two-way street.

Ideal Offerings for Yemaya

If you want to be in the good graces of Yemaya, the trick is to be generous with your offerings. A detailed chapter will discuss the various offerings you can leave her. Make sure that you visit the ocean or some river frequently to make these offerings. While it's okay to perform the rituals at your house and pray at the altar you've created, your spells and prayers will be most effective when you're close to water.

Ideal offerings for Yemaya can include sea shells, salt water, charms, flowers, fruits, herbs, and even food items. The best way to show reverence for her is to leave offerings that speak to her personality traits and associated elements. You could sing sacred songs or compose a unique prayer for her. Or, you could chant her name and use the vibrations of your voice to connect with her energy. Some people even make food dishes to pay tribute to the goddess.

Other Important Aspects of Connecting/Talking with Yemaya

According to Yoruba legends, Yemaya is considered to be the queen of the ocean and the mother of all living beings. She is considered to have many offspring whom she nurtures and protects. She loves her children more than anything else and is thus very kind and generous. Therefore, you should always approach her with reverence and respect. This is especially important for people not familiar with Yoruba practices and traditions. Suppose you feel interested in connecting with Yemaya. In that case, it's important that you first take the time to study the lore, traditions, and culture associated with her. You should remember that connecting with the Orisha is not something to be taken lightly and requires a lot of effort. Therefore, you need to always be respectful of the relationship you form with an Orisha deity.

Yemaya Meditation

Meditation is one of the most popular methods used to connect with Yemaya.
https://unsplash.com/photos/2pUP1Ts1bmo

Meditation practice is considered to be one of the best ways of connecting spiritually with an Orisha. Meditation helps ground you, cleanse your energy, and aligns it with the deity you favor – if done correctly. To practice meditation to connect with Yemaya, follow these steps:

1. Find a quiet, comfortable place in your house away from all sorts of distractions. Light seven white candles and place them in front of you (take care of fire safety). Use an oil diffuser or incense to create the perfect meditation environment.

2. Close your eyes and let your body relax. Take three slow, deep breaths, and set your intention for the meditation sessions. Open up your heart to Yemaya's energy, and chant in your mind, "I want to connect to Yemaya/Yemoja."

3. Now, imagine that you're on a beautiful island, completely surrounded by the deep blue ocean. The sky above is free of clouds, with the sun shining brightly. Feel the fresh, cool breeze on your face and enjoy the view.

4. Imagine playing in the water, splashing around in the cold, fresh waves. Now think about getting on a small boat, letting the

current take you out to sea. Focus on the feelings you have when surrounded by the ocean. Instead of feeling scared of the vastness of the sea, you'll feel at ease.

5. Envision the energy around you changing suddenly. You start to feel loved, cocooned in warmth, and look up to see a beautiful woman rising out of the sea. She looks at you and says, "*I am the Sea Goddess, Yemaya, Mother of all. I'm pleased that you have connected with me. Come with me, and let me show you who I am.*"

6. After this, imagine her taking you into her arms and into the sea. While you're with her, ask her questions and for blessings. Once you've finished connecting with her, say your goodbyes, take three deep breaths, and open your eyes.

7. Once you're back in your room, go over everything you've learned about her, and memorize how you feel right after the meditative session.

8. When trying to connect to Orisha deities, make sure you use the Orisha's name to invoke their presence. In this case, Yemaya's sacred name is Aquamarine, and her sacred water is Blue Agate. Also, make sure to use the goddess's name when presenting offerings to her.

Given below are some additional tips for connecting with Yemaya.

- To make meditative sessions more interesting, sit near a lake, river, sea, or even swimming pool and immerse your legs inside. The water will act as a conduit between you and Yemaya. While practicing this, you can also wear a flowing white skirt, which will sway around your legs when you're in the water, giving you a mermaid-like look.

- Another way you can better connect with Yemaya during these meditative sessions is by wearing a seashell. Seashells are her symbols and will make you feel her presence more strongly. You could also hold the seashell in your hand or near your ear to be able to hear the goddess.

Prayers for Yemaya

Stay in the good graces of the sea goddess by praying to her regularly, either in daily rituals, at occasional festivals, or in front of her altar.

Prayer 1:
>Yemaya, oh blessed queen of the seas,
>Let the sacred waters of the ocean wash over me.
>Hold me, oh mother, your child.
>Cleanse my soul, nurture my life, and sustain my spirit.
>Yemaya, oh, magnificent one.
>You who wear the seven sacred skirts of the seven seas,
>Move around me and surround me with your energy
>To wash away all negativity
>Oh, Yemaya, mistress of the tides and the moon,
>Bless me with your sacred light,
>and fill me with your energy.
>Help me to complete my purpose.
>Oh Yemaya, healing ocean mother,
>I ask you to fill me with your cleansing energy.
>Bless me with your pure waters,
>And let me heal with its regenerative energy

Prayer 2:
>Strange clouds and fragments of beauty.
>Envisioning shining stars of a story.
>Invoking you among the goddesses of the waters.
>You calm the storm with your joy.
>You bring calm with your kind words
>The sea breeze brings your energy to us,
>Oh, goddess of the sea and rivers
>You kiss the beautiful moon
>and bless us with your waves
>The waves carry beautiful flowers.
>Hidden in the waters.
>Their aromas are the hope that makes you
>the Goddess of the Ocean.

Prayer 3:

I sense the comfort and love of a mother as I gaze at your picture. I know you are close, guarding and directing your children. I lower my head in admiration and respect; I ask you for your graces. May God grant you permission to purify my soul and body with your divine waters, and may my Earthly path be illuminated by your divine light. Amen

Prayer 4:

Bring blessings and fortune to those who are in need, O magnificent Yemaya. We hope, dear Mother, that through your graces, we will achieve what we ask for in this prayer. Although we know that, due to our shortcomings, we do not merit what we ask for, we implore you to answer our prayers. Amen.

Prayer 5:

Queen who is Mother of All,

Goddess of the Ocean Depths,

defender of women

Ensure people are aware of your presence all over this holy place.

We who pray to you as Yemaya,

Our Mother, Our Womb of Formation,

ask that your love keeps rolling and washing over us

as the ocean waves, as the creeks from your breasts.

Yemaya, Mother of the Fish,

You who are solace, encouragement, and redemption,

We call you forth to enter our hearts and souls.

Prayer 6:

You are the force that ripples underwater,

She who binds the sea and the sky, the eternal mother who reclaims you.

Feel the sand under your toes, press the conch to your ear, and

gaze upon my blue,

and you know Me.

Submit your problem to Me,

Toss your worries into the ocean's core that is Me.
I'll take care of you, dry your tears, soothe your anguish
and shield you from the upcoming storms.
In your submission, I embrace your voice.
In the giving over, I become your liberty.
Daughter, return home and allow me
to make unified
everything that is fragmentary.

Prayer 7:

You who control the waters, pouring over humanity your protection, O Divine Mother, wash their bodies and their thoughts, performing a purging with your water and ingraining in their soul the regard and reverence due to the force of nature that it symbolizes. Let us safeguard your group of things and what they protect.

We beg strong Yemanja, Queen of the Waters, to receive this plea.

With goodness and love, give me the necessary capacity to withstand everything.

In your ocean of beauty and tranquility, I desire to live.

Keep my loved ones safe from harm and peril.

All hail Yemanja, Sea Queen!

Yemaya is considered to be one of the major Orisha deities mentioned in Yoruba legends. She is the mother of all and is thus easy to seek and connect with. Her spirit is nurturing and warm, which makes her entity all the more attractive to people. Yemaya devotees and worshippers are present worldwide and have different ways they pay homage to the Goddess of the Sea. People often seek her blessings and wisdom when they desperately need healing and protection in their lives. While many sources have mainstreamed the worship of Yemaya, her actual reverence stems from unique cultures and practices not known by many. For non-native devotees, it is incredibly hard to find authentic sources to understand how to properly connect with the goddess. The techniques provided in this chapter will hopefully help you connect more thoroughly with Yemaya.

Chapter 5: The Goddess of the Ocean and the Moon

The tides and the moon have always been interconnected. The water gravitates toward the moon, and it spins and turns with the moon's phases. Traditionally, Yemaya is seen as the goddess of the ocean and the moon. However, the public only acknowledges her rulership over water bodies. It fails to recognize or remember that she governs the moon as well.

Yemaya is also known as the goddess of the ocean and the moon.
https://unsplash.com/photos/8Gl7Ew-q6D8

The goddess Yemaya has many faces and a few reincarnations. In the beginning, when the oceans and the moon were first created, Olokun appeared and announced himself as the owner of the water's depths. He then dived into the water and created a splatter that evaporated into the skies. Immediately, the skies began to rain, and the droplets returned to the ocean. This was the moment when Yembo, the first incarnation of Yemaya, appeared. Yembo declared that her kingdom is "where the moon touches the waters."

Yemaya's full name is Ye Emo Eja, which directly translates to "the mother whose children are as numerous as the fish." It is believed that Yemaya gave birth to both the sun and the moon, as well as the first fourteen Orishas.

This chapter's main focus will be on Yemaya's connection with the moon. This includes various rituals that are done on certain moon phases as well as different prayers and spells that relate to the goddess and your connection with her.

Yemaya and the Phases of the Moon

The moon holds great power and affects everything around you, including yourself. Think of the way the moon affects the water or how most predators strike on the new moon. The moon's gravitational pull is so strong that it moves oceans and seas. It would be ridiculous to think that the moon can have this strong influence over the Earth but not affect humans in any way.

The phases of the moon affect humankind too. For instance, it is common knowledge that people's emotions are heightened during the full moon. This chapter will go in-depth about the different moon phases and what humans go through during each phase. However, before delving into the moon's phases, you need to understand Yemaya's role in all of this.

The first incarnation of Yemaya gave birth to the moon and the stars. She is the goddess of the night sky and waters. Yemaya created different moon phases to create order and harmony in life on Earth.

Every moon phase is associated with different themes in life. For instance, the new moon is linked to certain subjects, while other moon phases are associated with different themes. Why should you know this? Well, simply because the chances of receiving optimum results are higher when you pray or cast spells during relevant moon phases.

For instance, picture yourself praying for a new start. This is better accomplished during the new moon. Why? Each moon phase has powers, so asking for a new beginning will yield results during the new moon, but it will not be as powerful during a waning crescent. The waning crescent is associated with endings, so the power of your prayer and the waning crescent will clash. This is why it is better to cast spells or pray during phases that relate to what you are asking for or trying to manifest into existence.

Remember that the phases are divided into two groups: beginnings and endings. The first four phases are more about beginnings and new events, while the other four are more about endings and old situations. The full moon does not fall into either group and is considered a powerhouse by itself.

In spirituality, the moon is linked with the subconscious, intuition, femininity, fertility, magic, and psychic abilities. In Yoruban and Santerian traditions, Yemaya is also associated with these areas.

The goddess also rules over the realm of dreams. This includes prophetic and lucid dreams. This means that the goddess can respond to your calls and prayers through dreams. People who pray to Yemaya usually ask for her protection during pregnancy or ask that she help them with their fertility. Others ask her to guide their spiritual journey when they are practicing magic or casting spells. Spiritualists also ask Yemaya to guide and strengthen their intuition.

Yemaya is seen as the mother of all, so if you ever need to feel motherly love and protection, you can always pray to the goddess for just that. There are a million reasons to pray to her. It all comes down to what you need from the goddess.

If you would like to spark a connection, you should know that she responds when the time is right. This means that her response may not be instantaneous all the time. She will reply to you when you are ready to receive the answers or when the circumstances are right. She may appear in your dreams or send you direct messages that will be unquestionably from her. She will make sure that you understand that she is the sender, and the answer will be clear as the bright full moon in the sky.

New Moon

The new moon may be dark and indistinguishable from the night sky, but its powers surpass its appearance. This is the first moon phase. It brings about change, new beginnings, a new version of you, and a new page in your story. It has a child-like energy, and you will feel this enthusiasm if you connect with Yemaya during this phase.

This is the best time to bring your ideas to life. So before the new moon arrives, start a list of things you would like to begin or start with the new moon phase. When the sun sets and the moon rises, go to Yemaya's altar and invoke her.

Cleanse the altar, light the candles, and begin the invocation by saying, *"Queen of the Sea, Mother of life, I come to you this new moon night. In the reflection of your mirror, beneath your holy gaze, I give you honor, homage, and praise."*

You can use the same prayer on different moon phases; just make sure to say the correct moon phase. After your prayer, start communicating with the goddess. Share with her everything that you would like to start this month. Ask her to give you opportunities and guide you with your decisions.

During this period, if you receive invitations or come across a clear sign that the goddess heard your callings, answer them. It will be best if you do not reject invitations during this time. The goddess may send new people your way, unexpected invitations, or other opportunities that will create a path for what you want.

Waxing Crescent

The waxing crescent graces the sky two days after the new moon. During this moon phase, you will feel more confident in yourself and your abilities. You will feel a surge of bravery, making you more likely to take risks. It is essential to try to stay grounded during this phase because you might feel a bit impulsive.

This moon phase will not influence reckless or impulsive behavior, but people react to the moon differently. This means that if you are naturally impulsive, then you may feel more impulsive during this phase. If you are prone to recklessness, then consider asking the goddess to help you make wise decisions during this time.

Like the new moon, the waxing crescent brings fresh beginnings with it, but it also makes people feel more optimistic and confident enough to take on new tasks. It also weakens self-doubt, so if you are a person who second-guesses themselves a lot, you will feel more confident.

One of Yemaya's symbols is the crescent moon, so when you are praying to her during the waxing or waning crescent, make sure you have the crescent moon on the altar. When you pray to the goddess, tell her about the anxieties and fears you would like to eliminate during this time. Tell her about your new projects, but also tell her about what worries you. Ask her to give you confidence and comfort. The waxing crescent powers will give you confidence and trust in yourself, but the goddess can multiply them for you.

First Quarter

The first quarter and last quarter are known as the half-moon. In Santerian and Yoruban culture, the half-moon is a symbol of the goddess' perplexing knowledge and wisdom.

This moon phase pushes you to do better. In other words, it challenges you to overcome your fears of the unknown or the unseen. Why is that? Only the first half of the moon is visible, but the rest is not. This phase symbolizes the binary relationship and the sharp contrast between what you know and what you do not. The first quarter moon gives you strength and a deeper perspective.

During this time, you will be able to be more honest with yourself and reflect on various aspects that need to be worked on or fixed. You may feel anxious during this phase, and this is why you can burn Allspice as an offering to the goddess. This spice is used in various spells, but when it is burned on the first quarter moon as an offering, it sends your prayers to the goddess.

It is believed that burning this plant helps to reduce anxiety and stress, and it also makes you feel more relaxed. When you offer this spice to Yemaya, she will understand that you need immediate help with your fears and anxieties about the future.

You can burn this herb every first quarter moon as a ritual. Remember to cleanse the altar and invoke the goddess before you offer her any offerings.

Waxing Gibbous

The waxing gibbous moon is the last phase before the full moon. This placement makes this phase special. Why is that? Well, the full moon is considered to be the most powerful moon phase, so the waxing gibbous contains some of this power.

This moon phase brings positive opportunities and potential with it. During this time, you might feel like you are about to gain new experiences or manifest goals and dreams into reality. Trust your feelings and intuition during the waxing gibbous. If you feel like you are about to embark on a journey, you will be correct. This phase brings wealth, self-development, and successful manifestations with it.

The waxing gibbous will reward you even if you have been working for what you are trying to achieve. During this time, you can burn pine or Yemaya incense as an offering to the goddess and as a way to bless your financial gains within this period.

If you would like to add Yemaya incense to your workings, you can follow the recipe below.

Ingredients:
- Powdered star anise pods
- Rose petals
- Basil Leaf
- Powdered sandalwood
- Lemon verbena
- Meadowsweet

You will need the following:
- Dust mask
- Glass bowl
- Mortar
- Pestle

Steps:
1. Add herbs and plants to the mortar.
2. Put a dust mask on.
3. Crush ingredients with a pestle.
4. Add mixture into the bowl.

5. Pray to Yemaya over the ingredients.
6. Share with her your intentions and goals.
7. Place the bowl over Yemaya's altar.
8. Leave it there for 14 days.
9. Seal the powder in a container.
10. Burn the powder over charcoal.
11. Use during the waxing gibbous phase or when you are praying to the goddess.

Full Moon

The full moon is the most powerful of all the moon phases. This phase symbolizes the maternal figure that is Yemaya. She is considered the mother of all, and the full moon symbolizes her motherhood and all of her children.

You will be blessed with clarity and enlightenment on the first night of the full moon. You will receive emotional and mental clarity. You will not be doubting or second-guessing yourself, your choices, or your decisions. If you are feeling a bit emotional during this phase, then this is nothing to worry about. Almost everyone feels emotional under the light of the full moon. Your heightened emotions will bring you a lot of revelations. In other words, it will make you see what your subconscious may have been hiding from your conscious mind.

During this time, women are known to become more fertile, or there is a higher chance for them to conceive. If you intend to work with Yemaya during this time, then you will be very busy. There are various chants, prayers, and spells that you will be doing during this period.

If you want to work on your fertility with the goddess, then place a bowl of almonds on her altar and chant:

> "Today! Today, I'm going to sing!
> I will praise in the sand, at full moon, the mother Iemanjá!
> Rose of the sea, My blue sky star, It's not a fisherman's story
> That my love will give you.
> He leaves! Let the waves of the sea pass.
> Hear the song of the beautiful Odoiá.
> I wish he sent A big love From the bottom of the sea."

Begin by eating the almonds, given that they come from a separate bowl, not from the offering. Now, you may be wondering, why should I eat almonds? Well, almonds are known to help with fertility when you are working with Yemaya. They are considered to be a magical net in fertility spells as well.

If you want to seek Yemaya's protection, the best night is on a full moon. For this spell to work, you will need to take a trip to the beach, so get ready to pack a few things with you.

Ingredients:
- Holy oil
- Yemaya oil
- 7 quartz crystals
- 7 cubes of camphor
- 7 blue votive candles
- 7 silver fish hooks
- 7 silver coins
- 7 pennies
- 7 cubes of camphor
- 7 bluing balls
- 7 glass jars
- 3 keys
- Juice of 7 limes
- Blue cloth (square)
- White towel (clean)

Walk into the water during the high tide and stop when the water reaches your ankles. Now, ask the Eleggua to open the path for you and leave 3 keys as an offering. Count 7 waves and begin chanting the following to the goddess:

> *"Queen of the Sea, Mother of life, I come to you this Full Moon night. In the reflection of your mirror, beneath your holy gaze, I give you honor, homage, and praise."*

When you have finished, dip the jars in the ocean and then dry them with a clean towel. Fill the jars with crystals, fish hooks, bluing, camphor cubes, and coins. Make sure to put these ingredients in the same order and chant,

"I call the power of the sea, Keep my home safe and protect me."

Repeat the same chant every time you place 1 crystal or 1 key in the jar. When you have finished, you will have completed 35 chants.

Now, fill ⅔ of the jar with sea water and leave the pennies where the water meets the sand. When you are done, pack your jars and go home. Lay 7 plates on the ground and create a circle. Put each jar on every plate. Place the 7 candles next to the jars and anoint them with Yemaya oil. Fill your bathtub with water and add Florida water, sea salt, lime juice, and bergamot oil. Sit in the water for exactly 28 minutes. Make sure you set a timer. When the timer rings, pat yourself with a white towel. Remember to pat, and do not rinse. Put holy oil on your feet, hands, third eye, and heart.

Now, go back to the circle you created and cast an energetic spell. To do this, simply envision a white light forming a protective shield around you. Light each candle and say,

"Spirit of the sea, protect me."

Close your eyes and picture the water rising to protect you. Spend 28 minutes in meditation while keeping this image in your mind. When you have finished, say the following,

"Spirits of water, I thank you for lending your Ashé to this site. Return to your kingdom beneath the waves. Hail and farewell."

Close the circle and place your candles in random spots in your house. Do not blow them out; let the wax melt away. Store the seawater that is in the jars in another container and hang the talismans in a blue cloth. On the seventh day after the spell, pour the seawater in a clockwise motion around your house.

Waning Gibbous

The waning gibbous is the first phase of endings. This is the best time to shed away any self-sabotaging habits and self-destructive mindsets. You will likely meet parts of your shadow self during this time. When you do, do not reject these parts of you, you may not like how they make you feel about yourself, but accepting them is imperative. By accepting them, you will be releasing yourself from their tight grip.

Suppose you would like to shield yourself from your destructive habits. In that case, you might want to anoint candles with Yemaya oil on the goddess's altar or burn Yemaya oil and pray to her while inhaling the oil's sweet aroma.

Ingredients:
- 7 drops bergamot oil
- 7 drops sandalwood
- 2 drops lemon verbena
- 2 drops rose oil
- 1 oz. almond oil
- 1 pearl
- 4 drops magnolia
- Sea salt crystals

You will need the following:
- Reusable eye-droppers
- A small funnel
- Glass bottle
- Mortar
- Pestle

Steps:
1. Add almond oil to the jar.
2. Let it sit for 7 minutes.
3. Pour in the rest of the oils.
4. Use a dropper for the oils.
5. Cleanse the dropper with rubbing alcohol so you do not mix the oils.
6. Crush the pearl with your mortar and pestle.
7. Add the powdered pearl to the jar.
8. Swirl for 3 minutes.
9. Pray to the goddess for protection.
10. Add the sea salt crystal to the jar.
11. Seal the jar with its lid.
12. Leave on the altar for 7 days.
13. Use the oil for anointing yourself or candles. You can also burn the oil when you are praying for protection.

Last Quarter

Similar to the waning gibbous moon, the last quarter is also connected to the shadow self. This moon pushes you to work or fix your more negative traits or habits. It will draw your attention to the shadowy sides of you by making you confront it through friends, family, or people who are close to you.

You might be confronted with your negative habits. Do not be fazed when this happens. Try to be accepting of the situation and forgive yourself. Remember to befriend your shadow self and look at it as a pathway for your healing.

The best thing to do here is pray to the goddess and ask her to enlighten you and help you through this period with as much grace as possible. Remember that alone time is essential during this time, so grab your incense and sit by the beach. Connect with yourself and the ocean, and you will eventually feel better.

Waning Crescent

The waning crescent phase pushes you to pay attention to your needs. During this phase, you might feel exhausted. This usually happens to draw your attention to your energy levels and self-care. Suppose you have been straining yourself or spending most of your time worrying or caring for other people. In that case, this is the time to dedicate some of this care toward yourself.

Spend time by the ocean to connect with Yemaya and allow yourself to feel her love and care toward you. Make sure you meet your needs and do things that you genuinely enjoy, even if it means oversleeping or spending the whole day on the couch.

Dark Moon

The dark moon is the last phase, and it is the exact opposite of the new moon. The new moon is all about new beginnings, unlike the dark moon. During this time, you will feel nudged to end things that no longer serve you.

This is the time to cut off toxic friendships, end unfruitful relationships, or leave extremely taxing jobs. If you feel like the moon is telling you to eject a certain thing from your life, then take it as a sign.

However, you must reflect on what you are ending and your reasons for ending it. Do not end relationships or leave a job if you are unsure about your reasons.

It is best to offer a magnolia to Yemaya's altar or burn it by her altar if you want to gain wisdom during this challenging period.

Every moon phase contains power and energy that is unique to it. These energies affect you daily, whether you are conscious of it or not. However, now you know what they do and how Yemaya is connected to the moon and its phases. If you would like to work with the goddess, consider performing some spells or rituals during the relevant moon phases.

Chapter 6: Ritual Tools and Symbols

Yemaya is a generous and open-minded deity who usually accepts any kind of offering presented to her, given that the person's intentions are pure. However, it is best to present customized offerings and presents when trying to win the favor of any Orisha deity, and Yemaya is not an exception to this. Whether you present her with pearl-adorned combs, beautiful necklaces, fragrant perfumes, stunning paintings and depictions of her, flowers, seashells, stones, or food offerings, she'll happily accept your gifts and shower you with her blessings.

A lace fan is among the many offerings preferred.
https://unsplash.com/photos/ZdMg-ILt20A

Many people also leave her blue or white lace fans and feathered fans with duck or peacock feathers. As discussed before, these animals have special importance to the sea goddess. Thus any item representing them is deemed significant. Yemoja prefers small bells, fish nets, aquamarine gemstones, crystal beads, pearls, masks, and blue-colored glass – though the most popular offerings for Yemaya are observed to be food and flowers.

One of the most common symbols associated with Yemaya is conch shells. Most of her depictions portray her holding these cowrie shells. The legend associated with this symbolic item is that Yemeya would fill these shells with her comforting voice. Moreover, these shells have a narrow slit on one side, while the other looks like a pregnant belly, which connects them to the fertility goddess, Yemoja. According to legend, Yemaya fills these cowrie shells with the gift of fertility. The nurturing spirit wants all her offspring to be the most authentic versions of themselves, which is why she blesses the people on their path to find their meaning in life and pursue their dreams.

Cowrie shells are found all over the world but were considered to be sacred objects back in the day. People even used them as currency. Many women wore them as jewelry and traded them for spices and silk. These shells are incredibly versatile and are found in various shapes, sizes, and colors. As these shells were considered symbols of fertility back in the day, they were gifted to new brides or laboring mothers to ensure safe delivery. Today, many Yemaya worshippers wear cowrie necklaces and bracelets to channel their goddesses' energy. People keep the opening visible to signal their desire for a partner or might symbolize their strong opinions.

The Sacred Cowrie Shells

Since ancient times, cowrie shells have had supernatural significance in Yoruba and Santeria rituals and traditions. However, going into the full extent of those rituals is too complex to provide here. Instead, you can try a simple way to use these cowrie shells to connect with the divine. This is done by practicing a yes-no questions ritual, commonly known as Obi. There are about 5 possible answers that can be obtained from this practice. To perform the ritual, you will need 4 opened cowrie shells (the natural hump on the back of the shell should be cut off and sanded to result in a fairly flat surface). When the cut sides faces up during the reading, it means the shell is silent, whereas when the mouth-shaped side faces upward, the shell is speaking. Additionally, you'll need a simple cloth or mat to place on the ground or a table. This is where you'll be casting the shells. Make sure you pray to the spirits and ask them for their guidance before you cast the shells.

Cowrie shells have supernatural value in Yoruba and Santeria rituals.
Sodabottle, CC BY-SA 3.0 <https://creativecommons.org/licenses/by-sa/3.0>, via Wikimedia Commons https://commons.wikimedia.org/wiki/File:Cowrie_shells_-_sozhi_roll_of_3.jpg

Take the four conch shells in your hands while envisioning your question or the situation you're inquiring about. Focus solely on the question and slowly blow on the shells. Then, shake the shells in your hands, and roll them onto the mat like you would roll dice. Interpret the answers according to the following guidelines:

- If all four shells land with their mouth-shaped side facing up, it indicates that all four are speaking. This is considered a blessing, so the answer should be considered a yes. You'll be successful in what you asked about, more than you hope. You can do a second throw to see if your luck will last long.
- If three shells land with their mouth-shaped side facing upward, while one is downward, three will be speaking while one will be silent. This answer is less positive than the first one and can be considered a maybe. Although many people consider this answer a yes, the one silent shell creates doubt about the issue.

To further check for the answer, you can do a second throw. If the second throw yields all four shells speaking, then it translates to a yes. However, if you get one shell silent again, you should move on with your decision. For more than two silent shells, the answer should be considered to be no.

- If two shells land with their mouth sides facing upward while the other two are downward, this is considered a very positive response. This response tells you that everything is balanced, harmonious, and perfect. Throwing the shells a second time is not wise whenever you receive this answer.
- If you get one shell with the mouth upward and three of them downward, the silent shells outweigh the speaking ones. This is a clear no. It indicates that the thing you inquired about will be extremely difficult, if not impossible, to achieve.
- The last possible scenario is that you get all four shells facing downward or being silent. This response is an irrevocable no but is also a warning. It tells you that negative forces surround you and that you need to do spiritual cleansing as soon as possible.

Spirits and deities often commune in this pattern when called upon for guidance. However, extensive practice is required before you can master this art and interpret your answers correctly. You should make additional throws if you're not completely satisfied with your answer, but most experts suggest against more than two throws in a row.

Other Symbols and Associations

Although many of these have been discussed before, here's a list of symbols and associations connected to Yemaya which can be very helpful for your practices and rituals:

- **Days of the week** - Saturday is considered sacred to Yemaya, as discussed previously, but some stories also suggest that Friday is an important day of the week for the sea goddess.
- **Metals** - lead is the most commonly associated metal for Yemaya. It is the only metal that does not corrode easily in seawater and thus holds a special place for the sea goddess. She also accepts offerings made of silver and steel as well.

- **Colors** - the color blue holds a special place in Yemaya's heart. It is the color of the vast ocean she lives in. Different shades of blue should be used to present offerings. White is another favorite color of the goddess. It symbolizes the kindness and purity of the mother, Orisha. Some people also add green and red beads to the necklaces worn for festivals celebrating Yemaya.
- **Necklace** - beaded necklaces are common offerings for Yemaya. Her sacred necklace consists of seven white beads, succeeded by seven blue beads. This pattern is then repeated until the necklace is long enough to be worn. White beads can also be substituted by clear beads.

Floral Offerings

There's a widespread misconception that Yemaya only favors white roses as floral offerings. While it's true that white flowers are her favorites, and she does prefer roses, these are not the only varieties she likes. Yemaya loves any blue or white flowers but accepts flowers of all colors, particularly pink, yellow, red, or violet blooms. What matters the most when presenting floral offerings is the flowers' freshness, beauty, and fragrance. It's best to present them in groups of seven, if possible, to respect the goddess's sacred number. If you ever see beautiful flowers floating on the waves of the ocean, or some river, rest assured that someone else left them as presents for Yemaya. Never try to pick these flowers up or take them with you, even if they get washed up on shore.

Yemaya loves blue and white floral offerings in particular.
https://unsplash.com/photos/qzoSJlPxS9k

When presenting floral offerings to the mother goddess Yemaya, follow some guidelines to show your respect to her. Wear white flowing skirts or a dress, if possible. Let your feet soak in the water, but don't venture deeper than that. Before putting the flowers into the sea, bring them close to your heart and pray to the goddess. Ask for her blessings and guidance. At the end of the prayer, count seven waves before tossing the flowers into the sea. Wait for seven heartbeats and take seven steps backward before turning around and walking back to the beach. During this, ensure you do not turn your back toward the sea to show your respect to the goddess.

You can also make non-floral offerings at the seaside. However, make sure whatever you toss into the sea isn't toxic to marine life. Plastics are off-limits when throwing offerings into the sea. You could toss food items into the sea, but ensure you take the packaging off them first to avoid polluting.

Food Offerings

Many practitioners prepare food offerings for Orisha spirits to keep them nourished and happy. These offerings are commonly placed on their altars for a short time. People also prepare meals favored by these deities and eat them with their families to honor the Orisha. In Yemaya's case, she prefers her food offerings to be presented at the seaside if possible. You could also leave them at a lake or in a river. Yemaya is said to reign over all water, so you can make your offerings at any place convenient to you.

If none of these options are possible for you, you can always leave some food at her altar or at the roots of an old, large tree. Wherever you leave the offerings, be sure to clean up after yourself. It is essential to consider the environment when leaving out food as offerings. The food will eventually rot and degrade the environment with it. The spirits will not be offended if you let your offerings sit for a while before disposing of them responsibly.

Like every other Orisha deity, Yemaya has several food items she favors above all – which include goose, duck, ram, rooster, turtle, hen, swan, lamb, shellfish, and seafood. She also loves pork rinds, especially when freshly fried. Vegetarian offerings for the goddess can include blueberries, bananas, watermelon, seaweed, plantains, honeydew melon, cantaloupe, and lettuce. She also has a taste for scrumptious desserts filled with heavy cream and syrups. These can include cane syrup, saltwater taffy, molasses, sweets, white wine, and pound cake.

Cooking for Yemaya

While you can present ready-made food items to Yemaya as offerings, there's just something special about preparing a whole meal in the name of your favorite goddess and spiritual guide. Cooking is one of the best ways to show Yemaya how dedicated you are to her. Plus, she loves a creative spirit and will surely enjoy your attempt at making some of her favored dishes. You can either share this meal with your family or present it to Yemaya and then share it with your spiritual community.

Spicy Seafood Stew

This delicious recipe for a spicy seafood stew is savory, unique, and fits perfectly with Yemaya's personality. You can serve it with shrimp or add scallops.

You will need the following:
- 1 yellow pepper (chopped)
- 1 red onion (diced)
- 1 green pepper (chopped)
- 1 red pepper (chopped)
- ½ a stick of salted butter
- ½ lb. of clams
- ½ lb. of mussels
- 1 lb. of raw shrimp (shelled and cleaned)
- Salt and pepper (as needed)
- 1 tbsp flour
- 4 tbsp garlic (minced)
- 5 ounces oysters
- ½ cup of fish stock
- 1 tbsp of cajun (for seasoning)

Steps:
1. First, you will need to prepare the sauce. To do this, melt the butter in a medium-sized pan at high heat.

2. Once the butter is completely melted, add the onions and stir until they turn translucent.
3. When the onions are done, add the flour and mix thoroughly. Make sure there are no lumps form in the sauce.
4. The sauce will turn golden after a while, and this is when you will need to add the fish stock into the mix. Stir well.
5. Finally, add the rest of the chopped vegetables, garlic, and seasoning to the pan.
6. Let the mixture cook for about 10 minutes so that the peppers become soft. Once they're tender and soft, add the oysters to the pan and cook for another 5 minutes.
7. Next, add the clams and mussels to the mixture, and stir for 1 minute. Add the shrimp next, and cook until they turn pink and start to curl. Serve hot.

Coconut Macaroons

Don't confuse these macaroons with the fancy French delicacy most people think of, but rather sweet mounds of coconut and sugar. Almost every Orisha loves this dessert, and while it's easy to buy sweet treats from the market, baking them yourself will show a level of devotion not everyone has. Plus, these aren't that difficult to prepare and only require simple ingredients.

You will need the following:
- ½ tsp of vanilla extract
- ½ cup of sugar
- ⅛ tsp of salt
- 3 large eggs (whites)
- 14 ounces of coconut (sweetened)

Steps:
1. Preheat the oven to 300 degrees and start preparing the batter.
2. Mix the sugar, salt, and egg whites together in a small bowl until mixed completely.
3. When the egg whites start to get frothy, add the vanilla extract and then fold the batter into the sweetened coconut.

4. Use a spoon to scoop out the batter and place it onto a baking sheet in the shape of little mounds.
5. Place them in the oven, and bake for about 25 to 30 minutes. Periodically check to see if the edges have turned golden brown. That's when you'll need to remove them from the oven. Serve with caramel or chocolate sauce.

Coconut Shrimp

Coconut Shrimp.
https://unsplash.com/photos/ag8O-k-DzC0

This can easily become one of your favorite recipes and is loved by Yemaya as well. Keep in mind that this is a bit trickier than the other recipes, so if you're confused about any instructions, take a deep breath and center yourself, or ask a friend to help. These fragrant delicacies will transport you to the Caribbean beaches in no time.

You will need the following:
- ¾ cup of breadcrumbs
- ½ tsp of salt
- ⅓ cup of flour
- ½ tsp pepper
- 1 cup of coconut (shredded, sweetened)
- 1 tbsp vegetable oil
- 2 large eggs
- 1 lb. shrimp

Steps:

1. First, you need to peel the shrimp and remove all the veins, but be sure to leave the tail intact.
2. In a small bowl, mix the flour, salt, and pepper together.
3. In a separate bowl, whisk the two eggs until they start to froth.
4. In another bowl, place the breadcrumbs along with the sweetened coconut. Mix them thoroughly.
5. Now, place the bowls in sequence so that you can take the shrimp and roll it into the flour mixture first.
6. Then, dip it into the egg mixture and cover it completely. Finally, coat the shrimp with the breadcrumb and coconut mixture and place it on a plate.
7. Do this with all the shrimp, and then place them in a frying pan or skillet with medium heat.
8. Fry the shrimp for about 2 minutes on one side and another 2 minutes on the other. Remove the fried shrimp from the pan, and place them on paper towels to drain the oil.

Food offerings for Yemaya should be cooked in proper pots, pans, or ovens and then served on a sopera (the Spanish word for "tureen"). A sopera is a ritual tool dedicated to Orishas and is used to present food offerings to the deities. Each Orisha has a sopera dedicated to them, which is decorated according to their personality traits. For Yemaya, the sopera should be white in color but decorated with blue swirling, wave-like designs. You can get creative with the designs you want to paint onto the sopera or serving plate.

Tools and Sacred Objects

Ritual tools and objects hold a special power not understood by many. They are filled with the energy of specific Orisha and have quite an effect on a spell or ritual. These sacred objects symbolize deeper, hidden meanings associated with each Orisha and act similar to talismans or objects used in magic. In most Yoruba traditions, after someone is initiated into the ranks of the devotees, they are given sacred tools cast in lead. These can be used to channel Yemaya's energy when performing a ritual or spell. Below is a list of sacred ritual items you can use to channel Yemaya's Ashe, or energy, for a spell or ritual.

- Cowrie shells - tools for divination

- Full moon - symbolizes Yemaya's motherhood status
- Half moon - symbolizes Yemaya's wisdom
- Anchor - symbolizes stability
- Seven hoops or bracelets - symbolize Yemaya's wealth
- Mermaid charms - symbolize Yemaya's supernatural beauty
- Oars - represent the balance between good and evil (always in pairs of 2)

Rituals and spells are a common part of Yoruba practices and are performed throughout the culture. Symbols and ritual tools hold a special power that should never be underestimated. Making these tools a part of your practice will be highly beneficial for you. Try to get hold of the tools and charms associated with Yemaya, even if you've not been initiated into the ranks yet. However, always be respectful of the goddess and the practices you perform. Try not to disrespect any sacred objects or ritual tools particularly associated with Yemaya or, generally, Yoruba practices. Keep them situated at the altar you've created or in a cabinet somewhere. Furthermore, keep the goddess in your favor by offering her regular presents and flowers near a river or sea.

Chapter 7: Building a Holy Shrine

Although not everyone considers building a shrine a fundamental part of their practice, those who do agree that having a holy space has many advantages. Reading this chapter, you will learn about the benefits of building a shrine in or near your home and using this space to venerate Yemaya. You will be provided with numerous beginner-friendly tips for erecting a shrine to Yemaya, how to care for it, and how to use it for making offerings to the Orisha. The advice from this chapter should only serve as general guidelines. While certain elements are necessary to honor Yemaya, feel free to add your own personal touch to the space to fully empower your shrine. This will enable you to form a powerful bond with her, and she will help you achieve all your goals.

A shrine is needed for you to have a place to connect with the Orishas.
Greg Willis, CC BY-SA 2.0 <https://creativecommons.org/licenses/by-sa/2.0>, via Wikimedia Commons https://commons.wikimedia.org/wiki/File:Voodoo_Altar_New_Orleans.jpg

Benefits of Building a Shrine to Yemaya

A spiritual center for one's practice is a critical part of many pagan and non-pagan traditions. Having a sacred place dedicated to your practice has many benefits for your soul and your connection with your guides and the Orishas you worship. Below are a few of the greatest blessings you can gain by building a shrine to Yemaya.

Gaining a Place for Invoking the Orisha

Working with Orishas is a spirituality-based practice. Each item you place in your shrine becomes connected to your soul and the spirit of the Orishas you want to evoke. They represent emotions, intentions, and symbols of spiritual guides that can help you grow spirituality, access ancestral wisdom, and more. Yemaya is known for always being there for those in need. You will have a direct way of communicating with her through a shrine made in her honor. The more you use your shrine to call on her, the more spiritual power you garner throughout your practice. From the first stone you put onto the shelf to the first candle you see flickering in front of you, it will all nourish your spirit just like it's being nurtured by the mother goddess.

Water-based altar decorations, like the ones used to represent Yemaya, often include simple items that enhance the need for spiritual empowerment. Growing your connection with Yemaya involves using your shrine for several days, often placing new items on the holy surface each day. Whether you opt for exchanging the existing ones or adding new objects depends on the purpose of each individual practice. Either way, it will enhance the power of your spiritual work and deepen your connection to this Orisha. You can also share the shrine with other people. Their contribution to this common sacred space will fortify the spiritual bonds within your community. This will have a positive effect on your community's connection to Yemaya.

Inviting Plenty of Positive Energy

A shrine is a space where you can harness the goddess's spiritual energy (or ashe, depending on your religion). However, it can also be a valuable tool for inviting and retaining her nurturing energy in your home for an extended period. Yemaya has plenty of positive energy to share with her devotees. Setting up an altar or shrine for the mother goddess and taking care of it will ensure that positive energy keeps flowing through your space. It will follow you wherever you happen to be in your home.

Expressing Your Creativity

Building a shrine is an excellent way to express your creativity. While there are certain items you'll need to use, figuring out how to place them requires much creative thought, even if you have a guideline like the one provided in this chapter. You only need to learn how to take a creative approach to honor Yemaya through the shrine and how to maintain good care of it. At the same time, it allows you to build something unique and express your thoughts and emotions through your creation. Whether you honor Yemaya as an Orisha, a saint, or a goddess, you will always have several choices for venerating her and asking her for her blessings. Remember, Yemaya has many faces and can help you with different aspects of your life. She can bestow the gift of fertility in a multitude of areas, nurture your talents, grant you a safe voyage overseas, and much more. Whichever your goal is, there is a way to express it through the decorations you use for the shrine.

Replacing Negative Influences with Positive Energy

Negative experiences and influences can hinder your ability to be fertile and productive and cultivate self-love. If this is the case, Yemaya is the perfect person to turn to – and building a shrine to her is the first step in the right direction. By creating a shrine for Yemaya, you gain a space where you can do something about negative influences, regardless of their source. Whether the negativity comes from living beings or spirits, having a sacred place will empower you to fight them and keep them away from you and your life.

Learning Her Correspondences

There is no better way to learn the correspondences associated with an Orisha or saint than displaying them in a space you visit on a regular basis. And this applies not only to their colors and favorite items but to their preferred offerings too. Learning the correspondence of Yemaya will let you see firsthand how they work best. This information will help you understand what she likes and what to avoid when making offerings for her. It will allow you to form a much deeper connection with her during your daily practice.

Creating a Sacred Meditation Center

Shrines can be transformed to represent more than one Orisha or saint. However, even if you wish to dedicate your shrine exclusively to Yemaya, this space can be the perfect space for meditating with the goddess. By bringing together the right combination of elements, you can create a space where you can unwind after a busy day at work. As you evoke Yemaya's spirit and it permeates your senses, your body and mind relax, and your experience becomes deeper. If you're also making an inquiry, you can use incense and other tools known to help focus on a specific question or request. For relaxation, choose the ones that feel right to use in any situation. There is no better way to ground yourself than by meditating in front of the offerings dedicated to Yemaya, the goddess known for her calming essence and spiritually nurturing vibes.

Focusing on Your Intentions

You can call on Yemaya daily or only during the days associated with her and festivals. Either way, having a holy space can help you focus on your intent every time. Building the shrine is a great way to start focusing on whatever you want to ask the goddess. As you put things together, you leave mundane thoughts and worries behind. You're slowly transitioning into a thought process where there is only you, Yemaya, and tools that help you form a connection with her. If you practice magic with others, the shrine can bring each person's intentions or messages together and focus them toward the goddess. And if you are a solitary practitioner, you can tailor the space to your specific taste and preferences, which also helps enhance your spiritual powers.

Honoring Your Ancestors and Other Spirits

A shrine made for one Orisha (in this case, Yemaya) can also be used for seeking spiritual guidance from your ancestors and other spirit guides. Yemaya encourages you to nurture your familiar connections. This applies to both living relatives and those who are dead. You can always ask for Yemaya's guidance whenever you're in a difficult situation in life. However, don't be surprised if she tells you to turn to those who know you best - your family. Given her understanding and compassionate nature, she won't mind if you call on her and evoke your ancestors during the same ritual. You can also place offerings for her and the ancestors. Their collective wisdom can get you through even the most challenging situations. You can create a space where your devotion to Yemaya coexists with ancestral veneration. This will be a good reminder that you have several powerful forces supporting you.

Welcoming Nature

Establishing a connection with nature is another way to develop your spirituality and connection with Yemaya. Many devotees choose to grow medicinal herbs and plants for food, even if they only do this in a small corner of their home. By placing your harvest on the altar or shrine along with water, you can express gratitude for them. Some of these can be perfect for offerings – and prompt Yemaya to help you gain insight, cast a spell, or perform any other act that aligns with your traditions and culture. You will most likely leave the offerings on the altar for a number of hours and days. This allows the notice of their presence to be carried to Yemaya, and she will provide many blessings in return.

Sharing Your Devotion

Whether introducing someone to Yoruba or Santeria practices or wanting to find common ground with another devotee, building a shrine to Yemaya together can be a great way to share your spiritual beliefs. This is a common practice for celebrating her sacred days and festivals. Involving others in the building of the shrine or its preparation for the festivities is a great way to connect with your children or the children in your family/community. Yemaya has a special place in her heart for children, and nothing will make her happier than seeing them become valuable members of her community.

How to Create a Shrine for Yemaya

From where you place it to the items you put on it, there are a lot of details that go into building a shrine. Here are a few tips for creating a shrine for Yemaya in or near your home.

Shrine Placement

Before you start building a shrine, you must choose a suitable place for it, ideally in your home. However, if you'll share it with others or if you don't have space for it in your home, you can set it up near the house. This is a particularly great idea if you live near an ocean or sea, as this helps reinforce your effort for evoking Yemaya. Ideally, the shrine should be erected away from high-traffic areas or possible distractions. Otherwise, you won't be able to relax, let alone focus on your inquiry during your work. Many devotees opt for setting up their shrines in their home office or bedroom, as they spend most of their time in these rooms. Having a sacred place in your bedroom could also facilitate morning and evening prayers to the goddess, which are recommended to maintain a potent connection with her. If you don't have much space for a full table to serve as a shrine, you can always set up a smaller area on your dresser, vanity table, or even inside your closet. Alternatively, you can create a shrine on the windowsill. Leaving the door open and working under the moonlight is another excellent practice for keeping in touch with Yemaya. If you plan to practice meditation or similar techniques to communicate with the goddess, build the shrine in a room that can accommodate these activities too.

What to Use in the Shrine

Creating a shrine requires using all the items associated with this goddess. These are:

- Blue pieces of cloth - or one single piece, depending on how big the shrine will be
- Cowrie shells, or, if you can't find these, you can use any variety of sea shells
- Pearls, real ones, if possible
- A statute or picture of Yemaya
- Anything else that symbolizes Yemaya; pictures of dolphins, mermaids, waterfowl, and other sea creatures
- A sopera - a dish used for offerings made for Yemaya
- A blue gown (optional)
- A silver crown and other silver objects
- Fans
- A white candle
- A blue candle
- Incense; Yemaya incense or your favorite incense with a calming scent
- White or blue flowers or a bucket of colorful flowers
- A selection of offerings made from lettuce, seafood, watermelon, molasses, plantains, white wine, and coffee
- Ocean water; if you don't have this available, putting salt in water can be a good alternative

There are ready-made kits containing everything you need for setting up a shrine for Yemaya, but you're advised to also use your creativity. If you have godparents (*through the religion*), they can also help you figure out what you need. For example, which image you use will depend on what's traditionally used in the religion you follow. In Yoruba, she is depicted as an Orisha. In Santeria, her most common image is *La*

Virgen de Regla, but she can also be portrayed as the Sea Goddess.

After gathering your ingredients, you can start setting up the shrine:
1. Begin by draping the blue cloth over the surface of the base.
2. Place the image of the goddess in the center and scatter the shells, silver objects, pearls, fans, and the small items that symbolize Yemaya.
3. Place the sopera with the offerings and the bowl with the water in front of the main symbol.
4. Put one of the candles on the left side of the symbol and the other on the right.
5. Scatter the flowers between the other items.
6. Fold the dress (or leave it unfolded, depending on your space) and leave it on the far left side with the crown on top.
7. Place the incense on the left. Light it only before your practice, along with the candles.

How to Give Offerings and Clear Them

Before using the shrine, don't forget to bless it by dedicating a short prayer to the goddess. After this, you can start presenting the offerings. Be generous, and leave something every day. Say a prayer or do a quick meditation every time you do. If you're leaving food items, ensure they won't stay more than two or three days. Live flowers will also wilt, so you'll need to replace them. Non-perishable items can remain for as long as you need them or until you decide to replace them with other objects. Replace any burned-out candles as soon as possible.

Apart from the items listed above, you can also leave items that reflect personal needs and wants. If you play an instrument or sing, you can also use these talents to honor the Orisha. You can even leave small instruments in the sacred space. The number of the small items (like the silver objects, pearls, or shells) should be seven, as this is the number of seas she governs. If you feel that your space is getting too crowded, remove some items. You can always start adding new objects as you continue your daily veneration of the goddess.

You can also leave offerings when you seek Yemaya's wisdom, need a maternal figure, or a helping hand for healing from emotional trauma. Be polite when you make an offering at the shrine, and never leave an offering while asking for something harmful. Remember, she has a vengeful side too, and you don't want to anger her.

Additional Tips for Setting and Caring for Your Shrine

There are very few rules on how you can or cannot build a shrine for Yemaya. She is the goddess of many faces, and as long as you include some of the traditional elements associated with any of her traits, you can go on to personalize your space as you like. For newbies, it's generally recommended to have only a small shrine in your home. This will allow you to concentrate your power. It will also make it easier to nurture it with positive energy and take care of it in general. You'll need to keep it clean - physically and spiritually. The easiest way to do both is to cover it with a large piece of blue cloth when you aren't using it or have visitors who aren't familiar with your religion.

Occasionally you can remove everything, clean the dust and other debris, and put everything back onto your shrine. Make sure you cleanse it regularly with incense to ward off negative energies, as these can hinder your communication with the goddess. Not leaving perishable items on for too long is another way to keep negative energies away. Pay attention to Yemaya's clues, too, regarding the shrine and the offerings. Sometimes, she will tell you what to prepare next. Listen to her advice even if it sounds strange to you. She only wishes for you to find the balance you need.

Chapter 8: Spiritual Baths and Spells

As the mother of all Orishas and the patron of waters, Yemaya can help with various issues related to femininity and spiritual healing. Now that you've learned her correspondences, you can delve into using them to harness the goddess's essence. This chapter offers recipes for ritual baths and spells for self-love, fertility, and healing emotional wounds or trauma.

Ritual baths can be therapeutic and healing.
https://unsplash.com/photos/5PVLPi7oenA

Healing Bath from Yemaya's Hand

Taking a healing bath is a great way to use Yemaya's power for spiritual healing. This one will help you attract positive energy and spiritual prosperity, flush out negative energy, and ward it off in the future. You can take this easy-to-prepare bath at any time of the day.

You will need the following:
- 1 coconut soap only you use
- Sea water or regular water with sea salt added to it (as needed)
- Lavender perfume only you use
- Cane molasses
- A large blue candle (it has to be tall enough so the water doesn't cover its tip)
- A tall container
- Coconut water
- Blue or Indigo wash

Instructions:
1. Add the Indigo or Blue wash, lavender perfume, cane molasses, and coconut water to the container.
2. Pour in ¾ of the water and stir in a clockwise direction with your hands. While doing this, silently ask the goddess for prosperity, health, balance, abundance, peace, or anything you want.
3. Put the candle in the middle of the container and add more water if there is enough space, but be careful not to cover the candle.
4. Light the candle and gaze into its flame. Feel how the warmth radiates from it, filling you with love and care.
5. Ask Yemaya to empower the light to have an even more powerful effect when lighting your heart up.
6. When you feel ready, snuff out the candle. If there is any wax in the water, strain it.
7. Fill your bath with warm water by adjusting the temperature to your liking.

8. Place the container with the water blessed by Yemaya on the bathtub's edge.
9. Enter into the water and wash with coconut soap. It will purify your body from negative energies, and the scent of the soap will also attract positive energy.
10. Take the container and slowly pour the water over your body, starting from your neck and going downwards.
11. Reinforce your request for prosperity, health, balance, abundance, peace, or anything else you want.
12. If possible, allow the water to dry naturally and feel positivity coursing through your body. If you're cold, pat dry with a towel.
13. Don't forget to clean the bathtub after you're done to remove the negativity from your vicinity.
14. Take this bath every week (preferably on a Saturday), and you'll receive many blessings from Yemaya. The success you've asked for will soon begin.

Full Moon Bath Ritual

With the full moon bath ritual, you can call on the deepest power of the supreme mother goddess. It will help you heal through spiritual growth, self-love, and self-acceptance. You will need to take it at night when the moon is in the highest position.

You will need the following:
- 7 blue candles
- 7 white rose petals
- 1 moonstone or other lunar stone
- 7 pinches of sea salt
- 7 drops of peppermint, passionflower, or lavender essential oil

Instructions:
1. Start drawing a bath. While the tub is filling, place the candles around its edge and light them.
2. Gazing into the candlelight, take a few breaths and focus on the issue that needs to be eliminated from your mind so you can heal.

3. Add salt and essential oils to the bathwater. As you do, call on Yemaya and ask her to fill your heart.
4. Take a deep breath and enter the tub. As you immerse yourself in the water, feel the caring touch of the goddess, healing you.
5. Take as much time as you need soaking, and let her heal your deepest wounds.
6. Step out of the tub and pat yourself dry with a towel when you're ready.
7. Before you drain the water, place the rose petals on the edge of the tub as an offering to Yemaya while saying the following:

"Yemaya, our mother and the goddess of the water.

Come to this place and be with me.

Goddess of the rivers, lakes, and oceans,

Your beauty brings the flow of power.

I ask you to heal my soul, mind, and body.

With the help of your love, I will become whole again.

Ashe, great goddess."

Yemaya's Spell for Love

If you live near a large body of water (ocean, sea, lake, river, etc.), enacting Yemaya's love spell will be the perfect way to attract or deepen romantic feelings. And even if you don't, you can still perform a modified version of the spell. With the help of this spell, anyone can evoke Yemaya's power and attract love into their lives. It is particularly effective when enacted on a Saturday, Yemaya's sacred day. However, it only works if there is already attraction between you and the desired person.

You will need the following:
- 1 blue candle
- 1 melon
- Cane molasses
- Vanilla extract
- Brown sugar
- 2 blue ribbons

- Paper and a red pen

Instructions:
1. Place everything on your altar or shrine, and settle in front of it.
2. Light the candle and call on Yemaya.
3. Write down your name, the name of your love, and the date of birth for both of you seven times.
4. Turn the paper, and write what you need help with on the other side. For example, if you're already in a relationship, you can ask the goddess to strengthen your love for each other. If you aren't in a relationship with the person, you can ask the goddess to help either of you make the first step.
5. Cut off the top of the melon, and insert the paper into it.
6. Pour the sugar, vanilla extract, and cane molasses into the melon. Ask Yemaya to sweeten your heart as you're doing it with the melon.
7. Place the top of the melon back from where you cut it, and secure it into place by tying the ribbons around the melon. You can use a piece of tape to make it more secure.
8. Put the melon beside the candle, and keep it here until the candle burns down completely.
9. If you live by the water, carry the melon to the water and offer it to Yemaya. Place seven coins beside it and leave it there.
10. If you don't live near water, place the melon in your garden or outside your window. Leave it there for the goddess for a few days.
11. Walk away without looking back.
12. When you get home, give heartfelt thanks to the goddess by offering a prayer of gratitude.
13. Soon, the goddess will grant your request, and the love in your heart and the heart of your loved one will deepen.

New Moon Ritual

The goddess's power can also be harnessed around the new moon. During this period, you can ask her for new opportunities, fertility, or to help you move on from a traumatic experience and start a new chapter in your life.

You will need the following:
- The symbol of Yemaya
- 7 coins
- 1 blue candle
- Any offerings you want to give to Yemaya

Instructions:
1. Start by lighting the candle on the day of the new moon. The candle should be placed next to the symbol and any other offerings you want to make.
2. Hold a coin in your hands and call on Yemaya. Ask her for whatever you need for the new moon to bring.
3. Gaze into the candle flame and focus on your inquiry.
4. When you're ready, offer a prayer of gratitude to the goddess and put the coin down next to the other offerings before extinguishing the candle.
5. Repeat this for seven consecutive days, leaving a coin each time.
6. At the end of the seventh day, look at all the coins you've left for the goddess. Use them as a reminder of what inspired you to reach out to Yemaya.
7. The goddess will soon grant your wishes. When she does, you can remove the coins from the altar while expressing your gratitude once more.

Yemaya's Self-Confidence Ritual

This is another seven-day ritual dedicated to the mother goddess, except this one can be done at any time of the month. It invokes Yemaya's power with the help of seven candles and fills you with self-confidence and love.

You will need the following:
- 7 blue or white candles (pick whichever color resonates with you the most)
- 1 container

Instructions:
1. Place all the colors on the altar or shrine, and settle in front of it.
2. At nightfall, light one candle and call on Yemaya.
3. Focus your gaze on the flame, and envision how its warmth envelops you.
4. Visualize Yemaya's energy accompanying the warmth by forming a glowing orb around you.
5. Ask Yemaya to help you gain confidence in your ability to persevere and become the person you wish to be.
6. Let the candle burn out and leave it at the altar.
7. Repeat this for six more days.
8. On the seventh night, collect all the wax from the candles into a container.
9. Place the container on your windowsill to charge the wax with moonlight, which contains the goddess's essence.
10. You will soon start gaining confidence. Make sure you thank the goddess for her blessings.

Renewal Bath

This bath will help you recharge and fill your body and spirit with new, positive energy with the help of Yemaya. It only has a few simple ingredients and can be done any time of the week or month.

You will need the following:
- White flower petals
- 4 cups of water
- 1 teaspoon of cinnamon
- Dried raspberries or a splash of raspberry vinaigrette (if you're allergic to berries, omit this ingredient)
- 1 white candle

Instructions:
1. Pour the water into a pot and bring it to a boil.
2. Add the cinnamon, flower petals, and raspberries/vinaigrette into the boiling water.

3. Turn off the heat and let the water infuse with the rest of the ingredients for 15 minutes.
4. In the meantime, prepare a bath and light a candle you've placed on the edge of the tub.
5. Add the infused water to your bathwater, and mix it with your hand.
6. Immerse yourself in the water while calling on Yemaya.
7. Start focusing on what you need more energy for and tell this to the goddess.
8. Let her remove all the negativity from your body, mind, and soul and replace it with positivity.
9. As you relax and begin to feel renewed, say thanks to the goddess.
10. Leave the tub, snuff out the candle, and let yourself air dry.
11. You can follow up with your favorite beauty ritual, such as applying lotions, oils, serums, etc.

Spell for Recharging through Yemaya

This spell also works for recharging your energies with the help of the mother goddess. It allows you to form a deeper bond with Yemaya and tie yourself to her spiritually, which will go a long way for any healing or spiritual growth you need help with in the future.

You will need the following:
- 1 bowl of water
- A few drops of your favorite essential oil
- 1 symbol of Yemaya
- 1 blue candle

Instructions:
1. Place everything on your altar or shrine and prepare yourself for the ritual by taking a few deep breaths.
2. Add the essential oil to the water and light the candle.
3. Look at the symbol of the goddess and place one of your hands over it.
4. Place your other hand over the water. Visualize an energy channel being opened to receive positive energy.

5. Ask the goddess to bless you with positivity and help you chase away the negative influences by saying:

   "Mother Goddess, I ask you now for the renewal of my soul.

   Please send me your blessings and help me remain active and healthy."

6. Envision the positive energy traveling from the image of the goddess into the water.
7. When you feel you've channeled enough positivity into the water, immerse your hands in it.
8. Let your hand soak for half a minute, then pat it dry.
9. Repeat as often as you need to recharge yourself.

Yemaya's Self-Love Jar

With the help of a few items associated with Yemaya's power, you can create a jar full of positivity that will remind you of your best qualities. Anytime you feel a lack of self-love, you'll just have to look at the jar, and the goddess will remind you that you are worthy of love and compassion.

You will need the following:
- 1 large jar with a lid
- Sea salt
- Cane molasses
- Cinnamon
- Dried white flower petals
- 7 coins
- Small shells
- 1 blue candle
- 1 symbol of the goddess
- Dried seaweed
- Small figures of water creatures
- Paper and pen

Instructions:
1. Place everything on your altar in front of the divine symbol and light the candle.

2. Start putting everything into the jar. With each item, take a small break and say something positive about yourself.

3. On the paper, write what you're asking for from the goddess. For example, you can ask her to remind you of your self-worth, help you gain more confidence, or cultivate deeper self-love.

4. Place the paper into the jar and say a silent prayer to the goddess.

5. Close the jar, take the candle, and allow the wax to drip down around the lid while turning the jar.

6. As the wax hardens and forms a seal, say thanks for the goddess's blessing that you'll receive.

Fertility Ritual

This traditional Yoruba ritual has been used by young women who want to conceive a child. Apart from this, Yemaya can grant you fertility in many other aspects of life, such as art, work, and even cultivating relationships. The colors and seeds of the pumpkin symbolize her power over nature and fertility.

You will need the following:
- 1 pumpkin
- 1 blue candle
- 1 pencil
- 1 brown paper bag
- A representation of the Yemaya

Instructions:

1. Place the blue candle in front of the representation of Yemaya on your altar or shrine and light it.

2. Close your eyes and focus on manifesting your wishes. Saying them out loud often helps.

3. Open your eyes and carve a round opening in the pumpkin.

4. Take the pencil and write your wishes down on a piece of the paper bag.

5. Place the piece of paper inside the pumpkin, then pour candle wax on top of it.

6. After ensuring the pumpkin has been sealed with the wax, place it over your stomach, repeating your wishes.
7. When you feel your wishes have been heard, take the pumpkin to the nearest water source, and offer it to Yemaya. Alternatively, you can leave it on your windowsill so it can charge through the moon.

You may leave the candle burning for a short period after the ritual is completed. However, if you are going to leave it unattended, it's best to snuff it out. You can relight the candle any time you want to during the next seven days.

Yemaya's Healing Elixir

Not only is this simple elixir beneficial for your health, but you can also charge it with Yemaya's power. Prepare it on the night of the full moon, and you'll receive the benefits the next day.

You will need the following:
- Water - as needed (you can prepare several cups of the elixir and consume them one by one throughout the day)
- Cinnamon sticks
- 1 kettle
- 1 marker
- 1 glass jar

Instructions:
1. Draw a shell at the bottom of the jar to symbolize Yemaya. While doing this, focus on calling on her.
2. Fill the jar with as many cups of water as you want and ask for Yemaya's blessing.
3. Place the jar on the windowsill where it can bask in the moonlight and leave it overnight.
4. In the morning, pour the water from the jar into a kettle, bring it to a boil, and pour it back into the jar.
5. Place the cinnamon sticks into the water and visualize them releasing the positive energy Yemaya poured into them during the night.
6. Let the cinnamon infuse the water for 10 minutes, and your elixir will be ready to drink.

7. As you drink it, imagine Yemaya's love spreading through your body and healing you.

Disclaimer

The transfer of Yemaya's essence can have an incredibly powerful effect on the recipient of this nurturing energy. Using the goddess's power, you can balance out your spiritual energy, allowing you to become re-energized and helping you face life's challenges more easily. That being said, Yemaya's power can't cure any mental illness. If you suspect that you have any psychological condition, you should consult a relevant healthcare specialist regarding treatment. Once your doctor has established a diagnosis and conventional treatment plan, you can revisit the possibility of reaching out to the goddess to empower yourself through the healing process.

If you've already been diagnosed with a mental illness, wait until you feel strong enough to do any ritual evoking Yemaya. Receiving her healing energy can be an overwhelming experience, even for healthy minds. For beginners, her messages can be confusing, and her energy can be too powerful. If your mental well-being is not at its best, receiving spiritual messages can do more harm than good. Even if you can receive her messages, not being in the best mind frame can affect your ability to honor the goddess appropriately.

Chapter 9: Sacred Days and Festivals

Festivals and rituals are common ways to pay tribute to our beloved Orisha deities and have been taking place for years. Festivals honoring Yemaya are especially popular because of her prominence among the other orishas. After all, she is called the mother of all for a reason. Throughout history, the sea and ocean have remained sacred places for West Africans due to the many legends associated with them. There are several powerful female figures among the Orisha deities, among whom Yemaya is notable. She symbolizes a maternal relationship because of her association with water and fertility.

Furthermore, the ocean played a significant role in the forced crossings of the slave trade. Enslaved people who survived the journey set the custom of making offerings to the goddess and passed these practices down to their descendants. Thus originated the festivals celebrating the glorious Orisha of the oceans and sea, Yemaya.

Festivals and rituals are a wonderful way to pay tribute to the Orishas.
https://unsplash.com/photos/-p7amImLLqs

While one major Lemanja festival takes place on February 2nd in several places around the world, other smaller celebrations also occur throughout the year. The main celebration is held in Salvador and Sao Paulo and includes a variety of activities like dancing, singing, praying, feasting, and engaging in other rituals. During these festivals, it is customary to invoke Yemaya and ask for her blessings, using the themes and ritual tools covered in earlier chapters. This chapter will be a guide to understanding the various festivities associated with the goddess Yemaya and how you can participate in them.

Festival of Iemanjá in Salvador

Considered one of the most popular celebrations in Salvador, Bahia, the Iemanjá festival pays homage to the ocean goddess Yemaya and has been taking place since contemporary times. Over the years, it has retained its popularity and strength and is still one of the most essential manifestations of the city. The event, which is held on February 2, is filled with the fervor and zeal of the goddess's ardent devotees. It is not only filled with old traditions and practices but is also intense in the sense that numerous people partake in the activities with complete fervor. This festival is therefore regarded as an integral part of Salvador's heritage. It is safeguarded by the national registry to protect Afro-Brazilian cultures and other religious manifestations.

The biggest celebration usually takes place in the neighborhood of Rio Vermelho, located in the Fishermen's Colony. The place is decorated with charms and theme colors and is visited by people from all over the world who want to deliver gifts to Yemaya. Nowadays, most people only place flowers in the sea because other charms and offerings like mirrors, soaps, jewelry, or perfumes can cause damage to marine life. These are the guidelines you should follow if you're planning to attend the Yemaya festivities in Salvador, Brazil:

- The festivities of the Iemanjá celebration begin a day before the actual festival, on the night of February 1st. So, it's a good idea to arrive early at Casa de Iemanjá to fully explore the cultural heritage associated with the festival. People start by watching the sun rise while enjoying the sand between their toes and listening to the traditional Candomble and Umbanda drums playing in the background.
- The festivities officially begin at dawn with beautiful fireworks adorning the sky. People can leave offerings from early in the day to late at night.
- The celebration procession carries the offerings in boats to deliver them to Yemaya. This takes place at about 4 p.m. when the fishermen go out to sea. To join the procession, you should get there early and find a seat on one of the boats. You can hire a boat at any other time too, but leaving the procession with flower baskets will be a special experience.
- While there are no limitations to what you want to wear, it's best to wear something blue or white to show respect. This will portray your willingness to learn about the Yoruba culture, even if you're not one of the initiated.
- There are various recreational groups passing along the waterfront throughout the day, including capoeira, samba, and percussion groups. There are also many parties and shows filled with dancing, singing, and chanting in many places near the festival.

The Iemanjá Festival in Other Parts of the City

Salvador is a hub of celebrations in the name of Yemaya. She is a more beloved Orisha than any other female goddess and has an air of importance about her. Celebrations in other parts of the city include the

Solar de Unhao, which happens during the last week of January. People only present flower offerings to the goddess during this event and ask for her guidance.

Another festival happens in Itapua right before the Yemanja festival. It is known as Lavagem de Itapua and takes place on February 13th. During this celebration, the followers of Yemaya walk the streets dressed according to the theme for the occasion. They carry pots with flowers and fragrant water to cleanse the church's staircase. Many cultural groups roam the streets celebrating the Queen of the Sea and pay tribute to her legacy by offering various charms, singing songs, and dancing.

Yemoja Festival in Ibadan, Nigeria

Another prominent region where the goddess Yemaya is celebrated is in Nigeria, particularly Ibadan, New Oyo. Every year, Yoruba followers in Nigeria gather together and offer their thanks to the Goddess and Queen of the Sea, along with celebrating other Yoruba gods. They believe this is an essential practice in order to pay homage to their ancestral beliefs and traditional roots.

During this annual festival, the people start the day with a traditional dance, music, and some prayers invoking Yemaya. As Yemoja is considered the mother of all Orisha, she has more importance than any other Orisha. This prominent festival gains public attention based on the fact that it lasts 17 whole days and is said to be as old as the Yoruba culture. The celebration starts in October and ends on the last day of the month. The grand finale, which happens on October 31st, includes traditional dances in front of the temple of Yemoja.

Yemaya devotees perfect their dances before the celebration in order to correctly match the rhythm of the music. Inside the temple, there is a statue of Yemoja breastfeeding a baby. The dedicated followers of Yemaya sing songs, pray, chant, and give thanks to the mother goddess for her blessings. They thank the Orisha for keeping them healthy and prosperous during the past year and pray for her blessings for the coming year. Then, they move to the river to make their offerings.

Inside the temple of Yemoja, the chief of the village prepares the various offerings needed to be presented to the river goddess. In front of him is the statue of Ogunleki, next to which some hollowed-out calabashes are placed. Calabashes have a prominent role in Yoruba history and are thus considered sacred fruit. The chief drops the offerings into the calabashes while speaking sacred words of prayer to the mother goddess Yemoja.

Once these offerings have been prepared, the chief priest associated with Yemoja says a few prayers with his hands outstretched. The devotees respond to this prayer with *ase* (the traditional ending to prayer in Yoruba culture) and begin the procession. The procession starts from the temple and goes all the way to the river to present the offerings to Yemaya. The women are dressed in complete white and carry the food offerings in calabashes. Each calabash carries different food offerings, including cooked beans and rice, fruits, porridge, and other associated food items for Yemoja. The other participants follow the calabash carriers all the way to the river.

The river is considered to be inhabited by guiding spirits connected with Yemoja. Everyone makes pledges with the spirits, and during the next festival, they redeem their pledges by making different offerings to the spirits. This expression of gratitude helps the devotees plan and pray for the future as well. When the pledges and prayers at the river are completed, the chief priestess gathers some of the water from the river and sprinkles it on her fellow calabash carriers and Yemoja devotees. Some of this water is also collected and used for medicinal purposes and ritual baths.

The women play an integral part in the festivals of Yemoja – from carrying the calabashes to preparing the offerings and performing priestess duties; the female population has imperative roles in the sacred celebration. The processional celebration takes place over the next few days, along with a number of other traditional activities.

On the last day of the festival, the new initiates have to cut their hair and wear unique beads designed for new members. The jewelry is composed of blue and red beads that form a choker-like necklace. After a while, the new members are finally permitted to wear the long, white bead necklaces worn by other devotees. The procession concludes with the presentation of food offerings at the river's edge. Each item is put into the river one at a time and is taken away by the current.

Iemanjá Celebrations in Uruguay

Iemanjá celebrations also take place annually in Uruguay on February 2 and are considered to be one of the most festive occasions in the country. During this festival, many tourists are attracted to Ramirez

Beach. While festivities begin right after sunrise, noticeable crowds start to gather in the afternoon to enjoy the traditional music associated with Uruguayan people and Yoruba history. This involves rapid drumming sounds along with some fast music. Many street vendors line the edge of the beach, selling charms, necklaces, candles, posters, clothes, and food items relevant to Yemaya.

In the evening, the devotees start to prepare their altars dedicated to Yemaya. These structures are usually made with sand from the beach. People place all kinds of offerings to the goddess on this altar, along with a statue. The statue is surrounded by blue and white candles, which are lit after dusk. Some people also place handcrafted food or prepare food items that the goddess favors. After preparing the altar, the devotees sit down and look at the beautiful sunset from the beach while praying to the goddess. After sundown, the festivities increase. Uruguayan music spreads across the beach and lasts all night. The offerings are floated across the sea until they're swept away by the current.

Many people also take part in festive dances and whirling after nightfall. This is when the festival is at its peak. The participants in the dance often fall into a spiritual trance when whirling around frenetically. The devotees and any other participants dress in long, white, flowing skirts or dresses. They can be seen bowing to the queen of the sea and staying prostrate on the ground. Then, they walk slowly into the sea until the water comes up to their knees. Here, they present their offerings to Yemaya, say a few prayers, and walk back to shore without turning their backs as a sign of respect. Although there aren't many properly initiated worshippers of Yemaya, the festival usually attracts a large crowd of people who come to participate in the traditions. Most of them are just there to observe from the sidelines, while some take part in the activities and leave offerings for the goddess.

Yemaya Festival in Fernihurst, VIC

As you already know, the Yemaya festival has gained popularity all over the globe. Yoruba festivals and traditions aren't just practiced in native regions anymore but in various places all around the world. One of these major Yemaya festivals is celebrated at Fernihurst, Victoria, near Melbourne, Australia. The vibrant, multi-day event is a sight to see and is considered to be the experience of a lifetime. The festival is initiated with some prayers to the goddess, followed by an honorary celebration paying tribute to the traditional owners of the region. People pray to the goddess for blessings and cleansing of their spirits and hope to have the upcoming days full of familial and positive energy.

The devoted community celebrating this festival makes it possible for the event to be full of artistic possibilities and creative spirit. Celebrated along the Loddon River, the participants are given an open landscape to explore the water and nearby regions for self-exploration. As soon as you get there, you'll be immersed in a colorful world filled with music, dance, and celebratory spirit. The decor is unique and mesmerizing, complete with psychedelic patterns, warm lighting, abstract designs, and beautiful hanging charms.

This festival is unlike any other traditional Yemoja festival and consists of modern performances on the main stage. The unique aspect of this event is the incorporation of a modern twist into the traditional practices which are used to celebrate the goddess Yemaya. The pulsing rhythms make everyone move along with the music, which creates an almost trance-like state at the gathering. Devotees and guests are encouraged to move freely and become at one with the music. A special, fluid-like dance is commonly observed during these performances. Most of these musical performances symbolize personal transformation and help deepen your connection with the goddess, Yemaya. During the day, upbeat pop music plays across the speakers, whereas trance-like, mind-bending music takes over the festival once the sun sets.

If you're a part of the festival to self-explore and connect yourself with the goddess, it will hardly benefit you if you're a fly on the wall. Although there's nothing against observing the festivities, it will do you some good to actually participate in the dances and other practices to feel a part of the culture. The locals and festival organizers encourage the participants to take part in the visual and performing arts. The festival's open space gives participants the advantage of adding a spark to the music. Guests even have the option of creating their own music by jamming with anyone looking to work an instrument.

The guests can further feed their creative impulses by working with arts and crafts supplies to create unique treasures that can be later presented as offerings to the goddess or used to decorate her altar. This Yemaya festival can prove to be a wonderful bonding experience encouraging collaborative effort, peace, harmony, and unconditional love. Even if you're somewhat of a wallflower, try to throw yourself into the mix of this festival to enjoy the full experience. Treat everyone like a big family, and you'll be surprised to see how you're welcomed with open arms.

Yemaya Festivities in Pelotas

Another birthplace for traditional festivals celebrating the sea goddess, Yemaya, is Pelatos, Rio Grande. It is customary for the picture of Nossa Senhora to be carried across the city to the port of Pelatos on February 2nd. The boat brings aboard Yoruba practitioners who carry the image of Yemoja before the end of the Catholic feast, which is watched by thousands of people.

Festa da Conceição da Praia

One of the oldest religious festivals taking place in Brazil, the *Festa da Conceiço da Praia*, pays homage to the glorious patroness of Bahia. The theme of the party relates to the Immaculate Conception, which refers to a theme of the church but is also often related to the mother goddess, Yemoja. With the basilica's choir singing in the background, a procession of priests, seminarians, and other people march across the city, paying tribute to Nossa Senhora da Conceicao.

Preparations for the festival start at 5 in the morning, but the main celebrations start after 9 a.m. If you want to get a good view of the procession, it's best to arrive early. The musical performances are incredible and include many traditional aspects. The procession leaves Conceicao da Praia at 10:30 a.m. and returns after about 12 hours. After that, a huge celebration ensues, which includes baskets of offerings to the goddess, food stalls, and many other activities.

Other Yemaya Festivals in Sao Paulo

Sao Paulo also hosts a few Iemanjá festivals and feasts to pay tribute to the goddess of the sea. These usually take place during the first two weeks of December. During these festivals, many cars are decorated with Yoruba charms and colors. For Yemaya, the colors blue and white are most prominent in every decoration. Some of these cars travel hundreds of miles from the Sao Paulo Mountains to the beach. On the Praia Grande beach, numerous people gather near the statue of Yemoja.

New Year's Celebrations in Brazil

Many people also pray to Yemoja at the beginning of the New Year to ask for her blessings for the coming year. Rio de Janeiro, in particular, sees millions of devotees dressed in religious attire which matches the color themes of Yemaya. These people usually gather on the Copacabana beach to watch fireworks and make offerings to the goddess. These offerings can include flowers, food items, fruits, charms, etc. Some people send their offerings to Yemoja in small, wooden toy boats. Many shops sell beautiful paintings of the goddess, depicting her rising from the sea as a mermaid. Leaving floating candles along the coast is also a pretty common practice during this time.

Yemaya, the glorious goddess of the rivers, sea, and fertility, is celebrated all around the world. There are countless devotees who make meaningful offerings every year at these festivals. Whether it's the annual Iemanjá festival in Salvador, Bahia, or the Iemanjá festival in Ibadan, both locals, and foreigners celebrate these occasions with full zest. The more modern festivals are also carried out with great zeal, albeit a bit differently than the traditional events. The practices carried out during these festivals help many people get more familiar with their roots, connect with their spirituality, and honor the Orisha goddess Yemaya. No matter what stage of your spiritual journey you're at, celebrating Yemaya with your best intentions will get you one step closer to making a true connection with the Mother Goddess.

Chapter 10: Daily Rituals to Honor Yemaya

There are a number of different rituals and practices you can incorporate into your daily life if you're looking to honor Yemaya.

As Yemaya is the Orisha of the sea, many of these rituals involve water or items associated with water. Additionally, as the Orisha of motherhood, many of the rituals to honor her are fertility rituals.

In this last chapter, we'll look at ways you can honor Yemaya in your everyday life, helping you to create a long and lasting relationship with her. Some of these rituals include making offerings to the sea, creating an altar for Yemaya, taking a spiritual bath, conducting a healing ritual, and more.

Making Offerings to the Sea

If you live near the sea or plan on visiting the seaside, one of the most effective daily rituals to Yemaya is to make your offerings directly to the sea. These offerings can take the shape of a range of items, including:

- Fish
- Fruit
- Candles
- Flowers
- Honey

- Mirrors
- Foods
- Statues of Yemaya

If you plan on immersing your offerings in the sea, make sure that they are biodegradable and will do no damage to the waters they will be immersed in. For example, if you're going to immerse an idol, make sure that it and any paint on it are eco-friendly. The last thing you want is to unwittingly do further damage to the oceans while trying to honor Yemaya.

Another way to make offerings directly to the sea is to make a small vessel out of paper or paper mache. You can decorate the vessel with symbols of Yemaya, fill it with small offerings, and allow the boat to float away on the water.

Once you have made your offering, light a candle and set it in the sand. Then send out a prayer to Yemaya, offering your gratitude for the good luck and blessings that she has brought into your life.

After offering your prayer, make sure you extinguish the candle and take it home with you so that it does not accidentally injure another visitor at the beach.

Create an Altar and Make Your Offerings

If you don't live near the sea (or are unable to visit frequently), there's no reason to worry. You can also build an altar to Yemaya in your own home and make your offerings at the altar.

The altar you build should be populated with representations of Yemaya. This can include an image of her, cowrie shells and other types of shells, a sopera, blue cloth, and more.

Once you have constructed and are satisfied with your altar to Yemaya, the next step is to make your offerings. When you make your offerings at the altar, make sure to light a candle and offer a prayer to the Orisha. After you finish your prayer, you can either extinguish the candle or leave it to burn off on its own.

Conduct a Cowrie Ritual

Cowrie shells are intrinsically linked to Yemaya, and most altars to the Orisha hold at least a few of these shells. If you have access to cowrie shells, you can use them to conduct a ritual to Yemaya.

Tiger Cowrie Ritual

You will need the following:
- 1 tiger cowrie shell
- Frankincense oil

This ritual should be conducted when you're ready to start a new project. It is a way of honoring Yemaya as the Orisha of motherhood while also calling on her to bless your new undertaking.

To conduct the ritual, you should insert something representative of your project into the belly of the tiger cowrie shell. Some ideas include:

- A piece of paper on which you have written your goals for the project.
- A crystal chip to represent the energy you want to imbue your project with.
- A small item that is representative of the project – for example, if you're starting a new sewing project, you may place a scrap of fabric inside the shell.

Once you place the item in the belly of the shell, you should rub the entrance with the frankincense oil. This protects the energy you have imbued the shell with. After rubbing the oil into the shell, say a prayer to Yemaya, asking for good luck in your project.

On the night of the new moon, place the shell with the item in it on a windowsill. The new moon is the ideal time to begin your new project, and the cowrie shell with your chosen item inside it represents creativity. The shell is "pregnant" with a seed, and the new moon is the perfect time to allow it to grow.

Small Cowrie Ritual

Small cowries are the ones that are usually bought in bulk. These are generally easy to source, making this ritual one that anyone can perform.

You will need the following:
- 2 containers of the same size
- Enough small cowrie shells to fill one container

To perform this ritual, you should first fill one container to the brim with cowries. Then, each day, take out one cowrie. Facing the east, hold it so that the mouth of the shell is facing you.

Keeping Yemaya and your devotion to her in your mind, speak out loud to the shell. What you tell the shell differs from person to person – it may be an articulation of your dreams, values, hopes, or anything else. The shell essentially serves as a connection to Yemaya, and speaking to the cowrie is a way of speaking to Yemaya.

Once you have finished speaking and filled the shell with your voice, place it in the second container. Repeat this ritual daily.

When you have run out of cowries, cleanse the filled cowries using fresh water, and allow them to dry. The water will carry your words to Yemaya, and you can reuse the cowries to continue this ritual.

Conduct a Venus Comb Murex Ritual

Aside from cowrie shells, you can use any other shell to connect with Yemaya. The Venus Comb Murex is a popular option because of the association of the shell with combs (as its name indicates), grooming, beauty, and women. This ritual is a way of honoring aspects of yourself that often aren't recognized or appreciated the way they should be.

You will need the following:
- 1 shell of any kind
- 1 Venus Comb Murex. If you cannot source a physical shell, an image of one will do
- 1 bottle or pitcher of water
- 1 blue bowl
- 1 container of salt
- Blue and white beads – 7 or more
- 12 inches of string
- Glue
- 1 hair comb
- 2 glasses of drinking water
- Goldfish crackers
- Music associated with Yemaya – this can be ocean sounds or devotional music created to honor her

For this ritual, you should wear blue and white and follow the steps below:

1. Place the shell in front of the bowl.
2. Position yourself comfortably – you can also do this ritual sitting down if you prefer.
3. Take three deep breaths.
4. Gently pour the water into the bowl.
5. Once you have poured the water into the bowl, add salt into the water one pinch at a time.
6. Pick up one bead. Hold it in your hands and imbue it with a part of yourself that you feel isn't recognized or appreciated. You can do this by making a statement out loud. For example, you might say, *"I'm good at working in a team."* Once you imbue the bead with your energy, place it in the water.
7. Repeat the above step for each bead.
8. Once you've placed all the beads in the water, swirl the water clockwise with your fingers, allowing energy to build in the bowl, water, and beads. As you do this, imagine your words being transmitted to Yemaya.
9. One at a time, pull the beads from the water and string them on your thread. Tie a knot, and reinforce it with a drop of glue once the beads and thread have dried.
10. Look at the (picture of the) Venus Comb Murex and comb your hair, imagining Yemaya helping you while you do so. This act of self-care is a way to build up your self-esteem.
11. Once the bracelet and glue have dried, slip it onto your hand. Your bracelet, now imbued with Yemaya's power, is a reminder that while you cannot control how other people think and act, you can control how you think about yourself and present yourself to the world.
12. Play music and dance, allowing your energy to fill the room. Afterward, ground yourself by consuming a few goldfish crackers.
13. Take a drink from one glass of water, blessing your ritual and praying to Yemaya while you do so.

14. Finish by making an offering to Yemaya. You can do this by incorporating the other glass of water into your altar, or you can simply put it into the earth (the soil from a potted plant will work). Alternatively, you can take a shower and pour the glass of water on yourself as part of your shower.

Take Part in a Bath Ritual

Bath rituals are a powerful way to connect with and honor Yemaya, given how intrinsically connected they are to water. You can conduct bath rituals in your own bathroom or in a body of water.

Home Bath Ritual

You will need the following:
- A bathtub
- An altar to Yemaya
- ¼ cup of sea salt
- 7 drops of eucalyptus oil

Instructions:

1. First, create an altar for Yemaya in your bathroom. You can do this by bringing in a small side table and covering it with a blue cloth. Then, fill the altar with an image of Yemaya and ocean-related objects, such as seashells, pearls (real if possible), ocean-inspired art, and so on. You can also add some blue and white flowers to the altar.
2. Next, fill your bathtub with warm water.
3. Add the sea salt and eucalyptus oil to the water, gently mixing to incorporate them fully.
4. While praying to Yemaya, immerse yourself in the water. You can pray out loud or silently – Yemaya will hear you either way. This prayer can take the form of anything you wish – you can take the opportunity to speak with Yemaya about your fears and worries, vocalize your regrets, or thank her for your blessings. Next, ask her to remove any blocks that are preventing you from reaching your true potential and moving forward in life. Conclude your prayer by thanking her for her love and compassion.

5. When you have finished praying, remove the drain plug and allow the water in the bathtub to drain away. As the water drains, it will take all the negativity you released in your prayer along with it.

Sea/Ocean/River Bath Ritual

If you live near an accessible body of water, you can try this ritual. For this bath ritual, you will need the following:

- Cane molasses
- Offerings to Yemaya – a good option is an offering of blue and white flowers. Make sure that the offerings you choose are eco-friendly and can be immersed in a body of water without causing damage to the ecosystem.

Instructions:
1. Walk into the water and allow the water to rinse the molasses away from your body. As the water washes away the molasses, think of yourself being cleansed and purified by the power of Yemaya.
2. As the water is washing away the molasses, release your offerings into the water and thank Yemaya for her love and compassion.

Ritual to Return Energy and Heal the Natural Waters

One of the biggest concerns facing followers of Yemaya, and indeed, the world as a whole, is the state of the world's oceans. Plastic pollution and marine litter are threatening the world's waters at unprecedented rates. This ritual is one that is designed to provide healing energy to the natural waters of the world.

You will need the following:
- 7 shells – cowrie shells are best, but any shells work
- 7 blue and white flowers

This ritual can be conducted next to a natural body of water or in your home. If you're conducting the ritual in your home, you will also need the following:

- 1 large bowl of the freshest water possible. Distilled or spring water is ideal. Additionally, the bowl should at least be large enough for you to stand in. You can also fill a bathtub with water and immerse yourself in it.

Instructions:

1. Stand near the water (but not in it yet) and meditate on your aim for the ritual, taking the time to connect with your inner self. Think about the energy you want to share with the waters of the world and what you want to release into them.

2. Walk into the water. This is a way to physically connect to the waters of the world.

3. Call on the deities you believe in. Then, call to Yemaya and Oshun, the two Orishas associated with waters. You can also call on any other river deities that you believe in.

4. Holding the seven shells in your hand, call out to the ancestors of the shells that lived in the oceans at a time when the waters of the world were unpolluted and full of life. Ask them to bring that balance to the present so that the waters of the world can be healed.

5. Immerse the shells in the water. While you do so, say,

"Yemaya, I offer you these shells and their ancient energy to help restore your energy, heal you, and heal the damage the world has done to you."

Leave the shells in the water as an offering. If you're conducting the ritual at home, place them in a small bowl of salt water and place the bowl on your altar to Yemaya. Allow them to sit in the water until the full moon is over.

6. Next, take the seven flowers in your hands and call to Yemaya, Oshun, and any other water goddesses you believe in. Thank them for bringing fertility and life and giving the world the waters that nourish and cleanse all living beings. Ask the Orishas and goddesses for their blessings and ask them to help you cleanse yourself from head to foot. Feel the water moving across your feet, ankles, and the rest of your body if you are immersed in the water. Feel the cool freshness of the water, and the water helping you release everything you wish to cleanse yourself of, which will be carried away by the water.

7. Release the flowers in the water, feeling the water healing you. As you do so, thank Yemaya and the other goddesses and Orishas by saying,

   "Yemaya, I offer you these flowers as thanks for your love, compassion, healing, and protection. I offer you my thanks for the waters that nourish us and the air that sustains us."

8. Take time to connect with the wisdom of Yemaya and reflect on how thankful you are for her gifts to the world. Give your thanks to the oceans and the waters of the world, as well as to Yemaya, Oshun, the other deities of water you pray to, and the ancestors.

Clean and Conserve the Waters

Aside from providing the waters of the world with healing energy, you should also take a more proactive role in helping heal the waters of the world. You can do this by looking for organizations in your area that are taking a leading role in cleaning local bodies of water.

Ask them if you can volunteer with them and help pick up trash from the waters and beaches. If there is no water body in your local area, look for organizations that are doing work protecting the water and donate time or money to helping them in any way you can.

You can also write letters to members of your government to advocate for policies that protect the waters or help out organizations that are already working on doing so. If no such organization exists in your area, you can also consider starting one yourself.

Additionally, you can take steps to conserve water where possible. Work to reduce water waste and take steps to collect and use rainwater to reduce your water usage. You can also look at the actions your area is taking to recycle wastewater and look for ways to contribute. Some steps you can take to reduce your water usage include:

- Take shorter showers or bucket baths instead of bathing in the bathtub
- Only run the washing machine when you have a full load of clothes
- Reuse greywater from your laundry in your garden
- Turn off the tap when not in use – for example, when brushing your teeth or washing fruit and vegetables

- Only run the dishwasher when you have a full load
- Use drip irrigation instead of sprinklers in your garden
- Use collected rainwater to water your garden
- Remove turf on your lawn and replace it with water-efficient plants

Conclusion

The fact that you've chosen to worship Yemaya out of every other Orisha shows that you already have a spiritual connection with her. It doesn't matter if you've not been initiated yet. You're bound to get there in no time with just a bit of practice and consistency. Hopefully, the guidance provided in this book will prove to be helpful to your practice.

Whether you choose to worship Yemoja with spells and magic or simple offerings and prayers depends completely on you. Just remember that magic, in its natural state, is everywhere. You don't have to be a uniquely special person to be able to access the magic connecting you to the Goddess of the Sea. She is indeed kind and generous to those wanting to connect with her. Similarly, whether you decide to make the charms, candles, incense, and other offerings from scratch or buy them from the market depends completely on you.

Keep in mind that the worship of an Orisha deity is deeply personal and can be unique to every individual. There are no strict rules limiting the practices carried out for their worship. There is no wrong or right way. Simply practice the way that you feel reflects your inner feelings about the goddess. This is why you'll find very few rituals that are identical. The important part is to find your own path when worshiping the Mother Goddess, Yemaya.

The path to finding Yemaya can be long and hard if you begin without any guidance. This can be especially difficult for people who do not have the same cultural heritage as people from traditional African religions. Plus, these traditions and practices are usually very secretive, making it difficult for a non-native to learn about them. While the internet is a great resource for these things, there are not enough accurately-presented sources of information about this topic. Many of the sources online are misleading, but if you are successful in finding an authentic source of information, you should never hesitate to learn more about the mystical world of the Orisha.

There is no exclusive path you need to walk on in order to reach Yemaya. She traveled around the world with Obba Nani, leaving a part of herself everywhere she went. Therefore, it's safe to assume that her blessings do not only extend to the people who are a part of her religion but also to anyone who would want to join her devotees.

Building an altar for Yemaya should be no different than for any other Orisha. Just make sure you follow the color theme associated with the goddess, as explained in the book. Moreover, the offerings and charms should also be relevant to the information provided in the book about the goddess's likes and dislikes. Finally, the prayers should be said with complete devotion, but there's no hard and fast rule about following the prayers to the word. So you can make any alterations you want.

Here's another book by Mari Silva that you might like

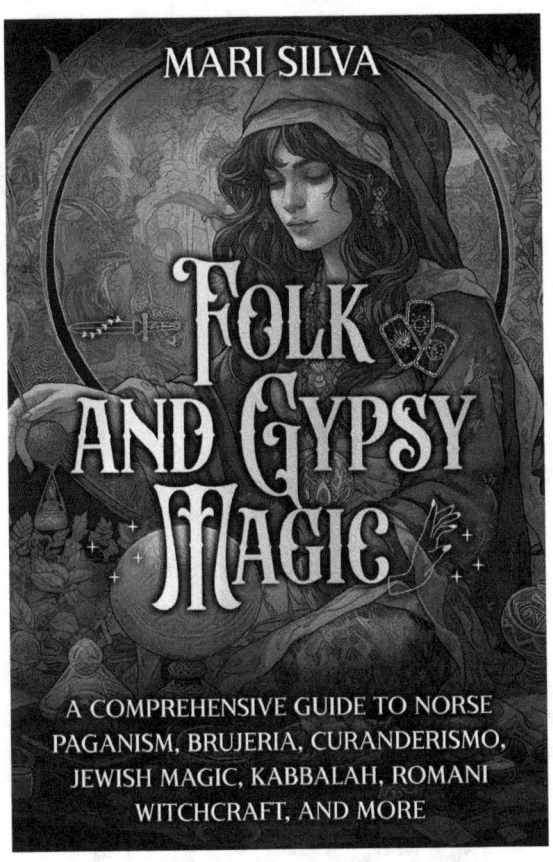

Your Free Gift
(only available for a limited time)

Thanks for getting this book! If you want to learn more about various spirituality topics, then join Mari Silva's community and get a free guided meditation MP3 for awakening your third eye. This guided meditation mp3 is designed to open and strengthen ones third eye so you can experience a higher state of consciousness. Simply visit the link below the image to get started.

https://spiritualityspot.com/meditation

Or, Scan the QR code!

References

Hoodoo in st. Louis: An African American religious tradition (U.s. national Park service). (n.d.). Nps.gov. https://www.nps.gov/articles/000/hoodoo-in-st-louis-an-african-american-religious-tradition.htm

Louissaint, G. (2019, August 21). What is Haitian Voodoo? The Conversation. https://theconversation.com/amp/what-is-haitian-voodoo-119621

The kemetic orthodox religion. (n.d.). Kemet.org. https://www.kemet.org/

The Santeria religion a story. (2009, September 8). African American Registry. https://aaregistry.org/story/from-africa-to-the-americas-santeria/

Wigington, P. (2019, November 29). Yoruba religion: History and beliefs. Learn Religions. https://www.learnreligions.com/yoruba-religion-4777660

42 laws of Maat under Kemet law. (n.d.). Blackhistoryheroes.com. http://www.blackhistoryheroes.com/2013/02/42-laws-of-maat-under-kemet-law-and.html

Ask-Aladdin. (n.d.). Ma'at Egyptian god - Ma'at the god of justice - AskAladdin. Egypt Travel Experts. https://ask-aladdin.com/egypt-gods/maat/

Cressman, D. (2021, October 5). A brief guide to the 7 principles of ma'at - Daniella Cressman. Medium. https://daniellacressman.medium.com/a-brief-guide-to-the-7-principles-of-maat-8ed2faf0fe7c

Elliott, J. (2010, January 1). 3 ways to go on a spiritual journey. WikiHow. https://www.wikihow.com/Go-on-a-Spiritual-Journey

Emily. (2021, October 10). What happens on a spiritual journey? 5 stages you'll experience. Aglow Lifestyle. https://aglowlifestyle.com/what-happens-on-a-spiritual-journey/

Ganguly, I. (2019, October 31). Spiritual journey - complete guide. TheMindFool - Perfect Medium for Self-Development & Mental Health. Explorer of Lifestyle

Abisoye. (2021, August 11). Olodumare, the god with no images, shrines. Plus, TV Africa. https://plustvafrica.com/olodumare-the-god-with-no-images-shrines/

Beyer, C. (2010, February 20). Bondye, the good god of vodou. Learn Religions. https://www.learnreligions.com/bondye-the-good-god-of-vodou-95932

Olódùmarè and the concept of god of the Yoruba people. (2020, March 25). Métissage Sangue Misto. https://metissagesanguemisto.com/olodumare-and-the-concept-of-god-of-the-yoruba-people/

Barrett, O. (2022, February 4). Spirits born out of blood: The lwa of the voodoo pantheon. TheCollector. https://www.thecollector.com/voodoo-lwa/

Beyer, C. (2009, June 4). Vodou Spirits. Learn Religions. https://www.learnreligions.com/spirits-in-african-diaspora-religions-95926

Beyer, C. (2010, February 1). An introduction to the basic beliefs of the vodou (Voodoo) religion. Learn Religions. https://www.learnreligions.com/vodou-an-introduction-for-beginners-95712

Beyer, C. (2012a, June 11). The Orishas. Learn Religions. https://www.learnreligions.com/who-are-the-orishas-95922

Beyer, C. (2012b, June 14). The Orishas: Orunla, Osain, Oshun, Oya, and Yemaya. Learn Religions. https://www.learnreligions.com/orunla-osain-oshun-oya-and-yemaya-95923

demo demo. (2016, September 20). Who are the Orishas? DJONIBA Dance Center. https://www.djoniba.com/who-are-the-orishas/

Gardner, L. (2009, September 29). Cult of the Saints: An Introduction to Santeria. Llewellyn Worldwide. https://www.llewellyn.com/journal/article/2048

"Santeria": La Regla de Ocha-Ifa and Lukumi. (n.d.). Pluralism.Org. https://pluralism.org/%E2%80%9Csanter%C3%ADa%E2%80%9D-the-lucumi-way

Emancipation: The Caribbean Experience. (n.d.). Miami.Edu. https://scholar.library.miami.edu/emancipation/religion1.htm

Regla De Ocha, Candomble, Lucumi, Oyo, Palo, Palo, M., Santeria, M., & Ifa, Y.(n.d.). Orisha Worshippers. Bop.Gov. Retrieved February 10, 2022, from https://www.bop.gov/foia/docs/orishamanual.pdf

mythictreasures. (2020, May 10). Introduction to 7-day candles. Mythictreasures. https://www.mythictreasures.com/post/into-to-7-day-candles

How to invoke the energy of yorube goddess Oshun. (n.d.). Vice.Com. https://www.vice.com/en/article/3kjepv/how-to-invoke-oshun-yoruba-goddess-orisha

admin. (2020, February 1). Fèt Gede - the Haitian Day of the Dead · Visit Haiti. Visit Haiti. https://visithaiti.com/festivals-events/fet-gede-haitian-day-of-the-dead/#:~:text=Every%20year%2C%20on%20November%201

Egun / The ancestors - The Yoruba Religious Concepts. (n.d.). Sites.google.com. https://sites.google.com/site/theyorubareligiousconcepts/egungun-the-ancestors

Herukhuti, R. A. (2022, January 27). Why Africans Honor Ancestral Spirits. https://www.afrikaiswoke.com/the-true-nature-of-african-ancestral-spirits/

Ost, B. (n.d.). LibGuides: African Traditional Religions Textbook: Ifa: Chapter 5. Our Ancestors Are With Us Now. Research.auctr.edu. https://research.auctr.edu/Ifa/Chap5Intro

Voodoo devotees eat GLASS and sacrifice goats during bizarre celebrations held to mark Haiti's day of the dead. (2016, November 2). The Sun. https://www.thesun.co.uk/news/2101053/voodoo-devotees-eat-glass-and-sacrifice-goats-during-bizarre-celebrations-held-to-mark-haitis-day-of-the-dead/

What is Santeria ? - The Yoruba Religious Concepts. (n.d.). Sites.google.com. https://sites.google.com/site/theyorubareligiousconcepts/what-is-santeria

Herb Magic Catalogue: Sampson Snake Root. (n.d.). Www.herbmagic.com. https://www.herbmagic.com/sampson-snake-root.html

High John the Conqueror Root: A Staple of Hoodoo Magic. (n.d.). Original Botanica. Retrieved November 17, 2022, from https://originalbotanica.com/blog/high-john-the-conqueror-root-a-staple-of-hoodoo-magic/ (This website was my main resource for this chapter)

JimsonWeed: History, Perceptions, Traditional Uses, and Potential Therapeutic Benefits of the Genus Datura - American Botanical Council. (n.d.). Www.herbalgram.org. https://www.herbalgram.org/resources/herbalgram/issues/69/table-of-contents/article2930/

SAW PALMETTO. (n.d.). Star Child. https://starchild.co.uk/products/saw-palmetto?variant=12527087550535

Altars of the Yoruba religion. (n.d.). Excelencias.com. https://caribeinsider.excelencias.com/index.php/en/news/altars-yoruba-religion

Dorsey, L. (2014, March 23). Creating ancestor Altars in Santeria, vodou, and voodoo. Voodoo Universe. https://www.patheos.com/blogs/voodoouniverse/2014/03/creating-ancestor-altars-in-santeria-vodou-and-voodoo/

Helena. (2021, January 24). How to build an altar at home for spiritual self-care. Disorient. https://disorient.co/build-an-altar/

LibGuides: African traditional religions textbook: Ifa: Chapter 5. Our ancestors are with us now. (2021). https://research.auctr.edu/Ifa/Chap5Intro

Bradley, J., & Coen, C. D. (2010). Magic's in the bag: Creating spellbinding Gris Gris bags and sachets. Llewellyn Publications.

Caro, T. (2020, September 14). Mojo Bag vs Gris-Gris [the difference & how to use them]. Magickal Spot. https://magickalspot.com/mojo-bag-vs-gris-gris/

How to make your own mojo bags. (n.d.). Nui Cobalt Designs. https://nuicobaltdesigns.com/blogs/daily-astrology-reports/16564821-how-to-make-your-own-mojo-bags

How to: What is a mojo bag and how do I use it? (n.d.). Livejournal.com. https://ldygry.livejournal.com/4248.html

Chery, D. N. (2016, July 29th). AP PHOTOS: Voodoo festival transforms Haitian village. Associated Press.

Feast of the Beautiful Valley. (2021, May 1st). Kemetic Temple UK. https://kemetictemple.uk/t/feast-of-the-beautiful-valley/618

Festival of the wag. (n.d.). Historyofegypt.net. https://historyofegypt.net/?page_id=980

Festivals. (n.d.). Kemet.org. https://www.kemet.org/community/festivals

Alston, D. D. "Ifa Reading of the Year 2022-2023." Last modified June 10, 2022. https://www.daydreamalston.com/blog/tag/isese

Atla LibGuides. "African Traditional Religions: Ifa." Last modified December 15, 2022. https://atla.libguides.com/OER_Ifa

Spiritual Doctor AFI. "Virgo Season and the Orishas." Last modified September 7, 2019. https://spiritualdoctorafi.com/blog/tag/isese

Africa Update Archives. (n.d.). Ccsu.edu. https://web.ccsu.edu/afstudy/supdt99.htm

Barrett, O. (2022, January 23). Voodoo: The revolutionary roots of the most misunderstood religion. TheCollector. https://www.thecollector.com/voodoo-history-misunderstood-religion/

Beyer, C. (2010, February 1). An introduction to the basic beliefs of the vodou (Voodoo) religion. Learn Religions. https://www.learnreligions.com/vodou-an-introduction-for-beginners-95712

Mark, J. J. (2021). Orisha. World History Encyclopedia. https://www.worldhistory.org/Orisha/

Murphy, J. M. (2022). Santería. In Encyclopedia Britannica.

Rudy, L. J. (2019, July 30). What is candomblé? Beliefs and history. Learn Religions. https://www.learnreligions.com/candomble-4692500

Asante, M. K., & Mazama, A. (Eds.). (2009). Encyclopedia of African religion. SAGE Publications.

AU press - digital publications. (n.d.). AU Press - Digital Publications. https://read.aupress.ca/read/sharing-breath/section/c53bd62e-abaf-4bd3-859d-20cf02db467a

Codingest. (n.d.). Orí: The significance of the head in Yoruba. Positive Psychology Nigeria. https://positivepsychology.org.ng/ori-the-significance-of-the-head-in-yoruba

Dopamu, A. (2008). Predestination, destiny, and faith in Yorubaland: Any meeting point? Global Journal of Humanities, 7(1 & 2), 37-39.

AU press - digital publications. (n.d.). AU Press - Digital Publications. https://read.aupress.ca/read/sharing-breath/section/c53bd62e-abaf-4bd3-859d-20cf02db467a

Balogun, O. (2013). The Concepts of Ori and Human Destiny in Traditional Yoruba Thought: A soft deterministic interpretation. https://www.academia.edu/3550807/The_Concepts_of_Ori_and_Human_Destiny_in_Traditional_Yoruba_Thought_A_Soft_Deterministic_Interpretation

Taiwo, P. O. (2018). Ori: The Ifa Concept of the Evolution of the earth. https://www.academia.edu/37623959/Ori_The_Ifa_Concept_of_the_Evolution_of_The_Earth

(N.d.-a). Researchgate.net. https://www.researchgate.net/publication/280495301_Predestination_and_Free_will_in_the_Yoruba_Concept_of_a_Person_Contradictions_and_Paradoxes_Philosophy_Culture_and_Traditions

(N.d.-b). Researchgate.net. https://www.researchgate.net/publication/237832774_The_Concepts_of_Ori_and_Human_Destiny_in_Traditional_Yoruba_Thought_A_Soft_Deterministic_Interpretation

A west African folktale of the story of oshún's flight to olodumare. (n.d.). Blackhistoryheroes.com. http://www.blackhistoryheroes.com/2015/10/a-west-african-folktale-of-story-of.html

An Illustration Studio. (2013). Creation Stories. Createspace.

Asante, M. K., & Mazama, A. (Eds.). (2009). Encyclopedia of African religion. SAGE Publications.

AU press - digital publications. (n.d.). AU Press - Digital Publications. https://read.aupress.ca/read/sharing-breath/section/c53bd62e-abaf-4bd3-859d-20cf02db467a

Hardy, J. (2022, July 2). 12 African gods and goddesses: The Orisha pantheon. History Cooperative; The History Cooperative. https://historycooperative.org/african-gods-and-goddesses/

Mark, J. J. (2021). Orisha. World History Encyclopedia. https://www.worldhistory.org/Orisha/

Ogbodo, I. (2022, March 17). Yoruba mythology: The orishas of the Yoruba religion. African History Collections. https://medium.com/african-history-collections/yoruba-mythology-the-orishas-of-the-yoruba-religion-f411c3db389d

Awakening to Your Divine Self: What is Ori Consciousness? (2017, September 20). Ayele Kumari, PhD / Chief Dr. Abiye Tayese. https://ayelekumari.com/ifayele-blog/awakening-to-your-divine-self-what-is-ori-consciousness/

How to align with your Ori? (n.d.). Infinity-Charm. https://infinity-charm.com/blogs/news/how-to-align-with-your-ori

Ibori – learn how to feed your Ori – babalawo Orisha. (n.d.). Babalawoweb.com.

Original Products. (2019, September 10). Creating an Orisha altar. Original Botanica; www.originalbotanica.com#creator. https://originalbotanica.com/blog/creating-an-orisha-altar-/

Ancestors. (2022, February 4). The Spiritual Community of the Òrìṣà - Energies of Nature. https://orisa.si/en/ancestors/

Egbe Òrun Complete. (n.d.). Scribd. https://www.scribd.com/document/494770885/Egbe-Orun-Complete

Egun / The ancestors - The Yoruba Religious Concepts. (n.d.). Google.com. https://sites.google.com/site/theyorubareligiousconcepts/egungun-the-ancestors

Isaad, V. (2021, October 23). Beginner's guide to spiritual practices to start connecting with your ancestors. HipLatina; HipLatina.com. https://hiplatina.com/connecting-ancestors-guide/

Baron, E. (2017, March 14). Beginning ancestor meditation. Nature's Sacred Journey. https://www.patheos.com/blogs/naturessacredjourney/2017/03/beginning-ancestor-meditation/

Connect. Collaborate. Express. (n.d.). RoundGlass. https://roundglass.com/living/meditation/articles/connect-to-your-ancestors

Evolve your ancestral story to heal & create change. (n.d.). Theshiftnetwork.com. https://theshiftnetwork.com/Evolve-Your-Ancestral-Story-Heal-Create-Change

How to build an Ancestor (Egun) shrine. (2017, September 20). Ayele Kumari, PhD / Chief Dr. Abiye Tayese. https://ayelekumari.com/ifayele-blog/how-to-build-an-ancestor-egun-shrine/

Onilu, Y. (2020, May 29). EGBE: "spiritual doubles" or "heavenly comrades." Chief Yagbe Awolowo Onilu; Yagbe Onilu. https://yagbeonilu.com/egbe-heavenly-mates/

Egbe Òrun Complete. (n.d.). Scribd. https://www.scribd.com/document/494770885/Egbe-Orun-Complete

Egbetoke, V. A. P. by. (2018, November 28). Ori, Egbe Agba, Egungun, Destiny, just to start knowing about. White Calabash. https://whitecalabash.wordpress.com/2018/11/28/ori-egbe-agba-egungun-destiny-just-to-start-knowing-about/

Ekanola, A. B. (2006). A naturalistic interpretation of the Yoruba concepts of Ori. Philosophia Africana, 9, 41+. https://go.gale.com/ps/i.do?id=GALE%7CA168285830&sid=googleScholar&v=2.1&it=r&linkaccess=abs&issn=15398250&p=AONE&sw=w&userGroupName=anon%7Ed19920da

Fruin, C. (2021). LibGuides: African Traditional Religions: Ifa: Hermeneutics. https://atla.libguides.com/c.php?g=1138564&p=8384978

Metalgaia. (2013, August 27). The Basics of Yoruba – An African Spiritual Tradition. Metal Gaia. https://metal-gaia.com/2013/08/27/the-basics-of-yoruba/

Wigington, P. (n.d.). Yoruba Religion: History and Beliefs. Learn Religions. https://www.learnreligions.com/yoruba-religion-4777660

Sawe, B. E. (2019, April 17). What Is The Yoruba Religion? Yoruba Beliefs and Origin. WorldAtlas. https://www.worldatlas.com/articles/what-is-the-yoruba-religion.html

Anzaldua, G. (2009). Yemayá. In A. L. Keating, W. D. Mignolo, I. Silverblatt, & S. Saldívar-Hull (Eds.), The Gloria Anzaldúa Reader (pp. 242–242). Duke University Press.

Beyer, C. (2012a, June 11). The Orishas. Learn Religions. https://www.learnreligions.com/who-are-the-orishas-95922

Beyer, C. (2012b, June 14). The Orishas: Orunla, Osain, Oshun, Oya, and Yemaya. Learn Religions. https://www.learnreligions.com/orunla-osain-oshun-oya-and-yemaya-95923

Brandon, G. (2018). orisha. In Encyclopedia Britannica.

Celebrate eleguá~eshu, Orisha of Destiny. (2022, September 26). New York Latin Culture Magazine TM; New York Latin Culture Magazine. https://www.newyorklatinculture.com/elegua-orisha-of-the-crossroads/

Beyer, C. (2012, July 27). Ebbos in Santeria - Sacrifices and Offerings. Learn Religions. https://www.learnreligions.com/ebbos-in-santeria-sacrifices-and-offerings-95958

Borghini, K. (2010, June 9). Offerings and sacrifices: Honoring our ancestors helps us give thanks. Goodtherapy.org Therapy Blog. https://www.goodtherapy.org/blog/offerings/

Cuba, A. pa mi. (2020, July 26). How to invoke Obatala? Prayers and prayers to the Orisha. Ashé pa mi Cuba. https://ashepamicuba.com/en/como-invocar-a-obatala-oraciones-y-rezos-al-orisha/

Dokosi, M. E. (2020, March 20). How Orisha veneration by the Yoruba and Ewe crossed over as Santería in the Americas. Face2Face Africa. https://face2faceafrica.com/article/how-orisha-veneration-by-the-yoruba-and-ewe-crossed-over-as-santeria-in-the-americas

Egbe Òrun Complete. (n.d.). Scribd. https://www.scribd.com/document/494770885/Egbe-Orun-Complete

February. (2017, February 9). Must read: Classes of egbe (heavenly mate of every human). Blogspot.com. https://fayemioye.blogspot.com/2017/02/must-read-classes-of-egbe-heavenly-mate.html

November. (2017, November 14). Ways to communicate to egbe effectively. Blogspot.com. https://fayemioye.blogspot.com/2017/11/communicate-with-egbe-through-these.html

Agbo, N. (2020, February 9). Significance of Egungun in Yoruba cultural history. The Guardian Nigeria News - Nigeria and World News; Guardian Nigeria. https://guardian.ng/life/significance-of-egungun-in-yoruba-cultural-history/

Issa, N. M., Tomé, J., Sturgeon, L., & Coyoli, J. S. (n.d.). Oro a egún. ReVista. https://revista.drclas.harvard.edu/oro-a-egun/

LibGuides: African Traditional Religions: Ifa: Appendix B: Categories of spiritual forces; Spiritual forces; And praise names. (2021). https://atla.libguides.com/c.php?g=1138564&p=8385027

Egungun Masquerade Dance Costume: Ekuu Egungun. (n.d.). Africa.si.edu. https://africa.si.edu/exhibits/resonance/44.html

Kalilu, R. O. R. (1991). The role of sculptures in Yoruba egungun masquerade. Journal of Black Studies, 22(1), 15-29. https://doi.org/10.1177/002193479102200103

United Nations High Commissioner for Refugees. (2002). Refworld: Information on refugees and human rights. United Nations.

How to build an Ancestor (Egun) shrine. (2017, September 20). Ayele Kumari, PhD / Chief Dr. Abiye Tayese. https://ayelekumari.com/ifayele-blog/how-to-build-an-ancestor-egun-shrine/

Kule, P. (2010, December 28). How to create a spiritual altar. HubPages. https://discover.hubpages.com/religion-philosophy/How-to-Create-a-Spiritual-Altar

Ancestor veneration: What is it, and why is it important? (n.d.). Urban Lotus Jewelry. https://www.urbanlotusjewelry.com/blogs/musings/how-to-connect-with-your-ancestors

16 Truths of IFA. (2013, December 4). Oyeku Ofun Temple. https://oyekuofun.org/16-truths-of-ifa/

How to Connect to Your Ancestors. (n.d.). RoundGlass. https://roundglass.com/living/meditation/articles/connect-to-your-ancestors

Akin-Otiko, A. (n.d.). The reality of reincarnation and the traditional Yoruba response based on odù ifá. Uwi.edu. http://ojs.mona.uwi.edu/index.php/cjp/article/viewFile/4627/3382

Anālayo, B. (n.d.). Rebirth and the west. Buddhistinquiry.org. https://www.buddhistinquiry.org/article/rebirth-and-the-west/

Cheng, C. (n.d.). Reincarnation in Hinduism. Emory.edu. https://scholarblogs.emory.edu/gravematters/2017/02/17/reincarnation-in-hinduism/

Wachege, P. (n.d.). CURSES AND CURSING AMONG THE AGĨKŨYŨ: SOCIO-CULTURAL AND RELIGIOUS BENEFITS. https://profiles.uonbi.ac.ke/patrickwachege/files/curses_and_cursing_among_the_agikuyu.pdf

Why Generational Curses Are So Hard To Break And How To Do It. (n.d.). The Traveling Witch. https://thetravelingwitch.com/blog/why-generational-curses-are-so-hard-to-break-and-how-to-do-it

Nigeria, G. (2019, November 24). The Orisha Ogun in Maleficent. The Guardian Nigeria News - Nigeria and World News; Guardian Nigeria. https://guardian.ng/life/the-orisha-ogun-in-maleficent/

Ogun. (n.d.-a). Encyclopedia.com. https://www.encyclopedia.com/humanities/news-wires-white-papers-and-books/ogun

Ogun. (n.d.-b). Mythencyclopedia.com. http://www.mythencyclopedia.com/Ni-Pa/Ogun.html

Ogun, god of war. (n.d.). Africanpoems.net. https://africanpoems.net/gods-ancestors/ogun-god-of-war/

Olive senior's gardening in the tropics. (n.d.). Torontomu.Ca. https://www.torontomu.ca/olivesenior/poems/ogun.html

Origin of Ogun – god of iron. (2016, December 30). Ondo Connects New Era. http://www.ekimogundescendant.org/origin-of-ogun-god-of-iron/

XoticBrands. (2020, December 4). Ogun, God of Iron and Rum…Who was he in 3 mins? Medium. https://xoticbrands.medium.com/ogun-god-of-iron-and-rum-4e68172f9af7

31 Days of Revolutionary Women, #16: Oshun. (2017, March 16). South Seattle Emerald. https://southseattleemerald.com/2017/03/16/31-days-of-revolutionary-women-16-oshun/

Baltimore Sun - We are currently unavailable in your region. (n.d.). Baltimoresun.com. https://www.baltimoresun.com/maryland/bs-md-african-faiths-20190315-story.html

Beyer, C. (2012, June 14). The Orishas: Orunla, Osain, Oshun, Oya, and Yemaya. Learn Religions. https://www.learnreligions.com/orunla-osain-oshun-oya-and-yemaya-95923

Brandon, G. (2018). orisha. In Encyclopedia Britannica.

Cuban Santeria tradition and practices. (n.d.). Anywhere.com. https://www.anywhere.com/cuba/travel-guide/santeria

Imoka, A. (2019, April 11). Who is Oshun Santeria? El Viejo Lazaro. https://www.viejolazaro.com/blogs/news/who-is-oshun-santeria

Imoka-Ubochioma, C. (2021, December 8). The Yoruba story of creation. Linkedin.com. https://www.linkedin.com/pulse/yoruba-story-creation-dr-chizoba-imoka-ubochioma/

Jeffries, B. S. (2022). Oshun. In Encyclopedia Britannica.

Mark, J. J. (2021b). Oshun. World History Encyclopedia. https://www.worldhistory.org/Oshun/

Mesa, V. (2018, April 20). How to invoke Oshun, the Yoruba goddess of sensuality and prosperity. VICE. https://www.vice.com/en/article/3kjepv/how-to-invoke-oshun-yoruba-goddess-orisha

Murphy, J. M. (2022). Santería. In Encyclopedia Britannica.

Ochún. (n.d.). AboutSanteria. http://www.aboutsanteria.com/ochuacuten.html

Oshun - Yoruba deity and goddess of the river. (n.d.). Realmermaids.net. http://www.realmermaids.net/mermaid-legends/oshun/

What is Santeria? (n.d.). AboutSanteria. http://www.aboutsanteria.com/what-is-santeria.html

Wigington, P. (2011, November 15). What is the Santeria religion? Learn Religions. https://www.learnreligions.com/about-santeria-traditions-2562543

Wigington, P. (2019, November 29). Yoruba religion: History and beliefs. Learn Religions. https://www.learnreligions.com/yoruba-religion-4777660

Yoruba. (n.d.). Everyculture.com. https://www.everyculture.com/wc/Mauritania-to-Nigeria/Yoruba.html

Children of Oshun – see the characteristics and find out if you are one of them! (2022, September 27). Love Magic Works. https://lovemagicworks.com/children-of-oshun-see-the-characteristics-and-find-out-if-you-are-one-of-them/

Church, S. (n.d.). The head or guardian, Orisha. Santeria Church of the Orishas. http://santeriachurch.org/head-or-guardian-orisha/

Oshun: The Yoruban goddess of love. (2013, March 18). The Broom Closet. https://broomcloset.wordpress.com/2013/03/19/oshun-the-yoruban-goddess-of-love/

Rogers, M. R. (2022, July 6). How to find your Orisha mother and father? Classified Mom. https://www.classifiedmom.com/how-to-find-your-orisha-mother-and-father/

Terrio, S. J. (2019). Whose child, am I?: Unaccompanied, undocumented children in U.s. immigration custody. University of California Press. https://doi.org/10.1525/9780520961449

Abisoye. (2021, August 13). The mythological powers of Oba's ears. Plus, TV Africa. https://plustvafrica.com/the-mythological-powers-of-obas-ears/

Amarachi. (2017, December 10). Orisha: The Legend of Sango & his Wives. Travel with a Pen Nigerian Travel Blog. https://www.travelwithapen.com/orisha-legend-sango-wives/

Celebrate obatalá, the Orisha who made the world and people. (2022, September 26). New York Latin Culture Magazine TM; New York Latin Culture Magazine. https://www.newyorklatinculture.com/obatala/

Control of the seasons in the new kingdom - The Yoruba Religious Concepts. (n.d.). Google.com. https://sites.google.com/site/theyorubareligiousconcepts/control-of-the-seasons-in-the-new-kingdom

Nut_Meg, O. (n.d.). Oshun. Obsidianportal.com. https://god-touched.obsidianportal.com/characters/oshun-1

Ochún. (n.d.). AboutSanteria. http://www.aboutsanteria.com/ochuacuten.html

Oshun loses her beauty. (n.d.). Uua.org. https://www.uua.org/re/tapestry/children/signs/session13/oshun

Prince_miraj. (n.d.). How oshun lured ogun from the forest. Wattpad.com. https://www.wattpad.com/522478079-nigerian-tribe-myth%27s-african-how-oshun-lured-ogun

Roy, M. (2020, May 7). Eshu, Yoruba trickster god. Minute Mythology. https://medium.com/minute-mythology/eshu-yoruba-trickster-god-a09fd22ca48c

Santos, E. (2020). Oxum. Solisluna Editora.

The birth of Oshun ibu yumu - the Yoruba Religious concepts. (n.d.). Google.com. https://sites.google.com/site/theyorubareligiousconcepts/the-birth-of-oshun-ibu-yumu-1

The Editors of Encyclopedia Britannica. (2015). Eshu. In Encyclopedia Britannica.

Wikipedia contributors. (2022, December 22). Aganju. Wikipedia, The Free Encyclopedia.
https://en.wikipedia.org/w/index.php?title=Aganju&oldid=1128829112

Yemaya abandons Arganyu in Oshuns Ile - The Yoruba Religious Concepts. (n.d.). Google.com.
https://sites.google.com/site/theyorubareligiousconcepts/yemaya-abandons-arganyu-in-oshuns-ile

Yemaya offers Oshun marriage with Arganyu - The Yoruba Religious Concepts. (n.d.). Google.com.
https://sites.google.com/site/theyorubareligiousconcepts/yemaya-offers-oshun-marriage-with-arganyu

Aletheia. (2018, March 4). Divine Masculine: 9 ways to awaken your inner Shiva ★ LonerWolf. LonerWolf.

Anusara School of Hatha Yoga. (2022, August 28). 6 easy ways to connect with the divine feminine. Anusara School of Hatha Yoga.
https://www.anusarayoga.com/6-easy-ways-to-connect-with-divine-feminine/

Davis, F. (2021, October 8). How to embody your divine feminine qualities. Karma and Luck. https://www.karmaandluck.com/blogs/news/divine-feminine-qualities

Divine Feminine: Meaning, origins, and more. (n.d.). Tiny Rituals.
https://tinyrituals.co/blogs/tiny-rituals/divine-feminine

Tiodar, A. (2021, June 1). 11 amazing qualities of the Divine Feminine explained. Subconscious Servant. https://subconsciousservant.com/divine-feminine-qualities/

What the "divine feminine" is all about & 9 ways anyone can embody it. (2021, March 22). Mindbodygreen. https://www.mindbodygreen.com/articles/divine-feminine

Rodríguez, C. (2020, August 23). 10 representative plants of Oshún. Ashé pa mi Cuba. https://ashepamicuba.com/en/plantas-de-oshun/

Goddess Oshun. (2012, January 21). Journeying to the Goddess.
https://journeyingtothegoddess.wordpress.com/2012/01/21/goddess-oshun/

My Yoruba. (n.d.). Tumblr.
https://myoruba.tumblr.com/post/82996905534/oshuns-herbs

Rhys, D. (2022, November 6). Oshun – Symbolism of the Yoruba Goddess. Symbol Sage. https://symbolsage.com/african-goddess-of-love/

Kaufman, A. (2022, October 31). Oshun Offerings: What are the Offerings to Oshun to Ask for Help? Digest From Experts.
https://digestfromexperts.com/4516/oshun-offerings/

Universe, V. (2014, September 8). Oshun's Butternut Squash Soup Recipe. Voodoo Universe. https://www.patheos.com/blogs/voodoouniverse/2014/09/oshuns-butternut-squash-soup-recipe/

View all posts by Simone Soulel Co. (2019, September 10). Oshun's Feast Day Recipes: Honey Yams ! The Bruja Encyclopedia. https://coven90210.wordpress.com/2019/09/10/oshuns-feast-day-recipes-honey-yams/

Scott-James, N. (2020, October 30). Ori Ye Ye O: Honoring the Yoruba Goddess Oshun. The Alchemist's Kitchen. https://wisdom.thealchemistskitchen.com/ori-ye-ye-o-yoruba-goddess-oshun/

Siren Says. (2009, May 11). Siren Says. https://sirensays.wordpress.com/2009/05/11/oshun-altar/

How to Invoke the Energy of Yorube Goddess Oshun. (2018, April 20). Vice.Com. https://www.vice.com/en/article/3kjepv/how-to-invoke-oshun-yoruba-goddess-orisha

Urošević, A. (2015, September 23). Spiritual Cleansing in Ifá: "Sour" and "Sweet" Baths. Amor et Mortem. https://amoretmortem.wordpress.com/2015/09/23/spiritual-cleansing-in-ifa-sour-and-sweet-baths/

Lousfey, D. (n.d.). Love Spells. SHUBHAM

Oshun Ritual with Yeye Luisah Teish for Love and Prosperity presented by the Neighborhood Story Project. (n.d.). P.5 Yesterday We Said Tomorrow. https://www.prospect5.org/programs/pp46cnl2n50rmcbjegutylqka9e4tx

Botanica, Y. [@YeyeoBotanica]. (2019, August 29). Oshun Fertility Ritual | Yeyeo Botanica. Youtube. https://www.youtube.com/watch?v=RFAZQSWRIp4

Botanica, Y. [@YeyeoBotanica]. (2017, January 30). Oshun Protection & Special Request | Yeyeo Botanica. Youtube. https://www.youtube.com/watch?v=RFAZQSWRIp4

No title. (n.d.). Twinkl.Co.In. https://www.twinkl.co.in/event/osun-festival-nigeria-2023

Rankin, L. M. (2019, July 3). A goddess for giving and receiving love. Human Parts. https://humanparts.medium.com/a-goddess-for-giving-and-receiving-love-7541cb73ad65

Sacred journeys with Bruce feiler. (n.d.). SACRED JOURNEYS WITH BRUCE FEILER. https://www.pbs.org/wgbh/sacredjourneys/content/osun-osogbo/

Regla De Ocha, Candomble, Lucumi, Oyo, Palo, Palo, Santeria, M. & Ifa, Y. (n.d.). Regla de Ocha Candomble Lucumi Oyo Palo Mayumbe Palo Monte Santeria Vodun Yoruba Ifa Religious Practices. Bop.gov. https://www.bop.gov/foia/docs/orishamanual.pdf

Top 10 oshun prayer ideas and inspiration. (n.d.). Pinterest. https://www.pinterest.com/ideas/oshun-prayer/899688434063/

About: Babalawo. (n.d.). DBpedia. https://dbpedia.org/page/Babalawo

About: Ori (Yoruba). (n.d.). DBpedia. https://dbpedia.org/page/Ori_(Yoruba)

Ajogun. (n.d.). Wiktionary.org. https://en.wiktionary.org/wiki/Ajogun

Alamy Limited. (n.d.). Osun Osogbo Monarch: Ataoja of Osogbo wearing his sacred crown on Osun Day. Alamy.com. https://www.alamy.com/osun-osogbo-monarch-ataoja-of-osogbo-wearing-his-sacred-crown-on-osun-day-image425916626.html

Dopamu, A. (2008). Predestination, destiny, and faith in Yorubaland: Any meeting point? Global Journal of Humanities, 7(1 & 2), 37–39. https://www.ajol.info/index.php/gjh/article/view/79372

Facebook. (n.d.). Facebook.com. https://web.facebook.com/StJohnsSpiritualBaptistChurch/posts/omi-tutu-that-is-water-that-calmsthis-ritual-is-very-oldthere-are-many-reasons-f/1874345729265590/?_rdc=1&_rdr

LibGuides: African Traditional Religions: Ifa: Chapter 5: Our ancestors are with us now. (2021). https://atla.libguides.com/c.php?g=1138564&p=8384925

Recio, S. (2019, February 14). What have I done? And other answers to your questions –. Sili Recio. https://silirecio.com/blog/what-have-i-done-and-other-answers-to-your-questions

The Ataoja of Osogbo land. (n.d.). Google Arts & Culture. https://artsandculture.google.com/asset/the-ataoja-of-osogbo-land/JwEH7uuwlNpEeQ?hl=en

The Spiritual Attorney. (2019, September 24). Ase': What it is & why it's important. TheSpiritualAttorney. https://www.thespiritualattorney.com/post/manage-your-blog-from-your-live-site

(N.d.). Blackpast.org. https://www.blackpast.org/global-african-history/ile-ife-ca-500-b-c-e/

(2019, December 25). Oshun: African Goddess of Love and Sweet Waters. Ancient Origins Reconstructing the Story of Humanity's Past; Ancient Origins. https://www.ancient-origins.net/myths-legends-africa/oshun-african-goddess-love-and-sweet-waters-002908

Anzaldua, G. (2009). Yemayá. In A. L. Keating, W. D. Mignolo, I. Silverblatt, & S. Saldívar-Hull (Eds.), The Gloria Anzaldúa Reader (pp. 242-242). Duke University Press.

Beyer, C. (2012a, June 11). The Orishas. Learn Religions. https://www.learnreligions.com/who-are-the-orishas-95922

Beyer, C. (2012b, June 14). The Orishas: Orunla, Osain, Oshun, Oya, and Yemaya. Learn Religions. https://www.learnreligions.com/orunla-osain-oshun-oya-and-yemaya-95923

Brandon, G. (2018). orisha. In Encyclopedia Britannica.

Canson, P. E. (2014). Yemonja. In Encyclopedia Britannica.

Cuban Santeria tradition and practices. (n.d.). Anywhere.com. https://www.anywhere.com/cuba/travel-guide/santeria

Eze, C. (2022, September 25). Yoruba mythology: The Orishas of the Yoruba race. The Guardian Nigeria News - Nigeria and World News; Guardian Nigeria. https://guardian.ng/life/yoruba-mythology-the-orishas-of-the-yoruba-race/

Mark, J. J. (2021). Orisha. World History Encyclopedia. https://www.worldhistory.org/Orisha/

Merten, P. (2018, July 31). In Cuba, Santería flourishes two decades after ban was lifted. The GroundTruth Project. https://thegroundtruthproject.org/cuba-santeria-catholicism-religion-flourish-two-decades-freedom-granted/

Murphy, J. M. (1988). Santeria: An African religion in America. Beacon Press.

Rhys, D. (2020, December 1). Yemaya (yemoja) – Yoruba Queen of the sea. Symbol Sage. https://symbolsage.com/yemaya-queen-of-the-sea/

Rituals and customs. (n.d.). BBC. https://www.bbc.co.uk/religion/religions/santeria/ritesrituals/rituals.shtml

Santeria deities. (n.d.). BBC. https://www.bbc.co.uk/religion/religions/santeria/beliefs/orishas.shtml

Sawe, B. E. (2019, April 17). What is the Yoruba religion? Yoruba beliefs and origin. WorldAtlas. https://www.worldatlas.com/articles/what-is-the-yoruba-religion.html

Snider, A. C. (2019, July 9). The history of Yemaya, santeria's queenly ocean goddess mermaid. Yahoo Life. https://www.yahoo.com/lifestyle/history-yemaya-santeria-apos-queenly-144630513.html

What is Santeria? (n.d.). AboutSanteria. http://www.aboutsanteria.com/what-is-santeria.html

Wigington, P. (2011, November 15). What is Santeria? Learn Religions. https://www.learnreligions.com/about-santeria-traditions-2562543

Wigington, P. (2019, November 29). Yoruba religion: History and beliefs. Learn Religions. https://www.learnreligions.com/yoruba-religion-4777660

Yoruba. (n.d.). Everyculture.com. https://www.everyculture.com/wc/Mauritania-to-Nigeria/Yoruba.html

Yoruba creation myth. (n.d.). Gateway-africa.com. https://www.gateway-africa.com/stories/Yoruba_Creation_Myth.html

(N.d.). Teenvogue.com. https://www.teenvogue.com/story/the-history-of-yemaya-goddess-mermaid

Amata. (2016, August 5). Sacred stories of the Orishas. Journey of a 21st Century Afrikan Queen. https://giramatans.wordpress.com/2016/08/05/sacred-stories-of-the-orishas/

Control of the seasons in the new kingdom - The Yoruba Religious Concepts. (n.d.). Google.com. https://sites.google.com/site/theyorubareligiousconcepts/control-of-the-seasons-in-the-new-kingdom

Goddess wisdom: Yemaya's story. (2013, July 18). Self-Love Rainbow; Blessing Manifesting. https://www.selfloverainbow.com/2013/07/goddess-wisdom-yemayas-story.html

Importance of mythology. (n.d.). Prezi.com. https://prezi.com/remyxkfdbc4o/importance-of-mythology/

In Search of Myths & Heroes. What is a Myth? (n.d.). Pbs.org. https://www.pbs.org/mythsandheroes/myths_what.html

Marriage of Oba Nani and Shango - the Yoruba Religious concepts. (n.d.). Google.com. https://sites.google.com/site/theyorubareligiousconcepts/marriage-of-oba-nani-and-shango

Rhys, D. (2020a, December 1). Olokun – Orisha of the depths of the ocean. Symbol Sage. https://symbolsage.com/olokun-sprit-of-waters/

Rhys, D. (2020b, December 1). Yemaya (yemoja) – Yoruba Queen of the sea. Symbol Sage. https://symbolsage.com/yemaya-queen-of-the-sea/

The separation of Oya and Yemaya - The Yoruba Religious Concepts. (n.d.). Google.com. https://sites.google.com/site/theyorubareligiousconcepts/marriage-of-oba-nani-and-shango/the-separation-of-oya-and-yemaya-1

Turnbull, L. (2022, October 28). Yemaya, the Santeria goddess of the ocean. Goddess Gift; The Goddess Path. https://goddessgift.com/goddesses/yemaya/

Yemaya abandons Arganyu in Oshuns Ile - The Yoruba Religious Concepts. (n.d.). Google.com. https://sites.google.com/site/theyorubareligiousconcepts/yemaya-abandons-arganyu-in-oshuns-ile

Yemaya becomes the Apetebi (woman) of Orula - The Yoruba Religious Concepts. (n.d.). Google.com. https://sites.google.com/site/theyorubareligiousconcepts/yemaya-becomes-the-apetebi-woman-of-orula-1

Yemaya offers Oshun marriage with Arganyu - The Yoruba Religious Concepts. (n.d.). Google.com. https://sites.google.com/site/theyorubareligiousconcepts/yemaya-offers-oshun-marriage-with-arganyu

Beyer, C. (n.d.). Syncretism - What Is Syncretism? Learn Religions. https://www.learnreligions.com/what-is-syncretism-p2-95858

Snider, A. C. (2019, July 9). The History of Yemaya, Santeria's Queenly Ocean Goddess Mermaid. Teen Vogue. https://www.teenvogue.com/story/the-history-of-yemaya-goddess-mermaid

Viarnés, C. (n.d.). All Roads Lead to Yemayá: Transformative Trajectories in the Procession at Regla. Hemisphericinstitute.Org. https://hemisphericinstitute.org/en/emisferica-5-1-traveling/5-1-essays/all-roads-lead-to-yemaya-transformative-trajectories-in-the-procession-at-regla.html

Gardner, L. (2009, September 29). Cult of the Saints: An Introduction to Santeria. Llewellyn Worldwide. https://www.llewellyn.com/journal/article/2048

Chai, S. C. (2021, November 9). The Virgin Mary and Blue: What is the Significance? – F O R M F L U E N T. F O R M F L U E N T. https://formfluent.com/blog/the-virgin-mary-and-blue-what-is-the-significance

Dorsey, L. (2015, September 7). How to create A sacred space for Yemaya. Voodoo Universe. https://www.patheos.com/blogs/voodoouniverse/2015/09/how-to-create-a-sacred-space-yemaya/

Jorgenson, J. (2019, July 13). Exploring the yorùbá goddess Yemaya. Exemplore. https://exemplore.com/wicca-witchcraft/Exploring-the-Yorb-Goddess-Yemaya

Kaufman, A. (2022, September 3). How to connect with Yemaya? Goddess Yemaya altar setup, offerings, & more. Digest From Experts. https://digestfromexperts.com/4361/how-to-connect-with-yemaya-altar-offerings/

Prayers for Yemaya - powerful & uplifting words for prayer. (n.d.). Prayerist.com. https://prayerist.com/prayer/yemaya

Toni. (2019, February 14). Connecting with Yemaya – . In the Key of Soul. https://www.inthekeyofsoul.com/mainblog/yemaya

Zeeshan. (2022, January 30). How to connect with Yemaya. Digital Global Times. https://digitalglobaltimes.com/how-to-connect-with-yemaya/

Morgaine, R. (2021). Yemaya: Orisha, Goddess, and Queen of the Sea. Weiser Books.

Kaufman, A. (2022, September 3). How To Connect With Yemaya? Goddess Yemaya Altar Setup, Offerings, & More. Digest From Experts.

https://digestfromexperts.com/4361/how-to-connect-with-yemaya-altar-offerings/

Quinn, A. (2018, September 28). Life-Changing Benefits of Home Shrines. Abbeygale Quinn. https://abbeygalequinn.com/benefits-of-home-shrines/

Creating an Orisha Altar. (n.d.). Original Botanica. https://originalbotanica.com/blog/creating-an-orisha-altar-

Learning to Surrender: The Sacred Lessons of Yemayá. Atmos. https://atmos.earth/ocean-conservation-santeria-yemaya-lessons/

PURIFICATION BATHS WITH YEMAYA. (2021, May 20). BOTANICA OCHUN. https://botanicaochunco.com/purification-baths-with-yemaya/

Gomez, A. R. (2010, March 29). Spell: Yemaya Bath Ritual. Llewellyn Worldwide. https://www.llewellyn.com/spell.php?spell_id=4038

Nana. (2014, December 7). BIGGEST SECRET ON YEMAYA LOVE SPELL REVEALED. TRUTH. Love Spells. https://lovespell.tips/yemaya-spells-for-love-that-works/

Crawshaw, E. (2021, October 26). 8 Spells and Rituals for Self-Love. Mysticum Luna. https://mysticumluna.com/blogs/blog/10-spells-and-rituals-for-self-love

Amogunla, F. (2020, December 6). Dance, water, and prayers: Celebrating the goddess Yemoja. Al Jazeera. https://www.aljazeera.com/features/2020/12/6/dance-water-and-prayers-celebrating-the-goddess-yemoja

Celebrating Yemaya: The mother of the ocean and sea in African diasporic traditions. (n.d.). Daily Kos. https://www.dailykos.com/stories/2022/7/10/2108414/-Celebrating-Yemaya-The-mother-of-the-ocean-and-sea-in-African-diasporic-traditions

Grimond, G. (2017, June 30). Brazil's goddess of the sea: Everything you need to know about festival of Iemanjá. Culture Trip; The Culture Trip. https://theculturetrip.com/south-america/brazil/articles/brazils-goddess-of-the-sea-everything-you-need-to-know-about-festival-of-iemanja/

Slama, F. (2020, January 23). Iemanjá Festival. Salvador - Bahia - Mix It Up. https://www.salvadordabahia.com/en/iemanja-festival/

Zelenková, B. (n.d.). Iemanja: A Uruguayan celebration of the Yoruba goddess of the sea. Ethnologist.Info. https://ethnologist.info/2019/04/25/iemanja-a-uruguayan-celebration-of-the-yoruba-goddess-of-the-sea/

A ritual to Yemaya – mother whose children are the fish. (2018, January 31). Judith Shaw - Life on the Edge. https://judithshaw.wordpress.com/2018/01/31/a-ritual-to-yemaya-mother-whose-children-are-the-fish/

Atmos. (2022, June 21). Learning to surrender: The sacred lessons of Yemayá. Atmos. https://atmos.earth/ocean-conservation-santeria-yemaya-lessons/

Celebrant Institute. (2011, December 23). A goddess water ritual for new year's eve. Spirituality & Health. https://www.spiritualityhealth.com/blogs/spirituality-health/2011/12/23/celebrant-institute-goddess-water-ritual-new-years-eve

Episode 51- Yemaya, the Yoruba Orisha "mother of all" – part 2 of seashells and ocean goddesses. (n.d.). Moonriverrituals.com. https://moonriverrituals.com/episode-51-yemaya-the-yoruba-orisha-mother-of-all-part-2-of-seashells-and-ocean-goddesses/

Original Products. (2018, December 31). Yemaya: The goddess of the New Year. Original Botanica; www.originalbotanica.com#creator. https://originalbotanica.com/blog/yemaya-the-goddess-of-the-new-year

Ratcliffe, D. (2017, June 7). A healing ritual for Yemaya (and YOU) on World Oceans Day. Inner Journey Events Blog. https://innerjourneyevents.wordpress.com/2017/06/07/a-healing-ritual-for-yemaya-and-you-on-world-oceans-day/

Reduce water consumption at home. (2012, January 24). Sswm.Info; seecon international gmbh. https://sswm.info/taxonomy/term/2658/reduce-water-consumption-at-home

Yemanja feast day: Uruguans flock to the beach to pay ode to sea goddess. (n.d.). https://www.outlookindia.com/ . Retrieved November 28, 2022, from https://www.outlookindia.com/international/yemanja-feast-day-uruguans-flock-to-the-beach-to-pay-ode-to-sea-goddess-photos-66798?photo-1

www.ingramcontent.com/pod-product-compliance
Lightning Source LLC
Chambersburg PA
CBHW072157200426
43209CB00052B/1327